Merging Artificial Intelligence With the Internet of Things

Muhammad Usman Tariq
Abu Dhabi University, UAE & University College Cork, Ireland

IGI Global
Scientific Publishing
Publishing Tomorrow's Research Today

Vice President of Editorial	Melissa Wagner
Director of Acquisitions	Mikaela Felty
Director of Book Development	Jocelynn Hessler
Production Manager	Mike Brehm
Cover Design	Phillip Shickler

Published in the United States of America by
IGI Global Scientific Publishing
701 East Chocolate Avenue
Hershey, PA, 17033, USA
Tel: 717-533-8845
Fax: 717-533-7115
Website: https://www.igi-global.com E-mail: cust@igi-global.com

Library of Congress Cataloging-in-Publication Data

Names: Tariq, Muhammad Usman, 1988- editor
Title: Merging artificial intelligence with the internet of things / edited by Muhammad Usman Tariq.
Description: Hershey, PA : IGI Global, [2025] | Includes bibliographical references and index. | Summary: "This book aims to provide a comprehensive exploration of AIoT, delving into its technical foundations, practical applications, and future trends"-- Provided by publisher.
Identifiers: LCCN 2024052948 (print) | LCCN 2024052949 (ebook) | ISBN 9798369385470 h/c | ISBN 9798369385517 s/c | ISBN 9798369385487 ebook
Subjects: LCSH: Artificial intelligence--Industrial applications | Internet of things--Industrial applications
Classification: LCC TA347.A78 M4695 2025 (print) | LCC TA347.A78 (ebook) | DDC 006.3--dc23/eng/20250730
LC record available at https://lccn.loc.gov/2024052948
LC ebook record available at https://lccn.loc.gov/2024052949
British Cataloguing in Publication Data
A Cataloguing in Publication record for this book is available from the British Library.

Table of Contents

Preface xiv

Chapter 1
Integrating AI With IoT: Challenges and Solutions 1
Poornima Pandian, Sri Sai Ram Engineering College, India
Anu Disney D., Sathyabama Institute of Science and Technology, India
Lavanya Devi S., Sri Sai Ram Engineering College, India
Gowri Manohari R., Sri Sai Ram Engineering College, India

Chapter 2
Shaping Intelligent Connectivity Using AI and IoT 33
Mitra Tithi Dey, Netaji Nagar Day College, India & University of Calcutta, India
Suman Patra, Netaji Nagar Day College, India & University of Calcutta, India
Sucharita Mitra, Netaji Nagar Day College, India & University of Calcutta, India

Chapter 3
Exploring the Role of AIoT in Data Privacy and Security 75
Sushil Bhardwaj, RIMT University, India
Indu Sharma, Chandigarh University, India
Shivani Mahendru, Chandigarh University, India
Ramandeep Kaur, Chandigarh University, India
Surbhi Sharma, RIMT University, India

Chapter 4
Integrating AI With Blockchains for Securing Cloud-Based IoT Networks: Benefits, Issues, and Challenges 103
Mohamadi Begum Y., Swami Vivekananda Yoga Anusandhana Samsthana University, Bangalore, India
Aashna K. Nishad, Presidency University, Bengaluru, India
Harshavardhan Vilas Kurtkoti, Presidency University, Bangalore, India

Chapter 5
My Walking Pal: An AI-Driven Smart Stick Using IoT for Enhanced Mobility to Empower Visually Impaired Individuals 135
Margaret T. A. Swetha, Stella Maris College, India
Devi D. Renuka, Stella Maris College, India

Chapter 6
Case Study Successful Artificial Intelligence (AI) and the Internet of Things (IoT) (AIoT) Implementation in Smart Cities 167
Bhanu Dwivedi, Manav Rachna International Institute of Research and Studies, Faridabad, India
Rachna Behl, Manav Rachna International Institute of Research and Studies, Faridabad, India

Chapter 7
A Study on AI-Driven Internet of Battlefield Things (IoBT)-Based Decision Making: KSK Approach in IoBT.. 203
Kutubuddin Sayyad Liyakat Kazi, Brahmdevdada Mane Institute of Technology, Solapur, India

Chapter 8
AIoT-Enabled Smart Homes Solution to Security, Comfort, and Energy Efficiency 239
Anubha Anubha, Jaipuria Institute of Management, Ghaziabad, India
Daviender Narang, Jaipuria Institute of Management, Ghaziabad, India
Ankit Raj, Jaipuria Institute of Management, Ghaziabad, India

Chapter 9
AIoT in Healthcare and Remote Monitoring: A Case Study 269
Anuska Dutta, Brainwre University, India
Diya Biswas, Brainware University, India
Piyal Roy, Brainware University, India
Shivnath Ghosh, Brainwre University, India
Saptarshi Kumar Sarkar, Brainwre University, India

Chapter 10
AIoT in Smart Education Systems 299
Ishani Maity, Brainware University, India
Arkadip Mandal, Brainware University, India
Piyal Roy, Brainware University, India
Saptarshi Kumar Sarkar, Brainware University, India

Chapter 11
AIoT in Environmental Sustainability 329
Rushda Sharf, Integral University, India
Yusra Sharf, Aligah Muslim University, India

Chapter 12
Revolutionising Agriculture: The Role of AIoT in Disease and Pest Management for Global Food Security 361
R. Monisha, KPR Institute of Engineering and Technology, India
K. S. Tamilselvan, KPR Institute of Engineering and Technology, India
A. Sharmila, Bannari Amman Institute of Technology, India

Chapter 13
Application of AIoT in Smart Retailing and Consumer Insights 397
Shikha Mittal, Raj Kumar Goel Institute of Technology, Ghaziabad, India
Manisha Singhal, Teerthanker Mahaveer Institute of Management and Technology, India
Mani Dublish, Ajay Kumar Garg Engineering College, Ghaziabad, India
Shaista Noor, Teesside University, UK

Chapter 14
The Evolution of Civil Engineering Field With the Emergence and Incorporation of Artificial Intelligence and Internet of Things 431
Aditya Singh, Amrita Vishwa Vidyapeetham, India

Compilation of References 487

About the Contributors 561

Index 567

Detailed Table of Contents

Preface... xiv

Chapter 1
Integrating AI With IoT: Challenges and Solutions.. 1
Poornima Pandian, Sri Sai Ram Engineering College, India
Anu Disney D., Sathyabama Institute of Science and Technology, India
Lavanya Devi S., Sri Sai Ram Engineering College, India
Gowri Manohari R., Sri Sai Ram Engineering College, India

One of the most popular technologies of the modern day is the Internet of Things (IoT), which has a big impact on our lives in many different ways, including societal, commercial, and economic ones. The current and next IoT technologies are significant in terms of digitization, productivity, and customer comfort in a variety of application areas, such as smart cities and education have a lot of potential to raise the standard of living for people in general. However, in the Internet of Things context, risks and cyberattacks have a significant impact on smart applications .Delivering a constantly upgraded and current security system for the next generation IoT system requires using artificial intelligence (AI) capabilities, particularly machine and deep learning solutions. IoT is considered as a technology for developing smart environments, including intelligent building management systems, intelligent cities, and intelligent healthcare systems.

Chapter 2
Shaping Intelligent Connectivity Using AI and IoT 33
Mitra Tithi Dey, Netaji Nagar Day College, India & University of Calcutta, India
Suman Patra, Netaji Nagar Day College, India & University of Calcutta, India
Sucharita Mitra, Netaji Nagar Day College, India & University of Calcutta, India

This chapter explores the transformative impact of intelligent connectivity, driven by the convergence of Artificial Intelligence (AI) and the Internet of Things (IoT). It highlights how these technologies, coupled with 5G, edge computing, and blockchain, enable adaptive, context-aware systems that enhance efficiency and innovation. AI empowers decision-making and automation through data analysis, while IoT provides real-time data streams, creating a synergistic loop for continuous optimization. Applications span smart cities, homes, healthcare, industrial IoT, and transportation, delivering improved quality of life, operational efficiency, and resource management. Key challenges include data privacy, scalability, interoperability, and ethical considerations, with solutions like encryption, standards, and inclusive policies being crucial. The chapter also examines emerging trends such as AIoT, 5G, edge computing, and AI-driven IoT platforms, which promise real-time processing, autonomous systems, and scalability. This chapter also covers case studies on AI and IOT based systems.

Chapter 3
Exploring the Role of AIoT in Data Privacy and Security 75
Sushil Bhardwaj, RIMT University, India
Indu Sharma, Chandigarh University, India
Shivani Mahendru, Chandigarh University, India
Ramandeep Kaur, Chandigarh University, India
Surbhi Sharma, RIMT University, India

The convergence of Artificial Intelligence (AI) and the Internet of Things (IoT), known as AIoT, is transforming industries by creating autonomous systems capable of real-time decision-making. However, this integration also poses significant data privacy and security challenges. The primary objectives of this chapter are (a) To understand the intersection of AIoT and data privacy/security (b) To identify the key privacy and security challenges posed by AIoT (c) To explore strategies for enhancing data privacy and security in AIoT and (d) To discuss the future of AIoT in the context of privacy and security. The chapter also discusses regulatory and policy recommendations to ensure a balance between innovation and data protection, presenting case studies and future trends. This comprehensive analysis provides valuable insights for researchers and professionals navigating the evolving landscape of AIoT.

Chapter 4
Integrating AI With Blockchains for Securing Cloud-Based IoT Networks: Benefits, Issues, and Challenges 103
Mohamadi Begum Y., Swami Vivekananda Yoga Anusandhana Samsthana University, Bangalore, India
Aashna K. Nishad, Presidency University, Bengaluru, India
Harshavardhan Vilas Kurtkoti, Presidency University, Bangalore, India

IoT network is a collection of vast number of objects or devices which can sense and generate data for further processing that aids decision-making in real time applications. Connecting such IoT devices to cloud servers helps in faster and easier data storage and processing. Integrating Artificial Intelligence (AI) with Blockchain technologies is a potential solution for all the security threats in an IoT network. The IoT cloud has got its own limitations in terms of storage, bandwidth and is more likely to get affected due to malicious attacks happening at multiple layers of IoT architecture. This chapter examines the need for securing IoT cloud using blockchain technology and enhancements made to the same by integrating AI with Blockchain. The benefits due to this integration of technologies also bring in a few challenges which are discussed in this chapter.

Chapter 5
My Walking Pal: An AI-Driven Smart Stick Using IoT for Enhanced Mobility to Empower Visually Impaired Individuals 135
Margaret T. A. Swetha, Stella Maris College, India
Devi D. Renuka, Stella Maris College, India

Visually impaired individuals often face significant challenges when navigating both indoor and outdoor environments, frequently requiring assistance. The unpredictable conditions of roadways further exacerbate these challenges, making it essential for them to remain vigilant to avoid hazardous situations such as colliding with stationary or moving obstacles, navigating staircases, or slipping on wet surfaces. To address these issues, a Smart stick has been designed and developed utilizing modern technologies, including the Internet of Things (IoT) and Artificial Intelligence, to provide a clear and safe path for users in their surroundings. The proposed design is a patented model for its design clarity and innovation. The model integrates multiple IoT sensors and AI-driven modules, all controlled by a microcontroller system. These sensors are employed to detect obstacles, while the AI component enhances the system's ability to adapt to varying environments and predict potential hazards. Additionally, the stick is equipped with a mechanism to send alerts about the user's location

Chapter 6
Case Study Successful Artificial Intelligence (AI) and the Internet of Things (IoT) (AIoT) Implementation in Smart Cities 167
Bhanu Dwivedi, Manav Rachna International Institute of Research and Studies, Faridabad, India
Rachna Behl, Manav Rachna International Institute of Research and Studies, Faridabad, India

This chapter investigates the integration of Artificial Intelligence (AI) and the Internet of Things (IoT) within smart city projects, emphasizing their practical applications and outcomes. It demonstrates how AIoT technologies improve urban infrastructure, resource management, and public services through comprehensive case studies from diverse cities. The chapter showcases the significant effects of AIoT on traffic management, energy efficiency, and public safety, and provides insights into best practices and strategies for addressing challenges such as data privacy, interoperability, and infrastructure investment. It highlights the convergence of AI and IoT as essential for advancing smart cities, enhancing quality of life, and fostering sustainable growth. Key elements for successful implementation include strong leadership, strategic vision, robust data privacy, and security measures. The chapter concludes with actionable recommendations for scaling AIoT solutions, positioning this integration as a fundamental shift toward more sustainable and resilient urban environments.

Chapter 7
A Study on AI-Driven Internet of Battlefield Things (IoBT)-Based Decision Making: KSK Approach in IoBT 203
Kutubuddin Sayyad Liyakat Kazi, Brahmdevdada Mane Institute of Technology, Solapur, India

The sensors that fuel the Internet of Body Technology (IoBT) provide essential information that improves situational awareness, decision-making, and combat performance. Despite challenges, the continuous development and integration of these technologies will transform combat, defining the character of conflict and changing the landscape of future battlegrounds. An array of sensors that continuously provide real-time data to intelligent computers will enable commanders to make well-informed decisions at the speed of light. The outcomes of every classifier employed in the KSK (Kutubuddin S Kazi) Approach are analyzed in the following scenarios: target acquisition and tracking, environmental condition, health, remote operations, and disaster relief. The accuracy range for the recommended KSK approach in IoBT is 90% to 96%, whereas the ranges for recall and precision are 89% to 95% and 90% to 95%, respectively.

Chapter 8
AIoT-Enabled Smart Homes Solution to Security, Comfort, and Energy Efficiency 239
Anubha Anubha, Jaipuria Institute of Management, Ghaziabad, India
Daviender Narang, Jaipuria Institute of Management, Ghaziabad, India
Ankit Raj, Jaipuria Institute of Management, Ghaziabad, India

Thanks to developments in Artificial Intelligence (AI) and the Internet of Things (IoT), the once-futuristic idea of smart houses is now a reality. These cutting-edge technologies are transforming regular houses into intelligent, networked spaces that improve security, comfort, and energy efficiency. These technologies including AI and IoT, automate such homes and control various systems and devices. At the core of the smart home lie their capabilities to automate routine tasks like adjusting lighting and temperature to locking doors and managing security cameras. This creates an ecosystem that is adaptable to suit the requirements and preferences of its occupants. In the era characterized by artificial intelligence (AI) and the Internet of Things (IoT), almost everything including homes is automated and smart. The smart home market valued at $ 79.16 billion in 2022 is expected to grow at a CAGR (Compound Annual Growth Rate) of 27.07% from 2023 to 2030 (Grandview Research Report, 2024). Accordingly, the present chapter aims to explore the potential of AIoT in home automation.

Chapter 9
AIoT in Healthcare and Remote Monitoring: A Case Study 269
Anuska Dutta, Brainwre University, India
Diya Biswas, Brainware University, India
Piyal Roy, Brainware University, India
Shivnath Ghosh, Brainwre University, India
Saptarshi Kumar Sarkar, Brainwre University, India

Integration of AI and IoT has contributed a lot to improve healthcare and real-time patient monitoring and predictive analysis of patients' health. This chapter focuses on AI and IoT-based telehealth devices that assess essential health parameters from a distance thus improving quality of the patient care and minimizing the risks of spreading diseases. These systems are intelligently implemented by cloud computing and machine learning and they foresee health anomalies and help in treatment plans. One of the innovations reported is the CNN for screening the arrhythmias in wearable devices while the athletes are in action to offer real-time results with a high level of precision. The chapter also explores transition from conventional methods of aircraft health monitoring towards the AIoT systems that employ real-time data in the maintenance as well as safety enhancements. The prospect of the use of AI is revealed with focus on its utilization in the identification of hazardous compounds and consideration of the health of the environment.

Chapter 10
AIoT in Smart Education Systems 299
Ishani Maity, Brainware University, India
Arkadip Mandal, Brainware University, India
Piyal Roy, Brainware University, India
Saptarshi Kumar Sarkar, Brainware University, India

Convergence of Artificial Intelligence (AI) and the Internet of Things (IoT) has given rise to AIoT (Artificial Internet of Things), a transformative force shaping various industries, including education. We provide a comprehensive overview of AIoT, focusing on its applications, challenges, and future potential in education. It highlights how AIoT can enhance the efficiency and intelligence of educational systems by leveraging data generated by IoT devices, resulting in more personalized and effective learning experiences. Key challenges, such as privacy and security concerns, data management, ethical considerations, and the integration of traditional education systems, are also examined. The chapter further explores emerging AIoT technologies and their role in transforming smart cities and educational environments. It concludes by offering predictions and speculations about future trends, emphasizing the potential impact on educational outcomes and equity.

Chapter 11
AIoT in Environmental Sustainability 329
Rushda Sharf, Integral University, India
Yusra Sharf, Aligah Muslim University, India

To address the majority of environmental sustainability issues, like transportation, energy, water management, and biodiversity, artificial intelligence (AI) has grown in importance. The primary focus areas in energy are area neural networks, expert systems, fuzzy logic models, and pattern recognition. This chapter assesses how the use of AI could improve the environment by reducing the effects of agriculture, climate change, water resources, weather forecasting, ocean health, and disaster resilience. The impact of AI on the environment and its sustainable applications are examined in this chapter using qualitative analysis. With an emphasis on AI's role in advancing environmental sustainability, the chapter's main goal is to identify applications of AI for environmentally friendly practices. It can help stakeholders understand international initiatives to improve environmental sustainability by utilizing AI.

Chapter 12
Revolutionising Agriculture: The Role of AIoT in Disease and Pest Management for Global Food Security.. 361
R. Monisha, KPR Institute of Engineering and Technology, India
K. S. Tamilselvan, KPR Institute of Engineering and Technology, India
A. Sharmila, Bannari Amman Institute of Technology, India

Pests and diseases affecting the plants lead to diminished crop yield worldwide. To address this, researchers have employed Industry 4.0 to modernise agriculture by incorporating advances such as Internet of Things (IoT), and Artificial Intelligence (AI). The IoT connects physical objects to the internet for data collection and exchange. As the count of those devices expanded, they began generating huge data. Consequently, extraction of actionable insights is required for effective decision-making. Thus, AIoT—the fusion of AI and IoT—addresses this scenario, where AI handles the huge data created by IoT devices by analysing and interpreting them. AIoT is applied to numerous sectors, including agriculture, where they assist in estimating crop yields, conserving soil, and identifying pests and diseases. AIoT also aids with crop disease diagnosis and pest management by providing real-time monitoring and predictive analytics. This chapter provides basics of AIoT and the potential of AIoT in disease and pest management. It highlights the challenges and future of AIoT.

Chapter 13
Application of AIoT in Smart Retailing and Consumer Insights 397
Shikha Mittal, Raj Kumar Goel Institute of Technology, Ghaziabad, India
Manisha Singhal, Teerthanker Mahaveer Institute of Management and Technology, India
Mani Dublish, Ajay Kumar Garg Engineering College, Ghaziabad, India
Shaista Noor, Teesside University, UK

Rapid developments in technology are causing a revolution in retail. In order to remain competitive and enhance the shopping experience for customers, retailers are utilizing new technologies. These technical advancements are helping retailers to stay ahead of the competition, retailers are increasingly using Artificial Intelligence of Things (AIoT) to help them comprehend the millions of data points that are present in their stores and transform them into useful information that will enable them to align the business more quickly and effectively for the required changes. At a staggering CAGR of 21.8%, the smart retail market is expected to rise at a quick pace, from roughly \$35.4 billion in 2023 to \$140.6 billion by 2030. This chapter illustrates how retail establishments can benefit from a potent digital transformation experience through the combination of AI & IoT (AIoT). Additionally, this chapter explores the advantages, difficulties, and prospects of AIoT in consumer insights and smart retailing, emphasizing its influence on the direction of the retail sector.

Chapter 14
The Evolution of Civil Engineering Field With the Emergence and Incorporation of Artificial Intelligence and Internet of Things 431
Aditya Singh, Amrita Vishwa Vidyapeetham, India

Civil Engineering is the oldest branch of engineering which was essential in the development of any civilization in the human history and eventually led to the development of other branches of engineering with the progress of any civilization in the pages of history. The same goes for the current times, but technological developments and implementation are usually seen at a slower rate in this branch of engineering compared to current existing branches of engineering. Over the recent decade, AI & IoT have developed at a very fast pace. Their applications and effect could be noticed in the field of civil engineering as well, which will be covered in this chapter. Then, some important new developments in this area because of AI and IoT will be discussed in order to understand the evolution and future developments of the mentioned field. Then, graphical analyses based on the available data will be performed to support the study and in understanding the future prospects.

Compilation of References 487

About the Contributors 561

Index 567

Preface

INTRODUCTION

The intersection of Artificial Intelligence (AI) and the Internet of Things (IoT) represents one of the most transformative developments of the 21st century. This fusion—often referred to as AIoT—is not just a technical convergence but a paradigm shift reshaping the very fabric of industries, societies, and daily human life. The book *Merging Artificial Intelligence With the Internet of Things* provides a timely and comprehensive exploration of how AIoT is revolutionizing key sectors including healthcare, transportation, agriculture, manufacturing, education, retail, civil engineering, environmental sustainability, and beyond.

The motivation behind this edited volume is rooted in the recognition that while AI and IoT have evolved significantly on their own, their integration is unlocking novel capabilities and creating intelligent, adaptive, and connected systems. These systems can make real-time decisions, learning from vast datasets, and optimizing outcomes with minimal human intervention. However, this evolution also brings forth complex legal, ethical, and technical challenges that must be addressed through collaborative global frameworks.

Through seventeen interdisciplinary chapters contributed by leading researchers and practitioners from around the world, this book offers readers not only conceptual foundations but also real-world applications and forward-looking perspectives. Each chapter dives into a unique domain, presenting use cases, innovations, challenges, and future directions of AIoT technologies.

CHAPTER OVERVIEW

- **Chapter 1** explores intelligent mobility in *autonomous vehicles* by integrating IoT to foster smarter, more sustainable urban environments. It highlights reduced emissions, improved traffic flow, and shared mobility systems as pathways to resilient cities.
- **Chapter 2** presents *My Walking Pal*, an AI- and IoT-powered smart stick that enhances mobility and safety for visually impaired individuals. The chapter showcases how assistive technologies can empower inclusivity through intelligent systems.
- **Chapter 3** delves into real-time object detection in *self-driving vehicles* under *rainy conditions*, detailing an embedded AI system that maintains accuracy and reliability despite environmental challenges.
- **Chapter 4** focuses on AIoT in *agriculture*, examining how it aids in pest and disease management, soil conservation, and yield prediction—thus playing a pivotal role in global food security.
- **Chapter 5** emphasizes the impact of AI in *clinical care*, detailing its applications in diagnostics, virtual assistants, patient engagement, and administrative efficiencies that collectively enhance patient outcomes.
- **Chapter 6** outlines the evolution of *intelligent connectivity* enabled by AI, IoT, 5G, and edge computing, showcasing how these technologies are transforming smart cities, industries, and consumer experiences.
- **Chapter 7** evaluates the traditionally slower adoption of AIoT in *civil engineering*, mapping its recent progress and future potential to reshape infrastructure design, maintenance, and monitoring.
- **Chapter 8** presents a deep dive into the *integration of AI, IoT, and robotics in healthcare*, emphasizing their collective role in remote monitoring, elder care, and surgical advancements.
- **Chapter 9** addresses the *legal challenges* posed by AIoT in *autonomous vehicles*, offering comparative insights from several countries and proposing frameworks for global governance.
- **Chapter 10** introduces an AI-based solution for *leather defect detection* in footwear manufacturing, highlighting its contributions to quality control and industrial efficiency.
- **Chapter 11** examines the convergence of AI and *blockchain* to secure *cloud-based IoT networks*, analyzing their potential in mitigating data vulnerabilities and improving trust.
- **Chapter 12** discusses the use of IoT in enabling *autonomous and intelligent devices*, backed by case studies that showcase practical implementations and innovation paths.

- **Chapter 13** showcases a novel application of IoT in *fish smoking*, optimizing traditional practices with temperature monitoring and automation to enhance efficiency and product quality.
- **Chapter 14** focuses on AIoT in *smart retailing*, explaining how data-driven consumer insights reshape customer experiences and operational strategies in retail businesses are.

CONCLUSION

This book is intended for researchers, engineers, policymakers, educators, and industry professionals who seek to understand the emerging landscape of AIoT. It provides not just theoretical grounding but also actionable knowledge that can inform both academic inquiry and practical implementation. As AIoT continues to evolve, we hope this collection will serve as both a foundational text and a catalyst for further innovation and interdisciplinary collaboration.

Chapter 1
Integrating AI With IoT: Challenges and Solutions

Poornima Pandian
https://orcid.org/0000-0002-5751-0859
Sri Sai Ram Engineering College, India

Anu Disney D.
https://orcid.org/0000-0001-5812-1874
Sathyabama Institute of Science and Technology, India

Lavanya Devi S.
https://orcid.org/0000-0002-3544-0079
Sri Sai Ram Engineering College, India

Gowri Manohari R.
https://orcid.org/0000-0001-7844-657X
Sri Sai Ram Engineering College, India

ABSTRACT

One of the most popular technologies of the modern day is the Internet of Things (IoT), which has a big impact on our lives in many different ways, including societal, commercial, and economic ones. The current and next IoT technologies are significant in terms of digitization, productivity, and customer comfort in a variety of application areas, such as smart cities and education have a lot of potential to raise the standard of living for people in general. However, in the Internet of Things context, risks and cyberattacks have a significant impact on smart applications .Delivering a constantly upgraded and current security system for the next generation IoT system requires using artificial intelligence (AI) capabilities, particularly machine and deep learning solutions. IoT is considered as a technology for developing smart environments, including intelligent building management systems, intelligent cities,

DOI: 10.4018/979-8-3693-8547-0.ch001

and intelligent healthcare systems.

INTRODUCTION

The dispersed and transparent services provided by the Internet of Things (IoT) are becoming a new, ubiquitous network paradigm. A vast number of smart gadgets, including sensors, smartphones, and other smart devices, are connected via the Internet of Things. These smart gadgets can exchange information and communicate with one another. As to the IDC statistics analysis, the global IoT device count exceeds 50 billion, and by 2020, it is expected to generate more than 60 ZB of data. The construction of complex systems to improve quality of life, such as machine condition diagnosis, human body activity monitoring, health monitoring, localization, and structural monitoring, is made possible by gathering data from these Internet of Things devices and analysing it to sense and understand the environment. As IoT grows in popularity and usage, a vast array of sensors and devices produces enormous amounts of data, and a variety of IoT apps are being created to provide customers with more precise services. Such Big data from IoT devices may be further processed and analysed to give consumers and IoT service providers information. To effectively use massive IoT sensing data, the rising IoT applications require several data-driven analytical techniques. AI algorithms have lately been included into IoT data analysis processes. With the development of cloud computing, graphics processing unit (GPU) computing, and other hardware advancements during the last ten years, artificial intelligence (AI) has achieved remarkable success. The most used AI algorithm is machine learning, which has been used in a variety of domains including computer vision, computer graphics, speech recognition, natural language processing (NLP), decision-making, and intelligent control. In a similar vein, computer networks may also benefit from machine learning (Sood and Mahajan, 2017).

The primary technology for autonomous smart/intelligent network management and operation has been identified as machine learning. In particular, the majority of IoT systems are growing more sophisticated, diverse, and dynamic; managing such IoT systems is challenging. To draw in additional users, these IoT systems' offerings also need to be enhanced in terms of efficacy and variety. Numerous research has advanced the use of machine learning on the Internet of Things. We may thus conclude that IoT can gain from utilising machine learning support. Because machine learning may offer workable ways to mine the information and features buried in IoT data, its application to the Internet of Things (IoT) enables users to gain deep insights and construct effective intelligent IoT applications (Cui et al., 2018).The IoT idea has developed into a significant focus on the primarily private end user in modern practice. The objectives of facilitating simplicity of use, which include straightforward implementation and connectivity, aid this. As a result, the majority of IoT devices fall into the consumer electronics category, which includes wearables, entertainment, and home appliances. Smart TVs, smart watches, and smart appliances are differentiated from their traditional or "dumb" equivalents by having an Internet connection. In general, the word "smart" has come to mean IoT capabilities. However, as demonstrated by the Mirai botnet, whereby (IoT) devices were adopted by taking advantage of default passwords and used as a platform for extensive distributed denial of service assaults, this intelligence also comes with new security dangers. Connectivity to a smartphone app or online interface that enables remote access, control, and even maintenance is a common feature of smart or Internet of Things devices. From the standpoint of the user, it makes it easier to utilise the device in any application environment and in a standalone configuration. Since it connects the user to the vendor's product ecosystem, it also improves customer retention, which is another desirable outcome from the vendor's point of view. An IoT-enabled gadget is frequently only functional when connected to a server that is managed by the item's manufacturer (Tariq, 2025).

The Industrial IoT (IIoT), which adapts the IoT idea to the demands of industrial operational technology (OT), is one example of an application domain that finds them intriguing due to their low pricing and ease of deployment, despite their primary consumer market design. These applications frequently use IoT-enabled sensors or cameras for monitoring machinery and plants. Wearable sensors are becoming more and more popular for worker safety surveillance in dangerous environments. IoT devices are used in smart farming to keep an eye on environmental conditions and adjust irrigation systems, for example, as necessary. Lastly, smart renewable energy systems also incorporate IoT ideas, especially when it comes to managing end-user components like PV systems, battery storage units, or electric car chargers. One of the most crucial technologies for creating intelligent systems is Artificial Intelligence (AI), which is regarded as a component of the Fourth Industrial Revolution (4IR). Therefore, by applying our understanding of AI, especially machine and deep learning, we can identify irregularities or undesired harmful activity on the Internet of Things and, therefore, provide a dynamic security solution that is always updated and enhanced. To extract valuable insights or intriguing data patterns from the security data, machine or deep learning models usually consist of a collection of rules, techniques, or intricate transfer functions. The resulting security models may therefore be used to teach machines to anticipate attacks or hazards early on or to spot IoT abnormalities to create a suitable defensive strategy.

BACKGROUND

Without the need for explicit programming, machines can learn on their own due to a technique called machine learning. Rather than relying on a rule-based system, machine learning focusses on using sophisticated algorithms and statistical approaches to access data and make accurate predictions. One of the main elements of machine learning accuracy prediction is the dataset. This makes the forecast more accurate and the facts more relevant. Several industries, including banking, retail, and healthcare, have made use of machine learning. More chances for illness detection and therapy are presented by the growing application of machine learning in healthcare. One excellent characteristic of machine learning is its ability to continuously enhance data for precise categorisation and prediction in illness analysis. As more data is collected, the prediction model will learn to make better decisions for more accurate predictions. Machine learning algorithms may be used to extract relevant data from patient datasets stored in electronic health records. By evaluating data and applying disease-causing factors from electronic health records, machine learning algorithms can assist in the diagnosis of diseases and anticipate their underlying causes. For the analysis and integration of vast quantities of complex healthcare data, machine learning has become more popular than the conventional biostatistical technique in classification, prediction, and clustering tasks. Reconstruction of medical pictures, segmentation of brain tumours, classification of interstitial lung illnesses, and identification of bodily parts from medical images are only a few of the tasks in which machine learning has lately shown exceptional results (Tariq, 2025). Dimensionality Reduction Algorithm (DRA) is a collection of algorithms, including principal component analysis (PCA) and linear discriminant analysis (LDA), that take in large data sets as input, find correlations and patterns in them, and output a much smaller data set (in terms of number of dimensions) while preserving all the previously provided crucial information. This gets rid of the data's strongly linked characteristics, redundant information, and inconsistencies. The stages involved in reducing dimensionality are outlined as follows:

1) Standardisation: Mean of all variables of the feature divided by standard deviation of all variables of the feature equals new variable D (original variable). This scales each data point.
2) Compute the matrix of covariance:

   $$[\text{Feature}][\text{Feature}]^T$$
3) Calculate the eigenvalues and eigenvectors.
4) Calculate the Principal components.

Combining IoT with DRA, like LDA, has shown great potential for the detection of Parkinson's illness and breast cancer. The existing research has extensively addressed the need of combining IoT with DRA to improve diagnostic capabilities.

Discriminate Analysis

Discriminant analysis is an important type of DRA in which data points are projected onto a lower-dimensional space such that classes are suitably divided into non-overlapping groupings. In the case of two groups, this type of categorization is comparable to multiple regression; however, it becomes more intricate when there are more groups involved. Applications of discriminant analysis in healthcare mostly include assessing a patient's disease prognosis and severity. A broad multiple discriminant analysis extends the same to a non-linear space, whereas LDA classifies by identifying a linear combination of characteristics.

Linear Regression

A linear method is used in the modelling technique known as linear regression to determine the connection between one or more independent variables and a dependent variable. In situations where there are simply continuous independent variables, it is desirable. While there are other methods for creating a linear regression model, the gradient descent approach and basic least squares are the most often employed. In the former case, the coefficients are found by directly minimising the sum of squared error values; in the latter case, the sum of squared residuals is minimised by an iterative process (Khodayar and Wu, 2015).

Logistic Regression

Logistic regression is a probability-based technique that uses the sigmoid function as the cost function, with a value between 0 and 1. There are two forms of logistic regression. Binary logistic regression is used to classify observations into two categories, whereas multinomial logistic regression is needed for more than two classes. Logistic regression is particularly useful when dealing with a dichotomous dependent variable (Tariq, 2025).

Support Vector Machine (SVM)

This technique employs the notion of a classifying hyperplane. The goal is to find a plane that splits the dataset into two groups with the maximum separation between data points. This hyper-plane is said to have the greatest range. The number of features determines data points on various sides of the hyperplane are assigned to distinct groups. The hyperplane's dimensions. For features with a count of 2 or fewer, the hyper-plane is essentially a line. For 3 characteristics, it converts to a 2-D plane, but for more, it gets difficult to visualize. SVMs have a high resilience to overfitting difficulties, making them beneficial. SVMs may classify datasets using both linear and non-linear kernels. The authors (Ginantra et al. 2020) have found that an SVM classifier outperformed other classifiers in recognising influenza-like illnesses (ILI), also known as acute respiratory infections. SVM is the most reliable method for position verification and does not require channel characteristics data for operation. SVMs were utilized to create algorithms for classifying medical implant materials (Kim et al., 2016).

K-Nearest Neighbor (KNN)

KNN is a supervised learning system that classifies items based on their similarities to specified properties of other objects in their category. Distances, often Euclidean, are calculated based on the object's category and the nearest points. Next, voting determines which group most of the closest objects belong to. The value of k is decided by parameter adjustment. To prevent numerous categories from receiving equal votes, the number of votes is often an odd number that is close to the square root of the total number of neighbours. The distance between neighbours is calculated by summing up the differences between their characteristics. KNN is useful for labelled data classification, even with tiny training sets, and is frequently utilized in numerous applications. The authors (Ahmed, 2017) utilized KNN using IoT data to predict cardiac attacks. The method was used to data from 20 Kinect sensors to determine joint locations in the body. The user's current activity was predicted using KNN classifiers that employed Euclidian and Minkowski distances. This has enormous potential for application in fitness measurement once classified for various activities. The researchers (Azimi et al. 2019) have proposed using repeated KNN imputations to estimate lost or missing data points from monitoring pregnant women. This application is reliable for both medical B2C services and maternal health research. The authors in (Hossain et al. 2018) used LoRaWAN sensors and accelerometers to identify activity using KNN, achieving an 80% accuracy rate.

K-Means Clustering

K-means classifies items based on whether they fit into a specific category. Therefore, the categorization categories are confined to "similar" and "dissimilar". category's centroid is determined using Euclidean distances, and a new item is classified based on its distance from the clusters. This approach has applications in web engines and WSN systems. K-means classification is applied in a variety of fields, including deploying wearable sensor networks to identify injuries among troops during wartime and monitoring patients' ECGs using wearable IoT nodes. In this work (Sood & Mahajan, 2017), the authors presented remote diagnostics for chikungunya utilising fog computing and fuzzy k-means to monitor illness spread. This approach has been tried and might be expanded to include COVID-19 tracking. Kim *et al.* 2016 found that using k-means clustering on MRI images can improve brain tumour identification.

Decision Tree

A decision tree has three components: core nodes, branches, and leaf nodes. These represent characteristics, decision rules, and outcomes, respectively. The Gini index and entropy are popular strategies for data classification. The authors (Cho, 2017) utilized decision trees to monitor individuals' whereabouts during a pandemic. The authors (Xie et al. 2019) developed a decision tree-based system to detect premature ventricular contraction (PVC) and diagnose arrhythmia based on heartbeat amplitudes and intervals.

Decision trees adapt based on the training data. Changing the training data can significantly impact the decision tree's output. The algorithm is computationally intensive. When splitting occurs, it is impossible to return to a local optimal state. The random forest approach solves these constraints (Xie et al. 2019). This model trains many decision trees simultaneously to create a single result. Bagging refers to the process of integrating decision trees. The researchers (Al Hossain et al. 2020) used a random forest model to forecast influenza infections in public locations with 95% accuracy, outperforming previous models.

Convolutional Neural Network (CNN)

CNN is a feed-forward network used for classification purposes. The input is broken down into constituents and sent to a convolution layer. The convolution layer combines these parts to create patterns. A ReLU layer maps input images against patterns to create a rectified feature layer, which is subsequently passed to a pooling layer. The pooling layer reduces the map to create a pooled feature map. Then it is transformed into a linear vector and fed into a fully connected network for categorization (Machinda et al., 2015).

Artificial Neural Network (ANN)

An artificial neural network (ANN) is a machine learning model that simulates the human brain's learning process. It consists of an input layer, multiple layers for data processing, and an output layer. In ANNs, hidden layers receive intermediate inputs, assign random weights and biases, and calculate weighted sums. These sums are then passed through layers until they reach the final layer, which determines the output using an activation function. Incorrect outputs are transmitted back to previous layers (back propagation) using a cost function to adjust weights until accurate answers are received (Tariq, 2025).

Reinforcement Learning

Reinforcement learning mimics how infants interpret their surroundings. The learner, or agent, starts from a given state in the environment (S0). The agent performs an action (A0), and the state changes to S1. If the action was correct, the environment would reward the agent with R1. This continues until the prize is maximized. It consists of algorithms like Monte Carlo and Q Learning.

Natural Language Processing (NLP)

Natural language processing (NLP) uses machine learning techniques to interpret human language, speech, and text. Its linguistic extraction capabilities make it simple to process and quantify unstructured data. The algorithm takes the following method.

1) Word categorization by stemming and tokenization.
2) Semantic analysis and disambiguation involve extracting the literal meaning of words and deconstructing them into context and intent.
3) Topic modeling involves understanding the conversation's context.

Scikit-learn, NLTK, spaCY, and TextBlob are the most used NLP libraries nowadays. NLP applications, which extract information from text or images, are employed in a variety of applications, including food intake and nutrition tracking, as well as evaluating patient emotional responses to medicine ingestion (Cui et al. 2018). Figure.1 represents various machine learning algorithms.

Figure 1. Types of machine learning algorithms

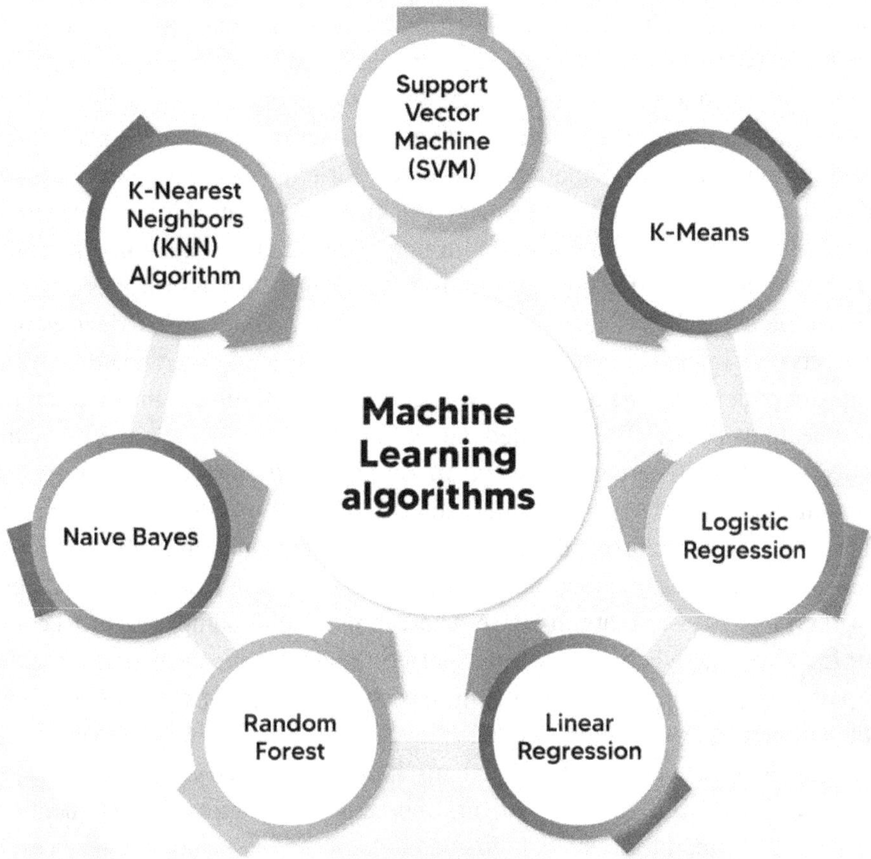

Healthcare IoT

The Internet of Things (IoT) allows smart devices such as smartphones, sensors, and Raspberry Pi to sense, monitor, and respond to their surroundings. This approach connects many devices to the internet at the same time, allowing for a larger range of connectivity. Thus, both human-machine and machine-to-machine interactions are possible. Humans can engage with machines to undertake healthcare jobs like surgery, patient monitoring, and real-time monitoring of hospital facilities and environment. Machines communicate with each other to store and retrieve information, such as sending data to a cloud system for temporary storage. Traditional IoT-enabled healthcare infrastructure. The hospital is the initial component that serves healthcare practitioners and patients. IoT solutions allow hospital management to monitor out-patients well-being and rehabilitation in their homes in real time. This can be accomplished with wearable or implantable medical bodies. Sensor signals are analyzed using machine learning, application software to generate meaningful information and to let hospital workers visualize an outpatient's health at home. If an out-patient's health deteriorates or becomes serious, they are quickly taken to the hospital ward by an emergency vehicle. Out-patients who are not under close surveillance or have recovered from their sickness may receive IoT-enabled assistive living devices. The ambient assisted living gadget enables real-time management of well-being for outpatients and individuals. For example, it tracks and reports on calorie expenditure, sugar levels, and heart rate. Assistive IoT devices provide patients with information to address potential health risks. Smart healthcare aims to improve patient well-being and provide caregivers with timely information for the best health services. IBM unveiled the notion of "Smart Planet" in 2009, which is where smart healthcare got its start. An intelligent infrastructure that uses sensors to gather data is referred to as the "Smart Planet." The information is processed into relevant information at the Cloud Data Centre and made available to authorised patients and healthcare practitioners after being transferred via IoT-related devices. Furthermore, the idea that consumers want prompt, high-quality care from healthcare professionals anywhere at any time spurred the development of smart healthcare. Smart healthcare has been defined by several writers as patient-centered facilities that are part of an ecosystem in which healthcare services are provided at various sites, such as hospital wards and patients' homes (Tariq, 2025).

Affective contact between patients and healthcare facility management can be facilitated by smart healthcare. It guarantees high-quality healthcare services, helps healthcare stakeholders make informed decisions, and permits the sensible distribution of healthcare resources. Additionally, an advanced method of data interpretation for medical reasons is referred to as "smart healthcare". On the other hand, heterogeneous computing is a type of healthcare management service that is enabled by IoT. Handsets that detect brainwaves, clothing with embedded sensors, blood pressure (BP) monitors, glucose monitors, Electrocardiogram (ECG) monitors, and pulse oximeters are a few examples of smart healthcare application prospects. Sensors found in medical equipment, dispensing systems, surgical robots, device implants, and any wearable technology are further application areas. Ably Medical Centre in Norway's supply of a smart bed is an excellent illustration of smart healthcare. The sensors included into the smart bed may measure all the blood pressure, weight, heart rate, and vital signs. It can let medical professionals know how a patient's condition is doing right now—whether it's getting worse or getting better with therapy. Furthermore, it keeps patients from collapsing or rotating them to relieve pressure spots on their bodies without others help. Collaboration across various IoT architectures can lead to advancements in the smart healthcare system. IoT-driven apps can be helpful in examining a patient's health status by generating a complete entity through the convergence of many devices. As a result, the Internet of Things system enhances both the hospital administration system's present technology and all medical operations. The ease with which medical experts and healthcare professionals may be contacted is rapidly improving. Medical data is more accurate and larger in scope when it is collected from a wide range of real-world circumstances. Furthermore, adding more contemporary technology to the hospital administration system improves the accuracy of healthcare delivery (Almotairi,2023). Figure. 2 shows typical IoT in healthcare.

Figure 2. IoT in healthcare

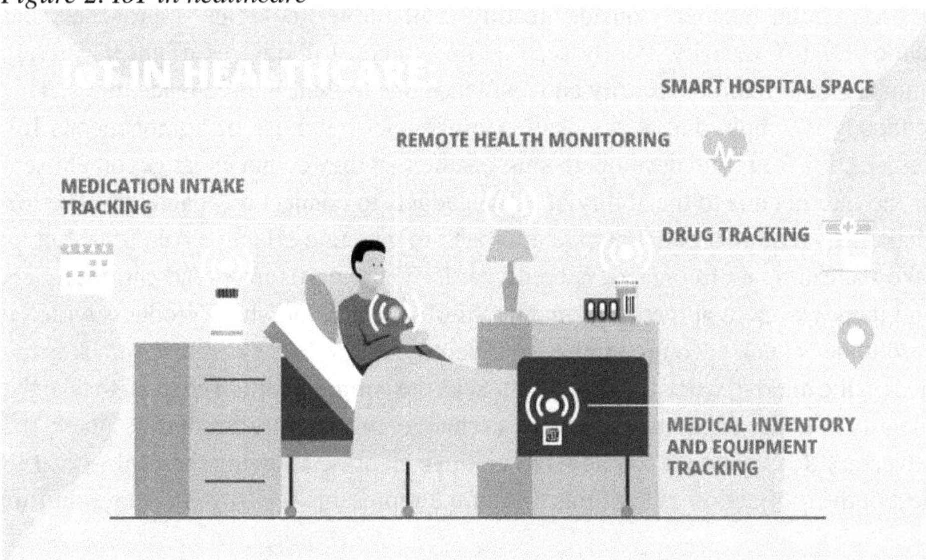

Security Challenges in IoT

The Internet of Things has provided users with numerous benefits; nevertheless, it has also presented certain drawbacks. Researchers and security specialists are primarily concerned with cybersecurity and privacy risks. These two are providing significant challenges for many commercial and public entities. Prevalent high-profile cybersecurity breaches have exposed the weaknesses of IoT devices. The interconnectedness of networks on the Internet of Things creates a vulnerability to anonymity and untrustworthiness, necessitating unique security solutions. Security and privacy are the most obstacles affecting IoT adoption. Unfortunately, users typically fail to see the security risks until a breach occurs, resulting in significant damage and loss of critical data. Consumers are becoming less willing to tolerate weak security due to recurrent breaches that jeopardize their privacy. A recent privacy and security analysis found that consumer-grade Internet of Things performed poorly. The IoT differs from traditional computers and computing devices, making it more exposed to security concerns in a variety of ways. The Internet of Things includes devices geared for large-scale deployments. Sensors are a great example of this. Typically, IoT deployments consist of similar gadgets with similar features. This similarity magnifies any security risk, potentially affecting many. Similarly, several organizations have developed guidelines for conducting risk assessments. This phase indicates an unparalleled number of connections between IoT devices. Many devices can automatically connect and communicate with other devices in an irregular manner. Consider readily available technologies, approaches, and tactics for IoT security. Poorly secured and linked IoT devices might negatively impact global Internet security and resilience due to their interconnectedness. This tendency is simply due to the challenge of widespread use of homogeneous IoT devices. IoT users and developers must ensure that they do not endanger other users or the Internet due to the ability of some gadgets to connect mechanically. The IoT challenges require a collaborative approach to generate effective solutions. Let us take the example of contactless credit cards. These cards may read card numbers and names without authentication, allowing hackers to purchase products with the cardholder's bank account number and identity. In the IoT, a common attack is the man in the middle, when a third party hijacks the communication channel to fake the identity of nodes engaging in network exchange. In a man-in-the-middle attack, the adversary does not need to know the victim's identity, allowing the bank server to accept the transaction as legitimate. Figure.3 represents security challenges in IoT.

Figure 3. Security challenges in IoT

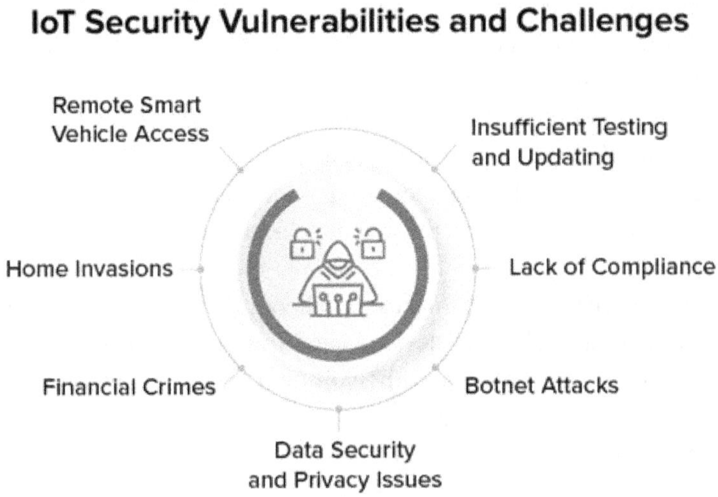

Privacy Challenges in IoT

The efficacy of Internet of Things (IoT) depends on its ability to respect individuals' privacy preferences. Concerns about privacy and other dangers associated with IoT may be substantial impediments to broad adoption. Respecting user privacy is crucial for building trust and confidence in the Internet of Things, linked devices, and services. The IoT is redefining privacy issues, including more surveillance and tracking. Privacy concerns arise from the widespread usage of intelligence-enabled objects in IoT, where information may be collected and distributed from anywhere. The ease of accessing personal information from anywhere in the world is facilitated by ubiquitous Internet connectivity.

Several variables may undermine the security of Internet of Things devices (Tawalbeh et al. 2020), such as:

- Occasional Updates: IoT makers typically provide security patches quarterly. Operating system versions and security fixes are also upgraded in a similar manner. Hackers have enough time to breach security protocols and grab important data.
- Saved Passwords: IoT devices hold integrated passwords, allowing support staff to remotely diagnose and apply OS updates. However, hackers could use the capability to breach device security.

- Automation: IoT solutions are often used by organizations and end-users to automate data collection and simplify business processes. If harmful sites are not mentioned, integrated AI can access them, potentially introducing dangers into the system.
- Remote Access Protocols: IoT devices use network protocols such as Wi-Fi, ZigBee, and Z-Wave to provide remote access. Specific restrictions to avoid cybercrime are typically not addressed. As a result, hackers can swiftly establish a hostile connection via these remote access protocols.

The current Internet paradigm makes it challenging to deploy privacy-preserving measures to a protected physical device. The limitations of IoT devices and their antiquated cryptographic challenge with traditional Internet to save the environment. To prevent possible risks, most computer devices have three fundamental limitations: computational power, battery life, and access control.

Battery Life

Heavyweight features may cause the battery to drain, and the majority of IoT devices lack the processing power necessary for system security design. Three potential approaches to addressing the security flaws have been suggested by the researchers. To take a risk-driven strategy, the first one makes use of the device's least secure features. Dealing with sensitive data, such as government, military, and healthcare, is not advised, nevertheless. The second suggestion evaluates the device's security features based on its small size and charging/battery capacity. Consequently, additional space may be made available to offer backup power or to expand battery backup in order to handle a difficult work. Lastly, the third suggestion is that the generation of energy from natural sources such as heat, light, wind, and vibration improve the hardware and financial expenses.

Computational Power

Traditional cryptography techniques are not appropriate for IoT devices due to their limited memory capacity and resource constraints. Furthermore, the devices lack the processing and storage capacity necessary to carry out sophisticated encryption. As a result, several studies have been proposed to use security techniques that investigate important computing device operations using devices with limited resources. To provide system security and dependable connection, physical layer authentication, for example, uses signal processing to allow secure authentication at the receiver's end that authenticates the communication parties. Additionally, an antenna's specific analogue characteristic allows for an efficient encoding of analogue information, which addresses the repeatability problem. The inconsistency acts as a distinguishing feature since it cannot be foreseen or controlled throughout the production process. Device authentication uses radio signals to save energy overhead and satisfy mobile IoT security standards.

Access Control

It prevents IoT devices from accessing backbone technology, ensuring information security against numerous security threats. Access control aims to effectively monitor resource access and prevent unauthorized information flow. IoT ecosystems enable continuous data transmission and sharing between people and devices. IoT domains are vulnerable to attacks such as password guessing and node capture, which can cause hardware failure. Malicious users may use deployed nodes to commit cybercrimes. Distinguishing between malicious and genuine nodes in a network can be challenging. When deploying a new computing equipment, a standard access control mechanism is preferable. It may stop malicious nodes and prevent unauthorized changes in IoT environments. Access control, including authentication and key setup, is crucial for protecting devices from malware assaults. Trusted organizations can create valid private keys using "certificate less" or "certificate-based" authentication mechanisms.

Applications

The Internet of Things has evolved beyond the definition and the data for the Internet of Things is just as crucial as electrons for energy. This section examines ML developments in IoT and classifies IoT applications. More than half of the world's population lives in cities due to greater work opportunities, education, healthcare, and living circumstance. This puts significant pressure on municipalities, urban development agencies, and governments to provide adequate resources. The "smart city" concept has gained popularity among governments globally, particularly in established and developing economies. Smart cities are a crucial aspect of urban development planning. There is no official definition of a smart city. Accelerated development and improved information technology aim to improve citizens' socio-economic conditions and quality of life.

Internet of Things (IoT) connects physical devices to the internet for efficient information sharing. Smart cities require technological support from IoT, often known as "urban IoT". Urban IoT generates significant amounts of data from "things." ML can help solve the challenge of extracting valuable insights from data.

Smart Grids

Smart grids improve energy availability and efficiency for cities, municipalities, and companies by eliminating waste, lowering faults, and optimizing supply to meet high demands. Although power-grid failures are uncommon, they can cost millions of dollars, cause blackouts, and disrupt social activities. Smart grids provide power in a dispersed and flexible manner. IoT can enable smart grids for better power management. ML will make a significant impact on the success of smart grids, going beyond current capabilities. The energy-space sector is where MLAs are accelerating the "data to knowledge to action" paradigm. IoT-based smart grids pose security problems. Using available data and MLAs, we may identify electricity usage patterns and consumer preferences. This will enhance power grid dependability and provide valuable insights for customers and power corporations to upgrade infrastructure for future difficulties. Figure 4 shows the structure of smart grid based IoT. Electricity demand forecasting (EDF) is a crucial part of power firms' strategic planning. According to the researchers (Khodayar & Wu,2015), EDF has an impact on operating decisions in smart grids. EDF relies on machine learning algorithms (MLAs) to learn from and forecast data. EDF in traditional power systems relies on previous usage data. Smart grids result from combining IoT with electricity grids.

Figure 4. Smart grid

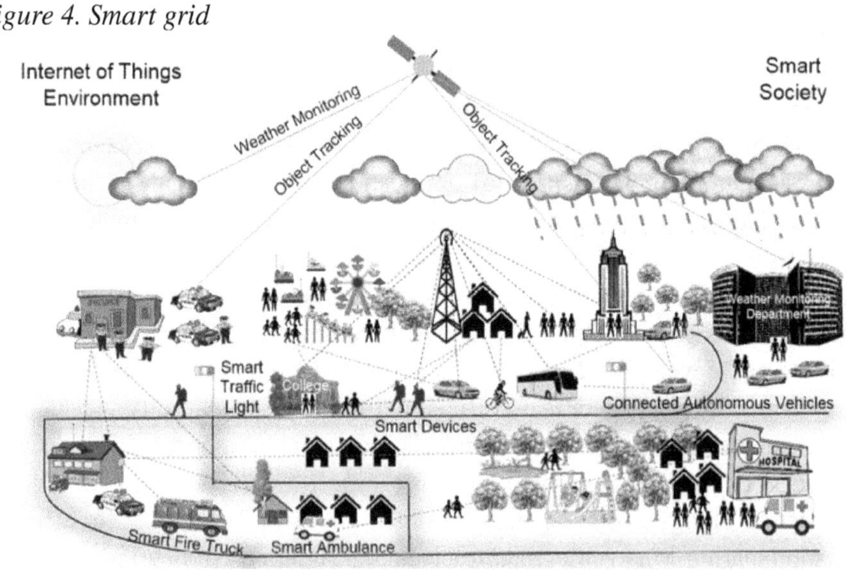

Smart Healthcare

The internet of things (IoT) is transforming healthcare by connecting smart sensors to the internet and providing real-time data. Islam et al. provided a complete explanation of IoT in healthcare, including platforms, applications, and market trends for smart healthcare solutions. Smart healthcare apps aim to improve access to treatment, enhance quality, and reduce costs. The automated evaluation of individual wellness and alerting others to potential health risks for patients is a frequently explored issue. A machine learning-based technique predicts activity quality and assesses cognitive health accordingly. SVM, PCA, and logistic regression MLAs are used to measure activities and predict cognitive health. Dawadi et al. use machine learning to automate cognitive health assessments. ML scoring models, both supervised and unsupervised, are utilized to measure and define activity performance classes and cognitive evaluations. IBM Watson offers an IoT-enabled cognitive health-care solution for a larger patient population. This approach leverages healthcare data and MLAs to provide novel insights. ML-enabled IoT health-care solutions improve proactive and preventive interventions while lowering costs. Cognitive care enables healthcare specialists to connect with patients, improving diagnostic accuracy and reducing errors. IoT-based healthcare systems can provide information to improve global healthcare quality.

Smart Supply Chain and Logistics

The Internet of Things (IoT) generates vast volumes of data and utilises advanced connectivity technologies. Real-time data analytics enable firms to satisfy customer needs in emerging economies. Supply-chain management (SCM) exemplifies the influence of IoT on the industrial sector. Ellis et al. proposed that IoT-enabled analytics will transform supply chain management (SCM). This work (Barun, 2014) highlights several immediate benefits of IoT in SCM, including:

- IoT "things" can interact quickly and provide real-time location information.
- IoT-enabled object tracking improves asset and fleet management, leading to better scheduling, routing, and timely product delivery.
- IoT allows for better management over mobile assets, including understanding their location and usage patterns.
- Downtime will be continuously monitored in real time.
- It improves logistical transparency.
- These benefits combine to improve the efficiency and sophistication of supply chain management.

Counterfeiting refers to the fraudulent imitation of packaging and products. This is a serious issue for global supply systems. In this work (Gai et al. 2013), the authors proposes an anti-counterfeit deterministic prediction model (ADPM) to address this issue. The Monte Carlo (MC) MLA helps ADPM identify counterfeit products. ADPM analyses product qualities by calculating correlation coefficients across objective features. In another study (Machida et al. 2015), the scientists used machine learning and statistical approaches to detect counterfeits.

Pandemic Management

The globe is currently seeing the catastrophic effects of the COVID-19 pandemic. The WHO has said that the global response might be far better than what is now being implemented. Healthcare systems in wealthy nations like Italy and the US, as well as emerging ones like India and Brazil, were often inadequate and overworked. IoT technology can efficiently monitor and manage the COVID-19 epidemic. IoT infrastructure and intelligence can handle difficulties such as lockdowns, social distance, contact tracking, healthcare monitoring, prescreening, remote meetings, and 24/7 accessibility (Singh et al. 2020). IoT can provide widespread access to virtual health-care technologies and telemedicine, ultimately contributing to Healthcare 4.0 objectives. Smart Field Hospital in Wuhan utilized IoT and AI solutions to promote relaxation among healthcare personnel. Robots and IoT devices enabled contactless body temperature monitoring, cleaning, and disinfection.

Autonomous Vehicles

IoT will connect AVs and assist in the development of driving cognition. The development of connected AVs is still in its early stages, relying on adopters' willingness to accept change, pricing, and issues such as pedestrian detection, intersection navigation, communications, collision avoidance, and security. The system improves its grasp of driving scenes by leveraging connected car data and prediction. TAAWUN's main idea may be expanded to utilise IoT infrastructure and sense data for prediction. AVs have lately had fatal crashes while testing. This indicates that the ML algorithms utilized by AVs are not yet ready for real-world situations. Following TAAWUN, there are some statements about the advantages of networked AVs. The authors (Elliott et al. 2019) examined current advancements in linked AVs, emphasising five key areas: intersection navigation, pedestrian recognition, collision avoidance, communication, and security. Safety is a major priority for any autonomous technology.

Figure 5. IoT and edge computing

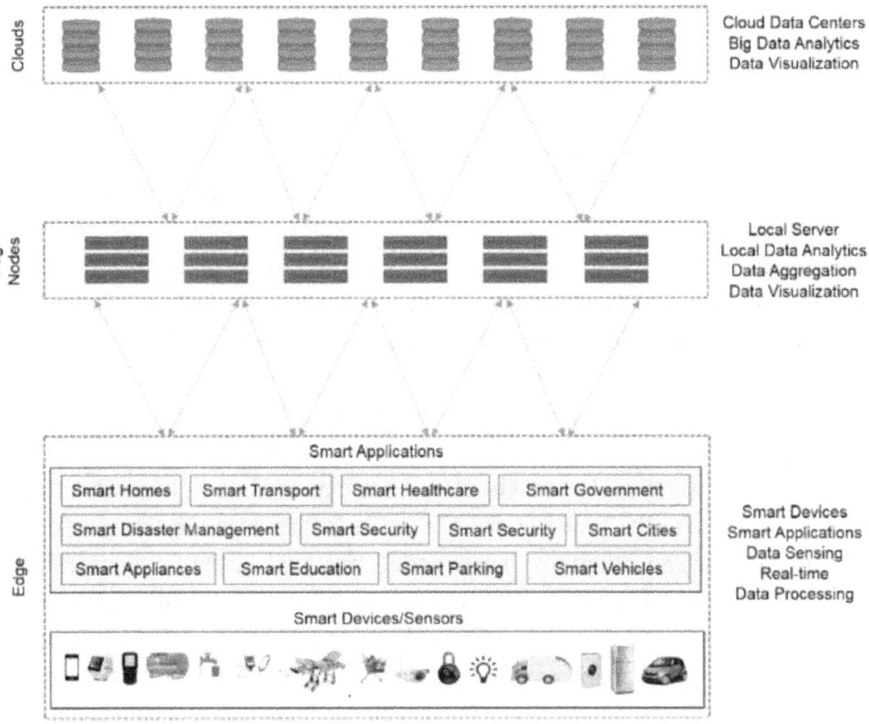

Figure 5 illustrates how edge and fog computing bring data intelligence and processing closer to the nodes where it is detected or required. Edge computing puts processing capacity closer to sensor data, rather than transferring it to a faraway cloud. This leads to faster data transfer for devices and applications. Fog computing, an emerging architecture, is a subset of the edge computing paradigm. Fog computing brings the cloud closer to data-generating items and actuators. It establishes standards for computing, data transport, storage, processing, and networking. Edge and fog computing enables IoT infrastructure to support smart applications and promote smart cities globally.

Challenges in IoT Deployment

The widespread deployment of IoT technologies is still a distant prospect. However, they are gradually being adopted globally. The Internet of Things combines four key technologies: sensing, networking, actuators, and security. The world is still experiencing connection troubles. Mobile connectivity and internet availability are challenges, especially in low-income nations. The lack of cross-platform functionality in current IoT platforms has led to delayed adoption. The current client-server architecture in IoT is unsuitable for the future due to increased latency, high energy consumption, single point of failure, and security concerns. Edge and fog computing solutions address network bandwidth, latency, accessibility, control, and management concerns. Security concerns are a major barrier to widespread use of IoT technologies. The Internet of Things (IoT) involves decentralised edge devices that might be vulnerable to cyberattacks due to their interconnectedness. The lack of universal authentication and authorization standards for IoT devices leads to additional security concerns. IoT success hinges on addressing security concerns. Many IoT simulators do not fully capture mobility, a crucial aspect of the Internet of Things. Most tools have inadequate mobility modelling capabilities, which emphasizes how urgently sophisticated simulators are needed. Particularly for intricate simulation settings like wearables, smart cars, and people on the go, these sophisticated simulators ought to be able to faithfully capture the dynamic nature of IoT topologies. Future simulators are expected to include advanced mobility models due to the growing use of mobile IoT devices. To simulate complex mobility patterns and situations, these models may make use of real-time data and predictive analytics. It is critically necessary to construct sophisticated simulators that can more fully and precisely capture the dynamic and mobile character of IoT installations. This may involve including real-world mobility data or using machine learning to forecast mobility trends. Furthermore, the recent incorporation of SDN into already-existing simulators draws attention to a research need. Simulators must be able to handle SDN and Network Function Virtualisation (NFV) natively to provide a comprehensive understanding of network dynamics and management as these technologies become more and more integrated into IoT networks. IoT simulators that do not support these technologies might miss out on important insights regarding SDN-centered IoT paradigms.

Because smart city infrastructures come from a variety of sources, including sensors, cameras, and traffic systems, they constantly produce enormous volumes of data that vary not just in volume and pace but also in format. Making sure that simulators can handle, analyse, and understand this diverse data with ease is a major task. Furthermore, real-world data is frequently lacking, necessitating the use of strong preprocessing and validation procedures in the simulators. Because data is frequently time-stamped and geo-tagged, there are additional temporal and geographical complexities to consider, necessitating that simulators effectively handle both dimensions. Vehicular Cloud Computing (VCC) has made it possible for cars to communicate, work together, and more efficiently use their combined processing capacity. VCC uses the computing, storage, and sensor power of cars to provide real-time, context-aware services by turning them into nodes of a dynamic cloud. This big shift puts the function of traditional cloud infrastructure in jeopardy as cars now create, consume, and save material. Rather, it is made up of an adaptable, self-organising cloud structure that changes according to the availability and proximity of nearby cars. Considering this, a significant trend for IoT simulators is starting to take shape: the requirement for precise simulation of automotive settings.

Mobility, IoT devices, heterogeneity, and battery management may all be seamlessly integrated in extremely dynamic and heterogeneous contexts by simulating Vehicular Ad-hoc Networks (VANET) scenarios using IoT simulators in conjunction with traffic simulators. As far as we are aware, Simulator Bridger is the only simulator that investigates this. There is an urgent need for more thorough and varied research because of the scant examination of this confluence between IoT and VANET modelling. More study is necessary because of VANETs' enormous potential and growing significance in contemporary urban environments. There are significant privacy and data security concerns when real-world data is included into IoT simulators. Since a simulator must cover both battery and communication models, none of them, as far as we know, can simulate threats like battery depletion. Numerous studies have been conducted on the detection of assaults on log files that are not simulated in real time with a real attacker utilising a real communication infrastructure. But as the Internet of Things ecosystem grows, several security risks appear, necessitating the use of simulators to faithfully replicate these vulnerabilities.

Data from IoT installations, including smart city infrastructures, is frequently sensitive by nature. This data may include traffic patterns, energy usage indicators, citizen personal information, and more. Such data breaches or unauthorized access can have serious repercussions for both individual privacy and larger infrastructure operations. Researchers will need to devote more time and energy to creating IoT simulators that are targeted at these problems to overcome this obstacle. Data anonymisation and sanitisation procedures should also be used when simulators include real-world data to guard against the loss of personally identifying information. In addition to protecting data, simulators should be able to replicate different threat situations. By modelling possible attack paths, vulnerabilities, and related mitigation techniques, researchers may get insight into how real-world IoT installations can react to security threats. More robust IoT systems in the real world may result from this proactive strategy, which identifies and fixes any vulnerabilities in a simulated setting.

Security Aspects of IoT

In this section, the security aspects of IoT are discussed. The most challenging aspect of IoT is security. IoT application data can be industrial, enterprise, consumer, or personal. Application data should be secure and protected to prevent theft and tampering.IoT apps can store patient health and shopping data. The Internet of Things (IoT) enhances device connectivity, yet challenges remain in scalability, availability, and responsiveness. Security is an issue when data is transmitted safely via the internet. When transmitting data across international borders, regulatory regulations like the Health Insurance Portability and Accountability Act (HIPA) may apply. In process automation, affordable IoT devices like webcams may be used to monitor plant parts and provide extra information outside the existing SCADA system, rather than for access control. Third-party IoT devices and services can be used to monitor machine conditions or for temporary installation during repair activities. These apps exist outside of OT and offer extra monitoring capabilities. Implementing network segmentation using virtual LANs, separate networks, or DMZs is a simple and effective countermeasure for current systems. For a recent research project, we installed additional equipment in a petrochemical facility to collect measurement data. The operator opted for a separate mobile connection for data transfer, even though the long-term measurement campaign could have been integrated into the company's IT/OT infrastructure. Some major firms have a policy that prohibits third-party devices used for engineering, commissioning, or maintenance from connecting to the company network for security concerns, which may appear counterintuitive. To incorporate IoT devices into plant networks, network segmentation is a crucial step in establishing a perimeter and implementing a defense-in-depth strategy. To enhance security, device authentication with MAC addresses or stronger cryptographic protocols, such https, is necessary. Deep packet inspection and intrusion detection systems (IDS) can monitor traffic and detect malicious or unfamiliar nodes. Proper white-listing technique is crucial for identifying permitted devices. However, network segmentation is simply the first step, as hijacked devices can still access the network.

Even if network segmentation is used, it may be bypassed by standard setups. Modern PV systems for residential and industrial customers generally link to an in-house IT network. The device connects to the vendor's server to upload operational data, including measurement values and status information, in addition to local network services like Modbus-TCP, Telnet, and rudimentary web server. The installation research created creates a tunnel over the firewall, allowing for software and firmware upgrades without the owner's knowledge. It connects to the Internet via port 80, which is open in most firewalls and not restricted by Internet providers. This channel can bypass network segmentation and provide full access to the local network, as it ends behind the firewall.

Device Hardening

Security measures should be applied at all levels, including hardware, software, and network connections. To prevent unauthorized access, device hardware must be designed with security consideration. Security modules, like Infineon's SLM 76 or ISO/IEC 11889 Trusted Platform Module, provide a safe foundation for storing credentials and API tokens, performing sophisticated cryptographic tasks, and serving as the foundation for further security measures. Encrypted devices can be used to store sensitive data. Code signing and secure boot routines can prevent unauthorized program installations. This is crucial for devices with physical access, including building and home automation systems.

To harden APIs, basic ideas such as deactivating unneeded ports, protocols, and services and verifying messages beyond access control are frequently sufficient. It is also necessary to check the none-used or reserved bits, as well as length values. This helps avoid attacks like buffer overflows. An IoT device should have a single point of access to request or store data or services, reducing the attack surface and allowing for more thorough security analysis. Device authentication and authorization need fine-grained implementation. Role-based access and public key infrastructures are recommended for network authentication and access control.

To secure a system, start by reducing the attack surface. Each connection or service creates new opportunity for attackers to exploit flaws. Deactivate specialized development access and services, including Telnet, SSH, or a debug terminal interface, to ensure security. Security modules are the second key stage. Today's microcontrollers often feature security modules that are still often utilized. eSIMs integrate a detachable SIM card onto a printed circuit board (PCB), making it difficult to remove and protect the user's identity. Using 5G for communication requires no extra effort.

Privacy and Confidentiality Enhancement

While IIoT focusses on machine-to-machine communication, privacy and secrecy are crucial for automation systems. The public expects appropriate data processing in domains including building, home automation, and healthcare. The report also found that customers want improved help and information from providers regarding their data usage.

Industrial automation challenges are similar, but they focus on processing data rather than human data. Threats include data manipulation or hijacking, such as man-in-the-middle attacks, which require encryption and integrity protection. However, there is a concern about rivals gaining access to crucial manufacturing expertise. Companies are concerned about both direct espionage and “unintended” information transfers. During recent discussions with the paper and cardboard sector, we discovered that sensor and monitoring data are extremely proprietary, even though the manufacturer might optimize machine functioning by accessing it. The client was concerned that the manufacturer's optimization of a certain portion of the machine may provide competitors with an unfair advantage. Mosaic assaults can collect seemingly insignificant data to obtain insight into an organization or extract key process knowledge.

Generative Adversarial Network (GAN)-Based IoT Security

GANs use adversarial settings to revolutionize machine learning methodologies. Two neural networks compete in a zero-sum game, eventually reaching equilibrium. Neural networks include two components: generators and discriminators. A discriminator is trained using a specific training set. The generator network generates candidate data, while the discriminator determines whether it is appropriately classified (e.g., by mapping characteristics to labels). The generator aims to intentionally deceive the discriminator, while the discriminator aims to strengthen itself against the generator, leading to network convergence. The generator tries to trick the discriminator into thinking the input data came from a real sample, while the discriminator tries to determine if it came from a generator. For a centralized GAN, all IoT device data points need be accessible. As a result, it can risk private information. In distributed GAN, IoT nodes communicate weights, not data. Therefore, the GAN is a generic solution, it might be tailored for IoT applications. ML can improve accuracy in hostile circumstances, but it can also pose a risk to the learning process. To improve training results, it's crucial to focus on positive aspects and minimize the impact of adversarial circumstances on inputs.

Federated Learning and IoT Security

Federated Learning is a framework for developing AI models that are spread across edge and mobile devices. It offers highly tailored and secure models while respecting client/user privacy. Basically, in FL model development, training, and evaluation is done without direct access to the user data. Smartphones, such as the Samsung S9 and Apple X, now contain advanced semiconductor architecture and cellular technologies, allowing for tremendous processing and AI capabilities. Most of the machine learning models are compatible with mobile smart devices.

FL computing design allows devices to download and run local models, which are improved by learning from stored data. Model parameters and weights are commonly used to describe changes in better models. Updates are encrypted and delivered to the master device (or cloud/central server). Similarly, all devices in the FL architecture will provide updates. All modifications are then averaged to improve the shared model. Distributing heavy analytics and computations across smart devices, as opposed to centralized computing systems, offers several benefits. FL is a great choice for mobile and distributed networks (e.g., IoT) due to its privacy and efficiency benefits, but it also has some challenges. Achieving rapid and timely contributions from participating devices in a pervasive environment requires adequate communication bandwidth, which can be tough to obtain. As a result, communication becomes a bottleneck instead of computation. Insufficient communication capacity can cause latency and slow down the FL model's convergence time.

Recent Trends in Adversarial Machine Learning Based IoT

Machine learning has both benefits and drawbacks. While it can enhance the value of data, it can also be misused by attackers. Adversarial Machine Learning (AML) is a branch of machine learning. AML attacks the system by exploiting machine learning features. Research has been conducted by manipulating training parameters to get the system to learn the opposite of its intended behavior. Deep Learning (DL) approaches are vulnerable to adversarial modifications in input data, which can lead to intrusion and DoS attacks. In object recognition, perturbation occurs when changes to classifiers lead to incorrect item identification. Recent research suggests that if DL methods are not effectively safeguarded in susceptible IoT networks, they may backfire. It's crucial to study the impact of AML in IoT networks and address related difficulties.

The sophistication of a security mechanism is determined by the device's capabilities and the system in use. The limits of IoT devices present a significant difficulty in implementing advanced security systems. Sophisticated security systems require extensive computer, storage, and communication resources. It's crucial to choose the appropriate location for ML and DL logic in the network. In-depth analysis is necessary to ensure the efficiency of security systems utilizing ML and DL approaches. Investigate low-cost and efficient security mechanisms for IoT, leveraging ML and DL.

IoT networks utilize resource-constrained devices, from home appliances to personal gadgets. These gadgets are typically easy targets for cyber-attacks. These devices create significant amounts of data, which can be utilized by ML and DL algorithms for many applications. Compromising these devices will negatively impact application outcomes. Compromise in smart home applications may not be as critical as critical infrastructure or medical applications. Compromise of data will render these applications vulnerable to ML and DL systems' findings. It could even risk human life. Ensuring device safety and data quality is crucial for ML and DL systems. Attackers could use compromised devices as bots to conduct other attacks.

To ensure the safety of ML and DL systems, IoT device security and data quality must be prioritized. Recent cyber assaults on low-power and resource-constrained devices raise concerns for IoT networks. Advancements in machine learning, like distributed learning and generative adversarial learning-based games, are gaining popularity. However, due to cyber threats and active attacks, these models may favor attackers.

For example: The policy challenges for self-driving cars will impact supporting technology such as IoT. Furthermore, the data produced by these technologies will be required for the ML mechanism to learn and simulate various behaviors. ML-based solutions may not be suitable for sensitive or personal data, such as that from healthcare applications or financial institutions. Validating and certifying IoT components, such as Body Area Network (BAN), remains a barrier for investors and will also impact ML-based solutions. The introduction of General Data Protection Regulation (GDPR) and regulations on cryptographic methods import and export pose substantial hurdles to IoT security.

Regulations for various IoT applications, such as smart homes and e-health, vary across nations, making a single security solution (conventional or ML-based) ineffective in several places. Currently, governments in the United States, Europe, and Asia are developing legislation that meets the needs of both customers and service providers, including in terms of security. Legislative measures are expected to shape consumer adoption of new technology.

Challenges in ML-Based IoT Networks

Creating ML models for IoT networks might be tough due to the variety of data sources. Labeling input data effectively might be challenging. In healthcare applications, correct training models are crucial for extracting the right characteristics from data and efficiently learning. False positives can have serious effects. Reliability of ML models is crucial for mission-critical IoT applications, which are prone to anomalies such as misclassifications caused by ML or DL algorithms. Reinforcement Learning (RL) has instability and divergence from not using all feasible action-reward combinations in a particular circumstance. ML models must be tailored to specific use-cases, IoT technology, and unique characteristics. To deploy ML and DL models on resource-constrained IoT devices, it's crucial to minimize processing and storage overhead (Ahmed, 2017). Deep learning models are highly specialized and trained for certain application domains. These models are limited to solving a specific sort of problem. When a problem's description, status, or nature changes, the model must be re-assessed and retrained, even if the new problem is comparable to the previous one. When using DL algorithms for multitasking, the model architecture must be restructured. Real-time IoT applications have challenges in updating and retaining

DL models with dynamic input data. Future research should focus on multitasking DL models. ML models used in IoT networks can provide domain specialists with insights into the decision-making process, in addition to precise forecasts. The model's interpretability is crucial for gaining deep insights into machine learning. Powerful models like deep learning and neural networks are challenging to grasp and interpret. Further study is needed to create smart models that are both accurate and interpretable. The demand for explainability in ML models pushes the use of simple models like decision trees. Experimentation is crucial for strengthening the theoretical basis of deep learning. DL models' performance may be quantified using parameters including computational complexity, learning efficiency, and accuracy (Al Hossain et al., 2020). Training ML models requires a large quantity of data and comes at a high cost. Training costs are especially important in real-time IoT applications. Updating machine learning models is crucial for accurate predictions over time. Manually retraining a model in the same way, it was taught is time-consuming. Continuous learning involves automating the evaluation and retraining of current models. Both strategies require a well-designed system model that considers both initial training and model maintenance.

CONCLUSION

Although most IoT deployments nowadays are closed ecosystems and data silos, the trend is moving towards specialized IoT platforms that handle the infrastructure and relieve the operator of lifecycle management. Platforms like Amazon's AWS IoT, Siemens' Mindsphere IoT, and Bosch's Ditto IoT offer IoT infrastructures and platforms as a service (IaaS, PaaS), making it easier to deploy, operate, and decommission IoT devices. Standardised security procedures and automated key exchange, authentication, and updating processes raise the security level from a security perspective. However, since every IoT device only communicates with the platform, if a security flaw is discovered, the effects are extensive. Additionally, the platform compromises the transmitted data's end-to-end security. Usually, a new secure connection is established for the application access by altering the security protocol at locations like edge devices, data concentrators, or database servers, like the LoRaWAN application server. Other security methods, such as watermarks incorporated into the sensor data, can prevent this break in the security chain and offer complete end-to-end protection in such systems.

REFERENCES

Ahmed, F. (2017). An Internet of Things (IoT) application for predicting the quantity of future heart attack patients. *International Journal of Computer Applications, 164*(6), 36–40. DOI: 10.5120/ijca2017913773

Al Hossain, F., Lover, A. A., Corey, G. A., Reich, N. G., & Rahman, T. (2020). FluSense: A contactless syndromic surveillance platform for influenza-like illness in hospital waiting areas. *Proceedings of the ACM on Interactive, Mobile, Wearable and Ubiquitous Technologies, 4*(1), 1–28. DOI: 10.1145/3381014 PMID: 35846237

Almotairi, K. H. (2023). Application of Internet of Things in healthcare domain. *Journal of Umm Al-Qura University for Engineering and Architecture, 14*(1), 1–12. DOI: 10.1007/s43995-022-00008-8

Azimi, I., Pahikkala, T., Rahmani, A. M., Niela-Vilén, H., Axelin, A., & Liljeberg, P. (2019). Missing data resilient decision-making for healthcare IoT through personalization: A case study on maternal health. *Future Generation Computer Systems, 96*, 297–308. DOI: 10.1016/j.future.2019.02.015

Bharadwaj, H. K., Agarwal, A., Chamola, V., Lakkaniga, N. R., Hassija, V., Guizani, M., & Sikdar, B. (2021). A review on the role of machine learning in enabling IoT based healthcare applications. *IEEE Access : Practical Innovations, Open Solutions, 9*, 38859–38890. DOI: 10.1109/ACCESS.2021.3059858

Cho, S. B. (2016). Exploiting machine learning techniques for location recognition and prediction with smartphone logs. *Neurocomputing, 176*, 98–106. DOI: 10.1016/j.neucom.2015.02.079

Cui, L., Yang, S., Chen, F., Ming, Z., Lu, N., & Qin, J. (2018). A survey on application of machine learning for Internet of Things. *International Journal of Machine Learning and Cybernetics, 9*(8), 1399–1417. DOI: 10.1007/s13042-018-0834-5

Elliott, D., Keen, W., & Miao, L. (2019). Recent advances in connected and automated vehicles. [English Edition]. *Journal of Traffic and Transportation Engineering, 6*(2), 109–131. DOI: 10.1016/j.jtte.2018.09.005

Gai, K., Qiu, M., Zhao, H., & Dai, W. (2015, November). Anti-counterfeit scheme using Monte Carlo simulation for E-commerce in cloud systems. In *2015 IEEE 2nd International Conference on Cyber Security and Cloud Computing* (pp. 74–79). IEEE. DOI: 10.1109/CSCloud.2015.75

Ginantra, N. L. W. S. R., Indradewi, I. G. A. D., & Hartono, E. (2020, February). Machine learning approach for acute respiratory infections (ISPA) prediction: Case study Indonesia. []. IOP Publishing.]. *Journal of Physics: Conference Series*, *1469*(1), 012044. DOI: 10.1088/1742-6596/1469/1/012044

Hossain, T., Ahad, M. A. R., Tazin, T., & Inoue, S. (2018, October). Activity recognition by using LoRaWAN sensor. In *Proceedings of the 2018 ACM International Joint Conference and 2018 International Symposium on Pervasive and Ubiquitous Computing and Wearable Computers* (pp. 58–61).

Khodayar, M. E., & Wu, H. (2015). Demand forecasting in the smart grid paradigm: Features and challenges. *The Electricity Journal*, *28*(6), 51–62. DOI: 10.1016/j.tej.2015.06.001

Kim, J., Lee, S., Lee, G., Park, Y., & Hong, Y. (2016). Using a method based on a modified K-means clustering and mean shift segmentation to reduce file sizes and detect brain tumors from magnetic resonance (MRI) images. *Wireless Personal Communications*, *89*(3), 993–1008. DOI: 10.1007/s11277-016-3420-8

Machida, T., Yamamoto, D., Iwamoto, M., & Sakiyama, K. (2015, January). Implementation of double arbiter PUF and its performance evaluation on FPGA. In *The 20th Asia and South Pacific Design Automation Conference* (pp. 6–7). IEEE. DOI: 10.1109/ASPDAC.2015.7058919

Singh, R. P., Javaid, M., Haleem, A., & Suman, R. (2020). Internet of Things (IoT) applications to fight against COVID-19 pandemic. *Diabetes & Metabolic Syndrome*, *14*(4), 521–524. DOI: 10.1016/j.dsx.2020.04.041 PMID: 32388333

Sood, S. K., & Mahajan, I. (2017). Wearable IoT sensor based healthcare system for identifying and controlling chikungunya virus. *Computers in Industry*, *91*, 33–44. DOI: 10.1016/j.compind.2017.05.006 PMID: 32287550

Tariq, M. U. (2025). Integrating ICT for Enhanced Organizational Resilience: Strategies and Case Studies. In Carvalho, L., Reis, L., Neves de Almeida Baptista Figueiredo, A., & Russo, N. (Eds.), *Leveraging Technology for Organizational Adaptability* (pp. 59–80). IGI Global Scientific Publishing., DOI: 10.4018/979-8-3693-6045-3.ch004

Tariq, M. U. (2025). Navigating Public Administration 5.0: Embracing AI for Smarter Governance. In Wongmahesak, K., Ahmad, J., & Mustanir, A. (Eds.), *Public Governance Practices in the Age of AI* (pp. 167–186). IGI Global Scientific Publishing., DOI: 10.4018/979-8-3693-9286-7.ch008

Tariq, M. U. (2025). AI-Enhanced Project-Based Learning: Revolutionizing Commerce Education With Generative AI. In ElSayary, A. (Ed.), *Prompt Engineering and Generative AI Applications for Teaching and Learning* (pp. 125–142). IGI Global Scientific Publishing., DOI: 10.4018/979-8-3693-7332-3.ch008

Tariq, M. U. (2025). Unlocking Competitive Edge: Harnessing the Power of Collaborative Innovation. In Martínez-Falcó, J., Sánchez-García, E., & Marco-Lajara, B. (Eds.), *Open Innovation Strategies for Effective Competitive Advantage* (pp. 315–344). IGI Global Scientific Publishing., DOI: 10.4018/979-8-3693-9266-9.ch011

Tariq, M. U. (2025). Empowering Patients With AI-Ethical Digital Tools for Health Data Management and Decision. In Pesqueira, A., & de Bem Machado, A. (Eds.), *Navigating Privacy, Innovation, and Patient Empowerment Through Ethical Healthcare Technology* (pp. 197–216). IGI Global Scientific Publishing., DOI: 10.4018/979-8-3693-7630-0.ch008

Tariq, M. U. (2025). Leveraging Libraries and Information Centers for Startup Innovation and Growth. In Gupta, V., & Gupta, C. (Eds.), *Navigating Strategic Partnerships for Sustainable Startup Growth* (pp. 1–28). IGI Global Scientific Publishing., DOI: 10.4018/979-8-3693-4066-0.ch001

Tawalbeh, L. A., Muheidat, F., Tawalbeh, M., & Quwaider, M. (2020). IoT privacy and security: Challenges and solutions. *Applied Sciences (Basel, Switzerland), 10*(12), 4102. DOI: 10.3390/app10124102

Xie, T., Li, R., Zhang, X., Zhou, B., & Wang, Z. (2019, October). Research on heartbeat classification algorithm based on CART decision tree. In *2019 8th International Symposium on Next Generation Electronics (ISNE)* (pp. 1–3). IEEE. DOI: 10.1109/ISNE.2019.8896650

ADDITIONAL READINGS

Braun, G. (2014). The internet of things and the modern supply chain. C3 Solutions, 1–13.

Bzai, J., Alam, F., Dhafer, A., Bojović, M., Altowaijri, S. M., Niazi, I. K., & Mehmood, R. (2022). Machine learning-enabled Internet of Things (IoT): Data, applications, and industry perspective. *Electronics (Basel), 11*(17), 2676. DOI: 10.3390/electronics11172676

KEYTERMS AND DEFINITIONS

Internet of Things: The Internet of Things (IoT) refers to a network of physical devices, vehicles, appliances, and other objects that are embedded with sensors, software, and other technologies to collect, exchange, and process data over the internet. These "smart" devices can communicate with each other and with centralized systems without human intervention, enabling automation and more efficient operations across various industries.

Security Challenges in IoT: The Internet of Things (IoT) presents significant security challenges due to its widespread adoption, the variety of connected devices, and the interconnected nature of these systems. Since IoT devices are often deployed in critical infrastructure, healthcare, homes, and industrial settings, any security vulnerabilities can have serious consequences.

Privacy in IoT: Privacy in the Internet of Things (IoT) is a critical concern due to the large amounts of sensitive data that IoT devices collect, store, and transmit. As these devices become more pervasive, they gather information about individuals' habits, locations, health, and personal preferences, which can lead to potential privacy risks if not managed properly.

ML-Based IoT: Integrating Machine Learning (ML) with Internet of Things (IoT) brings a new dimension of intelligence and automation to IoT devices and networks. While IoT provides the infrastructure for collecting vast amounts of data, ML enables devices to analyze, learn from, and make decisions based on that data. This synergy unlocks numerous possibilities for optimizing performance, enhancing security, and creating more efficient systems.

Chapter 2
Shaping Intelligent Connectivity Using AI and IoT

Mitra Tithi Dey
https://orcid.org/0009-0002-1373-8787
Netaji Nagar Day College, India & University of Calcutta, India

Suman Patra
https://orcid.org/0009-0006-6483-7477
Netaji Nagar Day College, India & University of Calcutta, India

Sucharita Mitra
https://orcid.org/0000-0003-1144-9965
Netaji Nagar Day College, India & University of Calcutta, India

ABSTRACT

This chapter explores the transformative impact of intelligent connectivity, driven by the convergence of Artificial Intelligence (AI) and the Internet of Things (IoT). It highlights how these technologies, coupled with 5G, edge computing, and blockchain, enable adaptive, context-aware systems that enhance efficiency and innovation. AI empowers decision-making and automation through data analysis, while IoT provides real-time data streams, creating a synergistic loop for continuous optimization. Applications span smart cities, homes, healthcare, industrial IoT, and transportation, delivering improved quality of life, operational efficiency, and resource management. Key challenges include data privacy, scalability, interoperability, and ethical considerations, with solutions like encryption, standards, and inclusive policies being crucial. The chapter also examines emerging trends such as AIoT, 5G, edge computing, and AI-driven IoT platforms, which promise real-time

DOI: 10.4018/979-8-3693-8547-0.ch002

processing, autonomous systems, and scalability. This chapter also covers case studies on AI and IOT based systems.

INTRODUCTION

Intelligent connectivity is essentially a sophisticated version of radical transformation in the ways through which systems, devices, and technologies are related and operated within a digitally flourishing environment. A notion more profound than simply connecting devices, it therefore involves a conjunction of communication networking that leads to data analysis, along with artificial intelligence, enabling an adaptive and smart system. Intelligent connectivity is the backbone of emerging smart technologies, such as smart cities, intelligent transport, Industry 4.0, and IoT- all of which rely on seamless real-time communication, data sharing, and decision-making. This implies that intelligent connectivity allows systems to make context-sensitive decisions in real time, thereby augmenting their efficiency, responsiveness, and flexibility in highly dynamic environments. This change is of great importance in our times, considering how devices are multiplying rapidly, data is proliferating in the same way, and technological growth is accelerating. The increasing demand for better, scalable, and reliable solutions drives the need for intelligent connectivity, particularly in sectors such as healthcare, transportation, manufacturing, and urban infrastructure. From an economic point of view, it offers new business models and opportunities. It promotes the automation of processes, enhances operational effectiveness, and enables data-driven decision-making, which is crucial for sectors aiming to maintain competitiveness in the digital era. Additionally, it supports sustainability initiatives by streamlining resource utilization and reducing waste. It will help narrow the digital divide and facilitate the availability and accessibility of data and services for all sectors of society, including remote and underserved areas, in a developing, digitally infrastructure-oriented society.

The Convergence of AI, IoT, and Other Emerging Technologies to Create Intelligent Systems

The technology of intelligent connectivity is not based on one but rather on the convergence of several technologies in line. AI and IoT form the heart of such convergences. Some other emerging technologies help develop intelligent connectivity, including 5G networks, edge computing, cloud computing, and blockchain, which provide augmentations to the capabilities of connected systems. It is shown pictorially in Figure 1.

- **Artificial Intelligence (AI).** allows for automated governance in decision-making and problem-solving capabilities across connected systems. These systems analyze vast amounts of datasets to determine trends, build predictions, and make decisions based on information without human interference. Intelligent connectivity means that AI allows for quick analysis and interpretation of data so that systems can operate intelligently and not necessarily wait for human decisions or interventions.
- **The Internet of Things (IoT).** This will be a collective set-up of devices as well as sensors connected through the web to each other and eventually to the center systems, allowing access from physical machine data, hence important within AI systems to actually produce a kind of insight. So, in essence, they are the "eyes and ears" for cognitive systems that enable it to appreciate, measure, and operate upon the reality.

This convergence of AI and IoT would probably transform devices, systems, and networks into something entirely new in a more dramatic way because it constantly gathers data from thousands of sources, and AI uses the same to conclude by analyzing that data. Therefore, continuous learning with optimization of the feedback system helps it make better, smart decisions throughout. For instance, emerging technologies like **5G** offer ultra-low latency and high bandwidth, therefore making them critical in enabling the operation of real-time communications and AI-driven IoT applications (Siddiqi et al.., 2019). Edge computing allows the processing of data closer to the source, reducing latency and improving capabilities for making decisions in real time (Khan et al., 2019). Lastly, blockchain technology gives a secure and decentralized approach for keeping the integrity of data, hence becoming very important in an IoT ecosystem, where security considerations will always be paramount (Dai et al., 2019).

The interplay between these technologies creates "intelligent systems," which can perceive and act in autonomous ways that are learned without human supervision and adapt to changing circumstances without human intervention (Najafabadi et al., 2015). Most of these are already within many applications, such as self-driving automobiles, predictive maintenance in industrials, and real-time measurement of health metrics in medicine.

Figure 1. Interconnectivity between different technologies and their applicability to create an intelligent system

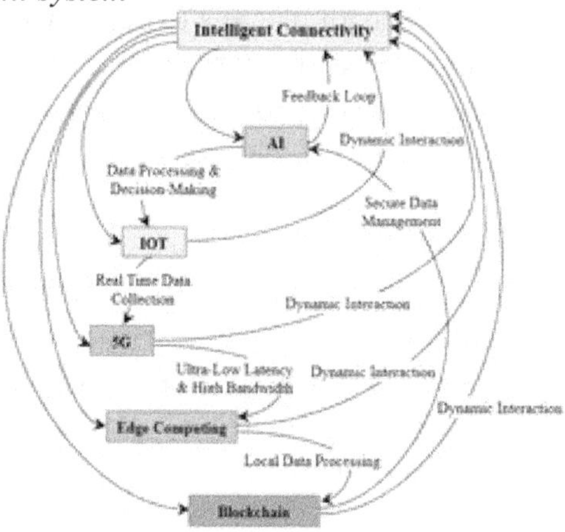

The Role of AI and IoT in Enhancing Connectivity

The relationship of AI with IoT is symbiotic, each enhances the other in important ways. Thus, IoT enables the collection of real-time data with the use of connected devices, whereas AI processes such data to derive intelligent decisions that might even optimize the operations, improve efficiency, or deliver the experiences specific to tastes and preferences. It is their dynamic interaction that has made the two a powerful enabler of intelligent connectivity.

- **AI's Contribution to IoT**: AI brings intelligence to the raw data gathered by these IoT devices. IoT generates a huge amount of data, but it is just raw and unstructured at times (Gubbi et al.., 2013). AI models- in particular, machine learning algorithms- are used for the analysis to extract actionable insights from all this data. AI contributes toward real-time interpretation of data streams, which enables immediate response in terms of triggering alerts and adjusting the system parameters or initiating predefined actions. IoT sensors, for instance, in smart buildings can monitor temperature, humidity, and occupancy. The same could even be analyzed by AI to come out with the optimization parameters, further improving the functioning of HVAC, reducing consumption, and enhancing comfort to its occupants.
- **IoT's Contribution to AI**: Data is the source for AI to learn from or base decisions on, depending on the source or learning model. IoT can be considered a source; it can be a set of environmental conditions, like temperature and

light, air quality, or operational conditions, like machine performance, traffic, or energy usage. For example, for a model, it predicts events in real-time, identifies anomalies, and sometimes even suggests action based on what has been learned. Thus, for instance, with IoT sensors attached to manufacturing plant machines, data can constantly be given about the health of machines; AI algorithms might use those data to predict failure and allow for timely scheduling of maintenance or optimizations in a production schedule (Pani et al., 2024; Tariq, 2025).

The Evolution from Basic Connectivity to Intelligent, Context-Aware Systems

This is something of a watershed change in the functions of connected environments from simple, dumb connectivity to sophisticated, context-aware systems. While traditional connectivity only gives the ability to communicate between devices and systems, intelligent connectivity adds additional complexity since it allows systems to infer context, predict needs, and respond without human intervention.

- **Basic Connectivity**: At its most basic level, connectivity permits devices to pass information or signals to each other. The first generation of wireless networks, Wi-Fi, Bluetooth, and cellular technologies, all extended the concept of fundamental connectivity, which permitted devices to connect to share information (Cheruvu et al., 2019). However, they did not understand the meaning of the information being exchanged. Devices would just broadcast information without a deep understanding of the environment in which they operated.
- **Context-Aware Systems**: Intelligent connectivity goes beyond the simple communication layer by incorporating contextual awareness (Dey & Boleng, n.d.). Contextual awareness refers to the ability of a system to understand the situation and context within which a given interaction occurs, including spatial, temporal, and environmental factors, as well as individual behavior. By incorporating AI, connected devices are endowed with the ability to assess those factors and further make judgments. For example, in a smart home, AI systems can learn about user behaviors- for example, when someone usually gets home or adjusts the thermostat, automatically changing home conditions without demanding input from the user.
- **Autonomous Decision Making**: The final development of intelligent connectivity is that of systems that are not just responsive to real-time inputs but anticipate future needs and function independently. Thus, these systems can be enabled with artificial intelligence to make possible autonomous decision-

making support to work with historical data and predictive models. In transportation, AI-driven traffic management systems can analyze, in real-time, how traffic flows and adjusts their local control over the traffic signals that could also predict traffic congestion before its occurrence, minimizing delays and improving mobility in an urban setting (Lv et al., 2014; Tariq, 2025).

Intelligent, contextual systems change industries and the way societies operate through increases in efficiency, personalization, and autonomy. Neither require manual input nor function under simple rules; in contrast, they learn iteratively and evolve to account for specific individual needs on top of environmental changes as they occur. In short, intelligent connectivity via the convergence of AI with IoT is changing how related technologies interact and function as it does today. This is what gives the cognitive capacity to process, analyze, and, importantly, extract meaningful interpretations from the immense volumes of data generated by the Internet of Things. For its part, IoT provides all the real-world data required to make these AI-based systems work. This trajectory of evolution- from connectivity to complex, context-sensitive systems- poses enormous possibilities for a vast portfolio of interconnected technologies in several different sectors, including healthcare and transportation. Such a transition is at the heart of the synergy between artificial intelligence and the Internet of Things (Tariq, 2025). This is the base upon which intelligent connectivity systems are now poised to impact future change

Understanding the Basics: AI and IoT

Artificial intelligence is the act of imitation of human-like cognitive abilities in machines that are built to be able to have thought processes, reason, learn, and even solve problems. These machines can be given the algorithms that enable them to carry out tasks that humans can perform using their intellects. AI systems can be developed to perform numerous kinds of tasks, from processing data to detecting patterns, language understanding, predictive modeling, and even making decisions without human intervention.

AI is not one technology but rather a collection of many techniques and methods, with each adding its unique capability to the overall concept. The main constituents of AI are:

1. **Machine Learning (ML).**: Machine learning is one of the variants of artificial intelligence, for which it focuses on the kind of ability of machines to find knowledge from data and therefore enhance their performance step-wise without explicit programming. One main difference between using pre-specified rules is

that algorithms machine learning looks for data in a pattern to produce related predictions or decisions.

- **Supervised Learning**: The algorithm trains when supervised learning is used for training by an input data set with known or labeled data and their correct outputs (Sen et al.., 2019). An algorithm learns to establish correct output associations with the inputs to produce output values for new, unseen values of inputs.
- **Unsupervised Learning**: In unsupervised learning, the algorithm works with unlabeled data and must find the patterns or structures that exist in the data itself (Usama et al., 2019). Some common applications of unsupervised learning include clustering, which groups similar data points, and dimensionality reduction, which simplifies the data to its most important features.
- **Reinforcement Learning**: Reinforcement learning is an agent that acts within its environment and learns from the outcomes of actions it undertakes (Barto, 2012). The agent gets rewarded or penalized in a particular way depending on what action is undertaken, and its aim is to maximize cumulative rewards over time. It is mostly used in robotics and game-playing AI.

2. **Neural Networks**: A neural network is a model for computation based on the structure and function of biological neural networks, specifically in the way information is processed (Indolia et al., 2018). It has layers of nodes; each node performs some math operation on the data passing through. Neural networks prove particularly adept with complex pattern recognition problems, especially at image recognition and natural language processing. They can be used for large dataset feature identification, so complex features can be trained by them.
3. **Deep Learning**: Deep learning is a type of machine learning that specifically deals with deep neural networks and is built on the concept of multiple layers of neurons to solve complicated problems (Sarker, 2021). The models learn through big datasets and can identify features without any human intervention. Deep learning is particularly effective in the domain of image and speech recognition, where other models of machine learning generally struggle. Popular deep learning methods include CNNs for image processing and RNNs for sequential data, such as time series analysis or language translation.

The Role of AI in Data Analysis, Decision-Making, and Automation

Modern analytics works are artificial, relying more on processing gigantic amounts of data by machines. People used to perform all data analysis work as they searched for dataset patterns and trends before finding human-driven decisions; the new development of AI has decreased all those processes significantly and therefore allowed people to make data easy to access and scalable easily (Tariq, 2025).

- **Data Analysis**: AI algorithms are much more efficient in processing large datasets than a human analyst would be. They can determine patterns, correlations, and anomalies that may otherwise remain hidden. For example, AI can scan sensor data from IoT devices and detect trends in temperature, humidity, or machine performance that may predict a problem before it happens (Mukhopadhyay et al., 2021).
- **Decision-Making**: AI makes the decision-making process easier because decisions are based on information. They rely on the processed information to indicate what can occur in the future or suggest actions to be taken. For instance, in the health industry, AI can be utilized to aid in the determination of the diagnosis of an illness from patient data and signs of symptoms or biomarkers showing certain conditions (Afzal et al., 2024). This would serve the purpose of improving corporate decision-making, such as what is the optimum inventory level or what marketing strategy.
- **Automation**: This is one of the biggest impacts AI has, namely, automation. It implies that AI can substitute human labor with repetitive processes. For instance, in manufacturing, automation systems powered by AI can run production lines and monitor equipment (Gao et al., 2024). AI automation systems can even repair and maintain equipment, thus decreasing the risk of human errors. In customer service, AI-powered chatbots can take in requests and answer them without a human being around 24/7.

This has improved the efficiency of operations, reduced costs, and provided insightful information that allows for informed strategic decision-making in many industries.

Internet of Things (IoT). Overview

IoT is a linkage system of physical objects, or "things," with sensors, software, and diverse technologies that collect data and transmit those data over the Internet and/or any other network. In such a system, the same objects are permitted to transmit data and may receive the same; as such, control or exploitation enables the solution of numerous tasks of the decision-making domain.

The key components of IoT are:

1. **Sensors**: The fundamental building blocks of IoT devices, sensors are the ones that make it possible to collect data from the physical world (Kumar & Mallick, 2018). The list of parameters that sensors can measure is very long: from temperature and humidity to motion and pressure and light. Temperature sensors monitor room conditions in a smart home; motion sensors determine whether a person is in a room.
2. **Actuators**: The components in an IoT device execute operations due to actions as instructed from actuators or through sensed information sent to the devices from various external sources (Choudhary, 2024). An actuator, for example, in a factory environment might make use of a robot arm and could perform work of component picking or assembly. On the other side, in the smart home, an actuator might control something that could be considered smart and would have on light control, heating, and on locks on doors according to some sensed data.
3. **Connectivity**: This refers to the medium through which devices or networks interact with each other or even a central system. In connecting IoT devices, a great range of communication protocols may be adopted: Wi-Fi, Bluetooth, Zigbee, LoRa, and 5G, among others. Their selection depends on variables like distance coverage, power consumption, and data transfer rate. The remote location and lower-powered devices may adopt either Zigbee or LoRa; in contrast, higher speeds would include autonomous vehicles with their very-low-latency 5G communications (Augustin et al., 2016).

THE ROLE OF IOT IN CREATING INTERCONNECTED DEVICES AND SYSTEMS

The core role of IoT is to build interconnected environments wherein devices can share information, monitor conditions, and act in real time by communicating with each other. This enables devices to exchange data, which creates an ecosystem of smart, connected systems that work in tandem to enhance efficiency, safety, and user experience.

- **Smart Homes**: IoT-connected devices, such as thermostats, lighting systems, and security cameras, form an environment for a smart home in which the owner can control and monitor his home from a smartphone or any other device. The IoT-enabled thermostat, for example, adjusts the home temperature according to the resident's schedule, while smart security cameras alert the homeowner of probable intrusions (Stopps & Touchie, 2021).

- **Smart Cities**: IoT enables the creation of smart cities, where infrastructure and services are optimized for efficiency and sustainability. IoT applications in smart cities include intelligent traffic management systems, where traffic signals adjust in real-time based on traffic flow, or smart waste management systems that monitor trash levels and optimize collection routes (Elassy et al., 2024).
- **Industry and Manufacturing (IIoT).**: Industrial settings for the IoT are key to predictive maintenance and process optimization. The sensors embedded into machinery are used to track performance so potential failures may be discovered early (Soori et al., 2023). The proactive strategy of maintenance this fosters reduces downtime and lowers repair costs. More so, IoT technology assists in the automation of industrial activities that ensure better efficiency and safety.

Synergy Between AI and IoT

While the true power of IoT is data acquisition and transmission, most of that data would lie in the dark without AI. AI adds an important layer to IoT by enabling real-time analytics, decision-making, and prediction capabilities. When combined with IoT, systems become more intelligent, responsive, and self-capable of adapting to the environment they are in.

- **Real-Time Analytics**: AI algorithms can process the sensor data in real time within IoT devices. This provides their systems with the capacity to respond promptly based on the latest developments. For example, smart production might use AI algorithms to evaluate data coming from sensors monitoring the health of machines. A strange pattern indicating wear or malfunction can trigger an immediate report to maintenance personnel (Selvarani et al., 2023). Its analytics allow decision-makers constant access to the freshest data to respond fast before things get worse.
- **Predictive Capabilities**: AI models, especially machine learning, can predict future trends or behaviors using historical data from IoT devices. For example, in the health sector, IoT devices can collect data on patients, and AI can analyze it to predict the probability of a medical condition so early intervention can be done (Rejeb et al., 2023). Similarly, in logistics, AI can use data from connected vehicles and warehouses in IoT to predict delivery times or

potential delays so supply chain management can be enhanced (Idrissi et al., 2024).

How IoT Data Fuels AI Systems to Make Intelligent Decisions

IoT devices, therefore, constitute the source of information for the AI system. The outputs of these IoT devices- sensor readouts, environmental conditions, or operational statistics- essentially power AI models to make smart, data-based decisions. This mutualism between IoT and AI makes intelligent connectivity possible.

- **Data for Learning**: IoT devices produce massive amounts of data, acting as a training ground for AI algorithms. Feeding an AI system with large amounts of real-world data can help train machine learning models to make highly accurate predictions and decisions. For example, in autonomous vehicles, camera, radar, and sensor data are used to train AI systems to recognize people on the road, other cars, and traffic signs for safe navigation.
- **Feedback Loop**: AI uses IoT data to make decisions, and this decision may or may not have an impact and influence the action of its IoT devices. For example, in any smart grid, IoT monitors the amount of energy consumed, then predictive algorithms by AI base on that to distribute appropriately. It is a constant feedback loop; the whole process is being improved whereby IoT devices get new info based on decisions taken using AI.

Table 1. How AI enhances IoT and vice versa

Aspect	Role of AI	Role of IoT	Combined Impact
Real-Time Data Analysis	AI algorithms analyze real-time data for insights and predictions.	IoT devices provide continuous data streams.	Enables real-time decision-making, predictive maintenance, and optimized processes.
Predictive Analytics	AI uses historical and real-time data to forecast future trends.	IoT devices collect and transmit data over time.	AI can predict equipment failure, health issues, or traffic patterns based on IoT data.
Automation	AI systems can autonomously control devices based on data insights.	IoT systems collect and transmit data to devices.	Automation of homes, factories, and transportation systems with real-time adjustments.

continued on following page

Table 1. Continued

Aspect	Role of AI	Role of IoT	Combined Impact
Personalization	AI tailors experiences based on data from IoT devices (e.g., personalized settings).	IoT devices collect personal data from users.	Creates personalized environments in smart homes, healthcare, and urban planning.
Efficiency & Optimization	AI processes large amounts of data to improve operational efficiency.	IoT devices provide granular data on system performance.	Enhanced operational efficiency and cost savings in industries like manufacturing, logistics, and healthcare.

In summary, AI and IoT are two of the key technologies driving the evolution of intelligent connectivity. AI is seen to analyze, predict, and automate processes to take advantage of the enormous volume of real-time data coming from IoT devices. In totality, these technologies provide systems with the capability of becoming smarter, more efficient, and responsive to changing environments, which are, in turn, the foundation of what will be intelligent, context-aware systems shaping the future. Table 1 shows the combined impact of AI and IOT.

KEY APPLICATIONS OF AI AND IOT IN INTELLIGENT CONNECTIVITY

Smart Cities

The concept of smart cities is based on the use of IoT devices and AI technologies for the optimization of resource use and improvement of quality of life, thus providing more sustainable and efficient urban environments. In the case of smart cities, interconnected devices collect data processed by AI systems to provide actionable insights and enable intelligent decision-making. Continuous monitoring of urban infrastructure leads to autonomous or real-time optimization actions, ranging from traffic management to waste disposal.

1. **Traffic Management**: One of the most persistent problems in modern cities is traffic congestion, which leads to delays, fuel waste, and increased pollution. AI and IoT are crucial for optimizing traffic flow, reducing congestion, and enhancing road safety. IoT-enabled sensors are placed along roads, traffic lights, and intersections to monitor traffic conditions in real time. These sensors collect data on vehicle flow, traffic density, and congestion levels. Artificial intelligence systems analyze this information to determine modifications to traffic signals in real time, redirect vehicles, or deliver instantaneous notifications to motorists.

Consequently, this practice minimizes delays at junctions and facilitates a more seamless movement of traffic throughout the urban environment.

Besides real-time traffic management, AI and IoT systems predict the patterns of traffic through records of history, weather, and social events (Duraipandi et al., n.d.). This is an area where cities may change and deploy resources based on the areas that need attention before trouble arises. For example, traffic lights can be regulated based on events that are occurring in specific locations, or additional public transportation can be provided to ease congestion. In the long term, AI-based traffic management systems can lead to reduced emissions, lessened fuel consumption, and improved road safety.

2. **Smart Lighting**: Another area of significant infrastructure is in the lighting sector. Most ordinary streetlights use fixed or prescheduled timers and draw current all day and night when nobody is there to watch. Smart lighting, using the power of IoT and AI, can be an even more energy-efficient endeavor: adjusting the light based on real-time ambient illumination and traffic/pedestrian traffic (Chiradeja & Yoomak, 2023). The IoT sensors inside streetlights sense movement and send information to the AI systems so that the appropriate brightening and dimming are performed when needed. Further, this system identifies when lights fail and informs maintenance personnel so the necessary rectifications are completed promptly.

Intelligent lighting systems play a critical role in making energy efficiency and sustainability achievable by reducing the unnecessary usage of power. For instance, in a residential area with minimal pedestrian movement at night, the light levels can be reduced to save energy while ensuring safety. Furthermore, smart lighting systems can be integrated with other systems, such as traffic control mechanisms, to make the overall infrastructure of a city more efficient.

3. **Waste Management**: There is another such area where AI and IoT will make waste management much more efficient in cities. IoT sensors are mounted in trash bins and collection points that report the fill levels in these bins. Whenever the fill levels in the bins reach a specified threshold, it alerts the trash collection services so that it can plan the pick-ups only when needed (Ahmed et al., 2024). The number of trucks on the roads decreases, hence reducing fuel usage. The use of AI will further strengthen the system in predicting waste generation patterns and optimizing collection routes, ultimately reducing the operational costs.

Further, AI systems can analyze waste composition data to help towns improve their recycling programs better with more resources being distributed to focused sectors like electronic and paper wastes, as well as plastics. Using these practices will enable cities to significantly reduce their carbon imprint, increase recycling percentages, and simplify mechanisms for waste management. These actions together help in sustaining the built environment.

Enhancing Citizen Services and Improving Quality of Life Through Intelligent Systems

Smart cities do more than just make efficient infrastructure; they upgrade the lives of citizens with new services and improvements in the existing ones. Governments can provide more intelligent and responsive services using AI and IoT.

1. **Public Safety and Security**: Public safety and security are much improved through the usage of video surveillance systems, which are based on artificial intelligence and IoT technologies. It takes the real-time process of data collated by the public cameras, sensors, and myriad other devices connected to make alerts in case unusual behaviors or events that may befall them, such as a bag left in an open space or overnight convergence of persons in a venue, then concerned ones can take steps in time (Fontes et al., 2022). The same areas will also be able to forecast the crime trends using AI-driven predictive analytics, thus helping in proper resource allocation by the concerned law enforcement agencies.
2. **Environmental Monitoring**: IoT sensors are diffused in the cities that monitor the air quality, temperature, humidity, noise pollution, etc. All this data is passed through AI algorithms to get real-time reports about environmental conditions in a place. For example, spikes in pollution levels or extreme climatic conditions are alerted to the citizens and officials concerned with that city (Olawade et al., 2024). Such awareness enables citizens to decide whether they should stay indoors during high-pollution days. In return, governing institutions can come up with efficient ways of addressing environmental concerns.
3. **Urban Planning**: With IoT and AI, cities can gather data regarding their traffic pattern, movement of pedestrians, energy consumption, and other such activities for better planning (Ullah et al., 2023). Urban planners can thus design efficient, sustainable, and informed decision-making strategies for developing the infrastructure of a city or allocating lands and resources based on needs. For example, high traffic congestion zones can be identified, roads redesigned or public transport measures taken to curb congestion.

Different applications of AI and IOT in urban infrastructure are shown in Table 2.

Table 2. AI and IoT applications in urban infrastructure

Application Area	IoT Technology Used	AI Role	Benefits
Traffic Management	Traffic sensors, cameras, GPS	Predictive traffic flow, dynamic signal adjustments	Reduced congestion, optimized traffic flow
Smart Lighting	IoT-enabled street lights, motion sensors	Adaptive lighting control, energy optimization	Energy savings, improved safety
Waste Management	Smart bins, waste level sensors	Predictive analytics, route optimization	Reduced waste collection costs, better recycling
Environmental Monitoring	Air quality sensors, weather stations	Data analysis for pollution prediction	Real-time environmental alerts, better air quality control

Smart Homes

Smart homes leverage the potential of artificial intelligence combined with the Internet of Things to make homes more comfortable, efficient, and safe concerning life at home. Modern systems in household appliances and equipment allow automating everyday chores, saving energy consumption, and boosting home security.

1. **Energy Management**: This is one of the most widely used applications between AI and IoT. IOT devices, such as Smart thermostats, lighting controls, and appliances, collect data on energy usage, which these AI systems analyze to manage consumption. For example, a smart thermostat learns the preferences of the household for temperatures over time and adjusts them according to periods of occupancy, outdoor weather conditions, etc. This method saves on energy and decreases utility costs while ensuring an acceptable degree of comfort.

The smart control lighting systems really hold a key place in the energy management plans. Another advanced lighting solution includes making necessary adjustments in brightness as and when the situations exist or people are there within it. Artificial intelligence further allows it to even recognize times and places with high power consumption and act correspondingly to reduce overall usage around the world. The smart plugs and IoT-enabled devices will give knowledge to its users about which gadgets utilize more energy; hence, their users can see which one needs improvement and implement a change accordingly (Albraheem et al., 2023).

2. **Security**: One of the significant concerns for homeowners is security, and smart homes help minimize risks and enhance protection by offering solutions. Devices under IoT include smart locks, cameras, motion sensors, and doorbell cameras to provide real-time surveillance and monitoring. AI algorithms can detect suspicious activity in video feeds and send instant alerts to either the homeowner or the police department.

AI-based facial recognition and object detection can even identify residents, guests, and intruders and can improve the accuracy of security, further reducing false alarms. (Kuppuswamy et al., 2023). Another aspect is how AI predictive analytics can contribute towards forecasting security breaches by analyzing the patterns emerging from past incidents in that neighborhood so that homeowners would be better prepared to counter such intrusions.

3. **Personalized Environments**: Smart homes can set up customized settings based on unique individual preferences. AI systems learn the habits and inclinations of home dwellers and automatically adjust the environment to their needs. For example, AI can control lighting, climate, and even pick favorite music or media based on the time of day, weather conditions, or what the residents are doing.

IoT devices, such as voice assistants, can create a seamless interface about controlling lighting, temperature, and entertainment at home (Torad et al., 2022). These systems only grow increasingly intuitive and effective concerning learning their occupants' routines, leading to the creation of a personalized experience for living in such space.

Case Studies of Smart Home Ecosystems

Many companies and projects implemented artificial intelligence and the Internet of Things in smart homes successfully, offering practical applications to users, as shown in Table 3:

1. **Google Nest**: It is a system from Google that enables IoT and AI to house thermostats, cameras, smoke detectors, and doorbell cameras. For example, a Nest thermostat learns people's preferences over time, then controls the home's temperature to lower energy consumption yet maintain comfort. In contrast, AI-based Nest cameras and doorbell cameras boost security because they allow the homeowner to know about unusual occurrences.

2. **Amazon Alexa**: The Amazon Alexa is the most widely used voice-activated smart home assistant from Amazon's Alexa ecosystem. It is integrated with a vast range of IoT devices, such as smart lights, thermostats, security cameras, and much more. Alexa uses AI to understand natural language commands, adjust home settings, and give responses to queries in real time. With time, Alexa learns the preferences of the user and makes recommendations, accordingly, making the home more responsive and intuitive.

Table 3. AI and IoT applications in smart homes

Application Area	IoT Devices Used	AI Role	Benefits
Energy Management	Smart thermostats, smart plugs, lighting	Optimizing energy consumption based on usage patterns	Reduced energy bills, improved efficiency
Home Security	Smart cameras, motion detectors, locks	Real-time threat detection, facial recognition	Enhanced security, reduced false alarms
Personalized Environments	Smart speakers, lighting systems, sensors	Customizing home settings based on preferences	Increased comfort, better home ambiance

Industrial IoT (IIoT).

Industrial IoT, also known as IIoT, refers to the utilization of IoT technologies in the industrial world to improve operations and productivity and reduce costs. With AI integration, IoT applications are achieving tremendous improvements in areas like predictive maintenance, process optimization, and safety monitoring, as shown in Table 4.

1. **Predictive Maintenance**: In the more conventional approach to maintenance, scheduling is either based upon rigid schedules or reactive techniques, which is too routine because equipment is serviced either in an over-maintenance regimen or after it has failed. Predictive maintenance operates differently, relying on real-time IoT sensor data embedded directly within machines and equipment to always report on their health. AI analyzes such data to detect early signs of deterioration, such as vibrations, changes in temperature, or diminished performance.

Predictive maintenance systems based on artificial intelligence predict the probability of potential failure in machinery so that an organization can schedule the need for repairs only based on necessity (Hosseinzadeh et al., 2023). This further leads to decreasing downtime, extending the equipment's life, and saving on maintenance costs. The same has been used very effectively in manufacturing, oil and gas, and the energy sector, where delay means massive losses.

2. **Process Optimization**: IoT sensors and AI-based technologies optimize industrial process variables by monitoring real parameters such as temperature, pressure, flow rates, and even material quality. AI algorithm scans these in real-time to detect inefficiency or mismatch in the overall process. For instance, an AI in a factory plant may detect bottlenecks or operational inefficiencies and may propose changes in production lines that can enhance throughput levels and minimize waste (Subramaniyan et al., 2021).

This will monitor the parameters of the IIoT system and then bring them to peak levels that increase productivity while bringing down costs. AI may use supply chain optimization for smooth and cost-effective operation, along with correct inventory management and demand predictions.

3. **Safety Monitoring**: The industrial environment calls for the safety of workers in industries such as mining, construction, and manufacturing. IoT devices such as wearables, cameras, and environmental sensors can monitor many safety-related parameters, which may include temperature, gas levels, and worker movement (Dian et al.., 2020). AI algorithms can then process the data to conclude dangerous conditions in real time and alert the workers and the management to take necessary steps.

The system can monitor employee fatigue and detect dangerous behaviors, thus alerting people promptly to prevent accidents or injuries. The use of artificial intelligence and the Internet of Things in safety oversight is a basic approach for industries to ensure improvement in workplace safety, reduce incidents, and meet safety regulations.

TRANSFORMING MANUFACTURING AND SUPPLY CHAIN OPERATIONS

It also includes AI and IoT with smarter factories and logistics networks. The ability to track goods and materials in a supply chain in real time by applying IIoT results in better management of the inventory with shorter lead times. A business's operation may be improved toward responding more dynamically toward changes in the market if equipped with AI usage in the elements of demand forecasting, inventory management, and optimization for logistics.

Table 4. Key IIoT applications

Application Area	IoT Devices Used	AI Role	Benefits
Predictive Maintenance	Vibration sensors, temperature sensors, RFID tags	Detecting faults before they occur, maintenance scheduling	Reduced downtime, extended equipment lifespan
Process Optimization	IoT sensors in manufacturing lines	Analyzing real-time data for efficiency improvement	Increased production, reduced waste
Safety Monitoring	Wearable devices, environmental sensors	Real-time alerts for unsafe conditions	Enhanced worker safety, reduced accidents
Supply Chain Optimization	GPS, RFID, IoT-enabled inventory systems	Predictive analytics for stock levels and demand forecasting	Improved inventory management, cost reduction

HEALTHCARE

AI and IoT in Telemedicine, Patient Monitoring, and Personalized Healthcare

The health sector is fundamentally transformed by the advent of technological advancements, particularly those associated with artificial intelligence and the Internet of Things. Such innovative medical practices facilitate a greater emphasis on patient-centered care and promote data-driven methodologies in treatment strategies. Applications of AI and IOT in Healthcare are shown in Table 5.

1. **Telemedicine**: This is one of the services that enable the consultancy of a patient by any health care provider with the least visits made to the individual physically. AI and IoT play an essential role in the provision of telemedicine services. The IoT devices, including the health monitoring through wearable apparatus and diagnostic devices at home, collect his/her health data continuously, and such include heart rate, blood pressure, and glucose level (Haghi et al., 2017). This information can, therefore, be processed by some AI algorithms for the providers of health care, hence making good decisions about the care.

Artificial intelligence-driven chatbots and virtual assistants are of great support to the telemedicine process through their prompt response to patient queries, appointment scheduling, and health advice based on patient medical history.

2. **Patient Monitoring**: Real-time monitoring of a patient by IoT-enabled devices, such as fitness trackers, ECG monitors, and glucose meters, even when a healthcare professional is not nearby. These devices transmit the continuous data of the patient's vital signs, and AI analyzes the data, detecting early signs of medical conditions or deteriorating health.

For example, in chronic disease patients, such as those with diabetes or cardiovascular disease, monitoring may be able to identify abnormalities before they progress into serious complications. Artificial intelligence algorithms can alert both the patients and healthcare providers about abnormal readings, thus creating a window for timely intervention that may prevent adverse outcomes (Alowais et al., 2023).

3. **Personalized Healthcare**: The most promising aspect of AI and IoT applications in healthcare is personalized medicine. Combining data from IoTs, such as from wearables and genetic tests, with the help of AI will assist a healthcare provider in tailoring treatments based on every unique patient's respective health profile (Zovko et al., 2023). Thus, each patient is given the most efficient and effective treatment for his or her health condition with fewer side effects and maximum positive effects.

For instance, AI can scrutinize the genetic data of a patient and predict which patient would be more receptive to a specific type of drug, thereby enabling very precise, individualized prescriptions of drugs. AI can also propose lifestyle modifications by taking real-time information from IoT devices. These may include alterations to an exercise or diet program to mitigate specific medical conditions.

Improving Healthcare Outcomes through Connected Medical Devices and AI-Driven Analytics

This can be achieved through the integration of interconnected medical devices with artificial intelligence- driven analytics, which can revolutionize healthcare outcomes by providing superior diagnostic instruments, customized treatment alternatives, and improved patient surveillance. Healthcare practitioners can identify trends and insights that may otherwise be missed by using extensive data sets produced by Internet of Things devices and analyzed by artificial intelligence.

Table 5. AI and IoT applications in healthcare

Application Area	IoT Devices Used	AI Role	Benefits
Telemedicine	Wearable health monitors, smart stethoscopes	Remote diagnosis, virtual consultations	Improved access to healthcare, reduced hospital visits
Patient Monitoring	ECG monitors, glucose monitors, wearable trackers	Continuous health monitoring, early detection of anomalies	Timely interventions, reduced hospital readmissions
Personalized Healthcare	Genetic testing kits, smart wearables	AI-driven treatment customization based on data	More effective treatments, fewer side effects

TRANSPORTATION AND LOGISTICS

AI and IoT are shaping the transportation and logistics space by improving traffic management, streamlining vehicle fleet operations, and enabling completely autonomous transport systems. These technological advances streamline transportation, curbing the emission of harmful greenhouse gases. They also make traveling safe, convenient, and friendly for travelers. Applications of AI and IOT in transportation and logistics are shown in Table 6.

1. **Autonomous Vehicles**: Autonomous vehicles, from Self-driving cars to Trucks, involve the use of IoT and artificial intelligence to make real-time decisions regarding traveling (Din et al., 2024). IoT sensors, comprising the cameras, radar, lidar, and GPS, allow instant data regarding the environment. AI processes this data by understanding obstacles, pedestrians, vehicles, and road signs. Then, use the data to come back with driving decisions to reach or travel safely and efficiently.

With the help of AI-powered autonomous vehicles, human error will be minimized, and traffic safety will improve along with the optimal routing for travel. In logistics, self-driving trucks are being tested for long-haul transport in order to save costs and optimize supply chains.

2. **Traffic Optimization**: AI and IoT are also used to optimize the traffic flow and reduce congestion in urban areas. ITS makes use of the IoT sensors that monitor the traffic situation and then changes the traffic lights, signs, and signals accordingly. With AI, the data helps in predicting the traffic and optimizes the flows that help in reducing the congestion and minimizing the time to travel

(Sayed et al., 2023). This technology can be integrated into public transport systems to allow passengers to have real-time updates and optimized bus and train schedules.

Except for real-time traffic management, the AI algorithms may use past historical data to analyze future traffic and advise alterations in the infrastructure of the roads by creating new lanes or roads that would satisfy the growing demands of traffic.

3. **Fleet Management**: In the logistics sector, IoT devices and AI are used to optimize fleet management. IoT sensors placed on vehicles provide data on location, fuel consumption, tire pressure, and driver behavior (Pourrahmani et al., 2022). This data is analyzed by AI systems to identify inefficiencies, monitor driver performance, and predict maintenance needs.

AI-powered fleet management systems can also reduce the consumption of fuel, travel time, and operational costs from real-time optimization in delivery routes. With AI, operated fleets will help logistics companies execute timely deliveries and also minimize carbon footprint.

Enhancing Logistics and Supply Chain Efficiency with AI and IoT

Another domain that AI and IoT revolutionize is logistics and the supply chain. Real-time tracking of goods, inventory, and shipments is now enabled with IoT devices, and by employing AI algorithms, companies are better able to predict demand and optimize inventory management (Idrissi et al., 2024b). Furthermore, these technologies also provide more visibility into the movement of goods and materials within a supply chain, enhancing efficiency in supply chains, minimizing waste, and reducing delays.

AI-driven predictive analytics help companies predict demand so that they can optimize their stock levels and minimize excess inventory. This makes for more efficient supply chains, reduces costs, and provides customer satisfaction through the assurance of products being available at the right time.

Table 6. AI and IoT applications in transportation and logistics

Application Area	IoT Devices Used	AI Role	Benefits
Autonomous Vehicles	Cameras, LiDAR, GPS, radar	Vehicle navigation, decision-making	Increased safety, reduced accidents
Traffic Optimization	Smart traffic lights, GPS	Predictive traffic management, real-time adjustments	Reduced congestion, improved travel time
Fleet Management	GPS trackers, vehicle sensors	Route optimization, performance monitoring	Cost reduction, improved fleet efficiency
Supply Chain Optimization	RFID tags, IoT-enabled inventory systems	Demand forecasting, supply chain optimization	Reduced delays, better resource allocation

In summary, AI and IoT have been revolutionizing some of the most important industries, including smart cities, healthcare, industrial processes, transportation, and logistics. From traffic management, personalized health care, and self-driving cars to optimized fleets, there are many applications of the same technology that would transform efficiency, safety, and sustainability of critical systems, hence bettering the quality of life for citizens and businesses.

Challenges in Shaping Intelligent Connectivity

The integration of Artificial Intelligence and the Internet of Things forms the intelligent connectivity that is transformative in improving lifestyles and revolutionizing industries. Still, its full realization depends on overcoming a few critical challenges: data security, scalability, interoperability, and ethical considerations. These challenges are pivotal in shaping a sustainable future for interconnected systems.

Data Privacy and Security

A core concern in the AI-IoT ecosystem is data privacy and security. Such systems are inherently about the massive collection, processing, and dissemination of sensitive data and, hence, are exposed to breaches and unauthorized access. This protection of the data becomes even more complex in a highly interconnected environment. Most AI models need large datasets to learn and make decisions, while IoT devices like smart home systems and wearable technologies gather real-time data about the habits, health, and locations of users. If such data is compromised, it could result in identity theft, financial fraud, or personal harm to the individual involved (Alaba et al., 2017). Additionally, many IoT devices have limited computational resources, making them easy targets for cyberattacks. Some of the possible threats, such as Distributed Denial of Service (DDoS). attacks and ransomware, have already proven the devastating impacts of these vulnerabilities. For example, the Mirai botnet attack in 2016 utilized open IoT devices to launch large-scale DDoS attacks, causing internet outages across the globe (Stergiou et al., 2018). To mitigate these risks, a range of strategies has been implemented. End-to-end encryption safeguards communication channels between devices, while multi-factor authentication (MFA). adds an extra layer of security for system access. Regular firmware updates address known vulnerabilities, ensuring device resilience against emerging threats. Regulatory frameworks, such as the General Data Protection Regulation (GDPR). and the California Consumer Privacy Act (CCPA)., provide a legal impetus for organizations to prioritize data privacy (Voigt & Bussche, 2017). These are the major challenges that have to be faced in establishing a secure and trustworthy AI-IoT ecosystem, realizing the transformational potential of intelligent connectivity (Tariq, 2025).

Scalability and Integration

It is very challenging to Scale AI and IoT systems to accommodate extensive deployments. A smart city, for example, may involve millions of interconnected sensors for monitoring traffic, energy usage, and public safety. Such systems produce enormous amounts of data that require robust processing and storage infrastructures. Cloud computing and edge computing have appeared as solutions. Cloud computing provides centralized resources to manage data, but long-time inactivity can be an issue for time-sensitive applications. Edge computing brings processing power closer to the source of data, reducing inactivity. However, maintaining consistency across these architectures is also a challenge (Ratasich et al., 2019). Integration with legacy systems is another concern. Many industries still rely on outdated technology, which may not easily connect with new intelligent systems. Renovating these systems is not only expensive but also time-consuming. Middleware solutions and APIs (Application Programming Interfaces). help to connect these gaps. It also allows legacy systems to communicate with modern IoT networks. Despite this, ensuring seamless functionality across diverse platforms remains a difficult task (Borgia, 2014).

Interoperability

Interoperability ensures that various IoT devices and AI systems can seamlessly communicate and share data. This is much required for intelligent connectivity, where heterogeneous systems often need to collaborate with each other. For example, in healthcare, IoT sensors in patient monitoring devices must share data with hospital management systems and AI tools for diagnostics. Therefore, synchronization between all these systems is essential for uninterrupted service. However, a major challenge is the lack of common standards and protocols in those systems. Different

IoT device manufacturers often use patented technologies which are exclusively used by the company itself creating silos that hamper interoperability. Without interoperability, IoT systems become fragmented, limiting their scalability and hindering the development of innovative applications and services. To address the interoperability challenge in IoT, several standards and frameworks have been developed. These initiatives aim to establish common protocols, data formats, and communication standards, enabling interoperability between devices from different manufacturers and across various IoT platforms. That is where Standardized communication protocols are being adopted to address the issue (Siva Daniel et al. 2021). For example, OPC UA (Open Platform Communications Unified Architecture)., a data exchange standard for machine-to-machine or PC-to-machine communication, becomes necessary. On the other hand, MQTT (Message Queuing Telemetry Transport)., which is a lightweight open messaging protocol, offers a resource-constrained network to distribute telemetry information in poor-network environments. Industry alliances, such as the Open Connectivity Foundation (OCF). and the Industrial Internet Consortium (IIC)., are working towards establishing guidelines for interoperability. These initiatives aim to ensure that devices, regardless of their origin, can exchange information effectively, paving the way for truly intelligent connectivity (Ray, 2018).

Ethical and Social Implications

The widespread adoption of AI and IoT in different sectors raises considerable ethical and social questions that should be taken into consideration. Ethical Considerations: In most cases, AI models are decision-making and hence often face criticism due to prejudice and lack of transparency. For example, if biased algorithms are used in recruitment processes or in credit approval systems, it is very possible that the outcomes will be unfair. So, transparency is essential for such cases. Transparent AI models, where the reasoning behind decisions is clear, are essential to address these issues (Jobin et al., 2019). Successful implementation of intelligent connectivity in various sectors can lead to job displacement as automation replaces human roles in such industries as manufacturing and logistics. That raises concerns about unemployment and the need for frequent training and the skilled upliftment of workers. Another challenge will be the digital gap between rural and urban areas. While the urban areas might enjoy the most updated AI-IoT systems, the rural and underprivileged communities will be left behind, and the inequalities will be accentuated. Inclusive growth requires ensuring affordable access to these technologies. Policymakers will need to address this divide through subsidized technologies and digital literacy programs (Bessen, 2019). Balancing innovation with ethical and social responsibilities will determine the success of intelligent connectivity in the long term.

FUTURE TRENDS IN AI AND IOT FOR INTELLIGENT CONNECTIVITY

AIoT (Artificial Intelligence of Things)

Artificial Intelligence of Things (AIoT). depicts the intersection of Artificial Intelligence (AI). and the Internet of Things (IoT). to create a more intelligent, autonomous, and efficient ecosystem. AIoT combines the sensing and communication capabilities of IoT with AI's data processing, learning, and decision-making abilities. This integration enables enhanced decision-making, automation, and predictive analytics, unlocking new possibilities across industries.

AIoT

The emerging concept of AIoT means combining AI and IoT for enhanced decision-making and automation.

Key Features of AIoT

- Data-Driven Intelligence - AIoT utilizes real-time and historical data for informed decision-making, which improves operational efficiency and enables proactive responses (Huang et al., 2025).
- Edge AI Processing - With AI models deployed at the edge, AIoT reduces latency, enhances privacy, and minimizes data transfer requirements (Sibanda et. al., 2023).
- Autonomous Operations - AI algorithms enable IoT devices to operate autonomously, reducing human intervention and enhancing reliability (Alahi et. al., 2023).
- Scalability and Adaptability - AIoT systems are designed to scale with evolving data requirements and adapt to new use cases (Forkan et. al., 2024).

Applications for AIoT

- Smart Cities - AIoT enables intelligent energy optimization, traffic management, waste management, public safety enhancements, etc (Omrany et al., 2024).
- Industrial Automation - Supply Chain Management, Process optimization, Predictive maintenance and benefit from AIoT technologies (Awaisi et al., 2024).
- Healthcare - AIoT improves remote patient monitoring, diagnostics, and personalized treatment recommendations. (Ibrahim et. al., 2022).

- Agriculture - Precision farming, soil monitoring, and automated irrigation systems leverage AIoT for efficiency and sustainability (Langa et. al., 2024).
- Retail - AIoT powers inventory management, personalized customer experiences, and cashier-less stores (Shekhawat et. al., 2023).

5G and Beyond

5G and Beyond represent the next generation of connectivity, providing ultra-fast, low-latency, and highly reliable networks that empower intelligent systems. The advanced capabilities of 5G, such as ultra-reliable low-latency communication (URLLC)., massive machine-type communication (MMTC)., enhanced mobile broadband (eMBB)., etc, are pivotal in enabling seamless integration of AI and IoT. The addition of terahertz communication, AI-native networking, and quantum security in 6G may transform AIoT ecosystems in terms of automation, scalability, and real-time decision-making (Silva et. al., 2020)., (Kim et. al., 2024)., (Wang et. al., 2020)., (Chatterjee et. al., 2022).

Edge Computing

Edge Computing is a transformative paradigm that shifts data processing and computation nearer to the source of data gathering, like sensors, IoT devices, smart gateways, etc. Traditional cloud computing relies on centralized data centers, but edge computing distributes processing tasks across local nodes, enabling faster response times and compromising reliance on high-bandwidth connections. It supports real-time analytics, decision-making, and automation while minimizing latency and optimizing bandwidth usage. This approach is particularly beneficial for latency-sensitive applications like autonomous vehicles, industrial robotics, health-care monitoring, and smart grids. In these applications, even a very little delay can impact performance. Additionally, edge computing boosts data security and privacy, limiting data transmission to centralized servers and thereby addressing compliance concerns. It plays a main role in IoT systems by enabling the seamless integration of AI models for predictive analytics, anomaly detection, and autonomous operations at the edge (Raj et al., 2021)., (Oh et. al., 2022)., (Sui et. al., 2023)., (Kuo et. al., 2023)., (Hua et. al., 2023).

AI-Driven IoT Platforms

AI-driven IoT Platforms represent the next stage in IoT evolution, integrating Artificial Intelligence to enhance decision-making, automation, and adaptability. These platforms incorporate machine learning algorithms, neural networks, and advanced analytics to process huge amounts of real-time data, incorporating predictive maintenance and anomaly detection and optimizing operations. The integration of AI transforms IoT systems into intelligent, self-learning networks capable of making autonomous decisions without human intervention. Such platforms continuously learn and improve from data patterns, allowing for smarter responses to dynamic environments. In the future, AI-driven IoT platforms are expected to support fully autonomous ecosystems, where interconnected devices not only communicate but also collaborate intelligently. Applications span across smart cities, healthcare, agriculture, and industrial automation, unlocking new levels of efficiency, scalability, and innovation (Salama et. al., 2022)., (Talukder et. al., 2021)., (Panduman et. al., 2024).

CASE STUDIES

Case Study 1: Smart City Implementation in Barcelona, Spain (Bolici et al., 2016)

The goals were to transform Barcelona into a citizen-centric, sustainable, and technologically advanced city by integrating smart technologies across various urban domains like transportation, energy management, environmental monitoring, and public safety and to improve quality of life and optimize resource utilization.

Key Technologies Used

Internet of Things (IoT).: Sensors deployed all over the city collect real-time data on traffic situations, water usage, noise levels, air quality, etc.

Artificial Intelligence (AI).: Algorithms for predictive modeling, data analysis, and decision-making to optimize traffic light timings, energy consumption, waste management, etc.

Cloud Computing: A centralized platform for storing data, processing, and accessing various city departments.

Mobile Applications: Apps for citizens for real-time information on public transportation, parking availability, and environmental conditions.

Key Outcomes

The key outcomes of Barcelona's smart city strategy through the Social Innovation for Communities project can be discussed as follows (Ferrer, 2017).:

- Initiatives aimed at reducing environmental impact, such as smart lighting, e-vehicle mobility solutions, and efficient residual energy management through heating and cooling networks.

- Promotion of community-driven projects and technologies that address social challenges and improve the quality of life for residents.
- Development of eco-friendly transportation options and infrastructure supporting electric vehicles for cleaner and more efficient urban mobility.
- Implementation of networks that reuse residual energy, reducing waste and contributing to a more sustainable energy system.
- Active involvement of communities in shaping smart solutions for addressing real societal needs.

Role of AI and IoT in Achieving Intelligent Connectivity

In Barcelona, AI and IoT play a crucial role in achieving intelligent connectivity across urban infrastructure by enabling real-time data collection from sensors embedded in various city elements like streetlights, waste bins, and parking spaces, etc. Those data are analyzed by AI algorithms to optimize operations, improve efficiency, and enhance citizen experience across areas like energy consumption, traffic management, public safety, etc, making Barcelona a leading example of a smart city.

Data Collection and Analysis

IoT sensors gather continuous data from across the city, which is then processed by AI algorithms to generate insights and actionable information for city management.

Predictive Modeling

AI algorithms can predict future trends like traffic patterns or energy demand, which helps in better resource allocation.

Real-time Optimization

Using AI, dynamic adjustments to city systems like traffic lights, etc, based on live data from IoT sensors can take place.

Citizen Engagement

Mobile apps utilizing IoT data provide citizens with personalized information and enable them to participate actively in the smart city ecosystem.

Case Study 2: Harley Davidson: IoT in Manufacturing (Ivan Muts, 2023)

With the installation of sensors or other automation devices, Harley-Davidson made a few fully IoT-enabled plants. The company has significantly transformed its manufacturing processes by leveraging AI and IoT through the implementation of predictive maintenance systems in their York plant, which resulted in a dramatic reduction in production time from 21 days to just 6 hours per motorcycle. A significant decrease in operational costs and improved production efficiency were achieved. This showcased the power of connected devices and data analysis in optimizing manufacturing operations within the motorcycle industry.

Key points about Harley-Davidson's AI and IoT success story

Predictive Maintenance

Harley-Davidson uses AI and IoT for predictive maintenance, where sensors on machines collect real-time data on equipment health to detect faults and plan repairs to minimize downtime.

Production Optimization

By evaluating data from linked equipment, Harley-Davidson can optimize production schedules, detect bottlenecks, and alter operations in real time, speeding up production and increasing throughput.

Impact on Production Time

One of the most notable achievements is the reduction of motorcycle production time from 21 days to 6 hours at their York plant, which significantly enhanced delivery times and customer satisfaction.

Cost Savings

The implementation of AI and IoT has resulted in substantial cost savings by reducing unplanned downtime, optimizing resource utilization, and minimizing waste.

Lessons Learned From Harley-Davidson's Experience

The success of AI and IoT relies heavily on comprehensive data collection from various sources. A robust system is required to integrate and analyze those data efficiently.

Change Management

Implementing new technology requires careful change management strategies to train employees and address potential resistance to new workflows.

Continuous Improvement

Harley-Davidson's approach emphasizes ongoing monitoring and refinement of its AI and IoT systems to continually identify areas for optimization.

Collaboration

Effective collaboration between engineers, IT teams, and production personnel is crucial to ensure the successful integration and application of AI and IoT solutions.

Case Study 3: AI and IoT in Healthcare at Cleveland Clinic, Mayo Clinic, Johns Hopkins Hospital

Cleveland Clinic (Business Wire, 2022)

A well-known healthcare institution often cited for successful AI and IoT applications is the Cleveland Clinic.

Key points about the use of AI and IoT

Personalized Healthcare Plans

They partnered with IBM to leverage AI to analyze vast patient data for treatment plans based on individual needs.

Predictive Analytics

The clinic utilizes AI to identify high-risk patients in critical care settings, which enables proactive interventions.

Operational Efficiency

AI is also used to optimize workflows within the hospital using streamlined processes like patient scheduling and resource allocation.

Other notable healthcare institutions with prominent AI and IoT implementations include:

Mayo Clinic: Mayo Clinic is known for extensive research and development in AI-powered diagnostics and treatment planning across various specialties (Mayo Clinic, 2025).

Johns Hopkins Hospital: Successfully implemented AI solutions to improve patient flow and reduce waiting times (Johns Hopkins Medicine, 2020).

REAL-WORLD APPLICATION OF INTELLIGENT CONNECTIVITY IN HEALTHCARE

Intelligent connectivity, powered by AI, IoT, and 5G, is transforming healthcare by enabling real-time monitoring, predictive analytics, and seamless communication across devices. Remote patient monitoring systems track vital signs, alerting clinicians to potential issues, thereby improving early diagnosis and preventive care. Smart hospitals leverage IoT-enabled devices for automated workflows, enhancing operational efficiency and reducing errors. AI-driven analytics optimize treatment plans, contributing to personalized care and better health outcomes. These technologies not only streamline resource management but also support telemedicine, making healthcare more accessible and cost-effective globally. (The Sun, 2023).

CONCLUSION

This chapter has presented the powerful combination of Artificial Intelligence (AI). and the Internet of Things (IoT). that shape intelligent connectivity. They work together to make other systems in different fields smarter and more efficient. In smart cities, the combination of AI and IoT will improve traffic management, energy use, and waste handling in order to make urban areas more livable. They create customized environments at home, making life more convenient and secure. Industries are being transformed by predictive maintenance and optimized supply chains. Better patient monitoring and telemedicine have also helped improve healthcare. Transportation and logistics have been made smarter with autonomous vehicles and real-time tracking. Challenges remain. Data privacy and security are constant concerns. Scalability and integration demand robust solutions for large-scale deployments. Interoperability between diverse systems and devices is essential but difficult. Ethical and social implications, like job displacement and accessibility, also require attention.

The Road Ahead

The future of intelligent connectivity should have an immense potential. The convergence of AI and IoT will grow stronger with emerging technologies like AI IoT (Artificial Intelligence of Things)., where these systems will act autonomously, making real-time decisions. The role of 5G and beyond will provide faster, more reliable, and efficient connections; further, it helps solve complex applications. Also, edge computing will make systems more responsive by processing data closer to its source. Research and development (R&D). should focus on overcoming the existing challenges, such as improving security and ensuring ethical usage. It is also vital to create an inclusive system that bridges the digital division. As AI and IoT continue to evolve, they will not only transform connectivity but also redefine the ways we live, work, and interact with the world.

The journey of intelligent connectivity is just beginning, and its possibilities are boundless.

REFERENCES

Afzal, M., Sah, A. K., Agarwal, S., Tanzeel, A., Elshaikh, R. H., Alobeidli, F. A., Alfeel, A. H., Choudhary, R. K., & Choudhary, A. (2024). Advancements in the treatment of autoimmune diseases: Integrating artificial intelligence for personalized medicine. *Trends in Immunotherapy*, *8*(2), 8970. DOI: 10.24294/ti8970

Ahmed, K., Dubey, M. K., Kumar, A., & Dubey, S. (2024). Artificial intelligence and IoT driven system architecture for municipality waste management in Smart Cities: A review. *Measurement. Sensors*, *101395*, 101395. Advance online publication. DOI: 10.1016/j.measen.2024.101395

Alaba, F. A., Othman, M., Hashem, I. A. T., & Alotaibi, F. (2017). Internet of Things security: A survey. *Journal of Network and Computer Applications*, *88*, 10–28. DOI: 10.1016/j.jnca.2017.04.002

Alahi, M. E. E., Sukkuea, A., Tina, F. W., Nag, A., Kurdthongmee, W., Suwannarat, K., & Mukhopadhyay, S. C. (2023). Integration of IoT-enabled technologies and artificial intelligence (AI). for smart city scenario: Recent advancements and future trends. *Sensors (Basel)*, *23*(11), 5206. DOI: 10.3390/s23115206 PMID: 37299934

Albraheem, L., Alajlan, H., Aljenedal, N., Alkhair, L. A., & Gwead, S. B. (2023). An IoT-based smart plug energy monitoring system. *International Journal of Advanced Computer Science and Applications*, *14*(10). Advance online publication. DOI: 10.14569/IJACSA.2023.0141038

Alowais, S. A., Alghamdi, S. S., Alsuhebany, N., Alqahtani, T., Alshaya, A. I., Almohareb, S. N., Aldairem, A., Alrashed, M., Saleh, K. B., Badreldin, H. A., Yami, M. S. A., Harbi, S. A., & Albekairy, A. M. (2023). Revolutionizing healthcare: The role of artificial intelligence in clinical practice. *BMC Medical Education*, *23*(1), 689. Advance online publication. DOI: 10.1186/s12909-023-04698-z PMID: 37740191

Augustin, A., Yi, J., Clausen, T., & Townsley, W. (2016). A Study of LoRa: Long Range & Low Power Networks for the Internet of Things. *Sensors (Basel)*, *16*(9), 1466. DOI: 10.3390/s16091466 PMID: 27618064

Awaisi, K. S., Ye, Q., & Sampalli, S (2024). A Survey of Industrial AIoT: Opportunities, Challenges, and Directions. IEEE Access.

Barto, A. G. (2012). *Intrinsic motivation and reinforcement learning*. https://people.cs.umass.edu/~barto/IMCleVer-chapter-totypeset2.pdf

Bessen, J. (2019). *AI and jobs: The role of demand.* National Bureau of Economic Research., DOI: 10.3386/w24235

Bolici, R., & Mora, L. (2016). The development process of smart city strategies: the case of Barcelona. In RE-CITY Future City-Combining Disciplines (pp. 155-181). Juvenes print.

Borgia, E. (2014). The Internet of Things vision: Key features, applications, and open issues. *Computer Communications*, *54*, 1–31. DOI: 10.1016/j.comcom.2014.09.008

Business Wire. (2022). PathAI and Cleveland Clinic announce collaboration to build digital pathology infrastructure and evolve the use of AI-powered pathology algorithms in research and clinical care. Business Wire. Retrieved January 6, 2025, from https://www.businesswire.com/news/home/20220310005017/en/PathAI-and-Cleveland-Clinic-Announce-Collaboration-to-Build-Digital-Pathology-Infrastructure-and-Evolve-Use-of-AI-Powered-Pathology-Algorithms-in-Research-and-Clinical-Care

Chatterjee, P., Bhadoria, R. S., & Pathak, Y. (Eds.). (2022). *5G and beyond: the future of IoT*. CRC Press. DOI: 10.1201/9781003045809

Cheruvu, S., Kumar, A., Smith, N., & Wheeler, D. M. (2019). Connectivity Technologies for IoT. In *Apress eBooks* (pp. 347–411). DOI: 10.1007/978-1-4842-2896-8_5

Chiradeja, P., & Yoomak, S. (2023). Development of a public lighting system with smart lighting control systems and internet of things (IoT). technologies for smart city. *Energy Reports*, *10*, 3355–3372. DOI: 10.1016/j.egyr.2023.10.027

Choudhary, A. (2024). Internet of Things: A comprehensive overview, architectures, applications, simulation tools, challenges and future directions. *Discover Internet of Things*, *4*(1), 31. Advance online publication. DOI: 10.1007/s43926-024-00084-3

Dai, H., Zheng, Z., & Zhang, Y. (2019). Blockchain for Internet of Things: A survey. *IEEE Internet of Things Journal*, *6*(5), 8076–8094. DOI: 10.1109/JIOT.2019.2920987

Dey, A., & Boleng, J. (n.d.). *An Introduction to Context-Aware Computing (Suzanne Miller, Interviewer)*. SEI Podcast Series. In Carnegie Mellon University Software Engineering Institute., https://insights.sei.cmu.edu/documents/4992/2015_016_100_439312.pdf

Dian, F. J., Vahidnia, R., & Rahmati, A. (2020). Wearables and the Internet of Things (IoT)., Applications, Opportunities, and Challenges: A survey. *IEEE Access : Practical Innovations, Open Solutions*, *8*, 69200–69211. DOI: 10.1109/ACCESS.2020.2986329

Din, I. U., Almogren, A., & Rodrigues, J. J. P. C. (2024). AIOT integration in autonomous vehicles: Enhancing road cooperation and traffic management. *IEEE Internet of Things Journal*, *11*(22), 35942–35949. DOI: 10.1109/JIOT.2024.3387927

Duraipandi, S., Divyadharshini, R., Janani, M., & Samyuktha, P. (n.d.). *Smart Traffic Management System using IoT*. https://api.semanticscholar.org/CorpusID:264557309

Elassy, M., Al-Hattab, M., Takruri, M., & Badawi, S. (2024). Intelligent transportation systems for sustainable smart cities. *Transportation Engineering*, *16*, 100252. DOI: 10.1016/j.treng.2024.100252

Ferrer, J.-R. (2017). Using edge computing for real-time processing in IoT systems. OpenEdition. Retrieved January 9, 2025, from https://journals.openedition.org/factsreports/4367

Fontes, C., Hohma, E., Corrigan, C. C., & Lütge, C. (2022). AI-powered public surveillance systems: Why we (might). need them and how we want them. *Technology in Society*, *71*, 102137. DOI: 10.1016/j.techsoc.2022.102137

Forkan, A. R. M., Kang, Y. B., Marti, F., Banerjee, A., McCarthy, C., Ghaderi, H., Costa, B., Dawod, A., Georgakopolous, D., & Jayaraman, P. P. (2024). Aiot-citysense: Ai and iot-driven city-scale sensing for roadside infrastructure maintenance. Springer. *Data Science and Engineering*, *9*(1), 26–40. DOI: 10.1007/s41019-023-00236-5

Gao, R. X., Krüger, J., Merklein, M., Möhring, H., & Váncza, J. (2024). Artificial Intelligence in manufacturing: State of the art, perspectives, and future directions. *CIRP Annals*, *73*(2), 723–749. DOI: 10.1016/j.cirp.2024.04.101

Gubbi, J., Buyya, R., Marusic, S., & Palaniswami, M. (2013). Internet of Things (IoT).: A vision, architectural elements, and future directions. *Future Generation Computer Systems*, *29*(7), 1645–1660. DOI: 10.1016/j.future.2013.01.010

Haghi, M., Thurow, K., & Stoll, R. (2017). Wearable devices in medical Internet of Things: Scientific research and commercially available devices. *Healthcare Informatics Research*, *23*(1), 4. DOI: 10.4258/hir.2017.23.1.4 PMID: 28261526

Hosseinzadeh, A., Chen, F. F., Shahin, M., & Bouzary, H. (2023). A predictive maintenance approach in manufacturing systems via AI-based early failure detection. *Manufacturing Letters*, *35*, 1179–1186. DOI: 10.1016/j.mfglet.2023.08.125

Hua, H., Li, Y., Wang, T., Dong, N., Li, W., & Cao, J. (2023). Edge computing with artificial intelligence: A machine learning perspective. *ACM Computing Surveys*, *55*(9), 1–35. DOI: 10.1145/3555802

Huang, Y. P., & Khabusi, S. P. (2025). Artificial Intelligence of Things (AIoT). Advances in Aquaculture: A Review. MDPI. *Processes (Basel, Switzerland)*, *13*(1), 73. DOI: 10.3390/pr13010073

Ibrahim, H. T., Mazher, W. J., & Ucan, O. N. (2022, December). AIoT in healthcare: a systematic mapping study. In *2022 International Conference on Artificial Intelligence of Things (ICAIoT)*. (pp. 1-6). IEEE. DOI: 10.1109/ICAIoT57170.2022.10121743

Idrissi, Z. K., Lachgar, M., & Hrimech, H (2024a). Blockchain, IoT and AI in logistics and transportation: A systematic review. *Transport Economics and Management*. DOI: 10.1016/j.team.2024.09.002

Idrissi, Z. K., Lachgar, M., & Hrimech, H (2024b). Blockchain, IoT and AI in logistics and transportation: A systematic review. *Transport Economics and Management*. DOI: 10.1016/j.team.2024.09.002

Indolia, S., Goswami, A. K., Mishra, S., & Asopa, P. (2018). Conceptual understanding of Convolutional Neural Network- a deep learning approach. *Procedia Computer Science*, *132*, 679–688. DOI: 10.1016/j.procs.2018.05.069

Jobin, A., Ienca, M., & Vayena, E. (2019). The global landscape of AI ethics guidelines. *Nature Machine Intelligence*, *1*(9), 389–399. DOI: 10.1038/s42256-019-0088-2

Johns Hopkins Medicine. (2020). Practical uses for artificial intelligence in health care. Johns Hopkins Medicine. Retrieved January 6, 2025, from https://www.hopkinsmedicine.org/news/articles/2020/02/practical-uses-for-artificial-intelligence-in-health-care

Khan, W. Z., Ahmed, E., Hakak, S., Yaqoob, I., & Ahmed, A. (2019). Edge computing: A survey. *Future Generation Computer Systems*, *97*, 219–235. DOI: 10.1016/j.future.2019.02.050

Kim, B., & Shin, K. S. (2024). Integration of Beyond 5g and Artificial Intelligence of Things (Aiot). with Non-Terrestrial Networks (Ntn).: Access to 5g and Low Earth Orbit (Leo). Telecommunications Facility in Korea. Available at *SSRN* 4978353. DOI: 10.2139/ssrn.4978353

Kumar, N. M., & Mallick, P. K. (2018). The Internet of Things: Insights into the building blocks, component interactions, and architecture layers. *Procedia Computer Science, 132*, 109–117. DOI: 10.1016/j.procs.2018.05.170

Kuo, Y. H., & Wu, E. H. K. (2023). Advanced, innovative AIoT and edge computing for unmanned vehicle systems in factories. *Electronics (Basel)*, *12*(8), 1843. DOI: 10.3390/electronics12081843

Kuppuswamy, A., Rajan, P. V., Selvaraj, S. K., Sankarappan, S., & Subramaniam, M. (2023). Object detection and facial recognition for the blind using deep learning and IoT. *AIP Conference Proceedings*, *2854*, 020044. DOI: 10.1063/5.0153559

Langa, R., Moeti, M. N., & Maubane, T. (2024). An AIoT-Based Automated Farming Irrigation System for Farmers in Limpopo Province. [JINITA]. *Journal of Innovation Information Technology and Application*, *6*(1), 12–27. DOI: 10.35970/jinita.v6i1.2187

Lv, Y., Duan, Y., Kang, W., Li, Z., & Wang, F. (2014). Traffic flow prediction with Big Data: A Deep learning approach. *IEEE Transactions on Intelligent Transportation Systems*, •••, 1–9. DOI: 10.1109/TITS.2014.2345663

Mayo Clinic. (2025). Artificial intelligence and informatics - Overview. Mayo Clinic. Retrieved January 6, 2025, from https://www.mayo.edu/research/departments-divisions/artificial-intelligence-informatics/overview

Mukhopadhyay, S. C., Tyagi, S. K. S., Suryadevara, N. K., Piuri, V., Scotti, F., & Zeadally, S. (2021). Artificial Intelligence-Based Sensors for next generation IoT Applications: A review. *IEEE Sensors Journal*, *21*(22), 24920–24932. DOI: 10.1109/JSEN.2021.3055618

Muts, I. (2023). IoT in manufacturing: Revolutionizing production processes. Euristiq. Retrieved January 6, 2025, from https://euristiq.com/iot-in-manufacturing/

Najafabadi, M. M., Villanustre, F., Khoshgoftaar, T. M., Seliya, N., Wald, R., & Muharemagic, E. (2015). Deep learning applications and challenges in big data analytics. *Journal of Big Data*, *2*(1), 1. Advance online publication. DOI: 10.1186/s40537-014-0007-7

Oh, J., Lee, J., Park, Y., & Park, Y. (2022, December). A secure data processing system in edge computing-powered AIoT. In *2022 IEEE Asia-Pacific Conference on Computer Science and Data Engineering (CSDE)*. (pp. 1-4). IEEE. DOI: 10.1109/CSDE56538.2022.10089302

Olawade, D. B., Wada, O. Z., Ige, A. O., Egbewole, B. I., Olojo, A., & Oladapo, B. I. (2024). Artificial intelligence in environmental monitoring: Advancements, challenges, and future directions. *Hygiene and Environmental Health Advances*, *100114*, 100114. Advance online publication. DOI: 10.1016/j.heha.2024.100114

Omrany, H., Al-Obaidi, K. M., Hossain, M., Alduais, N. A., Al-Duais, H. S., & Ghaffarianhoseini, A. (2024). IoT-enabled smart cities: A hybrid systematic analysis of key research areas, challenges, and recommendations for future direction. Springer. *Discover Cities*, *1*(1), 2. DOI: 10.1007/s44327-024-00002-w

Panduman, Y. Y. F., Funabiki, N., Fajrianti, E. D., Fang, S., & Sukaridhoto, S. (2024). A Survey of AI Techniques in IoT Applications with Use Case Investigations in the Smart Environmental Monitoring and Analytics in Real-Time IoT Platform. *Information (Basel)*, *15*(3), 153. DOI: 10.3390/info15030153

Pani, S., Pattnaik, O., & Pattanayak, B. K. (2024, February 2). *Predictive maintenance in Industrial IoT using Machine Learning approach.* https://www.ijisae.org/index.php/IJISAE/article/view/4689

Pourrahmani, H., Yavarinasab, A., Zahedi, R., Gharehghani, A., Mohammadi, M. H., Bastani, P., & Van Herle, J. (2022). The applications of Internet of Things in the automotive industry: A review of the batteries, fuel cells, and engines. *Internet of Things : Engineering Cyber Physical Human Systems*, *19*, 100579. DOI: 10.1016/j.iot.2022.100579

Raj, E., Buffoni, D., Westerlund, M., & Ahola, K. (2021, October). Edge mlops: An automation framework for aiot applications. In 2021 IEEE International Conference on Cloud Engineering (IC2E). (pp. 191-200). IEEE.

Ratasich, D., Khalid, F., & Geissler, F.. (2019). A roadmap to resilient IoT for cyber-physical systems. *IEEE Access : Practical Innovations, Open Solutions*, *7*, 13260–13283. DOI: 10.1109/ACCESS.2019.2891969

Ray, P. P. (2018). A survey on Internet of Things architectures. *Journal of King Saud University. Computer and Information Sciences*, *30*(3), 291–319. DOI: 10.1016/j.jksuci.2016.10.003

Rejeb, A., Rejeb, K., Treiblmaier, H., Appolloni, A., Alghamdi, S., Alhasawi, Y., & Iranmanesh, M. (2023). The Internet of Things (IoT). in healthcare: Taking stock and moving forward. *Internet of Things : Engineering Cyber Physical Human Systems*, *22*, 100721. DOI: 10.1016/j.iot.2023.100721

Salama, A. K., & Abdellatif, M. M. (2022, December). AIoT-based Smart Home Energy Management System. In *2022 IEEE Global Conference on Artificial Intelligence and Internet of Things (GCAIoT)*. (pp. 177-181). IEEE.

Sarker, I. H. (2021). Deep Learning: A comprehensive overview on techniques, taxonomy, applications and research directions. *SN Computer Science*, *2*(6), 420. Advance online publication. DOI: 10.1007/s42979-021-00815-1 PMID: 34426802

Sayed, S. A., Abdel-Hamid, Y., & Hefny, H. A. (2023). Artificial intelligence-based traffic flow prediction: A comprehensive review. *Journal of Electrical Systems and Information Technology*, *10*(1), 13. Advance online publication. DOI: 10.1186/s43067-023-00081-6

Selvarani, S., Ganeshan, M. K., & Vethirajan, C. Ashok Kumar, & Arumugam, U (2023). Artificial intelligence and machine learning in smart manufacturing in industry 4.0. In *International Journal of Research Publication and Reviews* (Vol. 4, Issue 11, pp. 2053–2058). https://ijrpr.com/uploads/V4ISSUE11/IJRPR19316.pdf

Sen, P. C., Hajra, M., & Ghosh, M. (2019). Supervised Classification Algorithms in Machine Learning: A Survey and review. In *Advances in intelligent systems and computing* (pp. 99–111). DOI: 10.1007/978-981-13-7403-6_11

Shekhawat, S. (2023). Smart retail: How AI and IoT are revolutionising the retail industry. Journal of AI. *Robotics & Workplace Automation*, *2*(2), 145–152. DOI: 10.69554/TCLG1264

Sibanda, M., Bhero, E., & Agee, J. (2023, January). Ai edge processing-a review of distributed embedded systems. In 2023 31st Southern African Universities Power Engineering Conference (SAUPEC). (pp. 1-6). IEEE. DOI: 10.1109/SAUPEC57889.2023.10057624

Siddiqi, M. A., Yu, H., & Joung, J. (2019). 5G Ultra-Reliable Low-Latency Communication Implementation Challenges and Operational Issues with IoT Devices. *Electronics (Basel)*, *8*(9), 981. DOI: 10.3390/electronics8090981

Silva, D., Inocêncio, L., Soares, J., & Sofia, R. (2021). A Performance Analysis of Internet of Things Networking Protocols: Evaluating MQTT, CoAP, OPC UA. *Applied Sciences (Basel, Switzerland)*, *11*(11), 4879. DOI: 10.3390/app11114879

Silva, M. M. D., & Guerreiro, J. (2020). On the 5G and Beyond. MDPI. *Applied Sciences (Basel, Switzerland)*, *10*(20), 7091. DOI: 10.3390/app10207091

Soori, M., Arezoo, B., & Dastres, R. (2023). Internet of things for smart factories in industry 4.0, a review. *Internet of Things and Cyber-Physical Systems*, *3*, 192–204. DOI: 10.1016/j.iotcps.2023.04.006

Stergiou, C., Psannis, K. E., Kim, B. G., & Gupta, B. (2018). Secure integration of IoT and cloud computing. *Future Generation Computer Systems*, *78*, 964–975. DOI: 10.1016/j.future.2016.11.031

Stopps, H., & Touchie, M. F. (2021). Residential smart thermostat use: An exploration of thermostat programming, environmental attitudes, and the influence of smart controls on energy savings. *Energy and Building*, *238*, 110834. DOI: 10.1016/j.enbuild.2021.110834

Subramaniyan, M., Skoogh, A., Bokrantz, J., Sheikh, M. A., Thürer, M., & Chang, Q. (2021). Artificial intelligence for throughput bottleneck analysis – State-of-the-art and future directions. *Journal of Manufacturing Systems*, *60*, 734–751. DOI: 10.1016/j.jmsy.2021.07.021

Sui, Q., & Liu, X. (2023). Edge computing and AIoT based network intrusion detection mechanism. *Internet Technology Letters*, *6*(5), e324. DOI: 10.1002/itl2.324

Talukder, A., & Haas, R. (2021, June). AIoT: AI meets IoT and web in smart healthcare. In Companion Publication of the 13th ACM Web Science Conference 2021 (pp. 92-98).

Tariq, M. U. (2025). Harnessing Technology to Combat Bias: Innovative Tools and Techniques in HR. In Kanwal, S. (Ed.), *Navigating Bias in Human Resource Management* (pp. 155–184). IGI Global Scientific Publishing., DOI: 10.4018/979-8-3693-7132-9.ch006

Tariq, M. U. (2025). Co-Living With Augmented Digital Beings-Navigating the Intersection of AI and Everyday Life. In Moutinho, L., & Martins, L. (Eds.), *Impacts of Sensetech on Society* (pp. 187–206). IGI Global Scientific Publishing., DOI: 10.4018/979-8-3693-7147-3.ch009

Tariq, M. U. (2025). Revitalizing Pedagogy: Integrating Indigenous Knowledge and Practices Into Higher Education Disciplines. In Kgari-Masondo, M. (Ed.), *Indigenous Teaching Disciplines and Perspectives for Higher Education* (pp. 379–400). IGI Global Scientific Publishing., DOI: 10.4018/979-8-3693-9296-6.ch018

Tariq, M. U. (2025). Bridging Cultures and Languages: Innovative Literacy Strategies for Inclusive and Engaged Classrooms. In Tussey, J., & Haas, L. (Eds.), *Supporting Cultural Differences Through Literacy Education* (pp. 257–282). IGI Global Scientific Publishing., DOI: 10.4018/979-8-3693-9271-3.ch010

The Sun. (2023). World's first AI hospital unveiled in China with robot doctors who 'can treat 3,000 patients a day & will save millions'. The Sun. Retrieved January 6, 2025, from https://www.thesun.co.uk/tech/28190601/worlds-first-ai-hospital-china/

Torad, M. A., Bouallegue, B., & Ahmed, A. M. (2022). A voice controlled smart home automation system using artificial intelligent and internet of things. *Telkomnika*, *20*(4), 808. DOI: 10.12928/telkomnika.v20i4.23763

Ullah, A., Anwar, S. M., Li, J., Nadeem, L., Mahmood, T., Rehman, A., & Saba, T. (2023). Smart cities: The role of Internet of Things and machine learning in realizing a data-centric smart environment. *Complex & Intelligent Systems*, *10*(1), 1607–1637. DOI: 10.1007/s40747-023-01175-4

Usama, M., Qadir, J., Raza, A., Arif, H., Yau, K. A., Elkhatib, Y., Hussain, A., & Al-Fuqaha, A. (2019). Unsupervised machine learning for networking: Techniques, applications and research challenges. *IEEE Access : Practical Innovations, Open Solutions*, *7*, 65579–65615. DOI: 10.1109/ACCESS.2019.2916648

Voigt, P., & Bussche, A. v. d (2017). *The GDPR: Principles, rights, and obligations*. Springer. DOI: 10.1007/978-3-319-57959-7

Wang, C. X., Di Renzo, M., Stanczak, S., Wang, S., & Larsson, E. G. (2020). Artificial intelligence enabled wireless networking for 5G and beyond: Recent advances and future challenges. *IEEE Wireless Communications*, *27*(1), 16–23. DOI: 10.1109/MWC.001.1900292

Zovko, K., Šerić, L., Perković, T., Belani, H., & Šolić, P. (2023). IoT and health monitoring wearable devices as enabling technologies for sustainable enhancement of life quality in smart environments. *Journal of Cleaner Production*, *413*, 137506. DOI: 10.1016/j.jclepro.2023.137506

KEY TERMS AND DEFINITIONS

Intelligent Connectivity: The fusion of AI, IoT, and high-speed networks enabling systems to make real-time, context-aware decisions autonomously.

Context-Aware Systems: Digital systems that interpret environmental, temporal, and behavioural data to make informed and adaptive responses.

Edge Computing: A decentralised computing model that processes data closer to the source, reducing latency and enabling real-time decision-making.

5G Networks: Next-generation wireless communication infrastructure providing ultra-low latency and high bandwidth essential for real-time, intelligent applications.

Autonomous Decision-Making: The capability of intelligent systems to make predictive, independent choices without human input by leveraging AI and contextual data.

Chapter 3
Exploring the Role of AIoT in Data Privacy and Security

Sushil Bhardwaj
https://orcid.org/0000-0001-5184-3866
RIMT University, India

Indu Sharma
Chandigarh University, India

Shivani Mahendru
Chandigarh University, India

Ramandeep Kaur
Chandigarh University, India

Surbhi Sharma
RIMT University, India

ABSTRACT

The convergence of Artificial Intelligence (AI) and the Internet of Things (IoT), known as AIoT, is transforming industries by creating autonomous systems capable of real-time decision-making. However, this integration also poses significant data privacy and security challenges. The primary objectives of this chapter are (a) To understand the intersection of AIoT and data privacy/security (b) To identify the key privacy and security challenges posed by AIoT (c) To explore strategies for enhancing data privacy and security in AIoT and (d) To discuss the future of AIoT in the context of privacy and security. The chapter also discusses regulatory

DOI: 10.4018/979-8-3693-8547-0.ch003

and policy recommendations to ensure a balance between innovation and data protection, presenting case studies and future trends. This comprehensive analysis provides valuable insights for researchers and professionals navigating the evolving landscape of AIoT.

INTRODUCTION

In the rapidly advancing digital landscape, the fusion of Artificial Intelligence (AI) and the Internet of Things (IoT) has given rise to a new frontier in technological innovation: the Artificial Intelligence of Things (AIoT). This concept refers to the integration of AI's computational capabilities with IoT's vast network of connected devices, enabling these devices to collect, analyze, and act upon data autonomously. AIoT allows for real-time decision-making, transforming sectors like healthcare, smart cities, manufacturing, and beyond into interconnected systems that operate intelligently and efficiently (Ruhela et al., 2021).

The Internet of Things (IoT) has become a key element of today's digital infrastructure (Huang, 2022). The exponential growth of IoT devices—ranging from smart home appliances to industrial sensors—has led to an unprecedented increase in data generation (Singh et al., 2023). These devices continuously collect, transmit, and sometimes store vast amounts of data, much of which is sensitive in nature. With billions of devices connected worldwide, IoT enables the smooth sharing and analysis of data across various industries (Wei et al., 2022). While IoT has improved operational efficiency, its widespread use has also highlighted serious weaknesses, especially regarding data privacy and security (Mandez et al., 2017) due to factors such as inadequate encryption, poor device management, and lack of standardization. The integration of AI with IoT, creating AIoT, offers potential solutions to these challenges by enabling more sophisticated data analysis, anomaly detection, and automated threat response. In the realm of security, AIoT can play a pivotal role in identifying and mitigating threats (Prathima et al., 2021). AI algorithms can analyze vast amounts of data generated by IoT devices to detect anomalies and predict potential security breaches (Moussa et al., 2018; Tariq, 2024). For example, in smart home systems, AIoT can monitor patterns of behavior to identify unusual activities, such as unauthorized access or potential intrusions, thereby enhancing overall security (Deep et al., 2020).

Data privacy and security have become major concerns in today's digital world (Kumar et al., 2021). IoT devices produce large amounts of data, much of which is personal or sensitive, leading to heightened risks of data breaches, unauthorized access, and cyberattacks (Singh et al., 2020). Smart home devices, such as internet-connected security cameras, are prime examples of IoT devices that generate vast amounts of sensitive data. These cameras often record video feeds from homes and store them on cloud servers for remote access. If these systems are not properly secured—whether through weak encryption or default passwords—they become vulnerable to hackers. A breach could allow unauthorized access to live feeds, enabling malicious actors to invade users' privacy, observe daily routines, or even commit crimes like burglary by monitoring when a home is vacant. This underscores the importance of robust security measures, including regular firmware updates, encryption, and strong authentication protocols to mitigate risks. The integration of AI into IoT, known as AIoT, increases these risks due to its advanced data processing capabilities. AI systems rely on extensive data to function properly, which naturally heightens the exposure of sensitive information (Tariq, 2025).

AIoT systems function in real-time, continuously gathering and processing data from diverse inputs. This uninterrupted stream of data presents several security challenges. For instance, if encryption or protective measures are insufficient, cybercriminals may intercept the data mid-transmission or even control devices remotely (Hasan et al., 2023). As a result, safeguarding data privacy and fortifying the security of AIoT systems is vital to prevent such breaches. Moreover, the use of AI for automated decision-making raises ethical questions about data usage and accountability. AIoT systems can learn user behaviors and predict actions, which may lead to decisions that impact privacy directly (Ahmad et al., 2020) . In some instances, these systems could unintentionally reveal personal information or make ethically questionable choices without human oversight (Abuladel et al., 2020). Consequently, it is crucial to address these concerns during the development and implementation of AIoT technologies.

AIoT systems can analyze data and make decisions autonomously, which raises questions about accountability and transparency. The "black box" nature of AI algorithms makes it difficult to understand how decisions are made, leading to trust issues among user (Said et al., 2021). The "black box" nature of AI algorithms refers to their complexity and lack of transparency, making it difficult to understand how they arrive at specific decisions or predictions. Even though AI models, especially deep learning systems, can perform highly accurate tasks, their internal workings are often opaque, even to developers. This lack of interpretability raises concerns in critical areas like healthcare and finance, where understanding the reasoning behind AI-driven decisions is crucial for trust, accountability, and ethical compliance (Tariq, 2024). Additionally, the current regulatory environment presents challenges since existing data protection laws, such as the General Data Protection Regulation (GDPR) in UK and Digital Personal Data Protection Act, 2023 (DPDP Act) in India, may not fully address the complexities unique to AIoT systems (Barani et al., 2022). These protections Act regulates the processing of digital personal data while ensuring the protection of individuals' privacy rights. The fast-paced evolution of technology requires ongoing updates to regulatory frameworks to protect user privacy while encouraging innovation. Tackling these challenges is essential for the responsible implementation of AIoT technologies.

To enhance data privacy and security in AIoT systems, several strategies can be implemented. One key approach is the use of advanced encryption techniques that ensure data is protected throughout its lifecycle, from collection to storage. Additionally, AI-driven security solutions can be leveraged to identify and respond to anomalies in real-time, significantly reducing the window of vulnerability (Ahmad et al., 2023). Privacy-preserving AI techniques, such as federated learning and differential privacy, can also be employed to minimize the exposure of sensitive data during processing (Sharghivand et al., 2021). Furthermore, developing comprehensive regulatory frameworks can guide organizations in implementing robust privacy and security measures while ensuring compliance with data protection laws (Tariq, 2025).

BACKGROUND

AIoT (Artificial Intelligence of Things) faces following key data privacy and security challenges due to its interconnected nature.

Data Vulnerabilities

A significant challenge in data privacy and security within AIoT systems is the heightened risk of data vulnerabilities stemming from the continuous flow of information between IoT devices and AI algorithms. This ongoing exchange generates numerous points of potential exposure, making these systems more vulnerable to interception, manipulation, or theft by malicious actors (Giordano et al., 2022).

The interconnected nature of AIoT systems means that if one device is compromised, it can serve as an entry point for attackers to access other devices and networks. One notable example of data vulnerability in AIoT systems is the case of smart home devices, such as security cameras and smart locks. These devices continuously collect and transmit sensitive data, such as video feeds and access logs. If a hacker gains access to a poorly secured camera, they could intercept the video stream or manipulate the lock's functionality, potentially allowing unauthorized entry into a home. Such breaches not only compromise the privacy of individuals but can also lead to physical security risks, emphasizing the urgent need for stronger security measures in AIoT devices

Another significant example of data vulnerability in AIoT systems can be seen in connected medical devices, such as insulin pumps and heart monitors. These devices continuously collect critical health data and communicate with healthcare providers (Jawad et al., 2024) for real-time monitoring (Pise et al., 2022). If a malicious actor exploits a security weakness in these devices, they could potentially gain unauthorized access to sensitive patient information or even manipulate the device's functioning. For instance, an attacker could alter insulin dosage levels, posing severe health risks to the patient. Such incidents not only compromise patient safety but also raise serious concerns about data privacy and trust in healthcare technology, highlighting the urgent need for stringent security protocols (Khokhar et al., 2022). Moreover, the rapid evolution of AI technologies adds to these vulnerabilities. AI algorithms require vast amounts of data to learn and improve, which often includes personal information (Mseer et al., 2023). This reliance on extensive data makes it critical to implement robust security measures throughout the data lifecycle, from collection to storage and analysis (Alzoubi et al., 2022). Without these measures, the risks associated with data vulnerabilities in AIoT systems can lead to severe consequences, including privacy violations and significant financial losses. Addressing these challenges is essential for ensuring the secure and responsible deployment of AIoT technologies.

AI-driven Decisions and Ethical Implications

One of the key challenges of data privacy and security in the context of Artificial Intelligence and the Internet of Things (AIoT) is the ethical implications of AI-driven decision-making.

AI-driven decisions pose significant challenges to data privacy and security within AIoT systems. As these systems analyze vast amounts of data to make autonomous choices, they often operate without human oversight, which raises ethical concerns about accountability and transparency. For example, in smart healthcare applications, AI can recommend treatments based on patient data. If these algorithms are biased due to incomplete or unrepresentative datasets, they may lead to unequal healthcare outcomes, negatively impacting certain demographic groups. Furthermore, the "black box" nature of AI makes it difficult to understand how decisions are made, increasing the risk of unintentional privacy violations. When users cannot comprehend how their data is used or how decisions are reached, trust in the system diminishes. Addressing these issues is crucial for ensuring that AI-driven decisions in AIoT are ethical, transparent, and respectful of individuals' privacy rights (Nozari et al., 2022). AIoT systems analyze large amounts of data to make independent decisions that can significantly affect individuals and communities. While this capability can improve efficiency and outcomes, it also raises concerns about accountability, transparency, and potential biases in the algorithms used.

AI-driven decisions can lead to ethical dilemmas when systems make choices that impact people's lives without human oversight. For example, in smart city infrastructure, AI algorithms can analyze traffic patterns to optimize traffic signals. While this can help reduce congestion and improve public transport efficiency, these algorithms might unintentionally favor certain neighborhoods over others, leading to unequal access to resources (Badr et al., 2021). If these decisions are made without clear explanations, affected residents may not understand how the choices were made, which can undermine trust in the system and raise fairness concerns. Another example is found in healthcare, particularly in predictive analytics used for patient care. AI algorithms can analyze a patient's historical data to predict health risks and suggest treatments. However, if these systems are based on biased training data, they may provide recommendations that disproportionately affect certain demographic groups. For instance, if a system is mainly trained on data from one ethnic group, it might suggest a treatment that is less effective for others, leading to unequal healthcare outcomes. This highlights the importance of developing AI algorithms using diverse and representative datasets to reduce bias and ensure fair healthcare access.

One more instance of ethical challenges in AIoT systems can be seen in autonomous vehicles. These vehicles use AI algorithms to analyze data from sensors and make driving decisions (Mahmud et al., 2022). However, in critical situations—such as an unavoidable accident—how the AI decides whom to prioritize can raise serious ethical questions. For instance, should the vehicle protect its passengers at all costs, or should it consider the safety of pedestrians? Such scenarios highlight the need for clear ethical guidelines to govern AI decision-making in real-time situations. Moreover, the rapid advancement of AI technologies increases the risk of ethical missteps. As AIoT systems become more integrated into daily life, it is crucial to make ethical decisions that respect individual rights and promote fairness. Addressing the ethical implications of AI-driven decisions in AIoT systems is vital for ensuring responsible and equitable use of technology. By examining these challenges and including diverse perspectives in AI development, stakeholders can work towards solutions that protect privacy while encouraging innovation

Autonomy and Accountability

Autonomy and accountability are two key challenges in the context of data privacy and security within AIoT (Artificial Intelligence of Things) systems. AIoT systems are designed to operate autonomously, making decisions based on real-time data from interconnected IoT devices (Liu et al., 2022). While this enhances efficiency and responsiveness, it also introduces risks concerning accountability and transparency. With autonomous decision-making, it becomes harder to trace actions to specific entities, raising concerns about who is responsible when things go wrong, especially when privacy is violated or security is compromised.

The increasing autonomy of AIoT (Artificial Intelligence of Things) systems introduces significant challenges regarding accountability, particularly in the areas of data privacy and security. As these systems become more capable of making decisions without human intervention, it becomes difficult to pinpoint responsibility when something goes wrong, such as a data breach or privacy violation. This lack of clarity around accountability can lead to situations where individuals or organizations are unsure who is responsible for protecting sensitive data or fixing system errors.

One major issue is the lack of transparency in AI decision-making, often referred to as the "black box" problem . AI algorithms used in AIoT systems process data in complex ways that are not easily interpretable. When an autonomous system makes a decision that results in a privacy breach or compromised data, it becomes challenging to trace the decision-making process or hold the appropriate party accountable. This lack of transparency makes it harder to identify and address security vulnerabilities.

Additionally, AIoT systems raise ethical concerns about decisions made without human intervention. In smart healthcare devices, for example, if an autonomous system makes an incorrect diagnosis or misadjusts medication, it can have serious consequences. Identifying responsibility for these errors—whether it lies with the device manufacturer, the AI system developer, or the healthcare provider—becomes complicated.

One major issue in AIoT is the difficulty of holding someone accountable for actions taken by autonomous systems. As these systems collect, analyze, and act on large volumes of data independently, it can be challenging to determine responsibility when the system makes an error or behaves in an unintended manner. A prominent example of autonomy and accountability issues in AIoT is autonomous vehicles. These vehicles rely on AI to process data from various sensors, making decisions in real time. In the event of an accident, it can be challenging to determine who is at fault: the manufacturer, the AI developer, or the vehicle's owner. If the vehicle makes an incorrect decision due to a flaw in the AI, this raises legal and ethical questions about accountability. For instance, if an autonomous car fails to recognize a pedestrian, leading to an accident, it may not be clear whether the fault lies in the data processing algorithms or the design of the IoT sensors. This lack of clarity in responsibility makes it difficult to ensure justice and compensation for affected parties.

In healthcare, AIoT systems, such as smart medical devices, present another example of autonomy and accountability challenges. Devices like insulin pumps and heart monitors can autonomously make adjustments based on patient data, but errors in these systems can have life-threatening consequences. For instance, if a smart insulin pump delivers an incorrect dosage due to a data processing error, who is held accountable? The device manufacturer, the AI system developer, or the healthcare provider? This uncertainty complicates the process of identifying who is responsible for any harm caused by the system's decisions.

An example of autonomy and accountability challenges in AIoT related to customer feedback can be found in AI-driven review analysis systems. Many retail platforms use AI to autonomously analyze customer feedback and reviews to improve products or services. However, if the AI misinterprets feedback—such as flagging positive reviews as negative due to language nuances—it could lead to inappropriate business decisions, such as discontinuing a successful product. In such cases, accountability is unclear: should the retailer be responsible for blindly trusting the AI, or is the fault with the AI developer for creating a system that doesn't properly understand customer sentiment?

To address these challenges, clear frameworks for accountability must be developed, ensuring that responsibility for the actions of autonomous systems is traceable. Additionally, increasing transparency in AI decision-making processes is essential. Users and developers should be able to understand how decisions are made, and there should be mechanisms in place to audit and review AIoT systems to ensure data privacy and security are maintained (Tariq, 2024).

Regulatory and Compliance Issues

As AIoT devices collect, process, and analyze vast amounts of data, they often operate in a legal gray area, where existing regulations may not fully address the complexities of this emerging technology. Regulatory and compliance issues arise because of outdated laws, jurisdictional conflicts, and the evolving nature of AI technologies (Tariq, 2025). One of the key challenges is the regulatory gap in addressing AIoT-specific issues. Current data privacy laws, such as the General Data Protection Regulation (GDPR) in the European Union, were designed primarily with traditional data management systems in mind. These laws may not fully address the unique challenges posed by AIoT, where data is constantly exchanged between interconnected devices and AI systems. For example, AIoT systems can autonomously collect, analyze, and share data without explicit user consent, potentially violating privacy regulations. This leads to challenges in enforcing compliance, as AIoT systems may not provide sufficient transparency or mechanisms for users to control how their data is handled. An example of regulatory challenges in AIoT can be seen in smart cities, where AIoT systems are used to optimize traffic flow, monitor public safety, and manage utilities (Manickam et al., 2020).

These systems rely on real-time data collection from IoT devices like cameras, sensors, and connected vehicles. While this data can improve city management, it also raises concerns about privacy violations, particularly when surveillance systems are involved (Dayana et al., 2024). In many cases, the use of facial recognition technology in public spaces conflicts with data protection laws, as individuals are often unaware that their data is being collected. This creates a regulatory dilemma, as local governments may struggle to ensure compliance with privacy laws while still benefiting from AIoT innovations. Another major issue is the challenge of cross-border data transfers. AIoT systems often operate globally, with devices and data spread across multiple countries. This creates complications in complying with varying national data protection laws. For instance, a company using AIoT devices in multiple regions may face difficulties ensuring that data collected in one country is handled according to the laws of another, particularly when data moves across borders. Differences in privacy standards between regions, such as between the GDPR in Europe and less stringent regulations in other parts of the world, exacerbate these challenges. Companies must navigate a complex web of regulations to ensure compliance across jurisdictions, which can be costly and time-consuming.

In the healthcare industry, AIoT devices such as smart wearables that monitor patient health data face significant regulatory hurdles. These devices collect sensitive personal information, such as heart rate, glucose levels, and sleep patterns, which must comply with strict healthcare data regulations like the Health Insurance Portability and Accountability Act (HIPAA) in the U.S. However, if data from these devices is shared with AI systems located in countries with weaker privacy protections, it could violate HIPAA or similar laws. Ensuring compliance across different jurisdictions becomes a complex task for healthcare providers and device manufacturers, raising concerns about how data is stored, transferred, and used.

The fast-paced evolution of AIoT technologies often outpaces the ability of existing legal frameworks to keep up. Addressing these challenges requires updating data protection laws to reflect the unique needs of AIoT systems and fostering international cooperation to harmonize regulations across borders.

STRATEGIES FOR ENHANCING DATA PRIVACY AND SECURITY IN AIOT

Enhancing data privacy and security in AIoT requires the following approaches:

Advanced Encryption and Data Protection Techniques

As AIoT (Artificial Intelligence of Things) systems grow in complexity and scale, the need for robust data privacy and security measures becomes increasingly urgent. These systems collect and process vast amounts of data, much of it sensitive, making them attractive targets for cyberattacks (Sithembiso et al, 2022). A critical strategy for enhancing data privacy and security in AIoT is the use of advanced encryption and data protection techniques. These techniques safeguard data from unauthorized access, interception, and manipulation, ensuring that the integrity of the information is maintained throughout its lifecycle (Tariq, 2024).

Encryption as a First Line of Defense: Encryption is one of the most fundamental and effective methods of protecting data in AIoT systems. By converting readable data into a coded form, encryption ensures that even if attackers intercept the data, they cannot understand or use it without the correct decryption key. In AIoT, encryption is essential at every stage of data transmission—from IoT devices collecting data to AI systems analyzing it. For example, AIoT systems used in healthcare must encrypt sensitive patient data, such as health metrics and medical records, to comply with regulations like HIPAA and prevent data breache. AIoT systems often operate in highly distributed environments, with multiple devices sharing data across networks. This increases the number of potential entry points for attackers. As a result, traditional encryption methods alone may not be sufficient. Advanced encryption techniques, such as homomorphic encryption, allow AIoT systems to perform computations on encrypted data without needing to decrypt it first. This provides an added layer of security, as sensitive data remains protected even during processing.

Data Encryption in Motion and at Rest: AIoT systems generate data that can be either in motion or at rest, and protecting both is crucial for maintaining security. Data in motion refers to data being transmitted between devices and systems, such as IoT sensors sending data to cloud-based AI systems for analysis. To protect this data, AIoT systems can implement Transport Layer Security (TLS) or Virtual Private Networks (VPNs) to secure communications. These technologies create encrypted tunnels through which data is transmitted, preventing unauthorized interception. On the other hand, data at rest—stored on devices, cloud servers, or local databases—must also be protected. Advanced encryption techniques like Advanced Encryption Standard (AES) are commonly used to safeguard stored data. By encrypting data before it is stored, even if an attacker gains access to the storage medium, the information remains inaccessible without the decryption key. Moreover, AIoT systems can leverage key management services to ensure secure storage and use of encryption keys, further protecting data from unauthorized access.

End-to-End Encryption and Zero-Trust Models: End-to-end encryption (E2EE) is an advanced encryption strategy that provides security throughout the entire data journey, from the point of data collection to its final destination. In AIoT, E2EE ensures that data is encrypted when generated by an IoT device, transmitted securely, and remains encrypted until accessed by an authorized recipient. This minimizes the risk of data being exposed at any point in the transmission process. AIoT systems implementing E2EE can prevent potential security breaches, especially in industries like finance and healthcare, where data sensitivity is high. In addition to E2EE, the zero-trust security model is gaining traction as a strategy for enhancing data protection in AIoT systems. The zero-trust approach assumes that no entity, whether inside or outside the network, can be trusted by default. Instead, every user and device must be authenticated and authorized before gaining access to the network or its data. For AIoT systems, this means continually verifying the identity and integrity of IoT devices, AI algorithms, and users. This model reduces the risk of insider threats and ensures that only legitimate actors have access to sensitive information.

Example: A practical example of advanced encryption techniques in AIoT can be found in smart grids. These systems use IoT devices to monitor and control energy usage, while AI algorithms optimize grid operations in real time. Given the critical nature of the energy infrastructure, securing smart grid data is vital. By using advanced encryption techniques, such as homomorphic encryption and AES, smart grids can ensure that data collected from energy meters is securely transmitted to central control systems. These techniques protect the grid from cyberattacks that could disrupt energy supply or compromise consumer privacy.

Advanced encryption and data protection techniques are essential strategies for enhancing the security and privacy of AIoT systems. As these systems become more interconnected and handle increasingly sensitive data, the need for robust encryption methods—such as homomorphic encryption, end-to-end encryption, and zero-trust models—becomes paramount. By implementing these techniques, AIoT developers can safeguard data at every stage of its lifecycle, reducing the risk of cyberattacks and ensuring compliance with stringent data protection regulations. In the fast-evolving AIoT landscape, advanced encryption remains a cornerstone of secure and responsible technological growth.

AI-Driven Security Solutions

AIoT systems are increasingly tasked with handling large volumes of sensitive data across various sectors. This interconnected landscape offers significant advantages but also heightens the risks of data breaches and security weaknesses. To tackle these issues, AI-driven security solutions have emerged as an effective strategy for improving data privacy and security within AIoT systems (Sithembiso et al, 2022). By harnessing the advanced capabilities of AI—such as real-time threat detection, predictive analytics, and automated response mechanisms—these security solutions can effectively reduce risks and maintain the integrity of AIoT environments.

AI-Enhanced Threat Detection and Response: One of the most critical benefits of AI in AIoT security is its ability to detect and respond to cyber threats in real-time. Traditional security measures often rely on pre-programmed rules and signature-based detection, which can struggle to identify new and evolving threats. In contrast, AI-driven solutions can analyze large datasets, recognize patterns, and detect anomalies that may indicate malicious activities. By using machine learning (ML) algorithms (Ortega et al., 2023), AI can learn from past cyberattacks and adapt to new tactics employed by hackers, providing a dynamic defense against ever-evolving threats. For example, AI can monitor traffic between IoT devices and identify unusual patterns that suggest an impending attack, such as a distributed denial-of-service (DDoS) attempt. Once a threat is detected, AI-driven security systems can take immediate action by isolating the compromised device or blocking the malicious traffic, significantly reducing the response time and limiting potential damage.

Predictive Analytics and Risk Management: AI-driven security solutions also leverage predictive analytics to anticipate potential security risks before they occur. By continuously analyzing data from various IoT devices and networks, AI can identify vulnerabilities and weak points that cybercriminals might exploit. For instance, AI can detect outdated software versions or insecure communication protocols within a network (Ji et al., 2022), providing alerts for necessary updates or security patches. This proactive approach enables organizations to address security flaws before they are exploited, thus reducing the likelihood of a successful attack. Moreover, AI can predict the likelihood of future attacks based on historical data and current trends. This capability is particularly useful in industries such as healthcare and finance, where the stakes of a data breach are high. By integrating AI-driven risk assessment tools, organizations can prioritize their security investments and focus on protecting the most vulnerable aspects of their AIoT infrastructure.

AI for Automated Incident Response: In addition to threat detection and risk management, AI-driven solutions play a crucial role in automating incident response processes. In many AIoT environments, responding to security incidents manually can be slow and prone to human error. AI-driven automation helps streamline these processes, enabling faster and more accurate responses to cyber threats. For example, AI can automatically isolate compromised IoT devices from the network, apply security patches, or trigger alerts to security teams for further investigation. This automation is particularly valuable in large-scale AIoT systems, such as smart cities or industrial IoT networks, where manual intervention would be inefficient and time-consuming. By automating key security functions, AI not only enhances the speed and accuracy of incident response but also frees up human resources to focus on more complex security challenges.

Example 1: AI-Driven Security in Autonomous Vehicles: A practical example of AI-driven security in AIoT is found in autonomous vehicles. These vehicles rely on IoT devices and AI algorithms to navigate, communicate, and make decisions in real-time. The vast amount of data generated by sensors, cameras, and other connected devices presents an attractive target for cybercriminals. By using AI-driven security solutions, autonomous vehicle systems can continuously monitor for cyber threats, such as attempts to hack the vehicle's control systems or manipulate data streams. In the event of an attack, AI can swiftly isolate compromised components and prevent further damage, ensuring passenger safety.

Example 2: AI-Driven Security in Smart Homes: Another example of AI-driven security is in smart home systems. AI-enhanced security cameras and devices can monitor user behavior, identify unusual activities, and flag potential threats, such as unauthorized access to a home's network or devices. AI-driven solutions also enable the system to automatically lock doors, alert homeowners, or notify authorities in the case of a breach, providing real-time protection and reducing the risk of intrusions.

By leveraging AI's capabilities in real-time threat detection, predictive analytics, and automated response, organizations can better protect their AIoT environments from cyberattacks and ensure the privacy of sensitive data. As AIoT continues to evolve, adopting AI-driven security measures will be crucial to maintaining trust and safeguarding the integrity of these interconnected systems.

Privacy-Preserving AI

Privacy-preserving AI techniques have emerged as critical strategies for safeguarding data privacy and security in AIoT systems. Privacy-Preserving AI techniques are methods that help protect personal data while still allowing AI to learn from it (Khowaja et al., 2021). For example, in federated learning, the AI trains on data without sharing it, and with differential privacy, small changes are made to data to keep it anonymous. These techniques ensure data stays private during AI training.

The key Privacy-preserving AI techniques are:

Federated Learning: Federated learning (Alam, 2022) is an AI technique that enables machine learning models to be trained across multiple decentralized devices or servers without needing to transfer raw data to a central location. In the context of AIoT, federated learning allows devices, such as smart sensors, wearables, or other IoT devices, to collaboratively learn from local data while keeping that data on the device. Instead of sending raw data to a centralized server for analysis, only the updated model parameters are shared. This reduces the risk of data breaches since sensitive information never leaves the device. For example, in healthcare AIoT systems (Rahi et al., 2023), federated learning allows medical devices like wearables to learn from patient data without transferring personal health information to a central server. This technique not only enhances data privacy but also ensures compliance with regulations like the Health Insurance Portability and Accountability Act (HIPAA).

Differential Privacy: Differential privacy is another powerful tool for ensuring data privacy in AIoT systems. It involves adding a certain level of noise or randomness to data before it is analyzed by AI algorithms. The goal of differential privacy is to obscure individual data points, making it difficult to trace any particular piece of information back to its original source while still allowing useful insights to be extracted from the dataset as a whole. This is particularly useful in AIoT systems where large datasets are analyzed to detect trends or patterns, such as in smart city infrastructure or industrial IoT environments. By applying differential privacy, AIoT systems can protect sensitive user information, such as location data or behavioral patterns, while still performing accurate analysis and decision-making processes. This helps mitigate risks associated with data re-identification or misuse, improving overall data security.

Example 1: Smart Homes: In smart home environments, various IoT devices like smart thermostats, security cameras, and voice assistants collect a significant amount of personal data. Privacy-preserving AI techniques can ensure this data remains secure and private. For example, federated learning allows these devices to learn and improve without sending sensitive user data (e.g., video or audio recordings) to a central server. This helps protect user privacy while maintaining the functionality of the smart home system. Differential privacy can also be applied to obscure specific details in user data, such as exact locations, while still allowing AI systems to optimize energy use or security alerts.

Example 2: Retail Industry: In retail, AIoT systems are used to track customer behavior, manage inventory, and improve customer experiences. Privacy-preserving AI can help retailers analyze data such as shopping habits or customer preferences without exposing individual identities. For instance, using differential privacy, AI models can analyze purchasing trends from IoT devices like smart shelves or point-of-sale systems without revealing specific customer data. This ensures customer privacy is respected while enabling retailers to make informed business decisions. Federated learning also allows retailers to improve product recommendations by learning from customer data on their devices without transmitting sensitive information to a central database.

While privacy-preserving AI offers significant advantages in protecting data privacy within AIoT systems, several challenges remain. Implementing techniques like federated learning and differential privacy requires careful balancing of privacy and utility (Wang et al., 2021). Too much noise added through differential privacy could reduce the accuracy of AI models, while federated learning may require significant computational resources, especially in resource-constrained IoT devices.

Another challenge is ensuring the scalability of privacy-preserving AI techniques in large-scale AIoT systems, such as smart cities or industrial IoT networks. As these networks grow, the complexity of managing decentralized data and ensuring its privacy will also increase. Further research and development into more efficient algorithms and techniques will be essential to overcoming these challenges.

Regulatory and Policy Recommendations

Regulatory and policy frameworks must be established and strengthened to protect data privacy and enhance security in AIoT environments. The following sections explore key regulatory and policy recommendations to ensure the responsible deployment of AIoT technologies.

Data Privacy Laws and Regulations: One of the foundational steps in protecting data privacy in AIoT systems is the development and enforcement of robust data privacy laws and regulations. Regulatory frameworks such as the European Union's General Data Protection Regulation (GDPR) and the California Consumer Privacy Act (CCPA) provide models for how data protection should be approached in the context of AIoT. These regulations emphasize user consent, transparency, and accountability, requiring organizations to inform users about data collection and seek explicit consent before using personal data. To enhance privacy in AIoT systems, regulators must adapt and expand these frameworks to cover the unique challenges posed by AI-driven automation and connected devices. AIoT systems often involve real-time data processing, continuous monitoring, and autonomous decision-making, which may not be fully addressed by existing laws. Therefore, policymakers should introduce specific guidelines to regulate how AI systems handle personal data, ensuring that AIoT applications operate in compliance with privacy laws (Demertzi et al., 2023).

Mandating Strong Security Standards: To safeguard AIoT systems from cyberattacks, regulatory bodies should mandate the implementation of strong security standards. Organizations must be required to adopt industry best practices, such as encryption, secure data storage, and regular security audits, to minimize the risks of data breaches. Additionally, multi-factor authentication (MFA) and regular software updates should be mandated to ensure that devices and networks are protected against emerging threats. For example, the National Institute of Standards and Technology (NIST) in the United States has developed the Cybersecurity Framework (Nazar et al., 2020), which provides guidelines for improving the security of critical infrastructure, including AIoT systems. Regulatory authorities can build upon frameworks like NIST's to create specific guidelines for AIoT security, ensuring that organizations follow robust security protocols in the design and operation of connected devices.

Ethical Use of AI and Transparency: A major concern with AIoT systems is the ethical use of data and AI-driven decision-making. As AI systems process large amounts of data and make autonomous decisions, there is a risk of bias, discrimination, or unethical use of personal information. Regulatory policies should address the ethical implications of AI in AIoT, ensuring transparency in how AI algorithms make decisions and handle sensitive data. Policymakers can promote transparency by requiring organizations to explain how AI models work, especially when they affect individual rights or personal data. AI systems in AIoT should be audited for fairness and accuracy to prevent bias and ensure that AI-driven decisions comply with ethical standards. Furthermore, organizations should be required to conduct regular ethical reviews of their AI systems to ensure that AIoT applications are used responsibly and with respect for user privacy.

Data Minimization and Purpose Limitation: One key principle that should guide regulatory policies in AIoT is data minimization, which means that organizations should only collect and process the minimum amount of data necessary for a specific purpose. This principle can help reduce the risk of data breaches, as less data is exposed to potential attackers. Additionally, purpose limitation requires organizations to use data only for the purposes specified at the time of collection and prohibits the use of data for unrelated or secondary purposes without user consent. Regulators should ensure that AIoT systems follow these principles to avoid unnecessary data collection and misuse. By enforcing strict rules on data minimization and purpose limitation, policymakers can help protect users' privacy and prevent the exploitation of personal information in AIoT environments.

Cross-Border Data Transfers: In many cases, AIoT systems involve data transfers across national borders, particularly when cloud-based services are used to store or process data. This creates additional challenges for ensuring data privacy and security, as different countries have varying levels of protection and regulatory requirements. To address this, policymakers should establish international agreements and standards that facilitate secure cross-border data transfers while respecting national sovereignty and privacy regulations. For instance, the EU-U.S. Data Privacy Framework was created to regulate data flows between the European Union and the United States while ensuring that privacy standards are upheld. Similar frameworks can be developed to regulate data transfers in the context of AIoT, ensuring that data remains protected even when processed outside the user's home country.

Example 1: Wearable Devices: In the healthcare sector, wearable devices collect sensitive health data, such as heart rate, sleep patterns, and activity levels. Regulatory policies should ensure that this data is encrypted and only used for its intended purpose. By mandating regular security audits and compliance with data privacy laws, such as HIPAA in the U.S., regulators can protect sensitive patient data and ensure that wearable devices operate securely.

CASE STUDIES OF AIOT APPLICATIONS IN TERMS OF DATA PRIVACY AND SECURITY

Case Study 1: AIoT in Smart Cities - Barcelona Smart City Project

Barcelona has been a leader in smart city innovations, integrating AIoT systems to enhance urban management, sustainability, and quality of life for its residents. The city has deployed thousands of IoT sensors across public infrastructure, including smart streetlights, air quality monitors, and traffic management systems. AI processes this data in real-time, optimizing energy consumption, improving traffic flow, and providing residents with real-time information on public transportation and environmental conditions.

Potential: The AIoT systems in Barcelona have led to significant benefits, including reduced energy consumption through smart lighting systems that adjust based on activity levels, improved air quality monitoring, and reduced traffic congestion. The AI algorithms analyze data from IoT sensors to make autonomous decisions that improve urban efficiency, helping Barcelona meet its sustainability goals while improving the overall quality of life for its citizens.

Risks and Challenges: However, the massive amount of data collected from various sensors, including cameras, traffic sensors, and environmental monitors, raises serious concerns about privacy. Citizens' movements, activities, and even personal health indicators can be tracked, leading to concerns about surveillance and data misuse. Ensuring that personal data remains private and secure is a major challenge, particularly given the complexity of real-time data transfers across multiple systems. Additionally, protecting this data from cyberattacks is crucial. If attackers were to gain access to these systems, they could disrupt essential city services like traffic lights or public transportation. Barcelona has had to implement strong data protection measures, including encryption, secure cloud storage, and compliance with data privacy laws such as the GDPR.

Case Study 2: AIoT in Indian Agriculture - Precision Farming with Stellapps

Stellapps, an Indian startup, has developed an AIoT-enabled solution specifically for the dairy industry. This system uses IoT sensors, data analytics, and AI-driven insights to optimize dairy farming practices, improve productivity, and streamline the supply chain from farm to consumer. The platform, called *SmartMoo*, is used by dairy farmers across India to monitor cattle health, milk quality, and supply chain logistics in real-time.

Potential: Stellapps' AIoT system helps small-scale dairy farmers in India enhance productivity by using IoT devices to monitor cattle health, feeding schedules, and milk output. The platform collects data from sensors attached to the cattle and milking equipment, which is then analyzed by AI algorithms to detect health issues, optimize feeding practices, and ensure milk quality. The AI system also provides predictive analytics, offering farmers insights into potential health risks or production inefficiencies before they become critical issues. Additionally, Stellapps integrates the supply chain by tracking milk from the farm to the retail outlet, ensuring transparency and traceability. This enhances the quality control process, reduces waste, and helps ensure that consumers receive fresh, safe milk.

Risks and Challenges: Despite the benefits, Stellapps' AIoT system faces challenges related to data privacy and security. As the system collects sensitive data about cattle health, farm operations, and supply chain activities, the risk of data breaches or misuse becomes significant. For instance, unauthorized access to a farm's operational data could lead to economic losses if sensitive business information, such as production yields or supply chain inefficiencies, is exposed to competitors.

FUTURE DIRECTIONS AND CONSIDERATIONS FOR DATA SECURITY AND PRIVACY IN AIOT

As the AIoT (Artificial Intelligence of Things) ecosystem continues to evolve, the future of data security and privacy will be shaped by advancements in technology, regulatory updates, and growing public awareness. While AIoT offers tremendous potential for innovation and efficiency across various sectors, the increasing complexity of interconnected devices and AI systems also introduces new vulnerabilities and risks. To mitigate these challenges, future directions will focus on advancing security techniques, evolving regulatory frameworks, and fostering ethical AI development.

Emerging Security Techniques

The future of data security in AIoT will likely be driven by the continuous development of advanced security techniques that can keep pace with the increasing scale and complexity of AIoT networks. As these systems generate and process massive amounts of data, protecting that information from breaches, unauthorized access, and malicious attacks will require more sophisticated security approaches.

Quantum Encryption: One of the most promising future directions is the adoption of quantum encryption techniques. Quantum encryption leverages the principles of quantum mechanics to create virtually unbreakable encryption keys. As quantum computing advances, it is expected to offer higher levels of security, especially in protecting AIoT data from quantum-based cyberattacks.

Homomorphic Encryption: This technique allows data to remain encrypted even during processing, allowing AI systems to analyze and compute encrypted data without needing to decrypt it. As AIoT systems handle sensitive personal data, homomorphic encryption will play a crucial role in ensuring that data privacy is preserved, even during real-time analysis.

Federated Learning and Edge AI: Federated learning allows AI models to be trained across decentralized devices without the need to transfer raw data to a central server. This technique minimizes the risk of data breaches, as sensitive information remains stored on local devices. As edge computing grows, enabling AI processing closer to data sources, federated learning will be crucial for maintaining privacy while enhancing AI's capabilities.

Zero-Knowledge Proofs: Future AIoT systems may increasingly employ zero-knowledge proofs, a cryptographic method that allows one party to prove knowledge of a piece of information without revealing the actual data. This technique could be highly beneficial in scenarios where verifying user identity or data authenticity is necessary, but without exposing sensitive details.

Evolving Regulatory Frameworks

As AIoT systems become more pervasive, regulatory bodies will need to adapt existing data privacy and security regulations to address the unique challenges presented by these interconnected devices. Current regulations, such as the General Data Protection Regulation (GDPR) and the California Consumer Privacy Act (CCPA), provide a solid foundation for data protection, but they may need to be expanded or reinterpreted to effectively govern AIoT environments.

AI Transparency and Accountability: Future regulatory frameworks will likely focus on AI transparency, requiring organizations to disclose how AI algorithms make decisions and process data. This is particularly important for AIoT systems that make automated decisions based on real-time data. Governments may introduce laws requiring organizations to ensure that AI-driven decisions are explainable, fair, and accountable.

Data Sovereignty and Localization: As AIoT systems span across international borders, data sovereignty and localization issues will become increasingly relevant. Future regulations may require organizations to store and process AIoT data within specific geographic boundaries, ensuring compliance with local data protection laws.

Cross-border Data Sharing: AIoT networks will continue to involve multiple devices and systems operating in different jurisdictions. Regulatory bodies will need to develop standardized guidelines for cross-border data sharing, ensuring that data privacy and security are maintained even as AIoT systems operate across different regulatory environments.

Balancing Innovation and Privacy Protection

One of the most significant challenges for the future of AIoT will be balancing the need for technological innovation with the need for privacy protection. As AIoT systems become more powerful and widespread, there will be ongoing tension between enabling innovation and ensuring that privacy rights are safeguarded.

Privacy by Design: Moving forward, organizations developing AIoT systems will need to embrace a "privacy by design" approach, integrating privacy and security features into their products and services from the ground up. This means considering data minimization, encryption, and user consent mechanisms at every stage of AIoT development, rather than treating privacy as an afterthought.

Public Awareness and Ethical AI Development: In the future, the role of public awareness in shaping AIoT technologies will become increasingly important. Users will need to be informed about how their data is being collected, stored, and used by AIoT systems. As AIoT technologies expand, the importance of ethical AI development will also grow, with a focus on ensuring that AIoT systems are designed and implemented in ways that respect individual rights and avoid reinforcing biases.

Broader Societal Implications

The future of AIoT extends beyond technical and regulatory considerations. AIoT systems will have profound impacts on society, influencing how we interact with technology, how businesses operate, and how governments function. While AIoT offers the potential to enhance convenience and efficiency, it also raises concerns about surveillance, data misuse, and the erosion of personal privacy.

Surveillance Concerns: As AIoT systems collect and analyze vast amounts of data in real-time, there is a growing concern that these technologies could be used for widespread surveillance. Governments and private organizations will need to address these concerns by developing safeguards that prevent the misuse of AIoT for invasive monitoring while ensuring that legitimate security needs are met.

Ethical AI Governance: In the future, ethical AI governance will be crucial to ensuring that AIoT systems are used responsibly. This includes developing ethical guidelines for AI decision-making, promoting fairness in algorithmic processes, and ensuring that AIoT systems do not perpetuate discrimination or bias.

CONCLUSION

In this chapter, we have explored the rapidly evolving landscape of AIoT (Artificial Intelligence of Things) and its profound impact on data privacy and security. The fusion of AI and IoT technologies offers immense potential for innovation across numerous industries, from healthcare and manufacturing to transportation and smart homes. However, as this integration deepens, the challenges associated with safeguarding data and ensuring privacy become more pronounced. The conclusion provides a synthesis of the critical points discussed throughout the chapter, focusing on the challenges, strategies, and future directions for AIoT in the realm of data privacy and security.

One of the central challenges posed by AIoT is the sheer volume of data generated by interconnected IoT devices and the reliance on AI systems to process and make decisions based on this data. This vast data flow creates numerous vulnerabilities, as sensitive information is constantly being transmitted, analyzed, and stored. Without robust encryption and security measures, AIoT systems can become prime targets for cyberattacks, data breaches, and unauthorized access. As outlined in the chapter, one key strategy for addressing these vulnerabilities is the adoption of advanced encryption techniques, such as homomorphic encryption and quantum cryptography, which ensure data security even in complex, decentralized networks. Moreover, the chapter has highlighted the ethical and privacy concerns associated with AI-driven decision-making. AI systems, when integrated with IoT, have the capacity to autonomously analyze data and make decisions that can significantly impact individuals' lives. This raises critical questions about accountability, transparency, and fairness. Techniques such as explainable AI and privacy-preserving AI models, including federated learning and differential privacy, offer promising solutions for mitigating these ethical risks. However, the development of these technologies must be accompanied by strong governance frameworks to ensure that AIoT systems operate in a manner that respects individual rights and societal values.

The evolving regulatory landscape is another important factor in the future of AIoT. While existing regulations like the GDPR and CCPA provide a foundation for data protection, they were not designed with the complexities of AIoT in mind. As AIoT technologies continue to advance, there is a clear need for updated regulatory frameworks that can address issues such as cross-border data sharing, AI transparency, and the accountability of autonomous systems. Policymakers must strike a delicate balance between encouraging innovation and enforcing stringent data protection measures to ensure that AIoT technologies do not compromise privacy or security.

Looking ahead, the future of AIoT is filled with both promise and challenges. Technological advancements in fields such as edge computing, blockchain, and AI-driven cybersecurity will play a crucial role in enhancing the privacy and security of AIoT systems. At the same time, the ongoing tension between innovation and privacy protection will require ongoing attention from researchers, industry leaders, and regulators alike. Public awareness and engagement will also be essential in shaping the future of AIoT, as users need to understand both the benefits and risks associated with these technologies. In conclusion, this chapter has provided a comprehensive examination of the role of AIoT in data privacy and security, offering valuable insights for researchers, policymakers, and industry professionals. By addressing the challenges and outlining key strategies for enhancing security, the chapter contributes to a deeper understanding of how AIoT can be harnessed to create secure, privacy-conscious systems that benefit society. As we move forward into an increasingly interconnected world, the responsible development and deployment of AIoT technologies will be essential to ensuring that they serve the public good while minimizing risks to privacy and security.

REFERENCES

Abuladel, A., & Bamasag, O. (2020). Data and location privacy issues in IoT applications. *2020 3rd International Conference on Computer Applications & Information Security (ICCAIS)*, Riyadh, Saudi Arabia, 2020, pp. 1-6. https://doi.org/DOI: 10.1109/ICCAIS48893.2020.9096837

Ahmad, B., Syed, J. S., Shah, M. A., Khan, M., Khan, A., Hasnain, B., & Mumtaz, T. (2022). Security threats and research challenges of IoT -. *RE:view*, 1–10. Advance online publication. DOI: 10.1109/ICETECC56662.2022.10069706

Ahmed, E., Islam, A., Ashraf, M., Chowdhury, A. I., & Rahman, M. M. (2020). Internet of Things (IoT): Vulnerabilities, security concerns and things to consider. https://doi.org/DOI: 10.1109/ICCCNT49239.2020.9225283

Alam, T., & Gupta, R. (2022). Federated learning and its role in the privacy preservation of IoT devices. *Future Internet*, *14*(9), 246. Advance online publication. DOI: 10.3390/fi14090246

Alzoubi, Y. I., Al-Ahmad, A. S., Kahtan, H., & Jaradat, A. (2022). Internet of Things and blockchain integration: Security, privacy, technical, and design challenges. *Future Internet*, *14*(7), 216. Advance online publication. DOI: 10.3390/fi14070216

Badr, Y., Zhu, X., & Naser, M. (2021). Security and privacy in the Internet of Things: Threats and challenges. https://doi.org/DOI: 10.1007/s11761-021-00327-z

Barani, B. S., Pandey, A., Abiko, A. T., Vijaykumar, J., Rastogi, U., Genale, A. H., & Karthika, P. (2022). Analysis of machine learning data security in the Internet of Things (IoT) circumstance. https://doi.org/DOI: 10.1007/978-981-16-2126-0_20

Dayana, D. S., Shanthi, T., Wali, G., Pramila, V. P., Sumitha, T., & Sudhakar, M. (2024). Enhancing usability and control in artificial intelligence of things environments (AIoT) through semantic web control models. In *Advances in Web Technologies and Engineering Book Series*. https://doi.org/DOI: 10.4018/979-8-3693-1487-6.ch009

Deep, S., Zheng, X., Jolfaei, A., Yu, D., Ostovari, P., & Bashir, A. K. (2020). A survey of security and privacy issues in the Internet of Things from the layered context. https://doi.org/DOI: 10.1002/ett.3935

Demertzi, V., Demertzis, S., & Demertzis, K. (2023). An overview of privacy dimensions on the industrial Internet of Things (IIoT). *Algorithms*, *16*(8), 378. Advance online publication. DOI: 10.3390/a16080378

Giordano, G., Palomba, F., & Ferrucci, F. (2022). On the use of artificial intelligence to deal with privacy in IoT systems: A systematic literature review. *Journal of Systems and Software, 193*, 111475. Advance online publication. DOI: 10.1016/j.jss.2022.111475

Hasan, N., Chamoli, A., & Alam, M. (2020). Privacy challenges and their solutions in IoT. https://doi.org/DOI: 10.1007/978-3-030-37468-6_11

Huang, Z. (2022). Research on artificial intelligence-related technologies for Internet of Things applications. https://doi.org/DOI: 10.1109/IIoTBDSC57192.2022.00029

Jawad, L. A. (2024). Security and privacy in digital healthcare systems: Challenges and mitigation strategies. https://doi.org/DOI: 10.1177/09702385241233073

Ji, B., Liu, Y., Xing, L., Li, C., Zhang, G., Han, C., Wen, H., & Mumtaz, S. (2022). Survey of secure communications of Internet of Things with artificial intelligence. *IEEE Internet of Things Magazine, 5*(3), 92–99. Advance online publication. DOI: 10.1109/IOTM.001.2100178

Khokhar, R. (2022). Internet of Things privacy security protection access control research. https://doi.org/DOI: 10.1109/ITOEC53115.2022.9734497

Khowaja, S. A., Dev, K., Faseeh, M. N., Khuwaja, P., & Foschini, L. (2021). Towards industrial private AI: A two-tier framework for data and model security. *arXiv: Cryptography and Security*.

Kumar, N., Madhuri, J., & ChanneGowda, M. (2017, May). Review on security and privacy concerns in Internet of Things. In 2017 International Conference on IoT and Application (ICIOT) (pp. 1-5). IEEE.

Liu, Q., Wang, G., Hu, J., & Wu, J. (2022). Preface of special issue on artificial intelligence: The security & privacy opportunities and challenges for emerging applications. *Future Generation Computer Systems, 133*, 169–170. Advance online publication. DOI: 10.1016/j.future.2022.03.021

Mahmud, U., Hussain, S., Sarwar, A., & Toure, I. K. (2022). A distributed emergency vehicle transit system using artificial intelligence of things (DEVeTS-AIoT). *Wireless Communications and Mobile Computing, 2022*, 1–12. Advance online publication. DOI: 10.1155/2022/9654858

Manickam, S., & Kooy, A. (2020). Internet of Things for smart cities: Challenges, security, and privacy issues. *Social Science Research Network*. https://doi.org/DOI: 10.2139/SSRN.3713677

Mendez, D. M., Papapanagiotou, I., & Yang, B. (2017). Internet of Things: Survey on security and privacy. *arXiv: Cryptography and Security*. https://doi.org/DOI: 10.1080/19393555.2018.1458258

Moussa, W., & Konstantas, D. (2018). IoT and security-privacy concerns: A systematic mapping study. *International Journal of Network Security & its Applications, 10*(6), 25–33. Advance online publication. DOI: 10.5121/ijnsa.2018.10603

Mseer, N. I., & Ahmed, S. M. (2023). Artificial intelligence and security challenges. https://doi.org/DOI: 10.1007/978-3-031-35828-9_13

Nazar, W., He, X., & Usman, M. (2020). Security & privacy in IoT using machine learning & blockchain: Threats & countermeasures. *arXiv: Cryptography and Security*.

Nozari, H., Szmelter-Jarosz, A., & Ghahremani-Nahr, J. (2022). Analysis of the challenges of artificial intelligence of things (AIoT) for the smart supply chain (Case study: FMCG industries). *Sensors (Basel), 22*(8), 2931. Advance online publication. DOI: 10.3390/s22082931 PMID: 35458916

Ortega, A. (2023). A survey of machine and deep learning methods for privacy protection in the Internet of Things. *Sensors (Basel), 23*(3), 1252. Advance online publication. DOI: 10.3390/s23031252 PMID: 36772292

Pise, A., Almuzaini, K. K., Ahamed, T., Ahanger, A., Farouk, A., Pant, K., Kumar, P., Pareek, P., & Nuagah, S. J. (2022). Enabling artificial intelligence of things (AIoT) healthcare architectures and listing security issues. *Computational Intelligence and Neuroscience, 2022*, 1–14. Advance online publication. DOI: 10.1155/2022/8421434 PMID: 36911247

Prathima, K. M., & Navya, B. S. (2021). AIoT - Artificial Intelligence of Things. https://doi.org/DOI: 10.48175/IJARSCT-V4-I3-013

Rahi, P., Sood, S., Dandotiya, M., Kalhotra, S. K., & Khan, I. R. (2023). Artificial intelligence of things (AIoT) and metaverse technology for brain health, mental health, and wellbeing. In *Advances in Healthcare Information Systems and Administration Book Series*. https://doi.org/DOI: 10.4018/978-1-6684-8913-0.ch019

Ruhela, S., Chaudhary, P., Shrivas, R., & Chopra, D. (2021). AIoT application for food recommendation based on emotion analysis. https://doi.org/DOI: 10.48175/IJARSCT-928

Said, S., Rowan, I., Hesham, O., Abou Tabl, I., Nu, M., Youssef, S. M., & Elagamy, M. (2021). AIOT-Arch: Furthering artificial intelligence in big data IoT applications. *IOP Conference Series. Materials Science and Engineering*, *1051*(1), 012008. Advance online publication. DOI: 10.1088/1757-899X/1051/1/012008

Sharghivand, N., & Derakhshan, F. (2021). Data security and privacy in industrial IoT. In A. B. Editor & C. D. Editor (Eds.), *Industrial IoT: Challenges, Design Principles, Applications, and Business Models* (pp. 35–50). Springer. DOI: 10.1007/978-3-030-76613-9_3

Singh, R., Prabha, C., & Sharma, N. (2023). Artificial internet of things (AIoT) and its momentous impact and challenges in modern agriculture. In Proceedings of the *2023 International Conference on Intelligent Computing and Information Systems* (pp. 123–130). IEEE. DOI: 10.1109/icicis56802.2023.10430232

Singh, S., & Kumar, D. (2020). Perceptions of security and privacy in Internet of Things. In Proceedings of the *2020 International Conference on Information and Communication Technology* (pp. 45–52). IEEE. DOI: 10.1109/ICICT48043.2020.9112462

Sithembiso, S., Kekana, T. A., & Sibiya, A. (2022). Strategies for Internet of Things data privacy and security using systematic review. In *Advances in Cyber-Physical Systems and Security* (pp. 78–85). ECCWS., DOI: 10.34190/eccws.21.1.194

Tariq, M. U. (2025). Leveraging Artificial Intelligence to Enhance Diversity and Drive Business Innovation. In Margaretha van der Poll, H., Andrew van der Poll, J., & Ngwakwe, C. (Eds.), *Diversity, AI, and Sustainability for Financial Growth* (pp. 79–96). IGI Global Scientific Publishing., DOI: 10.4018/979-8-3693-6011-8.ch004

Tariq, M. U. (2025). Empowering Learning Through Networked and Connected Education: Case Studies in Digital Engagement. In Gierhart, A. (Ed.), *Cases on Enhancing P-16 Student Engagement With Digital Technologies* (pp. 169–198). IGI Global Scientific Publishing., DOI: 10.4018/979-8-3693-5633-3.ch007

Tariq, M. U. (2025). Quantum Algorithms and Predictive Analytics: Revolutionizing Consumer Insight. In Gajbhiye, P., Kannan, H., Rodriguez, R., & Rojas-Méndez, J. (Eds.), *The Quantum AI Era of Neuromarketing* (pp. 173–202). IGI Global Scientific Publishing., DOI: 10.4018/979-8-3693-7673-7.ch008

Tariq, M. U. (2025). Enhancing Pandemic Preparedness With AI-Driven Risk Prediction Models. In Shah, I., Sial, Q., & Fateh, S. (Eds.), *Generative AI Techniques for Sustainability in Healthcare Security* (pp. 77–94). IGI Global Scientific Publishing., DOI: 10.4018/979-8-3693-6577-9.ch005

Tariq, M. U. (2024). Integrating AI and Blockchain in EV Charging: Innovations and Challenges. In L. D., N. Nagpal, N. Kassarwani, V. Varthanan G., & P. Siano (Eds.), *A Sustainable Future with E-Mobility: Concepts, Challenges, and Implementations* (pp. 253-269). IGI Global Scientific Publishing. DOI: 10.4018/979-8-3693-5247-2.ch013

Tariq, M. U. (2024). Smart Transportation Systems: Paving the Way for Sustainable Urban Mobility. In Munuhwa, S. (Ed.), *Contemporary Solutions for Sustainable Transportation Practices* (pp. 254–283). IGI Global., DOI: 10.4018/979-8-3693-3755-4.ch010

Tariq, M. U. (2024). Application of blockchain and Internet of Things (IoT) in modern business. In Sinha, M., Bhandari, A., Priya, S., & Kabiraj, S. (Eds.), *Future of customer engagement through marketing intelligence* (pp. 66–94). IGI Global., DOI: 10.4018/979-8-3693-2367-0.ch004

Tariq, M. U. (2024). The role of AI ethics in cost and complexity reduction. In Tennin, K., Ray, S., & Sorg, J. (Eds.), *Cases on AI ethics in business* (pp. 59–78). IGI Global., DOI: 10.4018/979-8-3693-2643-5.ch004

Wang, C., Ma, C., Li, M., Gao, N., Zhang, Y., & Shen, Z. (2021). Protecting data privacy in federated learning combining differential privacy and weak encryption. In M. X. Editor & Y. Z. Editor (Eds.), *Federated Learning: Advances and Applications* (pp. 101–115). Springer. DOI: 10.1007/978-3-030-89137-4_7

Wei, W., Piuri, V., Pedrycz, W., & Ahmed, S. H. (2022). Special issue on Artificial Intelligence-of-Things (AIoT): Opportunities, challenges, and solutions-Part II: Artificial-intelligence-powered Internet of Things. *Future Generation Computer Systems*. Advance online publication. DOI: 10.1016/j.future.2022.07.019

KEY TERMS AND DEFINITIONS

AIoT (Artificial Intelligence of Things): AIoT integrates AI capabilities into IoT devices, enabling smart devices to autonomously analyze data, make decisions, and enhance functionalities. This combination leverages IoT's data collection and AI's processing power, facilitating real-time decision-making and automation across various applications, such as smart homes, healthcare, and industrial automation.

Data Privacy: Data privacy refers to the proper handling, processing, and storage of personal data to ensure it is not misused or accessed without consent. It focuses on safeguarding individuals' personal information from unauthorized access, breaches, or exploitation, and is governed by laws like GDPR or the DPDP Act, aiming to provide individuals control over their data.

AI-Driven Security: AI-driven security uses artificial intelligence to enhance cybersecurity by detecting threats, identifying vulnerabilities, and responding to attacks in real-time. AI algorithms can analyze large volumes of data for patterns, predict risks, and automate defense measures, making security systems more efficient and capable of adapting to new cyber threats.

Advanced Encryption: Advanced encryption involves using sophisticated cryptographic techniques to protect data by converting it into unreadable code during transmission or storage. Only authorized users with the correct decryption key can access the data. Advanced encryption methods, like AES (Advanced Encryption Standard), are critical in securing sensitive information, especially in AIoT systems, where data flows constantly.

Data Privacy Laws: Data privacy laws regulate the collection, processing, and storage of personal information to protect individuals' privacy rights. These laws, such as GDPR (Europe) or the DPDP Act (India), require organizations to obtain user consent, secure personal data, and offer individuals rights to access, correct, or delete their data. Non-compliance can lead to legal penalties, ensuring that companies handle personal data responsibly and transparently.

Differential Privacy: Differential privacy is a technique used to protect individual privacy in datasets. It adds random noise to data queries, ensuring that the privacy of any single individual's data is not compromised while still providing accurate aggregate insights. This method is widely applied in statistical analysis and machine learning, balancing data utility with privacy protection, especially in sensitive areas like healthcare or social datasets.

Predictive Analysis: Predictive analysis uses statistical algorithms and AI techniques to analyze historical data, identify patterns, and make future predictions. It is widely applied in industries like healthcare, finance, and manufacturing to forecast trends, risks, and opportunities, enabling proactive decision-making and problem-solving.

Federated Learning: Federated learning is a decentralized approach to machine learning where models are trained across multiple devices or servers without transferring raw data. Instead of centralizing data, devices share only updates to the model, ensuring data privacy. This method is particularly useful in AIoT, where sensitive data from multiple devices can be used for training while maintaining privacy and security.

Chapter 4
Integrating AI With Blockchains for Securing Cloud-Based IoT Networks:
Benefits, Issues, and Challenges

Mohamadi Begum Y.
https://orcid.org/0009-0000-0186-2890
Swami Vivekananda Yoga Anusandhana Samsthana University, Bangalore, India

Aashna K. Nishad
https://orcid.org/0009-0005-5607-7175
Presidency University, Bengaluru, India

Harshavardhan Vilas Kurtkoti
https://orcid.org/0009-0003-7002-2969
Presidency University, Bangalore, India

ABSTRACT

IoT network is a collection of vast number of objects or devices which can sense and generate data for further processing that aids decision-making in real time applications. Connecting such IoT devices to cloud servers helps in faster and easier data storage and processing. Integrating Artificial Intelligence (AI) with Blockchain technologies is a potential solution for all the security threats in an IoT network. The IoT cloud has got its own limitations in terms of storage, bandwidth and is more likely to get affected due to malicious attacks happening at multiple layers of IoT architecture. This chapter examines the need for securing IoT cloud using blockchain technology and enhancements made to the same by integrating

DOI: 10.4018/979-8-3693-8547-0.ch004

AI with Blockchain. The benefits due to this integration of technologies also bring in a few challenges which are discussed in this chapter.

INTRODUCTION

The collection of data from smart devices and its transfer over the Internet for storage and further processing are the fundamental tasks associated with the Internet of Things (IoT) (Li et al., 2015). IoT devices rely on the cloud for handling large volumes of data that cannot be managed by local systems that lack storage and processing capabilities. Further, the cloud also provides economy, flexibility, and scalability. Hence, IoT devices get connected to the servers present in the cloud, and this brings in questions of security, privacy, and trust concerns. These concerns are of significance, especially when the applications are sensitive, and it is the cloud architecture that determines how well these concerns can be addressed. Apart from designing a secure cloud architecture, it also holds good to provide in-built security for the devices themselves. Securing the IoT environment has two primary goals: one is to ensure all data from the devices is gathered, stored, processed, and communicated securely; secondly, the various vulnerabilities in IoT components need to be detected at the appropriate time and should be handled properly. There are several approaches to protect the cloud environment from malicious attacks and security breaches. However, many of these approaches and practices involve a shared responsibility for the cloud provider and the consumers. It becomes challenging for the participating devices and the networks, which have inherent capability constraints to handle the same.

There are multiple dimensions to IoT cloud security. Confidentiality, availability, and integrity of data refer to secured data in cloud-based IoT, while adherence to legal and non-legal norms ensuring data protection and confidentiality of personal information constitute what is called privacy. Trust refers to the assurance achieved when security and privacy expectations are met. Various authentication and authorization mechanisms help build a secure information system, and the degree of security depends on how well the threats and risks are handled. The solutions to ensure security, privacy, and trust depend on the application requirements. The key issues must be analyzed to devise appropriate solutions based on how sensitive the application is. Several solutions (Li et al., 2015; Bhardwaj et al., 2016; Alghofaili et al., 2021; Eghtesadi et al., 2014) for securing the cloud are found in the literature, including firewalls, access control mechanisms, virtual private networks, etc. In a large-scale resource-sharing environment like the cloud, the multi-tenancy characteristic of the cloud allows the applications to have their data isolated and unavailable for other applications. Nevertheless, multiple access points for the users increase the threat of security breaches. An additional mechanism or an extra level of complexity for maintaining the cloud storage is required to avoid such breaches. A hacker getting access to the data may bring down the trust aspects considerably. The accounts, the privileges, and the business transactions should be managed to mitigate the effects of such security issues. The cloud security solutions vary depending on the type of cloud and the type of service it offers. Thus, IoT cloud security requires a different approach because the traditional solutions cannot be directly applied in such a dynamic environment where scalability issues are common (Sicari et al., 2015). IoT cloud security should focus on overcoming the challenges of data threats, including data breaches, data loss, unauthorized access, etc. There are many security recommendations for IoT devices, such as biometrics and two-factor authorization, and yet another potential solution is the use of blockchains. Blockchain, which is most familiar with Bitcoin and Ethereum, offers an intriguing solution for IoT security. Blockchain as a data structure organizes transactions as an ordered linked list with backlinks (Nofer et al., 2017). Thus, it creates a highly structured distributed ledger with serialized transactions for a given application. Each block in the ledger has multiple fields, including a set of transactions along with their timestamp apart from a hash of the previous block.

The use of AI is becoming common in providing cybersecurity solutions (Sarker et al., 2021). AI tools, by learning from past data, can help in the recognition of patterns indicating security breaches. Thus, integrating AI with blockchain for realizing IoT environments would be a choice for securing the same. The rest of the chapter is organized as follows. In the next section, a background to the problem is stated, and the subsequent section establishes how blockchain can be useful for securing IoT clouds. The process and approaches, as well as benefits of the resultant environment due to integration of AI with Blockchains for securing the IoT cloud, are discussed next, and in the last section, we conclude with research directions in these integrated technologies (Tariq, 2025).

BACKGROUND

The IoT architecture is built on wireless sensor networks and cloud data storage and processing technologies. Smart devices collect, store, and transfer data via IoT gateways or edge devices to the cloud. Advances in communication and Internet technologies have made it possible to collect real-time data from such devices and transmit it to a computing infrastructure for further processing to arrive at decision-making for a few applications. These applications range from small-scale ones like smart home automation to large-scale applications like disaster management. Each device we use in daily life, if equipped with sensors and actuators for capturing and transmitting relevant data, becomes an IoT device. The sensed data from the environment being periodically gathered is generally processed by a cloud computing infrastructure. The data generated from the IoT devices is large, complex, and diverse, for which no traditional storage mechanism will suffice. Therefore, it is sent to the cloud based on the device's connectivity. The various options available for the same include satellite, cellular, Wi-Fi, and direct connections, etc. The complete set of data generated, if sent to the cloud, can be expensive in terms of cost and time due to the volume of the data. Further, the data based on the application needs has to be processed without incurring any delay to give a real-time response. IoT-cloud convergence is undoubtedly the viable solution for resource-constrained IoT devices that cannot handle security issues.

Types of IoT Security

The security of IoT systems is inherently complex due to the diverse range of devices, protocols, and data flows. The security of IoT systems is multifaceted, requiring a layered approach to protect against threats (Obaidat et al., 2020; Gopinath et al., 2023). The entire IoT security system can be depicted as shown in Figure 1, where the different types of IoT security deal with security aspects at different levels and with overlapping. A foundational aspect is *device security*, which ensures that individual IoT devices are protected from unauthorized access and tampering. This includes implementing robust device authentication and authorization mechanisms to verify and validate the identities of users and devices interacting within the system. Authentication mechanisms, such as device certificates, token-based or password-based, or biometric verification, validate the identity of devices interacting in an IoT ecosystem (Zhao et al., 2023). Authorization frameworks determine what actions a device is allowed to perform. Encryption at the device level ensures data confidentiality and integrity, protecting sensitive information like sensor readings or control commands. Firmware security, including secure boot processes and signed updates, prevents attackers from injecting malicious code into devices.

Figure 1. IoT security layers

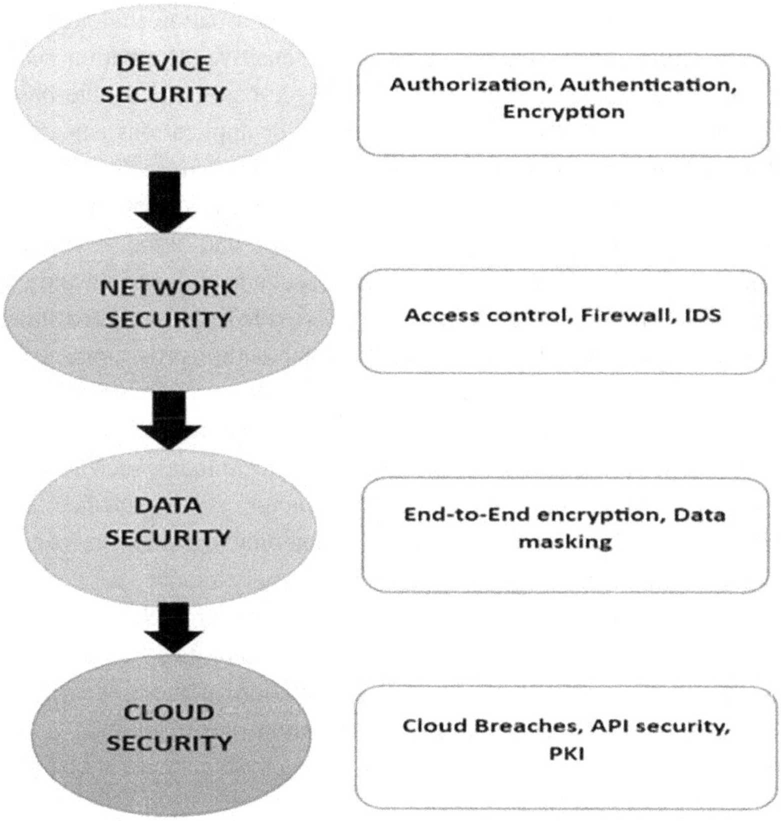

The devices in IoT networks transmit data via the internet, and hence, *network security* is vital for protecting the communication pathways that connect IoT devices. IoT systems often utilize diverse protocols like Message Queuing Telemetry Transport (MQTT), Constrained Application Protocol (CoAP), and Hypertext Transfer Protocol (HTTP), which may have varying levels of inherent security (Nikolov, 2020). Network access control mechanisms restrict unauthorized devices from joining the network, ensuring that only trusted devices participate in communication. Firewalls filter incoming and outgoing traffic, blocking malicious data packets, while intrusion detection systems (IDS) monitor network traffic for suspicious patterns indicative of cyberattacks. Given the distributed nature of IoT deployments, secure routing and encryption of network traffic are also critical components of network security. Another critical aspect is data security, which ensures the confidentiality, integrity, and availability of data generated by IoT devices (Chanal & Kakkasageri, 2020). Data transmitted across networks must be safeguarded using end-to-end encryption, ensuring that only authorized parties can access the information. In storage, techniques like data masking and tokenization anonymize sensitive information, reducing the risk of data breaches. Access controls, such as role-based or attribute-based access mechanisms, ensure that only authorized users or applications can interact with stored data. These measures are particularly significant in sectors like healthcare and finance, where IoT devices handle highly sensitive information subject to strict regulatory requirements. For systems that leverage cloud-based services, cloud security plays a pivotal role in mitigating risks associated with storing and processing IoT data offsite (Balogh et al., 2021). Cloud-based IoT platforms are vulnerable to attacks targeting the underlying infrastructure, application programming interfaces, or authentication mechanisms. Robust API security practices, including the use of secure API gateways and rate limiting, ensure secure communication between IoT devices and cloud platforms. Access management techniques, such as Multi-Factor Authentication (MFA) and Public Key Infrastructure (PKI), enhance the security of cloud-hosted IoT applications by ensuring that only legitimate users and devices access cloud resources. Together, the layers, namely, device, network, data, and cloud security, form a comprehensive framework for protecting IoT ecosystems. Each layer must be robust and adaptable, as vulnerabilities in any one layer can compromise the entire system. The implementation of these security measures requires a combination of technological solutions, organizational policies, and compliance with industry standards to ensure that systems remain resilient against evolving cyber threats (Tariq, 2025).

Security Issues in IoT

Threats in IoT (Sasi et al., 2024) are classified based on three aspects, namely, a. the physical nature of the smart objects from which data is sourced, b. their communication with one another, and c. confidential data getting intercepted by unauthorized parties. The last two categories of threats can be handled by using secure communication protocols and appropriate cryptographic algorithms, respectively (Cirani et al., 2013). These security threats occur at the various layers of the IoT architecture, namely, the perception, network, and middleware layers (Khan & Salah, 2018). The risk level of these threats is categorized in (Ivan et al., 2016). The medium risks happening at the middleware layer are very significant because this is the layer that is closer to the IoT application and where the IoT data gets stored and processed. Confidentiality refers to protecting privacy and access to data and is fundamental in any automated, networked applications (Sun et al., 2014). Confidentiality breaches in IoT networks are due to unauthorized access both at internal and external levels and data leaks (Shukla et al., 2022). Unauthorized access can adversely affect the functionality of the devices besides data leaks. Sensitive data, in particular, if not protected, can help attackers manipulate the data. Further, data in transit, if not encrypted properly, may also be exposed, leading to security threats. Not only weak encryption but also unencrypted communication channels result in potential threats. A strong intrusion detection system should be in place to protect these devices from threats, whether data at rest or in transit. Privacy gets compromised in cloud-based systems generally due to misconfigured access control mechanisms (Zuo et al., 2019). Thus, securing IoT devices becomes very crucial, especially for real-time as well as sensitive applications requiring high levels of security, privacy, and reliability. A few such applications include healthcare and medical devices, energy management, etc. Besides these common security threats, there are other inherent problems concerning the devices, like malicious software, limited update mechanisms, and improper storage.

Current Solutions for Security in Cloud-Based IoT Networks

Trust assessment of cloud services (Li et al., 2019) evaluates the cloud access and storage services for ensuring security and improved reputation. In the context of cloud-based IoT networks, scalability, latency, and data security challenges exist. Advanced solutions have been proposed and implemented to meet these requirements, combining concepts like edge computing, AI, and hybrid architectures.

Edge Computing

Edge computing brings the computational capabilities closer to IoT devices, reducing latency and bandwidth usage (Lim et al., 2023). This is especially useful for real-time monitoring applications, such as healthcare and smart city systems. Processing data locally at the edge also enhances privacy and ensures faster responses. However, the deployment of edge computing systems introduces vulnerabilities at the edge nodes, requiring robust security frameworks to safeguard sensitive data.

Hybrid Architectures: Cloud-Edge Orchestration

Hybrid architecture enables resource distribution of computations across cloud and edge layers for optimal usage. Cloud-edge orchestration (Wu, 2021) provides scalable solutions for low latency and high bandwidth IoT applications. For example, in the case of fog computing, intermediate layers between the cloud and edge help in reducing overhead on data transmission. However, this brings complexity into the picture due to increased layers that provide potential security gaps at the interface levels.

AI Integration in Edge and Fog Computing

AI integration into edge and fog computing further enables predictive analytics, real-time anomaly detection, and automated decision-making (Walia & Kumar, 2023). These features help predict security attacks in advance and optimize the IoT network efficiency. Nevertheless, AI systems can also be vulnerable to adversarial attacks and biased decisions. The robustness and transparency of AI algorithms are required (Tariq, 2025).

Blockchain for IoT Security

Blockchain is a decentralized security framework that secures data integrity and ensures secured communication between the IoTs. It is the foundation for cryptocurrencies like Bitcoin but has applications far beyond financial transactions. Data and transactions are digitally signed in a blockchain network. Reliability and security are guaranteed because of such encryption of both data and transactions. Blockchain operates using several key principles:

- **Decentralization**: Unlike traditional systems, which rely on a central authority, blockchain distributes data across a network of nodes. This eliminates single points of failure and enhances security.
- **Transparency**: All transactions are recorded in a public ledger, visible to participants within the network. This transparency ensures trust among users.
- **Immutability**: Once data is added to a blockchain, it cannot be altered or deleted. This feature ensures the integrity of records and prevents unauthorized modifications.
- **Consensus Mechanisms**: Blockchain relies on algorithms like Proof of Work (PoW), Proof of Stake (PoS), or Delegated Proof of Stake (DPoS) to validate transactions. These mechanisms ensure agreement among nodes and secure the network.
- **Smart Contracts**: These are self-executing contracts with terms directly written in the code. Smart contracts automate processes, reducing the need for intermediaries and enhancing efficiency.

In the context of IoT security, blockchain can address the following critical challenges:

- **Authentication**: Blockchain ensures that IoT data is tamper-proof, and devices and users can be authenticated through blockchain's decentralized identity management.
- **Secure Communication**: Peer-to-peer communication between IoT devices can be safeguarded without relying on a centralized server.
- **Audit Trails**: Blockchain maintains an immutable history of all interactions, allowing detailed auditing and tracking of device activity.

By integrating blockchain with IoT, organizations can enhance trust, reduce vulnerabilities, and create robust ecosystems for secure and scalable device communication (Krishnan et al., 2018). Smart contracts automatically execute processes and enforce security policies. Human interventions are thus reduced with blockchain. Blockchain solves the problem of trust and transparency but increases computation and storage complexity, and hence, it leads to scalability.

Zero Trust Security Models

Zero-trust security models involve continuous verification of the user and devices before granting them access. The process decreases the possibility of illegal entry by malicious agents and counteracts insider threats. However, the challenge remains to achieve zero trust across different IoT devices with varying capabilities and protocols. Zero Trust Security Models are designed with the principle that no user or device, whether inside or outside the network, should be trusted by default. Every access request must be continuously verified based on multiple factors, such as identity, device health, behavior patterns, and other contextual data. This approach significantly enhances security by minimizing the attack surface and reducing the risk of breaches.

Key Features of Zero-Trust Security Models

- **Continuous Authentication and Authorization**: Instead of granting broad, permanent access to users or devices once authenticated, Zero Trust requires constant validation of both the user's identity and the device's security status. This ensures that even if a user's credentials are compromised, an attacker cannot gain ongoing access.
- **Least Privilege Access**: Zero Trust implements the principle of least privilege, ensuring that users and devices are only granted the minimal level of access necessary for their specific roles or functions. This limits the potential damage that can occur in case of an attack.

- **Micro-Segmentation**: Network segmentation is taken to the next level in Zero Trust, where even within internal networks, different segments are isolated and protected. This containment strategy prevents lateral movement by attackers, ensuring that a breach in one part of the system does not expose the entire network.
- **Contextual and Behavioral Analysis**: Zero Trust security models use behavioral analytics and context-based access control to detect anomalies. By analyzing patterns such as login locations, access times, and device types, they can identify suspicious activities and restrict access in real time.
- **MFA**: MFA is a critical aspect of Zero Trust, ensuring that users authenticate through multiple layers of security (password, biometrics, hardware tokens, etc.). Even if one factor is compromised, attackers cannot access the system without passing the other layers of authentication.
- **End-to-End Encryption**: Data is encrypted at all stages—whether at rest, in transit, or use—making it difficult for unauthorized parties to intercept or manipulate the data. In the context of IoT, this protects the communications between devices and users from potential eavesdropping.

Enhancing IoT Security with Zero Trust

The application of Zero Trust in IoT environments is essential due to the unique challenges posed by the large number of devices with varying levels of security and different communication protocols (Li et al., 2022). Here's how Zero Trust enhances IoT security:

- **Device Authentication and Management**: Every IoT device is continuously authenticated and must meet security standards before it can communicate with the network. This ensures that unauthorized or compromised devices are detected and blocked from accessing the system. Devices are continuously monitored for health and compliance, minimizing risks associated with outdated or insecure devices.
- **Identity and Access Control for Devices**: Zero Trust solutions enable granular access control policies based on device identity, location, usage, and real-time data analysis. This reduces the risk of unauthorized devices gaining access to sensitive IoT networks or data.
- **Dynamic Policy Enforcement**: As IoT devices operate in various contexts (e.g., smart homes, industrial systems, healthcare networks), Zero Trust models dynamically enforce access policies tailored to each device's role, environment, and state. Policies adapt in real-time based on the context and trustworthiness of the device and user.

- **Mitigating Insider Threats**: Since Zero Trust treats every device and user as potentially compromised, it significantly reduces the risks posed by insider threats. Employees or devices with compromised credentials will face continuous scrutiny, limiting their ability to access sensitive information or systems.
- **Resilience to External Attacks**: Zero Trust models are designed to contain threats within defined segments, preventing attackers from exploiting vulnerabilities in one device to spread across the IoT ecosystem. This containment is critical for preventing large-scale, cascading attacks within complex IoT environments.

Challenges and Solutions in Implementing Zero Trust for IoT

The main challenge in applying Zero Trust to IoT is the diversity and heterogeneity of IoT devices and protocols. Many IoT devices have limited computational capabilities, making it difficult to implement traditional security measures such as strong encryption or continuous monitoring. Furthermore, the lack of standardization across IoT devices adds complexity to enforcing Zero Trust policies. Lightweight Security Protocols are proposed as a solution to overcome the above challenge. For devices with limited resources, lightweight encryption and authentication protocols can be designed to meet Zero Trust requirements without overloading the device's capabilities. Further, by processing data at the edge, closer to the devices, security measures such as real-time authentication, behavioral analysis, and anomaly detection can be offloaded from resource-constrained IoT devices, allowing for more efficient Zero Trust implementation. The development of standardized security frameworks for IoT, such as the IoT Cybersecurity Improvement Act, will facilitate the adoption of Zero Trust principles across diverse devices, helping to align various protocols and security measures. By addressing these challenges, Zero Trust security models can be effectively extended to IoT environments, ensuring robust protection against both external and internal threats while enabling secure, seamless device communication. There are several other general approaches that can be employed to enhance security in various environments, including IoT ecosystems. These approaches often focus on securing networks, systems, devices, and data using different methodologies. Here are some of the key security approaches:

- **Defense in Depth:** Defense in Depth (DiD) is a multi-layered security strategy (Mughal, 2018) that applies multiple layers of protection across a system, network, or application. The idea is that if one layer fails, others will continue to provide security, reducing the risk of a successful attack. Key components of DiD include firewalls, IDS, etc. As the first line of defense, endpoint security is taken care of by antivirus software that secures device configurations. Secure software development practices like vulnerability scanning and patch management ensure that applications are resistant to exploits. Encryption, tokenization, and backup strategies protect sensitive data from unauthorized access or loss. Employee training, role-based access control (RBAC), and strong authentication policies ensure that users follow security best practices. DiD is particularly effective in IoT environments because it allows for different security measures at various levels of the IoT ecosystem (e.g., devices, networks, applications).

- **Endpoint Security:** It focuses on securing individual devices (endpoints) within a network, such as computers, smartphones, IoT devices, and other connected systems. Given that each device can potentially be a target for attackers, endpoint security seeks to prevent, detect, and respond to malicious activity at the device level (Kamruzzaman et al., 2022). Techniques in Endpoint Security include Antivirus and Anti-malware software, device encryption, and patch management. Advanced tools that monitor and analyze the behavior of devices are used to detect unusual activities indicative of an attack. In IoT environments, endpoint security is critical, as many IoT devices have limited built-in security and may be more susceptible to compromise.
- **Network Segmentation:** It involves dividing a larger network into smaller, isolated segments to improve security. This approach (Baligodugula et al., 2024) limits the impact of security breaches by containing threats within a specific segment and preventing them from spreading throughout the entire network. Network segmentation can be done in a number of ways. Creating separate physical networks for different departments or systems is physical segmentation, while virtual segmentation refers to creating logical divisions within the same physical network infrastructure using VLANs (Virtual Local Area Networks) or SDN (Software-Defined Networking). More granular segmentation, often applied in cloud environments, has policies that control traffic between individual workloads, even within the same subnet, which is another type called micro-segmentation. In IoT systems, network segmentation is crucial as IoT devices can be vulnerable to cyberattacks, and isolating devices in different segments limits the spread of potential exploits.
- **Security Information and Event Management (SIEM):** SIEM is a security approach that involves collecting, analyzing, and acting upon data from various sources to detect, monitor, and respond to security threats. SIEM systems (González-Granadillo et al., 2021) aggregate logs and data from network devices, applications, and endpoints, providing security teams with real-time insights into the health and security posture of their environment.

Log management, real-time monitoring, and incident response are the key functionalities of SIEM.

- **Cloud Security:** As organizations increasingly rely on cloud services, securing cloud environments has become paramount. Cloud Security involves securing data, applications, and services hosted in cloud environments to ensure confidentiality, integrity, and availability. This ensures data encryption, identity and access management, multi-factor authentication, etc. Cloud security is especially important for IoT systems that rely on cloud infrastructure to store, process, or analyze IoT data. It ensures that sensitive information exchanged between IoT devices and cloud-based systems remains protected.
- **AI-Driven Security:** AI and ML are increasingly being integrated into security practices to enhance threat detection, response, and prevention (Abed & Anupam, 2022). These technologies can analyze large volumes of data, detect patterns, and predict potential threats or vulnerabilities in real time. Anomaly detection, automated responses, and predictive analysis techniques can help identify and mitigate threats in real time, especially in large-scale environments with thousands of devices. Assigning access rights based on the role or job function of the user or device and allowing users to access multiple systems with a single identity across different platforms are some widely adopted techniques.

LIMITATIONS IN IOT CLOUD SECURITY

Despite these solutions, many gaps still exist in the security of cloud-based IoT networks, which are as follows. Centralized systems are still vulnerable to single points of failure and thus susceptible to disruptions during outages or cyberattacks. Decentralized approaches are promising but have yet to achieve wide-scale scalability. Interoperability issues, wherein the IoT devices operate on different standards and protocols, make it challenging to integrate them seamlessly into unified security frameworks (Noura ct al., 2018). Since there is no standardization, uniform security practices are hard to implement. Interface vulnerabilities (Celesti et al., 2019) occur at the interface between cloud and edge layers and are unavoidable. Although edge computing offers an advantage in reducing latency, weak encryption or poor authentication mechanisms may make sensitive data open to attackers. AI vulnerabilities are yet another challenge. When AI systems are introduced into IoT networks, they can be attacked by adversarial attacks, thereby causing compromised prediction accuracy and decision-making. Ensuring AI robustness and explainability is still an open challenge. Although blockchain provides better security and trust, its high computational and storage requirements hinder its usage in resource-constrained

IoT devices. Data privacy laws like the General Data Protection Regulation (GDPR) lay very stringent requirements, and compliance is very challenging to achieve in globally deployed IoT networks. Therefore, there is a big trade-off between data utility and privacy, and innovatively federated learning may hold promise. There are several such limitations in the few existing solutions. Integrating AI with blockchain to secure the IoT cloud data is becoming popular due to the advantage of decentralization (Yu et al., 2018). The approaches to integrate IoT and Blockchain, the advantages and challenges are discussed in the following section.

Blockchains for Securing IoT Networks

Blockchain technology is all about building data structures that are inherently secure to ensure trust in transactions. A blockchain is basically a data structure resistant to hacking that follows a decentralized approach and uses cryptography and consensus techniques for incorporating security in applications, in particular those with risks of fraud and cyberattacks.

Key Advantages of Blockchain Technology

- **Enhanced Security:** Blockchain provides a high level of security due to its decentralized and cryptographic nature. Each transaction is cryptographically linked to the previous one, forming an immutable chain of blocks. The use of hash functions, public-private key encryption, and digital signatures ensures that transactions cannot be altered or tampered with without detection. Additionally, because the blockchain is decentralized, no single entity controls the entire network, making it difficult for hackers to alter or compromise the system.
- **Transparency and Accountability:** Blockchain provides transparency by recording all transactions in a publicly accessible ledger. Every participant in the network can view the transaction history, which ensures accountability. This transparency makes blockchain particularly useful for industries where traceability is crucial, such as supply chain management, financial services, and voting systems.
- **Decentralization:** Unlike traditional systems where a central authority controls data, blockchain operates on a decentralized network of nodes. Each node (or participant) in the network has a copy of the entire blockchain, and all decisions are made collectively through consensus mechanisms. This decentralization reduces the risk of fraud or corruption associated with central authorities and intermediaries.

- **Cost Efficiency:** Blockchain can lower costs by eliminating the need for intermediaries and automating processes through smart contracts. In traditional systems, third-party intermediaries such as banks, payment processors, and notaries are required to facilitate transactions. Blockchain removes the need for these intermediaries by enabling peer-to-peer transactions that are verified by the network itself.
- **Faster Transactions:** Blockchain can process transactions more quickly than traditional banking or payment systems, especially for cross-border payments. Traditional financial systems often involve intermediaries that slow down transactions, particularly across international borders. With blockchain, transactions can be completed almost instantly, especially when using digital currencies or cryptocurrencies.
- **Traceability:** Blockchain offers traceability by recording every transaction in a transparent and immutable ledger. This feature is especially beneficial in supply chain management, where it is important to track the movement of goods and verify their authenticity.
- **Increased Trust:** Because blockchain transactions are verifiable and immutable, participants in a blockchain network can trust that the data has not been altered or tampered with. This is particularly useful in environments where trust is critical, such as in financial transactions, voting systems, and contractual agreements.
- **Improved Data Integrity:** Blockchain ensures the integrity of data by using cryptographic hash functions and consensus algorithms. Each block in the blockchain contains a unique hash of the previous block, which makes it extremely difficult to modify the data without changing the entire blockchain. This ensures that the data stored on the blockchain is accurate and reliable.
- **Privacy and Confidentiality:** Blockchain can be designed to ensure privacy and confidentiality by allowing participants to maintain control over their data. While blockchain ensures transparency in transactions, sensitive data can be encrypted or stored off-chain. Additionally, blockchain networks can use pseudonymity, where participants use public keys instead of real-world identities to protect privacy.
- **Scalability:** While traditional centralized systems often struggle with scalability, blockchain systems are designed to handle a growing number of transactions and users. New advancements in blockchain technology, such as sharding and layer-2 solutions, aim to enhance scalability and improve transaction throughput, making blockchain suitable for large-scale applications.

Blockchain security fundamentally relies on cryptography and consensus to provide integrity, authenticity, and trust (Deepak et al., 2024; Commey et al., 2024). Most cryptography used by blockchain-based IoT systems is centered around the public-key approaches, specifically elliptic curve cryptography, which provides robust protection of exchanged data and transactions, ensuring both encryption and authentication. Data exchanges happen only after the authentication process is completed. More than that, hash functions such as SHA-256, which is used for securing the structure of a blockchain by creating unique hashes for data blocks and linking them securely with integrity checks, protect the IoT application by encrypting sensitive information and making data immutable.

The distributed blockchain network achieves secure transaction validation without a central authority by utilizing consensus mechanisms, either PoW or PoS. These mechanisms play a crucial role in ensuring the integrity and security of the blockchain by allowing decentralized participants to agree on the validity of transactions.

- **Proof of Work (PoW):** This is the original consensus algorithm used in Bitcoin and many other blockchains. It requires participants, known as miners, to solve complex mathematical problems to validate transactions and add them to the blockchain. This process is resource-intensive and requires significant computational power. PoW employs a mining process where the miners compete to solve a cryptographic puzzle by finding a noun (a random number). This process requires significant computing resources because the correct solution is difficult to find but easy to verify. PoW makes it extremely difficult for malicious actors to alter the blockchain because they would need to redo the computational work for all subsequent blocks. This ensures the immutability of the ledger. PoW has the advantages of security and decentralization despite having limited scalability and being energy intensive.
- **Proof of Stake (PoS):** This is an alternative consensus mechanism that is more energy-efficient than PoW. In PoS, validators (rather than miners) are chosen to create new blocks based on the amount of cryptocurrency they "stake" as collateral, rather than on their computational power. Here, participants (validators) lock up a certain amount of their cryptocurrency holdings as collateral (stake) to have the chance to validate transactions. Validators are chosen to create new blocks based on the size of their stake and the duration of the stake, often using a randomized selection process. If a validator behaves dishonestly (e.g., validating fraudulent transactions), they risk losing a portion of their staked cryptocurrency. This discourages malicious behavior. Since PoS does not require extensive computational resources, it is significantly more energy-efficient than PoW. It is scalable, too.

- **Hybrid Consensus Mechanisms:** This mechanism combines the advantages of PoW and PoS along with Delegated Proof of Stake (DPoS) for block creation and Practical Byzantine Fault Tolerance (PBFT) for block validation (Venkatesan & Rahayu, 2024). By taking advantage of individual mechanisms, we can improve scalability, security, and efficiency considerably.

Both PoW and PoS have their strengths and trade-offs, and the choice of consensus mechanism depends on the specific needs of the blockchain network, such as energy efficiency, scalability, and decentralization. These algorithms guarantee agreement among the participants in the network regarding whether the transactions are valid. For IoT applications, lightweight protocols for consensus are also getting attention in terms of energy and computations. For example, DPoS or PBFT can be used increasingly in IoT cases to ensure faster validation while having minimal overhead of computation. This makes blockchain integration in IoT environments efficient and secure against malicious actors. Integrating blockchain to IoT cloud enhances the security provided by the cloud environment and overcomes a few challenges stated in the previous section.

The Approach and Advantages

IoT devices, the clients generate data and create transactions. The participating IoT nodes in the blockchain network are responsible for maintaining all their transactions collaboratively on the blockchain (Reyna et al., 2018). These transactions are stored as a distributed database composed of blocks of data and get copied in every node. A list of transactions, along with their respective timestamp and a link to the previous block, constitutes one block in the blockchain. While the blockchain allows transparent information sharing within a network, it does not permit one to edit the same. This sort of immutable nature of the blockchain makes it useful in several business applications where data integrity and security are primary concerns. A secure IoT environment can be built easily by employing a unique key code to access the network. By doing so, every transaction would be accountable, leaving no room for unauthorized access. Attempts to make any changes can be traced back easily. Using blockchains, we can give locking access to IoT devices so that anyone intruding would be denied access to the data. Authentication of users can be ensured by Elliptic curve cryptography (ECC). ECC, which is a public key cryptography technique, is employed in blockchains to validate new transactions and hence to ensure that they are from an authorized user or not. In addition to ECC, blockchains use the SHA-256 hashing technique (Martino & Cilardo, 2020) for making the IoT application less vulnerable. SHA-256 is a powerful hashing technique for ensuring data authentication and integrity through its use in multiple stages of the blockchain

(Tariq, 2025). Primarily, each block in the database has a hash generated by SHA to refer to the preceding block of the chain. Every transaction caused by the IoT application needs to be validated by a consensus mechanism for it to be authenticated. To do so, all participating peers in the blockchain network reach a common agreement through a consensus mechanism, which is based again on SHA. The transaction information is hashed using SHA, which in turn is verified by the miners to validate the transaction. Thus, the blockchain has all blocks in it timestamped and validated by the miners to make it nearly impossible for security attacks, considering the computational capabilities required for causing alterations to the database.

Blockchain Security

The classical approaches of the blockchain-based authentication process are a little complex because of the limited capabilities of IoT devices (Ourad et al., 2018). The complexity increases also due to the centralized nature of the process. The simplest approach of securing by passwords is just not scalable where the devices are dynamic and large in number. Scalability issues can be solved by adopting a single sign-on policy. Public-key cryptography securely authenticates devices and users to ensure only legitimate entities participate and transact. The distributed authentication approach (Deepak et al., 2024) is an enhanced version that prevents a single point of failure in the process. Context-aware access control system allows users to dynamically define the contextual access rights in a smart contract (Sylla et al., 2021, Merlec & In, 2024). The contextual information usually includes user profile, resources, and other information relevant to acquiring access. Location-aware, role-based access control is an approach to having the resource owners send transactions to the blockchain. Thus, the blockchain manages the relationship between roles and permissions (Rahman et al., 2020).

Advantages

Several important benefits come from integrating blockchain into IoT. For one, it would improve data security through cryptographical techniques that ensure integrity as well as prevent unauthorized access to data. The decentralized approach of blockchain eliminates the threat of a single point of failure in IoT networks, making them more resilient against cyberattacks. It also guarantees that data is transparent and immutable so that all stakeholders can access a tamper-proof record of transactions. Smart contracts automate processes, reduce intermediaries, and make operations more efficient. Also, lightweight consensus mechanisms for IoT are designed with a balance between scalability and energy efficiency, tailored to resource-constrained devices.

Limitations and Challenges

Blockchain-based IoT cloud security, despite the above advantages, has certain limitations in terms of its implementation (Kumar & Mallick, 2018). The limitations are both open and related to IoT integration. These limitations are listed below.

Limited Scalability

The speed with which the transactions get validated and stored in the blockchain is primarily dependent on computational power. The mining process employed by blockchain is a compute-intensive task requiring more power and is certainly an inhibiting factor for the resource-constrained IoT devices. As the network grows while we want to increase the performance, we may have to trade-off between scalability, decentralization and security (Wang, 2021). This limitation has a severe impact, especially on real-time IoT applications, which cannot compromise on the speed and, hence, the performance of the blockchain.

Complex Authentication Process

Blockchain-based authentication of nodes overcomes the problem of single-point failure and certificate transparency prevalent in traditional public key infrastructure. Nevertheless, the authentication mechanism is complex due to the process of certificate management and usage. Although the authentication of nodes is essential for a secure environment, when done by a complex process, it will slow down the operations (Ao et al., 2019; Tian et al., 2020).

Increased Network Traffic Flow

A blockchain consensus protocol has various components, namely block proposal, block validation, information propagation, block finalization, and incentive mechanism (Xiao et al., 2020). These components of various consensus protocols (Bouraga, 2021; Wang et al., 2019) are time consuming as well as cause considerable network flow which impacts communication among the IoT devices.

Limited Storage

Since the blockchain maintains a distributed database, every node in the IoT network is required to record all transactional events. In contrast to a centralized IoT network, if the entire IoT network implements Blockchain technology, the total storage capacity is proportional to the square of the network size (Jhaveri et al., 2018). Thus, the limited storage capabilities of the devices make their direct participation in the blockchain difficult. System efficiency gets compromised when such data storage requirements exceed the actual storage available, and the resultant scalability issues must be addressed.

Compatibility

A majority of IoT applications are built around client-server architecture, relying on central servers for carrying out transactions. In principle, due to the decentralized nature of blockchains, care should be taken to configure the IoT sensors and other participants to be compatible with decentralization.

AI-ENABLED BLOCKCHAINS FOR IOT SECURITY

The emergence of AI and its Potential in IoT Cloud has impacted how security measures are devised. There is an important role of the emerging AI in the evolving landscape of IoT. IoT devices generate a large amount of complex data, which becomes impossible to process and derive insights from through traditional systems. AI provides the tools needed for analysis, interpretation, and real-time decision-making in highly unpredictable environments. It can predict model failures, such as network crashes or device malfunctioning, ahead of the event. With machine learning algorithms, IoT systems can learn from their history and become more accurate and adaptable in their predictions over time. Such predictive capabilities add to the reliability of IoT applications, especially when decision-making must be instantaneous in certain environments. AI-enabled blockchain security for IoT networks combines the advantages of the two technologies, AI and Blockchain, to offer enhanced security and transparency. As shown in Figure 2, AI helps create new business models by detecting and predicting anomalies and patterns, while blockchain makes it difficult for hackers to alter the records and, thereby, the transactions. Data management becomes seamless, and the risk of security breaches is reduced.

Figure 2. Convergence of Blockchain and AI

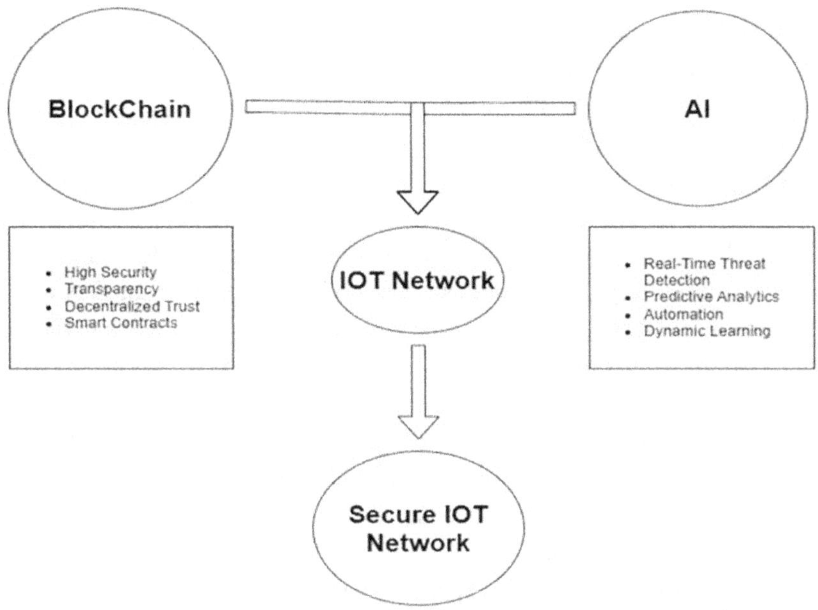

With AI integrated with IoT, the devices make self-determining decisions in highly complex, dynamic environments. For example, within an autonomous vehicle, an AI algorithm may make split-second decisions that rely on real-time data input from the vehicle's sensors, hence navigating through unpredictable traffic without harming its passengers. In industrial IoT, AI optimizes the operations of machines by using sensor data to identify potential failure or wear early on before expensive downtime. In addition, AI is an essential enabler of IoT cybersecurity. There are billions of connected devices in an IoT ecosystem, making the systems vulnerable to cyber-attacks. AI-based cybersecurity solutions monitor transactions, identify anomalies, and determine potential threats, providing ample opportunities for the prevention of fraud, data breaches, and malware attacks. This capability will ensure IoT networks are safeguarded from emerging cyber threats.

AI, blockchain, and IoT convergence led to a decentralized, secure, and intelligent ecosystem. AI can optimize the consensus mechanisms and transaction verification processes of blockchain networks, making them more scalable and energy efficient. For example, AI algorithms can predict the optimal path for transaction validation, improving the speed and reducing the computational overhead associated with blockchain operations. Furthermore, AI allows for the automation of complex processes such as access control, risk detection, and incident response. The integration of AI into blockchain networks allows IoT systems to operate autonomously, detect intrusions, and prevent malicious activities in real time. This approach using AI-enabled blockchain enhances the security, transparency, and reliability of IoT applications, making them more resilient to fraud and cyberattacks.

AI Integration

When AI is integrated into the Blockchain network of the IoT environment, it can create a decentralized network to operate without much manual intervention. The large number of IoT devices and the vast amount of data they generate require more computing power as well as time. AI algorithms and techniques can be built to analyze and interpret this data quickly and, hence, arrive at decisions in real time. The decision-making process thus can be automated, and recurring tasks can be done with ease. IoT security requires identifying and prioritizing risks associated with the generated data, its transactions, storage, and processing. In literature, we find many solutions proposed to overcome the limitations stated in the previous section. AI integrated into the blockchain can identify and prioritize risk, instantly spot any malware on a network, guide incident response, and detect intrusions before they start (Kaur et al., 2023). Various intrusion detection and prevention systems enabled by AI are reviewed in (Wiafe et al., 2020). The optimization processes of AI algorithms improve IoT security that is already taken care of by the nature of blockchains. Authentication and access control mechanisms can also be enhanced through AI (Bera et al., 2021; Fang et al., 2020), especially when coupled with machine learning techniques. Any intrusions in the network can also be detected, and more security layers can be added to the network. An AI-based access control framework for malicious attacks detection and mitigation (Bera et al., 2021) has been suggested to secure the IoT environment. Further, AI can also be used to generate secure smart contracts (Bai et al., 2018).

Smart contracts in a blockchain are executable codes to execute an agreement between untrustworthy parties without the involvement of a trusted third party. They enable users to codify their agreements and trust relations by providing automated transactions without the supervision of a central authority (Zheng et al., 2020). These contracts are generally not very secure and are prone to tampering despite being copied to each node in the network. Smart contract vulnerabilities and their security risks are summarized in Piantadosi et al. (2022), Praitheeshan et al. (2020), and Rouhani & Deters (2019). Security optimization-centric solutions with respect to vulnerability detection, transactional privacy, and trustworthy data feeding are presented in (Khan et al., 2021). By optimizing smart contracts, it would be possible to reduce potential vulnerabilities, and AI algorithms can be of help (Christidis & Devetsikiotis, 2016). Moreover, the detection of scams initiating malicious attacks on smart contracts can also be explored by employing AI.

Adaptive AI

AI solutions for enhancing security in IoT networks tend to distinguish authorized devices from unauthorized ones. In terms of network security, they must classify network behavior as normal or abnormal. An intelligent and automated detection mechanism followed by defense or corrective actions enhances IoT security (Wu et al., 2020). IoT security gets further enhanced when AI algorithms become adaptive. Instead of learning from the fixed rules and past data alone, these algorithms are capable of deriving insights on security threats and breaches in real time based on new data and experiences. Adaptive AI algorithms should consider the dynamic nature of IoT network, variety, and the limited computing power of the devices. Deviations from normal patterns or device behavior, termed as anomalies, need to be detected, and preventive actions should be recommended by AI algorithms.

Limitations in AI-Enabled IoT Security

IoT devices have limited computing power and are a bottleneck when it comes to deploying complex, resource-intensive AI models in them. This limitation is resolved using cloud and edge computing paradigms. However, to detect new attacks and threats, the learning needs to be continuous, and the same has to be updated regularly to make it effective. To balance the high computational overheads, if small data sets are used, it will result in bias and inaccuracy, which may lead to added vulnerabilities in the system. Furthermore, statistically significant findings are difficult to obtain. The emergence of ML-based approaches has made threat analysis more effective. However, the training data for these approaches is again from the devices that are heterogeneous with different capabilities and with different operating systems. Thus, the diversity of devices often results in complex models for security measures. The data generated by these devices also is in variety, many times unstructured, incomplete, and inconsistent. Overfitting and underfitting issues arise when the model learns from the data too closely or fails to capture the underlying patterns in the training data. Decision tree-based ML algorithms are widely used for intrusion detection in IoT networks. Features extracted from networks are fed to these algorithms, whose outcome is either 'intrusive' or 'normal.' These algorithms have limitations due to overfitting as the tree grows deeper. Noisy data can also lead to inaccurate results. Feature extraction needs to be carefully done, which is a time-consuming process. Deep Learning (DL) is a type of AI using advanced neural networks and algorithms.

Inherent dynamism and distribution in IoT networks are due to the addition, removal, and movement of the devices. Such dynamic and distributed IoT networks pose a bigger challenge; DL is particularly used when the data sets derived from complex sensor data are large and often employed for detecting advanced threats. Advanced threats are due to sophisticated risks that can compromise the integrity, confidentiality, and availability of data. DL enables accurate threat detection and predictive analytics but at the cost of latency and high processing time.

FUTURE DIRECTIONS AND CONCLUSION

Security breaches are common in networked applications, especially in a cloud, and current research focuses on how to overcome the challenges they bring in. One of the approaches is edge computing, which calls for data processing at the edges of the network (Shi et al., 2016) and addresses the problems of timely responses, limited bandwidth, and data safety and privacy. With more IoT applications moving toward edge computing, a distributed trusted authentication system (Guo et al., 2020) is becoming popular. The unique security and privacy requirements in cloud-based IoT (Zhou et al., 2017) and their respective countermeasures should consider next-generation mobile technologies too, since most of the devices are ubiquitous by nature. Various domains such as supply chain management, smart cities, healthcare, and agriculture, etc., require solutions for them to operate with efficiency and security. The convergence of IoT, AI, and Blockchain holds good for complete automation of applications in these key domains. IoT networks can be more secure if the solutions are decentralized. Federated learning (Zhang et al., 2021) is an enhanced ML technique that ensures the data privacy of each device during the training period where multiple clients collaborate. Although this technique is useful in domains such as healthcare and finance, it also is subjected to a few security attacks (Shaveta, 2024) that require further research on cryptography-based protections. Securing IoT networks based on fog computing integrated with 5G technologies is also a direction in the future for mitigating security threats. Energy efficiency is another key challenge in adopting solutions for securing IoT devices. A software-defined network (SDN) is a networking architecture where the entire network is controlled by a centralized software-based controller. Programmable SDN, being dynamic and pervasive, ensures energy efficiency, yet it is prone to anomaly and intrusion attacks (Rawat & Reddy, 2017). Thus, in addition to protecting from security breaches, any proposed solution to secure IoT networks needs to also ensure efficiency, scalability, resilience, energy efficiency, and many more essential features.

REFERENCES

Abed, A. K., & Anupam, A. (2022). Review of security issues in the Internet of Things and artificial intelligence-driven solutions. *Security and Privacy*, *6*(3), e285. DOI: 10.1002/spy2.285

Alghofaili, Y., Albattah, A., Alrajeh, N., Rassam, M. A., & Al-rimy, B. A. (2021). Secure cloud infrastructure: A survey on issues, current solutions, and open challenges. *Applied Sciences (Basel, Switzerland)*, *11*(19), 9005. DOI: 10.3390/app11199005

Ao, W., Fu, S., Zhang, C., Huang, Y., & Xia, F. (2019). A secure identity authentication scheme based on blockchain and identity-based cryptography. In Proceedings of *2019 IEEE 2nd International Conference on Computer and Communication Engineering Technology (CCET),* Beijing, China. DOI: 10.1109/CCET48361.2019.8989361

Bai, X., Cheng, Z., Duan, Z., & Hu, K. (2018). Formal modeling and verification of smart contracts. In *Proceedings of the 2018 7th International Conference on Software and Computer Applications,* Kuantan, Malaysia. DOI: 10.1145/3185089.3185138

Baligodugula, V. V., Ghimire, A., & Amsaad, F. (2024). An overview of secure network segmentation in connected IIoT environments. *Computing & AI Connect*, *1*(1), 1–12. DOI: 10.69709/CAIC.2024.193182

Balogh, S., Gallo, O., Ploszek, R., Špaček, P., & Zajac, P. (2021). IoT Security Challenges: Cloud and Blockchain, Postquantum Cryptography, and Evolutionary Techniques. *Electronics (Basel)*, *10*(21), 2647. DOI: 10.3390/electronics10212647

Bera, B., Das, A. K., Obaidat, M. S., Vijayakumar, P., Hsiao, K., & Park, Y. (2021). AI-enabled blockchain-based access control for malicious attacks detection and mitigation in IoE. *IEEE Consumer Electronics Magazine*, *10*(5), 82–92. DOI: 10.1109/MCE.2020.3040541

Bhardwaj, A., Subramanyam, G., Avasthi, V., & Sastry, H. (2016). Review of solutions for securing end user data over cloud applications. *International Journal of Advanced Computer Research*, *6*(27), 222–229. DOI: 10.19101/IJACR.2016.626005

Bouraga, S. (2021). A taxonomy of blockchain consensus protocols: A survey and classification framework. *Expert Systems with Applications*, *168*, 114384. DOI: 10.1016/j.eswa.2020.114384

Celesti, A., Fazio, M., Galletta, A., Carnevale, L., Wan, J., & Villari, M. (2019). An approach for the secure management of hybrid cloud–edge environments. *Future Generation Computer Systems*, *90*, 1–19. DOI: 10.1016/j.future.2018.06.043

Chanal, P. M., & Kakkasageri, M. S. (2020). Security and privacy in IoT: A survey. *Wireless Personal Communications, 115*(2), 1667–1693. DOI: 10.1007/s11277-020-07649-9

Christidis, K., & Devetsikiotis, M. (2016). Blockchains and smart contracts for the Internet of things. *IEEE Access : Practical Innovations, Open Solutions, 4*, 2292–2303. DOI: 10.1109/ACCESS.2016.2566339

Cirani, S., Ferrari, G., & Veltri, L. (2013). Enforcing security mechanisms in the IP-based Internet of things: An algorithmic overview. *Algorithms, 6*(2), 197–226. DOI: 10.3390/a6020197

Commey, D., Mai, B., Hounsinou, S. G., & Crosby, G. V. (2024). Securing blockchain-based IoT systems: A review. *IEEE Access : Practical Innovations, Open Solutions, 12*, 98856–98881. DOI: 10.1109/ACCESS.2024.3428490

Deepak, G., Gulia, P., Gill, N. S., Yahya, M., Gupta, P., Shukla, P. K., & Shukla, P. K. (2024). Exploring the potential of blockchain technology in an IoT-enabled environment: A review. *IEEE Access : Practical Innovations, Open Solutions, 12*, 31197–31227. DOI: 10.1109/ACCESS.2024.3366656

Eghtesadi, A., Jarraya, Y., Debbabi, M., & Pourzandi, M. (2014). Preservation of security configurations in the cloud. In *Proceedings of the 2014 IEEE International Conference on Cloud Engineering,* 17-26. DOI: 10.1109/IC2E.2014.14

Fang, H., Qi, A., & Wang, X. (2020). Fast authentication and progressive authorization in large-scale IoT: How to leverage AI for security enhancement. *IEEE Network, 34*(3), 24–29. DOI: 10.1109/MNET.011.1900276

González-Granadillo, G., González-Zarzosa, S., & Diaz, R. (2021). Security information and event management (SIEM): Analysis, trends, and usage in critical infrastructures. *Sensors (Basel), 21*(14), 4759. DOI: 10.3390/s21144759

Gopinath, V., Rao, K. V., & Rao, S. K. (2023). A comprehensive analysis of IoT security towards providing a cost-effective solution: A layered approach. *International Journal of Information Technology : an Official Journal of Bharati Vidyapeeth's Institute of Computer Applications and Management, 15*(7), 3813–3826. DOI: 10.1007/s41870-023-01405-5

Guo, S., Hu, X., Guo, S., Qiu, X., & Qi, F. (2020). Blockchain meets edge computing: A distributed and trusted authentication system. *IEEE Transactions on Industrial Informatics, 16*(3), 1972–1983. DOI: 10.1109/TII.2019.2938001

Ivan, C., Vujic, M., & Husnjak, S. (2016). Classification of security risks in the IoT environment. In *Proceedings of the 26th DAAAM International Symposium,* Vienna, Australia. DOI: 10.2507/26th.daaam.proceedings.102

Jhaveri, R. H., Patel, N. M., Zhong, Y., & Sangaiah, A. K. (2018). Sensitivity analysis of an attack-pattern discovery based trusted routing scheme for mobile ad-hoc networks in industrial IoT. *IEEE Access : Practical Innovations, Open Solutions, 6*, 20085–20103. DOI: 10.1109/ACCESS.2018.2822945

Kamruzzaman, A., Ismat, S., Brickley, J. C., Liu, A., & Thakur, K. (2022). A comprehensive review of endpoint security: Threats and defenses. In *Proceedings of the 2022 International Conference on Cyber Warfare and Security (ICCWS),* New York, USA. DOI: 10.1109/ICCWS56285.2022.9998470

Kaur, R., Gabrijelčič, D., & Klobučar, T. (2023). Artificial intelligence for cybersecurity: Literature review and future research directions. *Information Fusion, 97*, 101804. DOI: 10.1016/j.inffus.2023.101804

Khan, M. A., & Salah, K. (2018). IoT security: Review, blockchain solutions, and open challenges. *Future Generation Computer Systems, 82*, 395–411. DOI: 10.1016/j.future.2017.11.022

Khan, S. N., Loukil, F., Ghedira-Guegan, C., Benkhelifa, E., & Bani-Hani, A. (2021). Blockchain smart contracts: Applications, challenges, and future trends. *Peer-to-Peer Networking and Applications, 14*(5), 2901–2925. DOI: 10.1007/s12083-021-01127-0

Krishnan, K. N., Jenu, R., Joseph, T., & Silpa, M. L. (2018). Blockchain based security framework for IoT implementations. In *Proceedings of the 2018 International CET Conference on Control, Communication, and Computing (IC4)*, Trivandrum, India. DOI: 10.1109/CETIC4.2018.8531042

Kumar, N. M., & Mallick, P. K. (2018). Blockchain technology for security issues and challenges in IoT. *Procedia Computer Science, 132*, 1815–1823. DOI: 10.1016/j.procs.2018.05.140

Li, S., Iqbal, M., & Saxena, N. (2022). Future industry internet of things with zero-trust security. *Information Systems Frontiers*, •••, 1–14.

Li, S., Xu, L. D., & Zhao, S. (2014). The Internet of things: A survey. *Information Systems Frontiers, 17*(2), 243–259. DOI: 10.1007/s10796-014-9492-7

Li, X., Wang, Q., Lan, X., Chen, X., Zhang, N., & Chen, D. (2019). Enhancing cloud-based IoT security through trustworthy cloud service: An integration of security and reputation approach. *IEEE Access : Practical Innovations, Open Solutions, 7*, 9368–9383. DOI: 10.1109/ACCESS.2018.2890432

Lim, E. H., & Chai, Y., T., Muniandy, M. A., Fui Yong, T., Ooi, B. Y., & Lin, J. (2023). Edge computing and AI for IoT: Opportunities and challenges. In *Proceedings of the 2023 International Conference on Consumer Electronics - Taiwan (ICCE-Taiwan),* Pingtung, Taiwan. DOI: 10.1109/ICCE-Taiwan58799.2023.10226787

Martino, R., & Cilardo, A. (2020). Designing a SHA-256 processor for blockchain-based IoT applications. *Internet of Things : Engineering Cyber Physical Human Systems*, *11*, 100254. DOI: 10.1016/j.iot.2020.100254

Merlec, M. M., & In, H. P. (2024). SC-CAAC: A smart-contract-Based context-aware access control scheme for blockchain-enabled IoT systems. *IEEE Internet of Things Journal*, *11*(11), 19866–19881. DOI: 10.1109/JIOT.2024.3371504

Mughal, A. A. (2018). The Art of Cybersecurity: Defense in Depth Strategy for Robust Protection. *International Journal of Intelligent Automation and Computing*, *1*(1), 1–20.

Nikolov, N. (2020). Research of MQTT, CoAP, HTTP and XMPP IoT Communication protocols for Embedded Systems. In *Proceedings of the 2020 XXIX International Scientific Conference Electronics (ET)*, Sozopol, Bulgaria. DOI: 10.1109/ET50336.2020.9238208

Nofer, M., Gomber, P., Hinz, O., & Schiereck, D. (2017). Blockchain. *Business & Information Systems Engineering*, *59*(3), 183–187. DOI: 10.1007/s12599-017-0467-3

Noura, M., Atiquzzaman, M., & Gaedke, M. (2018). Interoperability in Internet of things: Taxonomies and open challenges. *Mobile Networks and Applications*, *24*(3), 796–809. DOI: 10.1007/s11036-018-1089-9

Obaidat, M. A., Obeidat, S., Holst, J., Al Hayajneh, A., & Brown, J. (2020). A comprehensive and systematic survey on the Internet of things: Security and privacy challenges, security frameworks, enabling technologies, threats, vulnerabilities and countermeasures. *Computers*, *9*(2), 44. DOI: 10.3390/computers9020044

Ourad, A. Z., Belgacem, B., & Salah, K. (2018). Using blockchain for IOT access control and authentication management. *Lecture Notes in Computer Science*, *10972*, 150–164. DOI: 10.1007/978-3-319-94370-1_11

Piantadosi, V., Rosa, G., Placella, D., Scalabrino, S., & Oliveto, R. (2022). Detecting functional and security-related issues in smart contracts: A systematic literature review. *Software, Practice & Experience*, *53*(2), 465–495. DOI: 10.1002/spe.3156

Praitheeshan, P., Pan, L., & Doss, R. (2020). Security evaluation of smart contract-based on-chain Ethereum wallets. *Lecture Notes in Computer Science*, *12570*, 22–41. DOI: 10.1007/978-3-030-65745-1_2

Rahman, M. U., Guidi, B., Baiardi, F., & Ricci, L. (2020). Context-aware and dynamic role-based access control using blockchain. *Advances in Intelligent Systems and Computing*, 1449-1460.

Rawat, D. B., & Reddy, S. R. (2017). Software defined networking architecture, security and energy efficiency: A survey. *IEEE Communications Surveys and Tutorials*, *19*(1), 325–346. DOI: 10.1109/COMST.2016.2618874

Reyna, A., Martín, C., Chen, J., Soler, E., & Díaz, M. (2018). On blockchain and its integration with IoT. Challenges and opportunities. *Future Generation Computer Systems*, *88*, 173–190. DOI: 10.1016/j.future.2018.05.046

Rouhani, S., & Deters, R. (2019). Security, performance, and applications of smart contracts: A systematic survey. *IEEE Access : Practical Innovations, Open Solutions*, *7*, 50759–50779. DOI: 10.1109/ACCESS.2019.2911031

Sarker, I. H., Furhad, M. H., & Nowrozy, R. (2021). AI-driven cybersecurity: An overview, security intelligence modeling and research directions. *SN Computer Science*, *2*(3), 1–18. DOI: 10.1007/s42979-021-00557-0

Sasi, T., Lashkari, A. H., Lu, R., Xiong, P., & Iqbal, S. (2024). A comprehensive survey on IoT attacks: Taxonomy, detection mechanisms and challenges. *Journal of Information and Intelligence*, *2*(6), 455–513. DOI: 10.1016/j.jiixd.2023.12.001

Shaveta, X. (2024). Federated learning in edge computing environments: Opportunities, challenges, and future directions. [IJSR]. *International Journal of Scientific Research*, *13*(9), 275–278.

Shi, W., Cao, J., Zhang, Q., Li, Y., & Xu, L. (2016). Edge computing: Vision and challenges. *IEEE Internet of Things Journal*, *3*(5), 637–646. DOI: 10.1109/JIOT.2016.2579198

Shukla, S., George, J. P., Tiwari, K., & Kureethara, J. V. (2022). Data ethics and challenges. In *Springer Briefs in Applied Sciences and Technology* (pp. 61–72). Springer Nature.

Sicari, S., Rizzardi, A., Grieco, L., & Coen-Porisini, A. (2015). Security, privacy and trust in Internet of things: The road ahead. *Computer Networks*, *76*, 146–164. DOI: 10.1016/j.comnet.2014.11.008

Sun, Y., Zhang, J., Xiong, Y., & Zhu, G. (2014). Data security and privacy in cloud computing. *International Journal of Distributed Sensor Networks*, *10*(7), 190903. DOI: 10.1155/2014/190903

Sylla, T., Mendiboure, L., Chalouf, M. A., & Krief, F. (2021). Blockchain-based context-aware authorization management as a service in IoT. *Sensors (Basel)*, *21*(22), 7656. DOI: 10.3390/s21227656

Tariq, M. U. (2025). Navigating Public Administration 5.0: Embracing AI for Smarter Governance. In Wongmahesak, K., Ahmad, J., & Mustanir, A. (Eds.), *Public Governance Practices in the Age of AI* (pp. 167–186). IGI Global Scientific Publishing., DOI: 10.4018/979-8-3693-9286-7.ch008

Tariq, M. U. (2025). AI-Enhanced Project-Based Learning: Revolutionizing Commerce Education With Generative AI. In ElSayary, A. (Ed.), *Prompt Engineering and Generative AI Applications for Teaching and Learning* (pp. 125–142). IGI Global Scientific Publishing., DOI: 10.4018/979-8-3693-7332-3.ch008

Tariq, M. U. (2025). Unlocking Competitive Edge: Harnessing the Power of Collaborative Innovation. In Martínez-Falcó, J., Sánchez-García, E., & Marco-Lajara, B. (Eds.), *Open Innovation Strategies for Effective Competitive Advantage* (pp. 315–344). IGI Global Scientific Publishing., DOI: 10.4018/979-8-3693-9266-9.ch011

Tariq, M. U. (2025). Leveraging Libraries and Information Centers for Startup Innovation and Growth. In Gupta, V., & Gupta, C. (Eds.), *Navigating Strategic Partnerships for Sustainable Startup Growth* (pp. 1–28). IGI Global Scientific Publishing., DOI: 10.4018/979-8-3693-4066-0.ch001

Tariq, M. U. (2025). Revolutionizing Retail: Enhancing Customer Experiences With the Metaverse. In Gonçalves Rodrigues, M., Carvalho, M., & Monteiro Pratas, J. (Eds.), *Cases on Metaverse and Consumer Experiences* (pp. 175–202). IGI Global Scientific Publishing., DOI: 10.4018/979-8-3693-7245-6.ch007

Tariq, M. U. (2025). AI-Driven Research Methodologies: Revolutionizing Data-Driven Discoveries in Engineering and Physical Sciences. In Basha, J., Alade, T., Al Khazimi, M., Vasudevan, R., & Khan, J. (Eds.), *Optimizing Research Techniques and Learning Strategies With Digital Technologies* (pp. 97–122). IGI Global Scientific Publishing., DOI: 10.4018/979-8-3693-7863-2.ch004

Tian, Z., Yan, B., Guo, Q., Huang, J., & Du, Q. (2020). Feasibility of identity authentication for IoT based on blockchain. *Procedia Computer Science*, *174*, 328–332. DOI: 10.1016/j.procs.2020.06.094

Venkatesan, K., & Rahayu, S. B. (2024). Blockchain security enhancement: An approach towards hybrid consensus algorithms and machine learning techniques. *Scientific Reports*, *14*(1), 1149. DOI: 10.1038/s41598-024-51578-7

Walia, G. K., Kumar, M., & Gill, S. S. (2024). AI-empowered fog/Edge resource management for IoT applications: A comprehensive review, research challenges, and future perspectives. *IEEE Communications Surveys and Tutorials*, *26*(1), 619–669. DOI: 10.1109/COMST.2023.3338015

Wang, L. (2021). The challenge and prospect of scalability of blockchain technology. In *Proceedings of the 5th International Conference on Computer Science and Artificial Intelligence,* Beijing, China. DOI: 10.1145/3507548.3507594

Wang, W., Hoang, D. T., Hu, P., Xiong, Z., Niyato, D., Wang, P., Wen, Y., & Kim, D. I. (2019). A survey on consensus mechanisms and mining strategy management in blockchain networks. *IEEE Access : Practical Innovations, Open Solutions*, *7*, 22328–22370. DOI: 10.1109/ACCESS.2019.2896108

Wiafe, I., Koranteng, F. N., Obeng, E. N., Assyne, N., Wiafe, A., & Gulliver, S. R. (2020). Artificial intelligence for cybersecurity: A systematic mapping of literature. *IEEE Access : Practical Innovations, Open Solutions*, *8*, 146598–146612. DOI: 10.1109/ACCESS.2020.3013145

Wu, H., Han, H., Wang, X., & Sun, S. (2020). Research on artificial intelligence enhancing Internet of things security: A survey. *IEEE Access : Practical Innovations, Open Solutions*, *8*, 153826–153848. DOI: 10.1109/ACCESS.2020.3018170

Wu, Y. (2021). Cloud-edge orchestration for the Internet of things: Architecture and AI-powered data processing. *IEEE Internet of Things Journal*, *8*(16), 12792–12805. DOI: 10.1109/JIOT.2020.3014845

Xiao, Y., Zhang, N., Lou, W., & Hou, Y. T. (2020). A survey of distributed consensus protocols for blockchain networks. *IEEE Communications Surveys and Tutorials*, *22*(2), 1432–1465. DOI: 10.1109/COMST.2020.2969706

Yu, Y., Li, Y., Tian, J., & Liu, J. (2018). Blockchain-based solutions to security and privacy issues in the Internet of things. *IEEE Wireless Communications*, *25*(6), 12–18. DOI: 10.1109/MWC.2017.1800116

Zhang, C., Xie, Y., Bai, H., Yu, B., Li, W., & Gao, Y. (2021). A survey on federated learning. *Knowledge-Based Systems*, *216*, 106775. DOI: 10.1016/j.knosys.2021.106775

Zhao, J., Hu, H., Huang, F., Guo, Y., & Liao, L. (2023). Authentication technology in Internet of things and privacy security issues in typical application scenarios. *Electronics (Basel)*, *12*(8), 1812. DOI: 10.3390/electronics12081812

Zheng, Z., Xie, S., Dai, H., Chen, W., Chen, X., Weng, J., & Imran, M. (2020). An overview on smart contracts: Challenges, advances and platforms. *Future Generation Computer Systems, 105*, 475–491. DOI: 10.1016/j.future.2019.12.019

Zhou, J., Cao, Z., Dong, X., & Vasilakos, A. V. (2017). Security and privacy for cloud-based IoT: Challenges. *IEEE Communications Magazine, 55*(1), 26–33. DOI: 10.1109/MCOM.2017.1600363CM

Zuo, C., Lin, Z., & Zhang, Y. (2019). Why does your data leak? Uncovering the data leakage in cloud from mobile apps. In *Proceedings of the 2019 IEEE Symposium on Security and Privacy (SP),* San Francisco, USA. DOI: 10.1109/SP.2019.00009

KEY TERMS AND DEFINITIONS

Internet of Things (IoT): A network of interconnected smart devices that collect, transmit, and process data through the Internet.

Cloud Computing: A model of delivering computing services over the Internet, offering scalable, flexible, and on-demand storage and processing power.

Confidentiality, Integrity, and Availability (CIA Triad): The foundational principles of information security ensuring data is protected from unauthorised access (confidentiality), remains accurate (integrity), and is accessible when needed (availability).

Multi-Tenancy: A cloud architecture feature allowing multiple users or organisations to share the same infrastructure while keeping their data isolated and secure.

Blockchain: A decentralised and tamper-resistant digital ledger that records transactions in sequential, cryptographically linked blocks, enhancing trust and security in data management systems.

Chapter 5
My Walking Pal:
An AI-Driven Smart Stick Using IoT for Enhanced Mobility to Empower Visually Impaired Individuals

Margaret T. A. Swetha
https://orcid.org/0000-0002-4693-8219
Stella Maris College, India

Devi D. Renuka
https://orcid.org/0000-0002-6525-1172
Stella Maris College, India

ABSTRACT

Visually impaired individuals often face significant challenges when navigating both indoor and outdoor environments, frequently requiring assistance. The unpredictable conditions of roadways further exacerbate these challenges, making it essential for them to remain vigilant to avoid hazardous situations such as colliding with stationary or moving obstacles, navigating staircases, or slipping on wet surfaces. To address these issues, a Smart stick has been designed and developed utilizing modern technologies, including the Internet of Things (IoT) and Artificial Intelligence, to provide a clear and safe path for users in their surroundings. The proposed design is a patented model for its design clarity and innovation. The model integrates multiple IoT sensors and AI-driven modules, all controlled by a microcontroller system. These sensors are employed to detect obstacles, while the AI component enhances the system's ability to adapt to varying environments and predict potential hazards. Additionally, the stick is equipped with a mechanism to send alerts about the user's location

DOI: 10.4018/979-8-3693-8547-0.ch005

INTRODUCTION

Visual impairment remains a significant global health issue, with profound social, economic, and personal impacts on affected individuals. The reliance on traditional navigation tools, such as the white cane, underscores the ongoing challenges faced by visually impaired individuals in their daily lives. While the white cane has been a long-standing aid, its limitations in detecting obstacles beyond physical contact necessitate the development of more advanced solutions. This paper presents the Smart Cane, an innovative device that incorporates IoT technologies to provide enhanced obstacle detection and alert mechanisms, offering a safer and more reliable alternative to traditional canes. The Internet of Things (IoT) has emerged as a transformative force across various sectors, including healthcare, transportation, and home automation. IoT's ability to connect devices and enable autonomous data exchange opens new possibilities for assistive technologies. By integrating sensors, microcontrollers, and communication modules, IoT-driven devices can offer real-time feedback and support, thereby improving the quality of life for users. The Smart Cane exemplifies this potential, utilizing IoT to create a connected system that proactively addresses the mobility challenges of visually impaired individuals (Tariq, 2024).

According to a comprehensive report jointly published by the World Health Organization (WHO) and the International Agency for the Prevention of Blindness (IAPB), there are currently an estimated 285 million people globally who are visually impaired, with 39 million of these individuals experiencing complete blindness. These individuals predominantly rely on their auditory senses and traditional white canes for navigation. However, the conventional cane provides limited protection against obstacles, posing significant safety risks. In response to this critical need, we have developed an innovative tool, the Smart Cane, which utilizes the Internet of Things (IoT) to assist and alert visually impaired individuals to potential obstacles in their environment. Preliminary evaluations indicate that this Smart Cane offers significant improvements over traditional navigation methods, providing enhanced safety and autonomy for the visually impaired community. The Smart Cane's design is grounded in a multidisciplinary approach that combines ergonomics, electronics, and software engineering to ensure user comfort, reliability, and effectiveness. At its core, the Smart Cane is equipped with multiple sensors, including ultrasonic sensors for obstacle detection, fire sensors for identifying heat sources, and water sensors for detecting wet or slippery surfaces. These sensors continuously scan the environment, feeding data into a microcontroller that processes the information in real-time. When an obstacle is detected, the microcontroller evaluates the proximity and potential risk, triggering an appropriate response. If the obstacle is deemed hazardous, the system generates an auditory alert through a voice playback module, enabling the user to take corrective action. Additionally, the Smart Cane's integration with GPS and GSM modules enhances its functionality by enabling location tracking and emergency communication. In situations where the user may require assistance, the Smart Cane can send a pre-programmed emergency message with the user's location to designated contacts.

The development of the Smart Cane presented several technological challenges, including the need for low-power consumption, robust data processing capabilities, and reliable communication protocols. Addressing these challenges required careful selection of components and optimization of the system's architecture. The microcontroller was chosen for its energy efficiency and processing power, while the sensors were selected based on their accuracy and durability in various environmental conditions. The communication modules were configured to operate seamlessly with the microcontroller, ensuring that alerts and emergency messages are transmitted promptly and accurately. Smart Cane represents a significant advancement in assistive technology for the visually impaired. By providing real-time obstacle detection and alerts, the Smart Cane enhances user confidence and independence, reducing the reliance on human assistance and traditional navigation aids. Early user feedback indicates that the Smart Cane is more effective at preventing accidents and facilitating safe mobility, particularly in unfamiliar or hazardous environments (Tariq, 2025).

Moreover, the Smart Cane's ability to communicate emergency information adds a critical layer of safety, offering peace of mind to both users and their families. The potential for widespread adoption of the Smart Cane is considerable, particularly in regions where access to advanced assistive technologies is limited. While the Smart Cane represents a significant leap forward in assistive technology, ongoing research and development are essential to further enhance its capabilities and user experience. Future iterations of the Smart Cane may incorporate additional sensors, such as cameras or infrared sensors, to provide more comprehensive environmental awareness. Advances in artificial intelligence and machine learning could also enable the Smart Cane to learn and adapt to individual user preferences, offering personalized assistance and improving overall effectiveness. The Smart Cane represents a sophisticated application of IoT principles, integrating the latest technological innovations to support the safe and independent movement of visually impaired individuals. This literature review examines the current state of research on the Smart Cane, focusing on the role of various IoT sensors—such as ultrasonic, fire, and water sensors—in detecting obstacles. When an obstacle is detected within the cane's operational range, the sensors relay the information to a microcontroller, which assesses the proximity of the hazard. If a potential danger is identified, the system activates an alert, typically through an auditory signal from a voice playback module. Additionally, the Smart Cane is equipped with GPS and GSM modules to send emergency notifications if necessary. This advanced assistive technology is designed to mitigate the challenges faced by visually impaired individuals, promoting a greater sense of safety and independence in their daily navigation (Tariq, 2024).

Additionally, expanding the Smart Cane's connectivity with other smart devices, such as smartphones or wearable devices, could further enrich the user experience by providing additional context and support. For example, integration with a smartphone app could allow users to receive detailed auditory descriptions of their surroundings or plan safe routes in real-time. The Smart Cane is a pioneering example of how IoT can be harnessed to improve the lives of visually impaired individuals. By integrating advanced sensor technologies, real-time data processing, and reliable communication systems, the Smart Cane offers a safer and more effective alternative to traditional navigation tools. As technology continues to evolve, the potential for further innovation in assistive devices is vast, promising even greater improvements in the quality of life for those living with visual impairments. This patented study and ideology highlights the critical role of interdisciplinary collaboration in developing the Smart Cane and underscores the importance of ongoing research and innovation in this field. As we continue to explore the possibilities of IoT and related technologies, the future holds tremendous potential for creating more inclusive and supportive environments for individuals with disabilities.

LITERATURE ANALYSIS

The advent of the Internet of Things (IoT) has significantly transformed assistive technologies for visually impaired individuals, offering innovative solutions to address mobility, safety, and navigation challenges. IoT-based devices integrate sensors, real-time data processing, and connectivity, providing users with intelligent systems capable of perceiving their surroundings and enhancing autonomy. Over the past decade, researchers have focused on developing and refining assistive tools, including smart canes, wearable devices, and smartphone-integrated systems, to meet the unique needs of visually impaired individuals. This survey synthesizes the existing literature, categorizing developments into wearable technology, handheld devices, voice-activated tools, and multifunctional systems, while addressing key challenges and future opportunities (Tariq, 2024).

The integration of IoT into assistive devices began with efforts to enhance traditional mobility aids like the white cane. Early research by Tang, Shi, and Lei (2016) introduced a low-consumption IoT framework for location tracking, showcasing the potential for energy-efficient systems tailored for real-world applications. Mala, Thushara, and Subbiah (2017) advanced this idea by developing navigation gadgets that relied on real-time data processing for obstacle detection and alerts. These early innovations laid the groundwork for subsequent advancements by demonstrating the feasibility of IoT in augmenting assistive devices. Wearable IoT technologies represent a promising area of research due to their compactness, ease of use, and hands-free operation.

Abusukhon (2023) proposed IoT-enabled bracelets designed specifically for indoor navigation. The device employed an array of sensors for obstacle detection, providing haptic feedback to guide the user through complex environments. This solution emphasized the potential for discreet wearable technology to complement or replace handheld aids in specific scenarios. Building on this concept, Nathan et al. (2023) developed a "Smart Walking Shoe" equipped with embedded sensors and vibration feedback mechanisms. The ergonomic design of this footwear not only ensured comfort but also enhanced safety by offering continuous obstacle awareness. Wearable devices like these highlight the versatility of IoT in addressing the diverse mobility needs of visually impaired individuals. However, challenges such as battery life, sensor durability, and environmental adaptability persist.

Smart canes have undergone significant evolution with the incorporation of IoT technology, transforming from simple obstacle-detection tools into multi-functional devices. Ahmed et al. (2022) introduced a cane equipped with ultrasonic, fire, and water sensors, alongside GPS and GSM modules. This design ensured real-time hazard detection and enabled the transmission of emergency alerts, showcasing the potential for multi-dimensional safety features in IoT-assisted devices. Another innovative development is the smartphone-integrated smart cane presented by Jasman et al. (2022). This system used sensors to detect obstacles and relayed alerts to the user's smartphone, which provided audio feedback for navigation. The integration of smartphones significantly expands the functionality of smart canes, offering users access to navigation maps and real-time updates. However, such systems often depend on internet connectivity, which can limit their reliability in remote or poorly connected regions.

Voice recognition systems and artificial intelligence (AI) have further enhanced the accessibility and adaptability of IoT-based assistive devices. Adil et al. (2020) demonstrated the efficacy of a voice-controlled blind stick, which allowed users to interact with the device using simple voice commands. This approach reduces the learning curve associated with complex device interfaces, making assistive technologies more user-friendly.

AI integration has added predictive capabilities to assistive devices, enabling systems to anticipate user needs and adapt to dynamic environments. For instance, AI algorithms can analyze environmental data to identify potential hazards, optimize navigation routes, and provide context-aware feedback. These advancements position AI as a critical enabler of next-generation IoT-based assistive devices.

The trend toward multifunctional devices reflects the growing demand for comprehensive solutions that address a wide range of challenges faced by visually impaired individuals. Raut et al. (2022) introduced an IoT-assisted smart device that combined GPS tracking with obstacle detection, offering real-time guidance and safety alerts. Similarly, Saisubramanyam and Rani (2020) emphasized the importance of emergency response capabilities in their GPS-enabled smart walking stick, designed for both visually impaired and elderly users.

These integrated systems underscore the potential of IoT to deliver holistic solutions that go beyond basic mobility aids. By combining multiple functionalities, such devices enhance user confidence and autonomy, although they require careful design to balance complexity and usability. One of the critical challenges in deploying IoT-based assistive devices is ensuring affordability and accessibility, particularly in developing regions. Ghosal et al. (2020) and Dabir et al. (2018) explored low-cost solutions by incorporating inexpensive components without compromising functionality. Such efforts aim to bridge the gap between technological advancements and widespread adoption, ensuring that these innovations benefit users across socio-economic layers. While affordability is a significant focus, accessibility also involves ensuring that devices are intuitive and easy to use. Studies like Adil et al. (2020) have highlighted the importance of user-centric design, including voice interfaces and tactile feedback, to cater to individuals with varying levels of technical proficiency.

The rapid evolution of IoT technology continues to drive innovation in assistive devices. Emerging trends include the integration of edge computing, which allows devices to process data locally, reducing latency and dependence on cloud connectivity. This is particularly relevant for real-time applications like obstacle detection and navigation. Another promising avenue is the use of advanced sensors, such as LIDAR, for precise environmental mapping. Nuanmeesri and Poomhiran (2020) demonstrated the potential of health monitoring systems integrated with assistive devices, expanding their functionality to include wellness tracking. This convergence of health and mobility solutions represents a significant step forward in holistic assistive technology design.

The adoption of 5G connectivity is expected to further enhance the performance of IoT-based devices by enabling faster data transmission and improved network reliability. Additionally, blockchain technology offers a secure framework for managing user data, addressing privacy concerns associated with IoT systems. Despite the significant progress in IoT-based assistive technologies, several challenges remain. The reliability of sensors and components is a critical concern, particularly in diverse environmental conditions. Energy efficiency is another key issue, as many devices rely on batteries that require frequent recharging or replacement. Interoperability between devices and platforms also poses challenges, as users often need to integrate multiple systems seamlessly. Standardization of protocols and interfaces can help address this issue, promoting compatibility and ease of use. Furthermore, user adaptability and acceptance remain crucial, as even the most advanced technologies may fail if they are not intuitive or accessible. The data analysis on IoT-based assistive devices for visually impaired individuals reflects a vibrant and rapidly evolving field, driven by advancements in sensor technology, connectivity, and artificial intelligence. From wearable devices and smart canes to voice-controlled systems and multifunctional tools, these innovations have significantly enhanced mobility, safety, and autonomy for visually impaired users.

While challenges related to cost, reliability, and user adaptability persist, ongoing research and technological advancements hold immense promise for the future. The integration of emerging technologies such as 5G, edge computing, and blockchain is expected to further revolutionize assistive devices, creating solutions that are not only functional but also inclusive and accessible. As researchers and developers continue to push the boundaries of what is possible, the focus must remain on ensuring that these innovations address the real-world needs of visually impaired individuals, fostering independence and improving quality of life.

GRID-STYLE BREAKDOWN OF THE COMPREHENSIVE ANALYSIS OF IOT-BASED ASSISTIVE TECHNOLOGIES FOR VISUALLY IMPAIRED INDIVIDUALS

Table 1. Grid-style breakdown of the comprehensive analysis for IoT based innovation for visually impaired

Category	Description	Key Studies	Technological Aspects	Challenges	Future Directions
Smart Canes	IoT-enhanced canes with sensors for obstacle detection and emergency alerts.	Ahmed et al. (2022), Raut et al. (2022), Ghosal et al. (2020), Adil et al. (2020)	Ultrasonic, fire, water sensors; GPS and GSM modules; auditory/haptic feedback.	Power consumption; sensor accuracy in adverse weather conditions.	Low-power solutions; AI/ML integration for adaptive feedback; enhanced sensor accuracy.
Smart Footwear	Shoes equipped with sensors to detect obstacles and provide vibration alerts	Nathan et al. (2023)	Vibration feedback, ergonomic design, integrated IoT sensors.	User comfort; limited market adoption.	Improved ergonomic designs; broader market adoption; multi-sensor integration.
Wearable IoT Devices	Wearables like bracelets providing real-time obstacle detection and guidance.	Abusukhon (2023)	Haptic feedback, indoor navigation, IoT sensor integration.	Limited outdoor applicability; battery life.	Extended use cases beyond indoor environments; integration with other devices.
Smartphone Integration	IoT devices connected to smartphones for enhanced functionality and monitoring	Pydala et al. (2023), Jasman et al. (2022)	Smartphone app interface; real-time auditory feedback; remote monitoring.	Dependence on smartphone functionality and connectivity.	Enhanced app features; cross-platform integration; real-time AI processing.
Early IoT Frameworks	Initial IoT applications in assistive technologies focusing on basic navigation.	Tang et al. (2016), Mala et al. (2017), Sathya et al. (2018)	Low-power IoT frameworks; basic obstacle detection; GPS tracking.	Limited functionality; nascent technology.	Building upon early frameworks; expanding IoT capabilities for real-world applications
Impact on Users	The effect of IoT devices on the mobility, safety, and autonomy of users.	Studies across all categories.	Real-time alerts; multi-functional devices; increased safety and confidence.	Adoption barriers; technological accessibility.	User-centered design improvements; education and outreach to increase adoption.

IMPACT AND USER EXPERIENCE

IoT-based assistive technologies have significantly enhanced the daily lives of visually impaired individuals by improving their safety, autonomy, and confidence in navigating various environments. The introduction of these smart devices has bridged critical gaps left by traditional mobility aids like white canes. Some of which is discussed below:

a. Increased Safety
    - **Real-Time Obstacle Detection:** IoT-enabled devices like smart canes and smart footwear offer real-time alerts for obstacles and environmental hazards, drastically reducing the risk of accidents. Ahmed et al. (2022) and Raut et al. (2022) emphasize how these devices can detect obstacles such as steps, potholes, and even fire or water hazards, alerting users instantly.
    - **Emergency Communication:** Integration with GPS and GSM modules allows these devices to send location-based alerts to caregivers or emergency services if the user encounters a dangerous situation, as shown in studies by Ahmed et al. (2022). This feature adds a critical layer of safety, especially for users navigating alone.

b. Enhanced Autonomy
    - **Navigation Without Assistance:** With advanced IoT devices, visually impaired individuals can navigate complex environments without the need for a human guide. This independence is especially valuable in urban settings where users must frequently encounter crowded or unfamiliar spaces.
    - **Customizable Alerts:** The ability to customize the type and intensity of feedback—whether through vibrations, sounds, or voice commands—allows users to tailor the devices to their personal preferences and comfort levels. This adaptability increases user satisfaction and makes the devices more user-friendly.

c. Improved Confidence
    - **Confidence in Exploration:** The reliable feedback from IoT devices encourages users to explore new environments, knowing that they have an effective tool for detecting potential hazards. This newfound confidence significantly improves their quality of life, enabling them to engage in activities they might have previously avoided due to fear of injury or disorientation.
    - **Positive Psychological Impact:** Studies have shown that the use of these technologies positively impacts the mental well-being of visually

impaired individuals. The sense of control and independence fosters a more positive outlook on life, as users feel less reliant on others for mobility.

User Experience With IoT-Based Devices

The user experience is a critical aspect of the effectiveness of IoT-based assistive technologies. The following factors contribute to the overall experience:

a. Ease of Use
    - **Intuitive Design:** Devices like smart canes and footwear are designed to be intuitive, requiring minimal training. For instance, the vibration feedback in smart footwear, as highlighted by Nathan et al. (2023), is natural and easy to understand, allowing users to quickly adapt to the technology.
    - **Minimal Maintenance:** These devices are typically low-maintenance, with long battery life and durable construction, making them practical for everyday use.

b. Comfort and Ergonomics
    - **Wearability:** Wearable IoT devices, such as bracelets and smart shoes, are designed with comfort in mind. The ergonomic design ensures that users can wear these devices for extended periods without discomfort, a crucial factor in adoption and continuous use.
    - **Lightweight and Discreet:** Many IoT devices are lightweight and discreet, which makes them less intrusive and more likely to be used consistently. This is particularly important for users who may feel self-conscious about carrying visible assistive tools.

c. **Accessibility**
    - **Affordability and Availability:** While the technology holds great promise, one of the challenges noted in various studies (e.g., Ghosal et al. (2020), Adil et al. (2020)) is making these devices affordable and accessible to a broader population, particularly in low-income regions.
    - **Language and Cultural Adaptations:** To increase accessibility, devices must accommodate different languages and cultural contexts. Voice commands and alerts, for example, need to be available in multiple languages to cater to diverse user bases.

d. **Feedback from Users:**
    - **User Satisfaction:** Studies generally report high levels of satisfaction among users of IoT-based assistive devices. The immediate feedback and increased sense of safety are often cited as the most valued features.

Feedback from users is crucial in the iterative design process, helping developers refine and enhance the functionality of these devices.

- **Areas for Improvement:** Some users have expressed a desire for even more advanced features, such as AI-driven obstacle detection that can predict potential hazards before they occur, or better integration with other smart home devices.

The impact and user experience of IoT-based assistive technologies for visually impaired individuals are overwhelmingly positive. These devices provide a level of independence and safety that was previously unattainable, contributing to the overall well-being and confidence of users. However, ongoing efforts are needed to address challenges related to accessibility, affordability, and the integration of more advanced features. As technology continues to evolve, the future of assistive devices promises even greater enhancements in the quality of life for visually impaired individuals.

My Walking Pal: An AI-Driven Smart Stick

The concept of the "My Walk Pal" smart stick emerges from a heartfelt commitment to addressing the unique challenges faced by visually impaired individuals and empowering them with a transformative tool for independent navigation. This innovative prototype represents a fusion of compassion, technology, and practicality, designed to redefine the way visually impaired individuals interact with their surroundings. Below is an elaboration of the key considerations that shape the vision of "My Walk Pal":

- **Addressing Daily Challenges for Visually Impaired Individuals**

Navigating everyday environments presents a formidable challenge for visually impaired individuals. Basic activities such as crossing streets, traveling to work, shopping, or even walking through a crowded area are fraught with obstacles and potential dangers that demand heightened vigilance. Traditional mobility aids like white canes are instrumental in helping detect nearby objects but are limited to tactile feedback and short-range detection. These tools do not provide real-time guidance for broader environmental awareness, such as changes in terrain, unexpected hazards like puddles, or directional assistance for specific destinations. The "My Walk Pal" bridges this gap by incorporating advanced IoT sensors that enable the smart stick to detect obstacles, sense environmental hazards (e.g., water or fire), and provide real-time auditory or haptic feedback to its user. This feature not only simplifies navigation but significantly reduces the cognitive burden, enabling users to focus on their journey with greater ease and confidence.

- **Enhancing Independence and Confidence**

Independence is a cornerstone of dignity and quality of life, yet it remains elusive for many visually impaired individuals due to their reliance on others for mobility and navigation. The "My Walk Pal" aims to restore this independence by offering features that go beyond obstacle detection. The integration of GPS and GSM modules allows the device to provide precise navigation to pre-set destinations, ensuring that users can confidently traverse unfamiliar locations. This functionality empowers visually impaired individuals to perform daily tasks like visiting a new market, attending social gatherings, or commuting to work without external assistance. Moreover, the intuitive design ensures that users can rely on the device even in high-stress or complex environments, boosting their confidence and fostering a sense of control over their mobility.

- **Utilizing IoT and Smart Technology for Practical Solutions**

IoT technology has revolutionized numerous industries, offering practical and efficient solutions to real-world problems. The "My Walk Pal" leverages the power of IoT to enhance the lives of visually impaired individuals. Its ultrasonic sensors detect objects within a certain range, enabling the device to alert users to obstacles that are not easily perceivable through traditional canes. Additional sensors like water and fire detectors increase situational awareness by alerting users to environmental hazards, such as spilled liquids or nearby fires. The microphone module enables voice command functionality, allowing users to interact with the device seamlessly and set navigation points without manual input. This combination of features transforms "My Walk Pal" into an intelligent companion, offering real-time insights that significantly improve navigation safety and ease.

- **Economic Accessibility and Practicality**

Economic accessibility is a key tenet of the "My Walk Pal" project, especially given the financial constraints faced by many visually impaired individuals, particularly those below the poverty line. By using cost-effective yet reliable components, the design ensures that the device remains affordable without sacrificing essential functionalities. For instance, the use of readily available sensors and open-source IoT modules keeps production costs manageable while maintaining high levels of reliability. The modular design of the device also facilitates repairs and upgrades, allowing users to replace components as needed without purchasing a new device. This focus on affordability and durability makes "My Walk Pal" a viable option for a wide demographic, extending its benefits to underserved communities.

- **Adaptability and Future Development**

The "My Walk Pal" is designed as a dynamic prototype that can evolve with advancements in technology and user feedback. For example, future iterations may include features like machine learning-based obstacle recognition, enhanced audio feedback systems, or even integration with smart city infrastructures for real-time traffic and environmental data. The adaptability of the design ensures that it can address the diverse needs of visually impaired users, whether they require advanced customization or simplified functionality. As user feedback and testing inform further refinements, the project aims to develop a robust, user-centric product that seamlessly blends functionality with ease of use.

- **Contribution to Social Inclusion and Equality**

At its core, the "My Walk Pal" embodies the principles of social inclusion and equality. By providing visually impaired individuals with an innovative tool that enhances their mobility and independence, the project contributes to levelling the playing field, allowing them to participate more fully in everyday life. The project aligns with global efforts to create an inclusive environment, enabling individuals with disabilities to access education, employment, and social opportunities with greater ease. Through the "My Walk Pal," visually impaired individuals can not only navigate their surroundings but also experience a renewed sense of freedom and equality, breaking down barriers to societal integration. The "My Walk Pal" smart stick is more than a technological innovation; it is a symbol of empowerment and inclusion for visually impaired individuals. By addressing their daily challenges, fostering independence, leveraging cutting-edge IoT technology, and prioritizing affordability, the device has the potential to transform lives. Its adaptability ensures that it can evolve to meet future needs, while its contribution to social equality underscores the project's commitment to creating a world where every individual can thrive, regardless of their abilities.

My Walking Pal: Patented Design

Individuals with good sight visualization and capabilities comparatively face a lot of challenges in day-to-day life. Certain activities which is part of our daily routine is still challenging when it comes to execution. However, we do manage on either way to efficiently get the job done since impaired vision is not criteria in terms of individuals with good sight visualization and capabilities. Looking on to the same comfort levels of a vision impaired individual, the daily tasks which is even consider as very basic one is a peak hike complexity to them. The complexity may reduce once they get accustomed to their works but still there will be certain about of discomforts and endurance that is invested will still be the same out difficulty that put in accomplishing the task. This could be anything as in like crossing roads, travelling, boarding vehicles etc. Eventually we also need to address that there are excellent innovations and Software's that are made available by both government as well as private sectors. But the question that is debateable is, how far it is made available to common people who are visually impaired and how economically it is made available to below poverty line cadre individuals.

Although blind individuals lead unique and fulfilling lives, they still encounter obstacles due to inaccessible infrastructure and societal barriers. Therefore, it is important for us to conduct a compassionate analysis of the issues and challenges faced by blind individuals in their daily lives. One of the biggest struggles for a visually impaired person, particularly those who have completely lost their sight, is navigating through unfamiliar places. Within the comfort of their own homes, blind individuals are able to move around confidently without assistance due to their familiarity with their surroundings. However, it is crucial for those living with or visiting blind individuals to be mindful of not rearranging or moving items without first informing or asking for their consent. Thanks to the use of tactile tiles, commercial spaces now have improved accessibility for the visually impaired. However, it is disheartening that not all places have implemented this accommodation. As a result, blind individuals face major difficulties when trying to navigate these environments. Sadly, this is just one of the many challenges that visually impaired people encounter in their daily lives, requiring them to constantly be vigilant to prevent any hindrances.

Figure 1. My walking pal: AI driven Smart stick (Indian patented design)

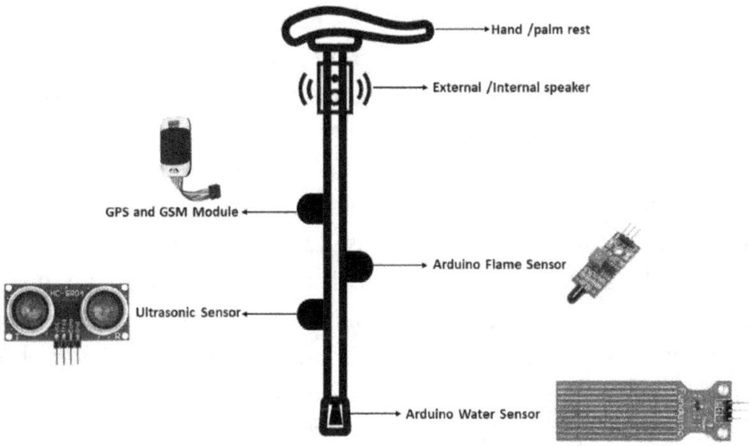

To address these peaking issues among visually impaired individuals, we have come up with a theoretical prototype called – My walking pal: the smart stick is intended to help them to assist in giving all walks of assistance while commute from one point to another. From the current framework, the smart stick is planned with various IoT sensors to recognize just the impediments and offers a caution hint to the person through the ringer sound or voice message. In this paper, we propose a solution in smart sticks (My walking pal) to help the individual to explore from source to objective utilizing google maps. The stick comprises of an ultrasonic sensor to distinguish the obstructions, a water sensor to recognize the water also puddles and a fire sensor is to distinguish the fire moreover it has a microphone to get the objective and with the assistance of Global positioning system (GPS) and Global System for Mobile Communications (GSM) module it will direct you the places through the speaker. My walking pal is smart stick which is quite easier to operate and it also aids the individual with finding the obstructions equally to its navigation to intended point of commute. Figure 1, My walking pal is a hypothetical prototype which is subjected to changes before implementation and testing. We may require changing the sensors based upon the actual usage and reality. My walking pal will be a very reasonable walking assistance to visually impaired in terms and very particularly to commute from one place to another.

AI-Driven Integration

Integrating AI into the "My Walking Pal" smart stick prototype is set to significantly enhance its capabilities, offering a more sophisticated and user-friendly experience for visually impaired individuals. The initial step involves gathering data from various sensors embedded in the smart stick, including ultrasonic sensors for detecting obstacles, water sensors for identifying puddles, fire sensors for hazard detection, and GPS for navigation. This data is then pre-processed to create a comprehensive dataset that will be used to train AI models. The preprocessing includes labelling and annotating data to distinguish different types of obstacles and environmental conditions. The core of the AI integration focuses on three key areas: obstacle detection, navigation guidance, and voice interaction. For obstacle detection, machine learning models will be trained to recognize and categorize obstacles based on sensor inputs, enabling the smart stick to provide accurate alerts about potential hazards. In terms of navigation guidance, AI algorithms will utilize GPS and map data to offer real-time, optimized route instructions, adapting to changing conditions and obstacles along the way. Voice interaction capabilities will be enhanced through natural language processing (NLP) to allow users to communicate with the smart stick using voice commands, making it easier to request information or give instructions.

Integration of these AI models will involve combining sensor data for improved accuracy and reliability. Real-time processing will be essential to ensure that the smart stick responds promptly to environmental changes, providing timely alerts and navigation cues. The user interface will include clear audio feedback and potentially haptic feedback to ensure that instructions are both effective and easy to understand. Succeeding the integration, extensive testing with visually impaired users will be conducted to assess the smart stick's performance and usability in real-world scenarios.

Figure 2. My walking pal: AI-driven approach with block representation

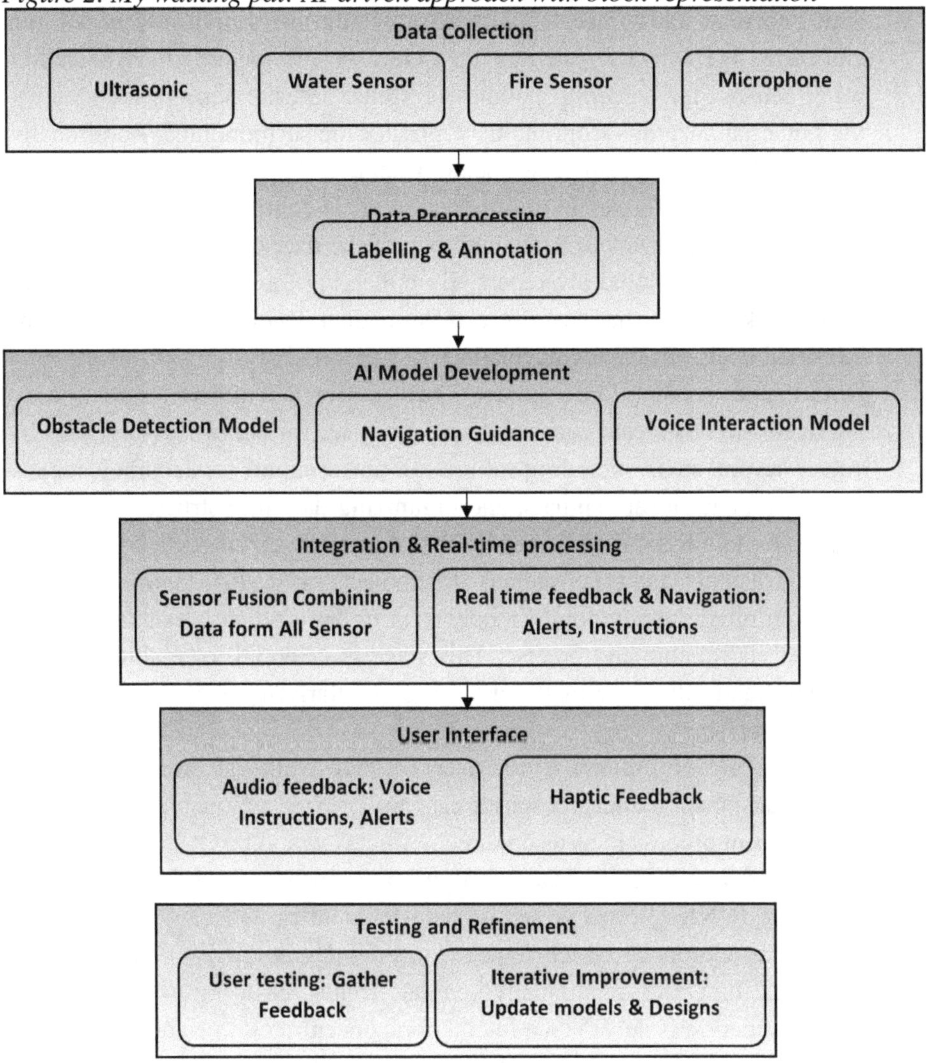

Feedback from these trials will be used to iteratively refine the AI models and overall design. The final prototype will then move into production, with considerations for cost-effectiveness and durability. Training and support will be provided to help users make the most of the smart stick, ensuring that it meets their needs effectively and affordably.

Overall, the incorporation of AI into "My Walking Pal" aims to provide a more intuitive and reliable navigation aid, helping visually impaired individuals navigate their environments with greater ease and confidence. Explanation of Graphical Elements are as follows

- **Data Collection:** The foundation of the "My Walk Pal" lies in its ability to gather accurate and comprehensive data about the user's environment. Various embedded IoT sensors—such as ultrasonic sensors for proximity detection, water sensors for detecting puddles or spills, and fire sensors for identifying potential hazards—continuously monitor the surroundings. Additionally, GPS modules provide precise location data, while a microphone captures voice commands for seamless interaction. This continuous data stream enables the device to create a detailed map of the user's environment, offering unparalleled situational awareness. By collecting this data in real time, the smart stick ensures that users receive immediate feedback to make safe and informed decisions during navigation.
- **Data Preprocessing:** Once the raw data is collected, it undergoes preprocessing to ensure it is clean, consistent, and ready for further processing. This involves several steps, including calibrating sensor inputs for accuracy, removing noise or irrelevant signals, and organizing data into structured formats. For example, obstacles detected by the ultrasonic sensor are labelled based on their distance and type, such as "low object" or "wall." Preprocessing not only optimizes the data for AI model training but also ensures that real-time feedback is reliable and precise. This stage is essential for maintaining the accuracy and efficiency of the device, particularly in diverse and dynamic environments.
- **AI Model Development:** At the heart of "My Walk Pal" are advanced AI models designed to interpret sensor data and provide actionable insights. The development process focuses on three key areas would be Obstacle Detection which works on Machine learning algorithms, such as Convolutional Neural Networks (CNNs), process sensor data to identify and classify obstacles. Navigation Guidance which focuses on AI integrates GPS data and environmental inputs to dynamically generate routes, ensuring users can reach their destinations safely. Voice Interaction concentrates on Natural Language Processing (NLP) models enable users to interact with the device using simple voice commands, enhancing its accessibility and ease of use. By developing specialized AI models for each function, the smart stick delivers a holistic solution that adapts to the user's needs and environment.
- **Integration & Real-time Processing:** The integration of AI models with IoT sensors allows the "My Walk Pal" to process data in real time. Sensor inputs are fed into the AI system, which analyzes the information and provides instantaneous feedback. For instance, if an obstacle is detected within a predefined range, the device generates an immediate audio or haptic alert, guiding the user around the hazard. Similarly, navigation instructions are adjusted dynamically based on changes in location or environmental conditions. Real-

time processing ensures that the smart stick remains responsive and reliable, even in complex or unfamiliar settings, offering users a seamless and intuitive experience.

- **User Interface:** The user interface of the "My Walk Pal" is designed to be straightforward and user-friendly. Audio feedback, delivered through an integrated speaker or earphones, provides real-time alerts and guidance. For instance, the device might inform the user about an obstacle ahead or provide turn-by-turn navigation instructions. Additionally, optional haptic feedback uses vibrations to signal the presence of nearby objects or hazards, offering an alternative communication channel for users who prefer tactile cues. By combining audio and haptic feedback, the device ensures that users receive clear and actionable information, tailored to their preferences and needs.
- **Testing & Refinement:** The development of "My Walk Pal" follows an iterative approach, with extensive testing and refinement at every stage. Prototypes are tested by visually impaired individuals in both controlled and real-world environments to evaluate performance, usability, and reliability. Feedback from these trials is invaluable, highlighting areas for improvement and guiding adjustments to the AI models, sensor configurations, and overall design. For instance, users might request enhanced sensitivity for certain sensors or suggest improvements to the audio feedback system. This iterative process ensures that the final prototype is not only effective but also aligns closely with user expectations and requirements.
- **Deployment & Support:** Once the prototype has been fully validated, the project moves into production, with a focus on cost-effectiveness and durability. By using affordable yet high-quality components, the smart stick remains accessible to a broad demographic, including individuals from economically disadvantaged backgrounds. Training programs and user manuals are provided to help users understand and utilize the device effectively. Additionally, ongoing support, including software updates and maintenance services, ensures that the device remains functional and up to date over time. These measures ensure a smooth transition from prototype to real-world deployment, maximizing the device's impact on users' lives.

The first stage in the "My Walking Pal" smart stick prototype involves the collection of raw environmental data through various sensors embedded in the device. This includes an ultrasonic sensor, a water sensor, a fire sensor, and a microphone. Each of these sensors serves a specific purpose: the ultrasonic sensor detects physical obstacles in the user's path, the water sensor identifies the presence of puddles or wet surfaces, the fire sensor detects heat or flames, and the microphone captures voice input from the user. The information gathered by these sensors is crucial for understanding the surroundings and ensuring the safety and navigation of the visually impaired individual. Once the raw data is collected, it undergoes preprocessing to prepare it for further analysis and AI model training. This stage involves cleaning and filtering the data to remove noise and irrelevant information, ensuring that only the most pertinent data is retained. Additionally, the data is labelled and annotated, which means that different types of obstacles and environmental features are categorized and tagged accordingly. This step is essential for enabling the AI models to accurately recognize and respond to various situations, ensuring that the smart stick can provide reliable feedback and guidance to the user.

The heart of the "My Walking Pal" smart stick lies in its AI-driven functionalities, which are developed during this stage. Three primary AI models are created: an obstacle detection model, a navigation guidance model, and a voice interaction model. The obstacle detection model is designed to recognize and classify different types of obstacles based on the sensor data, helping the user avoid collisions. The navigation guidance model utilizes GPS data and real-time sensor inputs to provide directional instructions, guiding the user safely to their destination. The voice interaction model, powered by natural language processing (NLP), allows the user to issue voice commands and receive spoken feedback, making the smart stick intuitive and easy to use. In this phase, all the data and AI models are integrated into a cohesive system that processes information in real time. The smart stick continuously analyses sensor data, applies the AI models, and delivers immediate feedback to the user. For instance, if the ultrasonic sensor detects an obstacle, the system quickly processes this information and triggers an audio alert or vibration to warn the user. Similarly, the navigation model provides turn-by-turn instructions based on the user's current location and surrounding environment. The integration of these elements ensures that the smart stick operates smoothly and efficiently, offering real-time assistance as the user navigates their surroundings. The user interface of the "My Walking Pal" smart stick is designed to be user-friendly and accessible, providing feedback through audio and, optionally, haptic signals. The audio feedback system delivers clear spoken instructions and alerts, guiding the user around obstacles and helping them follow the correct path. For users who prefer additional sensory input, haptic feedback (such as vibrations) can be incorporated to provide physical cues. This dual-feedback system ensures that users receive timely and comprehensible information, enhancing their confidence and independence while navigating.

Following the initial development, the smart stick undergoes rigorous testing with actual users to gather feedback and assess performance in real-world conditions. This stage is crucial for identifying any potential issues or areas for improvement. Based on user feedback, the AI models and overall design of the smart stick are iteratively refined to enhance functionality, accuracy, and ease of use. This continuous improvement process ensures that the device evolves to better meet the needs of its users, remaining effective and reliable over time. The final stage of the "My Walking Pal" smart stick prototype involves scaling the production and providing ongoing support to users. Once the design is finalized, the smart stick can be manufactured at scale, making it widely available and potentially more affordable. Additionally, training and support services are offered to ensure that users can effectively operate the device and take full advantage of its features. This stage also includes the distribution of updates and improvements, ensuring that the smart stick remains up-to-date with the latest technological advancements and continues to serve the needs of visually impaired individuals.

Figure:2., highlights the graphical representation of "My Walking Pal" smart stick prototype which outlines a comprehensive process, from data collection and AI model development to real-time processing, user interaction, and ongoing refinement. Each stage is interconnected, working together to create a smart, responsive, and user-friendly device that enhances the safety and independence of visually impaired individuals.

ADVANTAGES RENDERED TO THE SUPPORT IMPAIRED INDIVIDUALS

Integrating AI into the "My Walking Pal" smart stick offers numerous benefits for visually impaired individuals:

- **Enhanced Obstacle Detection:** AI-powered obstacle detection significantly improves the smart stick's ability to identify and categorize obstacles. Traditional sensors like ultrasonic, water, and fire sensors provide raw data about the environment, but AI algorithms process this data to discern the nature of obstacles. For instance, AI can distinguish between a solid object, a water puddle, and a potential fire hazard. This advanced classification enables the smart stick to issue more accurate alerts and warnings, reducing the likelihood of accidents and helping users navigate complex environments more safely.
- **Real-Time Navigation Assistance:** The integration of AI allows the smart stick to utilize GPS and map data for real-time navigation guidance. AI algorithms analyse the user's current location, planned route, and real-time environmental data to provide optimal navigation instructions. This includes adjusting routes based on detected obstacles or changes in the environment. For example, if a user encounters an unexpected barrier or a road is closed, the AI can recalibrate the route and guide the user accordingly, ensuring a smoother and more reliable navigation experience.

- **Voice Interaction:** With natural language processing (NLP), the smart stick can understand and respond to voice commands. This feature allows users to interact with the device hands-free, making it easier to request information, set destinations, or inquire about obstacles. For instance, a user could say, "Guide me to the nearest bus stop," and the smart stick would provide auditory directions. This capability enhances usability, especially for those who might find manual controls challenging or inconvenient.
- **Improved User Experience:** AI enhances the overall user experience by providing timely and relevant feedback. The smart stick offers clear audio instructions and, optionally, haptic feedback to ensure that users receive guidance in a manner that suits their preferences. The AI can tailor the feedback to the user's specific needs, such as adjusting the volume or tone of the audio cues based on the ambient noise levels. This personalized approach helps users stay informed about their surroundings and follow navigation cues more effectively.
- **Adaptability and Learning:** AI models in the smart stick can learn and adapt to individual users over time. By analyzing usage patterns and feedback, the smart stick can personalize navigation instructions and improve its performance based on the user's habits and preferences. For example, if a user frequently avoids certain types of obstacles or prefers specific routes, the AI can adjust its recommendations to align with these preferences, providing a more customized and efficient navigation experience.
- **Increased Independence:** The smart stick's advanced features contribute to greater independence for visually impaired individuals. By providing reliable obstacle detection, real-time navigation, and intuitive voice interaction, the smart stick enables users to move about more confidently without needing constant assistance. This enhanced autonomy can lead to a higher quality of life, as users can perform daily activities with greater ease and freedom.
- **Cost-Effectiveness:** Once the smart stick is developed and optimized, it can be produced at scale, potentially lowering costs. This makes it feasible to offer advanced assistive technology at a more affordable price point. Economically disadvantaged individuals, including those from below-poverty-line backgrounds, can benefit from such innovations, as cost-effective solutions become more accessible to a broader audience.
- **Continuous Improvement:** The iterative refinement process, driven by user feedback and performance data, ensures that the smart stick continues to evolve and improve. Regular updates and enhancements based on real-world usage help maintain the device's effectiveness and relevance. This commitment to ongoing improvement means that users will benefit from the latest

advancements in technology and AI, ensuring that the smart stick remains a valuable tool for navigating their environment.

Integrating AI into the "My Walking Pal" smart stick offers a range of benefits that enhance safety, navigation, usability, and overall quality of life for visually impaired individuals. The advanced features provided by AI not only improve the device's functionality but also contribute to greater independence and accessibility for the users.

LIMITATIONS: MY WALKING PAL

The "My Walking Pal" smart stick is designed to assist visually impaired individuals in navigating their surroundings, but it comes with several limitations. One key challenge is the accuracy and range of the sensors used, such as ultrasonic, water, and fire sensors, which may struggle in detecting small or transparent obstacles and can be affected by environmental conditions like rain or fog. Additionally, the AI models integrated into the device require extensive training data and significant processing power, which can be difficult to provide in a portable, compact device. This can impact the effectiveness of obstacle detection and navigation guidance. Some of the key takeaways with prospects to Walkin pal are as stated below:

Sensor Limitations

- **Accuracy**: The sensors embedded in the smart stick, such as ultrasonic and environmental sensors, may face difficulties in detecting certain types of obstacles. Small objects, such as curbs or narrow poles, and transparent obstacles, like glass doors or low-visibility hazards, pose significant detection challenges. The limitations in sensor resolution can occasionally lead to missed detections or false positives, impacting the reliability of the device. Enhancing sensor precision or integrating advanced imaging technologies could be potential solutions.
- **Range**: The detection range of sensors is inherently limited, which may reduce the warning time for fast-approaching obstacles like cyclists or vehicles. This is particularly problematic in high-speed or dynamic environments where immediate reaction is crucial. Expanding the range of sensors or incorporating predictive algorithms could improve responsiveness and safety.

Environmental Factors

- **Weather Conditions**: Adverse weather conditions such as heavy rain, fog, or snow can significantly impair the performance of sensors and GPS modules. For instance, water on the surface might interfere with ultrasonic sensors, while dense fog may obstruct hazard detection. Similarly, GPS signals can be affected by environmental obstructions, leading to inaccurate location tracking. Weather-resistant hardware and supplementary navigation methods, such as map preloading, could mitigate these challenges.
- **Noisy Environments**: In bustling urban settings or areas with high ambient noise, the effectiveness of the microphone for voice commands may be diminished. Users might struggle to interact with the device, and the device might fail to accurately interpret commands. Advanced noise-cancellation technologies or alternative interaction methods, such as tactile or gesture-based inputs, could offer improved performance in noisy surroundings

AI Model Limitations

- **Training Data**: AI models used for obstacle detection and navigation guidance require diverse and comprehensive training data to perform accurately across different scenarios. A lack of varied datasets can result in the models failing to recognize uncommon obstacles or environments. Expanding data collection efforts and incorporating edge-case scenarios into training can enhance the models' robustness.
- **Processing Power**: Real-time processing of sensor data and AI algorithms demands significant computational power. However, compact mobility devices have limited space to accommodate high-performance processors. This constraint can lead to slower response times or reduced functionality. Leveraging edge computing and efficient AI algorithms optimized for lightweight devices may address this issue.

Battery Life

- **Power Consumption**: The integration of multiple sensors, real-time data processing, and continuous feedback mechanisms leads to high energy consumption. Maintaining sufficient battery life without compromising the device's portability is a critical challenge. Energy-efficient sensors, low-power AI models, and adaptive power management systems can extend battery life.
- **Weight and Size**: The weight of the Smart Cane is a crucial consideration to ensure user comfort and ease of handling. Ideally, the cane should weigh

between 300 grams and 700 grams, striking a balance between durability and portability. A heavier design could lead to user fatigue, especially during extended use, while an excessively lightweight cane might compromise stability and robustness. To achieve this balance, lightweight materials such as aluminum alloys, carbon fiber, or reinforced plastics can be used. Aluminum alloys offer corrosion resistance and durability, while carbon fiber provides exceptional strength at minimal weight, albeit at a higher cost. Reinforced plastics present a more economical alternative suitable for broader accessibility.

The battery, a significant contributor to the cane's weight, can be optimized by using compact lithium-ion batteries, which are lightweight and efficient. A battery weighing approximately 150 grams would offer adequate power without significantly increasing the overall weight. Additionally, an ergonomic handle and a well-designed wrist strap can help distribute the weight evenly, minimizing strain on the user's hand. Usability testing with visually impaired individuals is essential to refine the weight and ensure the design meets practical needs, providing both comfort and reliability in daily navigation.

User Dependency

- **Learning Curve**: Adopting the device may require users to invest time and effort in learning how to operate it effectively. This includes understanding sensor alerts, voice commands, and navigation guidance. Providing comprehensive training, tutorials, and an intuitive interface can ease this transition.
- **Over-Reliance**: There is a risk of users becoming overly dependent on the device, potentially reducing their attentiveness to their surroundings. This could lead to unsafe situations if the device malfunctions. Encouraging users to complement the device with their own spatial awareness can help mitigate this issue.

Cost and Accessibility

- **Affordability**: Advanced technologies such as IoT sensors, AI models, and GPS modules may make the device expensive, limiting its accessibility to low-income individuals. Developing cost-effective components and exploring subsidies or partnerships with non-profits can make the device more affordable.
- **Availability**: Ensuring the widespread availability of the device, especially in remote or underdeveloped areas, poses logistical challenges. A robust dis-

tribution network and localized manufacturing units can improve reach and reduce costs associated with transportation and import duties.

Ethical and Privacy Concerns

- **Data Privacy**: Ensuring the widespread availability of the device, especially in remote or underdeveloped areas, poses logistical challenges. A robust distribution network and localized manufacturing units can improve reach and reduce costs associated with transportation and import duties.
- **Autonomy**: Ensuring the widespread availability of the device, especially in remote or underdeveloped areas, poses logistical challenges. A robust distribution network and localized manufacturing units can improve reach and reduce costs associated with transportation and import duties.

Adaptation to Diverse Environments

- **Urban vs. Rural Use**: Ensuring the widespread availability of the device, especially in remote or underdeveloped areas, poses logistical challenges. A robust distribution network and localized manufacturing units can improve reach and reduce costs associated with transportation and import duties.
- **Cultural and Language Barriers**: Ensuring the widespread availability of the device, especially in remote or underdeveloped areas, poses logistical challenges. A robust distribution network and localized manufacturing units can improve reach and reduce costs associated with transportation and import duties.

Maintenance and Durability

- **Wear and Tear**: Frequent use may lead to sensor degradation or physical damage. Regular maintenance or calibration will be necessary to ensure consistent performance. Developing durable hardware and providing affordable servicing options can address this challenge.
- **Environmental Durability**: The device must withstand exposure to various environmental conditions, such as heat, humidity, or dust, while remaining lightweight and user-friendly. Using robust, weather-resistant materials can increase the device's longevity without adding excessive weight.

CONCLUSION AND FUTURE DIRECTIONS

"My Walking Pal" smart stick offers a groundbreaking solution for visually impaired individuals, combining advanced sensors, AI-driven models, and real-time processing to significantly enhance mobility and safety. This device addresses the complex challenges that visually impaired individuals face daily, providing crucial assistance in navigating their environment. While the smart stick represents a significant leap forward in assistive technology, it is not without its limitations. Issues such as sensor accuracy, environmental adaptability, battery life, and the potential cost of the device underscore the need for further development and refinement. Despite these challenges, the "My Walking Pal" is a promising tool that has the potential to greatly improve the quality of life for those who need it most. Future versions of the smart stick should focus on enhancing sensor technology to improve obstacle detection accuracy and range, even in complex or adverse environments. Additionally, refining AI models to handle a wider variety of scenarios with greater efficiency will be essential. This includes improving the device's ability to learn from user behavior and adapting to individual needs over time. Reducing the power consumption of the device without sacrificing performance will be a crucial goal. This could involve exploring new battery technologies, optimizing the processing algorithms, or even integrating energy-harvesting technologies. Additionally, efforts should be made to keep the device lightweight, ergonomic, and easy to use, ensuring that it remains comfortable and convenient for daily use. Ensuring that the smart stick is affordable and accessible to all, including individuals from low-income backgrounds and those in remote or underserved areas, will be vital. This could involve partnerships with governments, NGOs, and private organizations to subsidize costs or create distribution networks that can reach the most vulnerable populations. Furthermore, producing a more economical version with essential features while maintaining effectiveness could broaden its reach.

To cater to a global audience, the device should be customizable for different languages, cultural contexts, and environments. This includes developing multilingual voice interaction systems and adjusting the AI models to account for regional variations in infrastructure and environmental conditions. Customization options can also extend to the level of feedback (audio, haptic, etc.) based on user preferences. Future designs should prioritize durability, especially in harsh environmental conditions, to ensure long-term reliability. This includes making the device resistant to water, dust, and physical shocks. Additionally, establishing a robust maintenance and support system, possibly through local service centres or mobile technicians, will ensure that users can keep their devices in good working condition over time. Ongoing user feedback will be crucial in guiding the evolution of the "My Walking Pal." Engaging with the visually impaired community to understand their experiences, preferences, and challenges will help developers make informed decisions about feature improvements and new functionalities. Pilot programs and real-world testing will provide valuable insights into the device's performance and areas for enhancement.

The future development of the smart stick could also explore integration with other assistive technologies, such as wearable devices or smart home systems, to create a more comprehensive support ecosystem. For example, linking the smart stick to a smartphone app could provide additional features like route planning, obstacle logging, or emergency alerts. By addressing these areas, the "My Walking Pal" smart stick can continue to evolve into a more powerful, reliable, and inclusive tool, helping visually impaired individuals navigate their world with greater confidence and independence. The ultimate goal is to contribute to a future where assistive technologies are seamlessly integrated into daily life, empowering all individuals to lead fulfilling, independent lives regardless of physical limitations.

REFERENCES

Abusukhon, A. (2023). IOT bracelets for guiding blind people in an indoor environment. *Journal of Communications Software and Systems*, *19*(2), 114–125. DOI: 10.24138/jcomss-2022-0160

Pathak, A., Adil, M., Rafa, T. S., Ferdoush, J., & Mahmud, A. (2020). An IoT based voice controlled blind stick to guide blind people. *Int. J. Eng. Invent*, *9*, 9–14.

Ahmed, S., ... (2022). An intelligent and multi-functional stick for blind people using IoT. In *2022 3rd International Conference on Intelligent Engineering and Management (ICIEM)*. IEEE. DOI: 10.1109/ICIEM54221.2022.9853012

Dabir, A., Solkar, R., Kumbhar, M., & Narayanan, G. (2018, April). GPS and IoT equipped smart walking stick. In *2018 International Conference on Communication and Signal Processing (ICCSP)* (pp. 322–326). IEEE. DOI: 10.1109/ICCSP.2018.8524472

Ghosal, A., Majumdar, A., Dhar, P., Kundu, A., Mondal, A., Biswas, A., & Ghosh, P. (2020). Smart Stick for Blind using IoT. *IJIRT*, *7*(5), 12–14.

Jasman, N., Jalil, M. F. I. M., Mukhtar, A., Sahari, K. S. M., & Rusli, M. E. (2022). IoT-based obstacle detection system for visually impaired person with smartphone module. *Journal of Advances in Information Technology*, *13*(4). Advance online publication. DOI: 10.12720/jait.13.4.368-373

Mala, N. S., Thushara, S. S., & Subbiah, S. (2017, February). Navigation gadget for visually impaired based on IoT. In *2017 2nd International Conference on Computing and Communications Technologies (ICCCT)* (pp. 334–338). IEEE. DOI: 10.1109/ICCCT2.2017.7972298

Nathan, S. S.Shelena Soosay NathanKuan Jung YingLim Hui WenLim Xin Weoi. (2023). Design of smart walking shoe for visually impaired people. *Journal of Advanced Research in Applied Mechanics*, *101*(1), 53–61. DOI: 10.37934/aram.101.1.5361

Nuanmeesri, S., & Poomhiran, L. (2020). Developing of intelligence walking stick and mobile application for elderly health care using the internet of things.

Pydala, B., Kumar, T. P., & Baseer, K. K. (2023). Smart_Eye: A navigation and obstacle detection for visually impaired people through smart app. [JAETS]. *Journal of Applied Engineering and Technological Science*, *4*(2), 992–1011. DOI: 10.37385/jaets.v4i2.2013

Raut, R., ... (2022). IoT-assisted smart device for blind people. In *Intelligent Systems for Rehabilitation Engineering* (pp. 129–150). DOI: 10.1002/9781119785651.ch6

Saisubramanyam, K., & Jhansi Rani, A. (2020). IoT based smart walking stick for blind or old aged people with GPS tracking location. *Journal of Engineering Science*, *11*(1), 501–505.

Sathya, D., Nithyaroopa, S., Betty, P., Santhoshni, G., Sabharinath, S., & Ahanaa, M. J. (2018). Smart walking stick for blind person. *International Journal of Pure and Applied Mathematics*, *118*(20), 4531–4536.

Tang, H., Shi, J., & Lei, K. (2016, June). A smart low-consumption IoT framework for location tracking and its real application. In *2016 6th International Conference on Electronics Information and Emergency Communication (ICEIEC)* (pp. 306–309). IEEE. DOI: 10.1109/ICEIEC.2016.7589744

Tariq, M. U. (2024). Streamlining Operations Insights and Innovations From the Gulf Cooperation Council (GCC). In Ayed, T., Ali, I., Abdelhamid, H., & Mohamed, A. (Eds.), *Utilizing Case Studies in Business Education* (pp. 188–216). IGI Global., DOI: 10.4018/979-8-3693-3779-0.ch010

Tariq, M. U. (2024). Smart Transportation Systems: Paving the Way for Sustainable Urban Mobility. In Munuhwa, S. (Ed.), *Contemporary Solutions for Sustainable Transportation Practices* (pp. 254–283). IGI Global., DOI: 10.4018/979-8-3693-3755-4.ch010

Tariq, M. U. (2024). Integration of IoMT for Enhanced Healthcare: Sleep Monitoring, Body Movement Detection, and Rehabilitation Evaluation. In Liu, H., Tripathy, R., & Bhattacharya, P. (Eds.), *Clinical Practice and Unmet Challenges in AI-Enhanced Healthcare Systems* (pp. 70–95). IGI Global., DOI: 10.4018/979-8-3693-2703-6.ch004

Tariq, M. U. (2024). Multi-Agent Models in Healthcare System Design. In Dall'Acqua, L. (Ed.), *Bioethics of Cognitive Ergonomics and Digital Transition* (pp. 143–170). IGI Global., DOI: 10.4018/979-8-3693-2667-1.ch008

Tariq, M. U. (2025). Leveraging Artificial Intelligence to Enhance Diversity and Drive Business Innovation. In Margaretha van der Poll, H., Andrew van der Poll, J., & Ngwakwe, C. (Eds.), *Diversity, AI, and Sustainability for Financial Growth* (pp. 79–96). IGI Global Scientific Publishing., DOI: 10.4018/979-8-3693-6011-8.ch004

Tariq, M. U. (2025). AI-Powered Breakthroughs: Revolutionizing Cognitive Psychology and Neuropsychology With Machine Learning. In Bansal, R., Maqableh, T., Shuklaa, G., Rabby, F., & Lathabhavan, R. (Eds.), *Transforming Neuropsychology and Cognitive Psychology With AI and Machine Learning* (pp. 65–92). IGI Global Scientific Publishing., DOI: 10.4018/979-8-3693-9341-3.ch003

Tariq, M. U., & Sergio, R. P. (2025). Ethical Considerations and Social Impact of AI and Computational Intelligence in Society 5.0. In Pandey, R., Srivastava, N., Prasad, R., Prasad, J., & Garcia, M. (Eds.), *Open AI and Computational Intelligence for Society 5.0* (pp. 225–248). IGI Global Scientific Publishing., DOI: 10.4018/979-8-3693-4326-5.ch010

ADDITIONAL READINGS

Ghani, F. A., & Zariman, A. (2019). Smart cane based on IoT. International Journal of Education. *Kexue Jishu Yu Gongcheng*, *2*(1), 12–18.

Nagarajan, S., & Dessai, S. (2020). IoT-based walking stick. In *Emerging Trends in Photonics, Signal Processing and Communication Engineering* (pp. 123–131). Springer. DOI: 10.1007/978-981-15-3477-5_16

KEY TERM AND DEFINITIONS

Visual Impairment: A condition characterised by partial or complete loss of sight that affects an individual's ability to navigate their environment.

Internet of Things (IoT): A network of interconnected devices that exchange data autonomously to enhance functionality and user experience.

Smart Cane: An advanced mobility aid integrating sensors, microcontrollers, and communication modules to provide real-time obstacle detection and alerts.

Obstacle Detection: The process by which sensors and algorithms identify potential hazards in the environment to prevent collisions.

Assistive Technology: Devices or systems designed to support individuals with disabilities in performing tasks more safely and independently.

Chapter 6
Case Study Successful Artificial Intelligence (AI) and the Internet of Things (IoT) (AIoT) Implementation in Smart Cities

Bhanu Dwivedi
https://orcid.org/0000-0002-7306-4414
Manav Rachna International Institute of Research and Studies, Faridabad, India

Rachna Behl
Manav Rachna International Institute of Research and Studies, Faridabad, India

ABSTRACT

This chapter investigates the integration of Artificial Intelligence (AI) and the Internet of Things (IoT) within smart city projects, emphasizing their practical applications and outcomes. It demonstrates how AIoT technologies improve urban infrastructure, resource management, and public services through comprehensive case studies from diverse cities. The chapter showcases the significant effects of AIoT on traffic management, energy efficiency, and public safety, and provides insights into best practices and strategies for addressing challenges such as data privacy, interoperability, and infrastructure investment. It highlights the convergence of AI and IoT as essential for advancing smart cities, enhancing quality of life, and fostering sustainable growth. Key elements for successful implementation include strong leadership, strategic vision, robust data privacy, and security measures. The

DOI: 10.4018/979-8-3693-8547-0.ch006

chapter concludes with actionable recommendations for scaling AIoT solutions, positioning this integration as a fundamental shift toward more sustainable and resilient urban environments.

INTRODUCTION

The concept of smart cities represents one of the most transformative developments in urban planning and governance. As urban populations grow at an unprecedented rate, cities face increasing challenges related to infrastructure, resource management, and quality of life. With the expansion of urbanization, governments and policymakers must seek innovative solutions to manage the complexities of modern cities while ensuring sustainability and livability for their citizens. The emergence of smart cities signifies the convergence of these technologies into a unified system that manages everything from energy consumption and transportation to healthcare and public safety. Smart cities rely on an intricate network of interconnected devices, sensors, and systems, all generating and collecting data in real-time. AI processes this vast amount of data to detect patterns, predict future outcomes, and make informed decisions (Shamsuzzoha et al., 2021). IoT, meanwhile, allows physical objects and infrastructure within a city to communicate with each other and with central management systems, ensuring efficient coordination and control. The combination of AI and IoT transforms traditional urban management into a highly optimized, responsive, and adaptive system capable of addressing the dynamic needs of its population. This chapter focuses on the successful implementation of AIoT in smart cities, analyzing how these technologies have been applied to solve critical urban challenges (Naphade et al., 2011). By examining a series of case studies from various smart cities worldwide, the chapter illustrates the tangible benefits of AIoT and explores the best practices for its deployment. These case studies highlight how AIoT technologies are already improving traffic management, energy distribution, public safety, environmental sustainability, and healthcare delivery. Through this analysis, the chapter provides practical insights into the strategies that have made AIoT projects successful and the challenges that remain to be addressed for future growth.

AIoT has emerged as a key enabler of the smart city concept, providing a technological foundation for more effective urban governance. Urban areas are facing unprecedented levels of stress due to rapid population growth, climate change, and increasing demand for services. Traditional methods of city management, which often rely on static and reactive approaches, are no longer sufficient to meet the demands of modern urban life (Dupont et al., 2015). Cities must become more adaptive and efficient in their operations to ensure sustainable growth and resilience in the face of evolving challenges. AIoT offers a solution to these pressing concerns by enabling cities to collect, analyze, and act on data in real-time, thereby optimizing their operations and reducing inefficiencies. AI-powered surveillance systems, for example, analyze video footage and sensor data in real-time to detect potential threats, suspicious activities, or accidents. AIoT systems can then automatically alert law enforcement or emergency responders, reducing the time it takes to address safety concerns. Similarly, IoT enabled health monitoring devices help track the well-being of residents and identify medical emergencies before they escalate, enabling quicker and more effective healthcare interventions. Through these applications, AIoT is not only transforming how cities function but also enhancing the overall quality of life for residents by creating safer, more efficient, and more sustainable urban environments (Ortega-Fernández et al., 2020). The integration of AI and IoT into a single system AIoT creates a synergistic relationship where the strengths of each technology complement and enhance the other. AI, with its advanced data analytics and decision-making capabilities, transforms the raw data collected by IoT devices into actionable insights. IoT devices, in turn, generate vast amounts of data from various urban systems, including traffic lights, air quality sensors, public transportation systems, and even waste management infrastructure. Without the connectivity and data generation provided by IoT, AI would lack the necessary input to perform its analysis and make informed decisions. Conversely, without AI's ability to analyze and interpret the data collected by IoT devices, cities would be overwhelmed by the sheer volume of information being generated, rendering it nearly impossible to act on in real-time (Shamsuzzoha et al., 2021). The convergence of these technologies allows cities to operate with unprecedented levels of intelligence and automation. AIoT systems continuously monitor and evaluate conditions in real-time, enabling city operators to optimize operations, identify potential problems before they occur, and respond quickly to emerging situations. For example, in a smart city equipped with AIoT technologies, the system could automatically detect a malfunction in a traffic light, reroute vehicles to avoid congestion, and alert maintenance teams to resolve the issue before it escalates. During natural disasters such as floods or hurricanes, AIoT systems can monitor weather conditions, predict the impact on infrastructure, and coordinate emergency responses in real-time, potentially saving lives and reducing damage (Yun et al., 2022). The case studies presented in this chapter highlight the successful implementation of AIoT technologies in various smart cities around the world. These case studies illustrate how AIoT is improving the efficiency, sustainability, and livability of urban environments, showcasing real-world applications in areas such as traffic management, energy efficiency, public safety, and environmental monitoring. One notable example is the city of Singapore, which has emerged as a leader in AIoT implementation. Singapore's smart city initiatives have integrated AI and IoT technologies across various sectors, including transportation, energy, and public safety. Through the use of AI-powered traffic management systems, the city has been able to significantly reduce congestion, optimize public transportation routes, and improve road safety. In the energy sector, AIoT-enabled smart grids have helped Singapore achieve greater energy efficiency by dynamically adjusting electricity distribution based on demand (Milovanovic & Pantovic, 2023; Tariq & Sergio, 2025)). Additionally, AI-driven surveillance systems have enhanced public safety by enabling real-time monitoring of public spaces and improving emergency response times. Another example is Barcelona, Spain, which has leveraged AIoT technologies to create a more sustainable and livable city. Barcelona's smart city strategy includes the deployment of IoT sensors to monitor air quality, waste management, and water consumption. AI algorithms analyze this data to identify patterns and predict future needs, enabling the city to optimize resource usage and reduce waste. In addition to these environmental initiatives, Barcelona has implemented AIoT solutions in its transportation system (Wu et al., 2019), using AI to analyze traffic data and IoT-enabled parking sensors to guide drivers to available parking spaces, reducing congestion and emissions. Data breaches or unauthorized access to sensitive information could have severe consequences, undermining the credibility of AIoT projects and potentially putting citizens at risk. Another challenge is the interoperability of AIoT systems. As cities adopt AIoT technologies from different vendors, ensuring that these systems can communicate and work together seamlessly becomes increasingly important (Alahi et al., 2023). The integration of AI and IoT technologies is driving a new era of urban transformation, enabling cities to become smarter, more sustainable, and more resilient. AIoT offers a powerful toolset for addressing the challenges of modern urban life, from optimizing traffic flow and energy consumption to enhancing public safety and environmental sustainability. The case studies presented in this chapter demonstrate the tangible benefits of AIoT and highlight the best practices for successful implementation. However, realizing the full potential of AIoT requires overcoming several challenges, including data privacy, interoperability, and infrastructure investment (Bibri, Huang, et al., 2024). By addressing these challenges and fostering collaboration across sectors, cities can harness the power of AIoT to create more intelligent, sustainable, and livable urban environments.

AIoT technologies provide innovative solutions to a variety of urban issues:

Traffic Management

By utilizing AI algorithms to analyze real-time data from IoT sensors on roads and vehicles, traffic flow is optimized, congestion is reduced, and travel times are minimized. Adaptive traffic lights adjust timings based on current conditions, while predictive analytics aid city planners in managing peak traffic periods more efficiently (Kuguoglu, van der Voort, & Janssen, 2021).

Public Safety

AI-driven surveillance systems, featuring facial recognition and behavior analysis, can detect unusual activities and notify authorities promptly. IoT devices like connected streetlights and safety sensors improve the monitoring of public areas, aiding in crime prevention and emergency responses.

Waste Management

Smart bins with IoT sensors monitor fill levels, optimizing waste collection routes and reducing operational costs. AI also helps predict waste generation trends, facilitating better planning and resource management.

AIoT technologies enhance the quality of life in smart cities by delivering more efficient and personalized services:

Energy Efficiency

AI systems leverage data from smart grids and connected devices to enhance energy distribution and consumption. This not only reduces energy costs for consumers but also lowers carbon footprints. AIoT-enabled smart buildings adjust HVAC systems based on occupancy and weather conditions.

Healthcare

Remote patient monitoring systems use IoT devices to gather health data, which AI algorithms analyze for early diagnosis and personalized treatment plans. This approach enhances healthcare access and outcomes, particularly for the elderly and those with chronic illnesses (Pise et al., 2022).

Public Transport

AIoT solutions improve the efficiency and user experience of public transportation. Real-time data from IoT devices aids in the scheduling and routing of buses and trains, while AI-powered applications offer passengers real-time updates and customized travel advice.

AIoT is crucial for advancing sustainability in urban settings:

Environmental Monitoring

IoT sensors track air and water quality, noise levels, and other environmental metrics. AI analyzes this data to identify pollution sources, forecast environmental changes, and suggest mitigation strategies, assisting city authorities in enforcing regulations and raising public awareness (Shamsuzzoha et al., 2021).

Resource Management

AIoT enhances the management of water and energy resources through predictive analytics and automated control systems. For example, smart irrigation systems utilize weather data and soil moisture levels to optimize water use in urban landscaping, conserving resources and cutting costs (Bibri, Krogstie, et al., 2024).

Urban Planning

AIoT technologies offer deep insights into urban dynamics, such as population movement and infrastructure utilization. This data-driven approach supports more informed decision-making in urban planning, ensuring sustainable growth. AI can also simulate the effects of proposed projects on traffic, the environment, and other factors, assisting planners in making well-informed decisions (Cardullo & Kitchin, 2019).

Develop Skilled Workforce and Continuous Learning

AIoT technologies require a skilled workforce familiar with both AI and IoT principles. Investing in training and development programs for city staff and engineers is crucial. Additionally, fostering a culture of continuous learning and innovation helps keep pace with rapid technological advancements (Alahi et al., 2023).

Monitor, Evaluate, and Adapt

Continuous monitoring and evaluation of AIoT initiatives are necessary to assess their effectiveness and impact. Key performance indicators (KPIs) should be established to measure progress toward goals. Flexibility in adapting strategies based on feedback and data analysis ensures that initiatives remain relevant and effective over time (Bibri, Alexandre, et al., 2023).

Case Studies of Successful AIoT Implementation Case Study

Singapore's Smart Nation Initiative: Singapore's Smart Nation initiative represents one of the most comprehensive and ambitious efforts to integrate Artificial Intelligence (AI) and the Internet of Things (IoT) into urban infrastructure, creating a highly connected and intelligent city. This case study examines the AIoT solutions deployed, the key factors contributing to their success, and the impact on urban living (Shamsuzzoha et al., 2021).

AIOT SOLUTIONS DEPLOYED

Smart Mobility

Singapore has implemented advanced traffic management systems that use AI and IoT to monitor and manage traffic flow in real-time. This includes intelligent traffic lights, automated toll collection, and a predictive maintenance system for public transport vehicles. The city also utilizes AIoT technologies to optimize public transportation routes and schedules based on data collected from various sensors and user applications.

Urban Environment Management

AIoT solutions are used to monitor environmental factors such as air quality, water levels, and waste management (Kaginalkar et al., 2021). IoT sensors placed throughout the city collect data, which AI systems analyze to predict and respond to environmental changes. This allows for proactive measures in addressing pollution, flooding, and waste management issues (Cardullo & Kitchin, 2019).

Public Safety and Security

The city has deployed a network of surveillance cameras equipped with AI-powered facial recognition and behavior analysis capabilities. These systems help monitor public spaces, detect potential security threats, and assist in crime prevention. Additionally, AIoT technology supports emergency response systems by providing real-time data and analytics.

Smart Homes and Buildings

Singapore's housing and commercial buildings incorporate AIoT technologies to improve energy efficiency and provide better living conditions. Smart meters, automated lighting, and climate control systems are managed through AI algorithms that adjust settings based on occupancy and environmental conditions.

KEY SUCCESS FACTORS

Government Vision and Support

The Singaporean government has played a crucial role in the success of the Smart Nation initiative. Strong leadership, clear vision, and substantial investment in infrastructure have been pivotal. The government has also established supportive policies and frameworks to encourage innovation and collaboration among private and public sectors.

Public-Private-Partnerships

Collaboration between government agencies, technology companies, and research institutions has been key to developing and implementing AIoT solutions. These partnerships have facilitated access to cutting-edge technologies, expertise, and funding (Dupont et al., 2015).

Data Governance and Privacy

Singapore has developed comprehensive data governance policies to ensure data privacy and security. This includes guidelines for data collection, sharing, and usage, which have been critical in gaining public trust and ensuring the responsible use of AIoT technologies (Noori et al., 2020) (Bernardo, 2019).

Focus on Scalability and Flexibility

The AIoT systems deployed in Singapore are designed to be scalable and flexible, allowing for the integration of new technologies and expansion to meet future needs. This adaptability has been essential in maintaining the city's position at the forefront of smart city innovation (Tariq, 2025).

Impact on Urban Living

The deployment of AIoT technologies in Singapore has had a profound impact on urban living. Residents enjoy improved transportation efficiency, reduced travel times, and enhanced safety and security. The smart management of environmental resources contributes to a cleaner and more sustainable city. Additionally, the integration of AIoT in homes and buildings enhances comfort, reduces energy consumption, and lowers costs.

Singapore's Smart Nation initiative showcases the potential of AIoT technologies in transforming urban environments (Shamsuzzoha et al., 2021). The strategic deployment of AIoT solutions, supported by strong government leadership, public-private partnerships, and a focus on data governance, has created a more efficient, sustainable, and livable city. This case study provides valuable insights for other cities aiming to implement similar smart city initiatives.

Barcelona: IoT and AI for Efficient City Management AIoT Solutions Deployed Key Success Factors Impact on Urban Living: Barcelona has emerged as a leading example of how the integration of Artificial Intelligence (AI) and the Internet of Things (IoT) can enhance city management and improve the quality of life for its residents. This case study explores the AIoT solutions implemented in Barcelona, identifies the key factors behind their success, and examines the impact on urban living. (Calzada, 2018)

AIOT SOLUTIONS DEPLOYED

Smart traffic and transportation management: Barcelona has implemented an AIoT-enabled traffic management system that includes smart traffic lights and real-time traffic monitoring. The system uses data from road sensors and connected vehicles to optimize traffic flow and reduce congestion. Additionally, the city's public transportation system leverages AIoT to provide real-time updates on schedules and occupancy levels, helping passengers make informed travel decisions (Noori et al., 2020).

Energy management and smart lighting: The city has deployed smart lighting systems that adjust streetlight intensity based on pedestrian and vehicle presence, time of day, and weather conditions. These AIoT-enabled lights help reduce energy consumption and improve safety. Moreover, Barcelona utilizes AI to manage energy usage in public buildings, optimizing heating, ventilation, and air conditioning systems to increase efficiency and reduce costs.

Waste management: Barcelona has implemented a smart waste management system that uses IoT sensors in waste bins to monitor fill levels. This data is analyzed to optimize waste collection routes, reducing the number of unnecessary collections and minimizing fuel consumption and emissions. AI algorithms also help predict waste generation patterns, enabling more efficient resource allocation (Cardullo & Kitchin, 2019).

Environmental Monitoring

The city uses a network of IoT sensors to monitor environmental factors such as air quality, noise levels, and temperature (Kaginalkar et al., 2021). AI systems analyze this data to identify trends and potential environmental hazards, allowing city officials to take proactive measures to address issues like pollution and heat islands (Bibri, Huang, et al., 2024).

- **Key success factors**

Strategic Vision and Planning

Barcelona's success with AIoT integration stems from a clear strategic vision for becoming a smart city. The city government has been proactive in setting objectives and implementing policies that promote technological innovation and sustainability.

Public-Private Collaboration

The collaboration between municipal authorities, private sector companies, and academic institutions has been crucial in deploying and maintaining AIoT systems (Dupont et al., 2015). These partnerships have provided access to the necessary technology, expertise, and funding.

Citizen Engagement and Transparency

Barcelona has placed a strong emphasis on involving citizens in its smart city initiatives. Public consultations, workshops, and open data platforms have helped build public trust and ensure that AIoT solutions are aligned with residents' needs and expectations (Noori et al., 2020).

Scalability and Innovation

The city has focused on scalable and modular solutions that can be expanded and upgraded as technology evolves. This approach allows Barcelona to continuously innovate and integrate new technologies into its existing infrastructure.

- **Impact on urban living**

The implementation of AIoT technologies in Barcelona has significantly improved urban living conditions. Residents benefit from reduced traffic congestion, more reliable public transportation, and enhanced public safety. The smart lighting and energy management systems contribute to lower energy consumption and a smaller carbon footprint. Moreover, the city's proactive approach to environmental monitoring and waste management has led to a cleaner and more sustainable urban environment (Calzada, 2018), (Noori et al., 2020).

- **Conclusion**

Barcelona's integration of AI and IoT technologies serves as a model for efficient city management. The city's strategic planning, emphasis on collaboration, and commitment to sustainability have enabled it to harness the potential of AIoT to improve urban living. This case study highlights the practical benefits of AIoT in smart cities and provides valuable insights for other municipalities aiming to adopt similar technologies.

Case Study: "Amsterdam's AI-Driven Sustainability: Amsterdam has positioned itself as a leader in using Artificial Intelligence (AI) and the Internet of Things (IoT) to drive sustainability efforts. This case study explores the AIoT solutions Amsterdam has deployed, the key factors contributing to their success, and the impact on urban living."

- **AIoT solutions deployed**

Smart Energy Management

Amsterdam has implemented AIoT solutions to optimize energy usage across the city. Smart grids, equipped with IoT sensors, collect data on energy consumption patterns, which AI algorithms analyze to balance energy supply and demand. This system helps reduce energy wastage and integrates renewable energy sources more effectively (Apanaviciene & Shahrabani, 2023).

Water Management

The city uses AIoT technology to manage its extensive canal system and water resources. IoT sensors monitor water quality, levels, and flow rates in real-time. AI analyzes this data to predict and manage flooding risks, ensuring timely responses to potential water-related issues. This system also supports efficient water usage and conservation.

Sustainable Mobility

Amsterdam has deployed AIoT solutions to promote sustainable transportation. Smart traffic lights, real-time public transport updates, and bike-sharing programs are all managed through an interconnected network of sensors and AI. This infrastructure reduces traffic congestion, encourages the use of public and non-motorized transport, and lowers carbon emissions (Kaginalkar et al., 2021).

Waste Management

The city's waste management system leverages AIoT to optimize collection schedules and routes based on data from IoT-enabled waste bins. AI predicts waste generation trends, helping the city allocate resources efficiently and reduce the environmental impact of waste collection (Shamsuzzoha et al., 2021).

KEY SUCCESS FACTORS

Government Leadership and Policy Support

Amsterdam's government has been proactive in creating policies and frameworks that support the integration of AIoT technologies. Strategic plans and regulations encourage innovation and ensure that sustainability remains a core focus.

Collaborative Ecosystem

Amsterdam's success is also attributed to the collaboration between government agencies, tech companies, research institutions, and citizens. This ecosystem fosters innovation and enables the sharing of knowledge and resources necessary for AIoT deployment.

Focus on Open Data

The city's commitment to open data has played a significant role in its smart city initiatives. By making data accessible to the public and developers, Amsterdam encourages transparency, citizen participation, and the development of new solutions and services.

Scalable and Adaptable Infrastructure

Amsterdam has invested in scalable and adaptable infrastructure, allowing it to integrate new technologies and expand existing ones. This approach ensures the city's AIoT systems remain relevant and effective as technology evolves (Kaginalkar et al., 2021).

Impact on Urban Living

The deployment of AIoT technologies has significantly improved the quality of life in Amsterdam. Residents benefit from a more sustainable and efficient energy system, enhanced water management, and improved mobility options. These advancements have led to a reduction in the city's carbon footprint, better resource management, and a cleaner, safer environment. Moreover, the city's focus on citizen engagement and open data has fostered a sense of community and involvement in sustainability efforts (Tariq, 2025).

CHALLENGES AND SOLUTIONS IN AIOT IMPLEMENTATION

Data Privacy and Security

The integration of Artificial Intelligence (AI) and the Internet of Things (IoT) in urban settings collectively termed AIoT brings forth remarkable opportunities to enhance the efficiency and effectiveness of smart city operations. However, this technological advancement is accompanied by significant challenges, particularly in the domains of data privacy and security. Given the volume of data that AIoT systems collect, process, and analyze, which often includes sensitive information about individuals and critical public infrastructure, addressing these concerns is of paramount importance.

Challenges

AIoT systems are designed to function through an extensive network of connected devices and sensors that continuously gather real-time data from various sources. This capability poses considerable risks, especially concerning data privacy and security. One major challenge is the unauthorized access to sensitive information, which can occur if adequate security measures are not in place. Such breaches can result in the exposure of personal data, leading to identity theft and privacy violations for individuals. With the involvement of multiple stakeholders ranging from government agencies to private companies ensuring that all parties adhere to stringent data protection regulations can be difficult. Inconsistent practices and varying levels of commitment to data security among stakeholders may lead to gaps in protection, further exacerbating privacy concerns. As smart cities expand their AIoT capabilities, addressing these challenges becomes increasingly urgent to safeguard citizens' data and maintain their trust (Yun et al., 2022).

Solutions

To effectively tackle the challenges associated with data privacy and security in AIoT systems, cities must adopt comprehensive data protection measures. One primary strategy is the implementation of robust encryption protocols that secure data during transmission and storage. Encryption ensures that even if data is intercepted or accessed without authorization, it remains unreadable and protected from misuse (Milovanovic & Pantovic, 2023). These measures help prevent unauthorized access and ensure that only those who genuinely need to interact with sensitive information can do so. Another critical aspect of safeguarding data privacy and security is the continuous updating of security protocols. Cyber threats evolve rapidly, necessitating a proactive approach to cybersecurity. Cities should invest in cybersecurity training for personnel, keeping them informed of emerging threats and best practices for data protection (Bernardo, 2019).

Mitigation Strategies Case Study

An exemplary case of effective data privacy and security management is Singapore's Smart Nation initiative. The city-state has prioritized data governance through comprehensive frameworks that address the privacy and security challenges associated with AIoT systems. Singapore employs strong encryption standards to protect data in transit and at rest, ensuring that sensitive information is shielded from unauthorized access. The combination of robust encryption, continuous monitoring, and stakeholder engagement exemplifies how cities can effectively address data privacy and security challenges. By learning from Singapore's proactive measures, other cities can adopt similar strategies to enhance their own AIoT initiatives, ensuring the safe and ethical use of technology in smart urban settings.

Interoperability and Standards

The integration of Artificial Intelligence (AI) and the Internet of Things (IoT) collectively referred to as AIoT has ushered in a new era of smart cities characterized by enhanced operational efficiencies and an improved quality of life for urban residents. This lack of standardization not only hampers the seamless operation of AIoT systems but also limits their scalability and potential to deliver integrated solutions.

Challenges

Interoperability issues are at the forefront of challenges faced during the integration of AIoT technologies in smart cities. The diversity of devices, protocols, and platforms can create silos within the infrastructure, where information exchange is impeded due to incompatible systems. This fragmentation leads to inefficiencies and complications when trying to implement a unified approach to city management. Moreover, the absence of widely accepted standards means that each vendor may prioritize proprietary technology over compatibility (Sharifi, 2019). This not only creates barriers to integrating new technologies but also complicates the process of upgrading or expanding existing systems. For example, if a city wishes to incorporate an innovative AI-based traffic management system, the inability of this new system to interface with the existing IoT infrastructure can lead to significant delays and increased costs.

Solutions

To overcome the challenges of interoperability, it is essential to adopt and adhere to international standards and protocols. Standardization facilitates seamless communication between devices and systems, enabling them to work together cohesively. By establishing common communication protocols, cities can ensure that devices from different manufacturers can exchange information and collaborate effectively. Cities should prioritize the use of open standards in their AIoT projects. Open standards allow for greater flexibility and adaptability, enabling cities to integrate new technologies more easily as they emerge.

Infrastructure and Investment

The successful implementation of Artificial Intelligence (AI) and the Internet of Things (IoT), collectively referred to as AIoT, in smart cities requires a solid foundation of infrastructure and a commitment to investment. This section explores the obstacles cities face regarding infrastructure and investment in AIoT initiatives, outlines potential solutions, and presents a case study highlighting effective funding strategies (Tariq, 2025).

Challenges

Developing and maintaining the infrastructure required for AIoT solutions can be both costly and resource-intensive. One of the primary challenges in infrastructure development is securing sufficient funding. Cities often operate within budget constraints, making it difficult to allocate financial resources for new technology initiatives. Justifying these investments to stakeholders such as city officials, community members, and investors can also be a complex process (Verrest & Pfeffer, 2019). This can create a dilemma for city planners and decision-makers, who must balance the costs of upgrading existing infrastructure against the potential benefits of implementing new technologies (Kaginalkar et al., 2021). The rapid pace of technological advancements further complicates the situation. As new AIoT technologies emerge, cities may struggle to keep up, leading to a mismatch between available infrastructure and the latest solutions. This issue can result in wasted investments and inefficiencies, as outdated systems may not integrate seamlessly with newer AIoT technologies.

Solutions

To overcome the challenges associated with infrastructure development and investment in AIoT, cities can explore various funding strategies and approaches. Public-private partnerships (PPPs) represent a promising avenue for financing AIoT initiatives. By collaborating with technology companies, research institutions, and other stakeholders, cities can share costs and risks while gaining access to cutting-edge technology and expertise. These partnerships allow for a more efficient allocation of resources and can expedite the deployment of AIoT solutions. Demonstrating the long-term benefits of AIoT investments is crucial for securing necessary funding. Cities should focus on articulating the potential returns on investment, including improved efficiency, cost savings, enhanced services, and better overall quality of life for residents. By presenting a comprehensive business case that highlights both short-term and long-term advantages, city planners can foster buy-in from stakeholders and increase the likelihood of securing funding. Successful pilot projects can serve as proof of concept, helping to build confidence among stakeholders and facilitate future investments.

Funding Strategies Case Study

A notable example of successful funding strategies for AIoT implementation is Amsterdam's approach to its smart city initiatives. The city has effectively leveraged public-private partnerships to finance various AIoT projects, resulting in a more innovative and resilient urban environment. Amsterdam's commitment to transparency and community engagement has played a crucial role in its funding success. By actively involving citizens in the planning and implementation of AIoT initiatives, the city has fostered trust and demonstrated the tangible benefits of these technologies. By learning from successful case studies like Amsterdam, cities can develop a roadmap for building the necessary infrastructure to support AIoT solutions. As urban areas continue to evolve, investing in AIoT technologies will be essential for creating smarter, more efficient, and sustainable cities that enhance the quality of life for all residents (Dupont et al., 2015).

Ethical and Social Implications

The deployment of artificial Intelligence (AI) and the Internet of Things (IoT) collectively referred to as AIoT has emerged as a cornerstone in the evolution of smart cities, providing a multitude of benefits in areas such as urban management, resource allocation, and public services. However, alongside these advancements, significant ethical and social concerns must be addressed to ensure that the implementation of AIoT technologies is both responsible and equitable. This section delves into the ethical and social implications associated with AIoT deployment, focusing on the challenges cities face, potential solutions, and a case study that highlights effective mitigation strategies.

Challenges

The integration of AIoT technologies raises a myriad of ethical and social concerns that must be carefully considered. One of the primary challenges is related to surveillance. Many AIoT applications involve the collection of vast amounts of data through sensors, cameras, and other devices. This data collection can lead to intrusive surveillance practices that infringe upon individuals' privacy rights. The fear of job loss can foster resistance to AIoT initiatives, particularly among workers in sectors likely to be affected, such as transportation and logistics. Without adequate measures in place to support those displaced, the adoption of AIoT could exacerbate existing social inequalities, further marginalizing vulnerable populations (Ahvenniemi et al., 2017). The risk of exacerbating social inequalities presents another challenge in the implementation of AIoT technologies. If access to the benefits of AIoT is unevenly distributed, certain segments of the population particularly low-income communities may be left behind. The digital divide can limit these communities' ability to leverage AIoT solutions, leading to disparities in access to resources and services. Such inequalities could hinder the overall effectiveness of AIoT technologies in improving urban living conditions.

Solutions

Addressing the ethical and social concerns related to AIoT technologies requires a multi-faceted approach that incorporates transparency, public engagement, and ethical guidelines. Cities must prioritize transparent decision-making processes, allowing residents to understand how AIoT technologies will be implemented and the implications for their daily lives. This transparency can foster trust among citizens, encouraging them to engage with and support AIoT initiatives. To mitigate potential job displacement, cities should develop retraining and upskilling programs aimed at helping workers transition to new roles created by AIoT technologies. By investing in workforce development, cities can alleviate fears of job loss and foster a more inclusive environment where all individuals can benefit from technological advancements (Barns, 2018). Amsterdam serves as a noteworthy case study for addressing ethical and social implications in AIoT implementation. The city has made concerted efforts to engage the public and consider ethical implications in its smart city projects. By establishing comprehensive ethical guidelines and frameworks, Amsterdam prioritizes responsible technology use that aligns with public interest and social equity (Batty et al., 2012). Furthermore, the city has implemented strict data governance policies to address issues of data ownership and privacy. By ensuring that data collected through AIoT technologies is handled transparently and securely, Amsterdam enhances public confidence in its smart city initiatives. The city's commitment to data ethics extends to ensuring that sensitive information is protected and that residents have control over how their data is used. Amsterdam's proactive approach to addressing potential job displacement is also commendable. The city collaborates with educational institutions and training organizations to develop programs that equip workers with the skills necessary for emerging roles in an AIoT-driven economy. The ethical and social implications associated with AIoT implementation in smart cities are complex and multifaceted. By acknowledging the challenges related to surveillance, data ownership, job displacement, and social inequality, cities can take proactive measures to mitigate potential risks.

Scalability and Adaptability

As urban populations continue to grow and technology advances at an unprecedented pace, cities must ensure that their Artificial Intelligence (AI) and Internet of Things (IoT) systems collectively known as AIoT are both scalable and adaptable. Scalability refers to the system's ability to handle increasing volumes of data, devices, and users, while adaptability involves the system's capacity to integrate new technologies and respond to changing urban needs. This section examines the challenges associated with scaling and adapting AIoT systems, explores potential solutions, and presents a case study that highlights best practices for achieving scalability and adaptability in a smart city.

Challenges

One of the primary challenges of AIoT implementation in smart cities is ensuring that these systems can scale and adapt to accommodate future growth. As cities expand, the number of connected devices, sensors, and users will increase significantly, leading to larger volumes of data that must be collected, processed, and analyzed in real-time. The infrastructure supporting these AIoT systems must be capable of handling this growth without compromising performance, reliability, or efficiency. Many cities operate under tight financial conditions, making it difficult to justify significant upfront investments in infrastructure without clear, demonstrable returns. The challenge is creating systems that are not only scalable but also economically viable over the long term.

Solutions

To overcome the challenges of scalability and adaptability in AIoT systems, cities must invest in flexible and modular infrastructure. This approach allows cities to expand their AIoT capabilities incrementally, as needed, without requiring costly overhauls or replacements. One key solution is adopting cloud computing and edge computing technologies, which offer enhanced flexibility and scalability for data processing and storage (Shamsuzzoha et al., 2021). Cloud computing allows cities to store and process large volumes of data in centralized data centers, reducing the need for local infrastructure investments. This approach is particularly beneficial for smart cities, as it enables real-time data processing and analytics without overwhelming local networks. Additionally, cloud-based systems are easily scalable, allowing cities to increase storage and computing power as needed. Cloud service providers typically offer pay-as-you-go models, which allow cities to scale their AIoT infrastructure cost-effectively. As new technologies and standards emerge, cities should ensure that their infrastructure is equipped to support the latest innovations. This includes upgrading communication networks, such as 5G, to handle increased data traffic and improve the overall speed and reliability of AIoT systems. By staying up-to-date with advancements in AI and IoT, cities can future-proof their infrastructure and ensure that their systems remain relevant and effective.

Barcelona, Spain, offers an exemplary model for scalable and adaptable AIoT infrastructure. The city has embraced both cloud and edge computing to manage its smart city initiatives efficiently. By leveraging cloud-based systems, Barcelona stores and processes vast amounts of data related to traffic, energy usage, and public services, ensuring that information is accessible in real-time for decision-making and resource allocation. The city has also invested in edge computing to enhance the performance of time-sensitive applications, such as its intelligent traffic management system. Edge devices installed throughout the city enable local data processing, reducing latency and ensuring that traffic signals and sensors can adjust in real-time to changing conditions (Caragliu et al., 2011). This combination of cloud and edge computing has provided Barcelona with a flexible and scalable infrastructure capable of supporting its growing urban population and increasing technological demands. The city has fostered collaboration between public and private sectors, ensuring that new AIoT solutions are developed in partnership with technology providers, research institutions, and local businesses. This collaborative approach has enabled the city to share resources, reduce costs, and accelerate the adoption of AIoT technologies (Harrison & Donnelly, 2011). By prioritizing open standards and interoperable platforms, Barcelona has ensured that its AIoT infrastructure can integrate new devices and technologies from a variety of vendors. This flexibility allows the city to adapt quickly to technological advancements and incorporate innovations without the need for extensive overhauls.

IMPACT AND BENEFITS OF AIOT IN SMART CITIES

Improved Urban Infrastructure

The integration of AIoT technologies significantly enhances urban infrastructure by enabling real-time monitoring and management of city systems. This includes water supply, waste management, electricity grids, and public utilities. AIoT helps optimize the maintenance and operation of infrastructure, reducing downtime and improving efficiency. Predictive analytics can forecast equipment failures, allowing for preemptive repairs and minimizing service interruptions. This leads to a more reliable and resilient urban infrastructure, ultimately improving the quality of life for residents (Tariq, 2025).

Transportation and Traffic Management

AIoT technologies revolutionize transportation and traffic management in cities by providing real-time data and intelligent traffic control systems.

These systems can reduce congestion, shorten travel times, and enhance the overall efficiency of public and private transportation networks. Smart traffic lights, real-time traffic updates, and adaptive traffic control systems help manage vehicle flow, reduce emissions, and improve road safety (Bibri, Krogstie, et al., 2024). Additionally, AIoT supports the development of smart public transport solutions, such as dynamic routing and real-time scheduling, which enhance the commuter experience.

Energy and Resource Management

AIoT enables more efficient management of energy and resources in cities, facilitating the transition to sustainable energy systems. Smart grids and meters allow for precise monitoring and control of energy consumption, leading to reduced waste and lower energy costs. AI algorithms optimize energy distribution, balance load demands, and integrate renewable energy sources. This contributes to energy conservation and supports environmental sustainability goals. In addition, AIoT technologies improve water and waste management, optimizing usage and reducing environmental impact.

Enhanced Public Services

AIoT technologies improve the delivery of public services, making them more efficient, responsive, and personalized. In healthcare, AIoT can enhance patient monitoring, enable remote diagnostics, and improve the efficiency of healthcare services. Public safety is also bolstered through AIoT applications such as smart surveillance, predictive policing, and disaster response systems (Dupont et al., 2015). These technologies help authorities respond more quickly to incidents and emergencies, thereby enhancing the overall safety and well-being of residents.

Healthcare Public Safety

AIoT plays a critical role in enhancing healthcare delivery and public safety in urban environments. In healthcare, AIoT enables continuous patient monitoring through wearable devices and remote sensors, providing real-time health data to medical professionals. This facilitates early detection of health issues and improves patient outcomes (Shamsuzzoha et al., 2021). For public safety, AIoT technologies such as AI-powered surveillance cameras and emergency response systems enhance the monitoring of public spaces, enabling quicker response times to incidents and emergencies, and improving overall safety.

Economic and Environmental Benefits

AIoT technologies contribute to economic growth and environmental sustainability in smart cities. The implementation of AIoT can lead to cost savings through more efficient resource use, reduced operational costs, and lower energy consumption. These technologies also support the development of new industries and job opportunities in the tech and data analytics sectors. Environmentally, AIoT helps reduce carbon footprints by optimizing energy usage, reducing waste, and supporting sustainable urban planning initiatives.

Job Creation

The deployment of AIoT in smart cities creates new job opportunities across various sectors. The demand for skilled professionals in AI, data science, and IoT technologies increases as cities adopt AIoT solutions. This includes roles in system design, data analysis, cybersecurity, and infrastructure management. Additionally, new business models and services emerge from the innovative use of AIoT, fostering entrepreneurship and economic diversification.

Sustainability and Environmental Conservation

AIoT technologies are integral to advancing sustainability and environmental conservation efforts in smart cities. AIoT facilitates the efficient use of resources, supports the integration of renewable energy, and promotes waste reduction. Environmental monitoring systems powered by AIoT provide real-time data on air quality, noise levels, and other environmental factors, enabling cities to take proactive measures to protect the environment (Shamsuzzoha et al., 2021). By optimizing resource management and reducing emissions, AIoT contributes to the development of greener, more sustainable urban environments.

Insights and Recommendations

This section provides a detailed analysis of the key insights derived from case studies, best practices for implementing AIoT (Artificial Intelligence and the Internet of Things) technologies in smart cities, future directions and emerging trends in the field, and policy recommendations for governments and city planners. The goal is to provide a comprehensive guide that city leaders, policymakers, and technologists can use to enhance the implementation of AIoT in urban environments.

Lessons Learned From Case Studies

Strategic Vision and Leadership

Case studies have shown that a clear strategic vision and strong leadership are crucial for the successful implementation of AIoT projects. For example, Singapore's Smart Nation initiative is driven by a well-defined national strategy that prioritizes technological innovation to improve urban living. Effective leadership provides direction, secures funding, and rallies stakeholders around a common goal.

Public-Private Partnerships

The success of AIoT projects often hinges on effective collaboration between public and private entities. Public-private partnerships (PPPs) can provide the necessary resources, including funding, technology, and expertise (Dupont et al., 2015). In Barcelona, such partnerships have enabled the deployment of innovative IoT solutions in areas like traffic management and public services, enhancing urban efficiency and quality of life.

Citizen Engagement

Engaging citizens is essential for ensuring that AIoT solutions meet the needs of the community and gain public acceptance. Cities like Amsterdam have implemented open data initiatives that encourage public participation and transparency. This approach not only builds trust but also fosters innovation by allowing developers to create applications that address real-world challenges.

Data Privacy and Security

Managing data privacy and security is a critical challenge in AIoT implementations. Case studies reveal that cities must adopt robust cybersecurity measures and transparent data governance policies to protect sensitive information (Yun et al., 2022). For instance, Singapore's approach to data privacy includes strict regulations and public education campaigns, ensuring that citizen's data is handled responsibly.

Scalability and Adaptability

AIoT solutions must be scalable and adaptable to evolving technological landscapes and growing urban populations. Successful projects often start with pilot programs that can be scaled up as needed. For example, Amsterdam's use of modular, scalable AIoT systems has allowed the city to expand its smart city infrastructure efficiently and cost-effectively.

BEST PRACTICES FOR SUCCESSFUL AIOT IMPLEMENTATION

Develop a Comprehensive Strategy

Cities should develop a detailed AIoT strategy that aligns with their broader urban development goals (Alahi et al., 2023). This strategy should include a clear roadmap with defined phases, milestones, and measurable objectives. Prioritizing areas where AIoT can have the greatest impact, such as transportation, energy management, and public safety, can optimize resource allocation and project outcomes.

Foster Collaboration and Knowledge Sharing

Cross-sector collaboration is vital for the success of AIoT projects. Governments should foster partnerships with private companies, academic institutions, and non-governmental organizations to leverage a wide range of expertise and resources. Knowledge sharing between stakeholders can accelerate innovation and help cities learn from each other's experiences.

Adopt Open Standards and Ensure Interoperability

To avoid vendor lock-in and ensure seamless integration of different technologies, cities should adopt open standards and promote interoperability (Wu et al., 2019). This approach facilitates the integration of various AIoT devices and systems, making it easier to scale solutions and incorporate new technologies as they become available.

Prioritize Data Security and Privacy

Cities must prioritize data security and privacy to protect citizens and maintain public trust. This includes implementing robust cybersecurity measures, such as encryption and secure data storage, as well as establishing clear data governance policies. Transparency in how data is collected, stored, and used is also crucial for gaining public acceptance of AIoT technologies (Naphade et al., 2011).

Invest in Infrastructure and Workforce Development

Building the necessary infrastructure, such as high-speed internet, sensors, and data centers, is fundamental to supporting AIoT applications. In addition to physical infrastructure, cities should invest in workforce development to ensure that there is a pool of skilled professionals capable of maintaining and managing AIoT systems. This includes providing training in areas such as data analytics, cybersecurity, and system integration.

FUTURE DIRECTIONS AND EMERGING TRENDS

Edge Computing

Edge computing is emerging as a critical component of AIoT systems, enabling real-time data processing closer to the source. This reduces latency and bandwidth usage, which is particularly important for applications like autonomous vehicles and real-time surveillance. Cities should consider incorporating edge computing capabilities into their AIoT infrastructure to enhance efficiency and responsiveness.

5G Connectivity

The deployment of 5G networks is expected to significantly enhance the capabilities of AIoT systems by providing faster, more reliable data transmission. This will enable the deployment of more complex AIoT applications, such as smart grids, advanced traffic management, and real-time public safety monitoring. Cities should plan for the integration of 5G technology to support the next generation of smart city solutions (Milovanovic & Pantovic, 2023), (Esenogho et al., 2022), (Hsiao, 2022).

AI-Driven Predictive Analytics

The use of AI for predictive analytics is growing, allowing cities to anticipate and mitigate issues such as traffic congestion, power outages, and public health crises. By leveraging predictive analytics, cities can optimize resource allocation, improve service delivery, and enhance urban resilience.

Sustainability and Environmental Conservation

There is an increasing focus on using AIoT technologies to promote sustainability and environmental conservation (Cardullo & Kitchin, 2019). This includes applications such as smart grids, water management systems, and environmental monitoring. Cities should prioritize AIoT projects that contribute to reducing carbon footprints and conserving natural resources.

Public Health and Safety

The COVID-19 pandemic has highlighted the potential of AIoT in public health monitoring and response. AIoT technologies can be used for real-time health data collection, monitoring public spaces, and managing healthcare resources. These applications can enhance public health infrastructure and improve emergency response capabilities.

POLICY RECOMMENDATIONS FOR GOVERNMENTS AND CITY PLANNERS

Develop Comprehensive AIoT Policies

Governments should develop comprehensive policies that provide a framework for AIoT deployment. These policies should address key issues such as data privacy, security, interoperability, and ethical considerations (Ortega-Fernández et al., 2020). A well-defined policy framework can guide the development of AIoT systems and ensure they are used responsibly.

Encourage Public-Private Partnerships

Public-private partnerships are essential for the successful implementation of AIoT projects. Governments can incentivize these partnerships through tax benefits, grants, and other financial incentives. These partnerships can help mobilize the necessary resources and expertise, facilitating the deployment of innovative AIoT solutions (Dupont et al., 2015).

Promote Inclusive and Equitable Access

To ensure that the benefits of AIoT technologies are widely shared, governments should promote inclusive and equitable access. This includes providing affordable technology and infrastructure in underserved communities and designing AIoT systems that are accessible to all, including people with disabilities and the elderly.

Invest in Education and Training

Governments should invest in education and training programs to develop a skilled workforce capable of managing and maintaining AIoT systems. This includes both technical training in areas such as data analytics and cybersecurity and broader education on the ethical use of AI technologies.

Support Sustainable Development

AIoT technologies can play a significant role in promoting sustainable development. Governments should support projects that prioritize environmental sustainability, such as smart grids and water management systems (Hui et al., 2023). Policies should also encourage the use of green technologies and sustainable practices in AIoT deployments.

CONCLUSION

In the final section of the chapter, we synthesize the key findings from the case studies and analysis, and we discuss the future trajectory of AIoT (Artificial Intelligence and the Internet of Things) in smart cities. This conclusion serves as a capstone to the comprehensive exploration of how AIoT technologies are transforming urban environments.

Pivotal Role in Urban Transformation

The case studies and analysis demonstrate that AIoT technologies play a pivotal role in transforming cities into more efficient, sustainable, and livable spaces. By integrating AI and IoT, cities can address a wide range of challenges, from traffic congestion and energy management to public safety and healthcare.

Strategic Leadership and Vision

Successful AIoT implementations are often underpinned by strong leadership and a clear strategic vision. City planners and policymakers who articulate a coherent strategy for smart city development, backed by robust policy frameworks and public-private partnerships, are more likely to achieve their goals.

Data Privacy and Security

Data privacy and security are critical considerations in the deployment of AIoT technologies. The effective management of data, including secure collection, storage, and usage, is essential for maintaining public trust and ensuring compliance with regulations.

Scalability and Interoperability

The ability to scale and integrate various AIoT systems is crucial for the long-term success of smart city initiatives. Cities that adopt open standards and prioritize interoperability can more easily expand their AIoT infrastructure and incorporate new technologies as they emerge (Ahvenniemi et al., 2017).

Community Engagement and Inclusion

Engaging the community and ensuring inclusive access to AIoT benefits are key factors in the successful adoption of these technologies. Public engagement not only fosters acceptance and trust but also ensures that AIoT solutions are responsive to the needs of all residents.

Sustainable Development

AIoT technologies offer significant potential for promoting sustainability in urban environments. From smart grids and waste management systems to environmental monitoring, these technologies help cities reduce their environmental impact and conserve resources (Kuguoglu, van der Voort, & Janssen, 2021).

THE FUTURE OF AIOT IN SMART CITIES

Continued Innovation and Integration

The future of AIoT in smart cities will be characterized by continued innovation and deeper integration of these technologies into urban infrastructure. As AI and IoT technologies evolve, we can expect more sophisticated applications, such as autonomous vehicles, advanced energy management systems, and smart healthcare solutions.

Greater Emphasis on Ethical and Social Implications

As AIoT technologies become more pervasive, there will be a growing emphasis on addressing the ethical and social implications of these systems. This includes considerations around data ethics, privacy, algorithmic transparency, and the potential for bias in AI systems. Policymakers and technologists will need to work together to ensure that AIoT deployments are ethical, fair, and beneficial to all segments of society (Nam & Pardo, 2011).

Expansion of Smart City Ecosystems

The ecosystem of smart cities will expand to include a broader range of stakeholders, including startups, research institutions, and civic organizations. This expansion will foster innovation, create new business opportunities, and promote a collaborative approach to solving urban challenges.

Resilience and Adaptability

As cities face increasing challenges from climate change, population growth, and economic pressures, the resilience and adaptability of AIoT systems will become increasingly important. Future AIoT implementations will likely focus on enhancing urban resilience, from disaster response systems to adaptive infrastructure that can respond to changing environmental conditions.

Global Adoption and Collaboration

The adoption of AIoT technologies will continue to grow globally, with cities around the world learning from each other's experiences and best practices. International collaboration and knowledge sharing will play a key role in advancing AIoT technologies and addressing common urban challenges.

Policy and Regulatory Evolution

As AIoT technologies evolve, so too will the regulatory frameworks that govern their use. Governments and international bodies will need to develop and refine policies that balance innovation with public safety, privacy, and ethical considerations (Verrest & Pfeffer, 2019). This regulatory evolution will be crucial for fostering a supportive environment for AIoT innovation while protecting citizens' rights and interests.

In summary, the conclusion of this chapter highlights the transformative potential of AIoT technologies in smart cities and underscores the importance of strategic planning, ethical considerations, and collaboration in realizing this potential. As cities continue to evolve, AIoT will be a key driver of sustainable and inclusive urban development, offering new opportunities to enhance the quality of life for all residents.

REFERENCES

Ahvenniemi, H., Huovila, A., Pinto-Seppä, I., & Airaksinen, M. (2017). What are the differences between sustainable and smart cities? *Cities (London, England)*, *60*, 234–245. DOI: 10.1016/j.cities.2016.09.009

Alahi, M. E. E., Sukkuea, A., Tina, F. W., Nag, A., Kurdthongmee, W., Suwannarat, K., & Mukhopadhyay, S. C. (2023). Integration of IoT-enabled technologies and artificial intelligence (AI) for smart city scenario: Recent advancements and future trends. *Sensors (Basel)*, *23*(11), 5206. DOI: 10.3390/s23115206 PMID: 37299934

Albino, V., Berardi, U., & Dangelico, R. M. (2015). Smart cities: Definitions, dimensions, performance, and initiatives. *Journal of Urban Technology*, *22*(1), 3–21. DOI: 10.1080/10630732.2014.942092

Apanavičienė, R., & Shahrabani, M. M. N. (2023). Key factors affecting smart building integration into smart city: Technological aspects. *Smart Cities*, *6*(4), 1832–1857. DOI: 10.3390/smartcities6040085

Barns, S. (2018). Smart cities and urban data platforms: Designing interfaces for smart governance. *City, Culture and Society*, *12*, 5–12. DOI: 10.1016/j.ccs.2017.09.006

Batty, M., Axhausen, K. W., Giannotti, F., Pozdnoukhov, A., Bazzani, A., Wachowicz, M., & Portugali, Y. (2012). Smart cities of the future. *The European Physical Journal. Special Topics*, *214*(1), 481–518. DOI: 10.1140/epjst/e2012-01703-3

Bernardo, M. D. R. M. (2019). Smart city governance: From e-government to smart governance. In *Smart cities and smart spaces: Concepts, methodologies, tools, and applications* (pp. 196–232). IGI Global. DOI: 10.4018/978-1-5225-7030-1.ch009

Bibri, S. E., Alexandre, A., Sharifi, A., & Krogstie, J. (2023). Environmentally sustainable smart cities and their converging AI, IoT, and big data technologies and solutions: An integrated approach to an extensive literature review. *Energy Informatics*, *6*(1), 9. DOI: 10.1186/s42162-023-00259-2 PMID: 37032812

Bibri, S. E., Huang, J., Jagatheesaperumal, S. K., & Krogstie, J. (2024). The synergistic interplay of artificial intelligence and digital twin in environmentally planning sustainable smart cities: A comprehensive systematic review. *Environmental Science and Ecotechnology*, *20*, 100433. DOI: 10.1016/j.ese.2024.100433 PMID: 38831974

Bibri, S. E., Krogstie, J., Kaboli, A., & Alahi, A. (2024). Smarter eco-cities and their leading-edge artificial intelligence of things solutions for environmental sustainability: A comprehensive systematic review. *Environmental Science and Ecotechnology*, *19*, 100330. DOI: 10.1016/j.ese.2023.100330 PMID: 38021367

Calzada, I. (2018). (Smart) citizens from data providers to decision-makers? The case study of Barcelona. *Sustainability (Basel), 10*(9), 3252. DOI: 10.3390/su10093252

Caragliu, A., Del Bo, C., & Nijkamp, P. (2011). Smart cities in Europe. *Journal of Urban Technology, 18*(2), 65–82. DOI: 10.1080/10630732.2011.601117

Cardullo, P., & Kitchin, R. (2019). Smart urbanism and smart citizenship: The neoliberal logic of 'citizen-focused' smart cities in Europe. *Environment and Planning C. Politics and Space, 37*(5), 813–830.

Dupont, L., Morel, L., & Guidat, C. (2015). Innovative public-private partnership to support smart city: The case of "Chaire REVES". *Journal of Strategy and Management, 8*(3), 245–265. DOI: 10.1108/JSMA-03-2015-0027

Esenogho, E., Djouani, K., & Kurien, A. M. (2022). Integrating artificial intelligence Internet of Things and 5G for next-generation smart grid: A survey of trends challenges and prospect. *IEEE Access : Practical Innovations, Open Solutions, 10*, 4794–4831. DOI: 10.1109/ACCESS.2022.3140595

Gupta, A., Gupta, S., Memoria, M., Kumar, R., Kumar, S., Singh, D., & Ansari, N. (2022, May). Artificial intelligence and smart cities: A bibliometric analysis. In *2022 International Conference on Machine Learning, Big Data, Cloud and Parallel Computing (COM-IT-CON)* (Vol. 1, pp. 540-544). IEEE. DOI: 10.1109/COM-IT-CON54601.2022.9850656

Harrison, C., & Donnelly, I. A. (2011, September). A theory of smart cities. In *Proceedings of the 55th Annual Meeting of the ISSS-2011*, Hull, UK.

Hsiao, S. J. (2022). Employing a wireless sensing network for AIoT based on a 5G approach. *Electronics (Basel), 11*(5), 827. DOI: 10.3390/electronics11050827

Hui, C. X., Dan, G., Alamri, S., & Toghraie, D. (2023). Greening smart cities: An investigation of the integration of urban natural resources and smart city technologies for promoting environmental sustainability. *Sustainable Cities and Society, 99*, 104985. DOI: 10.1016/j.scs.2023.104985

Kaginalkar, A., Kumar, S., Gargava, P., & Niyogi, D. (2021). Review of urban computing in air quality management as smart city service: An integrated IoT, AI, and cloud technology perspective. *Urban Climate, 39*, 100972. DOI: 10.1016/j.uclim.2021.100972

Kuguoglu, B. K., van der Voort, H., & Janssen, M. (2021). The giant leap for smart cities: Scaling up smart city artificial intelligence of things (AIoT) initiatives. *Sustainability (Basel), 13*(21), 12295. DOI: 10.3390/su132112295

Milovanovic, D. A., & Pantovic, V. (2023). 5G-AIoT artificial intelligence of things: Opportunity and challenges. In *Driving 5G Mobile Communications with Artificial Intelligence Towards 6G* (pp. 253–276). CRC Press. DOI: 10.1201/9781003205494-8

Nam, T., & Pardo, T. A. (2011, June). Conceptualizing smart city with dimensions of technology, people, and institutions. In *Proceedings of the 12th Annual International Digital Government Research Conference: Digital Government Innovation in Challenging Times* (pp. 282-291). DOI: 10.1145/2037556.2037602

Naphade, M., Banavar, G., Harrison, C., Paraszczak, J., & Morris, R. (2011). Smarter cities and their innovation challenges. *Computer*, *44*(6), 32–39. DOI: 10.1109/MC.2011.187

Noori, N., Hoppe, T., & de Jong, M. (2020). Classifying pathways for smart city development: Comparing design, governance and implementation in Amsterdam, Barcelona, Dubai, and Abu Dhabi. *Sustainability (Basel)*, *12*(10), 4030. DOI: 10.3390/su12104030

Ortega-Fernández, A., Martín-Rojas, R., & García-Morales, V. J. (2020). Artificial intelligence in the urban environment: Smart cities as models for developing innovation and sustainability. *Sustainability (Basel)*, *12*(19), 7860. DOI: 10.3390/su12197860

Pise, A. A., Almuzaini, K. K., Ahanger, T. A., Farouk, A., Pant, K., Pareek, P. K., & Nuagah, S. J. (2022). Enabling artificial intelligence of things (AIoT) healthcare architectures and listing security issues. *Computational Intelligence and Neuroscience*, *2022*(1), 8421434. DOI: 10.1155/2022/8421434 PMID: 36911247

Shamsuzzoha, A., Nieminen, J., Piya, S., & Rutledge, K. (2021). Smart city for sustainable environment: A comparison of participatory strategies from Helsinki, Singapore, and London. *Cities (London, England)*, *114*, 103194. DOI: 10.1016/j.cities.2021.103194

Sharifi, A. (2019). A critical review of selected smart city assessment tools and indicator sets. *Journal of Cleaner Production*, *233*, 1269–1283. DOI: 10.1016/j.jclepro.2019.06.172

Tariq, M. U. (2025). *AI-Driven Learning and Engagement in Higher Education*. IGI Global., DOI: 10.4018/979-8-3693-4074-5

Tariq, M. U. (2025). AI and Work-Life Balance: Transforming Employee Wellbeing in the Modern Workplace. In Ahmed, E., Babar, A., Samad, A., Ahmed, R., & Beydoun, G. (Eds.), *Strengthening Human Relations in Organizations With AI* (pp. 85–110). IGI Global Scientific Publishing., DOI: 10.4018/979-8-3693-6507-6.ch004

Tariq, M. U. (2025). AI and the Ethical Crossroads: Navigating Privacy, Personhood, and Autonomy in the Digital Age. In Chakraborty, S. (Ed.), *Human Values, Ethics, and Dignity in the Age of Artificial Intelligence* (pp. 49–72). IGI Global Scientific Publishing., DOI: 10.4018/979-8-3693-9035-1.ch003

Tariq, M. U. (2025). AI-Powered Business Process Automation: Revolutionizing Firm Management. In Derbali, A. (Ed.), *AI, Economic Perspectives, and Firm Business Management* (pp. 199–224). IGI Global Scientific Publishing., DOI: 10.4018/979-8-3693-7357-6.ch010

Tariq, M. U., & Sergio, R. (Eds.). (2025). *Convergence of AI, Education, and Business for Sustainability*. IGI Global., DOI: 10.4018/979-8-3373-1917-9

Verrest, H., & Pfeffer, K. (2019). Elaborating the urbanism in smart urbanism: Distilling relevant dimensions for a comprehensive analysis of smart city approaches. *Information Communication and Society*, *22*(9), 1328–1342. DOI: 10.1080/1369118X.2018.1424921

Wu, Y. C., Wu, Y. J., & Wu, S. M. (2019). An outlook of a future smart city in Taiwan from post–Internet of Things to artificial intelligence Internet of Things. In *Smart Cities: Issues and Challenges* (pp. 263-282). Elsevier. DOI: 10.1016/B978-0-12-816639-0.00015-6

Zanella, A., Bui, N., Castellani, A., Vangelista, L., & Zorzi, M. (2014). Internet of Things for smart cities. *IEEE Internet of Things Journal*, *1*(1), 22–32. DOI: 10.1109/JIOT.2014.2306328

KEY TERM AND DEFINITIONS

Smart Cities: Cities that utilize advanced digital technologies, including AI, IoT, and big data, to improve infrastructure, public services, and the overall quality of life through intelligent automation and efficient management.

AIoT (Artificial Intelligence of Things): The fusion of artificial intelligence (AI) and the Internet of Things (IoT), where AI processes and interprets data from IoT-connected devices to drive smart decision-making and automation in urban environments.

Internet of Things (IoT): A system of interconnected smart devices equipped with sensors and software that communicate with each other, facilitating real-time data collection and enabling the efficient management of urban infrastructure and services.

Urban Sustainability: A strategic approach to city planning that ensures the responsible use of resources to balance environmental, economic, and social factors, securing long-term livability for current and future residents.

Predictive Analytics: The application of AI-driven algorithms to evaluate past and present data, enabling city planners and decision-makers to anticipate trends, optimize resource allocation, and improve urban efficiency.

Chapter 7
A Study on AI-Driven Internet of Battlefield Things (IoBT)-Based Decision Making:
KSK Approach in IoBT

Kutubuddin Sayyad Liyakat Kazi
https://orcid.org/0000-0001-5623-9211
Brahmdevdada Mane Institute of Technology, Solapur, India

ABSTRACT

The sensors that fuel the Internet of Body Technology (IoBT) provide essential information that improves situational awareness, decision-making, and combat performance. Despite challenges, the continuous development and integration of these technologies will transform combat, defining the character of conflict and changing the landscape of future battlegrounds. An array of sensors that continuously provide real-time data to intelligent computers will enable commanders to make well-informed decisions at the speed of light. The outcomes of every classifier employed in the KSK (Kutubuddin S Kazi) Approach are analyzed in the following scenarios: target acquisition and tracking, environmental condition, health, remote operations, and disaster relief. The accuracy range for the recommended KSK approach in IoBT is 90% to 96%, whereas the ranges for recall and precision are 89% to 95% and 90% to 95%, respectively.

DOI: 10.4018/979-8-3693-8547-0.ch007

INTRODUCTION

The modern warfare is quite dynamic in terms of technology. The fundamental strategies of warfare are changing because of new ideas and frameworks. Thanks to the rapid advancement of drone technology, combat has never been the same. This very accessible and moderately priced technology has the potential to wreak massive harm when used in large enough quantities. The soldier on the ground will be simply overwhelmed by similar technological advances in the domains of communication, electronic warfare, and autonomous systems. Because of this, the soldier needs to be able to perceive things outside their senses. This can be done by modifying the concept of the Internet of Things to fit the sensors and gear used in warfare. These creatures or animals will need to maintain constant connection with the human fighters. These include firearms, ammo, vehicles, wearable technology for humans, and sensors like radars that are utilized in combat. The capabilities will include coordinated attacks to inflict damage that will hinder the enemy's ability to wage war, as well as data collecting and processing and interpretation for actionable intelligence. They will accomplish this by working together on a regular basis, exchanging ideas, organizing, and completing the assigned duties. A new technology called the Internet of Battlefield Things, or IoBT, has the potential to drastically alter modern warfare. By integrating battlefield operations with the Internet of Things (IoT), it gives armed forces a significant tactical advantage (Sayyad, 2024g). The key benefits of IoBNT are its capacity to improve soldiers' situational alertness. Through the connectivity of numerous sensors, tools, and machineries, IoBT delivers soldiers with real-time data and intuitions on the battlefield, enabling them to act more rapidly and resolutely. This may be vital in unpredictable, high-stakes warfare situations.

IoBT can also improve soldiers' communication and coordination. IoT devices make it simple for soldiers to communicate and exchange information. This could improve the overall effectiveness and efficiency of military operations. Another benefit of IoBT is its ability to reduce the risk to human soldiers. By utilizing autonomous vehicles, drones, and robots connected to Internet of Things devices, troops can decrease their exposure to risk and execute tasks that would be too dangerous for them to perform alone. This can be especially valuable in circumstances where the territory is tough or the atmosphere is aggressive (Sayayd, 2024j). However, like any innovative technology, IoBT has intrinsic drawbacks and possible hazards. That the network security is the main difficulties. Because IoBT depends so seriously on information and communication, a network hack could have hostile significances. Armed forces must implement vigorous security protocols to safeguard their data and impede cyberattacks (Sayyad, 2025; Sayyad, 2025c). Over-reliance on technology is an additional possible issue. Warriors can make sagacious decisions with the support of IoBT, but technology shouldn't substitute human decisions entirely. Even in the nonappearance of technology, soldiers still requisite to complete a rigorous training schedule and be primed to make acute decisions. Consequently, it may be said that IoBT can greatly improve military prowess and fight soldier safety. It is imperative that the risks be thoroughly considered, and the appropriate security measures put in place to ensure successful implementation. Taking everything into account, we believe that IoBNT should be further researched and developed because it has the potential to greatly enhance modern warfare. The "Internet of Battlefield Things" (IoBT) is an exhilarating concept that has the possibility to entirely transform current warfare. Through the incorporation of a vast setup of sensors, drones, robots, and other warfare resources, IoBT sees a forthcoming where information drifts effortlessly, enabling coordinated strikes, independent decision-making, and real-time situational consciousness. IoBT has enormous potential, but it also has far-reaching effects that should be properly evaluated (Sayya, 2025n). The Promise of IoBT is as follows:

- Enhanced Situational Awareness: A "common operating picture" that offers commanders with a real-time perception of the battlefield is industrialized through the incorporation of numerous sensors and strategies. Therefore, assessments can be made more quickly and efficiently.
- Precision Strikes: By amalgamation of information from numerous sources, it is possible to determine enemy objects with unprecedented accuracy, minimizing security damage and enhancing productivity.
- Autonomous Operations: By employing AI to execute tasks like combat and reconnaissance, robots and drones might reduce the risk to humanoid soldiers.
- Faster Reaction Times: Synchronized actions and quick reactions to exchanging threats are possible because information is instantaneously transmitted throughout the network.

The problems and troubles that still occur are as follows:

- Cybersecurity Vulnerabilities: IoBT is networked, making it vulnerable to cyberattacks. A breakdown in the network might have overwhelming consequences and even preclude military operations.
- Ethical Dilemmas: The increasing employment of sovereign weapons increases moral anxieties about humanoid decision-making in circumstances where inhabitant casualties or collateral damage are unavoidable.
- Technical Restrictions: AI and sensor technology might not be capable of buttoning the complexities of a real-world battlefield just yet.

- Cost and Complexity: A complete rollout of IoBT would entail a noteworthy disbursement for substructure, training, and technological expertise.

Notwithstanding its challenges, IoBT represents a significant shift in warfare. Research and development in this field are currently ongoing, and the results will likely influence future warfare tactics. However, we must use this technology sensibly, keeping moral considerations front and center, and prioritizing human review over machine learning when making choices. We will propose our KSK or KSK1 decision-making approach, as recommended in Kazi K S (2024). The IoBT has a lot of promise to enhance military capabilities, but it also has a lot of drawbacks. As with any new technology, a well-rounded approach that prioritises ethical considerations alongside responsible development and deployment is crucial. The future of IoBT will depend on how these problems are fixed and whether its potential benefits can outweigh its disadvantages. The Internet of Big Things (IoBT), an emerging technology, is revolutionizing modern warfare. IoBT improves situational awareness and provides soldiers with new capabilities by allowing diverse systems, sensors, and gadgets to be seamlessly integrated into the battlefield. IoBT enables real-time data sharing between soldiers, vehicles, and sensors. This comprehensive data fusion provides soldiers and commanders with a precise and comprehensive picture of the battlefield, empowering them to make well-informed decisions. Having access to real-time data helps commanders assess the situation, identify threats, and develop appropriate solutions more quickly and effectively. The Internet of Business Technology (IoBT) leverages advanced algorithms and machine learning to facilitate the processing of massive amounts of data and deliver actionable insights. Soldiers can access several extra capabilities with IoBT, including:

- Increased situational awareness: Information about the surroundings, friendly forces, and enemy locations is instantly available to soldiers.
- Improved communication: Soldiers can more easily plan and adjust to changing conditions thanks to IoBT's dependable and secure communication between units.
- Precision strikes: More precise and successful airstrikes result in fewer civilian casualties thanks to IoBT-connected sensors and advanced targeting systems.

The conclusion of "A Study on AI-Driven-Internet of Battlefield Things (IoBT) Based Decision Making" is that it addresses a significant frontier in the field of modern warfare. With its clearly articulated issue statement, well-defined aims, and well-structured objectives, it paves the way for considerable breakthroughs in the decision-making processes used by the military. The study can make a significant contribution to military strategy, operational effectiveness, and ethical issues in the application of technology in combat scenarios because it makes use of the synergies that exist between artificial intelligence and internet of things technologies. Research of this kind is essential in determining the future of war-fighting strategies and technology, ensuring that they are in line with both effectiveness and ethical responsibility. This is because the military landscape is constantly shifting, and research of this kind is extremely important. In the context of modern combat, the rapid expansion of technology has brought about a substantial transformation, and the combination of Artificial Intelligence (AI) and the Internet of Battlefield Things (IoBT) was recognised as a significant transformation. The research paper titled "A Study on AI-Driven Internet of Battlefield Things (IoBT) Based Decision Making" offers a thorough investigation into this cutting-edge junction, shedding light on the implications that this confluence has for the decision-making processes involved in military operations (Kutubuddin, 2024a).

A theoretical structure that emphasises the synergistic interaction between artificial intelligence and internet of things technology is successfully constructed by the study. The Internet of Battle Technology (IoBT) is a network of networked devices, sensors, and systems which collect and distribute real-time data within the setting of a battlefield, as the authors have expertly defined it. Using artificial intelligence algorithms to analyse this data, the research highlights the revolutionary potential of immediate decision-making that is driven by data in contexts with high stakes. Considering the ever-increasing complexity and fluidity of contemporary battlefields, which calls for sturdy frameworks to facilitate efficient strategic decision-making, the significance of the research is especially emphasised. An investigation into a variety of approaches to incorporating AI into IoBT systems is carried out in this work. The authors pinpoint the most significant operational obstacles and technology barriers by doing qualitative research, conducting case studies, and conducting a study of the technologies that are already available. They present convincing case studies that highlight successful applications of artificial intelligence-driven decision-making in military operations. These applications range from real-time tactical assessments to predictive maintenance in logistics for military operations. The potential for artificial intelligence to improve situational awareness is one of the most noteworthy discoveries. This would enable military commanders to make decisions based on accurate information more quickly. According to the findings of the research, artificial intelligence is capable of processing huge volumes of data from a variety of sensors. This enables the detection of trends and the forecasting of future risks, which eventually contributes to a proactive rather than reactive mindset. The findings of the study have significant repercussions, not just for military strategy but also for national policy and ethical considerations. There are concerns regarding accountability, transparency, and the ethical repercussions of machine-led combat that are brought up by the incorporation of artificial intelligence into decision-making processes. This paper does an amazing job of addressing these problems and advocating for the adoption of explicit norms and frameworks to control the use of artificial intelligence in military environments (Kutubuddin, 2024b).

In addition, the investigation of potential future possibilities reveals a promising path for the research that is being conducted in this vicinity. With the emphasis placed on the necessity of continual evolution alongside technical advancement, the authors recommend further research into the incorporation of emerging technologies with Internet of Things (IoBT) systems. Some examples of these technologies are quantum computing and machine learning. To summarise, "A Study on AI-Driven Internet of Battlefield Things (IoBT) Based Decision Making" is an important contribution to the ongoing conversation about the intersection of military technology and strategy. A well-structured analysis is presented by the writers, which not just elucidates the principles of artificial intelligence and internet of things technology but also addresses the ethical problems that are associated with such breakthroughs. For military strategists, policymakers, and researchers who are interested in understanding the future of warfare in a world that is becoming increasingly digital and networked, this paper is a vital piece of reading material. The insights that were presented provide a solid platform for further investigation into the dramatic changes that artificial intelligence and internet of things technology will cause to military operations and beyond.

INTERNET OF BATTLEFIELD THINGS (IOBT)

The Internet of Battlefield Things (IoBT) is a concept that marks a momentous transformation in the military scene. It combines the enhanced capabilities of the Internet of Things (IoT) with the actions that take place on the battlefield. As a result of the progression of modern warfare, the incorporation of intelligent technology into military strategy is progressively becoming not only advantageous but also critical. The implications, benefits, and difficulties connected with IoBT are discussed in this review. The review also highlights the potential of IoBT to rethink how we think about military operations and conflict. A linked collection of equipment, sensors, and algorithms on the battlefield that are meant to collect, distribute, and analyse data in real time is referred to as the Internet of Battlefield Things (IBT). This encompasses anything from drones, vehicles, and headquarters that are integrated with artificial intelligence and machine learning algorithms to wearable technology for veterans and service members. To enhance the overall efficiency for military operations, the overarching objective is to boost situational awareness, simplify decision-making processes, and streamline decision-making procedures.

Several benefits are as follows:

- The Internet of Things (IoBT) technologies capture real-time data from a variety of sources, which provides commanders with an in-depth understanding of the battlefield. This results in enhanced situational awareness. This capacity not only helps with making decisions about urgent tactical matters, but it also has an impact on planning for long-term strategic endeavours.
- Improvements in Communication: Armed forces personnel can communicate more effectively thanks to the interconnection of their gadgets, which guarantees that vital information is transmitted without any delay. This improved communication has the potential to reduce misunderstandings and errors, both of which could result in disastrous consequences.
- The integration of artificial intelligence and machine learning results in predictive analytics, which enables military organisations to analyse massive volumes of data in a short amount of time, thereby predicting probable threats and consequences. It is possible to significantly improve the success rates of missions by having the ability to anticipate and reduce hazards.
- Allocation of Resources: The Internet of Things has the potential to greatly improve both the logistical planning and resource allocation for the battlefield. The ability of military forces to optimise their operations, so decreasing waste and boosting efficiency, is made possible through the real-time tracking of supplies, personnel, and equipment.
- This allows soldiers to work at safer distances and reduce their exposure to danger. Wearable technologies and drones that provide reconnaissance are two examples of technologies that contribute to increased soldier safety. IoBT is designed to keep staff safe while also increasing their efficiency.

Obstacles in the development of IoBT systems:

- Risks to Cybersecurity: The interconnected structure of IoBT creates considerable concerns about cybersecurity: The possibility of hacking, data breaches, and even the manipulation of battlefield gadgets presents major hazards that can undermine missions and put lives in jeopardy.
- There is a lot of complexity involved with interoperability, which refers to the process of integrating diverse equipment and systems, particularly across different branches of the military and overseas partners. Even though achieving smooth interoperability is vital for the success of IoBT, it continues to be a substantial problem from a technological standpoint.

- IoBT can produce an excessive amount of data, which might lead to a situation known as "data overload." The large amounts of information that is available could make it difficult for military personnel to glean ideas that can be put into action if they do not have access to appropriate filtering and analysis tools.
- Considering ethical considerations, the use of modern technology in warfare creates ethical problems regarding the autonomy of robots when they are engaged in conflict. The possibility of an automated decision-making system raises questions regarding responsibility and the ethical implications of employing artificial intelligence in situations when life or death is at stake.
- It is necessary to make a significant financial investment in infrastructure, training, and maintenance to successfully implement IoBT technology. The challenge that military organisations face is a significant one: how to strike a balance between the restrictions of their budgets and the requirement for technological advancement.

The Internet of Battlefield Things is a revolutionary step forward in military strategy, offering levels of connectedness, efficiency, and situational awareness that have never been seen before. There is a large potential for benefits, but there are also a great deal of problems and threats. As nations continue to adopt and improve Internet of Things (IoBT) technology, it is necessary for military commanders, engineers, and policymakers to negotiate these complexity wisely. This will ensure that innovations serve to protect and empower rather than threaten. It is not only a technological advancement; the Internet of Things (IoBT) represents a paradigm shift that will have a significant impact on the future of warfare. As we work towards striking a balance between the advantages of technology and the responsibilities that come with its application in combat situations, the constant conversation that surrounds its consequences will be of the utmost importance.

PROBLEM STATEMENT

The Internet of Things (IoT) has brought about a transformation in several different industries, and its application in the military, which is referred to as the Internet of Battlefield Things (IoBT), brings about a set of difficulties and opportunities that are entirely unique. When it comes to improving decision-making processes on the battlefield, the current challenge is in the incorporation of artificial intelligence (AI) into the framework of the Internet of Battle Technology (IoBT). Historically, the process of making decisions in military operations has frequently been reactive and constrained by the cognitive capacity of humans, in addition to being constrained by the huge amounts of data created during violent scenarios. The study does a good job of pointing out the shortcomings of the traditional decision-making frameworks that are now in use. These frameworks may be overly slow or erroneous in situations that are constantly changing. In addition, the possibility of experiencing data overload during a variety of interconnected gadgets contributes to the difficulty of decision-making in strategic situations that occur on the battlefield.

GOAL

The fundamental objective of the project is to investigate the ways in which the incorporation of AI can revolutionise decision-making processes within the Internet of Things (IoBT) community. The purpose of this project is to enhance the precision, the speed, and the efficiency of judgements made by the military in real time by utilising artificial intelligence algorithms and analytics. Not only does this investigation seek to improve operational efficiency, but it also has the potential to save lives by optimising strategic responses to developing combat scenarios (Tariq, 2025a).

OBJECTIVES

The goals of the study are varied and well specified, and they are as follows:

- The purpose of this study is to examine the current state of artificial intelligence and internet of technologies, with the objective of determining the advantages and disadvantages of these technologies in connection to the process of military decision-making.
- A significant objective is to present a novel AI-driven framework that is targeted to Internet of Things applications that boost situational awareness and analytical capabilities for military leaders. This framework will be developed to develop an artificial intelligence framework.
- To evaluate the framework in simulated environments, the research project plans to build simulations that test the effectiveness and dependability of the proposed framework under a variety of battlefield scenarios. This will provide insights into the framework's ability to be successful in operational settings.
- As a result of the potential consequences that artificial intelligence could have in the field of combat, the purpose of this study is to analyse the ethical concerns that are linked with AI-driven decision-making. These concerns

include accountability, bias in decision-making, and the possibility of autonomous weapons systems.

- To make recommendations for best practices, the study intends to describe best practices for the deployment of artificial intelligence inside military operations. This will ensure not only the growth of technology but also compliance with international humanitarian standards.

AI BASED IoBT SYSTEMS

IoT device proliferation has created a demand for effective and intelligent management systems (Wale et al., 2019). One revolutionary approach to overcoming this difficulty is the fusion of IoT and Artificial Intelligence (AI), or IoBT. AI-powered IoBT is a game-changing technology that gives IoT devices sophisticated capabilities. IoBT systems improve connectivity, efficiency, security, and decision-making while cutting costs and opening new business prospects by utilizing AI algorithms. IoBT has the potential to transform several industries and influence connected technology going forward.

As seen in Figure 1, IoBT uses AI algorithms to deliver advanced capabilities, such as:

- Data Analysis and Prediction: To find trends, forecast future occurrences, and enhance device performance, AI algorithms examine enormous volumes of data gathered from IoT sensors.
- Automation of Decision-Making: AI-powered IoBT systems can automate decision-making procedures, minimizing the need for human intervention and guaranteeing quicker and more precise reactions to changing circumstances.
- Anomaly Detection and Response: By identifying abnormalities and deviations in IoT data, AI algorithms help prevent possible system failures and enable proactive maintenance.
- Real-Time Optimization: To ensure maximum efficiency and cut expenses, IoBT systems continuously monitor and optimize device performance in real time.

Figure 1. AI in IoBT capabilities

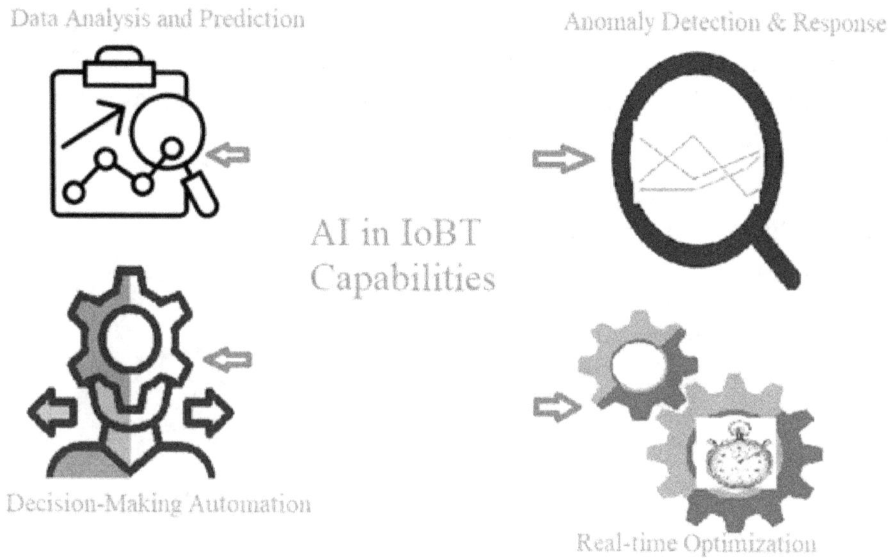

There are many advantages to IoT AI integration, including:

- Enhanced Connectivity and Efficiency: IoBT facilitates smooth communication and cooperation between IoT devices, enhancing overall network performance and efficiency.
- Enhanced Security: AI algorithms improve security by identifying and addressing possible threats, which lowers the likelihood of cyberattacks (Shinde et al, 2025).
- Cost Reduction: IoBT systems identify anomalies and enable preventive maintenance, which optimizes device performance and lowers maintenance costs.
- Enhanced Productivity: The proactive maintenance and automated decision-making free up human resources to work on higher-value projects (Kasat et al 2023; Neeraja et al., 2023).
- New Business Opportunities: IoBT creates new revenue streams and business models by enabling creative IoT solutions and offering insights into client behavior.

IoBT METHODOLOGY

The IoBT is a game-changing idea that uses networked sensors and gadgets to improve operations, safety, and situational awareness in contemporary warfare. This analysis explores the functions, limitations, and prospects of the several types of sensors used in this dynamic environment.

Figure 2. Difference sensors in IoBT

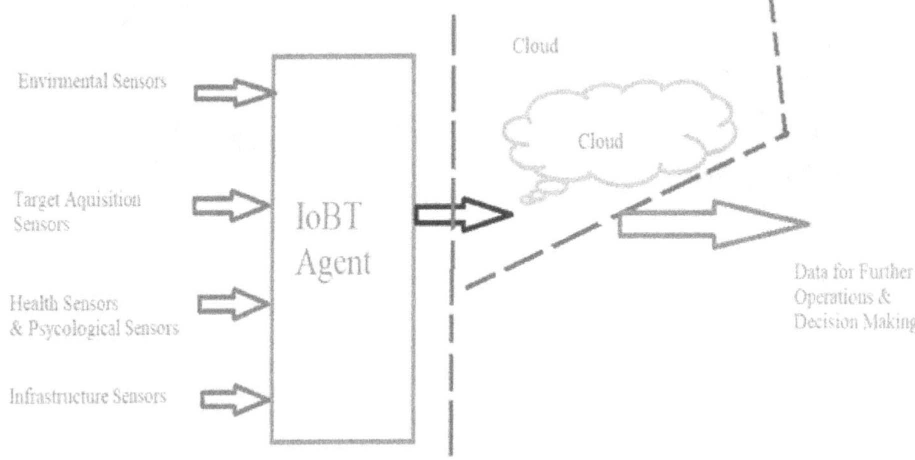

The Key Sensor Categories displayed in Figure 2 are as follows:

1. Environmental Sensors

These are essential for comprehending the conditions on the battlefield. Modern warfare is changing because of the deployment of environmental sensors on the battlefield. These gadgets, which can monitor a variety of environmental conditions, are said to provide tactical benefits by boosting troop safety, increasing operational efficiency, and supplying real-time situational awareness, according to Kassat et al. (2023). This evaluation examines the uses and effects of environmental sensors in combat, emphasizing both the advantages and difficulties associated with them. As examples, consider:

- Give current information on temperature, humidity, wind speed, and precipitation to help in weapon effectiveness and tactical decision-making. Sensors provide vital data for mission planning, including temperature, humidity, wind direction and speed, precipitation, and visibility. By assisting commanders in optimizing troop movements, aviation operations, and weapon system deployment, this data improves operational efficiency and reduces the hazards brought on by unfavorable weather (Tamboli et al, 2024; Kazi S,2025c).

- Sensors can detect aspects of the terrain such as soil type, vegetation cover, and elevation, which helps with target acquisition, obstacle identification, and route planning. This intelligence maximizes the effectiveness of troop and resource deployment by enabling more efficient use of them (Kazi K S, 2025; Kazi K,2024b; Odnala et al,2025).
- The sensors that can identify CBRN agents offer early warning and threat assessment, allowing for prompt countermeasures and personnel protection. This is especially important in situations where there are dangerous materials present, chemical attacks, or nuclear accidents (Priya, 2024; Khadake et al,2024).
- Sensors can give commanders and intelligence analysts' real-time situational awareness by keeping an eye on the surrounding environment and activity. This data aids in threat identification, adversary movement prediction, and efficient resource allocation.
- Commanders can attain more precise targeting by merging sensor data with weapon systems. This lessens collateral damage, decreases civilian casualties, and enhances operational efficacy (Sayyad, 2025a; Sayyd, 2025b).
- Assist in target identification as per Kutubuddin (2024e) and early warning systems, detect gunfire, explosions, and vehicle movements. These systems can identify hostile vehicles, aircraft, and even troop movements through the detection and classification of sound signatures (Sayyad, 2018).
- Keep an eye out for any biological, chemical, or nuclear dangers to ensure the protection of the troops and to guide countermeasures.
- Air quality sensors: These are essential for monitoring dangerous compounds and pollutants, which are necessary for evaluating health and safety.

One important development in contemporary warfare is the integration of environmental sensors on the battlefield. They provide several tactical benefits that improve soldier safety, operational effectiveness, and situational awareness. Reliability, interference, data management, and ethical issues are still problems, nevertheless. The use of environmental sensors will probably become much more common as technology advances, influencing how warfare is fought in the future.

2. Target Acquisition Sensors

A vital connection between successful action and battlefield knowledge is made possible by target acquisition sensors. These technologies have significantly changed the face of combat, starting with the first spotting telescopes and continuing through complex contemporary systems. This review examines the various applications, benefits, and drawbacks of target acquisition sensors in the contemporary battlefield.

The environment of the battlefield is dynamic and complicated, requiring a range of sensor types to handle various tasks and threats. Among them are:

- To identify and track targets, use imaging systems, cameras, and laser rangefinders. They provide precision aiming, day/night operation, and high-resolution imaging. Thermal cameras, scopes, and conventional binoculars provide visual identification and range estimation. Superior target recognition and tracking are achieved by advanced electro-optical systems that combine several sensors with image processing (Sayyad, 2025d).
- Radar sensors are incredibly useful for surveillance and early warning, these sensors can detect and track targets over great distances in a variety of weather situations. Radar offers long-range detection and identification, even in inclement weather, from airborne to ground-based platforms. Modern radar systems can follow and identify moving targets through various forms of camouflage, including foliage.
- Especially useful in naval warfare, these sensors are used to identify and track underwater targets.
- While laser designators pinpoint targets for precise strikes, rangefinders measure the distance to targets.
- These cutting-edge systems combine information from several sources to present a complete view of the combat zone, improving situational awareness, tracking, and target recognition.

Target acquisition sensors allow for quicker, more precise, and more efficient reactions to threats, making them an essential tool for modern military. Notwithstanding these obstacles, ongoing technological development and creative applications are reshaping warfare, improving battlefield awareness, and building a more capable and adaptable military. It is essential to guarantee the ethical and responsible development and application of these potent skills as the technology landscape changes (Altaf et al., 2024; Veema et al., 2023).

3. Health and Physiological Sensors

By incorporating health and physiological sensors into military gear and apparel, force protection might be greatly improved. The commanders can identify indicators of heat injury, hypothermia, and physical effort before they become critical by continuously monitoring vital signs like heart rate, blood oxygen levels, and body temperature. By enabling prompt action, this early warning system reduces the possibility of potentially fatal scenarios and lessens the effect of injuries on mission success (Upadhyaya et al, 2025; Priya et al., 2023) .

These sensors can also help soldiers perform at their best in the field. Military leaders can maximize soldiers' physical and cognitive ability by customizing training programs and operational methods based on individual soldiers' demands, which is achieved by measuring biomechanical data, sleep habits, and physical activity. Additionally, by using this data to inform equipment design, military gear can be made more physiologically appropriate for its users (Kazi, 2024b; Liyakat, 2025).

- These sensors track vital signs like heart rate, body temperature, and oxygen saturation, offering insights into soldier health and stress levels (Mulani et al,2025; Kazi K S, 2025; Kazi K,2024a).
- These devices keep track of the force and pressure exerted on exoskeletons to guarantee their correct operation and improve military performance (Kazi S,2024d).

  Future military healthcare could greatly benefit from the usage of physiological and health sensors. Medical practitioners can obtain important insights into the long-term effects of military duty by gathering thorough data on soldiers' health and performance throughout time. This data can then be used to inform people about the creation of more effective treatment and prevention programs. Furthermore, these sensors can support telemedicine and remote monitoring, enabling medical professionals to diagnose and treat injuries in real time—even in inhospitable or remote locations (Kazi S,2025; Kazi S,2025a).

4. Infrastructure Sensors

Armies are using infrastructure sensors to monitor terrain, detect enemy movement, and gather intelligence in a completely new way. Infrastructure sensors include a broad variety of equipment, such as:

- Structural Integrity Sensors: Keep an eye out for any damage or failure to buildings, bridges, and other infrastructure to ensure safe operations and logistics.
- Energy Monitoring Sensors: Monitor power distribution and consumption to improve resource management and lower attack susceptibility (Prashant,2023).
- Seismic sensors: Track the vibrations in the ground brought on by vehicles, artillery fire, and troop movements.
- Thermostatic sensors: Identify heat signatures coming from people, things, and machinery.
- Chemical sensors: Identify biological agents and potentially dangerous chemicals.
- Radar and lidar: Produce three-dimensional terrain maps and identify things in motion (Tariq, 2025b).

Infrastructure sensors have a bright future in the battlefield, notwithstanding their difficulties. These sensors' capabilities will be further boosted by technological advancements including downsizing, reduced power consumption, and improved data processing capabilities. Infrastructure sensors, with their real-time intelligence, target acquisition, early warning, and force protection capabilities, are revolutionizing the modern battlefield. These sensors will become more and more important for making decisions on the battlefield and completing missions successfully as technology advances (Kutubuddin 2024).

AI-Driven- IoBT Decision Making (KSK Approach)

The way we interact with the physical world has already been completely transformed by the Internet of Things (IoT), but the Internet of Behavior Things (IoBT) is set to take things even farther. This cutting-edge technology integrates IoT data with AI to do more than merely watch and respond to events—it can actively learn and make judgments based on real-time information (Liyakat,2025d; Kazi K S,2025). The possibilities of IoBT and its influence on AI-powered decision making are examined in this evaluation. The Internet of Battlefield Things (IoBT) is a concept that emerged from the rapidly expanding number of connected devices on the battlefield. With its extraordinary data output from sensors, drones, and other devices, this network has the potential to revolutionize military decision-making. Artificial intelligence (AI) is a key factor in realizing this promise and empowering commanders to make well-informed decisions in intricate and pressing circumstances (Prasad et al,2024; Liyakat,2023; Kazi K,2025). IoBT is more than just gathering data from devices that are connected. To facilitate wiser and more proactive decision making, it focuses on understanding behavior patterns and forecasting future results. This is accomplished by utilizing artificial intelligence (AI) algorithms that examine data streams from several sources, such as Internet of Things (IoT) sensors, user activity, social interactions, and environmental factors.

The processing of real-time data by traditional cloud-based AI techniques is frequently hindered by latency and bandwidth limits. By putting AI capabilities closer to the data source, IoBT strengthens edge computing. This makes it possible to analyze data more quickly, make decisions right away, and rely less on centralized systems. Within the IoBT, AI algorithms can combine data from many sources to provide a holistic image of the battlefield. This data consists of communications traffic, images, and real-time sensor readings. Commanders can spot patterns, irregularities, and possible dangers by examining these merged data streams that might go unnoticed otherwise. AI can use machine learning models to predict future events by using observations made in real time and previous data. These models may simulate possible situations, optimize supply systems, and anticipate adversary movements. Commanders can take proactive measures and obtain a substantial advantage over their opponents by projecting future developments (Kazi S,2024; Kazi S,2024a).

Certain IoBT tasks can be automated by AI-powered systems, freeing up commanders to concentrate on more strategic decision-making. AI, for instance, is capable of modifying network configurations, controlling sensors, and, in some predetermined scenarios, even participating in warfare. Commanders can assign tasks and become more aware of their surroundings because of their autonomy (Liyakat KS,2024). There are significant ethical issues with the use of AI in military decision-making. To avoid biases or unintentional harm, the development and implementation of autonomous AI systems must be governed by explicit ethical guidelines. The possible repercussions of employing data that might contain private or sensitive information must also be considered by commanders (Liyakat,2024; Pradeepa, et al,2022; Mahant,2025). On the battlefield, AI-driven IoBT is transforming decision-making. Artificial Intelligence provides commanders with previously unheard-of levels of intelligence and insight by automating jobs, combining data from many sources, and forecasting future occurrences. The IoBT's integration of AI will become ever more crucial for military effectiveness as technology develops. Nonetheless, to guarantee the ethical and advantageous application of this revolutionary technology, it is crucial to properly address ethical issues (Tariq, 2025c).

Figure 3. AI-driven-IoBT –KSK approach based proposed system

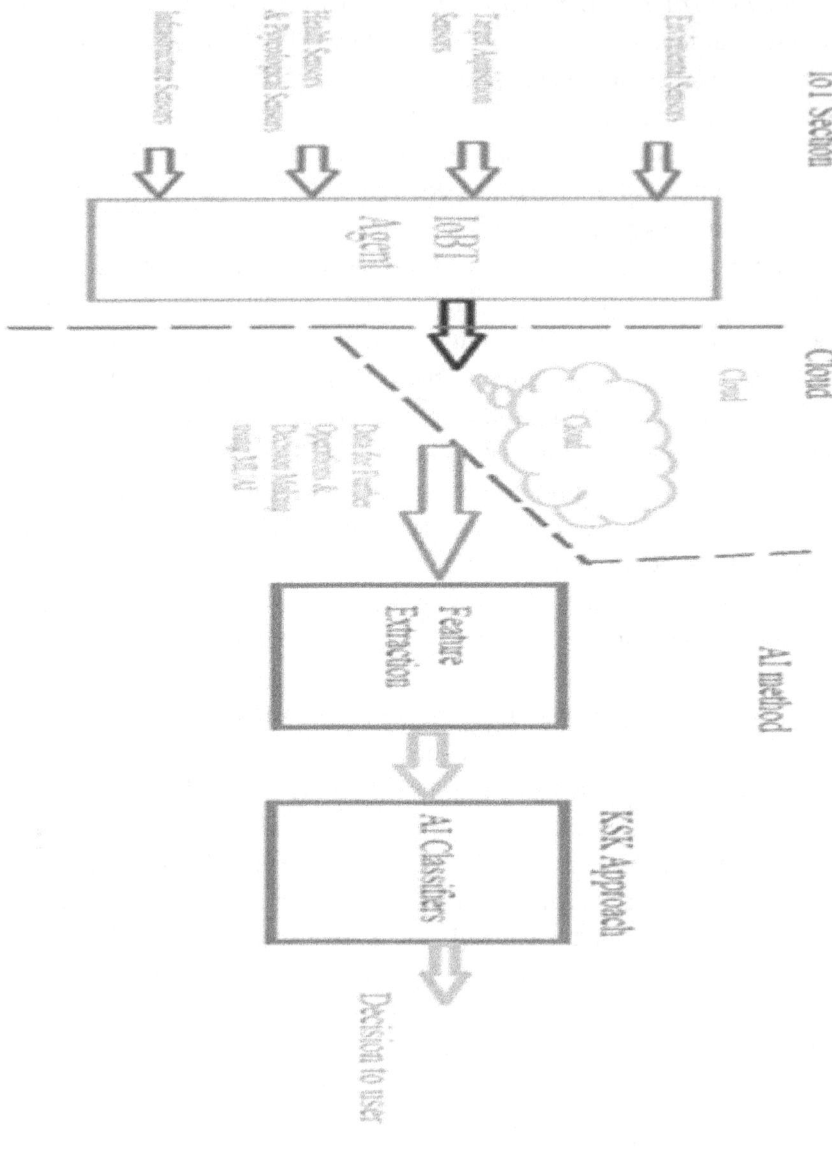

Figure 3 shows the AI-Driven IoBT based Decision Making system. It has three parts viz. IoT sections, Cloud section and Decision-making using AI. Hence this system is called as AI-Driven-IoBT Decision Making. For decision making we recommend KSK (Kutubuddin S Kazi) approach which employs ANN, K-NN and DT classifiers (Keerthana et al,2025; Kutubuddin,2024a). The performance of KSK approach is studied under the parameters like accuracy, recall and precision. Figure

4 shows the Confusion Matrix format for the proposed system. From this we studied the parameters Accuracy, Recall and Precision (Liyakat, 2023a; Liyakat,2025a; Tariq and Sergio, 2025a).

Figure 4. Confusion matrix format

Confusion Matrix		Target			
		Negative	Positive		
Model	Negative	K	A	*Negative Predictive Value*	*K/K +A*
	Positive	Z	I	*Positive Predictive Value*	*I/Z+I*
		Precision	Recall	Accuracy =(K + A)/ (K + A + Z + I)	
		K/K+Z	*I/A+I*		

The Final outcome of KSK approach is the better results occurred from above all classifiers. So, the KSK approach gives the outcome as Accuracy of KSK, Recall of KSK and Precision of KSK approach respectively.

Advantages of AI-Powered Decision Making with IoBT:

- Increased Efficiency: better resource allocation, less downtime, and optimized operations.
- Enhanced safety through proactive safety measures, real-time risk assessment, and predictive maintenance.
- Personalized Experiences: Personalized user interactions, specialized services, and suggestions.
- Data-driven Insights: A more thorough comprehension of consumer behavior, industry developments, and commercial prospects.
- Sustainable Solutions: Waste reduction improved environmental monitoring, and optimized energy use.

DISCUSSION

The IoBT is a new concept that aims to revolutionize modern fighting tactics. The basic idea behind this concept is to link soldiers to various military equipment, including vehicles, weapons, and wearable technology, through a network of sensors and actuators. The enhanced situational awareness and real-time data provided by this networked system would enable military personnel to make more informed judgments and cooperate more effectively. The main cause of the Internet of Business Technology (IoBT) is the widespread use of low-cost, small-sized electronic devices with networking and computing capabilities. These devices provide seamless data exchange and integration with a range of military armaments. For instance, sensors on vehicles measure soldiers' whereabouts and operational status, and wearable technology tracks soldiers' biometric data and health. Using networked sensors, devices, and technology, a developing idea called the IoBT enhances situational awareness and decision-making in military operations. This paper examines the most current research and advancements in IoBT and provides viewpoints on potential benefits and drawbacks (Tariq and Sergio, 2025b). By using the Internet of Things, the military can outperform adversaries in the battlefield by a large margin. The following are the Principal Findings of IoBT:

- Real-time data collection from several platforms and sensors is made feasible by IoBT, which enhances battlefield vision. Sensors that monitor unit movements, enemy positions, and climatic factors provide commanders with a comprehensive understanding of the operating environment.
- By combining data from many sources, IoBT enables data fusion and analysis. Artificial intelligence (AI) and complex algorithms can process this data to generate insights, predict outcomes, and recommend actions, improving the quality and speed of decision-making.
- IoBT enables precision targeting and engagement by providing real-time intelligence on opposing assets. Precise airstrikes, artillery fire, and other offensive operations are made possible by the target recognition and tracking capabilities of sensors.
- IoBT can streamline supply chain and logistics processes by monitoring inventory levels, predicting demand, and tracking equipment. Through optimization, inefficiencies are reduced, and the availability of essential resources is ensured.
- A few of the ways that IoBT enhances troop safety include through wearable sensors that monitor vital signs, recognize hazardous environments, and alert users to dangers. This information can be used by commanders to locate and protect people in dangerous situations.

IoBT can totally change military operations by improving situational awareness, decision-making skills, and soldier safety. However, problems with cost, interoperability, and data security need to be fixed before it can be fully utilized. As research and development continue, it is expected that IoBT will have a substantial impact on future military settings. For the security of IoBT/IoT devices, we will recommend the KK (Kutubuddin Kazi) approach, which was developed by Dr. Kutubuddin Kazi and is utilized for IoT security.

IoBT offers a lot of potential, but not without problems:

- The enormous volume of data generated by numerous sensors needs effective data processing and analysis.
- Secure data storage and transport are crucial to preventing unauthorized access and alteration.
- Encouraging seamless data exchange and communication among diverse sensor networks is essential.
- Sensors must be resilient enough to withstand extreme heat, shocks, vibrations, and difficult battle situations.

Obligations to sensors' capacity to precisely detect and track targets, precision strikes may be executed. When sensors discover hostile behavior early on, commanders can respond quickly. Sensors enhance force protection by detecting threats and providing early warning of oncoming attacks. Sensors provide detailed battlefield information, which helps with better mission planning and decision making.

- Surveillance and reconnaissance: Monitoring the enemy's positions, movements, and terrain. Precise target identification and localization maximizes combat effectiveness while minimizing collateral damage and augmenting armament system efficiency.
- Target acquisition and tracking: identifying and monitoring targets for artillery, airstrikes, and other operations. Less time and money must be spent on target acquisition while raising mission success rates, freeing up resources for other objectives.
- Force protection: identifying and monitoring threats such as snipers, roadside bombs, and chemical weapons. Early danger detection and identification enables proactive defense methods by reducing casualties and increasing operating safety.
- Remote Operations: Unmanned aerial vehicles (UAVs) and other remotely operated platforms with sensors lower the risk to humans by enabling target acquisition and reconnaissance in dangerous locations.

- Disaster relief: locating citizens who are stranded, identifying places that have been harmed, and assessing the ecosystem's condition.

RESULTS

The Outcome of proposed KSK (Kutubuddin S Kazi) Approach is studied by ANN, K-NN and DT Classifiers. The outcomes of all classifiers are studied under the conditions such as Environmental Condition, Target acquisition and tracking, Health, Remote Operations & Disaster relief(Infrastructure sensor output), the outcome of each classifier is shown in Figure 5,6,7, and Figure 8 respectively.

Figure 5. Performance for environmental condition

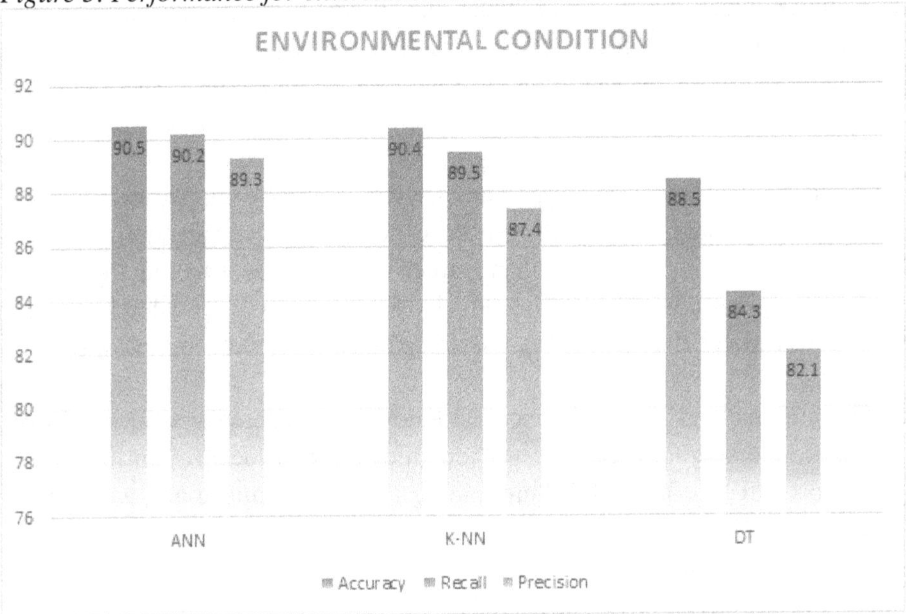

The environmental conditions are collected by sensors and processed by KSK appraoch, from Figure 5, where we get the maximum accuracy of 90.5% with ANN, recall of 90.2% with ANN and Precision of 89.3% with ANN. Hence we says that the Outcome of KSK approach is shown in Figure 9 for enviromental condition study.

Figure 6. Performance for target acquisition and tracking

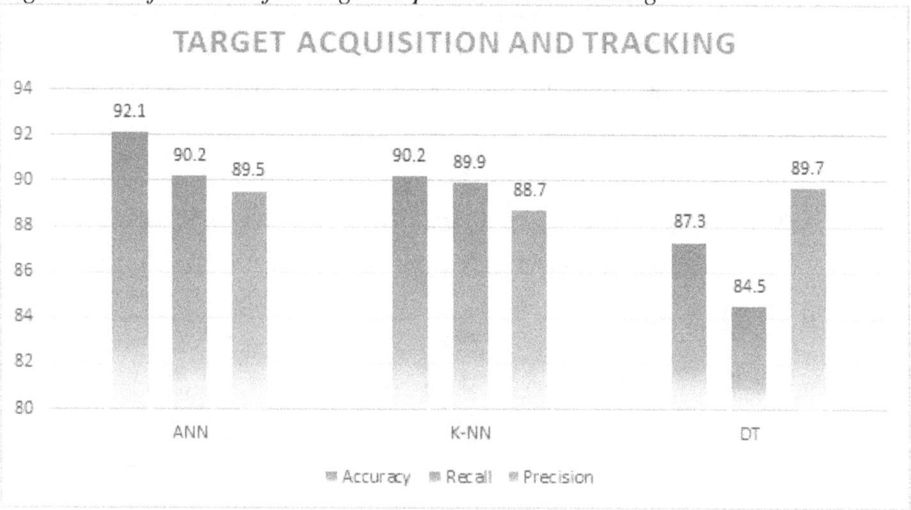

The Target acquisition and tracking are collected by sensors and processed by KSK appraoch, from Figure 6, where we get the maximum accuracy of 92.1% with ANN, recall of 90.2% with ANN and Precision of 89.7% with DT. Hence we says that the Outcome of KSK approach is shown in Figure 10 for Target acquisition and tracking study.

Figure 7. Performance for health and psychology

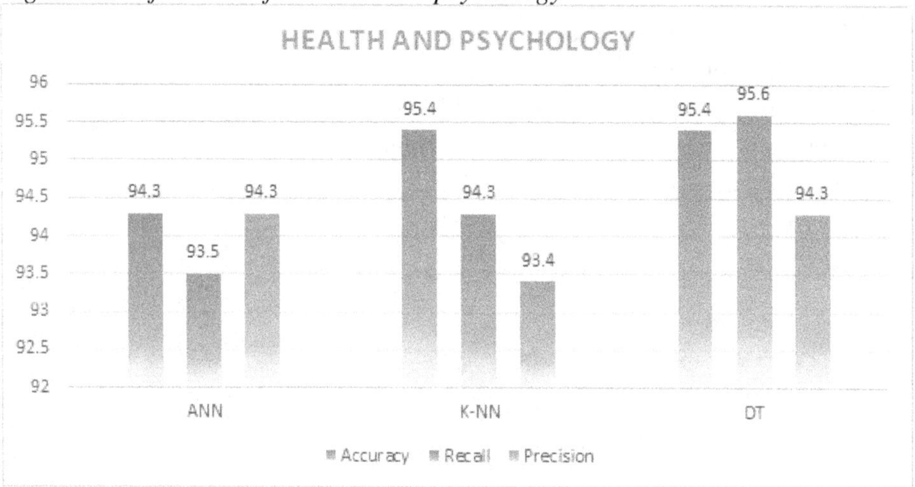

The Health and Psychology are collected by sensors and processed by KSK (Kutubuddin S Kazi) Approach, from Figure 7, where we get the maximum accuracy of 95.4% with K-NN & DT, recall of 95.6% with DT and Precision of 94.3% with ANN & DT. Hence we says that the Outcome of KSK approach is shown in Figure 11 for Health and Psychology study.

Figure 8. Performance for remote operations & disaster relief

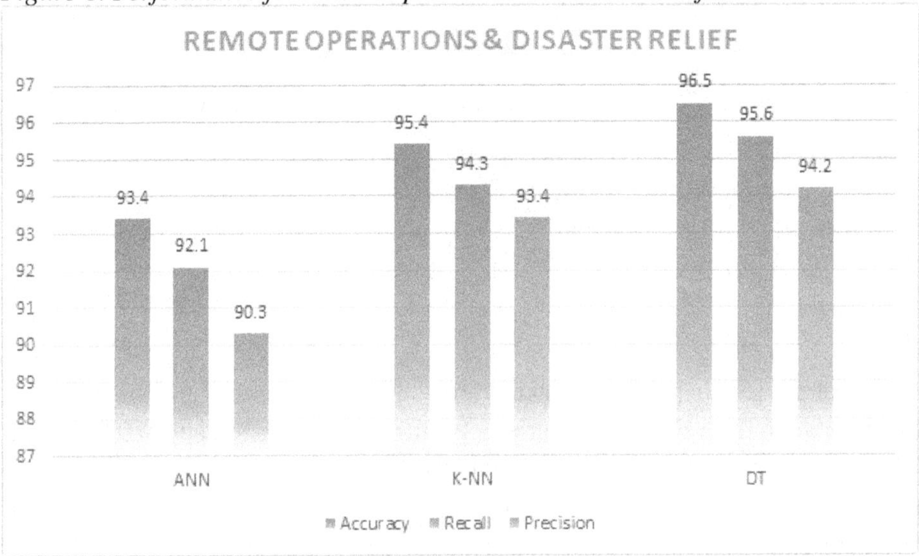

The Remote Operations are collected by sensors and processed by KSK appraoch, from Figure 8, where we get the maximum accuracy of 96.5% with DT, recall of 95.6% with DT and Precision of 94.2% with DT. Hence we says that the Outcome of KSK approach is shown in Figure 12 for Health and Psychology study.

Figure 9. KSK approach for enviromental condition study

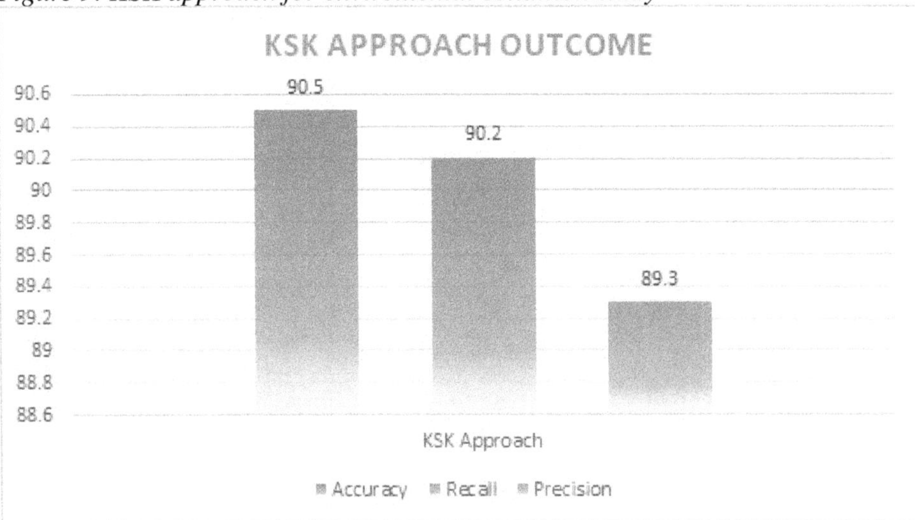

Figure 10. KSK approach for target acquisition and tracking

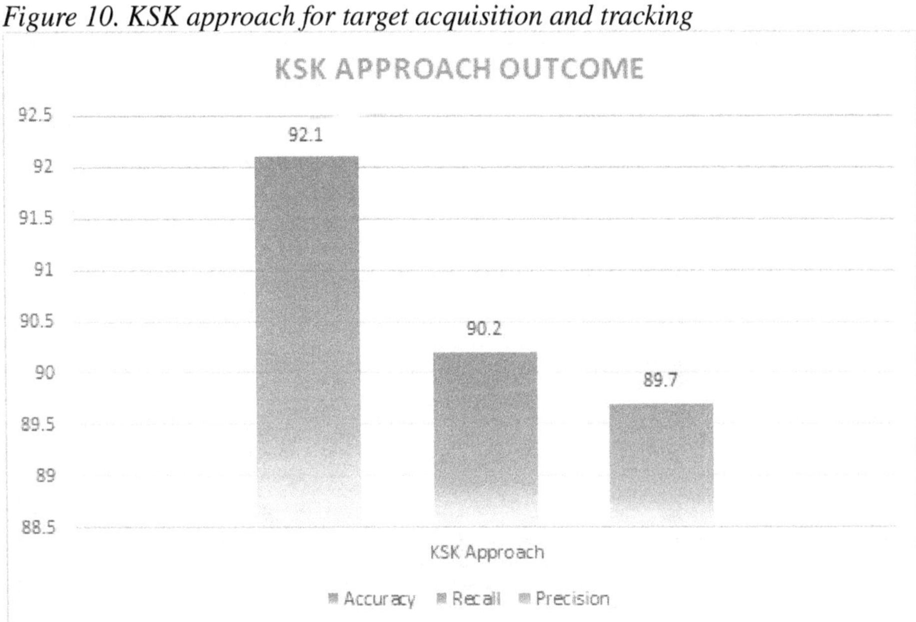

Figure 11. KSK approach for health and psychology

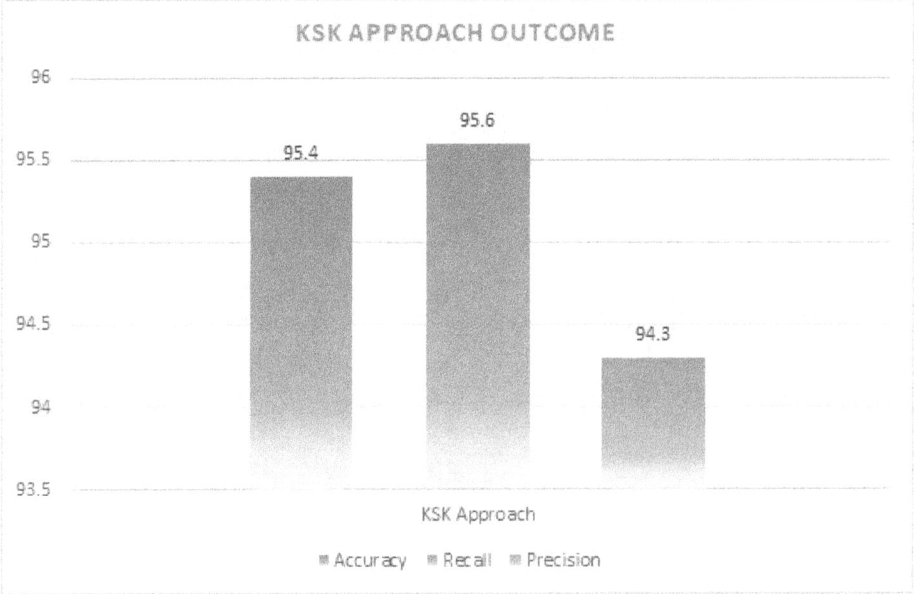

Figure 12. KSK approach for remote operations

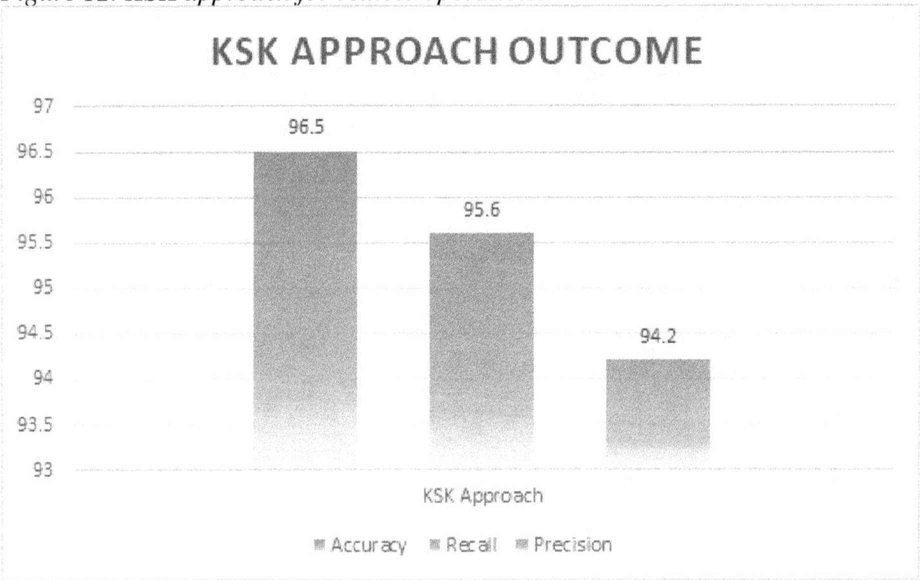

CONCLUSION

The battlefields of the future won't resemble those of the present. In contemporary warfare, the Internet of Battlefield Things, or IoBT, is revolutionary. Thanks to IoBT, which expands their skills, enhances their ability to make decisions, and heightens their situational awareness, the armed forces can function more effectively and efficiently. However, implementation, compatibility, and cybersecurity issues must be resolved for this ground-breaking technology to realize its full potential. The Internet of Combat Things is powered by sensors, which supply vital information for enhanced situational awareness, decision-making, and combat effectiveness. Notwithstanding obstacles, the ongoing advancement and incorporation of these technologies will revolutionize warfare, characterizing the nature of struggle and altering the terrain of upcoming battlegrounds. Commanders will be able to act quickly and intelligently by using a wide range of sensors that continuously feed real-time data to computers. The IoBT's remarkable situational awareness, autonomy, and capacity for focused actions have the potential to significantly alter combat. However, there are major challenges ahead, including those related to interoperability, security, data management, and ethical considerations. To ensure that the Internet of Big Things (IoBT) delivers on its promise of a safer, more effective, and responsible battlefield in the future, research and development must give priority to these challenges as technology improves. The accuracy range for the recommended KSK approach in IoBT is 90% to 96%, whereas the ranges for recall and precision are 89% to 95% and 90% to 95%, respectively.

REFERENCES

Kasat, K., Shaikh, N., Rayabharapu, V. K., & Nayak, M. (2023). *Implementation and Recognition of Waste Management System with Mobility Solution in Smart Cities using Internet of Things, 2023 Second International Conference on Augmented Intelligence and Sustainable Systems*. ICAISS., Available at https://ieeexplore.ieee.org/document/10250690/, DOI: 10.1109/ICAISS58487.2023.10250690

Kazi, K. (2024a). AI-Driven IoT (AIIoT) in Healthcare Monitoring. In Nguyen, T., & Vo, N. (Eds.), *Using Traditional Design Methods to Enhance AI-Driven Decision Making* (pp. 77–101). IGI Global., available at https://www.igi-global.com/chapter/ai-driven-iot-aiiot-in-healthcare-monitoring/336693, DOI: 10.4018/979-8-3693-0639-0.ch003

Kazi, K. (2024b). Modelling and Simulation of Electric Vehicle for Performance Analysis: BEV and HEV Electrical Vehicle Implementation Using Simulink for E-Mobility Ecosystems. *In L. D., N. Nagpal, N. Kassarwani, V. Varthanan G., & P. Siano (Eds.), E-Mobility in Electrical Energy Systems for Sustainability (pp. 295-320). IGI Global.* Available at: https://www.igi-global.com/gateway/chapter/full-text-pdf/341172DOI: 10.4018/979-8-3693-2611-4.ch014

Kazi, K. (2025). Machine Learning-Powered IoT (MLIoT) for Retail Apparel Industry. In Tarnanidis, T., Papachristou, E., Karypidis, M., & Manda, V. (Eds.), *Sustainable Practices in the Fashion and Retail Industry* (pp. 345–372). IGI Global Scientific Publishing., DOI: 10.4018/979-8-3693-9959-0.ch015

Kazi, K. S. (2025). AI-Driven IoT (AIIoT)-Based Decision-Making System for High BP Patient Healthcare Monitoring: KSK1 Approach for BP Patient Healthcare Monitoring. In Mzili, T., Arya, A., Pamucar, D., & Shaheen, M. (Eds.), *Optimization, Machine Learning, and Fuzzy Logic: Theory, Algorithms, and Applications* (pp. 71–102). IGI Global Scientific Publishing., DOI: 10.4018/979-8-3693-7352-1.ch003

Kazi, K. S. (2025). Advancing Towards Sustainable Energy With Hydrogen Solutions: Adaptation and Challenges. In Özsungur, F., Chaychi Semsari, M., & Küçük Bayraktar, H. (Eds.), *Geopolitical Landscapes of Renewable Energy and Urban Growth* (pp. 357–394). IGI Global Scientific Publishing., DOI: 10.4018/979-8-3693-8814-3.ch013

Kazi, S. (2024). Machine Learning-Based Pomegranate Disease Detection and Treatment. In Zia Ul Haq, M., & Ali, I. (Eds.), *Revolutionizing Pest Management for Sustainable Agriculture* (pp. 469–498). IGI Global., DOI: 10.4018/979-8-3693-3061-6.ch019

Kazi, S. (2024a). Computer-Aided Diagnosis in Ophthalmology: A Technical Review of Deep Learning Applications. In Garcia, M., & de Almeida, R. (Eds.), *Transformative Approaches to Patient Literacy and Healthcare Innovation* (pp. 112–135). IGI Global., Available at https://www.igi-global.com/chapter/computer-aided-diagnosis-in-ophthalmology/342823, DOI: 10.4018/979-8-3693-3661-8.ch006

Kazi, S. (2024b). IoT Driven by Machine Learning (MLIoT) for the Retail Apparel Sector. In Tarnanidis, T., Papachristou, E., Karypidis, M., & Ismyrlis, V. (Eds.), *Driving Green Marketing in Fashion and Retail* (pp. 63–81). IGI Global., DOI: 10.4018/979-8-3693-3049-4.ch004

Kazi, S. (2024d). Artificial Intelligence (AI)-Driven IoT (AIIoT)-Based Agriculture Automation. In Satapathy, S., & Muduli, K. (Eds.), *Advanced Computational Methods for Agri-Business Sustainability* (pp. 72–94). IGI Global., DOI: 10.4018/979-8-3693-3583-3.ch005

Kazi, S. (2025). Machine Learning-Driven Internet of Medical Things (ML-IoMT)-Based Healthcare Monitoring System. In Soufiene, B., & Chakraborty, C. (Eds.), *Responsible AI for Digital Health and Medical Analytics* (pp. 49–86). IGI Global Scientific Publishing., DOI: 10.4018/979-8-3693-6294-5.ch003

Kazi, S. (2025a). Transformation of Agriculture Effectuated by Artificial Intelligence-Driven Internet of Things (AIIoT). In Garwi, J., Dzingirai, M., & Masengu, R. (Eds.), *Integrating Agriculture, Green Marketing Strategies, and Artificial Intelligence* (pp. 449–484). IGI Global Scientific Publishing., DOI: 10.4018/979-8-3693-6468-0.ch015

Kazi, S. (2025c). AI-Driven-IoT (AIIoT)-Based Decision Making in Drones for Climate Change: KSK Approach. In Aouadni, S., & Aouadni, I. (Eds.), *Recent Theories and Applications for Multi-Criteria Decision-Making* (pp. 311–340). IGI Global., DOI: 10.4018/979-8-3693-6502-1.ch011

Keerthana, R. K. V., Bhagyalakshmi, K., Papinaidu, M. V. V., & Liyakat, K. K. S. (2025). Machine learning based risk assessment for financial management in big data IoT credit. SSRN *Electronic Journal*. DOI: 10.2139/ssrn.5086671

Khadake, S. B., Chounde, A. B., & Suryagan, A. A., M. H. M. and M. R. Khadatare, (2024). AI-Driven-IoT(AIIoT) Based Decision Making System for High-Blood Pressure Patient Healthcare Monitoring, *2024 International Conference on Sustainable Communication Networks and Application (ICSCNA)*, Theni, India, 2024, pp. 96-102, DOI: 10.1109/ICSCNA63714.2024.10863954

Kutubuddin (2024). Explainable AI in Healthcare. In: Explainable Artificial Intelligence in healthcare System, editors: *A. Anitha Kamaraj, Debi Prasanna Acharjya.* ISBN: 979-8-89113-598-7. DOI: https://doi.org/DOI: 10.52305/GOMR8163

Kutubuddin. (2024a). Machine Learning (ML)-Based Braille Lippi Characters and Numbers Detection and Announcement System for Blind Children in Learning, *In Gamze Sart (Eds.), Social Reflections of Human-Computer Interaction in Education, Management, and Economics, IGI Global.* https://doi.org/DOI: 10.4018/979-8-3693-3033-3.ch002

Liyakat, K. K. S. (2023a). Machine Learning Approach Using Artificial Neural Networks to Detect Malicious Nodes in IoT Networks. In Shukla, P. K., Mittal, H., & Engelbrecht, A. (Eds.), *Computer Vision and Robotics. CVR 2023. Algorithms for Intelligent Systems*. Springer., DOI: 10.1007/978-981-99-4577-1_3

Liyakat, K. K. S. (2024). Machine Learning Approach Using Artificial Neural Networks to Detect Malicious Nodes in IoT Networks. In Udgata, S. K., Sethi, S., & Gao, X. Z. (Eds.), *Intelligent Systems. ICMIB 2023. Lecture Notes in Networks and Systems* (Vol. 728). Springer., available at https://link.springer.com/chapter/10.1007/978-981-99-3932-9_12, DOI: 10.1007/978-981-99-3932-9_12

Liyakat, S. (2024g). Nanotechnology in BattleField: A Study. Journal of Nanoscience. *Nanoengineering & Applications*, *14*(2), 18–30p.

Liyakat, S. (2024j). Nanotechnology in BattleField: A Study. *Journal of Nanoscience. Nanoengineering & Applications.*, *14*(2), 18–30p.

Liyakat, S. (2024n). Impact of Nanotechnology on Battlefield Welfare: A Study. International Journal of Nanobiotechnology. 2024; 10(2): 19– 32p.

Liyakat. (2023). Detecting Malicious Nodes in IoT Networks Using Machine Learning and Artificial Neural Networks, *2023 International Conference on Emerging Smart Computing and Informatics (ESCI)*, Pune, India, 2023, pp. 1-5, . Available at: https://ieeexplore.ieee.org/document/10099544/DOI: 10.1109/ESCI56872.2023.10099544

Liyakat (2024). ChatGPT: An Automated Teacher's Guide to Learning. *In R. Bansal, A. Chakir, A. Hafaz Ngah, F. Rabby, & A. Jain (Eds.), AI Algorithms and ChatGPT for Student Engagement in Online Learning* (pp. 1-20). IGI Global. https://doi.org/DOI: 10.4018/979-8-3693-4268-8.ch001

Liyakat. (2025). IoT Technologies for the Intelligent Dairy Industry: A New Challenge. In S. Thandekkattu & N. Vajjhala (Eds.), *Designing Sustainable Internet of Things Solutions for Smart Industries* (pp. 321-350). IGI Global. https://doi.org/DOI: 10.4018/979-8-3693-5498-8.ch012

Liyakat, (2025a). Heart Health Monitoring Using IoT and Machine Learning Methods. In A. Shaik (Ed.), *AI-Powered Advances in Pharmacology* (pp. 257-282). IGI Global. https://doi.org/DOI: 10.4018/979-8-3693-3212-2.ch010

Liyakat. (2025d). AI-Driven-IoT(AIIoT)-Based Decision Making in Kidney Diseases Patient Healthcare Monitoring: KSK Approach for Kidney Monitoring. In L. Özgür Polat & O. Polat (Eds.), *AI-Driven Innovation in Healthcare Data Analytics* (pp. 277-306). IGI Global Scientific Publishing. https://doi.org/DOI: 10.4018/979-8-3693-7277-7.ch009

Mahant, M. A. (2025). Machine Learning-Driven Internet of Things (MLIoT)-Based Healthcare Monitoring System. In Wickramasinghe, N. (Ed.), *Digitalization and the Transformation of the Healthcare Sector* (pp. 205–236). IGI Global Scientific Publishing., DOI: 10.4018/979-8-3693-9641-4.ch007

Mulani, A. O., Bang, A. V., Birajadar, G. B., Deshmukh, A. B., & Jadhav, H. M. (2024). IoT Based Air, Water, and Soil Monitoring System for Pomegranate Farming. *Annals of Agri Bio Research*, *29*(2), 71–86.

Mulani, A. O., Liyakat, K. K. S., Warade, N. S., Patil, A., Kolte, M. T., Kinage, K., Rana, M., Salunkhe, S. S., Jadhav, V. S., & Nagrale, M. (2025). ML-powered Internet of Medical Things Structure for Heart Disease Prediction. *Journal of Pharmacology & Pharmacotherapeutics*, *0*(0), 0976500X241306184. Advance online publication. DOI: 10.1177/0976500X241306184

Neeraja, P., Kumar, R. G., Kumar, M. S., Liyakat, K. K. S., & Vani, M. S. (2024). *DL-Based Somnolence Detection for Improved Driver Safety and Alertness Monitoring. 2024 IEEE International Conference on Computing, Power and Communication Technologies (IC2PCT)*. Greater Noida., Available at https://ieeexplore.ieee.org/document/10486714, DOI: 10.1109/IC2PCT60090.2024.10486714

Nerkar, P. M., & Dhaware, B. U. (2023). Predictive Data Analytics Framework Based on Heart Healthcare System (HHS) Using Machine Learning, *Journal of Advanced Zoology*, 2023, Volume 44, Special Issue -2, Page 3673:3686. Available at: https://jazindia.com/index.php/jaz/article/view/1695

Odnala, S., Shanthy, R., Bharathi, B., Pandey, C., Rachapalli, A., & Liyakat, K. K. S. (2025). Artificial Intelligence and Cloud-Enabled E-Vehicle Design with Wireless Sensor Integration. SSRN *Electronic Journal*. DOI: 10.2139/ssrn.5107242

Pradeepa, M., ... (2022). Student Health Detection using a Machine Learning Approach and IoT, *2022 IEEE 2nd Mysore sub section International Conference (MysuruCon),* 2022. Available at: https://ieeexplore.ieee.org/document/9972445

Prasad, K. R., Karanam, S. R., Ganesh, D., Liyakat, K. K. S., Talasila, V., & Purushotham, P. (2024, May). AI in public-private partnership for IT infrastructure development. *The Journal of High Technology Management Research*, *35*(1), 100496. DOI: 10.1016/j.hitech.2024.100496

Prashant, K. Magadum (2024). Machine Learning for Predicting Wind Turbine Output Power in Wind Energy Conversion Systems, *Grenze International Journal of Engineering and Technology,* Jan Issue, Vol 10, Issue 1, pp. 2074-2080. Grenze ID: 01.GIJET.10.1.4_1 Available at: https://thegrenze.com/index.php?display=page&view=journalabstract&absid=2514&id=8

Priya Nerkar and Sultanabanu. (2024). IoT-Based Skin Health Monitoring System [IJBPAS]. *International Journal of Biology, Pharmacy and Allied Sciences, 13*(11), 5937–5950. DOI: 10.31032/IJBPAS/2024/13.11.8488

Sayyad, (2018). Significance of Projection and Rotation of Image in Color Matching for High-Quality Panoramic Images used for Aquatic study, *International Journal of Aquatic Science*, 9(2), pp. 130 – 145.

Sayyad, (2025). KK Approach for IoT Security: T-Cell Concept. In Rajeev Kumar, Sheng-Lung Peng, & Ahmed Elngar (Eds.), *Deep Learning Innovations for Securing Critical Infrastructures.* IGI Global Scientific Publishing.

Sayyad. (2025a). AI-Powered-IoT (AIIoT)-Based Decision-Making System for BP Patient's Healthcare Monitoring: KSK Approach for BP Patient Healthcare Monitoring. *In S. Aouadni& I. Aouadni (Eds.), Recent Theories and Applications for Multi-Criteria Decision-Making (pp. 205-238). IGI Global.*https://doi.org/DOI: 10.4018/979-8-3693-6502-1.ch008

Sayyad (2025b). AI-Powered IoT (AI IoT) for Decision-Making in Smart Agriculture: KSK Approach for Smart Agriculture. In S. Hai-Jew (Ed.), *Enhancing Automated Decision-Making Through AI* (pp. 67-96). IGI Global Scientific Publishing. https://doi.org/DOI: 10.4018/979-8-3693-6230-3.ch003

Sayyad (2025c). KK Approach to Increase Resilience in Internet of Things: A T-Cell Security Concept. In D. Darwish & K. Charan (Eds.), Analyzing Privacy and Security Difficulties in Social Media: New Challenges and Solutions (pp. 87-120). IGI Global Scientific Publishing. https://doi.org/DOI: 10.4018/979-8-3693-9491-5.ch005

Sayyad (2025d). Healthcare Monitoring System Driven by Machine Learning and Internet of Medical Things (MLIoMT). *In V. Kumar, P. Katina, & J. Zhao (Eds.), Convergence of Internet of Medical Things (IoMT) and Generative AI* (pp. 385-416). IGI Global Scientific Publishing. https://doi.org/DOI: 10.4018/979-8-3693-6180-1.ch016

Shinde, S. S., Nerkar, P. M., Kazi, S. S., & Kazi, V. S. (2025). Machine Learning for Brand Protection: A Review of a Proactive Defense Mechanism. In Khan, M., & Amin Ul Haq, M. (Eds.), *Avoiding Ad Fraud and Supporting Brand Safety: Programmatic Advertising Solutions* (pp. 175–220). IGI Global Scientific Publishing., DOI: 10.4018/979-8-3693-7041-4.ch007

Tamboli, D. A., & Sawant, V. A. M. H. M. and S. Sathe, (2024). AI-Driven-IoT(AIIoT) Based Decision-Making- KSK Approach in Drones for Climate Change Study, *2024 4th International Conference on Ubiquitous Computing and Intelligent Information Systems (ICUIS)*, Gobichettipalayam, India, 2024, pp. 1735-1744, DOI: 10.1109/ ICUIS64676.2024.10866450

Tariq, M. U. (2025a). Innovative Business Models: Integrating Social, Economic, and Environmental Goals in Rural Manufacturing. In Prabhakar, A., Yu, P., & Erokhin, V. (Eds.), *Rural Social Entrepreneurship Development: Network-Based Manufacturing System Model* (pp. 147–174). IGI Global Scientific Publishing., DOI: 10.4018/979-8-3693-7515-0.ch005

Tariq, M. U. (2025b). *AI-Driven Learning and Engagement in Higher Education*. IGI Global., DOI: 10.4018/979-8-3693-4074-5

Tariq, M. U. (2025c). AI and Work-Life Balance: Transforming Employee Wellbeing in the Modern Workplace. In Ahmed, E., Babar, A., Samad, A., Ahmed, R., & Beydoun, G. (Eds.), *Strengthening Human Relations in Organizations With AI* (pp. 85–110). IGI Global Scientific Publishing., DOI: 10.4018/979-8-3693-6507-6.ch004

Tariq, M. U., & Sergio, R. (Eds.). (2025). *Convergence of AI, Education, and Business for Sustainability*. IGI Global., DOI: 10.4018/979-8-3373-1917-9

Tariq, M. U., & Sergio, R. (Eds.). (2025). *Cases on AI-Driven Solutions to Environmental Challenges*. IGI Global, 2025. https://doi.org/DOI: 10.4018/979-8-3693-7483-2

Upadhyaya, A. N., Surekha, C., Malathi, P., Suresh, G., Suriyan, K., & Liyakat, K. K. S. (2025). Pioneering cognitive computing for transformative healthcare innovations. SSRN *Electronic Journal*. DOI: 10.2139/ssrn.5086894

Wale, A. D., & Dipali, R.. (2019). Smart Agriculture System using IoT. *International Journal of Innovative Research in Technology*, *5*(10), 493–497.

ADDITIONAL READINGS

Veena, C., Sridevi, M., Liyakat, K. K. S., Saha, B., Reddy, S. R., & Shirisha, N. (2023). *HEECCNB: An Efficient IoT-Cloud Architecture for Secure Patient Data Transmission and Accurate Disease Prediction in Healthcare Systems, 2023 Seventh International Conference on Image Information Processing*. ICIIP., Available at https://ieeexplore .ieee.org/document/10537627, DOI: 10.1109/ICIIP61524.2023.10537627

KEY TERMS AND DEFINITIONS

Battlefield: Traditionally, the battlefield refers to the physical space where armed conflict occurs, encompassing land, sea, and air. However, in the modern era, the definition is expanding to include the cyber domain and the information space.

Warfare: This encapsulates the organized and often violent conflict between states or other groups, involving the use of weapons, tactics, and strategies to achieve specific political objectives.

Internet of Things (IoT): The IoT refers to the vast network of interconnected devices embedded with sensors, software, and other technologies that enable them to collect and exchange data. These devices range from everyday objects like smart thermostats and refrigerators to industrial tools and medical equipment.

Internet of Battlefield Things (IoBT): A specialized subset of the IoT, the IoBT focuses on the application of IoT technology within a military context. It involves connecting a multitude of battlefield assets, including sensors, drones, vehicles, and even soldier wearables, to create a comprehensive and interconnected network.

Artificial Intelligence (AI): AI describes the development of computer systems capable of performing tasks that typically require human intelligence, such as learning, problem-solving, decision-making, and pattern recognition.

Automate Decision-Making: AI-powered decision support systems can analyze battlefield data and provide commanders with recommendations on optimal courses of action. This can significantly speed up the decision-making process, especially in fast-paced and complex environments.

Cybersecurity: A highly interconnected battlefield is vulnerable to cyberattacks. Adversaries could potentially disrupt IoBT networks, manipulate sensor data, or even take control of autonomous systems. Robust cybersecurity measures are essential to protect the IoBT from these threats.

Autonomous Systems: While fully autonomous weapons systems remain a subject of ethical debate, the IoBT is already facilitating the use of autonomous vehicles, drones, and robots for tasks like reconnaissance, surveillance, and even explosive ordnance disposal.

Chapter 8
AIoT-Enabled Smart Homes Solution to Security, Comfort, and Energy Efficiency

Anubha Anubha
https://orcid.org/0000-0002-2719-7697
Jaipuria Institute of Management, Ghaziabad, India

Daviender Narang
Jaipuria Institute of Management, Ghaziabad, India

Ankit Raj
Jaipuria Institute of Management, Ghaziabad, India

ABSTRACT

Thanks to developments in Artificial Intelligence (AI) and the Internet of Things (IoT), the once-futuristic idea of smart houses is now a reality. These cutting-edge technologies are transforming regular houses into intelligent, networked spaces that improve security, comfort, and energy efficiency. These technologies including AI and IoT, automate such homes and control various systems and devices. At the core of the smart home lie their capabilities to automate routine tasks like adjusting lighting and temperature to locking doors and managing security cameras. This creates an ecosystem that is adaptable to suit the requirements and preferences of its occupants. In the era characterized by artificial intelligence (AI) and the Internet of Things (IoT), almost everything including homes is automated and smart. The smart home market valued at $ 79.16 billion in 2022 is expected to grow at a CAGR (Compound Annual Growth Rate) of 27.07% from 2023 to 2030 (Grandview Research

DOI: 10.4018/979-8-3693-8547-0.ch008

Report, 2024). Accordingly, the present chapter aims to explore the potential of AIoT in home automation.

INTRODUCTION

As scientific and technological progress continues, the scope of the Internet of Things (IoT) has expanded beyond simple connections between people and devices. The current emphasis is on harnessing advanced data analytics and driving technological innovation, which are becoming key factors in the competitive dynamics of businesses. The rise of Artificial Intelligence (AI) has proven to be a crucial solution, addressing the challenges of managing the large volumes of data generated in IoT ecosystems (Afzal et al., 2018). As a result, the network layer has been transformed into an advanced data processing hub, coordinating high-level intelligent information analysis and supporting data collection and command execution at the terminal level (Yan, 2024).

AIoT is the integrated application of AI and IoT, where real-time data is gathered through IoT sensors and sophisticated data analytics are performed at the edge, terminals, or cloud, resulting in an intelligent ecosystem (Dong, 2020). In essence, AIoT is the convergence of AI and IoT technologies, blending IoT's sensor networks with AI's data processing power to achieve full digitalization and intelligent connectivity (Shafique et al., 2020; Hao, 2021). IDC forecasts that by 2025, there will be 55.7 billion IoT devices connected, producing almost 80 billion zettabytes of data (Hojlo, 2021). As businesses continue to digitize their internal processes across various functions, they are increasingly aware of the need to expand their ecosystems to meet market demands, improve customer satisfaction, and enhance flexibility and resilience. Given these insights, it is evident that AIoT has become a focal point in current research. Accordingly, the present chapter aims to explore the potential of AIoT in home automation. In other words, it intends to study the role of AIoT in home automation. This study will bring significant insights to researchers and key players in the smart home segment by exploring the potential benefits of AIoT in the home automation sector to have comfortable, secure, and energy-efficient smart homes. The chapter will also explain the risks and challenges in AI and IoT-based home automation.

LITERATURE REVIEW

When artificial intelligence (AI) and the Internet of Things (IoT) are combined, smart systems are produced that can gather, process, and react to data instantly, enabling a wide range of applications in various sectors like smart manufacturing, smart maintenance, smart energy utilization, smart quality control, smart retail, smart cars, smart cities, smart healthcare, wearable technologies, smart manufacturing including smart homes (Nazarevich, 2023). Businesses can use the industrial internet for things to gather data from production equipment, which enhances efficiency and decision-making. But frequently, the vast amount of data produced is unused and overwhelming. To overcome these problems, companies are capitalizing on the power of AIoT, which can help them in reducing their errors and human error in various industries. AIoT systems also offer improved security for smart homes' residents. AIoT systems have wider applicability in the transportation sector, too. These systems offer improved security and transit efficiency in self-driving cars by reading and scanning the sensor data. Next, AIoT has huge applications in medical domain. Due to their inherent ability to monitor individual patients' health conditions, AIoT can provide customized treatment for everyone. Today's AIoT-enabled wearable devices like Savemom[1] can collect the health data of a patient, which enables doctors to monitor the health condition of the patient in real time. The doctors can make suggestions about the treatment needed for a particular patient. In hospital administration, AIoT systems are also helpful as they can manage garbage more efficiently, take care of all transportation needs in the hospital, and optimize the consumption of energy. AIoT can offer personalized health insights to individuals through fitness trackers and smart watches. These smart gadgets show the different spectrum of AIoT applications like emergency alerts and location tracking. Though AIoT has many applications, as mentioned above, this chapter especially dwells on smart homes only.

RESEARCH METHODOLOGY

The study is descriptive, where the data is collected from secondary sources, including research papers, reports, newspapers, academic reports, government portals, websites, and videos by experts on the topic concerned. Therefore, the data used in the study is secondary. The analysis will focus on identifying the role of AIoT in home automation and the potential benefits of AIoT in the home automation sector. The chapter will also explain the challenges and risks in AIoT-based home automation.

Artificial Intelligence (AI)

Artificial intelligence is described as "a system's capacity to accurately interpret external data, learn from it, and apply that knowledge to achieve specific objectives and tasks through flexible adaptation" (Kaplan and Haenlein, 2019, p. 17). Kaplan and Haenlein (2019) categorize AI into three types: analytical, human-inspired, and humanized. Analytical AI focuses solely on cognitive intelligence. Human-inspired AI incorporates both cognitive and emotional intelligence, such as the ability to understand human emotions, and applies these insights in its decision-making processes. Humanized AI combines cognitive, emotional, and social intelligence and is capable of self-awareness in its interactions.

In other words, Artificial Intelligence (AI) is a branch of computer science focused on creating intelligent systems that can perform tasks and learn in ways akin to human behavior (Haenlein et al., 2019). AI involves the development of algorithms and models that enable machines to carry out functions such as natural language processing, image recognition, and decision-making. One of its primary benefits is automation, which drives greater efficiency. For example, AI can predict machine failures, enabling proactive maintenance that can minimize downtime and boost overall productivity (Guha, 2021; Sharma, 2024; Tariq, 2025).

Characteristics of AI

AI systems have several key characteristics. First, they demonstrate learning and adaptability, continuously improving from data over time, which enhances their efficiency and accuracy without explicit programming (McKinsey, 2024). AI also excels in automation, handling repetitive tasks to increase productivity and allow humans to focus on more complex activities (Chui et al., 2023). Additionally, AI is capable of pattern recognition, analyzing large datasets to uncover hidden patterns, making it essential for applications like fraud detection and personalized recommendations (Espina-Romero et al., 2024). AI supports decision-making by evaluating multiple factors to make informed choices (*ibid.*). Also, through natural language processing (NLP), AI enables intuitive human- device interactions via voice assistants, chatbots, and translation tools (Bender et al., 2023). Artificial Intelligence (AI) has revolutionized the way we solve problems and improve efficiency across industries. Autonomy is one of the important characteristics. It refers to the ability of AI to perform tasks independently without continuous human intervention. Autonomous systems leverage their algorithms to assess situations, make decisions, and execute actions, often in real time. This can be seen in automatic or self-driven cars. AI systems are increasingly capable of understanding and interpreting a situation and responding accordingly, which enhances decision-making. Context awareness allows

AI to process environmental cues effectively. AI can optimize energy consumption by understanding patterns in a house (Bender et al., 2023). By understanding the context, AI systems can deliver more personalized and effective results, making them integral to applications requiring adaptive functionality (Tariq and Sergio, 2025).

The solving ability of AI is one important characteristic. It tackles complex challenges by analyzing data, identifying possible solutions, and selecting the best course of action. AI's problem-solving ability has applications across various industries. For example, AI algorithms can identify optimal treatment paths by analyzing patient history and medical data. AI significantly reduces the time and resources needed for complex tasks. Next, emotional intelligence has become an important characteristic of AI. Emotional AI is also known as affective computing. It focuses on recognizing and responding to human emotions. Using tools like facial recognition and voice analysis, AI can measure emotions and tailor its interactions accordingly. For example, AI chatbots equipped with emotional intelligence can detect frustration or dissatisfaction in users' tone and respond with empathy.

The next important characteristic of Artificial Intelligence is scalability, which allows handling tasks and data at an enormous scale without compromising efficiency. Unlike human systems, which can be unhappy by increasing workloads, AI systems can be scaled seamlessly to accommodate larger data sets or more complex tasks. This characteristic is especially valuable in industries like e-commerce, where AI analyzes billions of transactions and customer interactions to optimize recommendations and pricing strategies.

Artificial Intelligence also has multimodal functionality. This refers to AI's ability to integrate and process information from various sources, such as texts, images, audio, and video, simultaneously. This characteristic enables AI to deliver richer and more comprehensive insights. For example, in autonomous vehicles, AI integrates inputs from cameras and sensors to understand the environment and make driving decisions. Similarly, in healthcare, AI systems combine medical imaging data with patient records to diagnose diseases with a creditable amount of accuracy.

With AI, creativity has emerged as one important feature that has the potential to generate original content across various domains. AI can create visual arts, songs, and videos. AI's ability to emulate human creativity has significant implications for industries such as advertising, where it generates innovative campaigns, and entertainment, where it personalizes user experiences. However, AI-generated creativity still relies on human-defined parameters. AI systems are exceptionally efficient in processing large volumes of data, extracting insights, and generating predictions in real time. Unlike traditional data analysis methods, which can be slow and cumbersome, AI utilizes advanced algorithms to process data at a very high speed. This characteristic is vital in many fields, like finance, where AI-powered systems analyze market data to predict trends. In scientific research, AI accelerates data analyses, enabling breakthroughs in areas such as genomics and climate modeling. The ability to process and analyze data with unparalleled efficiency makes AI indispensable in a data-driven world. AI systems are robust in design, operating reliably even in challenging conditions or when faced with incomplete data. A subset of robustness is fault tolerance, which ensures that AI systems can continue functioning with minimal disruption when errors occur. For example, autonomous drones maintain operations even when certain sensors fail, using alternative data sources to compensate. Similarly, AI in critical systems like power grids or medical devices ensures continuity and reliability, safeguarding against catastrophic failures. This characteristic makes AI suitable for applications where precision and dependability are paramount.

As with further improvements, AI systems have become more integral to decision-making processes. There is a growing emphasis on developing ethical and explainable AI. Ethical AI adheres to principles that prevent harm, ensure fairness, and protect user privacy. Explainable AI, on the other hand, focuses more on transparency, which allows users to understand how AI systems arrive at their conclusions. For instance, in legal or medical fields, explainable AI ensures accountability by providing clear and traceable reasoning behind decisions. These characteristics are crucial for building trust in AI systems.

Internet of Things (IoT)

The phrase *Internet of Things* (IoT) has gained a lot of traction in recent years and is currently very significant in the technology sector. An internet-connected network of gadgets that can "communicate" with one another is referred to as the Internet of Things (IoT) (Vermesan & Friess, 2014). These include wearables and smartphones, which are commonly used digital gadgets; smart meters, which are used in homes; and smart machines, which are used in factories. Gathering, sharing, and analyzing data allows these smart, networked devices to take appropriate action. IoT devices gather and analyze data from their surroundings by using sensors and processors. The information gathered by the sensors will be transmitted to other IoT devices or a gateway. After that, it will either be examined locally or transmitted to the cloud for analysis. It is anticipated that the volume of data generated by IoT connections will grow to an enormous 79.4 zettabytes by 2025 (Statista, 2016).

The devices might be as simple as household appliances, refrigerators, and light bulbs or as complex as industrial machines and vehicles (Kumar et al., 2019). It is rapidly becoming a key part of daily life, integrating a wide range of smart systems and devices. Advances in quantum and nanotechnology also enhance IoT's capabilities, improving storage, sensing, and processing speeds (Kumar et al., 2019). Research highlights IoT's potential to transform industries, though concerns about security, reliability, and interoperability remain (Chui et al., 2023). The prime objective of IoT is data aggregation, processing, and analysis of many data types from virtually all sources to offer knowledge and improvement cycles in decision-making (Khan et al., 2022; Tariq, 2025).

Characteristics of IoT

IoT is characterized by many features that make it more efficient. This section will detail all these characteristics of IoT. The first characteristic of IoT is its interconnectivity. Due to interconnectivity, communication is possible among smartphones, routers, and sensors, which allows them to perform their intended functions smartly (Soori et al., 2023; Sadhu et al., 2022). This inter-connectivity allows connection with global communication infrastructure and information. The second important characteristic of the Internet of Things is its capability to analyze data intelligently to offer meaningful insights from it. The third important characteristic of the Internet of Things is its capability to monitor in real time (Aouedi et al., 2024). This real-time monitoring enables various industries like manufacturing, transportation, and healthcare to track the work progress (Patel et al., 2016). This also helps them detect errors and irregularities, which can allow them to take timely action to prevent accidents, failures, and mistakes. For example, IoT-powered health monitoring systems can keep track of the vitals of patients (Li et al., 2021). The second example could be of today's smart factories, which apply the internet of things for predictive maintenance, which reduces the probability of machine and equipment breakdowns. The next characteristic of the Internet of Things is its capability of automation and control. Due to this, various devices can operate autonomously without human intervention. They only require some predefined set of instructions and conditions. For example, IoT-enabled automation allows smart homes to control security systems, heating, and lighting based on the environmental conditions and preferences of their residents (Nguyen et al., 2021; Li et al., 2015). In another example of the manufacturing sector, IoT-powered robotic process automation can optimize the overall production process by improving efficiency and reducing human intervention. Another characteristic of IoT is its scalability. Due to this, IoT networks can allow for a greater number of connected devices without sacrificing performance. The next characteristic of the Internet of Things is security (Mouha, 2021). IoT systems involve a huge amount of sensitive data and information that must be secured and must not be misused. For this, IoT devices and infrastructure must include features like regular software updates, access control, authentication, and encryption.

Artificial Internet of Things (AIoT)

AIoT (Artificial Intelligence of Things) is the integration of Artificial Intelligence (AI) with the Internet of Things (IoT), enabling devices to not only collect and transmit data but also to analyze and act on that data autonomously (Muhammed et al., 2024). The integration of AI technologies with IoT infrastructure is known as AIoT (Ahvar et al., 2023; Dia et al., 2022). By adding AI capabilities to IoT devices, AIoT enhances their functionality, allowing them to perform tasks like predicting outcomes, optimizing operations, and making real-time decisions without human input (Singh et al., 2021). This combination has the potential to transform industries by improving automation, efficiency, and user experience. Like traditional IoT, AIoT devices collect data from various sensors, which is then processed using AI techniques to extract valuable insights (Susan et al., 2023). Through machine learning (ML) and deep learning (DL), these devices can identify patterns, make predictions, and improve their performance over time (Baker & Xiang, 2023). AIoT systems can automatically make decisions, such as adjusting lighting or managing energy use in a smart building, without requiring user intervention (Varghese et al., 2020), thus enhancing operational efficiency.

AIoT (Artificial Intelligence of Things) is integrating more advanced AI capabilities into IoT systems, enabling them to process and analyze vast amounts of data generated by interconnected devices. By incorporating AI, IoT devices can autonomously learn about their environment and make decisions based on that knowledge without human intervention. These devices are capable of sensing and monitoring various environmental parameters like temperature, humidity, and pressure, as well as tracking human behavior, movement, and interactions with the surroundings (Muhammed et al., 2024). This allows for the automation of processes with minimal human involvement. For instance, AIoT systems can automatically adjust room temperature and lighting based on occupancy or ambient light levels or notify maintenance teams when a machine is at risk of failure based on performance data. In these applications, devices are equipped with sensors that detect real-time changes and actuators that respond by altering the physical environment. This intelligent feedback loop enables more efficient and autonomous systems, transforming everyday operations and enhancing decision-making (Parihar et al., 2023; Aslam et al., 2024).

Characteristics of AIoT

The AIoT system is defined by several important characteristics. First, it includes intelligent perception and data collection, where IoT devices, equipped with sensors, collect data from the environment. This data is then processed and analyzed (Wei et al., 2022). Next, AIoT leverages artificial intelligence to handle large datasets, extracting valuable insights and recognizing patterns. As the system processes more data, it becomes capable of autonomous decision-making, improving the intelligence and flexibility of IoT devices (Ahvar et al., 2023). Furthermore, AIoT systems support real-time interaction and communication, enabling devices to collaborate and coordinate tasks over the Internet. This connectivity ensures seamless cooperation among devices in a shared network (Matin et al., 2024). Other key characteristics include scalability, which allows AIoT systems to integrate additional devices and manage growing data volumes as the network expands (Gowda et al., 2024). Edge computing is another essential aspect, enabling local data processing at the device level or on the network's edge, reducing latency and bandwidth demands, which is crucial for applications requiring rapid response times (Qi et al., 2024). Additionally, AIoT systems have predictive capabilities, allowing them to anticipate future events based on past data, which is particularly useful for tasks such as predictive maintenance or resource optimization (Susan et al., 2023). Next, security and privacy protocols are embedded within AIoT systems to safeguard sensitive data and ensure secure communication between devices (Baker & Xiang, 2023).

The next significant characteristic of AIoT is its ability to process and analyze vast amounts of data intelligently. IoT devices generate enormous volumes of data from sensors, cameras, and other connected devices (Gowda et al., 2024). AIoT systems leverage AI algorithms, such as machine learning and deep learning, to process this data in real time, extract meaningful insights, and make informed decisions. Unlike traditional IoT systems that rely on cloud-based processing, AIoT often employs edge computing, enabling data processing closer to the source. This reduces latency and enhances efficiency (Baker & Xiang, 2023). AIoT systems can examine data streams in real time, allowing for expeditious responses to dynamic conditions (Qi et al., 2024). By recognizing patterns in historical data, AIoT can forecast future outcomes, enabling proactive decision-making. Further, AIoT systems are programmed to operate autonomously, reducing the need for human intervention. By integrating AI into IoT devices, these systems can make decisions faster based on the data they collect and analyze. For example, in a smart home, an AIoT-enabled thermostat can learn user preferences and adjust the temperature automatically without manual input (Susan et al., 2023).

Next, AIoT systems continuously learn from data and keep improving their decision-making capabilities over time to give an enhanced experience. These systems can adapt and act according to new information and changing environments, ensuring optimal performance and user satisfaction. Enhanced connectivity is another characteristic of AIoT. AIoT relies on seamless connectivity between devices, networks, and platforms (Wei et al., 2022). This characteristic guarantees that data can be transmitted and shared effortlessly across the ecosystem. AIoT systems tend to use advanced communication protocols, such as 5G, to enable high-speed connectivity (Susan et al., 2023). Furthermore, AIoT devices can communicate and work together in close synchronization even if they are from different manufacturers or use different technologies. AIoT systems can scale to accommodate a growing number of devices and users without compromising performance. Edge computing is an important characteristic of AIoT. Instead of sending all data to centralized cloud servers for processing, AIoT systems perform data processing at the edge of the network, closer to the source of data generation. This approach significantly reduces latency, minimizes bandwidth usage, and enhances privacy and security (Baker & Xiang, 2023).

Edge computing is another significant characteristic that ensures that decisions are made quickly, which is crucial for time-sensitive applications like autonomous vehicles and industrial automation. Next comes data privacy (Ahvar et al., 2023). By processing data locally, AIoT systems can reduce the risk of sensitive information being exposed during transmission (Baker & Xiang, 2023). AIoT systems leverage advanced machine learning (ML) and deep learning (DL) algorithms to analyze and interpret complex data sets and perform tasks that would be impossible for traditional IoT systems. These algorithms enable AIoT devices to identify patterns, classify data, and make predictions with relatively higher accuracy. AIoT devices can utilize deep learning to recognize images, faces, and speech, which enables applications like smart security systems and voice-activated assistants (Susan et al., 2023). AIoT systems can recognize unusual patterns or behaviors, such as equipment malfunctions or security breaches, and trigger appropriate responses (Gowda et al., 2024). AIoT systems are programmed to optimize energy consumption, making them more sustainable and cost-effective. By analyzing data from sensors and other sources, AIoT can identify inefficiencies and implement energy-saving measures.

Predictive Maintenance is the next important attribute of AIoT (Ahvar et al., 2023). By predicting when equipment is likely to fail, AIoT can prevent unnecessary energy consumption and reduce downtime. Security is a major and most talked-about concern in AIoT systems, as they are often vulnerable to cyberattacks. AIoT addresses this issue by integrating AI-driven security measures, such as anomaly detection, encryption, and authentication protocols. AIoT systems can detect and respond to security threats in real time, minimizing the risk of data breaches (Gowda et al., 2024). Further, AIoT affirms that data is encrypted during transmission and storage, protecting it from unauthorized access. Next are personalization and customization. AIoT systems can deliver tailor-made experiences by analyzing user behavior and preferences. This characteristic is particularly more important in consumer applications like wearable devices and personalized healthcare, including smart homes. AIoT can provide personalized recommendations based on user data, such as suggesting products, services, or content (Baker & Xiang, 2023). AIoT devices can adapt to individual users, enhancing convenience and satisfaction and enriching user experience, which further results in more loyal users (Susan et al., 2023).

AIoT Enabled Homes

The smart home industry has attracted significant investments from both venture capitalists and tech companies. AIoT-powered smart homes, in particular, have experienced rapid growth in recent years, fueled by advancements in artificial intelligence (AI) and the Internet of Things (IoT), along with a growing consumer demand for convenience, security, and energy efficiency. The global smart home market is expected to grow from USD 79.16 billion in 2021 to USD 209.71 billion by 2027, with a compound annual growth rate (CAGR) of 17.3% between 2021 and 2027 (Markets & Markets, 2022). The widespread adoption of AIoT technologies is a key driver behind this expansion. The concept of smarter homes has gained momentum, particularly with the rise of AI-powered energy management systems in smart homes. This has been a pivotal step in the evolution of home automation and AI technologies. Major tech companies like Google, Amazon, and Apple are investing heavily in AIoT innovations to enhance their smart home ecosystems, while smaller businesses and startups continue to drive innovation by focusing on niche solutions and markets (Forbes, 2023).

The landscape of Indian households is witnessing a major transformation on account of many factors, like the growing use of smartphones, widespread broadband access, rising disposable incomes, and a young, tech-savvy population (Anubha & Shome 2021). Together, these factors signal the beginning of a new era for smart home solutions in India, filled with potential for innovation and growth. A recent report from Statista (2023a) forecasts that the Indian smart home market will reach $6.5 billion by 2024, with household adoption set to double by 2028. This shows that more people are looking for the luxury and convenience that smart homes provide. The GfK Global Consumer Life Study 2023 also shows that interest in this technology is growing worldwide, with India becoming a strong user, even though there were initial concerns about cost, safety, and privacy (Yadav, 2024). The idea of a fully connected home with smart devices is exciting. Home automation aims to improve energy use, comfort, safety, and well-being by creating self-sustaining home systems. The home automation industry is expected to grow rapidly, with the pandemic and major life changes playing a big role in this growth. During the pandemic, 70% of people made changes to their living spaces because they spent more time at home, and 51% bought at least one smart home device.[2].

Benefits of AIoT-Enabled Smart Homes

Despite the fact that flying automobiles are still a way off, many of the futuristic ideas that people had for the twenty-first century are already evolving. A case in point is the rise of smart houses, which are outfitted with gadgets that automate routine chores. This section will examine the advantages of AIoT-enabled smart homes.

More Convenience

AIoT-enabled smart homes make life easier by allowing residents to control things with their voice or set automatic schedules. Devices like smart speakers (e.g., Amazon Echo[3]) and smart thermostats (e.g., Nest[4]) let you change things like lights, temperature, and security with just a command or a preset routine, saving time and effort.

Energy Savings

AIoT helps save energy by learning residents' habits and adjusting home systems to fit them. Smart thermostats and lighting systems reduce energy use without sacrificing comfort. For example, an AI thermostat like Ecobee[5] Adjusts heating and cooling based on people's schedules, helping lower energy bills and reduce environmental impact.

Better Security

AIoT improves home security by analyzing data from smart cameras, doorbells, and alarms. Devices like the Ring Video Doorbell use AI to recognize visitors or potential threats, reducing false alerts and improving safety. AI can also spot unusual activity and notify the residents quickly so that they can respond to security concerns faster. Further, AIoT powered cameras can recognize the people living in the home, and sensors can detect if someone is present. The system can send alerts if there's an intrusion or unusual activity. Though this may seem intrusive, it can also offer benefits like allowing access through face, biometric, or retinal scans. Additionally, AI can predict security threats and start recording automatically.

Preventative Maintenance

AIoT-powered devices can predict when appliances might break down or need maintenance, helping residents fix issues before they become big problems. For example, smart fridges and heating/cooling systems can monitor their own performance and alert residents about potential issues, saving them from expensive repairs and extending the life of their appliances.

Tailored Experience

AIoT learns residents' preferences over time and adjusts their home to suit them. Smart lights and entertainment systems, like Philips Hue and AI-powered soundbars, change settings based on residents' habits. This creates a more comfortable and personalized home environment that fits residents' unique needs and routines.

Lower Energy Bills

Smart devices in AIoT-enabled homes can monitor and adjust how appliances are used, from changing light brightness to controlling heating and cooling systems and tracking energy consumption. This helps reduce energy bills by using energy more efficiently.

Smart Lighting

Smart homes feature lighting systems that can be controlled with voice commands, remote controls, or mobile apps. These lights can be customized based on how each area of the house is used. In some cases, the lighting also acts as an interface for speakers and heating systems.

Intelligent Detection System

Homes with AIoT can predict problems and detect issues like water leaks in pipes, gas leaks, or electrical faults. If a problem is detected, the resident is notified, and the system can even shut off gas, water, or electricity to prevent further damage. These benefits offer peace of mind for smart home residents and make it easier for them to manage their homes. While saving on energy is a major advantage, AI in smart homes also improves the overall quality of life and convenience.

The Future of AIoT-Enabled Smart Homes

The integration of Artificial Intelligence of Things (AIoT) in smart homes is poised to revolutionize the way people live, work, and interact with their surroundings. AIoT, which combines the power of Artificial Intelligence (AI) with the Internet of Things (IoT), is emerging as a transformative force in the global technology landscape. In developing countries, the adoption of AIoT in smart homes is still in its nascent stages, but the growth potential is immense. With rapid urbanization, increasing disposable incomes, and a growing tech-savvy population, developing countries like India are becoming a fertile ground for the proliferation of AIoT-enabled smart home solutions.

Driving Factors for AIoT-Enabled Smart Homes

Rapid Urbanization and Smart City Initiatives: Developing countries like India are undergoing rapid urbanization with a tremendous amount of speed, with a significant portion of their population migrating to cities in search of better opportunities. The Indian government's Smart Cities Mission, launched in 2015, aimed to develop 100 smart cities across the country[6]. These smart cities are envisioned to leverage advanced technologies, including AIoT, to enhance urban living. Smart homes equipped with AIoT devices are a critical component of this vision. The integration of AIoT in smart homes can enable efficient energy management, enhanced security, and improved quality of life, aligning with the goals of the Smart Cities Mission.

Increasing Internet Penetration and Smartphone Usage: The developing countries like India have witnessed exponential growth in internet penetration with the introduction of Jio in Indian market and a significant rise in smartphone usage over the past decade. According to the Telecom Regulatory Authority of India (TRAI), India had over 800 million internet users as of 2024, with more than 500 million smartphone users[7]. This widespread connectivity is a key enabler for AIoT adoption in smart homes. AIoT devices rely on seamless connectivity to function effectively, and the availability of affordable smartphones and data plans has made it easier for consumers in developing countries like India to adopt smart home technologies. The proliferation of 4G and the upcoming rollout of 5G networks are expected to further accelerate the adoption of AIoT in smart homes.

Rising Disposable Incomes and Aspirational Middle Class: The growing middle class in developing nations, characterized by rising disposable incomes and an aspirational lifestyle, is driving demand for smart home solutions. According to a report published by the Brookings Institution, middle class in country like India is expected to grow to 475 million people by 2030, making it one of the largest consumer markets in the world. As more people in India move up the economic ladder, there is an increasing willingness to invest in technologies that enhance convenience, comfort, and security. AIoT-enabled smart home devices, such as smart thermostats, lighting systems, and security cameras, are becoming more accessible and affordable, making them attractive to middle-class consumers.

Government Support and Policy Initiatives: The government has been proactive and aggressively promoting the adoption of advanced technologies, including AI and IoT in developing countries including India. Initiatives such as the National Digital

Communications Policy (NDCP) 2018 and the Draft IoT Policy aim to create a conducive ecosystem for the growth of AIoT in India[8]. Additionally, the government's focus on digital transformation and the promotion of Make in India initiatives are expected to boost the domestic manufacturing of AIoT devices, making them more affordable and accessible to Indian consumers. The government's push for digital India and the development of smart infrastructure are also expected to drive the adoption of AIoT in smart homes.

Growing Awareness of Energy Efficiency and Sustainability: With rapid increase in the use of social media, the awareness of environmental issues and the need for sustainable living, consumers are becoming more conscious of their energy consumption. According to a report by the International Energy Agency (IEA), energy demand in India is expected to double by 2040[9], making energy efficiency a critical concern. Smart home-small-small-small-style solutions can play a crucial role in promoting energy efficiency by optimizing the use of electricity, water, and other resources. For instance, smart thermostats can adjust heating and cooling based on occupancy, while smart lighting systems can automatically turn off when rooms are unoccupied. These features not only reduce energy consumption but also lead to cost savings for homeowners.

Challenges to AIoT Enabled Smart Homes and a Way Out

Despite the promising growth prospects, the adoption of AIoT enabled smart homes in developing countries (for instance, India) faces several challenges that need to be addressed to unlock its full potential. Patel et al. (2016) pointed out that the major obstacles to adopting AIoT devices include expensive costs, low public awareness, and insufficient infrastructure, particularly in rural regions. Nevertheless, efforts like the Digital India and Smart Cities Mission are anticipated to fuel growth in the industry.

High Initial Costs: One of the primary barriers to the adoption of AIoT-enabled smart home solutions is the high initial cost. While the prices of AIoT devices have been declining, they are still relatively expensive for the average consumer in developing nations. According to a report, the average cost of a smart home system in India ranges from INR 20,000 to INR 1,00,000, depending on the complexity and features[10]. The cost of installing and maintaining smart home systems can be prohibitive, particularly for middle-income group and lower-income group households. To overcome this challenge, manufacturers and service providers need to focus on offering affordable and scalable solutions that cater to the diverse needs of consumers in developing nations.

Lack of Awareness and Technical Knowledge: Despite the growing popularity of smart home technologies, there is still a lack of awareness and technical knowledge among consumers of developing nations. Many people are unfamiliar with the benefits of AIoT and how it can enhance their daily lives. Additionally, the complexity of setting up and managing smart home systems can be intimidating for non-tech-savvy users. According to a survey by Deloitte, only 25% of Indian consumers are aware of smart home technologies, and even fewer understand how to use them effectively[11]. To address this issue, there is a need for extensive consumer education and awareness campaigns to highlight the advantages of AIoT and provide guidance on its usage.

Data Privacy and Security Concerns: The proliferation of AIoT devices in smart homes raises significant concerns about data privacy and security. AIoT devices collect and transmit vast amounts of personal data, making them vulnerable to cyberattacks and data breaches. In India, where data protection laws are still evolving, consumers are increasingly concerned about the safety of their personal information. According to a report by NortonLifeLock, 70% of consumers in developing nations are worried about the security of their smart home devices[12]. To build trust and encourage adoption, AIoT manufacturers and service providers must prioritize data security and implement robust encryption and authentication mechanisms.

Interoperability Issues: The lack of standardization and interoperability among AIoT devices is another challenge that hinders the seamless integration of smart home solutions. Different manufacturers often use proprietary protocols and platforms, making it difficult for devices from different brands to communicate with each other. This fragmentation can lead to a poor user experience and limit the functionality of smart home systems. According to a report by McKinsey, interoperability issues are one of the top barriers to the adoption of IoT technologies globally[13]. To address this issue, industry stakeholders need to collaborate on developing common standards and protocols that ensure interoperability across devices and platforms.

Infrastructure Limitations: While developing nations have made giant strides in improving its digital infrastructure, there are still gaps that need to be addressed to support the widespread adoption of AIoT in smart homes. Issues such as inconsistent internet connectivity, power outages, and limited broadband penetration in rural areas can hinder the performance of AIoT devices. According to the World Bank, only 34% of India's rural population has access to the internet, compared to 70% in urban areas. To overcome these challenges, there is a need for continued investment in digital infrastructure, including the expansion of high-speed internet and the development of reliable power supply systems.

Available Opportunities for AIoT Enabled Smart Homes: A Case Study of India

Despite the challenges, the Indian market presents numerous opportunities for the growth of AIoT in smart homes. These opportunities are driven by the unique characteristics of the Indian consumer base, the evolving technology landscape, and the supportive policy environment.

Customized Solutions for Consumers: The Indian market is highly diverse, with different needs and preferences across different regions and income groups. This diversity presents an opportunity for AIoT manufacturers and service providers to develop customized solutions that cater to the specific requirements of Indian consumers. For instance, smart home solutions that are designed to operate in low-bandwidth environments or are equipped with multilingual interfaces can appeal to a broader audience. Additionally, offering flexible pricing models, such as subscription-based services, can make AIoT-enabled smart home solutions more accessible to middle- and lower-income households.

Integration with Renewable Energy Solutions: India is making significant strides in the adoption of renewable energy sources, such as solar power. According to the Ministry of New and Renewable Energy (MNRE), India's installed solar capacity reached 70.10 GW in 2023, with a target of 100 GW by 2025[14]. AIoT can play a crucial role in optimizing the use of renewable energy in smart homes. For example, AIoT-enabled energy management systems can monitor energy consumption patterns and automatically adjust the use of solar power to maximize efficiency. This integration can not only reduce energy costs for homeowners but also contribute to India's broader sustainability goals.

Partnerships with Real Estate Developers: The Indian real estate sector is witnessing a significant surge in demand for smart homes, particularly in urban areas. Real estate developers are increasingly incorporating smart home technologies into their projects to attract tech-savvy buyers. According to "India Smart Home Market Outlook, 2026" report, the demand for smart homes in India is expected to grow at a CAGR of 35% between 2021 and 2026[15]. This trend presents an opportunity for AIoT manufacturers and service providers to collaborate with real estate developers to integrate AIoT solutions into new residential projects. Such partnerships can help drive the adoption of AIoT in smart homes and create a competitive advantage for developers.

Expansion of E-commerce Platforms: The significant growth of e-commerce in India has made it easier for consumers to access a wide range of products, including AIoT-enabled smart home devices. E-commerce platforms such as Amazon, Flipkart, and Tata Cliq are increasingly offering smart home products, making them more accessible to Indian consumers. According to a report by IBEF, India's e-commerce market is expected to reach USD 200 billion by 2026, driven by the increasing penetration of internet and smartphones[16]. Additionally, the availability of customer reviews, product comparisons, and online tutorials on these platforms can help educate consumers and drive adoption.

Emergence of Local Startups and Innovators: India's vibrant startup ecosystem is playing a key role in driving innovation in the AIoT space. Several Indian startups are developing innovative smart home solutions that are tailored to the needs of Indian consumers. These startups are leveraging AI and IoT technologies to create affordable, user-friendly, and energy-efficient smart home devices. According to NASSCOM, India is home to over 1,000 IoT startups, with a significant focus on smart home solutions[17]. The emergence of local innovators is not only driving competition but also fostering a culture of innovation that can accelerate the adoption of AIoT in smart homes.

Risks of AIoT-Enabled Smart Homes

Benefits aside, AIoT-enabled smart homes face significant risks. One of these is security and privacy risk. Data breach may be a kind of security and privacy risk which AIoT enabled homes may face. Due to interconnectivity, smart appliances become a quick point of entry for cyber-attacks, which in turn means data breaches and unauthorized access (Santhi et al., 2024). A hacker can seize a weak point in a smart thermostat that gains access into the home's Wi-Fi network and all connected appliances (ibid.). Another challenge is the attack by a malware. Smart devices can catch malware, so hackers can take control of them and then force them to do malicious actions (Sasi et al., 2024) For example, a malicious app used in a smart speaker could be exploited to eavesdrop on conversations or to launch attacks on other devices. Privacy issues are one of the major concerns in AIoT enabled smart homes. The collection and sharing of data by smart devices raise some concerns about their privacy since data is not always safe, especially people (Gowda et al., 2024). AIoT-enabled smart homes depend hugely on continuous data collection in order to function effectively. Devices such as smart thermostats, security cameras, and voice assistants gather loads and loads of data about user behavior, preferences, and daily routines. On one hand this data improves device functionality, but it also raises serious privacy concerns (Yan, 2024). For example, a smart home hub device may collect habits and preferences data from the consumer and sell it to third parties without letting the owner know (ibid.). Another significant security and privacy risk could be of surveillance (Bugeja et al., 2021). All the cameras and sensors mounted in these intelligent homes tend to pose a risk of surveillance, which may result in violated rights of privacy. For instance, a home security system may videotape visitors without their knowledge or consent (Bugeja et al., 2021).

Next, the data collected by smart home devices is frequently shared with third parties, such as device manufacturers, service providers, and advertisers. This sharing can lead to severe consequences, such as targeted advertising or data breaches (Buil-Gil et al., 2023). Further, the constant monitoring capabilities of AIoT devices can be exploited for surveillance by malicious actors or even governments, raising concerns about the misuse of personal data and the erosion of privacy (Tawalbeh et al., 2020).

Beyond digital threats, AIoT-enabled smart homes also face physical security risks. Hackers who gain control of smart locks or security cameras by any means can potentially gain physical access to a home, endangering the safety of residents. Cybercriminals can manipulate smart home devices to cause physical harm (Vardakis et al., 2024). For example, they could tamper with a smart thermostat to create unsafe living conditions or disable a smoke detector. Some hackers may use ransomware to lock out or lock in homeowners in their smart home systems, demanding payment to restore access. This can leave homeowners without control over critical systems, such as heating, cooling, or security (ibid.). One of the most common and significant risks facing AIoT-enabled smart homes is the lack of standardization across devices and platforms. This lack of standardization leads to interoperability issues, resulting in difficulty for homeowners to integrate different devices into a cohesive smart home ecosystem (Gowda et al., 2024). Interoperability could be in the form of device fragmentation. Different platforms and devices within the smart sphere of influence will not integrate well. For example, a thermostat from one manufacturer will not work with another's speaker (Albouq et al., 2022).

Regular software and firmware updates are most essential to maintain the security and functionality of smart home devices (Wijesundara et al., 2024). However, managing these updates can be challenging. Different devices may receive updates at different times, leading to inconsistencies in performance and security (Catuogno & Galdi, 2023). Some devices may stop receiving updates altogether, leaving them vulnerable to security threats. Updates to one device may cause compatibility issues with other devices in the smart home ecosystem, leading to reduced functionality or system failures (Raghu et al., 2025). For example, a gadget using a Zigbee protocol would not be compatible with another device using a Z-Wave protocol (Danbatta, & Varol, 2019).

AI algorithms used in AIoT-enabled smart homes can be subject to bias, leading to discriminatory outcomes including AI algorithms are only as efficient as the data they are trained on. If the training data is biased, the algorithms may produce biased results (Belenguer, 2022). For example, a smart home security system that uses facial recognition may be less accurate for certain demographic groups, leading to unfair treatment (Ferrara, 2023). Bias in AI algorithms can result in discriminatory practices, such as denying access to certain individuals or providing suboptimal service based on demographic factors. This raises ethical concerns about fairness and equality in smart home technology (Nazer et al., 2023).

The increasing automation of smart homes raises questions about the balance between convenience and user autonomy. This could be over-reliance on automation. As smart homes become more automated, homeowners may become overly reliant on AIoT devices to manage their daily lives (Gøthesen et al., 2023). This can lead to a loss of personal autonomy and a reduced ability to make independent decisions. The automation of critical systems, such as security and heating, can cause situations where human oversight is lacking. This can be problematic if the AIoT system makes an incorrect decision or fails to respond appropriately to a situation (Awaisi et al., 2024). AIoT devices may be required to make ethical decisions, such as prioritizing the safety of certain individuals over others in an emergency (Jnr, 2024). This raises complex ethical questions about how these decisions should be made and who should be held accountable.

Further, the production and operation of AIoT-enabled smart homes have significant environmental implications like e-Waste (Thapliyal et al., 2024). The rapid pace of technological advancement leads to frequent device upgrades, resulting in increased electronic waste. Many smart home devices are not designed for easy recycling, exacerbating the problem. Smart home devices, particularly those that operate continuously, consume significant amounts of energy. This can contribute to higher carbon footprints, especially if the energy is sourced from non-renewable resources (Stolojescu-Crisan et al., 2021). Last, the production of smart home devices requires the extraction of rare earth metals and other finite resources, which can have long-term environmental consequences (Balram, 2019).

CONCLUSION

AIoT enabled smart homes are offering unmatched security, comfort, and energy efficiency. These homes integrate AI with IoT, allowing interconnected devices to not only automate everyday tasks but also make smart decisions based on user preferences, behaviors, and external factors. AIoT systems can anticipate needs, optimize resource use, and enhance security by processing real-time data, shaping the future of residential living. In terms of security, AIoT systems provide advanced protection through AI-driven surveillance, motion detection, and facial recognition, offering proactive defense against unauthorized access and threats. The integration of AI and IoT also ensures personalized comfort, as devices can adjust lighting, temperature, and entertainment systems based on individual preferences. This level of automation changes how people interact with their homes, making life easier, more interactive, and enjoyable. One of the key advantages of AIoT smart homes is their ability to improve energy efficiency. AI-based thermostats, lighting, and energy meters monitor and regulate energy use, helping homeowners meet sustainability goals while reducing their carbon footprint. With increasing global focus on climate change, AIoT technology offers a powerful solution for creating eco-friendly, energy-efficient homes. Despite these benefits, challenges such as data privacy concerns, compatibility issues, and the cost of implementation remain. However, as AI and IoT technologies continue to evolve, these challenges are expected to be addressed, making smart home solutions more accessible and secure.

In summary, AIoT-enabled smart homes are transforming residential living by offering solutions for enhanced security, comfort, and energy efficiency. These homes will be more intuitive, sustainable, and responsive to the needs of future generations. Looking ahead, the future of smart homes in India is clear. The combination of traditional values with modern technology will create homes that are smarter and better suited to the needs of their residents. There will be a strong focus on sustainability, comfort, and efficiency, leading to a new era of home design that is both innovative and environmentally friendly. In addition, the growing importance of security and privacy, driven by advancements in biometric and surveillance technology, means that future smart homes will provide safety in both physical and digital ways. This balanced approach to home automation, blending advanced technology with user-centered design, will transform the idea of luxury living in India.

REFERENCES

Afzal, M. K., Zikria, Y. B., Mumtaz, S., Rayes, A., Al-Dulaimi, A., & Guizani, M. (2018). Unlocking 5G spectrum potential for intelligent IoT: Opportunities, challenges, and solutions. *IEEE Communications Magazine*, *56*(10), 92–93. DOI: 10.1109/MCOM.2018.8493125

Ahvar, E., Ahvar, S., & Lee, G. M. (2023). Artificial Intelligence of Things: Architectures, Applications, and Challenges. *Springer Handbook of Internet of Things*, 443-462.

Albouq, S. S., Abi Sen, A. A., Almashf, N., Yamin, M., Alshanqiti, A., & Bahbouh, N. M. (2022). A survey of interoperability challenges and solutions for dealing with them in IoT environment. *IEEE Access : Practical Innovations, Open Solutions*, *10*, 36416–36428. DOI: 10.1109/ACCESS.2022.3162219

Ali, Z. H., Ali, H. A., & Badawy, M. M. (2015). Internet of Things (IoT): Definitions, challenges and recent research directions. *International Journal of Computer Applications*, *128*(1), 37–47. DOI: 10.5120/ijca2015906430

Anubha, A., & Shome, S. (2021). Intentions to use travel eWOM: Mediating role of Indian urban millennials' attitude. *International Journal of Tourism Cities*, *7*(3), 640–661. DOI: 10.1108/IJTC-04-2020-0073

Aouedi, O., Vu, T. H., Sacco, A., Nguyen, D. C., Piamrat, K., Marchetto, G., & Pham, Q. V. (2024). A survey on intelligent Internet of Things: Applications, security, privacy, and future directions. *IEEE Communications Surveys and Tutorials*, 1. DOI: 10.1109/COMST.2024.3430368

Aslam, A., Qureshi, K. N., & Newe, T. (2024). Future Privacy and Trust Challenges for AIoT Networks. In *Artificial Intelligence of Things (AIoT)* (pp. 198–216). CRC Press. DOI: 10.1201/9781003430018-14

Awaisi, K. S., Ye, Q., & Sampalli, S. (2024). A Survey of Industrial AIoT: Opportunities, Challenges, and Directions. *IEEE Access : Practical Innovations, Open Solutions*, *12*, 96946–96996. DOI: 10.1109/ACCESS.2024.3426279

Baker, S., & Xiang, W. (2023). Artificial intelligence of things for smarter healthcare: A survey of advancements, challenges, and opportunities. *IEEE Communications Surveys and Tutorials*, *25*(2), 1261–1293. DOI: 10.1109/COMST.2023.3256323

Balaram, V. (2019). Rare earth elements: A review of applications, occurrence, exploration, analysis, recycling, and environmental impact. *Geoscience Frontiers*, *10*(4), 1285–1303. DOI: 10.1016/j.gsf.2018.12.005

Belenguer, L. (2022). AI bias: Exploring discriminatory algorithmic decision-making models and the application of possible machine-centric solutions adapted from the pharmaceutical industry. *AI and Ethics*, *2*(4), 771–787. DOI: 10.1007/s43681-022-00138-8 PMID: 35194591

Bender, E. M., Gebru, T., McMillan-Major, A., & Shmitchell, S. (2021, March). On the dangers of stochastic parrots: Can language models be too big? In *Proceedings of the 2021 ACM conference on fairness, accountability, and transparency* (pp. 610-623). DOI: 10.1145/3442188.3445922

Bugeja, J., Jacobsson, A., & Davidsson, P. (2021). PRASH: A framework for privacy risk analysis of smart homes. *Sensors (Basel)*, *21*(19), 6399. DOI: 10.3390/s21196399 PMID: 34640718

Buil-Gil, D., Kemp, S., Kuenzel, S., Coventry, L., Zakhary, S., Tilley, D., & Nicholson, J. (2023). The digital harms of smart home devices: A systematic literature review. *Computers in Human Behavior*, *145*, 107770. DOI: 10.1016/j.chb.2023.107770

Catuogno, L., & Galdi, C. (2023). Secure Firmware Update: Challenges and Solutions. *Cryptography*, *7*(2), 30. DOI: 10.3390/cryptography7020030

Chui, M., Yee, L., Hall, B., & Singla, A. (2023). The state of AI in 2023: Generative AI's breakout year.

Danbatta, S. J., & Varol, A. (2019). Comparison of Zigbee, Z-Wave, Wi-Fi, and bluetooth wireless technologies used in home automation. In *2019 7th International Symposium on Digital Forensics and Security (ISDFS)* (pp. 1-5). IEEE.

Dia, I., Ahvar, E., & Lee, G. M. (2022). Performance evaluation of machine learning and neural network-based algorithms for predicting segment availability in AIoT-based smart parking. *Network (Bristol, England)*, *2*(2), 225–238.

Dong, Y. (2020, November). Research on Logistics Talents Cultivation Strategy Against the Background of Artificial Intelligence and Internet of Things. In *2020 Conference on Education, Language and Inter-cultural Communication (ELIC 2020)* (pp. 1-6). Atlantis Press. DOI: 10.2991/assehr.k.201127.001

Espina-Romero, L., Gutiérrez Hurtado, H., Ríos Parra, D., Vilchez Pirela, R. A., Talavera-Aguirre, R., & Ochoa-Díaz, A. (2024). Challenges and Opportunities in the Implementation of AI in Manufacturing: A Bibliometric Analysis. *Sci*, *6*(4), 60. DOI: 10.3390/sci6040060

Ferrara, E. (2023). Fairness and bias in artificial intelligence: A brief survey of sources, impacts, and mitigation strategies. *Sci*, *6*(1), 3. DOI: 10.3390/sci6010003

Forbes (2023). Investment Trends in the Smart Home Industry. Retrieved from Forbes https://www.forbes.com/home-improvement/internet/smart-home-tech-trends/

Gartner. (2023). Top Strategic Technology Trends for 2023. Retrieved from Gartner https://www.gartner.com/en/articles/gartner-top-10-strategic-technology-trends-for-2023

Gøthesen, S., Haddara, M., & Kumar, K. N. (2023). Empowering homes with intelligence: An investigation of smart home technology adoption and usage. *Internet of Things : Engineering Cyber Physical Human Systems*, *24*, 100944. DOI: 10.1016/j.iot.2023.100944

Gowda, V. D., Kaur, M., Srinivas, D., Prasad, K. D. V., & Shekhar, R. (2024). AIoT Integration Advancements and Challenges in Smart Sensing Technologies for Smart Devices. In *AIoT and Smart Sensing Technologies for Smart Devices* (pp. 42–65). IGI Global. DOI: 10.4018/979-8-3693-0786-1.ch003

Grandview Research Report (2024). Smart Home Market Size, Share and Trends Report, 2030. Available at: https://www.grandviewresearch.com/industry-analysis/smart-homes-industry

Guha, A., Grewal, D., Kopalle, P. K., Haenlein, M., Schneider, M. J., Jung, H., Moustafa, R., Hegde, D. R., & Hawkins, G. (2021). How artificial intelligence will affect the future of retailing. *Journal of Retailing*, *97*(1), 28–41. DOI: 10.1016/j.jretai.2021.01.005

Haenlein, M., Kaplan, A., Tan, C. W., & Zhang, P. (2019). Artificial intelligence (AI) and management analytics. *Journal of Management Analytics*, *6*(4), 341–343. DOI: 10.1080/23270012.2019.1699876

Hao J. (2021). Outlook for the Future of the Internet of Things in the 5G Era. Application of Microcontrollers and Embedded Systems. 21 (7).

Hojlo, J. (2021). Future of Industry Ecosystems: Shared Data and Insights. Available at: https://blogs.idc.com/2021/01/06/future-of-industry-ecosystems-shared-data-and-insights/

Jnr, B. A. (2024). Artificial Intelligence of Things and Distributed Technologies as Enablers for Intelligent Mobility Services in Smart Cities-A Survey. *Internet of Things : Engineering Cyber Physical Human Systems*, •••, 101399.

Kaplan, A. (2022). Social Media Powered by Artificial Intelligence, Violence and Nonviolence. In Encyclopedia of Violence, Peace, & Conflict (Third Edition).

Kaplan, A., & Haenlein, M. (2019). Siri, Siri, in my hand: Who's the fairest in the land? On the interpretations, illustrations, and implications of artificial intelligence. *Business Horizons*, *62*(1), 15–25. DOI: 10.1016/j.bushor.2018.08.004

Khan, N., & Gupta, K. (2022, October). IOT: Applications, Challenges and Latest Trends. In *2022 1st IEEE International Conference on Industrial Electronics: Developments & Applications (ICIDeA)* (pp. 181-186). IEEE.

Kumar, S., Tiwari, P., & Zymbler, M. (2019). Internet of Things is a revolutionary approach for future technology enhancement: A review. *Journal of Big Data*, *6*(1), 1–21. DOI: 10.1186/s40537-019-0268-2

Li, S., Xu, L. D., & Zhao, S. (2015). The internet of things: A survey. *Information Systems Frontiers*, *17*(2), 243–259. DOI: 10.1007/s10796-014-9492-7

Li, Y., Zuo, Y., Song, H., & Lv, Z. (2021). Deep learning in security of internet of things. *IEEE Internet of Things Journal*, *9*(22), 22133–22146. DOI: 10.1109/JIOT.2021.3106898

Markets and Markets. (2022). Smart Home Market - Global Forecast to 2027. Retrieved from Markets and Markets https://www.marketsandmarkets.com/Market-Reports/european-smart-homes-market-1290.html

Matin, A., Islam, M. R., Wang, X., Huo, H., & Xu, G. (2023). AIoT for sustainable manufacturing: Overview, challenges, and opportunities. *Internet of Things : Engineering Cyber Physical Human Systems*, *24*, 100901. DOI: 10.1016/j.iot.2023.100901

McKinsey. (2024). What is AI (artificial intelligence)? Available at: https://www.mckinsey.com/featured-insights/mckinsey-explainers/what-is-ai

Mishra, N., & Pandya, S. (2021). Internet of things applications, security challenges, attacks, intrusion detection, and future visions: A systematic review. *IEEE Access : Practical Innovations, Open Solutions*, *9*, 59353–59377. DOI: 10.1109/ACCESS.2021.3073408

Mouha, R. A. R. A. (2021). Internet of things (IoT). *Journal of Data Analysis and Information Processing*, *9*(02), 77–101. DOI: 10.4236/jdaip.2021.92006

Muhammed, D., Ahvar, E., Ahvar, S., Trocan, M., Montpetit, M. J., & Ehsani, R. (2024). Artificial Intelligence of Things (AIoT) for smart agriculture: A review of architectures, technologies and solutions. *Journal of Network and Computer Applications*, *228*, 103905. DOI: 10.1016/j.jnca.2024.103905

Nazarevich, D. (2023). AI and IoT at the crossroads: the rise of AIoT and its impact on the future. Available at: https://innowise.com/blog/artificial-intelligence-of-things/

Nazer, L. H., Zatarah, R., Waldrip, S., Ke, J. X. C., Moukheiber, M., Khanna, A. K., Hicklen, R. S., Moukheiber, L., Moukheiber, D., Ma, H., & Mathur, P. (2023). Bias in artificial intelligence algorithms and recommendations for mitigation. *PLOS Digital Health, 2*(6), e0000278. DOI: 10.1371/journal.pdig.0000278 PMID: 37347721

Nguyen, D. C., Ding, M., Pathirana, P. N., Seneviratne, A., Li, J., Niyato, D., Dobre, O., & Poor, H. V. (2021). 6G Internet of Things: A comprehensive survey. *IEEE Internet of Things Journal, 9*(1), 359–383. DOI: 10.1109/JIOT.2021.3103320

Parihar, V., & Malik, A. Bhawna, Bhushan, B., & Chaganti, R. (2023). From smart devices to smarter systems: the evolution of artificial intelligence of things (AIoT) with characteristics, architecture, use cases and challenges. In AI models for blockchain-based intelligent networks in IoT systems: Concepts, methodologies, tools, and applications (pp. 1-28). Cham: Springer International Publishing.

Patel, K. K., Patel, S. M., & Scholar, P. (2016). Internet of things-IOT: definition, characteristics, architecture, enabling technologies, application & future challenges. *International journal of engineering science and computing, 6*(5).

Qi, W., Xu, X., Qian, K., Schuller, B. W., Fortino, G., & Aliverti, A. (2024). A Review of AIoT-based Human Activity Recognition: From Application to Technique. *IEEE Journal of Biomedical and Health Informatics*. PMID: 38809724

Raghu, N., Mahesh, T. R., Vivek, V., Kumaran, S. Y., Kannanugo, N., & Vishwanatha, S. (2025). IoT-Enabled Safety and Secure Smart Homes for Elderly People. In *Future of Digital Technology and AI in Social Sectors* (pp. 297–328). IGI Global.

Sadhu, P. K., Yanambaka, V. P., & Abdelgawad, A. (2022). Internet of things: Security and solutions survey. *Sensors (Basel), 22*(19), 7433. DOI: 10.3390/s22197433 PMID: 36236531

Santhi, V., Sabareesh, Y. N. S., Sudheer, P. P., & Krishna, V. P. S. (2024). Trends and Challenges in AIoT Implementation for Smart Home, Smart Buildings, and Smart Cities in Cloud Platforms. *Artificial Intelligence of Things (AIoT) for Productivity and Organizational Transition*, 240-319.

Sasi, T., Lashkari, A. H., Lu, R., Xiong, P., & Iqbal, S. (2024). A comprehensive survey on IoT attacks: Taxonomy, detection mechanisms and challenges. *Journal of Information and intelligence, 2*(6), 455-513.

Shafique, K., Khawaja, B. A., Sabir, F., Qazi, S., & Mustaqim, M. (2020). Internet of things (IoT) for next-generation smart systems: A review of current challenges, future trends and prospects for emerging 5G-IoT scenarios. *IEEE Access : Practical Innovations, Open Solutions, 8*, 23022–23040. DOI: 10.1109/ACCESS.2020.2970118

Sharma, S. (2024). Benefits or concerns of AI: A multistakeholder responsibility. *Futures*, *157*, 103328. DOI: 10.1016/j.futures.2024.103328

Singh, A., Kapoor, D., & Bose, R. (2021). Enhancing Home Security Using AIoT: A Case Study of Indian Households. *Indian Journal of Technology and Engineering*, *27*(3), 145–160.

Soori, M., Arezoo, B., & Dastres, R. (2023). Internet of things for smart factories in industry 4.0, a review. *Internet of Things and Cyber-Physical Systems*, *3*, 192–204. DOI: 10.1016/j.iotcps.2023.04.006

Statista (2016). Internet of Things (IoT) connected devices installed base worldwide from 2015 to 2025. Available at: https://www.statista.com/statistics/471264/iot-number-of-connected-devices-worldwide/

Statista (2023a). Smart Home – India. Available at: https://www.statista.com/outlook/cmo/smart-home/india

Statista. (2023b). Consumer Interest in Smart Home Solutions. Retrieved from Statista https://www.statista.com/statistics/1130403/smart-home-revenue-distribution-forecast-in-north-america-by-segment/

Stolojescu-Crisan, C., Crisan, C., & Butunoi, B. P. (2021). An IoT-based smart home automation system. *Sensors (Basel)*, *21*(11), 3784. DOI: 10.3390/s21113784 PMID: 34070717

Susan, J., Subashini, P., & Krishnaveni, M. (2023). Artificial Intelligence of Things for Smart Healthcare Development: An Experimental Review. *Handbook of Research on Deep Learning Techniques for Cloud-Based Industrial IoT*, 29-60.

Tariq, M. U. (2025). *AI-Driven Learning and Engagement in Higher Education*. IGI Global., DOI: 10.4018/979-8-3693-4074-5

Tariq, M. U. (2025). Smart Forecasting With AI: Revolutionizing Energy Consumption and Storage. In Derbali, A. (Ed.), *Integrating Artificial Intelligence Into the Energy Sector* (pp. 165–184). IGI Global Scientific Publishing., DOI: 10.4018/979-8-3693-7112-1.ch009

Tariq, M. U. (2025). Bridging Cultures and Languages: Innovative Literacy Strategies for Inclusive and Engaged Classrooms. In Tussey, J., & Haas, L. (Eds.), *Supporting Cultural Differences Through Literacy Education* (pp. 257–282). IGI Global Scientific Publishing., DOI: 10.4018/979-8-3693-9271-3.ch010

Tariq, M. U. (2025). Innovative Business Models: Integrating Social, Economic, and Environmental Goals in Rural Manufacturing. In Prabhakar, A., Yu, P., & Erokhin, V. (Eds.), *Rural Social Entrepreneurship Development: Network-Based Manufacturing System Model* (pp. 147–174). IGI Global Scientific Publishing., DOI: 10.4018/979-8-3693-7515-0.ch005

Tariq, M. U., & Sergio, R. (Eds.). (2025). *Convergence of AI, Education, and Business for Sustainability*. IGI Global. DOI: 10.4018/979-8-3373-1917-9

Tawalbeh, L. A., Muheidat, F., Tawalbeh, M., & Quwaider, M. (2020). IoT Privacy and security: Challenges and solutions. *Applied Sciences (Basel, Switzerland)*, *10*(12), 4102. DOI: 10.3390/app10124102

Thapliyal, S., Wazid, M., Singh, D. P., Chauhan, R., Mishra, A. K., & Das, A. K. (2024). Secure Artificial Intelligence of Things (AIoT)-enabled authenticated key agreement technique for smart living environment. *Computers & Electrical Engineering*, *118*, 109353. DOI: 10.1016/j.compeleceng.2024.109353

Vardakis, G., Hatzivasilis, G., Koutsaki, E., & Papadakis, N. (2024). Review of Smart-Home Security Using the Internet of Things. *Electronics (Basel)*, *13*(16), 3343. DOI: 10.3390/electronics13163343

Varghese, J. E. E. N. A., Vargheese, S. K., & Peter, E. L. D. H. O. (2020). A study on artificial intelligence of things: Techniques and applications. *A Journal of Composition Theory*, *8*(3), 888-896.

Vermesan, O., & Friess, P. (2014). *Internet of things applications-from research and innovation to market deployment*. Taylor & Francis.

Wei, Z., Zhu, M., Zhang, N., Wang, L., Zou, Y., Meng, Z., Wu, H., & Feng, Z. (2022). UAV-assisted data collection for Internet of Things: A survey. *IEEE Internet of Things Journal*, *9*(17), 15460–15483. DOI: 10.1109/JIOT.2022.3176903

Wijesundara, W. M. A. B., Lee, J. S., Tith, D., Aloupogianni, E., Suzuki, H., & Obi, T. (2024). Security-enhanced firmware management scheme for smart home IoT devices using distributed ledger technologies. *International Journal of Information Security*, *23*(3), 1–11. DOI: 10.1007/s10207-024-00827-x

Yadav, V. (2024). The future of smart homes: Trends and predictions for the next decade India. Available at: https://etedge-insights.com/technology/innovation/the-future-of-smart-homes-trends-and-predictions-for-the-next-decade-india/

Yan, J. (2024). AIoT in Smart Homes: Challenges, Strategic Solutions, and Future Directions. *Highlights in Science. Engineering and Technology*, *87*, 59–65.

Zhang, F., Pan, Z., & Lu, Y. (2023). AIoT-enabled smart surveillance for personal data digitalization: Contextual personalization-privacy paradox in smart home. *Information & Management*, *60*(2), 103736. DOI: 10.1016/j.im.2022.103736

KEY TERMS AND DEFINITIONS

Artificial Intelligence: Artificial intelligence (AI) refers to computer systems that are capable to perform complex tasks that historically only a human could do".

Internet of Things: Internet of Things (IoT) refers to an internet-connected network of gadgets that can "communicate" with one another.

Artificial Internet of Things: Artificial Intelligence of Things (AIoT) is the integration of AI) with IoT, enabling devices to not only collect and transmit data but also to analyze and act on that data autonomously.

Smart Home: It is a convenient home setup where devices and appliances can be controlled remotely and automatically from anywhere with an internet connection

ENDNOTES

1 https://www.jiovio.com/

2 https://www.prnewswire.com/news-releases/new-survey-finds-70-of-consumers-improved-home-during-covid-19-more-than-half-used-smart-devices-301201817.html

3 https://www.amazon.in/gp/help/customer/display.html?nodeId=GHRYQ6GHE4A5TUD2

4 https://www.amazon.in/Nest-Thermostat-Generation-Stainless-Compatible/dp/B0131RG6VK

5 https://www.ecobee.com/en-us/

6 https://pib.gov.in/PressReleasePage.aspx?PRID=2085711#:~:text=Smart%20Cities%20Mission%20in%20a,robust%20infrastructure%2C%20and%20sustainable%20solutions.

7 https://www.trai.gov.in/sites/default/files/2024-12/PR_No.94of2024.pdf

8 https://www.meity.gov.in/writereaddata/files/National_Digital_Communications_Policy%E2%80%932018.pdf

9 https://www.pv-magazine-india.com/2018/11/13/indias-energy-demand-will-more-than-double-by-2040-iea/

10 https://houssed.com/blog/home-decor/home-automation-costs

11 https://www2.deloitte.com/us/en/insights/industry/telecommunications/connectivity-mobile-trends-survey/2023/smart-home-industry-adoption-trend.html

12 https://www.crn.in/news/annual-nortonlifelock-cyber-safety-insights-report-finds-almost-4-in-10-indian-adults-experienced-identity-theft/

13 https://www.rinf.tech/interoperability-challenges-in-iot-and-how-to-solve-them/#:~:text=Lack%20of%20Standardization&text=A%20study%20by%20McKinsey%20highlighted,enable%20a%20seamless%20IoT%20ecosystem.

14 https://mnre.gov.in/en/solar-overview/

15 https://www.researchandmarkets.com/reports/5521845/india-smart-home-market-outlook-2026?srsltid=AfmBOooBuj3DpZA9Qmq40p0OH1zSGoyOjCD7F0uyamauCh2BvqXRxthR

16 https://www.ibef.org/research/case-study/india-s-e-commerce-market-to-grow-30-to-200-billion-by-2026-morgan-stanley

17 https://nasscom.in/product/171

Chapter 9
AIoT in Healthcare and Remote Monitoring:
A Case Study

Anuska Dutta
Brainwre University, India

Diya Biswas
Brainware University, India

Piyal Roy
https://orcid.org/0009-0007-5378-2789
Brainware University, India

Shivnath Ghosh
https://orcid.org/0000-0001-7368-7139
Brainwre University, India

Saptarshi Kumar Sarkar
https://orcid.org/0009-0004-1786-8284
Brainwre University, India

ABSTRACT

Integration of AI and IoT has contributed a lot to improve healthcare and real-time patient monitoring and predictive analysis of patients' health. This chapter focuses on AI and IoT-based telehealth devices that assess essential health parameters from a distance thus improving quality of the patient care and minimizing the risks of spreading diseases. These systems are intelligently implemented by cloud computing and machine learning and they foresee health anomalies and help in treatment plans. One of the innovations reported is the CNN for screening the arrhythmias

DOI: 10.4018/979-8-3693-8547-0.ch009

in wearable devices while the athletes are in action to offer real-time results with a high level of precision. The chapter also explores transition from conventional methods of aircraft health monitoring towards the AIoT systems that employ real-time data in the maintenance as well as safety enhancements. The prospect of the use of AI is revealed with focus on its utilization in the identification of hazardous compounds and consideration of the health of the environment.

INTRODUCTION

The objective behind this remote patient monitoring system is to construct a healthcare system that is more effective, efficient, and easily accessible to a larger population. Rapid sickness detection and accurate disease prediction are made possible by Artificial Intelligence (AI) and the Internet of Things. The primary goal of implementing AIOT for remote patient monitoring is to provide us with precise early warning signs for numerous serious illnesses, such as cancer and heart disease so that we can treat them effectively. Due to a dearth of doctors in some underdeveloped nations, care is not given appropriately because of time constraints. Patients and the elderly find it extremely difficult to keep appointments and receive the proper care from doctors when they have this illness. The prohibition on seeking medical attention during the pandemic is another issue (Prakash et al., 2024). When Patient care is integrated into AIoT in contemporary healthcare. Since the start of the pandemic, Key components that have garnered significant interest and traction include telemedicine and remote patient monitoring (RPM). RPM and telehealth make patient data easily accessible, contributing to the delivery of high-quality care at a lower cost. A model developed using machine learning is employed in the design of an Internet of Things (IoT)- equipped health surveillance device to monitor a patient's vital signs, such as body temperature and heart rate, as well as their behaviors, including jogging, running, sleeping, and exercising. This demonstrates how AIOT, by highlighting the importance of early identification, particularly for serious illnesses, can improve patient outcomes and contribute to the development of a more efficient and user-friendly healthcare system. In recent years, numerous machine learning and AI algorithms have been utilized to diagnose human illnesses.

Integration and Interoperability Challenges

Empowering all populations with access to high-quality healthcare is a key goal of modern economic systems and civilizations. Doctors are under a rising workload and time strain and often spend less time, even in the most advanced healthcare systems. Big Data, Web technologies, AI, and telemedicine are all crucial in boosting diagnostic accuracy and raising the standard of treatment. The COVID-19 epidemic has propelled the growing trend of telemedicine over the Internet. To enhance patient health statistics and differentiate between diseases, this study proposes a revolutionary smartphone-based care approach that gathers information about patients through progressive web apps (PWA), integrates that data with a range of medical information resources, and utilizes AI. Any AI- and IoT-powered health system can suggest the most effective treatment plan and available options for the individual in question. The smart care system, based on cutting-edge web technologies including PWA, Web Bluetooth, Web Language API, and Web USB, smoothly integrates into the concept of a smart medical facility (Norori et al., 2021). The acquired findings indicate that the proposed framework enhances reaction time while reducing uplink traffic. For real-time healthcare applications, this reduction in reaction time is substantial. The acquired findings indicate that the proposed framework enhances reaction time while reducing uplink traffic. For real-time healthcare applications, this reaction time improvement is substantial (Pise et al., 2022).

The digitization of health information is causing a rapid evolution in the healthcare sector, fundamentally transforming how medical data is collected, stored, and shared. Electronic health records (EHRs) originate from multiple sources, including laboratories, hospitals, IoT devices, mobile applications, and even social media platforms. These data sources collectively contribute to a patient's comprehensive medical history, encompassing details about diagnoses, treatments, medications, allergies, and lifestyle habits. However, to maximize the potential of EHRs and deliver high-quality healthcare, it is imperative to establish efficient mechanisms for the rapid, secure, and seamless transfer of EHR data across different healthcare facilities.

Interoperability plays a crucial role in ensuring that medical information can be shared among various stakeholders within the healthcare ecosystem. Syntactic interoperability enables data exchange between different healthcare systems by adhering to standardized formats and communication protocols. In contrast, semantic interoperability ensures that shared data can be meaningfully interpreted and utilized across diverse platforms. Without semantic interoperability, healthcare institutions risk miscommunication, data silos, and inefficiencies that hinder patient care. By fostering interoperability at both syntactic and semantic levels, medical professionals can access accurate and timely patient information, leading to more informed decision-making, reduced medical errors, and enhanced patient outcomes. The integration of advanced technologies such as data mining, big data analytics, and artificial intelligence further amplifies the benefits of semantically interoperable EHR systems. These technologies facilitate real-time analysis of vast amounts of health data, enabling predictive modeling, early disease detection, and personalized treatment plans. For example, AI-driven systems can analyze EHR data to identify patterns in patient histories, flag potential health risks, and recommend evidence-based interventions. Additionally, real-time decision support tools powered by big data analytics help clinicians make more accurate diagnoses, optimize treatment strategies, and improve overall patient safety.

Despite the promise of semantically interoperable EHR systems, several challenges remain. Technical barriers, such as variations in data formats and inconsistent standardization across healthcare institutions, can impede seamless data sharing. Privacy and security concerns also pose significant hurdles, as increased interoperability requires robust cybersecurity measures to prevent unauthorized access and data breaches. This chapter examines the current state of research on semantically interoperable Electronic Health Record (EHR) systems, highlighting their advantages, limitations, and future directions. It examines ongoing efforts to enhance interoperability through emerging technologies and regulatory initiatives, addressing key challenges that must be overcome to achieve widespread adoption. As healthcare continues to evolve in a digital landscape, ensuring the successful implementation of semantically interoperable EHR systems will be instrumental in improving patient care, streamlining healthcare workflows, and advancing medical innovation (Chadha & Chaudhary, 2023).

Data Silos: Since the healthcare industry generates many data and depends on it for its operations, collecting, handling, and sharing that data is crucial. Thanks to technological advancements, medical professionals can now save it digitally in a format known as electronic medical records (EMRs). Many stakeholders, including consumers, physicians, insurance companies, pharmacies, and providers, are given access to these records. It is essential to integrate new technologies in an area as sensitive as healthcare. Blockchain software has emerged as an immutable tool that can facilitate advancements in the healthcare industry due to its distributed nature and openness. Strict rules are in place to safeguard patient privacy, as healthcare data is highly sensitive. The medical field generates an enormous amount of data, which is essential for its operations, so gathering, managing, and disseminating that data is crucial. Physicians can now preserve it electronically in a format called EMRs, or electronic medical records, because of technical improvements. These records are accessible to a wide range of stakeholders, including patients, healthcare providers, the insurance industry, pharmacies, and other relevant parties. In a field as delicate as medical care, innovation must be incorporated. Blockchain innovation has emerged as an immutable tool that can facilitate advancements in the healthcare industry, thanks to its decentralized architecture and transparency. Because medical data is so sensitive, patients are subject to stringent regulations (Xu et al., 2024).

Figure 1. Data silos

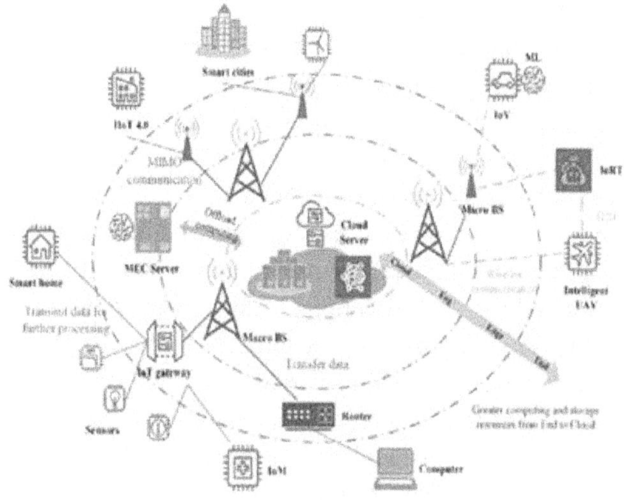

DATA PRIVACY AND SECURITY

Using AIoT in healthcare helps to hide the important data of patients. While there are undoubtedly many advantages to the Internet of Things, there are also significant security and privacy concerns regarding medical data. Nevertheless, a variety of attacks can seriously hinder the functionality of AIoT devices with limited resources. Perception, network, and application are the three layers that comprise the AIoT, and each is susceptible to security risks. These threats can originate from both within and outside the network, and they may exhibit either aggressive or passive characteristics. Replay, sniffing, and eavesdropping are just a few examples of IoT security vulnerabilities that can compromise network connectivity. Due to its ability to work with both current and emerging technologies and provide practical solutions to healthcare security problems, the AIoT application is likely to be investigated in this context. Furthermore, several potential issues and discrepancies with the AIoT approach are identified daily (Pise et al., 2022).

HIPAA and GDPR Compliance: Since the healthcare industry generates an immense volume of data and relies on it for efficient operations, the process of collecting, handling, and sharing such data must be meticulously managed. With technological advancements, medical professionals have transitioned from traditional paper-based records to digital storage formats known as electronic medical records (EMRs). These digital records enable seamless access and communication among various stakeholders, including patients, healthcare providers, insurance companies, pharmacies, and regulatory bodies.

The integration of emerging technologies in healthcare must be approached with caution, as any vulnerabilities in data security can have severe consequences. Blockchain technology, known for its decentralized nature and transparency, has emerged as a promising solution for enhancing data security, ensuring immutability, and preventing unauthorized alterations to medical records. By leveraging blockchain, healthcare institutions can establish a secure and tamper-proof environment for storing and sharing patient data, thereby reducing the risks of fraud, cyberattacks, and unauthorized data modifications. Additionally, blockchain can improve data interoperability, enabling different healthcare systems to communicate and exchange information efficiently while maintaining strict access control measures.

Given the highly sensitive nature of healthcare data, regulatory frameworks such as the Health Insurance Portability and Accountability Act (HIPAA) in the United States and the General Data Protection Regulation (GDPR) in the European Union have been established to enforce stringent data protection standards. These regulations are designed to minimize breaches of patient health data, ensure that individuals retain control over their personal information, and mandate strict compliance measures for organizations handling such data. Any technology, including blockchain, that seeks to be adopted in the healthcare sector, must align with these existing legal and ethical guidelines to be viable in real-world applications. Despite its potential, the integration of blockchain in electronic health record (EHR) systems presents both opportunities and challenges. While blockchain offers enhanced security, data integrity, and controlled access, its implementation must address concerns related to compliance, scalability, and governance. Regulatory bodies are continuously evaluating how blockchain-based solutions can be adapted to align with established privacy laws while maintaining their core benefits. This report delves into the various aspects of HIPAA and GDPR compliance in blockchain-based EHR solutions, examining potential areas for improvement and exploring how healthcare institutions can leverage blockchain while adhering to legal and ethical standards (Singha & Singha, 2024).

Risk of Cyberattacks: Data on threats enables companies and other organizations to strategically organize their digital defenses for the most effective and up-to-date security, as well as determine the necessary steps to combat cyber attacks. When combined with enhanced security examination, threat intelligence reduces the time between the detection of a breach and its mitigation. This is achieved by regularly sharing data and information on new and emerging cyber threats and vulnerabilities that affect businesses' networks. This article identifies and classifies the obstacles that organizations must overcome in order to invest in interoperable and effective cybersecurity information sharing. The obstacles are broken down into layers. It then offers an assessment of the current resources that disseminate cybersecurity knowledge. The ultimate objective of this research is to help enterprises enhance their cyber threat intelligence sharing, safety record, and ability to counter new and emerging attacks (Rantos et al., 2020).

Patient Consent: The virtual reality integration of scattered patient data via a consolidated health record has advantages, but it also has drawbacks, primarily in terms of practicality and authorization concepts. Our aim is to design and build an internet-based shared health record architecture focused on patient integration and authorization paradigms. The suggested methodology can partially replace message-based communications. High availability provision vaults for the virtualized standard EHR require advanced hardware and software, which is expected to drive up costs for medical professionals. For the recommended architecture to be approved, digital signing and document authentication must be integrated into work processes. The general shift from paper-based communications to a "pull model" requires more investigation (Bergmann et al., 2007).

Accuracy and Reliability of AI Algorithms

The use of AIoT in healthcare provides us with data accuracy and reliability. The healthcare industry is now offering more individualized, IoT- based healthcare services as a result of recent economic and technological advancements. These services are provided through control and monitoring apps, which are typically developed using algorithms based on AI and Machine Learning (ML). These apps play a crucial role in demonstrating the effectiveness of conventional healthcare systems. Occasionally, medical professionals struggle to consider multiple interconnected health issues, which can lead to an incorrect diagnosis that affects patients' long-term health and quality of life. AIoT technology is building upon past advancements in healthcare to address this issue. The goal of cutting-edge technology is a completely self-sufficient healthcare service that takes into account the interconnected nature of a patient's numerous health issues. In particular, we start by describing the essential requirements for fully personalized healthcare services (CPHS) within the framework of the current medical treatments IoT. This includes outlining flexibility and offering a sample use case scenario that functions as a stand-in for the current state of the Internet of Things. The most important CPHS criteria, in conjunction with their advantages and disadvantages when considering customized healthcare services, were examined in our second look at a basic three-layer design for IoT-based healthcare systems. Various artificial intelligence based and non-AI-based techniques were used to accomplish this. Third, we spoke about possible AI- and non-AI-based responses as well as the numerous security threats that every layer of the Network of The design of things confronts (Talukder & Haas, 2021).

Algorithmic Bias: AI has a lot to offer the medical sector. AI can aid in making medical decisions. A significant unsolved issue that has to be addressed before integrating AI into healthcare procedures is algorithmic bias. Large datasets are necessary for most AI systems to gain insight from, yet many human demographic groups have historically been either underrepresented or nonexistent in biological databases. AI is susceptible to bias reinforcement if the training data is not reflective of the population variability. Inaccurate diagnoses, poor results, and an absence of generalizability might result from this. Here, we describe the challenges of achieving more equity in AI systems and provide workable remedies for bias through the use of open scientific resources (Norori et al., 2021; Tariq and Sergio, 2025).

Model Validation: The past few years have seen a significant shift in the medical industry due to the implementation of AI in healthcare. Medical institutions have adopted AI technologies in an attempt to lower health risks and increase the precision of disease identification. AI applications have changed laws and policies concerning work ethics and medical practice. However, the field of developing trustworthy and comprehensible AI (XAI) for medical facilities is still very young. The European Union, in particular, has said that AI must be reliable and human-centered; nonetheless, low methodological quality and high bias risk have become major problems in the healthcare sector. The objective of this study is to give a systematic analysis of the comprehension and dependability of applications of artificial intelligence in healthcare, which will supplement previous research and lead to more accurate and definitive outcomes. It does this through incorporating assessments of data fusion, bias risk, and quality. Similarly, 64 recent contributions on the dependability of AI for medical applications were located from many databases using an extensive literature search method and selection criteria. The papers that were being considered were categorized using the following seven categories: digital health, understandable automated machinery, forecasts, assistance with decision-making, blockchain, transparency, and review. We have provided a thorough and methodical review of previous research in this work, and we have also outlined the obstacles, drives, and suggestions for further research, so creating a pathway for future investigations. This study also included a systematic scientific mapping analysis to address the challenges of objectivity and trustworthiness by reorganizing and summarizing the findings of previous investigations. Furthermore, this work has presented eight current state-of-the-art critical studies regarding those more pertinent research gaps, offering unambiguous evidence for the reliability of AI in healthcare. Additionally, to the best of our knowledge, this investigation is the sole attempt to examine the feasibility of employing trustworthy and XAI possibilities for the healthcare sector. It accomplishes this by fusing data-combining methods and tying together several critical pieces of information from AI algorithms and publically accessible healthcare statistics. Subsequently, relevant methodological features to improve the credibility of AI applications in the medical field were explored, and the analysis of the updated contributions revealed important implications for researchers and practitioners. The theoretical framework and contemporary applications of 17 XAI techniques in healthcare were covered one after the other. Lastly, a number of goals and recommendations were given to legislators in order to create electronic healthcare systems that prioritized obtaining important characteristics like robustness, morality, and legitimacy. This study focused on several forms of information fusion in healthcare, such as data, feature, image, decision, multimodal, hybrid, and temporal (Albahri et al., 2023).

Data Quality Impact: Data are an essential resource for companies and organizations because they constitute the foundation for informed decisions and strategic planning. In today's data-driven world, where ML and AI models are continually evolving and being applied across an extensive range of real-world applications, efficient data usage is more critical than ever. Organizations rely on data to gain insights, improve operational efficiency, and drive innovation, making data quality, security, and accessibility paramount (Tariq, 2025).

High-quality data play a pivotal role in the training of ML/AI algorithms, directly influencing the accuracy, reliability, and performance of the models. Poor-quality or biased data can lead to incorrect predictions, flawed decision-making, and unintended consequences, which can be particularly detrimental in sensitive fields such as healthcare, finance, and autonomous systems. Therefore, ensuring that data used in AI training are accurate, unbiased, and representative is a fundamental requirement for successful AI adoption.

In the healthcare industry, high-quality data are indispensable for achieving precise diagnostics, developing effective treatment plans, and ultimately improving patient outcomes. AI-driven applications such as predictive analytics, medical imaging interpretation, and personalized medicine rely on vast amounts of patient data to function effectively. The integration of AI in healthcare has the potential to revolutionize disease detection, optimize drug discovery, and enhance patient care by identifying patterns that may be imperceptible to human clinicians. However, this potential can only be realized if the data fueling these systems are meticulously curated and managed.

As AI and ML technologies continue to advance, the importance of ethical data management cannot be overstated. Addressing challenges related to data privacy, integrity, and bias will be key to fostering trust in AI systems and ensuring that they serve the best interests of society. By investing in data quality, security, and governance, businesses and institutions can unlock the full potential of AI while safeguarding individual rights and promoting responsible innovation (Enshaei & Naderkhani, 2024).

Technology Adoption and Resistance

Environmentally friendly smart healthcare (SHC) advances more quickly the more disruptive technologies—such as big data, blockchain, machine learning, AI, health record systems (EHRs), and the Internet of Things (IoTs)—evolve. This is true even though individual devices that are worn, devices, and applications are vulnerable to cyber-related threats. The AIoMT framework, or artificial intelligence aspect of the Internet of Medical Products, emerged from the merger of AI with IoMT. The application of AIoMT in smart medical care holds great potential. Several instances include its ability to alleviate the extreme stress on the healthcare industry caused by a scarcity of medical professionals, health problems created by a population growing older, a consistent increase in chronic illnesses, and the advent of worldwide health emergencies such as COVID-19. The capacity of AIoMTs to handle enormous amounts of patient data and their dynamic nature made them vulnerable to cyberattacks. AIoT technology is more safety for patient, less of fear to happen any knid of accident (Taimoor & Rehman, 2021).

Patient Trust in AI Systems: Telehealth, also known as remote patient monitoring (RPM), has become an essential aspect of modern healthcare, gaining widespread recognition and acceptance, especially since the onset of the COVID-19 pandemic. By making patient data readily accessible, RPM and telehealth contribute to the delivery of high-quality and cost-effective healthcare, bridging the gap between patients and medical professionals. This article introduces a Smart Distant Outpatient Movement Surveillance System designed to continuously monitor a patient's health indicators and physical movements in real-time through connected sensors. The system utilizes an IoT-enabled wellness tracking device that employs machine learning models to track and analyze an individual's vital signs, including heart rate, body temperature, and respiratory patterns, alongside their daily activities such as walking, running, sleeping, and training. By assessing respiratory conditions across various activities, machine learning algorithms play a crucial role in distinguishing between different patient states, with current capabilities limited to recognizing coughs and normal breathing patterns. Additionally, a web-based platform is developed to monitor and display real-time data collected from the connected devices, allowing healthcare providers to efficiently track patient health metrics remotely and intervene when necessary. This advancement in telehealth technology underscores the potential of AI-driven solutions in enhancing patient monitoring, improving clinical outcomes, and revolutionizing remote healthcare delivery (Tariq, 2025).

The use of AI is revolutionizing numerous industries, but it has a profoundly transformative effect on the healthcare system. AI can provide prognoses, diagnoses, and surgery results that are on par with or better than those provided by medical practitioners, according to recent studies and experiments. AI is being adopted by the healthcare industry, and its uses are revolutionizing it by cutting costs, improving diagnostic accuracy, and enhancing patient satisfaction. However, despite its potential, AI adoption in healthcare faces significant resistance due to various cultural, infrastructural, and regulatory challenges.

One of the most pressing issues in AI adoption is the reluctance of healthcare professionals to trust AI-driven systems. Many medical practitioners are skeptical of AI's ability to make critical decisions, as they believe that human expertise, intuition, and experience cannot be replaced by algorithms. The fear of losing professional autonomy and concerns about AI replacing human jobs contribute to this cultural resistance. Additionally, there is a widespread perception that AI may depersonalize healthcare by reducing doctor-patient interactions, which are crucial for effective treatment and emotional support.

Another major challenge is the lack of AI advocacy and structured efforts to promote awareness about the benefits of AI in healthcare. AI engineers and the health sector have lost out on significant yearly opportunity expenses due to the absence of AI advocacy and adoption (AIE). Many healthcare professionals, particularly in developing countries, lack proper training in AI applications, leading to resistance rooted in unfamiliarity and misconceptions.

Studies testing the interaction of barriers and their impact on AI adoption are scarce, particularly when considering developing nations such as India. Healthcare institutions in these regions often struggle with limited infrastructure, making it difficult to implement AI solutions effectively. Moreover, ethical concerns surrounding data privacy, security, and AI decision-making accountability further hinder its acceptance. This chapter investigates the obstacles to AI adoption in Indian healthcare by identifying and analyzing 250 barriers concerning technology adoption. After an in-depth review of prior research and multiple focus group discussions (FGDs), the number of barriers was refined to the 16 most significant ones using the DELPHI approach and expert consultations. These barriers were then classified using analytical techniques such as interpretive structural modeling (ISM) and cross-impact matrix multiplication applied to classification (MICMAC) to assess their influence and relevance.

The results obtained from ISM and MICMAC indicate that the primary obstacles to AI adoption in healthcare are:

Lack of infrastructure – Many healthcare facilities lack the necessary digital systems, connectivity, and computational resources required to support AI-driven technologies (Biswas et al., 2024).
Regulatory and legal uncertainties – Inadequate regulatory frameworks and unclear guidelines regarding AI integration pose a major challenge. Healthcare providers hesitate to adopt AI due to concerns over liability and compliance.
Cybersecurity risks – AI applications in healthcare involve handling vast amounts of sensitive patient data, making them vulnerable to cyber threats, data breaches, and unauthorized access.
Resistance from healthcare professionals – Doctors and medical staff fear AI may replace their expertise or reduce their control over clinical decisions.
Financial constraints – The high initial investment required for AI implementation discourages healthcare institutions, particularly in resource-limited settings.
Ethical concerns – The use of AI in medical decision-making raises questions about accountability, bias in AI algorithms, and the transparency of machine-driven diagnoses.

To overcome these barriers, a multi-faceted approach is necessary. Increasing AI literacy among healthcare professionals through training and awareness programs can help build trust in AI-driven solutions. Policymakers must establish clear regulatory frameworks that provide guidance on AI ethics, data security, and liability. Additionally, investments in AI infrastructure and research will be critical for facilitating a smoother transition toward AI-integrated healthcare systems.

The findings of this study contribute to the broader discourse on technology adoption, offering a structured framework for businesses and healthcare stakeholders to evaluate and implement AI solutions effectively. By addressing cultural resistance and other barriers, AI can be harnessed to improve healthcare delivery, enhance patient outcomes, and optimize resource allocation in medical institutions. The successful adoption of AI will not only transform the healthcare industry but also set a precedent for its application in other critical sectors (Gupta & Srivastava, 2024).

Cost-Benefit Analysis

In healthcare using technology helps to reduce the cost. Where a dc charge for an operation for million there using AI technology it does not take that much charge. The utilization of smart technology in medicine, such as AI/ML, requires a telemedicine system that allows medical professionals to monitor patients even when they are geographically separated. By utilizing cutting-edge telemedicine methods built on the IoT and artificial intelligence, the number of patients who visit hospitals can be decreased. Through the acquisition of diagnoses and more accurate analysis, the application of IoT in the health industry improves the quality of service (Hussain et al., 2024).

Initial Setup Costs: IoT represents an advancement of IoMT within the domain of wellness and healthcare technology, with applications primarily aimed at delivering personalized care. IoMT uses a broad variety of this technology's capabilities in healthcare industries, such as home medical equipment, emergency kits, service apps, cell phones with sophisticated apps, and data generated by connected devices. IoMT has brought medicine closer to the public through a variety of means, including detectors, gadgets that can be worn, smart applications, and the gathering of data regarding symptoms and illnesses while patients are going about their daily lives. By tracking the course of an illness and directing remote tests and treatments, this data may be used to increase agility within healthcare through the application of AI technologies and machine learning. As a result, treating patients on-site no longer requires a full-time professionals medical staff. IoMT has thereby revolutionized the use of technologies that are disruptive. It has established a tremendous differentiation for communities confronting an overburdened medical sector that will only get more stressed as long consumers continue to act, thanks to its ground-breaking characteristic that includes real-time diagnosis and excellent health treatment. This chapter's objective is to provide an up-to-date summary of IoT and IoMT and what they mean for medical technology, with a particular emphasis on their field of application in relation to contemporary healthcare and in tandem with other emerging technologies. It's also crucial to recognize that this paper takes a novel approach to the problem, concentrating on how technology performs from modern perspectives and how to categorize and combine technology's possibilities (Shafik, 2024a).

Operational Efficiency: Sustainable smart healthcare (SHC) developments more quickly the more disruptive technologies—such as big data, blockchain, machine learning, AI, electronic health records (EHRs), and the Internet of Things (IoTs)—evolve. This is true even though individual's wearables, devices, and applications are vulnerable to cyber-related threats. The AIoMT paradigm—also known as Artificial Intelligence of the Internet of Medical Things—was created when AI and IoMT were combined. The application of AIoMT in smart healthcare holds great potential. Its ability to reduce the severe strain on healthcare facilities brought on by a lack of healthcare workers, health issues resulting from aging populations, a steady rise in ongoing illnesses, and the emergence of global health emergencies like COVID-19 are just a few examples. AIoMTs are vulnerable to cyberattacks as they are dynamic and may manage large amounts of patient data. In conjunction with cryptocurrency and data encryption frameworks, the chapter offers a methodology to guarantee a safe AIoMT ecosystem since medical endpoint devices (MePD) employ the AIoMT Cloud to move information handling from the user via AI algorithms to healthcare midstream devices (MiPD) (fog, mist, or edge). Finally, but just as importantly, including medical professionals and patients in the model-development approach will foster a culture of collaboration, acceptance, and mutual respect (Shafik, 2024).

Data Management and Quality

Data creation, storage, and analysis are occurring at previously unheard-of rates in the Big Data era. Recent research has demonstrated the prevalence of low-quality data in big databases and online. This is due to the fact that low-quality data can significantly affect how data analysis turns out. Thus, the significance of the fourth "V" reality of big data is becoming more widely acknowledged. Volume, speed, and variety—the first three Vs—are the main topics of this course. That presents numerous difficulties. Managing the truth in large-scale data Erroneous data must therefore be understood and (perhaps) repaired in a timely and scalable manner due to the sheer amount and pace of data. frequently with a range of data from many sources. As a result, data quality guidelines cannot be predetermined. To learn how data economics works, go to the "Speaks for itself" page. The most recent findings in large data quality management are presented in this course. Its two main focuses are (i) identifying quality problems directly from the data and (ii) business accuracy vs. efficiency. and identify a range of issues open to the community (Saha & Srivastava, 2014).

Figure 2. Overview and architecture of AIoT

Data Overload: With the help of embedded detection, identification, communication, and processing functions, physical, digital, and virtual objects can interact with one another as well as other devices connected to the internet and applications...What consumers need Utilization People's is meant to make life simple and more useful by providing items and applications. Moreover, the application of IoT technology in the automotive industry gave rise to the concept of the so-called

Industrial Internet of Things (IIoT), whom facilitates the use of electronic-physical systems in which people and machines interact. The incorporation of generated data is facilitated by an internal or architectural approach for IoT data management. Other solutions on the market provide indexing and archiving of both structured and unstructured data. NoSQL language compatibility is one of its characteristics. As a result, this article offers a more relevant perspective on IoT data management, analyzing recently proposed approaches, highlighting the most interesting ones, and proposing further contributions by areas on the basics indicated on unprepared courses (Diène et al., 2020).

Real-time Data Processing: The primary goals of cancer surveillance are data collection to evaluate the cancer burden and community-level implementation of public health initiatives for cancer avoidance and management. The quantity of human labor needed to collect cancer data is a major obstacle confronting the cancer monitoring community, as it can cause delays in assessment and data consumption. The Centers for Disease Prevention and Control A platform for cloud-based computing called cancer surveillance(CS-CBCP) has been created, developed, and tested in order to modernize and automate the collecting of oral cancer data and reporting. In addition to what had previously been unavailable, this system can retrieve real-time cancer data and offer cancer information that has been automated during collection. 19 As the need for ongoing coordination during the pandemic has been emphasized, CS-CBCP has the capacity to offer such a platform suitable for remote operation of centralized cancer registries (Jones et al., 2021).

Data Accuracy and Redundancy: Here, we proportion our expertise of constructing absolutely new smartphone apps from scratch in addition to developing apps for experts on iOS gadgets with an analog compass for controlled assessment and specialized subject applications. Additionally, we illustrate the connection between these metrics and satellite TV for PC observations. the usage of a hard and fast of 3700 iPhone statistics of coseismic subsurface breaks down that we collected in northern Chile all through the 2014 Mw8.1 Pisagua tragedy. Analogs distinguished from the magnetic enchantment field via contrasting strategies received through smartphones That breath is the conventional tool. It would be inaccurate to accept as true that our research demonstrates that iOS devices can control whatever, besides the most demanding workloads, for the reason that electric and steel components, which are magnetically vulnerable, are handled with more caution (Allmendinger et al., 2017).

Data Integration Complexity: Precision medicine's main objective is to link big businesses with research projects in libraries of molecular and environmental triggers so that personalized treatment plans and diagnostics can be created for specific illnesses. By applying machine learning and artificial intelligence techniques to it, analytical models of complex illnesses may be created. The term "environmental management" describes the requirement that these models take into consideration significant differences in people's genetic predisposition in addition to social and environmental factors. Processing, visualizing, and integrating massive datasets involving systems, unstructured systems, and computational techniques must be done efficiently in medicine. Different mysteries impose constraints on this, which should be enhanced in an integrated curriculum. Effective data integration and application in medical practice is essential for the successful implementation of computer intelligence techniques. Building a successful framework for informative medical research in the current environment presents many challenges because customized medicine requires work constrained by time, control, and bioethical considerations. Here, we will go over a few of these limitations and then discuss possible solutions to our problems (Martínez-García & Hernández-Lemus, 2022).

Legal and Regulatory Frameworks

The internet, the Internet of Things, or IoT, and the Web have gained increased popularity recently. By communicating to the internet, devices and systems may communicate with people and with one other thanks to the Internet of Things. It can manage and operate devices remotely by utilizing Internet networks. That being said, the Internet of Things is really driven by AI. Thus, it is possible to draw the conclusion that a smarter future may come sooner rather than later given the growing link between IoT and AI. Thus, it is clear that AIOT has the power to fundamentally alter the medical industry by rethinking the role that devices, applications, and human contact play in the provision of therapeutic solutions. Consequently, AIOT offers physicians and health care institutions the opportunity to improve the caliber and resources of their medical systems (Nozari et al., 2023).

Healthcare Regulations: AIoT revolutionizes patient care in the context of contemporary healthcare. This chapter examines the impact of AIOT on at-home patient care, emphasizing ways to enhance patient outcomes. Wearable AIoT technology enables "real-time assessment of your physical activity and mental wellbeing." Sensor hubs and machine learning are utilized to assess data related to heart rate, temperature, breathing, and blood oxygenation. The AIoT system gathers various biological data via RPM and sends it through the internet of thing cloud for improved illness monitoring. Many wearables, robotic surgery tools, anticoagulation devices, Link inhalers, dementia monitoring wrist watches, and IoT-related connections have all been studied for their ability to improve patient care. Eyeglasses and are The chapter highlights AIOT's significance in patient satisfaction and early identification, particularly in turmoil life-threatening species, demonstrating the technology's promise to provide more readily available and effective health care (Prakash et al., 2024).

Liability and Accountability: The COVID-19 epidemic is still causing havoc in 2021, affecting roughly 170 million people globally. Systems of healthcare are quite contagious. Fortunately, AI technologies like cloud computing and large data analysis, which are key to the fight against the COVID-19 pandemic, have made the IoT to be among the largest and most successful technologies in the smart world. AI and 5G technologies are starting to gain traction, enhancing the abilities and interconnectivity of IoT applications and progressively transforming IoT into more potent AI+IoT (AIoT), such as deep learning and machine learning based on AI technology. Health care providers may now make better medical judgments with greater safeguards for both clients and doctors personnel because to recent significant developments in medical device technology, which have also revolutionized companies with reduced patient interaction. The article offers full details on how to resist the COVID-19 pandemic & potential uses of the technology, as well as an overview of the most recent advancements in combating the virus utilizing IoT and AI (Chen et al., 2021).

Cross-border Data Transfers: The ability of AIoT to generate and capture commercial value is becoming progressively more embraced by the quickly developing IoT and AI methodologies. The application of AI and IoT-based technology to forecast potential outcomes and recommend appropriate course of actions is known as AIoT. However, there hasn't been much study done in this area, and the fundamental strategies for creating AIoT contextualized amenities remain inadequately well understood in practice. We expand our decrease in methods to AIoT-based commercial solutions in this sector. Law enforcement and AIoT by researching situational assessment of context-based systems, we attempt to close this gap. Thus, our contextual study identifies a philosophical framework that enables a police field section's AIoT to guarantee challenging contextual tasks. There is discussion of the consequences, constraints, and potential uses of creating intricate AIoT environment solutions (Huang et al., 2021).

Figure 3. Cross border monitoring

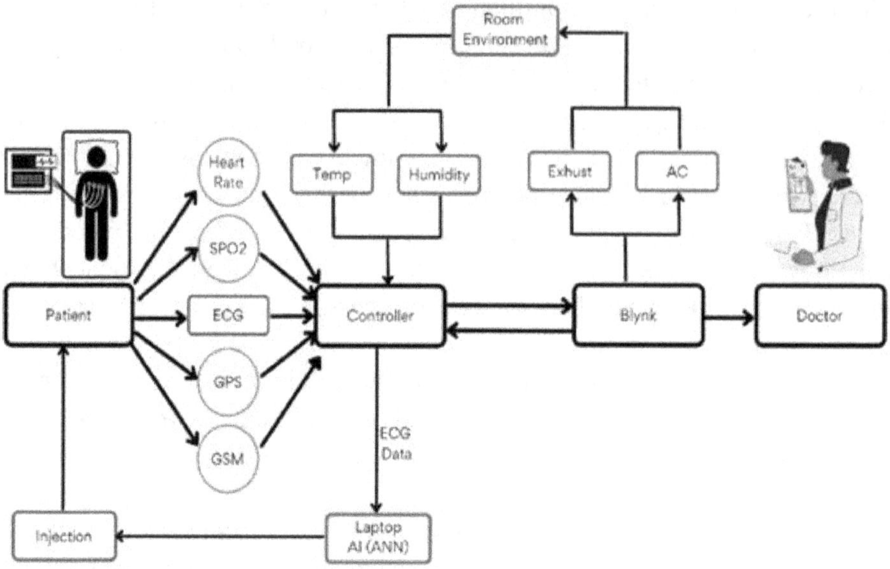

Ethical Considerations: Since the epidemic, videoconferencing and RPM (remote patient monitoring) have drawn a lot of interest as two crucial areas. RPM and videoconferencing make it easier for patients to retrieve their medical records and enable them obtain quality care at a reduced cost. This research proposes an intelligent remote healthcare tracking device that can monitor patients' behaviors and their relative importance based on linked sensors. Employing models developed with machine learning, an internet-connected IoT medical monitoring device was developed to monitor the body temperature of a person and heart rate—two essential parameters for activities like walking, running, sleeping, and exercising—as well as the manner in which they breathe during those endeavors. Simulations based on machine learning are employed for evaluating the patient's lung function in different ways and to identify disease events. Machine learning methods are now limited to identifying typical breathing and coughing patterns. Additionally, web apps have been created to monitor the data that the target devices upload.

Impact on Healthcare Workforce

Quick improvements in a variety of technology and procedures result in more specialized and effective solutions that support the healthcare sector. Tailored data management systems are needed by healthcare organizations and intelligence to store the diverse data that gets collected from sensors and apps due to the population's constant expansion. Combining different approaches Robots with artificial intelligence that operate in smart hospitals and are capable of performing surgery and analyzing medical pictures represent a significant advancement in the industry that will improve the long-term performance of smart hospital systems. sensors to check the condition of equipment, and Internet of Things-based temperature control systems for intelligent hospital administration systems; Additionally, there are a lot of applications available right now. Researchers have suggested a number of designs that aid in the development of smart cities, hospitals, and other development sectors in which they are becoming more and more active. Comparing these newer methods to previous ones, basic issues are solved more quickly, more effectively, and more simply. This paper's major goal is to demonstrate many elements and characteristics of AI and connected to the internet of modern hospital systems, as well as the role that healthcare plays in the development of the contemporary world by combining these specialized fields and achieving remarkable industrial outcomes. Additionally, we offer the limitations that come with creating sophisticated clinical management systems.

Job Automation: Floor monitoring systems using triboelectric sensors have shown to be efficient models for recording lots of knowledge from our daily actions without the privacy problems associated with cameras, enabling intelligent houses and related applications. However, the development of trustworthy ground monitoring systems is severely hampered by the drawbacks of dielectric sensors, namely their excellent water sensitivity and lack of long-term durability. For very reliable detection that is independent of technique and environmental factors, two quad encoding electrode have been organized and their outputs standardized about the reference electrode. Each floor mat can have unique coding, which enables simultaneous array connections and simplifies the output terminal system. In addition, profound learning-assisted analysis of information, smart floor monitoring, and communication for different smart home monitoring. The system is implemented, complete with automated control, identity detection, and position/trajectory tracking (Tariq, 2025). Thus, potential advancements in floor-sensing devices for smart home applications are demonstrated by the design of an affordable, wide-area, dependable, intelligent floor-monitoring system (Shi et al., 2021).

Workforce Augmentation: The world's population is aging faster than ever, and seniors' increasing desire to remain in place calls for answers. The person-environment (P-E) combination assumption is reorganized in this dissertation using the Ersatz Word of Things (AIOT) to emphasize the personal privacy-preserving solutions that allow elderly people to be continuously monitored for their well-being. We provide a complete P-E for AIP Visualization (PE4AIP) that evaluates aged well-being through three main measurements: human features, system characteristics, and interactions between people and their environments. This P-E is based on the basis of the P-E Fit theory. In order to measure the `fit' between seniors and their settings, the check finds name-sset markers such as gregarious interactions, environmental console, and toxic shift modus vivendi geometrical regularity. A PE4AIP-enabled AIP set up structure was created to put into practice this representation and provide guidance for developing AIP systems that prioritize privacy and customisation. Notably, the sophisticated construction uses contemporary technology to provide information and real-time viewing. The ing method uses non-intrusive light, particularly the unit that exploits proximity detectors and bound computing, as well as the amp alone notice unit that exploits 3-D life to pass along the circumstances of older adults to caregivers without compromising sensitive confidentiality. Experiments and investigations with an empirical approach Accept the structure and suggested representation's efficacy. The forward motion of the old inch point unit's (saips) implementation raises questions about the unit's applicability and legitimacy among elderly participants and their careers (Tariq and Sergio, 2025). The outcomes demonstrate how well the system predicts well-being, how unobtrusive it is, and how well-received the technology is generally. This search pushes GeronTech beyond providing amp on paper-based and via trial and error legitimate framework that enhances the prerequisite and spirit of the past. Our work's scope and depth represent a significant contribution to the creation of clever, useful, and successful aging-in-place solutions, with broad ramifications for the rapidly growing field of assistive technologies for senior citizens (Pise et al., 2022).

Redesign of Workflows: One of the innovations that is most assisting businesses in going digital is the Internet of Elements. The focus of attention for this engineering's diligence is inch unique (Sahoo et al., 2024). It analyzes in depth the answers related to the forward mill, forward logistics, problem iron, and forward lifecycle areas of scrutiny. The goal of the completed thesis work is to comprehend the primary paths for this technology's future expansion and to create a cutting-edge study of Internet of Elements Technology with the Industry 4.0 movement in Italy and outside. The data base for IoT projects that I was given outside of the Observatories IoT was enhanced by the inch rate at which the top head was completed, which was led by ampere nose count of the initiatives that have been mandated. Starting there, a report of the projects was created, concentrating on a number of variables such as the primary usage areas and the trend in the geographical distribution of the number of projects implemented over time. inch growth It was completed with a small assessment of Italian businesses that was sent to both large corporations and SMEs, and for which several variables related to the IIOT person were investigated. To get insight into potential future developments, an investigation was conducted to find the most innovative start-ups in the Internet of Things space that have surfaced in the last few years. Effectiveness, at this point the main tendencies in development were established. Finally, a specialized representation was created to look at one of these instances, the AIoT, in further depth (Paoletti, 2021).

Long-term Sustainability: The floor-watching technology with integrated triboelectric detectors has been demonstrated as an efficient paradigm to record the copious sensory data from our everyday activities without the privacy problems associated with cameras, thereby enabling smart houses and related purposes. Even with triboelectric sensors' inherent drawbacks—like their high susceptibility to humidity and extended periods of rest—a genuine base watching unit remains a compelling case. Here, we create a strong and intelligent floor-watching system by combining deep learning-assisted information analytics with incredibly dependable triboelectric coding mats. ii Several organizing electrodes for coding are arranged, and their outcomes are normalized using values ranging to the amp characterization electrode to a very high signal that is not affected by the nearby parameters and procedure protocols. Furthermore, all of the floor coverings can be screen-printed using a single mask because of the common electrode arrangement, which makes them easier and less expensive to produce. Extremely strong characteristic coding is imposed to each base flat completed unnecessary wiring, allowing the yield of connections and unit complexity to be degraded by the parallel-array link. A intelligent floor-watching apparatus has been realized for different smart home-watching and interactions, such as position/trajectory tracking, identity identification, and automated controls, further integrating with deep learning-assisted information analytics. The consequence is an impressive advancement in base perception engineering for inch ahead home purposes, as demonstrated by the mature, inexpensive, large-area genuine and forward-looking base watching unit (Shi et al., 2021).

Energy Efficiency: Wearable technology is becoming more widely used in a variety of industries, particularly sporting apparel that monitors and enhances the performance of athletes. This intense inch-go search is combined with affordable, actual low-power wearable equipment that can perform hyperbolic psychoanalysis. This work presents the convolutional nerve-related web (CNN) for an arrhythmia in the heart detection device that may be worn during sport teaching sessions, together with coupled energy-aware methodologies. An ultra-low-power microcontroller for nursing is equipped with the active force direction scheme (dpms), which when combined with an amplifier photovoltaic (pv) Sending Harvest (eh) beat, produces an amp battery-life reference that is comparable to the amp self-powered method. After scaling the picture and interpolating the data using a bicubic approach, the CNN-based evaluation filters categorize the electrocardiogram (ECG) output into both healthy and unhealthy categories. The eh-dpms reaches a penetration threshold for amplifier the amount of 1434% additional Transmission free, which translates to four consecutive 45-minute exercises without the need to manually reload it, according to check results. Furthermore, a 98.6% accuracy rate in detecting arrhythmias is attained in the experimental sessions with 55222 photos used for system training combining the MIT-BIH QT and for a long time ST database, and 1320 images deployed to a reusable system. As a result, the proposed wearable unit shifts from moderator associates in nursing to athlete check reduction. the possibility of abnormal eye disorders when participating in sports (Castillo-Atoche et al., 2022).

Maintenance and Upgrades: Aircraft health monitoring systems are undergoing a transformation because to incorporate the use of artificial intelligence and other components (AIoT), which combines sophisticated analytical tools with massive data collecting. This read suggests a powerful frame that enhances guard spell optimization, cost-saving care procedures, and prophetic truth. With the help of a three-tiered cloud architecture, the AIoT system makes it possible to gather data in real time from sensors integrated into aircraft systems. Machine learning techniques then analyze and interpret the data to support proactive decision-making. This search explores the evolution of traditional to AI-enhanced viewing, providing an overall organic framework with planet communication and 6G engineering. This work introduces the mathematical representations that quantify the advantages of enhanced diagnostic depth using AIoT, encompassing topics like safety enhancements and accuracy cost savings forecasting. The results highlight the significance of investing in IoT technology for improving efficiency and communication in air care and trade operations. Mark summarizes the transition from traditional health observation to proactive health guidance and inch of air (Kabashkin & Shoshin, 2024).

Environmental Impact: Finding dangerous materials in the natural world is essential to safeguarding public health and biodiversity. Thanks to recent technological advances, AI has become known as an attractive option for developing sensors that can detect and analyze these features. It also considers the problems with this change that will be anticipated and followed because the environment is dynamic. The combination of these systems drastically changes environmental policy and shapes our knowledge of how we can use a comprehensive approach to better manage the natural environment. Essential for well-being. As a result, we can accomplish demonstrate the transformational impact of these collaborative efforts on our understanding of the Earth as they address barriers, provide in-depth environmental assessments, and deal with issues over time, laying the foundation for a promising future (Arowolo et al., 2024).

CONCLUSION

Present a telehealth gadget in this article that allows for remote monitoring of a person's critical health indicators by sending them to the IBM cloud. By using these procedures, healthcare providers can reduce the chance that an infection will occur during an operation. In the field of healthcare, AI and IoT help to secure the information of patients. These contemporary methods improve efficiency, accuracy, and dependability. In this profession, the most recent technology always stands by patients who require round-the-clock monitoring. Patients' previous medical records might be stored in an online and offline database that is designed to assess vital signs. Future health-related challenges might benefit from the knowledge found in the database. Utilizing contemporary technology, doctors may obtain research updates and create personalized medication regimens for their patients. A gadgets health monitoring device that can be directly associated to the IoT was created using machine learning algorithms. Its purpose was to predict patient behaviors, such as running, strolling, sleeping, and exercising, as well as the associated impacts on breathing and body temperature. The identification of patient activities was done using machine learning algorithms. Machine learning algorithms can currently only identify cough and breathing patterns that are typical. Additionally, a web-based app was created to control the data that the suggested devices uploaded. The patient had no discomfort at all from the suggested health monitoring equipment created in this study. It may be simply uninstalled and reinstalled without help whenever necessary. The findings suggested that the suggested solution may be highly beneficial for providing remote patient care. We plan to expand the suggested devices to include other illness categories soon. Additionally, this paper makes no suggestions for machine learning algorithms. Thus, we will create an initial machine learning system and work to achieve the best outcomes.

REFERENCES

Albahri, A. S., Duhaim, A. M., Fadhel, M. A., Alnoor, A., Baqer, N. S., Alzubaidi, L., Albahri, O. S., Alamoodi, A. H., Bai, J., Salhi, A., Santamaría, J., Ouyang, C., Gupta, A., Gu, Y., & Deveci, M. (2023). A systematic review of trustworthy and explainable artificial intelligence in healthcare: Assessment of quality, bias risk, and data fusion. *Information Fusion*, *96*, 156–191. DOI: 10.1016/j.inffus.2023.03.008

Albahri, A. S., Duhaim, A. M., Fadhel, M. A., Alnoor, A., Baqer, N. S., Alzubaidi, L., Albahri, O. S., Alamoodi, A. H., Bai, J., Salhi, A., Santamaría, J., Ouyang, C., Gupta, A., Gu, Y., & Deveci, M. (2023). A systematic review of trustworthy and explainable artificial intelligence in healthcare: Assessment of quality, bias risk, and data fusion. *Information Fusion*, *96*, 156–191. DOI: 10.1016/j.inffus.2023.03.008

Allmendinger, R. W., Siron, C. R., & Scott, C. P. (2017). Structural data collection with mobile devices: Accuracy, redundancy, and best practices. *Journal of Structural Geology*, *102*, 98–112. DOI: 10.1016/j.jsg.2017.07.011

Arowolo, M. E., Aaron, W. C., Eteng, U. S., Divine, I. L. O. H., Aguma, C. P., & Olagunju, A. O.Modupe Ebunoluwa ArowoloWilliam Clement AaronAdeniyi olusegun kugbiyiUbi Solomon EtengDivine ILOHChimaoge Peace AgumaAdeyemi Oyetoro Olagunju. (2024). Integrating AI enhanced remote sensing technologies with IOT networks for precision environmental monitoring and predicative ecosystem management. *World Journal of Advanced Research and Reviews*, *23*(2), 2156–2166. DOI: 10.30574/wjarr.2024.23.2.2573

Bergmann, J., Bott, O. J., Pretschner, D. P., & Haux, R. (2007). An e-consent-based shared EHR system architecture for integrated healthcare networks. *International Journal of Medical Informatics*, *76*(2-3), 130–136. DOI: 10.1016/j.ijmedinf.2006.07.013 PMID: 16971171

Biswas, D., Dutta, A., Ghosh, S., & Roy, P. (2024). Future trends and significant solutions for intelligent computing resource management. In *Computational Intelligence for Green Cloud Computing and Digital Waste Management* (pp. 187–208). IGI Global. DOI: 10.4018/979-8-3693-1552-1.ch010

Castillo-Atoche, A., Caamal-Herrera, K., Atoche-Enseñat, R., Estrada-López, J. J., Vázquez-Castillo, J., Castillo-Atoche, A. C., Palma-Marrufo, O., & Espinoza-Ruiz, A. (2022). Energy efficient framework for an AIoT cardiac arrhythmia detection system wearable during sport. *Applied Sciences (Basel, Switzerland)*, *12*(5), 2716. DOI: 10.3390/app12052716

Chadha, R., & Chaudhary, A. (2023, December). Advancing patient care and monitoring through the fusion of artificial intelligence and the Internet of Things in healthcare. In *International Conference on Intelligent Systems Design and Applications* (pp. 472-480). Cham: Springer Nature Switzerland.

Chen, S. W., Gu, X. W., Wang, J. J., & Zhu, H. S. (2021). AIoT used for COVID-19 pandemic prevention and control. *Contrast Media & Molecular Imaging*, *2021*(1), 3257035. DOI: 10.1155/2021/3257035 PMID: 34729056

Diène, B., Rodrigues, J. J., Diallo, O., Ndoye, E. H. M., & Korotaev, V. V. (2020). Data management techniques for Internet of Things. *Mechanical Systems and Signal Processing*, *138*, 106564. DOI: 10.1016/j.ymssp.2019.106564

Enshaei, N., & Naderkhani, F. (2024). The role of data quality for reliable AI performance in medical applications. *IEEE Reliability Magazine*, *1*(3), 24–28. DOI: 10.1109/MRL.2024.3430192

Gupta, A. K., & Srivastava, M. K. (2024). Framework for AI adoption in health care sector: Integrated DELPHI, ISM-MICMAC approach. *IEEE Transactions on Engineering Management*, *71*, 8116–8131. DOI: 10.1109/TEM.2024.3386580

Huang, C. H., Chou, T. C., & Wu, S. H. (2021). Towards convergence of AI and IoT for smart policing: A case of a mobile edge computing-based context-aware system. [JGIM]. *Journal of Global Information Management*, *29*(6), 1–21. DOI: 10.4018/JGIM.20211101.oa2

Hussain, A., Iqbal, A., Irfan, M. A., Ahmed, I., & Khalil, A. (2024). AIoT-based telehealth system using Healthy Pi. In *Impact of Artificial Intelligence on Society* (p. 143).

Jones, D. E., Alimi, T. O., Pordell, P., Tangka, F. K., Blumenthal, W., Jones, S. F., Rogers, J. D., Benard, V. B., & Richardson, L. C. (2021). Pursuing data modernization in cancer surveillance by developing a cloud-based computing platform: Real-time cancer case collection. *JCO Clinical Cancer Informatics*, *5*(5), 24–29. DOI: 10.1200/CCI.20.00082 PMID: 33411623

Kabashkin, I., & Shoshin, L. (2024). Artificial intelligence of things as new paradigm in aviation health monitoring systems. *Future Internet*, *16*(8), 276. DOI: 10.3390/fi16080276

Martínez-García, M., & Hernández-Lemus, E. (2022). Data integration challenges for machine learning in precision medicine. *Frontiers in Medicine*, *8*, 784455. DOI: 10.3389/fmed.2021.784455 PMID: 35145977

Norori, N., Hu, Q., Aellen, F. M., Faraci, F. D., & Tzovara, A. (2021). Addressing bias in big data and AI for health care: A call for open science. *Patterns (New York, N.Y.)*, *2*(10), 100347. DOI: 10.1016/j.patter.2021.100347 PMID: 34693373

Nozari, H., Tavakkoli-Moghaddam, R., Ghahremani-Nahr, J., & Najafi, E. (2023). A conceptual framework for artificial intelligence of medical things (AIoMT). In *Computational Intelligence for Medical Internet of Things (MIoT) Applications* (pp. 175-189). Academic Press.

Paoletti, M. (2021). Industrial Internet of Things: State-of-the-art and directions of future development.

Pise, A. A., Almusaini, K. K., & Ahanger, T. A. (2022). Research article enabling artificial intelligence of things (AIoT) healthcare architectures and listing security issues.

Pise, A. A., Almuzaini, K. K., Ahanger, T. A., Farouk, A., Pant, K., Pareek, P. K., & Nuagah, S. J. (2022). Enabling artificial intelligence of things (AIoT) healthcare architectures and listing security issues. *Computational Intelligence and Neuroscience*, *2022*(1), 8421434. DOI: 10.1155/2022/8421434 PMID: 36911247

Prakash, A., Avasthi, S., Agarwal, K., & Hussain, M. (2024). Modern healthcare systems: Unveiling the possibility of AIoT for remote patient monitoring. In *Developments Towards Next Generation Intelligent Systems for Sustainable Development* (pp. 180–203). IGI Global.

Rantos, K., Spyros, A., Papanikolaou, A., Kritsas, A., Ilioudis, C., & Katos, V. (2020). Interoperability challenges in the cybersecurity information sharing ecosystem. *Computers*, *9*(1), 18. DOI: 10.3390/computers9010018

Saha, B., & Srivastava, D. (2014, March). Data quality: The other face of big data. In *2014 IEEE 30th International Conference on Data Engineering* (pp. 1294-1297). IEEE.

Sahoo, T., Mondal, A., Roy, P., & Podder, A. (2024). Artificial intelligence and its application in engineering: A comprehensive review. In *Emerging Engineering Technologies and Industrial Applications* (pp. 1-20). DOI: 10.4018/979-8-3693-1335-0.ch001

Shafik, W. (2024). Smart health revolution: Exploring artificial intelligence of internet of medical things. In *Healthcare Industry Assessment: Analyzing Risks, Security, and Reliability* (pp. 201–229). Springer Nature Switzerland. DOI: 10.1007/978-3-031-65434-3_9

Shi, Q., Zhang, Z., Yang, Y., Shan, X., Salam, B., & Lee, C. (2021). Artificial intelligence of things (AIoT) enabled floor monitoring system for smart home applications. *ACS Nano*, *15*(11), 18312–18326. DOI: 10.1021/acsnano.1c07579 PMID: 34723468

Singha, R., & Singha, S. (2024). AIoT concepts and integration: Exploring customer interaction, ethics, policy, and privacy. In *Artificial Intelligence of Things (AIoT) for Productivity and Organizational Transition* (pp. 26–51). IGI Global. DOI: 10.4018/979-8-3693-0993-3.ch002

Taimoor, N., & Rehman, S. (2021). Reliable and resilient AI and IoT-based personalised healthcare services: A survey. *IEEE Access : Practical Innovations, Open Solutions*, *10*, 535–563. DOI: 10.1109/ACCESS.2021.3137364

Talukder, A., & Haas, R. (2021, June). AIoT: AI meets IoT and web in smart healthcare. In *Companion Publication of the 13th ACM Web Science Conference 2021* (pp. 92-98).

Tariq, M. U. (2025). *AI-Driven Learning and Engagement in Higher Education*. IGI Global., DOI: 10.4018/979-8-3693-4074-5

Tariq, M. U. (2025). Navigating the Convergence of IoMT and Generative AI in Global Healthcare: Opportunities, Challenges, and Ethical Considerations. In Kumar, V., Katina, P., & Zhao, J. (Eds.), *Convergence of Internet of Medical Things (IoMT) and Generative AI* (pp. 513–534). IGI Global Scientific Publishing., DOI: 10.4018/979-8-3693-6180-1.ch022

Tariq, M. U. (2025). AI-Powered Breakthroughs: Revolutionizing Cognitive Psychology and Neuropsychology With Machine Learning. In Bansal, R., Maqableh, T., Shuklaa, G., Rabby, F., & Lathabhavan, R. (Eds.), *Transforming Neuropsychology and Cognitive Psychology With AI and Machine Learning* (pp. 65–92). IGI Global Scientific Publishing., DOI: 10.4018/979-8-3693-9341-3.ch003

Tariq, M. U., & Sergio, R. (Eds.). (2025). *Cases on AI-Driven Solutions to Environmental Challenges*. IGI Global, 2025. https://doi.org/DOI: 10.4018/979-8-3693-7483-2

Tariq, M. U., & Sergio, R. (Eds.). (2025). *Convergence of AI, Education, and Business for Sustainability*. IGI Global., DOI: 10.4018/979-8-3373-1917-9

Xu, H., Seng, K. P., Ang, L. M., & Smith, J. (2024). Decentralized and distributed learning for AIoT: A comprehensive review, emerging challenges and opportunities. *IEEE Access : Practical Innovations, Open Solutions*, *12*, 101016–101052. DOI: 10.1109/ACCESS.2024.3422211

KEY TERMS AND DEFINITIONS

Artificial Intelligence of Things (AIoT): The combination of AI and the IoT to enable smarter automation, decision-making, and data analysis across various industries.

Wearable Technology: Smart electronic devices worn on the body that collect and analyze data, often used in healthcare, fitness, and sports performance monitoring.

Convolutional Neural Network (CNN): A deep learning algorithm primarily used for image and pattern recognition, applied in this context for detecting heart arrhythmias from electrocardiogram (ECG) data.

Electrocardiogram (ECG): A test that records the electrical activity of the heart to monitor heart health and detect irregularities.

Energy Harvesting (EH): The process of capturing and storing energy from external sources (e.g., solar, kinetic) to power electronic devices, reducing the need for batteries.

Deep Learning: A subset of AI that uses neural networks with multiple layers to analyze and interpret large datasets, enabling applications such as smart monitoring systems and automated decision-making.

Telehealth: Use of digital communication and technology to provide remote healthcare services, including monitoring, consultation, and diagnosis.

Internet of Medical Things (IoMT): A network of connected medical devices that collect, transmit, and analyze patient data for healthcare applications.

Cloud Computing: A system of remote servers that store, manage, and process data, enabling real-time healthcare monitoring and data sharing.

Machine Learning (ML: A branch of AI that allows systems to learn from data and improve decision-making without explicit programming.

Smart Home Monitoring System: A network of sensors and AI-driven devices that track activities, detect anomalies, and enhance security and automation in residential environments.

Aircraft Health Monitoring System (AHMS): A system that uses AI and IoT to analyze aircraft data in real-time, improving maintenance, safety, and operational efficiency.

Big Data Analytics: Process of analyzing large volumes of data to uncover patterns, trends, and insights for better decision-making.

Edge Computing: A computing approach where data is processed closer to the source (e.g., IoT devices) instead of relying on centralized cloud servers, reducing latency and improving efficiency.

Cybersecurity in Healthcare: Measures and technologies used to protect healthcare data and systems from cyber threats, ensuring patient information remains secure.

Predictive Maintenance: Use of AI and IoT to monitor equipment performance and predict failures before they occur, reducing downtime and maintenance costs.

Environmental Monitoring: The use of AIoT systems to detect hazardous materials, analyze environmental changes, and improve ecological conservation efforts.

Data Interoperability: The ability of different information systems, devices, and applications to communicate and exchange data effectively.

6G Technology: The next-generation wireless communication technology expected to provide faster, more reliable connectivity for AIoT applications.

Digital Twin: A virtual model of a physical object or system that is continuously updated with real-time data, used for simulations and decision-making.

Chapter 10
AIoT in Smart Education Systems

Ishani Maity
Brainware University, India

Arkadip Mandal
Brainware University, India

Piyal Roy
https://orcid.org/0009-0007-5378-2789
Brainware University, India

Saptarshi Kumar Sarkar
https://orcid.org/0009-0004-1786-8284
Brainware University, India

ABSTRACT

Convergence of Artificial Intelligence (AI) and the Internet of Things (IoT) has given rise to AIoT (Artificial Internet of Things), a transformative force shaping various industries, including education. We provide a comprehensive overview of AIoT, focusing on its applications, challenges, and future potential in education. It highlights how AIoT can enhance the efficiency and intelligence of educational systems by leveraging data generated by IoT devices, resulting in more personalized and effective learning experiences. Key challenges, such as privacy and security concerns, data management, ethical considerations, and the integration of traditional education systems, are also examined. The chapter further explores emerging AIoT technologies and their role in transforming smart cities and educational environments. It concludes by offering predictions and speculations about future trends, emphasizing the potential impact on educational outcomes and equity.

DOI: 10.4018/979-8-3693-8547-0.ch010

INTRODUCTION

IoT is a critical driver of the design of smart space, within which physical classrooms and virtual classes can be administered. The move to smart education that encompasses internet of things and artificial intelligence into the education system is appealing because the system impacts students' motivation, attendance, participation and mastery. Teachers' facilitation, school management, assessment and last but not the least, classroom management are few of the challenges that traditional education face. Innovations of recent ICTs such as IoT, AI, and 5G have brought about many intelligent solutions regarding many aspects in life; however, those intelligent solutions are not yet totally implemented in the educational system. Covid-19 pandemic situation has especially brought the instinct for novel, smart solutions to the field of education. This chapter discusses the (i) issues with the conventional educational system and reviews related studies (Badshah et al., 2023). The fourth industrial revolution is coming, and instead of using technology piecemeal, it is necessary to create new value through convergence. In this way, the combination of IoT connectivity with AI's capacity for learning allows for the development of increasingly automated and intelligent systems. As a result, learning about AI in preparation for the hyper-convergence and hyper-connectivity age should go beyond simply using AI technology and comprehending its fundamentals to include experiencing a wider range of environments. Because of this, major nations all over the world are actively leading the way for data schooling, especially AI education, from school through middle and high school. They feel that young students should be able to access and use the newest technologies with ease (Hong & Kim, 2024).

BACKGROUND

In the past decade, there has been extensive research into the integration of healthcare with advanced AI technologies, particularly focusing on the application of medical technology, smart devices, and the AIoT. This interdisciplinary research holds transformative potential, especially for improving healthcare access and quality in isolated and rural areas by leveraging AIoT's connectivity. In the healthcare sector, these technological advancements have contributed significantly to enhanced efficiency, reduced costs, and greater utility, paving the way for more affordable and effective care options. Researchers have also explored both the advantages and limitations of implementing AIoT solutions in healthcare, weighing the potential improvements in patient care against challenges such as data privacy and security (Tariq, 2025).

Although the use of IoT in health care has these advantages, it brings major issues particular to the vulnerability of sensitive health care data. These challenges have emerged as IoT devices have become more central to health care organizations, thus presenting the need to develop a better way of protecting data. At the same time, Intelligent Artificial Network of Things has become present and redefine intelligent system area, and therefore, people need more creative ideas for data processing taking into consideration the issues of privacy and scalability. Modern decentralized and distributed learning methodologies are now rapidly substituting conventional centralized models, which give the ways to process the vast amounts of generated IoT data while maintaining the density of data privacy. Such distributed learning approaches are particularly relevant particularly since they enable data to be processed at its point of origin thereby avoiding the need to transfer data to central servers thus cutting on privacy risks. This shift not only helps in secure data storage and management but also works well with the present requirement of the industry, concerning the large amount of data generated by different connected health care devices (Pise et al., 2022; Xu et al., 2024).

Importance and Impact of AIoT in Education

The AIoT useful course was used in this study to conduct experimental teaching. This 4D (find, define, develop, deliver) doubling diamonds shape was utilized to create the course and plan the educational material in order to monitor the students' self-efficacy as well as instructional anxiety. The notion of the Technology Acceptance Model, also called the TAM, was employed to investigate the effectiveness and pleasure of learning. Thirteen weeks of two classes per week, for a total of thirty-six Upper One pupils from a Kaohsiung senior high school, were chosen to be the research subjects. In order to ascertain the relationship between students' self-efficacy, anxiety, conclusions, and degree of experience with the AIOT course after the reversed learning process, questionnaires and qualitative telephone conversations were employed (Tsai et al., 2021; Tariq, 2024).

Objectives of the Chapter

The purpose of this chapter is to describe the integration on AI and the Internet of Things in educational systems which is also called as AIoT. Thus, this chapter seeks to explore how the innovative AIoT technologies may transform smart education to operate more efficiently in terms of learning impact, teaching control, and bureaucratic work. Hence, its importance lies in the analysis of AIoT's effect on existent environments as well as various learning formats like personalized learning, data-based decision making at real-time, or learner's engagement. Furthermore, the chapter aims at examining some of the challenges as well as potentialities that teachers and institutions may encounter in implementing technologies such as AIoT including; data security, integration of AIoT systems, and the competency of teachers. Moreover, as most of the existing AIoT studies were reviewed on the basis of innovations at the end of 2020, this chapter also presents case studies and best practices for the education community to follow how AIoT can be applied to smart education. Finally, the chapter aims to propose a vision on how the AIoT could bring effective intelligent, responsive, and adaptive learning environments to education.

CONCEPT OF SMART EDUCATION SYSTEMS

Information technology advancements offer chances for innovative techniques, strategies, and resources for fresh or enhanced training and teaching methods. Moreover, a paradigm change in education is being made possible by new technologies. We created a Smart Learning Framework after looking into a variety of information technologies that promote smart education. The information technologies are theoretically organized in a tiered architecture by the framework. Based on the framework, we also created a clever approach to instructional design. Moreover, we demonstrate how to create a specific class or lecture design using the structure and design approach. We looked at smart education systems that have been published in the literature in order to confirm the smart education framework (Tariq, 2025).

Evolution of Education Technology

The evolution of education technology in visual arts, as illustrated in Figure 1, highlights the integration of technological standards, frameworks, and student expectations in modern art education. This article delves into the role of technological standards in the visual arts, arguing that such standards guide what art educators are expected to teach. The discussion includes an analysis of various influential frameworks, such as the National Visual Arts Standards, which lay out expectations for what students should know and be able to do in the visual arts. It also examines the NAEA's Contemporary Skills and Professional Guidelines for Visual Arts Educators, as well as the teaching practices of 26 college-level art education programs. These guidelines collectively emphasize the integration of technology as both a teaching tool and a creative medium. As such, they encourage art educators to adapt their methods and curricula to reflect evolving technological capabilities, recognizing that modern art education must increasingly include digital tools and media (Patton & Buffington, 2016). With the shift toward technology-enhanced learning, schools are under pressure to invest significantly in digital programs, which often require high-bandwidth infrastructure, skilled technicians, specialized professional development, and ongoing maintenance. This increased demand raises the question: why would universities pursue such funding for instructional technology when student performance outcomes in high-tech and low-tech environments often show minimal difference? The answer lies in students' evolving expectations. In today's world, learners demand more from their education than traditional lecture-based or correspondence-style learning. They seek engaging, interactive experiences that reflect the technologically rich environments they are accustomed to outside the classroom (Tariq, 2024).

Figure 1. Evolution of education technology in visual arts.

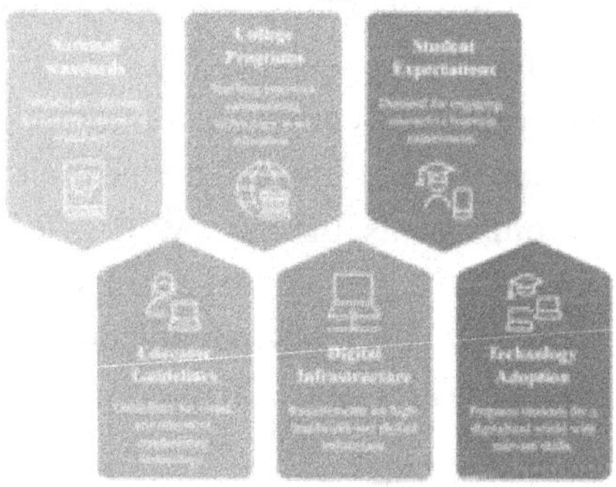

The adoption of technology in education thus transcends mere academic performance metrics. It addresses a broader mandate to prepare students for a digitalized world, aligning with their expectations and preparing them with relevant, practical skills. This approach ultimately aims to provide a learning experience that resonates with the digital culture in which students live, equipping them with the competencies they need to thrive in a technology-driven society (Rogers & Dhatariya, 2001).

Characteristics of Smart Education Systems

Throughout history, various efforts have been made to enhance the impact of education, aiming to improve both teaching methods and learning outcomes. In recent years, there has been a significant focus on the integration of newly developed technologies, particularly Information and Communication Technology (ICT), in education. This trend has garnered international attention as countries around the globe seek to incorporate these advancements into their educational systems. Despite these national initiatives, the supporting infrastructure to effectively implement and sustain such efforts remains inadequate. Addressing this gap, the Plug-in Integrated Education and Learning Assistance System has been developed, designed to harness the positive effects of ICT on education. Some of the features that are offered in this system include: Monitoring functionality for educators, students, and parents; tutoring capability; learning mechanisms; e-Portfolio; and ways of creating content meant to support a more effective and encouraging learning climate (Jo et al., 2014). Central to this article is, therefore, the question of which factors may serve as antecedent towards engendering meaningful learning in technologically supported contexts. The facts of the very fast rate of development of technologies, as well as the goals and objectives of modern cross-sectional educational theories, presuppose the profound transformation of the educational environment. These changes are described systematically in this article and the theoretical model of smart education is developed here to evaluate learning effectiveness and to help educators to support learning activities in technology supported environments. Within this framework, three key components are identified: teacher, learner, and technology. All of these elements are essential for learning activities, but on an individual level, they continue to be broken down even further to define their roles and relationships. Through specifying these components, the framework offers an overall template of how the learning and teaching processes can be promoted in technology enhanced environment and, therefore, how educators can enhance the use of technology in improving learning experiences (Zhu et al., 2016).

Key Components and Technologies

As far as long time ago, the idea was set that advanced computer technologies would be able to interpret natural language and to predict our requirements using contextual logical processing in order to perform necessary actions without reference to the user. With personal computers being so nicely integrated into daily use, with PCs getting more and more diminutive, the problem of how one comes to grips with machines has emerged as a critical question. In the last three decades, much has been invested in trying to build a strong Natural User Interface (NUI) that supports direct user interaction with computers. But appreciable advancement has been done in this area and what has been achieved is still some way off from becoming ubiquitous in daily use. Still, as the general challenges above have unraveled, improvements in voice recognition and machine learning have gone on, and the amount of well-formatted data that applications and content supply enables has risen, opening fresh doors to interaction and utility (Sarikaya, 2017). The purpose of this chapter is to provide some information on new technologies concerning structures of modular power converters, employed in electric vehicles. Whereas now a conventional electric drivetrain layout can be characterized as involving one inverter tightly coupled to the battery. This configuration also restricts the system to contain only a single high voltage battery module so that the dc-link voltage of the inverter together with the latter's apparent power and rating is defined by the battery voltage. For this reason, various new power converter architectures have been developed in recent years to improve the qualification and efficiency. These new architectures enable several battery modules and higher interconnection between the battery and the inverter and hence improving the overall performance and flexibility of the electric vehicles. These improvements not only contribute positively to the efficiency of electric drivetrain but also addresses the problem for electric vehicles to penetrate a market that is becoming competitive by making use sophisticated technology responsive to the drive towards sustainability (Stippich et al., 2017; Tariq, 2025).

AIOT TECHNOLOGIES IN SMART EDUCATION

An AIoT system created especially for educational reasons is examined in this article along with its uses. Three interesting case studies that test the AIoT system in diverse educational settings are presented. Figure 2 shows the integration of AI and IoT components, applications, benefits, and challenges in modern educational systems.

Figure 2. AIoT technologies in smart education.

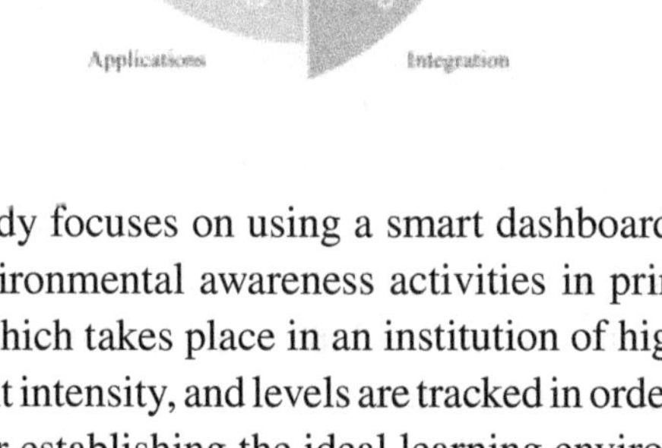

The first case study focuses on using a smart dashboard to track the condition of plants during environmental awareness activities in primary education. In the second case study, which takes place in an institution of higher learning, variables like temperature, light intensity, and levels are tracked in order to provide customized recommendations for establishing the ideal learning environment through modifications. The final case study investigates how plants may be able to detect human activity patterns and presence in educational settings. Plant data is analyzed using the AIoT system's capabilities to determine the presence of humans.

Overview of AI Technologies in Education

The holistic idea of this chapter is to impart a conceptual understanding about AI stemming from the basic notion of intelligence, its role and need in our daily life, and its necessity in business and education. AI has been part of our lives for a very long time and has now very subtly integrated into our daily lives to such an extent that we can now in many ways work efficiently only with the aid of this intelligence. There has been a slow transformation of their education systems from the earlier traditional system of education to outcome based education systems in the recent years. The uses of AI-based systems in the outcome based education is valuable in delivering tailored experience across different teaching-learning cohorts. Also, in this Covid-19 where education across the world is taught online the process can be managed more efficiently by incorporating the taste of AI. Our perspective in this chapter is to focus on scope, applications, and the future of AI in education (Bhise et al., 2022). Indeed, credit has shifted digital technologies into the internal part of our life. It alters the way we seek information, the way we relate to one another as well as how we conduct ourselves. Such a transformation is applicable in almost all the fields including education. The main objective of this article is to identify prospective impact of artificial technologies to the study process and to predict possible changes in educational landscape (Chassignol et al., 2018; Tariq, 2024).

Overview of IoT Technologies in Education

In the years past with the spread of the world wide web, global communication among people of the world is now attainable. However, with the help of the IoT, the human-to-human communication has been shifted to refer to human-to-human, human-to-machine, and machine-to-machine communications all together. Therefore, it has been possible for IoT to capture all aspects of human life such as security and privacy, health care, recycling, and keeping an eye on the environment, among others. In this chapter, we address the significance of IoT technology in the field of education in improving the efficiency of teaching and learning (Ramlowat & Pattanayak, 2019). The different ways in which technology will influence the process of learning in the following years is as follows: IoT still reinforces its relevant role with regard to Information and Communications Technologies and social advancement. By using IoT, institutions can develop better learning environments, increase organizational effectiveness and get immediate, valuable information on students. The aim of this study is to identify the benefits that can be realized from IoT in higher learning institutions and how to optimize on them while avoiding the costs associated with them. Further efforts are necessary for releasing the full potential of IoT systems and technologies (Aldowah et al., 2017).

Integration of AI and IoT in Educational Contexts

Artificial Intelligence and the Internet of Things have improved decision-making processes, efficiency, and allocation of resources in schools using a mixed-methods approach that combines statistical information through system log files and qualitative knowledge from discussions with school administrators (Ghosh et al., 2024). The outcomes show that the integration of these forms of technology has significantly increased operational efficiency and data-driven decision-making (Sahni & Singh, 2024). In order to improve student learning outcomes, a growing corpus of research is concentrating on the integration of computational thinking (CT) with AI. In this topic, numerous researchers have created educational activities that meet different learning objectives. It is unclear how instructional efforts lead to the incorporation of AI on CT in students' learning processes, despite the abundance of studies concentrating on instructional layout and student learning results. We carried out a thorough literature assessment of empirical research that combined AI and CT towards student development in order to fill this study vacuum (Weng et al., 2024).

APPLICATIONS OF AIOT IN EDUCATION

In this work, a set of smart environments IoT detection tools—such as "additional devices for ecological IoT detecting" and "ecological assessment systems incorporating artificial intelligence technology"—that use the Internet of Things for ecological education are presented (Sahoo et al., 2024). Supplemental tools for environmental Internet of Things detection gather the necessary data by means of various environmental detectors at the Internet of Things' foundational layer. These tools are then integrated into college students' living quarters. To help students better understand the shift in the environment trend at each time point, the environmental analysis system uses artificial intelligence technology in conjunction with data analysis to create a visual chart.

Personalized Learning

Education is a process that takes place throughout the individual's life and depends on people's experience, awareness, preferences, more or less unconsciously, cultural determination, and setting. Knowledge and learning have been defined as a relatively permanent change in behaviour or knowledge base of a learner. Education is irrespective of an individual interaction of knowledge or skill from others and or experience. Consequently, learning is a process which enables an individual to gain new information, modify his or her perceptions, develop new competencies, and increase his or her insight. This means that, particular learning models are capable of responding to individual requirements and aims. In addition, to specificity of individualization, there is the aspect of technology integration, which is highly effective. This chapter provides a review of the recent research literature on personalized learning as technology is changing how learning can be effectively personalized (Shemshack & Spector, 2020).

Adaptive Learning Platforms

The use of artificial intelligence or more commonly termed as machine learning is the leading factor that has culminated the fast development of e-learning platforms which bestow a revolutionary interest to the field of education. Against this background, there is the need to focus on how AI/ML is integrated into adaptive instructional technologies to improve the quality of learning. The purpose of this research is two-fold, which includes identifying the current state of the implementation of AI/ML in online education for adaptive learning; and defining the benefits and challenges that would aid in measuring AI/ML impact on students' performance, retention, and engagement levels. In light of this a literature review was conducted to seek knowledge on Machine Learning and Artificial Intelligence in e-learning, with special emphasis on articles from 2010 to the present. To reviewed 63 articles, systematic approach was used to evaluate the presence of adaptive algorithms for learning and their educational perspectives (Gligorea et al., 2023). A great number of modern e-learning environments include elements that can be helpful in adapting the delivered material to the learners in terms of the content they receive. Scientists from various nations have directed their attention towards this sphere and attempted to work out options that can help teachers to design the PC&LOs and learning objects D for forming of the individual content for definite learners, according to the purpose of the mentioned study is to review the works and publications concerning the adaptive learning, presented in the sphere of E-Learning platforms (Talaghzi et al., 2020).

Intelligent Tutoring Systems

ITSs can be considered one of the remarkable streams and applications of AI in the educational process that are aimed to deliver individualized learning with consideration of learner needs. As a prelude to the subsequent chapters, this introduction is intended to provide the reader with an easy-to-understand, technical overview of ITSs: what they are, why they exist, considerations in the historical evolution of ITSs, and how ITSs' basic architecture functions. Defining the ITS based on the ITS components involved, this chapter then explains how the current ITS can be differentiated from ITS converted from traditional Computer Assisted Instruction (CAI) systems, followed by a focus on a range of ITS architectures.

By their nature, Intelligent Tutoring Systems are meant to present learners with adapted lessons simulating individual tutoring. While using very natural pedagogical strategies, ITSs, based on AI technologies, have the ability to monitor students' performance in real time, demonstrating the content and providing feedback depending on students' achievements. It is most useful in a variety of learning environments with heterogeneous groupings as learners will come with different learning experiences and distinct learning modalities. The principle that stands behind the creation of ITSs is the intention to promote improvement of educational performance when specific focus is paid to those students who require additional assistance in terms of improved learning of a particular subject and comprehension of the material taught. The need for ITSs can be dated back to CAI and it is important to note that ITS is a vast improvement on CAI. While CAI was aimed at presenting pre-designed instructional content, ITSs made a further leap in adding certain algorithms that evaluate a student's responses and his/her learning patterns. This Increase signified a paradigm change in the educational technology because they created way of interaction between the learner and the system. The features of ITSs are based on cognitive theories of psychology and instruction, producing systems that not only transmit knowledge, but also invite students into meaningful learning experiences.

A 'typical' ITS consists of several key components: They include a domain model, a student model, a pedagogical model and the graphical user interface. Domain model depicts the content knowledge the system intends to ensure the learners master and holds the concept and skill requirement information. The student model, in contrast, records the learner's achievements, potential difficulties, and preferences which allows the system to adapt the lesson to the learner. The pedagogical model may refer to the techniques that the system uses in order to support learning, prescribed the most effective method to present content and evaluate comprehension. Lastly, the user interface serves to share the ways by which students effectively engage with the system and obtain content.

These first systems would subsequently set the stage for future ones and prove the concept of AI in education. Conducting a meta-analysis of the outcome data from 50 controlled research studies comparing intelligent tutoring systems to traditional classroom instruction, the chapter demonstrates significant benefits of ITS. Intelligent tutoring methods raised test scores in students by an average of 0.66 levels above the non-intelligent tutoring levels; this means that the students' scores improved and moved from 50% level to 75% level. That said, the study found differences in broad patterns of instructional use and learning outcomes, which depended greatly on the types of assessments made. The enhancements of ITSs were categorized in terms of enhancements captured by locally developed tests or norm referenced enhanced tests. Thus, this research underpins the work of bringing congruence between curriculum and fair goals, as well as of enhancing both testing instruments and the aims of education.

Classroom Management

Consequently, classroom management, abbreviated here as CRM, has been linked historically to notions of behavioral containment and students' misconduct in school environments. But this view only captures rudimentary aspects of what it means by EMS and MMS. Thus, CRM is not limited to the direct consideration of controversies in studying them as a range of interactions encompassing a proactive approach to create favorable conditions in reference to acceptable and productive behavior and learning. This change of view underscores the rationale of developing favourable classroom environment whereby students are motivated to take responsibility for their behaviours and as a result, receive better outcomes in their classes.

Studies conducted into CRM have time and time again revealed a positive relationship between teachers' managerial competencies and student conduct and academic results. A number of researchers who adopted the process- product research design in schooled contexts have found that managing teaching practices significantly enhance a more fruitful learning environment. The cases of disruptive behaviors owe much to proper management by teachers since they also reduce cases of disruptive behavior and enhance a secure learning environment with the learners. This research supports the central position that teachers occupy as effective agents in shaping the character and climate of classrooms as well as the students' academic experience.

Over the years, scholars have identified several key elements necessary for successful CRM. These elements include clear expectations for behavior, consistent enforcement of rules, effective communication, and the ability to build strong relationships with students. Together, these components form the foundation of an effective classroom management strategy that not only minimizes behavioral problems but also enhances student learning and engagement. Despite the wealth of research outlining best practices for CRM, there remains a gap in understanding how effectively these findings are translated into actual classroom practices. To date, no comprehensive surveys have been conducted to assess how current teachers apply research outcomes in their classrooms. Recognizing this gap, a survey was developed to explore the extent to which educators utilize established CRM strategies and principles in their daily practice (Little & Akin-Little, 2008). By collecting data directly from teachers, this survey aims to provide valuable insights into the relationship between research-based strategies and their practical implementation in the classroom, ultimately informing future professional development and educational policy. This inquiry into the application of CRM research outcomes is vital not only for enhancing teacher effectiveness but also for improving student experiences and outcomes in the classroom. By understanding how well teachers are able to integrate research findings into their management practices, educators, administrators, and policymakers can work collaboratively to support ongoing professional development and create environments that promote student success. Ultimately, this survey seeks to bridge the gap between theory and practice, ensuring that the benefits of classroom management research are realized in educational settings.

Smart Classrooms

This chapter elaborates on the theoretical possibilities and guidelines for the adoption of smart learning spaces in schools. Networks of learning resources are expanding students' potentiality of engaging in different types of formal and non-formal learning, in physical and/or virtual contexts, both within and beyond the classroom. Smart Pedagogy has to have a set of agreed upon definitions for knowledge and learning; it also has to engage in a more profound analysis of the learning process, thinking process and communication. It should provide actionable recommendations regarding the who, what, and why of teaching in a hybrid human–machine environment. Smart classrooms will be made up of several smart learning spaces, eventually employing some type of artificial intelligence (Lorenzo et al., 2021). Fast proliferation of various types of smart devices, smart systems, and smart technologies provides academic institutions, students and learners with enormous opportunities in terms of new approaches to learning technologies, education, learning processes and strategies, corporate training, user's personal productivity and efficiency, and faster and better quality of services provided (Uskov et al., 2015).

Automated Attendance and Monitoring

In our busy environment, the majority of the procedure is automated to minimize manual error and human interference. If we might automate many of the delicate, intricate daily tasks, it will be simple. This essay addresses an advanced attendance system which automatically keeps track of and regulates students' attendance in a learning environment. Additionally, this system automatically analyzes data and generates comprehensive reports on a weekly, monthly, and annual basis. The complete system is constructed with Arduino electronics as well as RFID scanners (Kovelan et al., 2019). Currently, the development of smartphones is on the rise, and it has also lighted the way to enhance the computational power, security and search and rescue with the help of smartphones. Most of the many organizations still use paper based system to update the attendance records. Such information management system as manual recording of attendance for employees has led to occurrence of challenges in information accuracy and workforce performance efficiency. In this chapter, reviewed and discussed various methods, applications and systems that can be used by the employer to monitor their staff attendance using fingerprint, Iris, RFID and GPS (Alagasan et al., 2021).

Administrative Efficiency

For nonprofit managers, the question of whether accounting metrics for managerial efficiency an impact on donations have is crucial. Extant literature is not conclusive. While some studies find no significant relationship, others discover a significant negative relationship. The authors look into a number of explanations for the earlier inconsistent outcomes. Donors appear to be cutting back on their contributions to organizations with higher cost of administration ratios when those ratios are most likely to be accurate and useful. The authors propose that the reason several previous studies did not uncover significant relationships is that they included a large number of organizations in their samples for whom their administrative ratios were either incorrect or not useful for donor purposes. Prior studies are also impacted by model specification flaws, but they are not as important as sample composition.

Data-Driven Decision Making

The advanced sensor infrastructure of Industry 4.0 is assisting decision-makers in manufacturing and maintenance by making it easier to apply algorithms that assess data, predict possible issues, and provide remedial actions. This chapter provides an overview of the literature on data-driven maintenance decision-making and makes recommendations for future research topics related to Industry 4.0 service applications. The primary research topics include utilizing the cloud as a continuum for most activities and integrating maintenance decision-making with other processes like scheduling and planning.

Resource Management

High involvement management (HIM) approach that is considered best practice and that may lead to the enhanced organizational performance has provided the stimulus for research in human resource management (HRM). However, there are still concerns that the general rule still holds true, that is, that THEM will only perform better under certain conditions and that the business plan of the company and the environment in which the HRM systems will operate should be in harmony. A flurry of studies aimed at determining if HIM is, in fact, globally relevant has been carried out since the 1990s. The studies are reviewed in this chapter. The intellectual underpinnings of the performance-HRM argument are initially presented in this study. This shows that there is more at stake than just a rivalry between universalism.

Student Engagement and Support

Academic advising, career counseling, and wellness services are examples of centralized student support that are crucial components of the a first-year student experience. Although a number of studies have looked into the relationship between using these services and student outcomes, there hasn't been much attention paid to how they might affect student involvement. This gap is addressed in the current work. A weekly interview was conducted with nineteen first-year students at a remote institution in Australia. A theoretical model of student participation was used to analyze the subgroup of data that reported how often students used support services. Results indicate that by enhancing students' feelings of wellbeing, self-efficacy, and belonging, support services may increase student engagement. They also present chances to interrupt patterns of disengagement (Picton & Kahu, 2022).

Virtual Classrooms and Augmented Reality

In this study, the teaching tactics in the virtual classroom are combined with the use of augmented reality (AR) to create a virtual learning application. The pedagogical models currently in use for higher education courses include virtual learning through the use of 3D models, thanks to this study. The Internet of Things, or IoT, course is intended to be taught to undergraduate students through the AR smartphone app. In order to help learners better understand ideas linked to hardware and embedded systems, an online 3D modeling environment has been built to teach the fundamentals of IoT lab experiments. The primary goal of this study project is to evaluate how well students perform in augmented reality courses that integrate with the current virtual classroom pedagogical style. The KNN and linear regression are used to analyze the student's performance (Maiti et al., 2021).

AI-Driven Student Support Systems

The application, views, and effects of Decision Support Systems, or DSS, in college administration are examined in this research. A cross-sectional study was carried out among administrators in higher education from different institutions, with an emphasis on DSS. Administrators indicate strong employment of DSS and commend its effectiveness and ease of use, underscoring its crucial role in higher education administration. According to the report, DSS has a favorable impact on initiatives for student success, enrolment management, the allocation of resources, and strategic planning. Furthermore, it illustrates the correlation between the implementation of DSS and good results, such as enhanced productivity and perceived advantages. But enduring problems including poor data quality, privacy difficulties, and opposition to change draw attention to the necessity of better data management techniques, moral issues, and change management methods (Zhang & Goyal, 2024).

CHALLENGES AND CONSIDERATIONS

In the era of the IoT, millions of sensors and gadgets gather and process environmental data, send it to cloud centers, and then use the Internet to get feedback for connectedness and perception. It is challenging to send vast volumes of heterogeneous data, interpret complicated situations from this data, and then act quickly to make wise decisions. AI, particularly deep learning, has demonstrated effectiveness in a number of fields, including natural language processing, speech recognition, and computer vision. Figure 3 illustrates the integration of AI and IoT, key challenges, benefits, and future considerations

Figure 3. Challenges and considerations in AIoT.

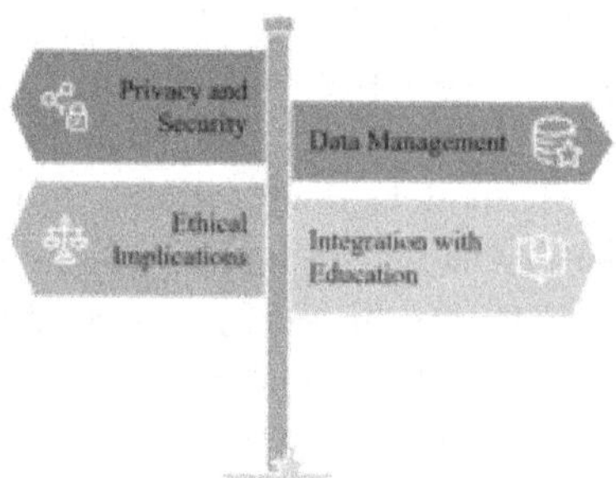

The advent of AI in the IoT marks the era of AIoT. In order to demonstrate how AI may enable the IoT to become quicker, smarter, greener, and safer, this article provides a thorough overview of AIoT.

Privacy and Security Concerns

Research extensively explores the interrelationship between security concerns (SC) and privacy concerns (PC), suggesting that while these constructs are recognized as distinct, they are often closely connected and, in some cases, treated as nearly synonymous. However, addressing the nuanced distinctions between SC and PC can provide a more comprehensive view of users' apprehensions regarding data security in online environments. To this end, this study introduces an Internet Users Data Transport Security Concern (IUITSC) scale, which builds upon the separate dimensions of SC and PC, offering a robust measure for assessing user concerns about data protection. By integrating this scale with an existing privacy concern (PC) scale, the proposed model encompasses a complete spectrum of security and privacy-related issues (SC–PC) as perceived by internet users. To validate the construct, the study employs a nomological network that incorporates factors of trust and personality traits, allowing for a rigorous evaluation of the relationships between these elements. The paper lays a theoretical foundation for various factor structures, exploring both several first-order factor models and a more complex second-order factor model, each contributing to an enriched understanding of user security and privacy concerns (Bansal, 2017).

In the context of e-commerce, consumer concerns surrounding security and privacy are prominent barriers to wider adoption, as these apprehensions often amplify the perception of risk associated with online transactions. Understanding how security and privacy concerns influence consumers' risk assessments can offer insights for mitigating these worries and encouraging broader e-commerce participation. This study also examines the connection between anonymity and safety by applying the theory of planned behavior, which provides a framework for investigating how perceptions of risk affect users' behavioral intentions in the online domain. Specifically, the research explores the interplay between trust, privacy, and security concerns, assessing their collective impact on consumers' perceived risk of e-commerce. The study validates its theoretical model with survey data, highlighting how fostering trust and addressing privacy and security concerns can influence e-commerce adoption. By delving into these relationships, the research offers a nuanced perspective on the factors shaping consumer attitudes toward online security and privacy, ultimately contributing to a deeper understanding of digital risk perception and its effects on behavior (Gurung & Raja, 2016).

Data Management and Quality

In complex e-business environments, empowering decision-makers with the autonomy to manage data quality is essential for making informed and accurate decisions. This research introduces a decision-support framework designed to help decision-makers evaluate data quality through two key lenses: objectively, or context-independently, and temporally, or in a context-dependent manner. At the core of this framework is the Information Products Map (IPMAP), a structured tool that leverages the data product approach to assess and maintain high data quality standards. This approach emphasizes completeness as a critical measure of data quality, illustrating how decision-makers can reliably evaluate data integrity. Furthermore, the research presents a decision-making tool, IPView, that integrates the proposed framework, allowing users to consistently uphold data quality by monitoring and assessing completeness and other relevant quality factors.

Data quality significantly impacts consumer perceptions, as many products and services are delivered through data-driven processes. Poor data quality can lead to unfavorable consumer experiences, diminishing the perceived value of these goods and services. This is particularly pertinent to large-scale companies like AT&T, which rely on data to operate their global cognitive network, manage daily functions, and support strategic decision-making across the enterprise. The article examines AT&T's strategic initiatives aimed at regulating and enhancing data quality. These efforts stem from the understanding that once inaccurate data is introduced into a database, correcting it can be an arduous and sometimes unfeasible task. Therefore, AT&T has implemented proactive measures to manage data quality from the outset, ensuring that high-quality data underpins its operations, ultimately leading to better business outcomes and customer satisfaction (Shankaranarayanan & Cai, 2006).

Ethical Implications

Traditional nursing ethics emphasize a high degree of care for the well-being of research subjects, setting rigorous standards for their protection and dignity. Initially, the establishment of ethical standards in nursing research was rooted in quantitative methodologies, with clear guidelines for ensuring participant safety. However, as qualitative research methods gain prominence, nurses are required to navigate additional ethical complexities. They must be vigilant about challenges associated with study design and planning, which include the risks of coercion, deception, and breaches of confidentiality. Moreover, qualitative research often brings about an "emergent design," where study protocols evolve over time. This demands a flexible approach to informed consent, as participants may need to be continually informed and reassured about any evolving risks and objectives of the study. This evolving nature of research collaboration calls for innovative strategies to safeguard research subjects while respecting the inherent subjective nature of qualitative inquiry.

Beyond nursing, the ethics of technology are evaluated in various fields, such as Science and Technology Studies (STS), engineering, computer science, management, and law. Although these disciplines explore the responsibilities associated with technological advancements, the role of businesses and executives in the creation, adaptation, and application of these technologies, especially within communities, is less well-documented. Businesses play a crucial part in technology development, often holding specific beliefs and visions about technology's role in society. However, their social obligations regarding the ethical progression and responsible deployment of technology remain underexplored. This chapter focuses on digital technologies and gadgets equipped with increasingly sophisticated sensing, data storage, and transmission capabilities, which pose significant ethical challenges by their ability to intrude into human activities and personal spaces. As these digital tools become more pervasive, it raises questions about the responsibility's businesses have in ethically developing and deploying these technologies and the standards they should uphold to protect societal welfare (Martin et al., 2022).

Integration with Traditional Education Systems

This chapter explores the role of both conventional and digital technologies in vocational education, analyzing current trends in development and modernization to assess their impact on training quality. The authors argue that integrating these technologies is essential for enhancing the overall standard of vocational education, as it allows for a more versatile and comprehensive approach to teaching and skill development. They propose a strategy where the unique strengths of conventional and digital technologies complement and reinforce each other, creating a unified approach to vocational training. By combining these tools, instructors can leverage traditional methods alongside innovative digital solutions, making the learning experience more dynamic and relevant to industry standards (Tariq, 2024).

To achieve this integration, the authors outline four key methods of technology incorporation: addition, replacement, development, and transformation. In the "addition" method, digital tools are introduced to supplement existing conventional techniques, enhancing the learning process without completely replacing traditional methods. "Replacement" involves substituting outdated practices with modern technologies, improving efficiency and engagement. The "development" approach focuses on advancing existing technologies to create a more cohesive learning experience, while "transformation" reimagines the entire educational framework to seamlessly incorporate both conventional and digital tools. The chapter also provides algorithms designed to guide the integration of these tools within specific subjects and educational initiatives, making it easier for instructors to implement these methods effectively. These strategies and algorithms serve as valuable resources for college instructors and administrators in secondary vocational education, helping them adopt an approach that fosters higher didactic productivity and aligns with the evolving demands of the workforce (Vetitnev et al., 2020).

FUTURE TRENDS AND INNOVATIONS

As the world's population continues to grow and the industrial sector develops, cities often suffer from their inability to offer a good quality of life to their residents due to the absence of proper smart technologies. This has however been dealt with by the World Wide Web of Things (Internet of Things) which links actual item through gadget, sensors, software or internet connections. This has shifted the infrastructure of smart cities by introducing various technologies that make work efficient, the environment better and residents of the city comfortable. AI can now be applied to the vast amount of data generated by IoT which is creating new opportunities for the construction of future smart cities. In this review chapter, we define smart cities, examine IoT architecture, and give an overview of these urban areas (Alahi et al., 2023).

Emerging Technologies in AIoT for Education

The emergence of the AIoT is profoundly shaped by the convergence of technologies like the Internet of Things (IoT) and artificial intelligence (AI), which collectively enable innovative applications across various sectors. The accelerating development and integration of these technologies are introducing novel challenges, demanding a comprehensive understanding and expansion of AI capabilities. As a result, there is an increased emphasis on cultivating AI competencies across industries, particularly in the industrial sector, where the need for professionals skilled in AI and IoT applications is rapidly growing. Recognizing this trend, academic institutions are intensifying efforts to promote AI education and ensure that students graduate with relevant, industry-ready skills. However, a significant barrier exists: many teachers lack adequate knowledge in AI, which impedes effective AI instruction in classrooms. Addressing this, it becomes crucial to not only train teachers in AI competencies but also to equip them with pedagogical strategies for teaching these skills. In this study, we propose an initiative known as Artificially Intelligent Internet of Things Professional Development (AIoT-PD), designed to support teachers' professional growth in AI and IoT domains, thereby preparing them to introduce AI competencies in their classrooms effectively (Kitcharoen et al., 2024).

AIoT has recently gained widespread attention, becoming one of the most discussed and researched topics in technological circles. Although many researchers are focused on exploring AIoT applications, there remains a gap in the healthcare sector, where technological advancements lag behind. The concept of a Smart Healthcare System is not new; however, integrating AI, IoT, and cloud computing to improve upon traditional healthcare services can revolutionize the industry. Such advancements could enhance patient care, streamline operations, and make healthcare systems more efficient and responsive to patient needs. By modernizing healthcare through AIoT, we can bridge the gap between current healthcare practices and future-ready solutions, fostering a system where intelligent, connected devices enable better health outcomes for individuals and communities alike.

Predictions and Speculations for the Future of Smart Education

In this work, we explore the intersection of big data and urban governance beyond the traditional frameworks associated with smart cities. While much research has focused on how data-driven systems are reshaping urban life within these "actually existing" smart cities, our focus extends to the implications of urban algorithms and the material-discursive activities shaping governance in the cities of the future. Rather than simply examining how data is used to manage current urban spaces, we delve into how data and algorithms actively participate in shaping the future vision of urban life. Through preemptive security measures, these algorithms forecast potential risks to public safety, ranging from the threat of human injury to possible urban disruptions. This approach anticipates and seeks to mitigate risks, enforcing a layer of security that predefines the needs and organization of urban life, effectively insuring it against anticipated threats (Leszczynski, 2016). These systems highlight the transformative potential of urban algorithms as both administrative tools and agents of change, shifting urban governance toward proactive, data-driven approaches.

Alongside urban governance, the integration of digital database technologies in education is transforming policy and administrative approaches in this sector. Schools and government bodies are increasingly adopting digital tools that serve as modern policy instruments, enabling new forms of data collection, analysis, and interpretation. This chapter provides two case studies that illustrate the influence of these digital policy tools in education. The first case is Pearson Education's Learning Curve, a vast online database that uses advanced data visualizations to interpret and draw insights from global educational data, offering a comprehensive view of educational systems worldwide. The second case examines 'knowledge analytics' platforms, which track and predict student performance through digital footprints, enabling educators and administrators to intervene more strategically based on predictive insights. These tools exemplify how digital database technologies are shaping education by allowing policymakers to better understand and manage educational processes. Together, these digital platforms underscore the role of big data and predictive analytics as central to the governance and future planning of both urban environments and educational systems (Williamson, 2016).

Potential Impact on Educational Outcomes and Equity

This chapter offers a critical review of the indicators used to measure equity in educational outcomes, focusing on their effectiveness in capturing disparities across different social and economic backgrounds. The study systematically assesses these indicators through multiple criteria, including their methodological rigor, the relevance of their application, and their ability to accurately reflect equity within educational contexts. By analyzing the structural impact of sample composition on equity measures, the study highlights how different sampling choices can influence the validity and reliability of equity metrics. The examination uses both empirical data from the German National Educational Panel Experiment and theoretical frameworks to evaluate the robustness of these indicators. Such an approach allows for a nuanced understanding of how socioeconomic factors, particularly achievement gaps linked to students' socioeconomic status (SES), affect educational outcomes in middle school environments.

A key finding of this study is the moderate to high validity convergence among various equity indicators, underscoring the reliability of these metrics in capturing SES-related achievement gaps. The research further indicates that longitudinal indicators, which track students' progress over time, provide a more comprehensive evaluation of student intake effects compared to cross-sectional indicators that capture a single time point. Additionally, the study finds that employing multilevel indicators can significantly reduce sampling error, making it easier to accurately assess equity within diverse educational settings. However, indicators derived from mean differences and regular least-squares regression analysis are noted for their practicality due to their standardization and interpretability. Such metrics allow researchers and educators to effectively compare educational outcomes across demographic groups while ensuring that the indicators remain accessible and informative. This research thus contributes valuable insights into the assessment of educational equity, demonstrating the importance of selecting appropriate indicators and methodologies to ensure that measurements of equity are both valid and interpretable (Nachbauer & Kyriakides, 2020).

CONCLUSION AND FUTURE SCOPE

This chapter has explored the transformative potential of integrating AI and IoT into education, highlighting the opportunities and challenges associated with smart learning systems. The integration of emerging technologies such as edge computing, digital tools, and AI competencies has the potential to revolutionize educational environments by enhancing personalization, improving data-driven decision-making, and fostering more equitable outcomes. However, concerns around privacy, security, and ethical implications remain critical, and careful consideration must be given to address these issues. Future work should focus on refining AIoT systems to better support teachers and learners, ensuring that technology integration aligns with educational goals, and developing robust frameworks to safeguard data integrity and equity. Further research is needed to assess long-term impacts on educational outcomes, refine AI training programs for educators, and explore innovative methods to bridge the gap between traditional and smart educational systems.

REFERENCES

Alagasan, K., Alkawaz, M. H., Iqbal Hajamydeen, A., & Mohammed, M. N. (2021). A review paper on advanced attendance and monitoring systems. In *2021 IEEE 12th Control and System Graduate Research Colloquium (ICSGRC)* (pp. 195–200). https://doi.org/DOI: 10.1109/ICSGRC53186.2021.9515249

Alahi, M. E. E., Sukkuea, A., Tina, F. W., Nag, A., Kurdthongmee, W., Suwannarat, K., & Mukhopadhyay, S. C. (2023). Integration of IoT-enabled technologies and artificial intelligence (AI) for smart city scenario: Recent advancements and future trends. *Sensors (Basel)*, *23*(11), 5206. DOI: 10.3390/s23115206 PMID: 37299934

Aldowah, H., Ul Rehman, S., Ghazal, S., & Naufal Umar, I. (2017). Internet of things in higher education: A study on future learning. *Journal of Physics: Conference Series*, *892*, 012017. DOI: 10.1088/1742-6596/892/1/012017

Badshah, A., Ghani, A., Daud, A., Jalal, A., Bilal, M., & Crowcroft, J. (2023). Towards smart education through Internet of Things: A survey. *ACM Computing Surveys*, *56*(2), 1–33. DOI: 10.1145/3610401

Bansal, G. (2016). Distinguishing between privacy and security concerns: An empirical examination and scale validation. *Journal of Computer Information Systems*, *57*(4), 330–343. DOI: 10.1080/08874417.2016.1232981

Bhise, A., Munshi, A., Rodrigues, A., & Sawant, V. (2022). Overview of AI in education. In *Artificial Intelligence in Higher Education* (pp. 31–62). https://doi.org/DOI: 10.1201/9781003184157-2

Chassignol, M., Khoroshavin, A., Klimova, A., & Bilyatdinova, A. (2018). Artificial intelligence trends in education: A narrative overview. *Procedia Computer Science*, *136*, 16–24. DOI: 10.1016/j.procs.2018.08.233

Ghosh, S., Roy, P., Sarkar, S. K., Podder, A., & Roy, B. (2024). Challenges and barriers to integrating AI in library environments. In *Applications of Artificial Intelligence in Libraries* (pp. 109–138). https://doi.org/DOI: 10.4018/979-8-3693-1573-6.ch005

Gligorea, I., Cioca, M., Oancea, R., Gorski, A.-T., Gorski, H., & Tudorache, P. (2023). Adaptive learning using artificial intelligence in e-learning: A literature review. *Education Sciences*, *13*(12), 1216. DOI: 10.3390/educsci13121216

Gurung, A., & Raja, M. K. (2016). Online privacy and security concerns of consumers. *Information and Computer Security*, *24*(4), 348–371. DOI: 10.1108/ICS-05-2015-0020

Hong, J., & Kim, K. (2024). Impact of AIoT education program on digital and AI literacy of elementary school students. *Education and Information Technologies*. Advance online publication. DOI: 10.1007/s10639-024-12758-0

Jo, J., Park, K., Lee, D., & Lim, H. (2014). An integrated teaching and learning assistance system meeting requirements for smart education. *Wireless Personal Communications*, *79*(4), 2453–2467. DOI: 10.1007/s11277-014-1765-4

Kitcharoen, P., Howimanporn, S., & Chookaew, S. (2024). Enhancing teachers' AI competencies through artificial intelligence of things professional development training. [IJIM]. *International Journal of Interactive Mobile Technologies*, *18*(02), 4–15. DOI: 10.3991/ijim.v18i02.46613

Kovelan, P., Thisenthira, N., & Kartheeswaran, T. (2019). Automated attendance monitoring system using IoT. In *2019 International Conference on Advancements in Computing (ICAC)* (pp. 376–379). https://doi.org/DOI: 10.1109/ICAC49085.2019.9103412

Leszczynski, A. (2016). Speculative futures: Cities, data, and governance beyond smart urbanism. *Environment and Planning A. Environment & Planning A*, *48*(9), 1691–1708. DOI: 10.1177/0308518X16651445

Little, S. G., & Akin-Little, A. (2008). Psychology's contributions to classroom management. *Psychology in the Schools*, *45*(3), 227–234. DOI: 10.1002/pits.20293

Lorenzo, N., Gallon, R., Palau, R., & Mogas, J. (2021). New objectives for smart classrooms from Industry 4.0. *Technology. Knowledge and Learning*, *26*(4), 719–731. DOI: 10.1007/s10758-021-09527-0

Maiti, M., Priyaadharshini, M., & Vinayaga Sundaram, B. (2021). Augmented reality in virtual classroom for higher education during COVID-19 pandemic. In *Intelligent Computing* (pp. 399–418). https://doi.org/DOI: 10.1007/978-3-030-80129-8_29

Martin, K., Shilton, K., & Smith, J. ery. (2022). Business and the ethical implications of technology: Introduction to the symposium. In *Business and the Ethical Implications of Technology* (pp. 1–11). https://doi.org/DOI: 10.1007/978-3-031-18794-0_1

Nachbauer, M., & Kyriakides, L. (2019). A review and evaluation of approaches to measure equity in educational outcomes. *School Effectiveness and School Improvement*, *31*(2), 306–331. DOI: 10.1080/09243453.2019.1672757

Nachbauer, M., & Kyriakides, L. (2019). A review and evaluation of approaches to measure equity in educational outcomes. *School Effectiveness and School Improvement*, *31*(2), 306–331. DOI: 10.1080/09243453.2019.1672757

Patton, R. M., & Buffington, M. L. (2016). Keeping up with our students: The evolution of technology and standards in art education. *Arts Education Policy Review*, *117*(3), 1–9. DOI: 10.1080/10632913.2014.944961

Picton, C., & Kahu, E. R. (2021). 'I knew I had the support from them': Understanding student support through a student engagement lens. *Higher Education Research & Development*, *41*(6), 2034–2047. DOI: 10.1080/07294360.2021.1968353

Pise, A. A., Almuzaini, K. K., Ahanger, T. A., Farouk, A., pant, K., Pareek, P. K., & Nuagah, S. J. (2022). pant, K., Pareek, P. K., & Nuagah, S. J. (2022). Enabling artificial intelligence of things (AIoT) healthcare architectures and listing security issues. *Computational Intelligence and Neuroscience*, *2022*, 1–14. DOI: 10.1155/2022/8421434 PMID: 36911247

Ramlowat, D. D., & Pattanayak, B. K. (2019). Exploring the Internet of Things (IoT) in education: A review. In *Information Systems Design and Intelligent Applications* (pp. 245–255). https://doi.org/DOI: 10.1007/978-981-13-3338-5_23

Rogers, R., & Dhatariya, K. K. (2021). Bilateral Charcot neuroarthropathy in pregnancy: A case report and review of the influence of pregnancy hormones on ligament laxity. *AACE Clinical Case Reports*, *7*(1), 57–60. DOI: 10.1016/j.aace.2020.11.015 PMID: 33851021

Sahni, V., & Singh, M. (2024). Smart Indian agriculture farm using an IoT dashboard. *Educational Administration: Theory and Practice*.https://doi.org/DOI: 10.53555/kuey.v30i5.3215

Sahoo, T., Mondal, A., Roy, P., & Podder, A. (2024). Artificial intelligence and its application in engineering. In *Emerging Engineering Technologies and Industrial Applications* (pp. 1–20). https://doi.org/DOI: 10.4018/979-8-3693-1335-0.ch001

Sarikaya, R. (2017). The technology behind personal digital assistants: An overview of the system architecture and key components. *IEEE Signal Processing Magazine*, *34*(1), 67–81. DOI: 10.1109/MSP.2016.2617341

Shankaranarayanan, G., & Cai, Y. (2006). Supporting data quality management in decision-making. *Decision Support Systems*, *42*(1), 302–317. DOI: 10.1016/j.dss.2004.12.006

Shemshack, A., & Spector, J. M. (2020). A systematic literature review of personalized learning terms. *Smart Learning Environments*, *7*(1), 33. Advance online publication. DOI: 10.1186/s40561-020-00140-9

Stippich, A. (2017). Key components of modular propulsion systems for next generation electric vehicles. *CPSS Transactions on Power Electronics and Applications*, *2*(4), 249–258. DOI: 10.24295/CPSSTPEA.2017.00023

Talaghzi, J., Bennane, A., Himmi, M. M., Bellafkih, M., & Benomar, A. (2020). Online adaptive learning. In *Proceedings of the 13th International Conference on Intelligent Systems: Theories and Applications*. https://doi.org/DOI: 10.1145/3419604.3419759

Tariq, M. U. (2024). Generative AI in Curriculum Development in Higher Education. In Fields, Z. (Ed.), *Impacts of Generative AI on Creativity in Higher Education* (pp. 227–258). IGI Global., DOI: 10.4018/979-8-3693-2418-9.ch009

Tariq, M. U. (2024). Harnessing Persuasive Technologies for Enhanced Learner Engagement and Motivation. In M. Sanmugam, D. Lim, N. Mohd Barkhaya, W. Wan Yahaya, & Z. Khlaif (Eds.), *Power of Persuasive Educational Technologies in Enhancing Learning* (pp. 30-62). IGI Global. https://doi.org/DOI: 10.4018/979-8-3693-6397-3.ch002

Tariq, M. U. (2024). Navigating the Personalization Pathway: Implementing Adaptive Learning Technologies in Higher Education. In Minh Tung, T. (Ed.), *Adaptive Learning Technologies for Higher Education* (pp. 265–291). IGI Global., DOI: 10.4018/979-8-3693-3641-0.ch012

Tariq, M. U. (2025). Gamification and Virtual Reality: Transforming Early Childhood Language Learning. In Manditereza, B. (Ed.), *Digital Pedagogy in Early Childhood Language Development* (pp. 25–52). IGI Global Scientific Publishing., DOI: 10.4018/979-8-3693-7437-5.ch002

Tariq, M. U. (2025). Integrating Theory and Practice: Transformative Approaches in Practice-Led Research for Professional Development. In Kwok, S., Yu, P., & Le Corre, J. (Eds.), *Exploring Practice-Led Research for Professional Development* (pp. 419–436). IGI Global Scientific Publishing., DOI: 10.4018/979-8-3693-6376-8.ch016

Tariq, M. U. (2025). Empowering Learning Through Networked and Connected Education: Case Studies in Digital Engagement. In Gierhart, A. (Ed.), *Cases on Enhancing P-16 Student Engagement With Digital Technologies* (pp. 169–198). IGI Global Scientific Publishing., DOI: 10.4018/979-8-3693-5633-3.ch007

Tariq, M. U. (2025). Beyond the Classroom: The Sustained Influence of Educators on Student Success. In West, E. (Ed.), *Former Educators' Roles in Supporting Student Growth and Learning* (pp. 321–346). IGI Global Scientific Publishing., DOI: 10.4018/979-8-3693-6427-7.ch013

Tsai, C.-C., Cheng, Y.-M., Tsai, Y.-S., & Lou, S.-J. (2021). Impacts of AIoT implementation course on the learning outcomes of senior high school students. *Education Sciences, 11*(2), 82. DOI: 10.3390/educsci11020082

Uskov, V. L., Bakken, J. P., & Pandey, A. (2015). The ontology of next generation smart classrooms. In *Smart Education and Smart E-Learning* (pp. 3–14). https://doi.org/DOI: 10.1007/978-3-319-19875-0_1

Vetitnev, A. M., Maznichenko, M. A., Lopatinskiy, D. B., & Aksenov, I. A. (2020). Traditional and digital technologies in professional education: Integration opportunities. *Journal of Physics: Conference Series, 1691*(1), 012135. DOI: 10.1088/1742-6596/1691/1/012135

Weng, X., Ye, H., Dai, Y., & Ng, O. (2024). Integrating artificial intelligence and computational thinking in educational contexts: A systematic review of instructional design and student learning outcomes. *Journal of Educational Computing Research, 62*(6), 1640–1670. DOI: 10.1177/07356331241248686

Williamson, B. (2015). Digital education governance: Data visualization, predictive analytics, and 'real-time' policy instruments. *Journal of Education Policy, 31*(2), 123–141. DOI: 10.1080/02680939.2015.1035758

Xu, H., Seng, K. P., Ang, L. M., & Smith, J. (2024). Decentralized and distributed learning for AIoT: A comprehensive review, emerging challenges, and opportunities. *IEEE Access : Practical Innovations, Open Solutions, 12*, 101016–101052. DOI: 10.1109/ACCESS.2024.3422211

Zhang, J., & Goyal, S. B. (2024). AI-driven decision support system innovations to empower higher education administration. *Journal of Computers. Mechanical and Management, 3*(2), 35–41. DOI: 10.57159/gadl.jcmm.3.2.24070

Zhang, J., & Tao, D. (2021). Empowering things with intelligence: A survey of the progress, challenges, and opportunities in artificial intelligence of things. *IEEE Internet of Things Journal, 8*(10), 7789–7817. DOI: 10.1109/JIOT.2020.3039359

Zhu, Z., Sun, Y., & Riezebos, P. (2016). Introducing the smart education framework: Core elements for successful learning in a digital world. *International Journal of Smart Technology and Learning, 1*(1), 53. DOI: 10.1504/IJSMARTTL.2016.078159

KEY TERM AND DEFINITIONS

Internet of Things (IoT): A network of interconnected devices that collect and exchange data to automate and optimise environments.

Artificial Intelligence (AI): The simulation of human intelligence in machines programmed to learn, reason, and solve problems.

AIoT: The integration of AI with IoT, enabling smart, autonomous systems that analyse data and adapt in real time.

Smart Education: An innovative educational approach that utilises advanced technologies like IoT, AI, and 5G to enhance learning and teaching.

Hyper-Connectivity: The state of pervasive digital interconnection that facilitates seamless data exchange and communication across devices and systems.

Chapter 11
AIoT in Environmental Sustainability

Rushda Sharf
https://orcid.org/0009-0004-3733-1054
Integral University, India

Yusra Sharf
https://orcid.org/0000-0001-7950-6212
Aligah Muslim University, India

ABSTRACT

To address the majority of environmental sustainability issues, like transportation, energy, water management, and biodiversity, artificial intelligence (AI) has grown in importance. The primary focus areas in energy are area neural networks, expert systems, fuzzy logic models, and pattern recognition. This chapter assesses how the use of AI could improve the environment by reducing the effects of agriculture, climate change, water resources, weather forecasting, ocean health, and disaster resilience. The impact of AI on the environment and its sustainable applications are examined in this chapter using qualitative analysis. With an emphasis on AI's role in advancing environmental sustainability, the chapter's main goal is to identify applications of AI for environmentally friendly practices. It can help stakeholders understand international initiatives to improve environmental sustainability by utilizing AI.

DOI: 10.4018/979-8-3693-8547-0.ch011

INTRODUCTION

Due to the global environmental issues of the 21st century, artificial intelligence (AI) has emerged as a crucial field of study essential to addressing many of the current environmental sustainability challenges (Prank, 2021). John McCarthy first defined AI in 1956 as the science and engineering of building intelligent machines. Essentially, AI is a branch of computer science that leverages prior knowledge to solve environmental problems more effectively. Artificial intelligence (AI) has therefore addressed the many limitations of human thought in the current digital era, opening a new field where intelligent machines with artificial brains are designed to coexist with human brains (Jha et al., 2019). Our knowledge of and capacity to manage the ecosystem could be significantly enhanced by the application of AI in environmental sustainability. While machine learning algorithms can be used in water science to forecast discharge and water levels and improve quality, AI-enabled technologies, such as drones and motion-sensing cameras, can be used to gather and analyze huge amounts of biodiversity data. Furthermore, the integration of machine learning, blockchain technology, and the Internet of Things can enhance urban water management. By anticipating and lessening the effects of natural disasters like earthquakes, hurricanes, and floods, AI can also be utilized to decrease the risk of disasters. AI can also lessen the environmental impact and increase the agricultural sector's resource efficiency. As AI applications continue to advance, it is crucial to think carefully about the moral ramifications of applying AI to environmental sustainability and make sure the technology is applied responsibly and openly. Although there are many different aspects to environmental sustainability, many common environmental issues can be readily resolved by igniting public interest, thanks to the development of artificial intelligence (AI). Sustainable agriculture, environmental asset conservation, pollution and waste management, pollution treatment, and monitoring are the four (4) primary areas into which the domains of artificial intelligence (AI) and environmental sustainability can be broadly separated (Nishant et al., 2020; Callicot & Mumford, 1998). Importantly, most of the current regional and global environmental troubles are addressed by AI in areas like water, transportation, energy, and biodiversity, though many of these areas have influenced every category and are always evolving. AI has been used in real-world applications in transportation and biodiversity in numerous developed countries. For example, preventing pollution in the ocean, conserving wildlife to boost biodiversity, and employing AI-powered autonomous garbage collection trucks to pick up electronic waste. In current times, artificial intelligence (AI) has gained a lot of attention. Advances in other cutting-edge technologies, like virtual reality, big data, the Internet of Things (IoT), and cloud computing, have made important progress in AI possible. AI has the potential to transform environmental sustainability in addition to its economic and social advantages. Given the volume and complexity of interactions that occur within an ecosystem, scientists argue that understanding how the ecosystem works is one of the main barriers to environmental sustainability. The human mind or traditional statistical methods can't analyze the vast amount of data that is available. To manage these complexities and make prompt decisions in uncertain and volatile situations, AI can assist in the analysis and creation of models from the huge amounts of data that sensors can gather.

Sustainable AI refers to artificial intelligence (AI) systems that follow moral business practices. There are practical solutions, even though many of the AI systems in use today are harmful to the environment. Experienced AI model developers and users are aware that training AI models is a time-consuming and energy-intensive process that inevitably produces emissions and air pollution (Nishant et al., 2020). AI models need to be made more effective to use less energy when being trained. An AI system's power consumption should be minimized by optimizing each component. By doing this, companies can create new approaches to AI modeling and optimization that lessen the negative environmental effects of their AI systems. A key component of sustainable AI is minimizing the detrimental effects of AI on the environment while simultaneously emphasizing the application of AI and machine learning as instruments to promote sustainable development across a range of sectors (Table 1). This entails using AI and ML to help businesses operate sustainably so that the achievements of the present do not endanger the future. In addition to reducing the adverse environmental effects of AI, sustainable AI highlights machine learning as an instrument to promote sustainable development across a variety of industries. To ensure that the accomplishments of today do not jeopardize the future, we must leverage AI and ML to assist organizations in operating sustainably. The foundation of sustainable AI is two key ideas. Above all, we must ensure that AI is environmentally friendly and sustainable. The second is using AI as a tool to promote sustainable development and decrease the harmful environmental effects of various industries. By focusing on both aspects of sustainable AI, we can cover the mode for a future that is more ecologically conscious and sustainable (Tariq, 2025).

Table 1. Generative AI market growth and adaptation trends

Consumer data	Timeline	Growth rate
Businesses using generative AI for synthetic customer data	2023vs 2026	Less than 5% to 75%
Industry/function specific/gene AI model	2023vs 2027	Approximately 1% to over 50%
Energy-conserving gene AI implementations	By 2028	30%

The Significance of AI

Organizations can minimize waste and determine which goods and services emit mainly carbon emissions by optimizing their resource use like water, energy, and materials through monitoring and analysis using AI systems. AI technology can assist with precision farming, air pollution, sustainable building design, and even lowering greenhouse gas emissions. However, AI systems themselves have a propensity to use a lot of energy. The AI sector may use as much energy as a nation the size of the Netherlands by 2027, according to a recent study, and some reports claim that global emissions from cloud computing release more carbon than commercial airlines. Along with strategies for lessening the effects of AI systems on the environment, it will also cover methods for measuring the AI system's environmental sustainability, including raw materials, energy efficiency, transportation, and water (Tariq and Sergio, 2025).

AI Domain and Levels

Three levels of artificial intelligence have been distinguished. Artificial Super Intelligence (ASI), Artificial General Intelligence (AGI), and Artificial Narrow Intelligence (ANI) are the three levels of Artificial Narrow Intelligence (ANI) distinct (Strelkova & Pasichnyk, 2017) as machines that are trained for a specific task and can make decisions in only one area. Weak AI is another name for ANI, and Google search is a common example. According to Wang et al. (2017), AGI, also mentioned to as Strong AI, is the "true synthetic intelligence." According to them, the stage of artificial intelligence development known as artificial general intelligence is when machines have the capacity for thought and decision-making like that of humans; autonomous vehicles are a common example. According to Cully et al. (2015), ASI is the stage or level of AI where the brain's capabilities are significantly superior to the best human brain in most domains, like social skills, general knowledge, and scientific inventiveness. Six domains in artificial intelligence address issues related to environmental sustainability. According to Jha et al.(2019), the first step in implementing any AI is to use machine learning (ML), which involves a variety of machine learning processes. ML aims to feed machines with historical data, experiences, and statistical information. These data aid in the completion of tasks that are assigned to address issues, especially those connected to the environment (Figure 1). As a result, machine learning employs a variety of mathematical techniques to make highly intelligent machines that can improve and aid in the improvement of more sophisticated technologies during the applications used for analysis (Jha et al., 2019).

Second, according to Jha et al. (2019), Artificial Neural Networks (ANN) are a perfect task-specific method or logic. Its operations also do not fall under the typical conventional computational task that is programmed, but slightly on an internal task. Because neural networks can be trained, they offer numerous advantages over traditional systems in place of extensive programming. For instance, it can forecast and predict water resource variables using parallel reasoning (Maier et al., 2000). Third, robotics combines various fields with human cognitive behavior, such as emotions and thought processes. Nishant et al. (2020) state that this enables artificial intelligence robots to carry out tasks utilizing human motions and other manipulations. One of the many fields where robotics is frequently used is farming. Examples of this include planting, seeding, harvesting, weeding, shepherding, irrigating, spraying, and fertilizing. Fourth, the application of Natural Language Processing (NLP) is a developing field whose primary function is closely linked to AI's ability to imitate human attention processes (Nishant et al., 2020; Szeliski, 2014), as well as its pursuit of diverse understandings and the creation of human language through text analysis (Nishant et al, 2020; Khurdi, 2017). Poria et al. (2017) and Nishant et al. (2020) reported that affective computing is produced when Computer Vision and NLP are combined to enable machines to be trained from speech and visual data. Fifth, Zadeh (1975) defines fuzzy logic (FL) as an approach to human reasoning that permits more values than the conventional binary Boolean logic. Sixth, Nishant et al. (2020) state that Expert Systems use databases and knowledge bases, including inference engines, to address multifaceted issues. Expert systems have used both fuzzy logic and machine learning models to assist in decision-making, according to recent studies (Nishant et al., 2020; Leokumar, 2019)

Figure 1. Hierarchy of artificial intelligence domain

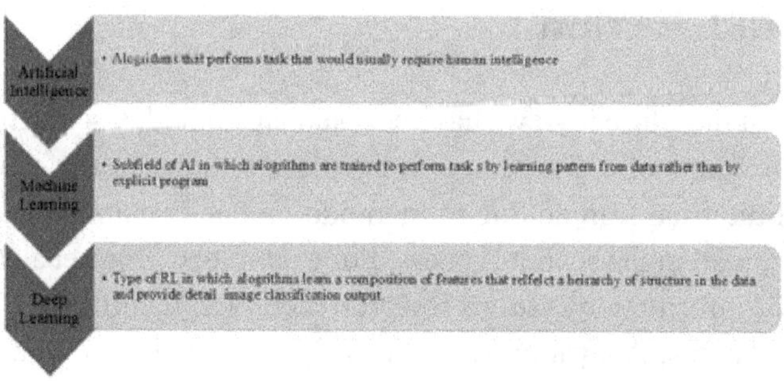

Background

Artificial Intelligence (AI) has emerged as a disruptive force, transforming industries, reshaping our lives and work, and significantly impacting businesses, institutions, and societies. Driven by advancements in machine learning and deep learning, as well as the exponential growth of available data, AI technologies have enabled machines to handle complex tasks such as natural language processing, image recognition, and decision-making (Shollo et al., 2022). The technology offers significant potential for businesses and society by improving efficiency, reducing costs, and providing better decision-making capabilities (Dwivedi et al., 2023; Ransbotham et al., 2017). Combined with big data, AI has the potential to surpass human decision-making and abilities across industries (Liu & Zeng, 2021). Recent developments in large language models, such as OpenAI's GPT-3, GPT-4, and ChatGPT, have expanded AI's capabilities and accessibility. These models use deep learning techniques to understand and generate human-like responses in natural language (Lund et al., 2023), with applications in virtual assistants, content generation, and sentiment analysis (Dwivedi et al., 2023). To conduct the review, we adopt a computational literature review (CLR) approach, using machine learning algorithms to analyze large volumes of literature (Antons et al., 2023; Mortenson & Vidgen, 2016). Specifically, we use structural topic modeling (Roberts et al., 2013, pp. 1–20) to analyze articles published in journals between 2010 and 2023 that reference "artificial intelligence". Our study further showcases the effectiveness of enrolling ChatGPT to support crucial aspects of the CLR process. To overcome the limitations of traditional and systematic literature reviews, researchers have turned to computational literature reviews (CLRs), which leverage machine learning algorithms to analyze larger volumes of literature, implying that researchers do not need precise scoping and search terms (Mortenson &Vidgen, 2016).

LITERATURE REVIEW

Several AI literature reviews have adopted an expanded scope to examine entire domains systematically. These articles typically range in the number of articles included in the final sample due to methodological decisions regarding years and journals included in the search process. For example, Collins et al. (2021) reviewed AI across the information systems research literature, identifying 91 studies to synthesize key themes; Anayat & Rasool (2022) undertook a bibliometric analysis of AI in marketing featuring 328 studies; and Verma et al. (2021) also examined AI in marketing but included 1580 articles with a focus on identifying author performance and citation network. Several reviews examine specific areas across domains like sustainable development goals (Di Vaio et al., 2020) or focus on two disciplines, like the adoption (traditionally studied in information systems) of AI in operations management (Grover et al., 2022). Other reviews look at AI and business more broadly. For example, Loureiro et al. (2021) consider 404 articles from which they identify 18 topics and consider future trends, and Arsenyan & Piepenbrink (2023) present an analysis of AI research in five management domains, examining 6324 articles published between 1990 and 2020. Both reviews found that AI research in management has grown significantly in recent years. AI research in management is also becoming increasingly interdisciplinary, drawing contributions from economics, computer science, and psychology. To address how AI is used to address environmental sustainability in domains like energy, biodiversity, transportation, and water, a systematic review was utilized in this chapter. Aside from other guidelines that are applied to all, the approach described in the Systematic Review of AI and environmental sustainability was utilized. The accepted international standards that rely on the work of other researchers have been adhered to when evaluating the Systematic Review (SR) framework due to its capacity to reveal validity in comparison to other analytical frameworks. The best framework is a systematic review since it facilitates the collection of objective secondary data. To ensure that the projected idea was appropriate, preliminary searches were conducted to help produce papers. This was done primarily to ensure that there were enough papers available for the review and to avoid any duplication of the addressed question. Furthermore, the search terms were centered on environmental sustainability and artificial intelligence, both trustworthy given the methodology used. However, Google Scholar searches were conducted using the terms environmental sustainability and AI to obtain answers to the questions posed to improve the retrieval of results and aid in gaining a deeper understanding (Tariq, 2025).

AI Applications for Sustainability Strategies

AI could be used in an organization's sustainability plan in the following ways:

- Emissions Monitoring and Reporting: Examine and monitor an organization's emissions data to identify improvement areas.
- Supply chain monitoring: Examining and observing suppliers' sustainable practices.
- Predictive upkeep: Forecast equipment failures and plan maintenance to reduce unscheduled downtime and energy waste.
- Intelligent transportation: To enhance logistics and transportation networks while lowering transportation-related emissions.

- Energy efficiency: To decrease energy consumption and carbon emissions, as well as to maximize the performance of buildings' HVAC, lighting, and other equipment

Table 2. Clinical application of artificial intelligence

Clinical workflow	Types of Application	Classes of uses cases
Triage scenario	Detection	For workflow optimization and quality assurance
Replacement scenario	Segmentation	Separate normal from not normal
Add on scenario	Classification	Grading and classification of image

AI Benefits for Environmental Sustainability

By anticipating usage trends and optimizing energy use, AI can help raise energy efficiency in industries and buildings (Fig. 2). It has been argued that AI has helped to lower the demands for natural resources and energy from human activities. For the research, the primary focus areas are neural networks, pattern recognition, expert systems, and fuzzy logic models (Demirci et al., 2019; Tyralis et al., 2019). These include energy generation and allocation, operations, and maintenance, which have been central areas of interest in the energy industry (Wang & Shrinivasan, 2017; Ordiano et al., 2018; Merizalde et al., 2019). When it comes to forecasting, most of these algorithms used by researchers integrate into fuzzy logic (FL) systems for decision support (Liu et al., 2018). Crucially, a variety of models yield more precise results, as do accepted combinations such as area neural networks (Wang et al., 2017). Google's DeepMind, for instance, has optimized the cooling systems in its data centers using AI to lower carbon emissions and energy consumption. Tesla optimizes driving patterns with artificial intelligence- driven autonomous driving features in its electric cars, which lowers emissions and increases energy efficiency (Tariq & Sergio, 2025).

Figure 2. Artificial intelligence in the energy industry

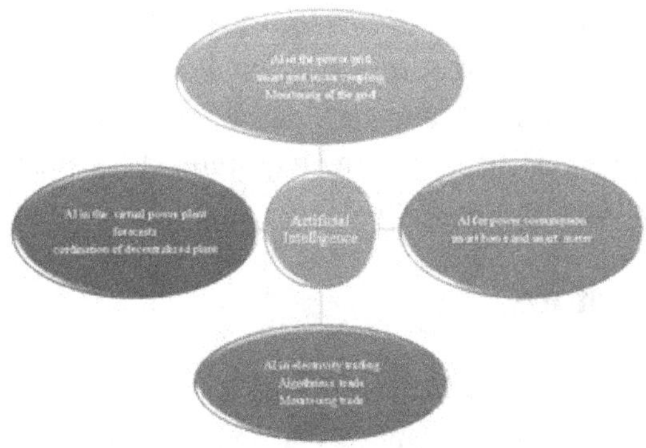

Fig 2. *Artificial intelligence in the energy industry*

Renewable Energy

By forecasting energy output, optimizing performance, and enhancing maintenance, AI can sustain the development of renewable energy sources like solar and wind. AI is used by GE Renewable Energy to improve the efficiency of its wind turbines. With the use of sensors and AI algorithms, these turbines can anticipate variations in wind conditions and modify their operation accordingly. This predictive ability guarantees that the turbines run as efficiently as possible while also optimizing energy output. AI-driven maintenance scheduling also lowers maintenance expenses and downtime by proactively identifying and resolving problems. The expansion and effectiveness of renewable energy sources, such as wind power, are aided by this AI application (Tariq, 2025).

SMART GRIDS

Artificial intelligence can evaluate data from sensors, meters, and other devices to help build smarter energy grids. This can lower energy waste, increase reliability, and assist utilities in better managing the supply and demand of electricity. Microsoft has set lofty sustainability targets, hoping to become carbon-negative by 2030, and has been utilizing AI to increase data center energy efficiency.

Sustainable Agriculture

By evaluating forecasting crop yields and soil data and spotting pest and disease outbreaks, artificial intelligence can sustain sustainable agricultural practices. By doing this, farmers can maximize crop yields while using fewer fertilizers and pesticides. By precisely identifying and eliminating weeds in agricultural fields with AI-powered robots, Farmwise lessens the requirement for chemical herbicides and encourages sustainable farming methods.

Precision Agriculture

By enabling farmers to make data-driven decisions, artificial intelligence (AI) is transforming agriculture, improving crop management, and raising sustainability and productivity. A more accurate and effective method of cultivation is made possible by the incorporation of sensors and data analytics into farming procedures. For instance, sensors mounted on equipment and in fields gather a variety of information about crop health, temperature, nutrient levels, and soil moisture. Machine learning models are then used to process this real-time data, giving farmers profound insights into the state of their soil and crops. Farmers can, therefore, maximize crop yield while using the fewest resources possible (Tariq, 2025).

Waste Management and Recycling

Waste management is being revolutionized by AI-driven systems that offer more intelligent and effective solutions. By analyzing historical data and real-time inputs, such as traffic patterns and bin fill levels, these systems can optimize waste collection routes (Fig.3). As a result, there are considerable financial savings, less fuel used, and fewer greenhouse gas emissions from collection vehicles. By spotting recycling and composting opportunities, AI helps cut down on landfill waste. To recover the partition of recyclables from non-recyclables and ultimately lower the amount of waste dumped in landfills, machine learning algorithms can sift through enormous volumes of data. AI can improve recycling procedures by sorting materials at recycling facilities more effectively, which will raise the recycling rate. The quality and value of recycled materials can be raised by using advanced robotics and AI vision systems to sort materials more precisely than manual labor.

Figure 3. Artificial intelligence waste management system

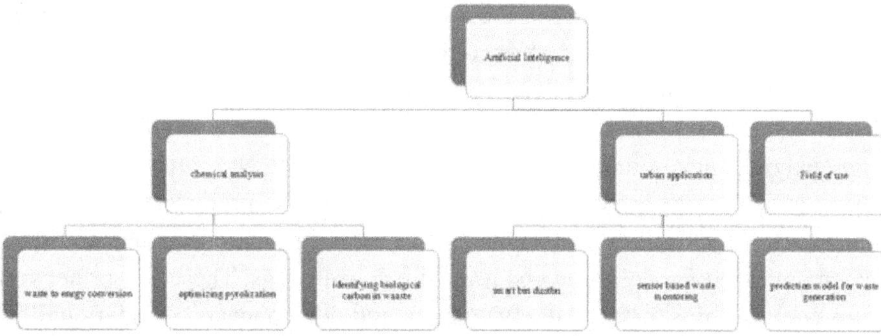

WATER MANAGEMENT

Applications of artificial intelligence (AI) in water resources maximize water conservation, a topic that has garnered a lot of research interest since 2015. The most widely used techniques in this field are genetic algorithms, artificial neural networks, particularly the adaptive neuro-fuzzy inference system, support vector machine as the main machine learning models, decision trees (particularly random forest), multiple regression, autoregressive moving average model (ARMA), and spline regression (Nishant et al., 2020; Sanz et al., 2016; Ochoa et al., 2017). Additionally, popular machine learning models merge genetic algorithms with area neural networks (ANN), such as ANFIS (Rodriguez-Soto et al., 2017). For example, stream flow can be predicted, and water quality parameters can be analyzed using machine learning (ML) models (Demirici et al., 2017). By analyzing data on water availability, quality, and usage, AI can help with water management. This can lower water waste, enhance water quality, and assist cities and municipalities in better managing their water resources. One initiative to help clean up marine environments is Ocean Cleanup, which uses AI-powered systems to monitor and gather plastic debris in the ocean (Tariq, 2025).

Air and Water Quality Monitoring

Despite a recent decrease in emissions, air pollution continues to pose the greatest threat to European public health, with an estimated 238,000 fatalities in 2020 alone. Numerous factors significantly affect the quality of water, most notably agricultural runoff that contains chemical pesticides and fertilizers that are harmful to humans and eutrophicate water supplies. A key component of the continuous endeavor to monitor and enhance the quality of the air and water is AI-driven sensor networks. These advanced systems provide a data-driven, real-time approach to environmental protection with numerous advantages for ecological sustainability and public health. In urban areas where air pollution is a major concern, networks of sensors continuously measure pollutants such as particulate matter, NO_2, and volatile organic compounds. This data is processed by AI algorithms to produce real-time maps of air quality, which allow authorities to modify industrial operations and traffic management to reduce pollution and issue timely warnings. These sensor networks monitor contaminants, dissolved oxygen, pH, and other aspects of water quality in aquatic environments. Safe drinking water sources and the preservation of aquatic ecosystems depend on AI's analysis of the data. Furthermore, prompt action can be taken to minimize damage when contamination events, such as chemical spills or algal blooms, are detected early.

Transportation

Research on applications of AI in connection to sustainable transportation is also available. Most papers published focus on machine learning (Abduljabbar et al., 2019). In addition, the use of computer vision to support decision-making has been noticed in public transportation, urban mobility, traffic management, and safety (Liyanage et al., 2019). Machine learning and other statistical and time series models are taken into consideration when applying AI to transportation for traffic control and planning, with computer vision techniques being used for road marking (Nishant et al., 2020).

CHANGE IN THE CLIMATE

By analyzing data on weather, greenhouse gas emissions, and other environmental factors, AI can aid in the fight against climate change. This can assist in guiding strategies and policies aimed at cutting emissions and decreasing the effects of climate change (Fig.4). IBM's Watson helps us understand and predict weather patterns and the climate change effects in a variety of applications, such as weather forecasting and climate modeling.

Climate Modeling and Prediction

Since 1880, the Earth's temperature has increased by 0.08^{0}C on average every ten years, and since 1981, the warming rate has more than doubled, posing a serious climate crisis. AI modeling and prediction could be a key device in the fight against climate change. Large datasets are analyzed by ML algorithms to get trends and produce more precise climate models. Additionally, it can use a variety of data points, such as greenhouse gas emissions, temperature, and ocean currents, that are impossible for humans to handle on their own. This, therefore, enables us to better comprehend the effects of climate change and make appropriate preparations for them.

Figure 4. Artificial intelligence solves climate change as per the process.

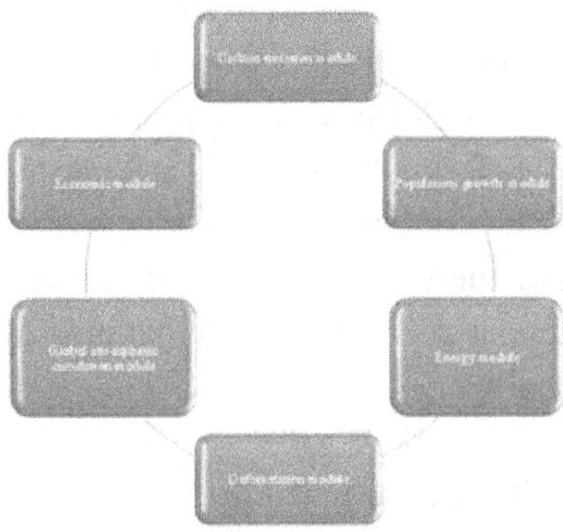

Fig. 4. *Artificial intelligence solves climate change as per the process*

CONSERVATION OF BIODIVERSITY

By analyzing data on species populations, threats, and habitats, artificial intelligence (AI) may support biodiversity conservation. This can enhance our comprehension of the intricate relationships that exist between various species and their environments and help guide conservation strategies. Additionally, numerous examples of artificial intelligence (AI) demonstrate how it is being used more and more to enhance biodiversity conservation and monitoring (Kwok et al., 2019). It is crucial to emphasize the need to refrain from overusing resources, which can lead to environmental problems, and information about the ecosystem and its diverse biodiversity, which could be addressed by access to AI-related data. Nishant et al. (2020) claim that biodiversity research produced useful techniques that would yield valuations or estimates of land-related service provisions. Similarly, a large portion of artificial intelligence-based biodiversity research can forecast ecosystem services through natural language processing or machine learning (Toivonen et al., 2019).

Marine Ecosystem Protection

Marine heat waves, biodiversity loss, increasing sea levels, and acidification are just a few of the many ways that marine ecosystems are currently declining. In the fight against these problems and to monitor and protect marine ecosystems, artificial intelligence is becoming a potent ally. Advanced artificial intelligence (AI)-enabled autonomous underwater vehicles (AUVs) are being used to investigate and record the condition of our oceans, supporting vital conservation initiatives. These AI-powered AUVs are capable of carrying out in-depth surveys of marine environments, gathering a significant amount of data, and taking high-resolution photos. They can identify minute alterations in coral reefs, which is essential for keeping an eye on the condition of these delicate ecosystems. AI assists conservationists in taking timely action to safeguard these vital habitats by detecting indicators of disease, damage, or bleaching.

Preparedness and Response to Disasters

The world has seen a 5 fold rise in natural disasters over the past 50 years caused by changes in the climate. The World Meteorological Organization (WMO) claims that AI is essential to developing early detection and warning systems for these catastrophes and tremendous weather conditions, which can help save lives. Artificial intelligence can analyze historical data, present conditions, and real-time data streams by utilizing sophisticated algorithms to generate early warnings and enable prompt, well-informed responses. This ability is essential for protecting human life and minimizing environmental harm. AI-driven systems, for example, can track environmental factors like temperature, humidity, wind speed, and past fire behavior in the event of a wildfire. To help authorities better allocate firefighting resources and enable the evacuation of at-risk communities before the fire reaches them, machine learning algorithms can generate extrapolative fire risk assessments.

Sequestration and Capture of Carbon (CCS)

AI technology plays a key role in carbon capture and sequestration (CCS) processes, which seek to absorb CO2 emissions and store them underground to stop their discharge into the atmosphere. By assisting in the capture materials selection and the adjustment of process conditions, artificial intelligence (AI) optimizes CCS procedures. To identify the best CCS strategy for each particular situation, machine learning models examine a variety of variables, including the geology of the storage location, the kind of industrial emissions, and operational parameters. By optimizing the solvent or adsorbent used to capture CO2, artificial intelligence's predictive capabilities increase carbon capture efficiency and guarantee that the most carbon is extracted from industrial emissions. Optimizing resource use not only lowers carbon emissions but also lessens the environmental impact of CCS. To guarantee the long-lasting integrity of the CO2 stored underground, AI also helps with the ongoing monitoring of storage locations. AI can assist in preventing leaks and guaranteeing secure, long-lasting captured carbon storage by analyzing sensor data and anticipating possible problems.

Impact of AI on the Ecosystem and Environmental Management

AI has a significant impact on solving environmental issues. AI is used in climate modeling and prediction to comprehend the intricate dynamics of climate change. AI-powered solutions maximize renewable energy sources, improving the energy sector's sustainability and efficiency. AI also controls energy use in smart buildings, which lowers expenses and emissions. Precision farming maximizes crop yields while preserving resources by utilizing sensors and data analytics (Table 3). AI can be used to monitor endangered species and protect their habitats in the field of wildlife conservation. Similarly, ocean health and related hazards are protected by AI-enabled marine ecosystem monitoring. AI-driven sensor networks improve air and water quality, safeguarding ecosystems and public health. Furthermore, recycling and waste management have been transformed, which has increased resource efficiency and decreased landfill waste. AI helps carbon capture and sequestration (CCS) by optimizing materials and conditions, which lowers carbon emissions and improves environmental sustainability (Fig. 5). Additionally, AI helps with early warning systems for disaster preparedness and response. In the end, AI technology is leading the charge to build a more sustainable and greener future, and it is crucial to hire the best talent to help make this happen. It is anticipated that technologies such as AI and the IoT will advance environmental and ecosystem management as well as the majority of ecology and biodiversity research.

Figure 5. Artificial intelligence-related environmental cost

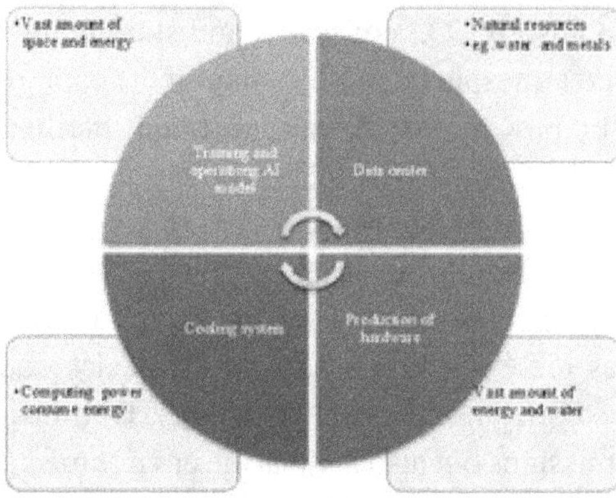

Table 3. Impact of AI on environmental application in each sector

	Expected impact on Global GDP in 2030 against baseline (% of baseline GDP)	Expected impact on Global GHG in 2030 against baseline (% of baseline emissions)
Agriculture	0.2% – 0.3%	- 0.1% to – 0.3%
Energy	1.6% – 2.2%	- 1.6% to – 2.2%
Transport	1.2% – 1.8%	0.3% to – 1.7%
water	0.04% – 0.2%	0.0% to 0.2%
All AI application studies	**3.1% – 4.4%**	**- 1.5% to – 4.0%**

IMPACT OF AI ON AGRICULTURE AS SMART FARMING

Soil content sensing, irrigation, crop yield and monitoring, crop establishment, and weeding are just a few of the agricultural processes where Artificial intelligence-based solutions can recover efficiency. In addition to improving output quality and guaranteeing a faster time to market for produced commodities, AI-based technological solutions may raise the sector's resource efficiency by lowering the use of land, fertilizers, pesticides, and water. Instead of using costly and fuel-polluting helicopters to monitor the fields, AI can use drones, cameras, and sensors to scan plantations, detect pests, identify areas that are either poorly or excessively irrigated, and intervene more quickly. Drones or robots can assist with early crop disease detection and field inspection, improving efficiency and guaranteeing future food security. Solar-powered robots that may recognize weeds and mechanically eliminate them (without the use of chemicals) can also greatly improve weed control. All these advancements are giving farmers the means to monitor, quantify, and evaluate their farms' requirements, enabling better resource management and a decrease in waste and environmental impact.

Applying AI to Environmental Sustainability Presents Challenges

Although it has been demonstrated that artificial intelligence can sustainably address environmental issues, they are hampered by machine learning's reliance on historical data. Because it is challenging to incorporate the variability of human behavior into machine learning models, artificial intelligence is unpredictable and constantly evolving. Therefore, it is challenging to estimate potential climate change because historical data from before any significant human activity reflects ages and climate cycles. An additional obstacle to using AI for environmental sustainability is the elevated risk of cybersecurity. Risk management for cybersecurity is critical when integrating data for artificial intelligence applications. Another issue with using AI for the sustainability of the environment is the deficiency of inaccurate performance metrics and the ambiguity of human behavioral responses to different AI-supported interventions (Nishant et al., 2020). The advancement of environmental sustainability depends on the measurement and tracking of interventions. Since the measurement is difficult and frequently ineffective, AI success for environmental sustainability is determined by integrating technical and analytical performance into an inclusive metric. Although AI applications are just as intelligent as humans when it comes to making decisions, their emphasis is very different from how humans react to those decisions. AI to prevent disaster: Many models and strategies for lowering the likelihood of disaster have already been tried and tested. So far, thcy have focused primarily on the response and rescue phases. For example, private companies tested a prototype of a blockchain-powered tsunami alert system that uses artificial intelligence in Sendai, Japan.

GDP Contribution and GHG Emission Mitigation Potential

AI for the environment has the potential to contribute to future global GDP by up to 4.4% while also reducing global greenhouse gas emissions by up to 40% by 2030 relative to the baseline. The previous studies reported that by 2030, environmental application of AI in agriculture, energy, transport, and water (hereafter referred to as "the four sectors") have the potential to generate future GDP gain of $ 3.6- USD 5.2 trillion relative to the baseline, or 3.1%-4.4%. This aligns with our previous research that suggests global GDP could be up to 14% higher (equivalent of an additional $ 15.7 trillion) in 2030 as a result of AI applications across all sectors of the economy. The previous studies reported that AI application in the four sectors has the potential to lower global GHG emission by 1.5%-4.0% in 2030, relative to the projected baseline.29 This would contribute to closing 7.9%-15.7% of the gap between our baseline projection of GHG emission and the trajectory required to meet the UN target by 2100. Beyond the benefits of higher productivity and GDP, the real power of AI tools lies in their potential to tackle some of the growing pressures on our planet by accelerating a low-carbon transition. The environmental application of AI can reduce GHG emissions via the following channels: reduction of GHG intensity, Higher efficiency of energy use, and change in energy mix in given sectors.

AI to Manage Hydrological Hazards

The ability of several cutting-edge modeling systems to predict drought events is being assessed. These models include support vector machines, artificial neural networks (ANN), genetic programming (GP), and adaptive neural-based fuzzy inference systems (ANFIS). The current drawback of applying AI to drought management is the dearth of "big data" required to create models with accurate forecasting capabilities.

Resilience to Natural Disasters From Storm and Flood Damage

AI can greatly lessen the effects of climate change, which is causing extreme weather events to occur more frequently and with greater intensity. Every year, flooding affects an estimated 250 million people. According to our analysis, between now and 2030, AI-enabled forecasting advancements could enable flood early warning systems, saving over 3,000 lives, reducing homelessness by 1.2 million, and mitigating $14 million in economic damages. Similar to this, more precise forecasting of storm damage in forestry using machine learning could assist management in enhancing storm resilience and thereby lowering forest wind damage, which currently accounts for about half of all forest damage in Europe, by 2 million m^3 (thereby preventing the loss of 800,000 tons of carbon uptake).

Preventing Unlawful Deforestation and Damage to Forests

Between 80,000 and 150,000 square kilometers, approximately. Human activity causes the loss of forests worldwide each year; illegal activities are responsible for up to 90% of tropical deforestation. To tackle this issue, 48 NGOs and tech firms have started utilizing AI to monitor and control forest disturbances faster and more effectively than in the past. AI can analyze ground-based sensors or satellite data to track forest conditions at scale and in real time, generating early warning systems for pattern recognition and priority research. By 2030, we predict that 32 million hectares of forest could be preserved worldwide if governments make the most of AI to support legislation.

AI to Improve Climate Change Assessment

To study the climate and pinpoint high-risk areas, a huge amount of data is required, including sensor data and photographs. ML algorithms can assist in mitigating and managing the effects of climate change by improving the accuracy of global climate models and projections. For instance, severe weather events like hurricanes and wildfires can be predicted using real-time data analysis from weather stations and satellite imagery. According to recent research, neural networks and artificial intelligence may also be used to study more complex, smaller-scale meteorological phenomena like the formation of convective clouds. As a result, they could potentially reduce the uncertainties in the current climate models.

Role of AI in Advancing Targets for Sustainability

Globally, economic, social, and environmental systems are being impacted by climate change, and these effects are predicted to persist for some time to come. Due to its ability to collect, analyze, and compile extensive and intricate datasets on emissions and climate impact, AI holds great promise for assessing, forecasting, and mitigating the effects of climate change. This allows for better solutions for well-informed decision-making.

Sustainable Development Goals (SDGs)

The 2030 Agenda for Sustainable Development, which included 169 targets and 17 goals, established the SDGs in 2015. All 134 SDG targets, which cover social, economic, and environmental concerns, can be made possible by AI.

Economic Outcomes

42 targets, like SDG 8 on well-mannered work and economic growth, SDG 9 on industry, innovation, and infrastructure, SDG 10 on reducing inequality, SDG 12 on accountable utilization and creation, and SDG 17 on partnerships for the aim, can benefit from the technological advancements made possible by AI. AI can be used to forecast human behavior, find the causes of inequality, and boost productivity.

AI and Environmental Outcomes

The environmental group has 25 targets that AI-based technologies can help achieve. It specifically alludes to SDGs 13 and 15 on climate action, life lowers the sea, and life on land, respectively. AI makes it possible to analyze vast, interconnected databases, which helps with the creation of cooperative environmental preservation initiatives. It can, for example, process vast quantities of satellite imagery to assist in environmental planning and decision-making to prevent desertification and reverse adverse trends. It can also assist low-carbon energy systems by combining energy efficiency and renewable energy. The capability to analyze vast, interrelated databases and produce collaborative actions to protect the environment could be one of AI's benefits. Regarding SDG 13 on climate action, there is proof that developments in artificial intelligence will help with understanding climate change and modeling its potential effects. To combat climate change, artificial intelligence will also help low-carbon energy systems that incorporate sources of renewable energy and efficiency of energy to a high degree(International Energy Agency 2017; WEF 2018; Vinuesa et al., 2016). AI has the potential to develop ecosystem health as well. AI can help achieve target 14.1, which calls for the prevention and significant decline of marine pollution of all types by using algorithms to automatically identify potential oil spills (Keramitsoglou et al., 2006). Neural networks and objective-oriented methods may be used to enhance the categorization of vegetation cover types based on satellite images, potentially processing huge volumes of images in a comparatively shorter amount of time (Mohamadi et al., 2016). By identifying the main drivers of desertification, these artificial intelligence techniques may assist in reversing trends or identifying information that is pertinent for environmental planning, decision-making, and management to prevent further desertification. They may also assist in identifying trends over large areas.

Established Links Between the SDGs and AI

According to our analysis of pertinent data, AI may help achieve 134 targets (79%) of the SDGs, typically through advancements in technology that might make it possible to get around some of the current restrictions. However, the advancement of AI may have a detrimental effect on 59 targets (35%, also across all SDGs). According to the three pillars of sustainable development, society, economy, and environment, we categorize the SDGs into three groups for this study (United Nations Economics and Social Council 2019; Stockholm Resilience Center SRC] 2016). An evaluation of artificial intelligence's (AI) impact on the Sustainable Development Goals is necessary, given its emergence and growing influence across numerous industries. In order to facilitate sustainable development, the rapid advancement of AI must be backed by the regulatory knowledge and supervision required for AI-based technologies. If this isn't done, there may be gaps in safety, ethics, and transparency.

How Artificial Intelligence is Addressing Environmental Issues

Jensen says there are several ways artificial intelligence may be used to address environmental issues, such as designing more energy-efficient buildings, monitoring deforestation, and determining the most effective way to use renewable energy sources. The World Environment Situation Room (WESR), in collaboration with several partners, collects, aggregates, and presents the best earth observation and sensor data available for use in near real-time analysis and future projections on a range of topics, including atmospheric CO2 concentration, sea level rise, and changes in glacier mass. Eventually, WESR is supposed to look like Earth's mission control center, where all of our critical environmental indicators may be readily monitored to direct our actions. The International Methane Emissions Observatory (IMEO), one of the UNEP-led projects within the WESR digital ecosystem, uses AI to transform the way methane emissions are monitored and mitigated. The platform functions as an international public database of methane emissions that have been empirically confirmed. To support data-driven decisions, it strategically connects this data with scientific action, transparency, and policy through the use of AI. Businesses and consumers can use it to make the best decisions possible by calculating the impact of products over their entire lifecycles and supply chains.

About the Significance of the Energy and Carbon Emissions

Kate Crawford claims that AI is to blame for 2% of the world's electricity use and greenhouse gas emissions and that this percentage is only expected to rise. To contextualize this, the industry's substantial energy use and carbon emissions are shown in the comparisons that follow. The AI industry's detrimental effects on the environment cannot be minimized or disregarded.

Synergistic Relation for a Greener Future

The issues of environmental degradation and climate change have grown more urgent in our time. Finding solutions that can lessen the impact of human activity on the environment is essential to addressing these issues. The synergy between artificial intelligence (AI) and sustainability initiatives is one promising partnership that has surfaced, providing a partnership for a more sustainable and environmentally friendly future. Through this collaboration, decision-making and resource management are enhanced by utilizing AI's data processing and analytical capabilities. Given that large corporations account for the majority of carbon emissions, this is particularly potent for businesses to use. AI-powered technologies are being used in a variety of industries, like manufacturing waste reduction and energy optimization. Organizations can enhance their operations and decrease their carbon footprint by integrating AI into sustainability initiatives. Furthermore, they can uncover new opportunities for eco-friendly innovations.

Approach to Ensuring the Long-Term Viability of AI

Reducing AI's environmental impact requires a multifaceted approach. First and foremost, financing the research and development of energy-efficient hardware and AI algorithms may significantly reduce energy consumption. Artificial intelligence (AI) systems can attain comparable efficiency while using less energy by optimizing their hardware and algorithms. It's also critical to promote ethical AI design standards, which include avoiding needless data collection and ensuring end-of-life considerations are taken into account. Additionally, a culture of transparency and accountability needs to be fostered. Stakeholders must give priority to supplying relevant data on AI models and data sources to assess their environmental impact. Governments and regulatory organizations should enact clear guidelines and regulations to guarantee the moral development, application, and disposal of AI technologies. It's also critical that companies, scholars, and legislators work together. By encouraging interdisciplinary research and knowledge sharing, researchers should develop solutions that emphasize environmental sustainability and technological advancements.

Research Gaps Regarding AI's Contribution to Sustainable Development

The more AI applications are used to support SDGs, from driverless cars (Bonnefon et al., 2016) to AI-powered medical devices (De Fauw et al., 2018) and intelligent electrical grids, the more crucial it is to fund the safety research required to maintain these systems' functionality and resilience against failure or hacking. Understanding disasters, which may be made possible by a structural flaw in AI technology, is an essential area of study for the safe integration of AI. For example, the incorporation of artificial intelligence in the financial sector (WEF 2018) raises such concerns in a current World Economic Forum (WEF) report. Raising awareness of the dangers of potential AI system failures is crucial in a society that is becoming more and more reliant on this technology. Second, long-lasting research may be needed to identify harmful aspects of AI, and as was already mentioned, there aren't many well-established assessment methodologies available to do so. The SDGs that correspond to the Environment group exhibit a bias towards publishing positive results. The creation of improved data-mining and machine-learning methods for the prediction of specific outcomes is the focus of substantive research and the application of AI technologies to SDGs happenings. Applications like predicting severe weather or recidivist offender behavior fall under this category. It is anticipated that this research will enable planning and reaction to a variety of situations. Institutions face several obstacles when implementing AI systems in their decision-making process, such as the requirement to put policies in place for cybersecurity and the requirement to safeguard citizens' data and privacy. Regarding the problems of monitoring, tracking, communication, and data storage, as well as the automation of procedures without strict ethical guidelines, both elements have an impact on human rights (Helbing et al., 2019). Furthermore, AI technologies have the potential to worsen existing problems if they are created for technologically advanced environments in less developed countries (such as in the production of food). This finding raises serious concerns about how advances in AI technologies may exacerbate inequality within and between nations, undermining the SDGs' overall goal. We urge scholars and investors to concentrate more on creating AI solutions that address regional issues in less developed countries and areas. Projects carrying out this kind of work should make sure that solutions aren't just imported from countries with high levels of technological advancement. To improve the chances of adoption and success, they ought to be created with a thorough awareness of the local area or culture.

In the Direction of Sustainable AI

While job displacement makes others worse off, the enormous wealth that AI-powered technology has the potential to create may primarily benefit those who are already wealthy and educated. Due to the unequal distribution of computing and educational resources worldwide, the growing economic significance of AI may lead to greater inequality. The aggravation of preexisting biases in the data used to train AI algorithms may lead to increased discrimination. Long-term effects of AI are possible (though unstudied) due to a lack of reliable research techniques, even though current scientific evidence denies the technological determinism of such fake news (Petit al., 2018). Thus, a paradigm change is necessary to promote cooperation and limit AI's ability to dictate how citizens behave. This will help guide AI's enormous potential toward the SDGs' accomplishment as well as the greatest possible benefit for people and the environment. A worldwide, science-driven discussion is needed to create common values and laws across countries and cultures to create a future where AI helps achieve all of the SDGs.

DISCUSSION

In today's rapidly evolving technological landscape, Artificial Intelligence (AI) stands out as the hottest topic of the moment. AI is a swiftly advancing technology reshaping numerous industries, and sustainability is no exception. With its potential to enhance efficiency, minimize waste, and foster innovation, AI emerges as a pivotal tool in addressing environmental challenges and steering us toward a sustainable future, making it a key player in AI for Environmental Sustainability. However, the potential risks and challenges associated with AI ensure that it is used responsibly and ethically. In recent decades, artificial intelligence has undergone transformative advancements, reshaping diverse sectors such as healthcare, transport, agriculture, energy, and the media. Despite the enthusiasm surrounding AI's potential, concerns persist about its potential negative impacts, including substantial energy consumption and ethical challenges. This paper critically reviews the evolving landscape of AI sustainability, addressing economic, social, and environmental dimensions. Among the most significant strengths identified is AI's capacity to process vast amounts of data and solve intricate problems that were previously deemed unsolvable without human intervention. This capability is particularly crucial in fields such as agriculture, where AI can markedly improve resource efficiency and crop yields through precision farming techniques. The ability of AI to learn from data with minimal prior knowledge of the underlying processes highlights its potential to drive innovations in sustainability in various sectors. However, this potential is tempered by significant weaknesses, primarily the high energy consumption associated with AI technologies. Training large AI models often requires substantial computational resources, leading to considerable carbon emissions. This paradoxically undermines the environmental benefits that AI aims to deliver. Addressing this challenge requires advances in energy-efficient AI technologies and the integration of renewable energy sources into data centers. The opportunities for AI in sustainability are expansive. The ability of AI to enhance climate change mitigation strategies through improved weather forecasting, disaster resilience, and optimization of renewable energy systems presents transformative potential. Additionally, AI can accelerate scientific research in fields critical to sustainability, such as materials science and chemistry, by providing advanced data analysis tools and predictive models.

Weaknesses

One of the most prominent challenges in the application of AI methods is the concern of explainability of the AI method implemented. The reason for the appearance of this problem is the perceived lack of understanding or representation of how recommendations or estimates resulting from AI methods are computed. Therefore, decision-makers may be reluctant to implement the recommendations of AI methods, despite their potential high quality. Another weakness of AI methods in terms of sustainability is the high power consumption that many of the methods cause. The energy consumption for developing and operating AI systems can negate some of the benefits of sustainability (Nicodeme, 2021). Above all, training large models, and thus, in most cases, particularly powerful models, causes significant computational effort and requires a considerable amount of energy. Furthermore, the vulnerability of AI methods to systemic risks should be highlighted. These include, for example, algorithmic bias and allocative harms. It is indicated that the results of complex AI methods can be strongly distorted by data bias (Bluemanstock, 2018). One major challenge is that most AI models are designed to optimize performance metrics such as accuracy, often at the expense of interpretability. This trade-off makes it difficult to provide explanations that are accurate and understandable in specific contexts, such as environmental sustainability, where stakeholders need to see how different environmental factors interact and contribute to the model outputs.

Strength of the Study

The first strength is the possibility of learning solutions purely from data and, in many cases, only relying on very little knowledge about the underlying process. This means that detailed knowledge of the natural sequence of the process to be depicted (relationship between input and output) is not necessarily required to train an AI model. While numerical methods usually try to represent or approximate this process mathematically, AI methods normally "do not care" how the actual process works (e.g., physically), as long as a sufficient amount of data to learn is available and a model structure appropriate for the complexity of the process is chosen. Therefore, AI can often find solutions to problems of unusually high complexity. For precision agriculture, AI algorithms could help support the growing process and significantly increase crop yields by managing controllable parameters such as irrigation or fertilization. AI can be used in biodiversity conservation through advanced data analysis and monitoring techniques. For example, AI algorithms can process large volumes of data from remote sensors, camera traps, and satellite imagery to monitor wildlife populations and track changes in ecosystems.

CONCLUSION

According to this proposal, artificial intelligence could considerably contribute to the improvement of environmental sustainability across several themes, including water, energy, transportation, and biodiversity. Even though there are promising technologies to address environmental sustainability issues, most of the issues must be resolved before their use can be sustained. To guarantee environmental sustainability and the full AI potential for present and future generations, more research is needed to address the challenges of utilizing each AI technology separately, like implementation. As a result, there is a chance that sustainable solutions will be used more frequently in industries like energy, water, transportation, and biodiversity. This chapter focused on the true value of AI in how it helps and supports environmental governance, and the pressing need to overcome the obstacles posed by the application of AI should be reflected in policy to ensure a sustainable future for both the present and future generations. Enhancing industrial environmental performance, environmental risk reduction, environmental safety, and environmental governance are among the advantages that AI offers. Any meaningful advancement toward environmental sustainability must be accompanied by prompt, accurate, and precise measurement and monitoring of interventions.

REFERENCES

Abduljabbar, R., Dia, H., & Kwok, S. R. (2019). AI empowers conservation biology. *Nature, 567*(7746), 133–135. DOI: 10.1038/d41586-019-00746-1 PMID: 30833739

Abduljabbar, R., Dia, H., Liyanage, S., & Bagloee, S. A. (2019). Applications of artificial intelligence in transport: An overview. *Sustainability (Basel), 11*(1), 189. DOI: 10.3390/su11010189

Anayat, S., & Rasool, G. (2022). Artificial intelligence marketing (AIM): Connecting-the-dots using bibliometrics. *Journal of Marketing Theory and Practice*, •••, 1–22.

Arsenyan, J., & Piepenbrink, A. (2023). Artificial intelligence research in management: A computational literature review. *IEEE Transactions on Engineering Management, 71*, 2088–5100.

Blumenstock, J. (2018). *Don't forget people in the use of big data for development.* Nature Publishing Group.

Bonnefon, J. F., Shariff, A., & Rahwan, I. (2016). The social dilemma of autonomous vehicles. *Science, 352*(6293), 1573–1576. DOI: 10.1126/science.aaf2654 PMID: 27339987

Callicott, J. B., & Mumford, K. (1998). Ecological sustainability as a conservation concept. In: *Ecological Sustainability and Integrity,* Concepts and Approaches. Springer; p. 31–45. DOI: 10.1007/978-94-017-1337-5_3

Collins, C., Dennehy, D., Conboy, K., & Mikalef, P. (2021). Artificial intelligence in information systems research: A systematic literature review and research agenda. *International Journal of Information Management, 60*, 102383. DOI: 10.1016/j.ijinfomgt.2021.102383

Cully, A., Clune, J., Tarapore, D., & Mouret, J. B. (2015). Robots that can adapt like animals. *Nature, 521*(7553), 503–507. DOI: 10.1038/nature14422 PMID: 26017452

De Fauw, J., Hughes, D. L., Coombs, C., Constantiou, I., Duan, Y., & Edwards, J. S. (2018). Clinically applicable deep learning for diagnosis and referral in retinal disease. *Nature Medicine, 24*(9), 1342–1350. DOI: 10.1038/s41591-018-0107-6 PMID: 30104768

Demirci, M., Ünes¸ F., & Korlü, S. (2019). Modeling of groundwater level using artificial intelligence techniques: a case study of Reyhanli region in Turkey.

Di Vaio, A., Palladino, R., Hassan, R., & Escobar, O. (2020). Artificial intelligence and business models in the sustainable development goals perspective: A systematic literature review. *Journal of Business Research, 121*, 283–314. DOI: 10.1016/j.jbusres.2020.08.019

Dwivedi, Y. K., Hughes, D. L., Coombs, C., Constantiou, I., Duan, Y., Edwards, J. S., Gupta, B., Lal, B., Misra, S., Prashant, P., Raman, R., Rana, N. P., Sharma, S. K., & Upadhyay, N. (2020). Impact of COVID-19 pandemic on information management research and practice: Transforming education, work and life. *International Journal of Information Management, 55*, 102211. DOI: 10.1016/j.ijinfomgt.2020.102211

Frank, B. (2021). Artificial intelligence-enabled environmental sustainability of products: Marketing benefits and their variation by consumer, location, and product types. *Journal of Cleaner Production, 285*, 125242. DOI: 10.1016/j.jclepro.2020.125242

Gonzalez Ordiano, J. A., Waczowicz, S., Hagenmeyer, V., & Mikut, R. (2018). Energy forecasting tools and services. *Wiley Interdisciplinary Reviews. Data Mining and Knowledge Discovery, 8*(2), e1235. DOI: 10.1002/widm.1235

Grover, P., Kar, A. K., & Dwivedi, Y. K. (2022). Understanding artificial intelligence adoption in operations management: Insights from the review of academic literature and social media discussions. *Annals of Operations Research, 308*(1–2), 177–213. DOI: 10.1007/s10479-020-03683-9

Helbing, D. (2019). *Towards Digital Enlightenment 73–98*. Springer International Publishing., DOI: 10.1007/978-3-319-90869-4

International Energy Agency. (2017). *Digitalization & Energy (International Energy, 2017)*. Agency.

Jha, K., Doshi, A., Patel, P., & Shah, M. (2019). A comprehensive review on automation in agriculture using artificial intelligence. *Artificial Intelligence Agriculture, 2*, 1–12. DOI: 10.1016/j.aiia.2019.05.004

Keramitsoglou, I., Cartalis, C., & Kiranoudis, C. T. (2006). Automatic identification of oil spills on satellite images. *Environmental Modelling & Software, 21*(5), 640–652. DOI: 10.1016/j.envsoft.2004.11.010

Kurdi, M. Z. (2017). *Natural Language Processing and Computational Linguistics 2: semantics, Discourse, and Applications, 2*. John Wiley & Sons. DOI: 10.1002/9781119419686

Leo Kumar, S. P. (2019). Knowledge-based expert system in manufacturing planning: State-of-the-art review. *International Journal of Production Research, 57*(15-16), 4766–4790. DOI: 10.1080/00207543.2018.1424372

Liu, Y., Yu, S., Zhu, Y., Wang, D., & Liu, J. (2018). Modeling, planning, application, and management of energy systems for isolated areas: A review. *Renewable & Sustainable Energy Reviews*, *82*, 460–470. DOI: 10.1016/j.rser.2017.09.063

Liu, Z., & Zeng, X. (2021). Hybrid intelligence in big data environment: Concepts, architectures, and applications of intelligent service. *Data and Information Management*, *5*(2), 262–276. DOI: 10.2478/dim-2020-0051

Loureiro, S. M. C., Guerreiro, J., & Tussyadiah, I. (2021). Artificial intelligence in business: State of the art and future research agenda. *Journal of Business Research*, *129*, 911–926. DOI: 10.1016/j.jbusres.2020.11.001

Lund, B. D., Wang, T., Mannuru, N. R., Nie, B., Shimray, S., & Wang, Z. (2023). ChatGPT and a new academic reality: Artificial Intelligence-written research papers and the ethics of the large language models in scholarly publishing. *Journal of the Association for Information Science and Technology*, *74*(5), 570–581. DOI: 10.1002/asi.24750

Maier, H. R., & Dandy, G. C. (2000). Neural networks for the prediction and forecasting of water resources variables: A review of modeling issues and applications. *Environmental Modelling & Software*, *15*(1), 101–124. DOI: 10.1016/S1364-8152(99)00007-9

Merizalde, Y., Hern'andez-Callejo, L., Duque-Perez, O., & Alonso-G'omez, V. (2019). Maintenance models applied to wind turbines. *A comprehensive overview*. *Energies*, *12*(2), 225. DOI: 10.3390/en12020225

Mohamadi, A., Heidarizadi, Z., & Nourollahi, H. (2016). Assessing the desertification trend using neural network classification and object-oriented techniques. *Journal ofFaculty.Istanbul University*, *66*, 683–690.

Nicodeme, C. (2021). Ai legitimacy for sustainability. In: 2021 IEEE Conference on Technologies for Sustainability (SusTech), pp. 1–5. IEEE, Ochoa, V., & Urbina-Cardona, N. (2017). Tools for spatially modeling ecosystem services: publication trends, conceptual reflections, and future challenges, *Ecosystem Servey, 26*, 155–169.

Nishant, R., Kennedy, M., & Corbett, J. (2020). Artificial intelligence for sustainability: Challenges, opportunities, and a research agenda. *International Journal of Information Management*, *53*, 102104. DOI: 10.1016/j.ijinfomgt.2020.102104

Petit, M. (2018). Towards a critique of algorithmic reason. A state-of-the-art review of artificial intelligence, its influence on politics, and its regulation. Quadratic Deletion CAC, 44.

Poria, S., Cambria, E., Bajpai, R., & Hussain, A. (2017). A review of affective computing: From unimodal analysis to multimodal fusion. *Information Fusion*, *37*, 98–125. DOI: 10.1016/j.inffus.2017.02.003

Ransbotham, S., Kiron, D., Gerbert, P., & Reeves, M. (2017). Reshaping business with artificial intelligence: Closing the gap between ambition and action. *MIT Sloan Management Review*, •••, 59.

Roberts, M. E., Stewart, B. M., Tingley, D., & Airoldi, E. M. (2013). The structural topic model and applied social science. *Advances in neural information processing systems workshop on topic models: Computation, application, and evaluation*

Rodriguez-Soto, C., Velazquez, A., Monroy-Vilchis, O., Lemes, P., & Loyola, R. (2017). A joint ecological, geographical and cultural approach to identify territories of opportunity for large vertebrates conservation in Mexico. *Biodiversity and Conservation*, *26*(8), 1899–1918. DOI: 10.1007/s10531-017-1335-7

Shollo, A., Hopf, K., Thiess, T., & Müller, O. (2022). Shifting ml value creation mechanisms: A process model of ml value creation. *The Journal of Strategic Information Systems*, *31*(3), 101734. DOI: 10.1016/j.jsis.2022.101734

Stockholm Resilience Centre's (SRC) contribution to the 2016 Swedish 2030 Agenda HLPF report (Stockholm University, 2017).

Strelkova, O., & Pasichnyk, O. (2017). Three Types of Artificial Intelligence, Khmelnytskyi National University: Khmelnytskyi, Salcedo-Sanz, S., Cuadra, L., & Vermeij, M.J.A. (2016). A review of computational intelligence techniques in coral reef-related applications. *Ecological Informatics*, *32*, 107–123.

Szeliski, R. (2014). *Concise Computer Vision: An Introduction Into Theory and Algorithms*. Springer London.

Tariq, M. U. (2025). *AI-Driven Learning and Engagement in Higher Education*. IGI Global., DOI: 10.4018/979-8-3693-4074-5

Tariq, M. U. (2025). Harnessing Technology to Combat Bias: Innovative Tools and Techniques in HR. In Kanwal, S. (Ed.), *Navigating Bias in Human Resource Management* (pp. 155–184). IGI Global Scientific Publishing., DOI: 10.4018/979-8-3693-7132-9.ch006

Tariq, M. U. (2025). Innovative Business Models: Integrating Social, Economic, and Environmental Goals in Rural Manufacturing. In Prabhakar, A., Yu, P., & Erokhin, V. (Eds.), *Rural Social Entrepreneurship Development: Network-Based Manufacturing System Model* (pp. 147–174). IGI Global Scientific Publishing., DOI: 10.4018/979-8-3693-7515-0.ch005

Tariq, M. U. (2025). Revolutionizing Communication: EEG-Based Brain-Computer Interface for Speech and Mood Detection. In Prabhakar, A., Yu, P., & Erokhin, V. (Eds.), *Rural Social Entrepreneurship Development: Network-Based Manufacturing System Model* (pp. 237–264). IGI Global Scientific Publishing., DOI: 10.4018/979-8-3693-7515-0.ch008

Tariq, M. U., & Sergio, R. (Eds.). (2025). *Cases on AI-Driven Solutions to Environmental Challenges.* IGI Global, 2025. https://doi.org/DOI: 10.4018/979-8-3693-7483-2

Tariq, M. U., & Sergio, R. (Eds.). (2025). *Convergence of AI, Education, and Business for Sustainability*. IGI Global., DOI: 10.4018/979-8-3373-1917-9

Toivonen, T., Heikinheimo, V., Fink, C., Hausmann, A., Hiippala, T., Jarv, O., Tenkanen, H., & Di Minin, E. (2019). Social media data for conservation science: A methodological overview. *Biological Conservation*, *233*, 298–315. DOI: 10.1016/j.biocon.2019.01.023

Tyralis, H., Papacharalampous, G., & Langousis, A. (2019). A brief review of random forests for water scientists and practitioners and their recent history in water resources. *Water (Basel)*, *11*(5), 910. DOI: 10.3390/w11050910

Verma, S., Sharma, R., Deb, S., & Maitra, D. (2021). Artificial intelligence in marketing: Systematic review and future research direction. *International Journal of Information Management Data Insights*, *1*(1), 100002. DOI: 10.1016/j.jjimei.2020.100002

Vinuesa, R., Fdez. De Arévalo, L., Luna, M., & Cachafeiro, H. (2016). Simulations and experiments of heat loss from a parabolic trough absorber tube over a range of pressures and gas compositions in the vacuum chamber. *Journal of Renewable and Sustainable Energy*, *8*, 342–354. DOI: 10.1063/1.4944975

Wang, P., & Goertzel, B. (2017). Introduction: aspects of artificial general intelligence, in Proceedings of the 2007 conference on Advances in Artificial General Intelligence: Concepts, Architectures, and Algorithms: Proceedings of the AGI Workshop 2007, 2006, pp. 1–16 Ukraine, pp. 1–4.

Wang, Z., & Srinivasan, R. S. (2017). A review of artificial intelligence based building energy use prediction: Contrasting the capabilities of single and ensemble prediction models. *Renewable & Sustainable Energy Reviews*, *75*, 796–808. DOI: 10.1016/j.rser.2016.10.079

World Economic Forum (WEF). 2018. Fourth Industrial Revolution for the Earth Series Harnessing Artificial Intelligence for the Earth.

Zadeh, L. A. (1975). Fuzzy logic and approximate reasoning. *Synthese*, *30*(3-4), 407–428. DOI: 10.1007/BF00485052

KEY TERMS AND DEFINITIONS

Environmental Sustainability: It is the ability to maintain an ecological balance in our planet's natural environment and conserve natural resources to support the wellbeing of current and future generations. Environmental sustainability is important for the wellbeing of current and future generations. Climate change presents a variety of complex environmental, social, and economic challenges for countries across the globe.

Artificial Intelligent: AI is a branch of computer science that relies on prior knowledge to determine how to solve environmental problems more successfully.

AIoT: AIoT refers to the Artificial Intelligence of Things; it merges the connectivity offered by the Internet of Things (IoT) with the insights derived from Artificial Intelligence (AI). This developing technology is centered around the incorporation of Artificial Intelligence into IoT systems.

Machine Learning (ML): Subfield of AI in which algorithms are trained to perform tasks by learning pattern from data rather than by explicit program

Chapter 12
Revolutionising Agriculture:
The Role of AIoT in Disease and Pest Management for Global Food Security

R. Monisha
https://orcid.org/0000-0002-4591-897X
KPR Institute of Engineering and Technology, India

K. S. Tamilselvan
https://orcid.org/0009-0009-5214-590X
KPR Institute of Engineering and Technology, India

A. Sharmila
Bannari Amman Institute of Technology, India

ABSTRACT

Pests and diseases affecting the plants lead to diminished crop yield worldwide. To address this, researchers have employed Industry 4.0 to modernise agriculture by incorporating advances such as Internet of Things (IoT), and Artificial Intelligence (AI). The IoT connects physical objects to the internet for data collection and exchange. As the count of those devices expanded, they began generating huge data. Consequently, extraction of actionable insights is required for effective decision-making. Thus, AIoT—the fusion of AI and IoT—addresses this scenario, where AI handles the huge data created by IoT devices by analysing and interpreting them. AIoT is applied to numerous sectors, including agriculture, where they assist in estimating crop yields, conserving soil, and identifying pests and diseases. AIoT also aids with crop disease diagnosis and pest management by providing real-time

DOI: 10.4018/979-8-3693-8547-0.ch012

monitoring and predictive analytics. This chapter provides basics of AIoT and the potential of AIoT in disease and pest management. It highlights the challenges and future of AIoT.

INTRODUCTION

Technological advancements have made rapid progress in transforming various sectors, with agriculture being no exception. According to future estimates, there is a high possibility that by 2050, the global population will reach 9.8 billion (Mok et al., 2020; Abbasi et al., 2022). In response to this, the food demand is expected to rise by approximately 59% to 98%; henceforth, agricultural production must increase by at least 70% (Blanco-Carmona et al., 2023). However, various challenges constantly threaten agricultural productivity, including water and resource scarcity, climate change, and crop diseases and pest attacks, which are responsible for nearly 40% of annual global production losses (Sarkozi, 2019; Karar et al., 2021). Crop diseases pose a serious threat to food security for high-risk and staple crops such as wheat, rice, and others, making it extremely difficult to meet the Sustainable Development Goals (Verma et al., 2024). The utilization of cutting-edge technologies is necessary to address the challenges, to optimize farming practices, and to ensure sustainable food production. Gleaned from the significant shifts in how food is cultivated and harvested, the agricultural industry has undergone several revolutions. The concept of settled farming laid the foundation for the Neolithic Revolution, followed by the Industrial Revolution, which introduced mechanical farming tools. The Green Revolution brought significant progress in irrigation, fertilizers, and yield-based crop selection, effectively boosting food production. Several decades later, the state-of-the-art transformation, termed Agriculture 4.0, powered by Industry 4.0 technologies, incorporates artificial intelligence (AI), the Internet of Things (IoT), robotics, and cloud computing to enhance efficiency, precision, and sustainability in agriculture (Aceto et al., 2019). Artificial Intelligence of Things (AIoT), the convergence of AI and IoT, is emerging as an effective power in modern agriculture. It enables the seamless integration of IoT-based sensor networks with AI-driven analytics, providing real-time insights and automotive capabilities that can revolutionize agricultural practices. AIoT helps by continuously monitoring yield factors such as crop health, soil moisture, and temperature, facilitating data-driven decision-making, early disease identification, and precision agriculture, ultimately reducing resource wastage and improving overall productivity (Khan et al., 2022).

When it comes to applications of AIoT in agriculture, its role in pest and disease management is inevitable. The traditional method of monitoring crops manually has several limitations, including time consumption, labor intensity, and proneness to human error. The drawbacks in manual monitoring emphasize the strong need to adopt AIoT-based solutions, which employ machine learning (ML) algorithms, computer vision, and satellite sensing technologies to detect diseases and pest infestations at an early stage. AIoT can analyze huge amounts of real-time data, thus providing farmers with actionable insights and enabling timely interventions that mitigate crop losses and enhance food security (Muhammed et al., 2024). In this chapter, the impact of AIoT in modern agriculture, especially in addressing the difficulties and challenges revolving around pest and disease management, is discussed. Initially, the chapter delves into the evolutionary history of smart farming technologies/ Agriculture 4.0, the integration of AI and IoT in agricultural systems, and the real-world applications transforming traditional farming practices. The nuances of Industry 4.0 and its applications in agriculture are briefly explained. Furthermore, the challenges and prospects of AIoT are highlighted, emphasizing the need for continuous innovation and widespread adoption to achieve sustainable agricultural development in the face of growing global food demands.

BACKGROUND

About the practice of how food is produced today, human history has witnessed four agricultural revolutions so far (Liu Y et al., 2020). Approximately 10,000 years ago, the first industrial revolution (IRN), named the *Neolithic Revolution*, signaled the shift from foraging to farming settlements. The action of domestication of plants and animals at that time led to a chain of events that served as the groundwork for modern agriculture. Later, between the 17th and 19th centuries, the second agricultural *Industrial Revolution* took place. The revolution introduced different farming concepts like crop rotation, invented mechanical tools for farming, and the application of fertilizers and pesticides. In the mid-20th century, the third, or *Green Revolution,* greatly increased food supply and helped avert famines in developing countries by inventing high-yielding crop species, synthetic fertilizers, and new irrigation techniques. The fourth revolution - *Industry 4.0-* reshaped industries through the incorporation of technological innovations like AI, big data (BD), IoT, and cloud computing (Aceto et al., 2019). The merging of these advanced techniques into farming has given rise to Agriculture 4.0 (*smart agriculture/ digital farming),* which is revolutionizing traditional practices. To address several issues related to agricultural food production, smart agriculture offers farmers a wide range of instruments. By utilizing real-time data and intelligent systems to optimize farming operations, this revolution promises to significantly improve yield, food safety, and sustainability (Tian et al., 2021). It also lessens the environmental impact and addresses the issues of a growing global population. Each revolution has built on the progress of its predecessor, continuously transforming agriculture to meet the evolving needs of society.

Emergence of AIoT

IoT and AI have emerged as cutting-edge technologies in recent years, greatly impacting environmental progress (Khan et al., 2022a). The IoT began as a concept focused on connecting devices and machines to the internet, permitting those devices to communicate, fetch, and trade data. The central objective of IoT was to fabricate a network of interconnected devices that could offer real-time data, leading to increased efficacity, automation, and finer decision-making (IBM 2024). As IoT devices proliferated, they began generating massive amounts of data (Nagaty 2023; Allioui & Mourdi 2023). However, this data was often underutilized due to its complexity and volume. Simply collecting data was no longer sufficient; there was a need to extract actionable insights from it to enhance the effectiveness of IoT systems. This is where Artificial Intelligence of Things comes into play, where AI handles the BD generated from IoT devices by analyzing and interpreting such huge amounts of data. AI focuses on creating systems capable of learning, reasoning, and making decisions, often replicating human cognitive functions. AI technologies enable autonomous systems to analyze large datasets, recognize patterns, make prognostications, and perform prescriptive decision analysis. Henceforth, the unification of AI and IoT allows systems to adapt and progress, bettering their performance continuously and spontaneously. This progression not only makes IoT processes more dynamic and reciprocal between humans and machines but also strengthens data management capabilities with analytics (Wikipedia 2024). The integration of AI inside IoT ecosystems enhances operational efficiency, improves risk management, stimulates superior products and services, and augments the scalability of IoT (Bzai et al., 2022; Fraga-Lamas et al., 2021).

Figure 1. Applications of AIoT.

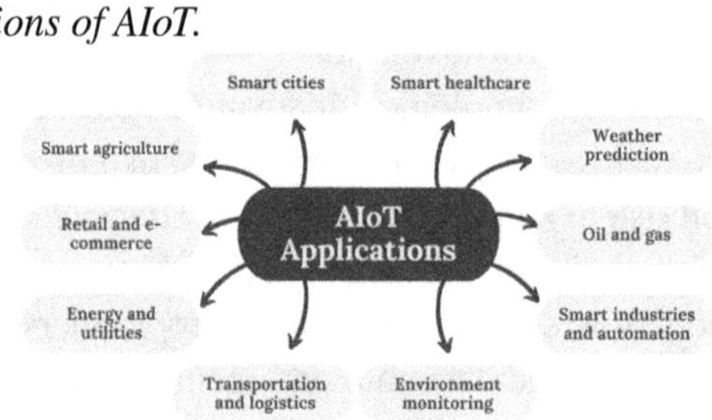

AIoT has numerous applications across different fields like smart cities, drug discovery, data mining and sharing, traffic management, automated vehicles, and agriculture, as depicted in Figure 1. From the technologies, AIoT has found its uses in agriculture in a variety of tasks such as supply chain management, disease and pest detection, water and soil preservation, and harvest rate estimation, as shown in Figure 2 (Muhammed et al., 2024). It also focuses on harvest management, greenhouse automation, and intelligent fertigation, allowing for more adaptive reactions to environmental changes. AIoT offers advanced monitoring and data collection using internet-connected sensors that are coupled with satellite systems over the farmlands.

Figure 2. AIoT applications in agriculture.

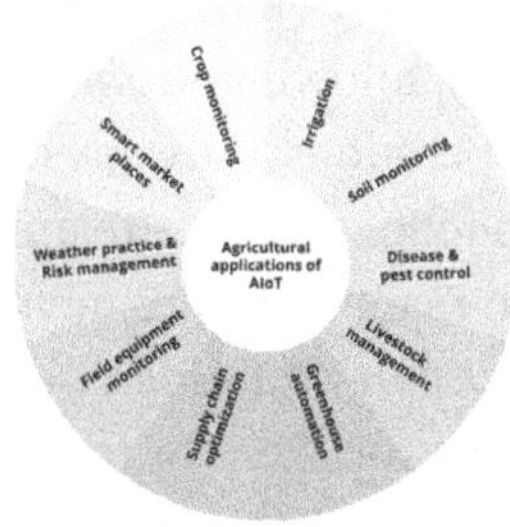

The traditional farming practices were either assisted with or replaced with real-time data and intelligent systems by employing AIoT. AIoT addresses several crucial concerns in the agricultural field, including maximizing resource efficiency, maintaining sustainability, and alleviating crop losses through tailored solutions. The diseases and pests affecting the crops have a significant impact on the quantity and quality of the yield. The speed of their outbreaks often outpaces conventional detection and control methods and becomes increasingly resistant to those treatments. These challenges are further compounded by climate change, which can alter pest and disease patterns, making them harder to predict and control. The complexity of these threats demands innovative, technology-driven solutions to protect global food security. Henceforth, the inclusion of AIoT in agriculture offers a promising solution in light of the significant challenges posed by pests and diseases. AIoT facilitates the early detection of diseases through continuous monitoring and predictive analytics.

The Emergence of Industry 4.0 (I4.0) in Agriculture

Historical Context of I4.0

The first IRN set about in the late 18th century from Britain ushered in a complete metamorphosis in production. The discovery of steam and water power lessened industrial reliance on human and animal labor, allowing for mass production. This revolution steered forward a new era of precision engineering, in which items were created using machines rather than being meticulously crafted by hand (Groumpos et al., 2021). The Second IRN occurred after a century, and it launched assembly lines and used new energy sources, including petroleum, gas, and electricity (*Industry 4.0: The Future of Manufacturing | SAP*, n.d..). These advances made technological instruments leaner and less bulky, allowing for mass production and some level of automation in manufacturing operations. Advanced communication technologies, such as the telegraph and telephone, greatly streamlined operations, and many of them continue to affect modern manufacturing methods (IBM, 2024a). The Third IRN set about in the mid-20th century, putting computers, improved telecommunications, and data analysis at the forefront of industry. This period saw the early development of factory automation and robotics, with the digitization of industries taking shape through the incorporation of programmable logic controllers into machinery (Cannavacciuolo et al., 2023). These advancements contributed to the automation of processes, data management and analysis, and the establishment of contemporary computerized business systems (Mohajan, 2021). The Fourth IRN (I4.0) is a transformative period in manufacturing that involves the integration of modern technology, smart machinery, and real-time data. Its primary goal is to improve performance and maintenance by allowing machines to be self-aware and self-learning, resulting in seamless interaction with their surroundings (Vaidya et al., 2018). This transition enables the creation of open, intelligent manufacturing platforms for industrial applications (Bahrin et al., 2016). I4.0 emphasizes real-time data monitoring, product tracking, and precise management of manufacturing operations (Almada-Lobo, 2015). I4.0 is typified by the convergence of multiple systems and technologies rather than by a single breakthrough. The chart visualizing the four revolutions is given in Figure 3.

Figure 3. The four IRNs.

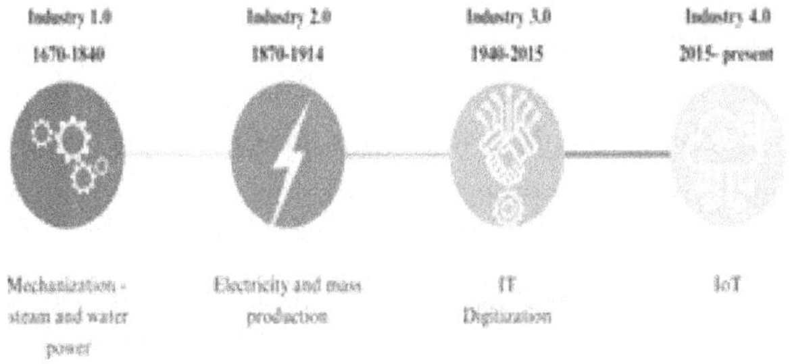

Definition of I4.0

As part of a strategic drive by the German government to modernize the manufacturing sector, the phrase "*Industrie 4.0*" was initially used in Germany at the 2011 Hannover Fair (Wu et al., 2024). By incorporating cutting-edge technologies into industrial processes, this effort sought to increase competitiveness, efficiency, and production. By 2014, Drath and Horch's seminal paper in IEEE Industrial Electronics Magazine had sparked broad academic interest (Drath & Horch, 2014; Schwab, 2017). In order to characterize this revolution as a worldwide phenomenon propelling the future of industrial production, the 2016 Industrie 4.0 Working Group highlighted important concepts, such as the incorporation of IoT and services into manufacturing environments.

There are various definitions of I4.0 in literature. It is essentially a confluence of technical advancements intended to open the door for intelligent and networked production systems (Culot, 2020). I4.0, according to World Economic Forum founder Klaus Schwab, is the combination of technologies that makes it harder to distinguish between the digital, biological, and physical realms. In his definition, he underlined its disruptive power across industries and its exponential rate of development (Schwab, 2017; Tariq, 2025).

I4.0 Technologies

Additive Manufacturing (3d Printing)

Additive manufacturing, also known as 3D (three-dimensional) printing or layered manufacturing, is an innovative approach that produces various structures and intricate geometries directly from 3D model data. Unlike subtractive manufacturing, additive manufacturing constructs products layer upon layer. According to ASTM, it is described as "the process of combining materials for constructing objects based on 3D model data, typically in a layer-by-layer manner, as compared with subtractive manufacturing approaches" (Ngo et al., 2018; Tariq, 2025).

Introduced to the world in 1984 by Charles W. Hull, this technology began with the development of a process called stereolithography. In this process, a digital 3D model, often created using computer-aided design software, is transformed into a stereolithography file, which can be interpreted by 3D printers (Jadhav & Jadhav 2022). 3D printing utilizes an array of materials, including polymers, metals, ceramics, and composites, with polylactic acid and acrylonitrile butadiene styrene being particularly prevalent to construct the object (Stankovic et al., 2021). However, the choice of material and the bonding mechanism between layers depend on the type of printer employed, such as selective laser sintering, fused deposition modeling, or stereolithography (Ngo et al., 2018). This technology supports the processing of smart and adaptive materials, enhancing their adaptability and functionality. Its rapid evolution can be attributed to factors such as decreasing costs of 3D printers, improvements in printing accuracy, an expanding variety of materials, and the expiration of key patents. This technology is transforming production lines and value chains by obviating conventional processes such as tooling and welding and facilitating the substitution of small production lines. It has found significant applications in industries such as healthcare and dentistry, where the demand for precision and customization is high (Stankovic et al., 2021).

The following are some possible applications for 3D printing in developing nations:

- Construction: By adopting a technique known as "contour crafting," 3D printing can rapidly and economically construct homes with floors, walls, plumbing, and electricity within a very short time, providing a solution to the housing scarcity in slums.
- Water and Sanitation: 3D printing makes toilets and rainfall collectors in response to deaths caused by water and sanitation.
- Disaster Relief: Where power infrastructure has been interrupted, 3D printers that can run on solar energy can be used to create vital medical supplies in disaster-affected areas.
- Shoes: To combat the jigger infestation, the University of Nairobi in Kenya is promoting the creation of 3D-printed shoes from recycled plastic, which also have the added advantage of being recyclable after worn out. (Ibrahim et al., 2015)

Artificial Intelligence

AI, a subfield of computer science, has grown in importance over the last ten years, and its uses are now widely accepted in society. At the 1956 Dartmouth Conference, John McCarthy put forth a generally recognized definition of AI, emphasizing the technology's objective of allowing robots to mimic intelligent human behavior (Anderson, 2024). AI aims to mimic and improve human intelligence so that machines can think and act similarly to people. It creates intelligent systems that can perceive, process, and react to inputs. Numerous disciplines are incorporated into it, including computer science, biology, philosophy, psychology, neuroscience, statistics, and mathematics. Its main objective is to develop transparent, interpretable, and explicable systems to resolve issues in the actual world (Ghosh, 2021). One of the pioneers of AI, Marvin Minsky, defined AI as "the science of enabling machines to perform tasks that would necessitate intelligence if executed by humans" (Stankovic et al., 2021). One important branch of AI is ML, which aims to make it possible for computers to replicate human learning. Deep learning, another subset of AI, which is based on artificial neural networks, imitates how the brain processes information such as text, sound, and images (Ltd, 2022). The sub-disciplines involved in AI are illustrated in Figure 4. AI is now regarded as a necessary component of contemporary life, impacting industries like media, healthcare, banking, and transportation.

Figure 4. Sub-disciplines of AI.

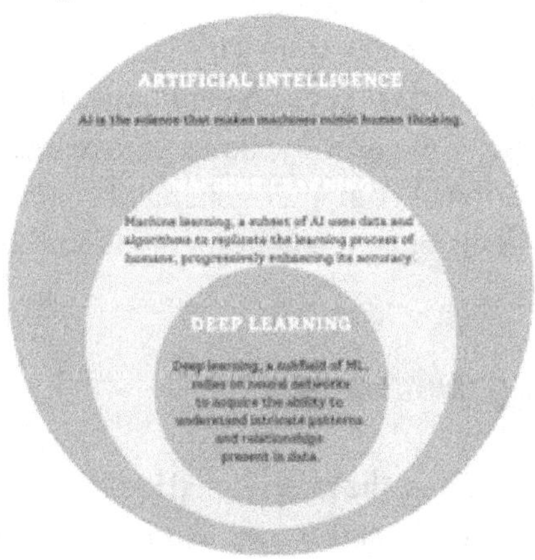

There are three categories of AI:

- Strong AI: This describes computers that possess human-like consciousness and self-awareness and are capable of reasoning and solving problems. These machines can think and make decisions on their own, coming up with the best answers to issues. Like living things, strong AI has its worldview and impulses. Strong AI might, in a way, signify a new kind of civilization.

- Weak AI: This term refers to robots that seem intelligent but are incapable of self-awareness or reasoning. Although these systems are capable of carrying out particular tasks, they lack the capacity for autonomous thought and problem-solving that distinguishes humans. The majority of modern applications employ weak AI.
- General AI: A machine that can carry out every cognitive work that a person can is said to have general AI. Although it is a long-term objective, this degree of AI has not yet been attained. General AI would be able to understand, reason, and adapt similarly to humans, maybe achieving a cognitive level that could compete with humans in a variety of tasks. (Ghosh, 2021)

Augmented Reality

In 1992, the word "augmented reality" (AR) was first devised by a Boeing researcher, Thomas Preston Caudell, while he developed an AR software for seeing assembly drawings. The multiple meaning of AR exists today, but the one given by Paul Milgram and Fumio Kishino is the most widely accepted. According to their theory, various forms of reality combine to form a continuum that leads from the real world to a completely virtual one. The core goal of AR is to create links between the data generated by a device or computer data and the physical environment, either directly or by man and device interaction. This situation allows users access to an interface for an electronic physical environment. Any display technology that can combine or overlay data with the user's vision of the real environment can employ this integration. The coalition of computer-generated content and real-world views, AR helps improve human vision and cognition in unexpected ways (Bogue, 2013; Arena et al., 2022).

Big Data, Data Mining, Data Analytics

In contemporary applications, the interrelated ideas of BD, data mining, and data analytics are crucial for organizing and extracting insights from enormous amounts of data. The three Vs—Volume (huge volumes of data created from sources like social media and IoT), Velocity (real-time data generation and processing), and Variety (different types of data, such as unstructured, semi-structured, and structured)—are what define BD, which refers to enormous, complicated databases. Such data may be processed and stored efficiently, thanks to technologies like Hadoop and Spark. Data mining uses methods like statistical analysis, ML, and AI to extract patterns, trends, and useful insights from these massive datasets. With applications in fields like fraud detection and client segmentation, it usually entails processes like data cleaning, integration, pattern recognition, and prediction. Building on these insights, data analytics interprets and presents results to help make well-informed decisions. It includes prescriptive analytics, which suggests actions; predictive analytics, which forecasts future events; and descriptive analytics, which summarizes historical data. Data visualization and interpretation are aided by programs like Tableau, Power BI, and Python libraries. They are essential in industries like marketing, banking, and healthcare because BD lays the groundwork, Data mining reveals the insights, and data analytics turns these insights into workable plans (Kudyba & Kudyba, 2014; Tariq, 2025).

Blockchain

Blockchain is a safeguarded, decentralized digital record invented by Haber and Stornetta in the early 1990s and popularized by Satoshi Nakamoto in 2008 (Nakamoto, 2008; Haber & Stornetta, 1991). Its primary characteristics—data integrity, security, decentralization, and trustworthiness—are intended to improve safety and trust. By fusing "database" and "network" concepts, blockchain—which was first created to digitally date, hash, and link data chronologically—has matured into a powerful tool for recording, registering, and transferring digital assets (Zheng et al., 2018). By dispersing its ledger over a decentralized network of complete nodes, which together use consensus procedures to validate and log transactions, blockchain removes centralized control. Because modifications necessitate the consent of the majority, this structure makes it transparent and safe from manipulation and tampering. The technology is widely used in a variety of sectors, including media, public services, healthcare, and finance. It makes it possible for value to be exchanged instantly and decentralized, boosting traceability, decreasing the need for middlemen, and increasing the effectiveness of procedures like payments, legal verification, patent establishment, and certification for renewable energy. Blockchain is a key component of contemporary digital innovation since it is revolutionizing the way value is exchanged (Kayikci & Khoshgoftaar, 2024).

Cloud Computing

Cloud computing presents numerous growth and development prospects for any sector. Software-as-a-Service, Platform-as-a-Service, and Infrastructure-as-a-Service are the three prototypes of cloud delivery. Cloud computing is a new technology that is both a technical and social reality. It is now impossible to predict what applications will move to this new paradigm and how its infrastructure will develop.

This technological transition, where users depend on services from massive data centers and keep private information and software on systems they do not control, is expected to have substantial economic, social, ethical, and legal ramifications (Marinescu, 2022).

Cyber Physical Systems (CPSs)

CPSs are advanced systems that seamlessly integrate computational and physical components, enabling interaction through sensing, computation, control, and networking (Schranz, 2021). Defined by the National Science Foundation as "engineered systems created from and rely on a seamless coordination of computing and physical components," CPSs are inherently transdisciplinary, merging principles from cybernetics, mechatronics, robotics, networking, and process science (Cyber-Physical Systems (CPS), 2024). They function through the integration of software and hardware via controlled mechanisms and algorithms, offering diverse applications in industrial control, smart grids, smart vehicles, medical devices, household systems, aerospace, and defense. These systems are composed of two key parts: the physical activity and the cyber system. The increasing interaction between these elements heightens the impact of cyber threats on physical systems, underscoring the need for robust security measures (Tyagi, 2021). CPSs represent a paradigm shift in connected systems, expanding the scope of traditional embedded and automated systems to address complex, interconnected challenges in various domains.

Internet of Things

Kevin Ashton invented the phrase "Internet of Things" when presenting it to Procter & Gamble in 1999. To provide improved services for society, IoT offers an infrastructure that binds both virtual and physical items (Kiran, 2019). Improved programmability, data storage space, and sensor-related potentialities are introduced, enabling intelligent, autonomous online communication from physical things. This would enable centralized, well-established systems to function in a disruptive, decentralized environment. Machine-to-machine (M2M), machine-to-infrastructure, and machine-to-environment communication are all included in the IoT (Stankovic et al., 2021).

Application of I4.0 in Agriculture

The merger of I4.0 with agriculture provides the chance to promote traditional farming to the next level, known as Agriculture 4.0 (De Clercq et al., 2018). This paradigm shift uses cutting-edge digital tools to improve agricultural production, sustainability, and efficiency. According to recent surveys, digital technologies that support "Agriculture 4.0" have reduced costs per hectare by 13% and the use of fuel, water, fertilizer, and pesticides by 30%. Additionally, a 15% decline in the crops' carbon footprint has been documented in terms of environmental sustainability (Osservatori, 2021). The size of the land has a huge impact on the espousal of I4.0 solutions; in fact, only 25% of farms under 10 hectares use 4.0 solutions, while 65% of farms over 100 hectares do so (ISTAT, 2020).

Smart agriculture gives farmers a variety of tools to tackle several issues related to agricultural food production. Key technologies and their applications include:

- ML and DL: Random Forest, support vector machines, regression models, and principal component analysis algorithms are widely used. DL methods like convolutional neural networks and recurrent networks contribute significantly to predictive analytics and pattern recognition.
- Sensor Technology: Wireless sensor networks and remote sensing are vital for monitoring soil conditions, climatic change, and crop health. Key metrics from satellite data, such as the normalized difference vegetation index and leaf area index, are commonly used to assess vegetation health and dynamics (Tariq, 2025).
- Robotics and Automation: Robotics, particularly unmanned aerial vehicles, play a vital role in tasks, namely crop monitoring, spraying, and planting. They are a frequent focus of research due to their efficiency in data collection and precision agriculture (Araújo et al., 2021).

These technologies' convergence gives farmers the means to make data-driven decisions, manage resources more effectively, and increase productivity. Even though there has been a lot of progress, adoption barriers—especially for smaller farms—showcase the need for scalable and reasonably priced solutions to guarantee that I4.0 ideas are applied more widely in agriculture.

UNDERSTANDING AIOT: THE CONVERGENCE OF AI AND IOT

The Role of IoT in Agriculture

IoT is a network of physical objects, such as devices, instruments, vehicles, and others, that are joined with sensors, software, circuits, electronics, and network connections (Alaba, 2024). One important aspect of the IoT is the internet itself, and the first major turning point in its history was the development of connectedness. In 1991, an Internet Toaster was created by John Romkey and Simon Hackett, shortly after the first IoT device was designed by David Nichols and his associates at MIT in 1989. The toaster was a huge milestone since the developers were able to turn it on and off remotely by successfully linking it to the internet. For the same reason that the smart vending machine was created, Dr. Quentin Stafford-Fraser and his associates at the University of Cambridge created the first online webcam. The first significant advancement in wearable technology was WearCam, developed by Steve Mann a year later. By this point, internet-connected devices were becoming commonplace. However, it was still the product of strange, dispersed experiments rather than a singular technique. This was altered in 1999 when Kevin Ashton, a co-founder of MIT's Auto-ID Labs, came up with the name "Internet of Things." Ashton was a strong proponent of RFID's potential and thought it was a necessary component of the IoT. The IoT became commercially viable in 2000 when LG unveiled the first smart refrigerator. The IoT gained popularity in less than ten years after the term was first used. In 2005, the United Nations released its initial study on the IoT, identifying it as one of the technologies with the greatest promise for globalization. Apple released the first iPhone in 2007, barely two years after the UN report's forecasts. Although the Simon Personal Communicator, developed by IBM in 1994, was the first smartphone, the iPhone was the device that made smartphones popular throughout the world, even though the first iPhone merely permitted internet browsing. By 2008, there were more linked gadgets than there were humans worldwide. Since there were officially enough connected devices for any data to be gathered globally, if necessary, this was the moment when the IoT took off. For IoT, the 2000s were exciting since several milestones were reached quickly. Modern smartwatches were made possible by this, the first wearable activity tracker. IoT milestones began to get increasingly specialized and technical after the 2010s. (Kulkarni, 2023).

IoT plays a crucial role in several sectors, including smart urban planning, traffic control, healthcare, and connected living spaces. The IoT has emerged as a key factor propelling innovation and modernization in agriculture. IoT gadgets, such as weather stations, crop health monitors, and soil moisture sensors, are transforming farming methods in fields all over the world. Farmers can make quick and well-informed decisions because of these technologies' ability to support real-time monitoring and data collection. For example, by detecting when crops require water, soil sensors ensure effective watering while reducing water waste. Real-time data collection from agricultural settings improves operational effectiveness and decision-making, promoting sustainable farming methods (Tariq, 2025).

Important IoT Uses in Agriculture

- Air Monitoring: To guarantee ideal crop growth, greenhouse gas levels and air quality are evaluated.
- To maximize soil health, characteristics like moisture, pH, and nutrient levels are measured.
- Water monitoring: keeping tabs on water quality and usage to guarantee sustainable irrigation methods.
- Disease monitoring is the process of using sensor data and imaging equipment to find early indicators of agricultural illnesses.
- Monitoring environmental conditions includes keeping an eye on humidity, temperature, and other elements that are vital to plant growth.
- Crop and Plant Growth Monitoring: Tracking growth stages and identifying stressors with IoT devices.
- Automation of greenhouses: regulating ventilation, temperature, and lighting to create ideal growing conditions.
- Fertilization and Pest Control: Using real-time data to automate and optimize the application of pesticides and fertilizers.
- Livestock tracking: Watching the whereabouts, condition, and behavior of animals in order to improve welfare and productivity.

Agriculture is unquestionably becoming a more data driven, robust, and efficient sector, thanks to the IoT. The potential of IoT to transform conventional farming methods through real-time data collection, effective resource management, and sophisticated decision-making skills is what makes it significant for the agricultural industry. Real-time crop management, soil, and environmental state using IoT-enabled equipment enables predictive analysis and well-informed decision-making to address problems before they become more serious. Demand-based watering, fertilizing, and robotic harvesting are examples of automated features that increase productivity and efficiency while minimizing resource waste. In order to address the expanding needs of urban populations, IoT also helps urban agriculture by enabling short food supply chains through innovations like rooftop farming, hydroponic systems, and IoT-powered greenhouses.

IoT minimizes environmental effects while promoting sustainability through precision farming, which maximizes the use of water, power, and fertilizers. Furthermore, IoT-powered smart farming produces cleaner, more organic goods by using less fertilizer and pesticide. Additionally, real-time monitoring improves farming agility by enabling prompt reactions to environmental hazards and weather variations, protecting crops. Furthermore, IoT systems increase the nutritional value of products and reproduce optimal growing circumstances by using drone surveillance, farm mapping, soil and crop sensors, and other technologies to improve product quality. Sensors, wireless networks (GSM, LTE, Wi-Fi), BD analytics, and cloud computing are some of the technologies that support these developments. By processing and analyzing the massive volumes of data produced, IoT can propel agriculture toward increased sustainability, efficiency, and adaptability.

The Role of AI in Agriculture

The concept and subtypes of AI were already discussed in Section 2.3.2. AI in agriculture signifies a change from conventional farming techniques to data-driven, precision-driven methods that improve production, sustainability, and efficiency. By facilitating real-time data analysis and decision-making, AI technologies—powered by ML, computer vision, and sensor-based systems—are revolutionizing the agriculture sector. This development makes it possible to use resources more wisely, produce more crops, and have a less environmental impact. Large-scale datasets produced by IoT devices are analyzed by AI-driven systems, which yield useful information for improving pest control, disease management, fertilization, and irrigation.

Precision agriculture has been transformed by adaptive AI technologies, in particular, which use self-learning algorithms that react dynamically to changing circumstances. For instance, resource-efficient farming is made possible by programs that use satellite imaging, drones, and ground sensors to monitor crop health, identify illnesses early, and adjust nutrition and irrigation plans. Furthermore, the combination of AI with IoT, commonly known as the AIoT, offers cutting-edge features like supply chain optimization, autonomous operations, and predictive analytics, which further lessen labor dependency and operational inefficiencies.

AI has the potential to transform agriculture, but there are a number of obstacles in the way. Small and medium-sized farms are less able to afford the high upfront expenditures of AI-enabled technologies, such as drones, sensors, and analysis tools. The bedrock of smart farming is real-time data collecting and processing, which is hampered by poor internet connectivity in rural locations. Furthermore, in order to optimize the use of AI systems, farmers and other agricultural personnel must receive specialized training due to their complexity. A complex strategy including infrastructure development, specialized education programs, and financial assistance systems is needed to overcome these obstacles. To give farmers the tools they need to embrace these technologies, governments, non-governmental organizations, and industry players must work together to offer subsidies, expand rural internet, and offer thorough training programs. In the future, developments in AI and other technologies will keep propelling agriculture's development. Accurate data analysis and reduced entry barriers will result from the creation of affordable, user-friendly tools and improved algorithms. Integrating cutting-edge technology like blockchain can improve supply chain transparency and increase the value of crops grown responsibly. AI will be able to contribute more significantly to the achievement of sustainable farming methods and global food security if present obstacles are overcome and innovation is encouraged.

The Synergy of AIoT

AIoT devices can interact directly or indirectly through M2M communication. When all the AIoT devices are connected to a single wireless coverage, then direct M2M communication takes place. Whereas when the device connections don't pertain to the same coverage range, then indirect M2M occurs. To forward messages, at least one router is needed. For instance, these devices pass messages to the server of IoT cloud, which forwards the messages to the devices connected to a single IoT platform. Owing to limited resources, at least three routers are required for AIoT devices to communicate with one another. To get to the IoT cloud server, AIoT devices first transmit messages to an edge router within wireless range. The edge router linked to the devices' destinations receives the messages from the IoT cloud server. Considering resource limitations, including energy, wireless bandwidth, and computer resources, this architecture enables the deployment of suitable wireless access mediums at the front-end layer.

The IoT platform consists of three layers: AIoT front-end devices, edge routers, and back-end cloud servers. AIoT devices amass real-world data, interact with their environment, and communicate with edge routers or the cloud. Edge routers manage, collect, and save AIoT sensory data, perform real-time data analytics, and communicate with AIoT local devices. The IoT cloud server performs long-term data analytics, storage, and decision-making.

To implement AIoT device safety and security, AIoT devices typically consist of four primary low-power components: - A processing unit and sensor interfaces based on a single-core or multicore MCU; Low-cost, low-power sensors, typically based on MEMS/NEMS sensors; a power management unit, which is necessary to extend the AIoT device's lifespan by reducing its power consumption; and wireless access media that can be either single or multiple wireless access mediums (Hou et al., 2023).

In addition to developments in the three essential elements, a variety of application fields have seen the proposal and development of domain-specific AIoT systems. In the healthcare industry, for instance, AIoT systems allow for remote patient monitoring, on-site disease detection, and assistive technology that benefits individuals with disabilities. AIoT systems make 3D tracking possible in the fields of augmented, virtual, and mixed reality to offer users engaging experiences. AIoT solutions have been created in the fields of video streaming and analytics to improve video quality and maximize processing efficiency. These created domain-specific technologies all show how AIoT has the potential to transform a variety of businesses (Siam, 2024).

IoT systems, where data analysis speed and accuracy are crucial, benefit greatly from AI's capacity to handle and analyze enormous volumes of data in real time. AIoT systems, for example, can track patients' vital signs in real time and provide predictive analytics that enable early intervention and individualized treatment programs in the healthcare industry. AI-enhanced IoT systems in manufacturing use predictive maintenance to optimize production operations, lowering downtime and increasing efficiency. AIoT is being utilized in smart cities to improve public safety, optimize energy use, and control traffic patterns, resulting in more sustainable and livable urban settings. Additionally, AIoT is transforming logistics in the transportation industry and opening the door for driverless cars, which have the potential to completely change how we carry people and things.

The following are some ways that AI improves IoT through data analysis, pattern recognition, and predictive analytics:

- Data Analysis: AI systems can instantly process and examine enormous volumes of data produced by IoT devices. Better comprehension of complicated systems and speedier decision-making are made possible by this. AI, for instance, may combine data from multiple sensors to find patterns or anomalies that would be challenging to find by hand. Optimizing irrigation schedules in agriculture may entail examining weather, temperature, and soil moisture data.
- Pattern Recognition: One branch of AI/ML excels at finding patterns in big datasets. AI models learn to identify particular behaviors or occurrences as a result of the constant data collection from IoT devices. For example, they can identify defective machinery in a factory or early indicators of crop disease in agriculture. AI can improve its capacity to identify these trends over time, increasing the precision and effectiveness of IoT systems.
- Predictive analytics: By utilizing historical and real-time data to estimate future trends or events, AI improves the IoT. AI can forecast events like equipment failures, maintenance requirements, or resource demand by utilizing ML algorithms. Predictive analytics, for example, may forecast traffic congestion patterns and recommend the best routes in smart cities. In the healthcare industry, it can use patient data to identify future health issues and enable early interventions.

Because AIoT systems are capable of continuous learning and adaptation, they can get better over time and react to conditions and surroundings that change. These capabilities operate as follows:

- Continuous Learning: AIoT systems are able to learn from newly generated data by utilizing ML techniques. AI models can be trained to adjust and improve their comprehension of the environment as IoT devices gather additional data. AIoT systems, for instance, are used in smart farming to continually monitor crop health and modify pest management, fertilization, and irrigation plans based on real-time data. As the system gains knowledge from fresh inputs, it gets better over time.
- Adjustment to Changing Circumstances: AIoT systems are made to adjust to changing surroundings. This flexibility is especially crucial in industries where conditions are often changing, like healthcare, transportation, and agriculture. For example, a healthcare system can modify its monitoring and warnings in reaction to patients' changing conditions, or an AIoT system in a smart city can modify traffic signal timings in response to fluctuating traffic numbers. Real-time data is continuously processed by AI algorithms, which then modify the system's behavior accordingly.
- Better Performance Over Time: Because AIoT systems are adaptive, they may learn from past actions and results to improve their performance over time. An AIoT system used in industrial predictive maintenance learns from past equipment performance data, increasing the accuracy of its failure predictions as it gathers more data over time. This continuous learning maximizes operating efficiency and minimizes downtime.

AIoT in Pest and Disease Management

As discussed in the Introduction section, pest attacks and plant diseases are common occurrences during crop cultivation. These incidents may or may not cause fatal damage depending upon the variety of the crop and the attacks. However, there is always a high chance of expecting an onslaught on the cultivated crops, which might lead to the destruction of those crops. In addition to the death of the crops, in more severe cases, the land may also be damaged. These situations lead to a chain of unfortunate events. The crops are damaged, the quantity and quality of production are affected, farmers lose a huge chunk of their investment and fail to reap any benefits, and the demand for the supply increases due to lesser output, which in turn affects the economy for the product. When the scale of disruption is large, the result might affect even the economy of the nation and struggle to attain the Sustainable Development Goals. In order to prevent any mishaps from happening, it is essential that proper diagnosis and damage control are performed. Early and accurate diagnosis of pests and diseases plays an important role in controlling the above-mentioned situations (Udutalapally et al., 2020). More detailed challenges experienced due to these issues are detailed in Figure 5.

Figure 5. Challenges faced due to disease and pest management.

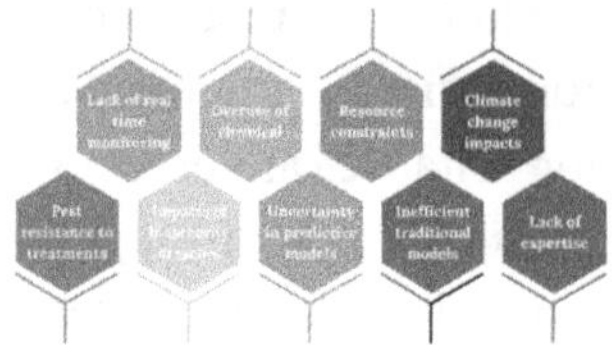

Currently, the amalgamation of AI and IoT offers favorable solutions for plant illness detection and reduction, pest attack cure, and prevention. Real-time photos of crops are captured by IoT-enabled field sensors or high-resolution cameras installed on drones. AI models that have been trained on large datasets examine these photos to find visual signs like leaf yellowing, wilting, or unusual patterns. AI ensures prompt interventions by detecting tiny indications of diseases that the human eye typically misses. Environmental elements that are critical to the spread of disease and pests, like temperature, humidity, and soil moisture, are continuously monitored by IoT sensors. By analyzing these data streams, AI models can detect outbreak-friendly situations and take preventative action. An abrupt increase in humidity, for example, could raise the possibility of fungal infections and necessitate a quick response. By pinpointing the precise location and extent of infestations, AIoT systems allow for precision pest management. Drones or automated sprayers with IoT devices apply pesticides to specific regions rather than applying them all at once. This keeps crops healthy while using fewer chemicals, saving money, and lessening the impact on the environment. Farmers are empowered with actionable insights thanks to the constant flow of data from AIoT systems. Visualizations of illness trends, pest hotspots, and treatment efficacy are available on user-friendly dashboards. Making well-informed judgments and increasing the quality and quantity of yields are made easier by these insights. Thus, it has been a focused research area in the past decade, and some of them are listed in Table 1. Out of all the research undertaken so far, some information can be summarized, and future directions are given below:

1. The usage of AI for image processing has become a trend, where CNNs were always known for their supremacy. But the introduction of transformers for computer vision has been a game changer. These transformers can be fully utilized in the AIoT scenario because it is well known that IoT devices generate an enormous amount of data when it is collected in real time. Transformers are famous for handling large datasets with ease and precision. So, the shift toward vision transformers and other transformer-based hybrid models is highly appreciated and welcomed.

2. On the other level, how images are collected will also experience a huge change. The usage of drones or cameras may not be feasible when they are applied to hectares of land. The cost and difficulty increase with the increase in area. Therefore, hyperspectral, multispectral, or RGB images from satellites serve as a better alternative compared to ground-based sensing.
3. Though there has been good acceptance and implementation of smart farming worldwide, it is not practiced widely. Only a few percent of farmers around the globe are aware of and practice them. Therefore, it is important that the new developments do not stay within theoretical research but are made into products that can be easily and efficiently used by locals and farmers for their benefit. These researches are undertaken for the benefit of laymen, but if it is not realized properly, its predominance in papers might gradually vanish.

Table 1. AIoT applications for pest and disease management.

Reference	**Description**	**Data type**	**Data source**
Jiang et al. (2019)	Rainbow, GoogleNet inception	images	common
Pallagani (2019); Udutalapally (2020)	CNN	images	common
Bhatia et al. (2021)	-	images	common
Li et al. (2022b)	InceptionV3, ViT, MobileNet	images	common
Chatterjee et al. (2021)	Fully-Connected Neural Network	disease symptoms, behavior changes	own
Chen et al. (2019)	CNN	rainfall, barometric pressure, temperature, humidity,	own
Antico et al. (2024)	FL, CNN,	images	common
Saberi Anari (2022)	Many SVM	images	common
Murugamani (2022)	SVM	images	own
Li et al. (2022a)	ViT	images	common
Liu et al. (2019)	CNN	images	common
Chen et al. (2020)	CNN, LSTM, YOLOv3	images	own
Guo et al. (2020)	RPN, Chan–Vese	images	common
Khan et al. (2022)	CNN, FL, ResNet50, ResNet-101,	images	common
Patel (2020)	KNN, SVM	soil types, pH, electric conductivity	own

Advancements and Challenges in AIoT for Agriculture

The integration of AI and IoT generates vast volumes of data, posing challenges in processing and analysis. IoT devices, often limited in computational power and memory, struggle to run complex AI algorithms, while transferring data to cloud services can lead to network overload, delays, and security risks (Tulkinbekov & Kim, 2022; Martsenyuk et al., 2021; Stanko et al., 2024). Edge computing offers a solution by processing data closer to the source, reducing latency and network loads, and enabling real-time decisions (Ezeugwa, 2024). Distributed processing systems like Hadoop and Spark facilitate efficient parallel data handling (Yang, 2024), while data optimization techniques, such as compression and filtering, minimize transmission loads (Bajic et al., 2023). To address energy constraints, specialized hardware like neuromorphic processors and the development of energy-efficient algorithms are crucial Samriya et al., 2023. Ensuring data security through encryption, anonymization, and compliance with regulations like GDPR also remains critical (Shen et al., 2021; Garg et al., 2019). Data latency presents another significant challenge, particularly in real-time AIoT applications like industrial control and medical systems. Limited bandwidth and reliance on cloud processing exacerbate delays, potentially impacting mission-critical operations (Devi et al., 2023; Shaik et al., 2024). Edge computing mitigates this issue by enabling localized data processing, reducing the need for data transmission to distant servers. High-speed networks, such as 5G, further reduce latency and enhance system performance (Spicher et al., 2021). Additionally, lightweight protocols like MQTT and CoAP are designed to improve data transmission efficiency in resource-constrained environments (Li & Ye, 2021), while resilient AI algorithms capable of handling outdated or missing data ensure robustness during delays (Shanthakumar et al., 2023).

Energy consumption is another major concern, as most IoT devices operate on limited power supplies. Adding AI functionality increases energy demands, creating a trade-off between performance and efficiency (Liu et al., 2022). Solutions include using specialized low-power hardware like neuromorphic processors and application-specific integrated circuits (Liu et al., 2023), lightweight AI models optimized with quantization and pruning techniques (Zhang et al., 2024), and edge computing to minimize energy-intensive cloud transmissions (Ren et al., 2023). System-level energy management strategies, such as dynamic CPU control and renewable energy integration, can further enhance device autonomy and sustainability (Rácz et al., 2022). Security and privacy issues also pose significant risks to AIoT systems, particularly regarding unauthorized access, data leakage, and malware attacks (More et al., 2023). Strong authentication mechanisms, including multi-factor authentication, cryptographic techniques, and secure key management, help prevent unauthorized access (Sharphathy et al., 2023). Ensuring the integrity of software updates and using AI to detect anomalies in network traffic can mitigate potential cyber threats (Ahmad et al., 2023). Privacy concerns, especially around sensitive user data, necessitate compliance with regulations like GDPR, implementation of transparent data policies, and the use of anonymization techniques to protect identities during analysis (Issaoui et al., 2023; Abd Razak et al., 2020). Regular audits and access controls are essential to address vulnerabilities and uphold data security (Davari & Bertino, 2019; Marques & Bernardino, 2020). Addressing these challenges with innovative hardware, software, and policy measures will ensure the efficient, secure, and sustainable deployment of AIoT systems across various domains.

The promise of AIoT lies in its immense potential to transform society and businesses positively. However, its adoption faces several challenges across various industries. A significant hurdle is the lack of experience and digital skills necessary for leveraging these technologies effectively, as many companies are new to connecting devices and systems through the internet (Ayaz, 2019). The rapid growth of internet-connected devices introduces complexities from a cyber-physical perspective, making the interrelation of connected systems challenging to manage (Nozari et al., 2022). Additionally, monetary constraints, such as the cost of purchasing tools and maintaining systems, coupled with limited knowledge and awareness, further hinder technology adoption. Trust in AIoT technology also plays a critical role in its adoption. A lack of confidence in the reliability and flexibility of AIoT systems can delay their implementation. For instance, farmers, often unfamiliar with technology, may rely entirely on experts to operate and interpret AIoT systems, which can complicate learning and adoption. The shortage of professionals with the necessary digital skills exacerbates this issue, making it difficult for industries to implement, operate, and maintain new systems. Privacy and security concerns pose another significant challenge, as AIoT systems collect and transmit vast amounts of data, increasing the risk of breaches and cyber-attacks. Organizations must address these risks by complying with applicable data preservation laws and regulations.

Proper infrastructure is essential for the successful deployment of AIoT, as inadequate systems can render companies reliant on outdated technologies. In agriculture, environmental uncertainties such as rainfall, humidity, sunlight, and temperature pose additional challenges for AIoT adoption. Robust AI models require large datasets, but agricultural data often depends on seasonal patterns, limiting real-time analysis. This constraint can affect the accuracy of AI models, with potential errors in predictions leading to significant costs, including the loss of crop production for an entire year, which impacts farmers and global food security. A strategic approach, such as using a small portion of farmland for AI-based data analysis before broader implementation, may help mitigate risks. Addressing these challenges requires a combination of technical, economic, and educational efforts to unlock the full potential of AIoT systems across diverse sectors.

The Future of AIoT in Agriculture

The future of AIoT in agriculture is poised to bring transformative changes, addressing critical challenges while unlocking new possibilities. With advancements in AI algorithms, IoT device capabilities, and communication networks, AIoT systems are expected to redefine agricultural practices, leading to improved productivity, sustainability, and resilience. One key aspect of the future is precision agriculture, where AIoT systems will enhance the monitoring and management of crops, soil, and weather conditions. Real-time data from sensors, drones, and satellite imagery will be combined with AI-driven analytics to make precise decisions on irrigation, fertilization, pest control, and harvesting. This will optimize resource usage, minimize waste, and increase yield while reducing environmental impact. Sustainable farming will also gain momentum with the integration of renewable energy sources and energy-efficient devices in AIoT systems. Solar-powered IoT sensors and edge computing devices will enable off-grid farming solutions, making advanced agricultural technology accessible even in remote areas. AIoT systems will support circular economy models by monitoring waste levels and promoting composting, recycling, and efficient resource management. Another promising trend is the rise of autonomous farming systems. AIoT-enabled robots, such as autonomous tractors and harvesters, will take over labor-intensive tasks, reducing dependency on manual labor and addressing workforce shortages. These robots will operate with greater precision and efficiency, guided by AI-powered control systems integrated with IoT devices.

The integration of blockchain with AIoT is expected to strengthen supply chain transparency and traceability. Farmers and consumers will benefit from real-time tracking of produce, ensuring quality, authenticity, and fair-trade practices. Blockchain will also help resolve data ownership and sharing issues, ensuring that farmers retain control over the information collected by IoT devices on their lands. AIoT systems are also likely to drive climate-resilient agriculture, helping farmers adapt to unpredictable weather patterns. AI-powered predictive analytics will provide early warnings for extreme weather events, disease outbreaks, or pest infestations, enabling proactive measures to protect crops and livestock. Lastly, the future of AIoT in agriculture will emphasize data democratization and user-friendly interfaces. Simplified tools and mobile applications will empower farmers, even those with limited technical knowledge, to benefit from advanced AIoT systems. Government policies, subsidies, and collaborations with the private sector will play a crucial role in scaling AIoT adoption and bridging the digital divide in agriculture.

CONCLUSION

This chapter has explored the transformative potential of AIoT in addressing critical challenges in agriculture, particularly in the context of pest and disease management. Beginning with an overview of global food security issues, it underscored the necessity for technological interventions to meet the growing food demand. The historical evolution of agriculture was discussed, highlighting how technological advancements have shaped modern practices, culminating in the emergence of 4.0 and Agriculture 4.0. AIoT was introduced as a convergence of IoT and AI, leveraging real-time data collection, intelligent analytics, and automated decision-making. Key applications in agriculture, such as precision farming, disease and pest detection, and resource optimization, were examined, showcasing their ability to enhance productivity, sustainability, and resilience. The integration of technologies like ML, sensors, drones, and blockchain further emphasized the depth of AIoT's impact. Challenges such as high implementation costs, data privacy concerns, and technical barriers were addressed alongside potential solutions, including edge computing, renewable energy integration, and policy interventions. The chapter also discussed future directions, emphasizing precision agriculture, autonomous systems, and data democratization as pivotal to achieving sustainable farming and global food security.

REFERENCES

Abbasi, R., Martinez, P., & Ahmad, R. (2022). The digitization of the agricultural industry–a systematic literature review on agriculture 4.0. *Smart Agricultural Technology*, *2*, 100042. DOI: 10.1016/j.atech.2022.100042

Abd Razak, S., Nazari, N. H. M., & Al-Dhaqm, A. (2020). Data anonymization using a pseudonym system to preserve data privacy. *IEEE Access : Practical Innovations, Open Solutions*, *8*, 43256–43264. DOI: 10.1109/ACCESS.2020.2977117

Aceto, G., Persico, V., & Pescapé, A. (2019). A survey on information and communication technologies for industry 4.0: State-of-the-art, taxonomies, perspectives, and challenges. *IEEE Communications Surveys and Tutorials*, *21*(4), 3467–3501. DOI: 10.1109/COMST.2019.2938259

Adli, H. K., Remli, M. A., Wan Salihin Wong, K. N. S., Ismail, N. A., González-Briones, A., Corchado, J. M., & Mohamad, M. S. (2023). Recent Advancements and Challenges of AIoT Application in Smart Agriculture: A Review. *Sensors (Basel)*, *23*(7), 3752. DOI: 10.3390/s23073752 PMID: 37050812

Ahmad, S., Arya, S. K., Gupta, S., Singh, P., & Dwivedi, S. K. (2023, May). Study of Cryptographic Techniques Adopted in Blockchain. In *2023 4th International Conference on Intelligent Engineering and Management (ICIEM)* (pp. 1-6). IEEE. DOI: 10.1109/ICIEM59379.2023.10166591

Alaba, F. A. (2024). Definition of IoT. In *Internet of Things: A Case Study in Africa* (pp. 19–40). Springer Nature Switzerland. DOI: 10.1007/978-3-031-67984-1_2

Allioui, H., & Mourdi, Y. (2023). Exploring the full potentials of IoT for better financial growth and stability: A comprehensive survey. *Sensors (Basel)*, *23*(19), 8015. DOI: 10.3390/s23198015 PMID: 37836845

Almada-Lobo, F. (2015). The Industry 4.0 revolution and the future of Manufacturing Execution Systems (MES). *Journal of innovation management, 3*(4), 16-21.

Anderson, M. M. (2024). AI as Philosophical Ideology: A Critical Look Back at John McCarthy's Program. *Philosophy & Technology*, *37*(2), 44. DOI: 10.1007/s13347-024-00731-1

Antico, T. M., Moreira, L. F. R., & Moreira, R. (2024). Evaluating the potential of federated learning for maize leaf disease prediction. *arXiv preprint arXiv:2412.07872*.

Araújo, S. O., Peres, R. S., Barata, J., Lidon, F., & Ramalho, J. C. (2021). Characterising the agriculture 4.0 landscape—Emerging trends, challenges and opportunities. *Agronomy (Basel), 11*(4), 667. DOI: 10.3390/agronomy11040667

Arena, F., Collotta, M., Pau, G., & Termine, F. (2022). An overview of augmented reality. *Computers, 11*(2), 28. DOI: 10.3390/computers11020028

Ayaz, M., Ammad-Uddin, M., Sharif, Z., Mansour, A., & Aggoune, E. H. M. (2019). Internet-of-Things (IoT)-based smart agriculture: Toward making the fields talk. *IEEE Access : Practical Innovations, Open Solutions, 7*, 129551–129583. DOI: 10.1109/ACCESS.2019.2932609

Bahrin, M. A. K., Othman, M. F., Azli, N. H. N., & Talib, M. F. (2016). Industry 4.0: A review on industrial automation and robotics. *Jurnal Teknologi, 78*, 6–13.

Bajic, B., Suzic, N., Moraca, S., Stefanović, M., Jovicic, M., & Rikalovic, A. (2023). Edge computing data optimization for smart quality management: Industry 5.0 perspective. *Sustainability (Basel), 15*(7), 6032. DOI: 10.3390/su15076032

Bhatia, G., Joshi, N., Iyengar, S., Rajpal, S., & Mahadevan, K. (2021). Crop Prediction Based on Environmental Conditions and Disease Prediction. In *Information and Communication Technology for Intelligent Systems:Proceedings of ICTIS 2020,* Volume 1 (pp. 335-344). Springer Singapore. DOI: 10.1007/978-981-15-7078-0_31

Blanco-Carmona, P., Baeza-Moreno, L., Hidalgo-Fort, E., Martín-Clemente, R., González-Carvajal, R., & Muñoz-Chavero, F. (2023). AIoT in Agriculture: Safeguarding Crops from Pest and Disease Threats. *Sensors (Basel), 23*(24), 9733. DOI: 10.3390/s23249733 PMID: 38139579

Bogue, R. (2013). Robotic vision boosts automotive industry quality and productivity. *The Industrial Robot, 40*(5), 415–419. DOI: 10.1108/IR-04-2013-342

Bzai, J., Alam, F., Dhafer, A., Bojović, M., Altowaijri, S. M., Niazi, I. K., & Mehmood, R. (2022). Machine learning-enabled internet of things (iot): Data, applications, and industry perspective. *Electronics (Basel), 11*(17), 2676. DOI: 10.3390/electronics11172676

Cannavacciuolo, L., Ferraro, G., Ponsiglione, C., Primario, S., & Quinto, I. (2023). Technological innovation-enabling industry 4.0 paradigm: A systematic literature review. *Technovation, 124*, 102733. DOI: 10.1016/j.technovation.2023.102733

Chatterjee, P. S., Ray, N. K., & Mohanty, S. P. (2021). LiveCare: An IoT-based healthcare framework for livestock in smart agriculture. *IEEE Transactions on Consumer Electronics, 67*(4), 257–265. DOI: 10.1109/TCE.2021.3128236

Chen, C. J., Huang, Y. Y., Li, Y. S., Chang, C. Y., & Huang, Y. M. (2020). An AIoT based smart agricultural system for pests detection. *IEEE Access : Practical Innovations, Open Solutions*, *8*, 180750–180761. DOI: 10.1109/ACCESS.2020.3024891

Chen, W. L., Lin, Y. B., Ng, F. L., Liu, C. Y., & Lin, Y. W. (2019). RiceTalk: Rice blast detection using Internet of Things and artificial intelligence technologies. *IEEE Internet of Things Journal*, *7*(2), 1001–1010. DOI: 10.1109/JIOT.2019.2947624

Culot, G., Nassimbeni, G., Orzes, G., & Sartor, M. (2020). Behind the definition of Industry 4.0: Analysis and open questions. *International Journal of Production Economics*, *226*, 107617. DOI: 10.1016/j.ijpe.2020.107617

Cyber-Physical Systems (CPS). (2024, June 3). NSF - National Science Foundation. https://www.nsf.gov/funding/pgm_summ.jsp?pims_id=503286

Davari, M., & Bertino, E. (2019, December). Access control model extensions to support data privacy protection based on GDPR. In *2019 IEEE International Conference on Big Data (Big Data)* (pp. 4017-4024). IEEE. DOI: 10.1109/BigData47090.2019.9006455

De Clercq, M., Vats, A., & Biel, A. (2018). Agriculture 4.0: The future of farming technology. *Proceedings of the world government summit,* Dubai, UAE, 11-13.

Devi, K. V. R., Koithyar, A., Lakhanpal, S., Parmar, A., Sethi, V. A., & Ftaiet, A. A. (2023, December). Edge Computing and 5G Integration for Real-time Analytics in Interoperable Smart Grids. In *2023 International Conference on Power Energy, Environment & Intelligent Control (PEEIC)* (pp. 419-424). IEEE. DOI: 10.1109/PEEIC59336.2023.10451199

Drath, R., & Horch, A. (2014). Industrie 4.0: Hit or hype? [industry forum]. *IEEE Industrial Electronics Magazine*, *8*(2), 56–58. DOI: 10.1109/MIE.2014.2312079

Eminify. (2023, April 12). An Introduction to Industry 4.0 | emnify Blog. *An Introduction to Industry 4.0.* https://www.emnify.com/blog/industry-4-0

Ezeugwa, F. A. (2024). Evaluating the integration of edge computing and serverless architectures for enhancing scalability and sustainability in Cloud-based Big Data Management. *Journal of Engineering Research and Reports*, *26*(7), 347–365. DOI: 10.9734/jerr/2024/v26i71214

Fraga-Lamas, P., Lopes, S. I., & Fernández-Caramés, T. M. (2021). Green IoT and edge AI as key technological enablers for a sustainable digital transition towards a smart circular economy: An industry 5.0 use case. *Sensors (Basel)*, *21*(17), 5745. DOI: 10.3390/s21175745 PMID: 34502637

Garg, S., Singh, A., Kaur, K., Aujla, G. S., Batra, S., Kumar, N., & Obaidat, M. S. (2019). Edge computing-based security framework for big data analytics in VANETs. *IEEE Network*, *33*(2), 72–81. DOI: 10.1109/MNET.2019.1800239

Ghosh, M., & Thirugnanam, A. (2021). Introduction to artificial intelligence. *Artificial Intelligence for Information Management: A Healthcare Perspective*, 23-44.

Groumpos, P. P. (2021). A critical historical and scientific overview of all industrial revolutions. *IFAC-PapersOnLine*, *54*(13), 464–471. DOI: 10.1016/j.ifacol.2021.10.492 PMID: 38620687

Guo, Y., Zhang, J., Yin, C., Hu, X., Zou, Y., Xue, Z., & Wang, W. (2020). Plant disease identification based on deep learning algorithm in smart farming. *Discrete Dynamics in Nature and Society*, *2020*(1), 2479172. DOI: 10.1155/2020/2479172

Haber, S., & Stornetta, W. S. (1991). *How to time-stamp a digital document*. Springer Berlin Heidelberg. DOI: 10.1007/3-540-38424-3_32

Hou, K. M., Diao, X., Shi, H., Ding, H., Zhou, H., & de Vaulx, C. (2023). Trends and challenges in AIoT/IIoT/IoT implementation. *Sensors (Basel)*, *23*(11), 5074. DOI: 10.3390/s23115074 PMID: 37299800

IBM. (2024, October 28). What is the IoT? *What is the IoT?*https://www.ibm.com/topics/internet-of-things#:~:text=The%20Internet%20of%20Things%20(IoT)%20refers%20to%20a%20network%20of,to%20collect%20and%20share%20data

IBM. (2024a, August 29). Industry 4.0. *What is Industry 4.0?*https://www.ibm.com/topics/industry-4-0

Ibrahim, A. M., Jose, R. R., Rabie, A. N., Gerstle, T. L., Lee, B. T., & Lin, S. J. (2015). Three-dimensional printing in developing countries. *Plastic and Reconstructive Surgery. Global Open*, *3*(7), e443. DOI: 10.1097/GOX.0000000000000298 PMID: 26301132

Industry 4.0: The Future of Manufacturing | SAP. (n.d.). SAP. https://www.sap.com/india/products/scm/industry-4-0/what-is-industry-4-0.html#:~:text=Industry%204.0%20definition&text=Industry%204.0%20allows%20for%20smart,manufacturing%20and%20supply%20chain%20operations

Issaoui, A., Örtensjö, J., & Islam, M. S. (2023). Exploring the General Data Protection Regulation (GDPR) compliance in cloud services: Insights from Swedish public organizations on privacy compliance. *Future Business Journal*, *9*(1), 107. DOI: 10.1186/s43093-023-00285-2

ISTAT. *Digitalizzazione e Tecnologia Nelle Imprese Italiane, Censimenti Permanenti Imprese*; Roma, Italy, 2020. Available online: https://www.istat.it/it/archivio/246548

Jadhav, A., & Jadhav, V. S. (2022). A review on 3D printing: An additive manufacturing technology. *Materials Today: Proceedings*, *62*, 2094–2099. DOI: 10.1016/j.matpr.2022.02.558

Jiang, P., Chen, Y., Liu, B., He, D., & Liang, C. (2019). Real-time detection of apple leaf diseases using deep learning approach based on improved convolutional neural networks. *IEEE Access : Practical Innovations, Open Solutions*, *7*, 59069–59080. DOI: 10.1109/ACCESS.2019.2914929

Karar, M. E., Alsunaydi, F., Albusaymi, S., & Alotaibi, S. (2021). A new mobile application of agricultural pests recognition using deep learning in cloud computing system. *Alexandria Engineering Journal*, *60*(5), 4423–4432. DOI: 10.1016/j.aej.2021.03.009

Kayikci, S., & Khoshgoftaar, T. M. (2024). Blockchain meets machine learning: A survey. *Journal of Big Data*, *11*(1), 9. DOI: 10.1186/s40537-023-00852-y

Khan, F. S., Khan, S., Mohd, M. N. H., Waseem, A., Khan, M. N. A., Ali, S., & Ahmed, R. (2022, October). Federated learning-based UAVs for the diagnosis of Plant Diseases. In *2022 International Conference on Engineering and Emerging Technologies (ICEET)* (pp. 1-6). IEEE. DOI: 10.1109/ICEET56468.2022.10007133

Khan, J. I., Khan, J., Ali, F., Ullah, F., Bacha, J., & Lee, S. (2022a). Artificial intelligence and internet of things (AI-IoT) technologies in response to COVID-19 pandemic: A systematic review. *IEEE Access : Practical Innovations, Open Solutions*, *10*, 62613–62660. DOI: 10.1109/ACCESS.2022.3181605

Kiran, D. R. (2019). Chapter 35-internet of things. *Production Planning and Control*, •••, 495–513.

Kudyba, S., & Kudyba, S. (2014). *Big data, mining, and analytics*. Auerbach Publications. DOI: 10.1201/b16666

Kulkarni, P. (2023, November 7). *Evolution of Internet of Things (IoT) - A Brief History*. Bytebeam. https://bytebeam.io/blog/a-brief-history-of-internet-of-things/

Li, H., Li, S., Yu, J., Han, Y., & Dong, A. (2022a, April). Plant disease and insect pest identification based on vision transformer. In *International conference on internet of things and machine learning (IoTML 2021)* (Vol. 12174, pp. 194-201). SPIE. DOI: 10.1117/12.2628467

Li, H., Li, S., Yu, J., Han, Y., & Dong, A. (2022b, January). AIoT platform design based on front and rear end separation architecture for smart agricultural. In *Proceedings of the 2022 4th Asia Pacific Information Technology Conference* (pp. 208-214). DOI: 10.1145/3512353.3512384

Li, X., & Ye, B. (2021). Latency-Aware Computation Offloading for 5G Networks in Edge Computing. *Security and Communication Networks, 2021*(1), 8800234. DOI: 10.1155/2021/8800234

Liu, C., Yang, Z., Zhang, X., Zhu, Z., Chu, H., Huan, Y., & Zou, Z. (2023). A Low-Power Hybrid-Precision Neuromorphic Processor With INT8 Inference and INT16 [-nm CMOS. *IEEE Transactions on Circuits and Systems I: Regular Papers.*]. *Online Learning : the Official Journal of the Online Learning Consortium*, •••, 40.

Liu, L., Wang, R., Xie, C., Yang, P., Wang, F., Sudirman, S., & Liu, W. (2019). PestNet: An end-to-end deep learning approach for large-scale multi-class pest detection and classification. *IEEE Access : Practical Innovations, Open Solutions*, *7*, 45301–45312. DOI: 10.1109/ACCESS.2019.2909522

Liu, Y., Chen, Y., Ye, W., & Gui, Y. (2022). FPGA-NHAP: A general FPGA-based neuromorphic hardware acceleration platform with high speed and low power. *IEEE Transactions on Circuits and Systems. I, Regular Papers*, *69*(6), 2553–2566. DOI: 10.1109/TCSI.2022.3160693

Liu, Y., Ma, X., Shu, L., Hancke, G. P., & Abu-Mahfouz, A. M. (2020). From industry 4.0 to agriculture 4.0: Current status, enabling technologies, and research challenges. *IEEE Transactions on Industrial Informatics*, *17*(6), 4322–4334. DOI: 10.1109/TII.2020.3003910

Ltd, H. T. C. (2022). *Artificial Intelligence Technology*. Springer Nature.

Marinescu, D. C. (2022). *Cloud computing: theory and practice*. Morgan Kaufmann.

Marques, J. F., & Bernardino, J. (2020). Analysis of Data Anonymization Techniques. In *KEOD* (pp. 235-241). DOI: 10.5220/0010142302350241

Martsenyuk, V. P., Klos-Witkowska, A., Sverstiuk, A., Bahrii-Zaiats, O., Bernas, M., & Witos, K. (2021). Intelligent Big Data System Based on Scientific Machine Learning of Cyber-physical Systems of Medical and Biological Processes. In *CMIS* (pp. 34-48). DOI: 10.32782/cmis/2864-4

Mohajan, H. (2021). Third industrial revolution brings global development.

Mok, W. K., Tan, Y. X., & Chen, W. N. (2020). Technology innovations for food security in Singapore: A case study of future food systems for an increasingly natural resource-scarce world. *Trends in Food Science & Technology*, *102*, 155–168. DOI: 10.1016/j.tifs.2020.06.013 PMID: 32834499

More, P., Sakhare, S., & Mahalle, P. (2023, December). Identity-Based Access Control in IoT: Enhancing Security through Mutual Cryptographic Authentication and Context Awareness. In *2023 3rd International Conference on Mobile Networks and Wireless Communications (ICMNWC)* (pp. 1-6). IEEE.

Murugamani, C., Shitharth, S., Hemalatha, S., Kshirsagar, P. R., Riyazuddin, K., Naveed, Q. N., Islam, S., Mazher Ali, S. P., & Batu, A. (2022). Machine Learning Technique for Precision Agriculture Applications in 5G-Based Internet of Things. *Wireless Communications and Mobile Computing*, *2022*(1), 6534238. DOI: 10.1155/2022/6534238

Nagaty, K. A. (2023). Iot commercial and industrial applications and AI-powered IoT. In *Frontiers of Quality Electronic Design (QED) AI, IoT and Hardware Security* (pp. 465–500). Springer International Publishing. DOI: 10.1007/978-3-031-16344-9_12

Nakamoto, S. (2008). *Bitcoin: A peer-to-peer electronic cash system.* Satoshi Nakamoto.

Ngo, T. D., Kashani, A., Imbalzano, G., Nguyen, K. T., & Hui, D. (2018). Additive manufacturing (3D printing): A review of materials, methods, applications and challenges. *Composites. Part B, Engineering*, *143*, 172–196. DOI: 10.1016/j.compositesb.2018.02.012

Nozari, H., Szmelter-Jarosz, A., & Ghahremani-Nahr, J. (2022). Analysis of the challenges of artificial intelligence of things (AIoT) for the smart supply chain (case study: FMCG industries). *Sensors (Basel)*, *22*(8), 2931. DOI: 10.3390/s22082931 PMID: 35458916

Osservatori.net. *Smart Agrifood: Condivisione e Informazione, Gli Ingredienti Per L'innovazione*; Politecnico di Milano: Milan, Italy, 2021; Available online: www .osservatori.net

Pallagani, V., Khandelwal, V., Chandra, B., Udutalapally, V., Das, D., & Mohanty, S. P. (2019, December). *DCrop: A deep-learning based framework for accurate prediction of diseases of crops in smart agriculture. In 2019 IEEE international symposium on smart electronic systems (iSES)(formerly inis).* IEEE.

Patel, K., & Patel, H. B. (2020). A state-of-the-art survey on recommendation system and prospective extensions. *Computers and Electronics in Agriculture, 178*, 105779. DOI: 10.1016/j.compag.2020.105779

Rácz, A., Veres, A., Hága, P., Borsos, T., & Kenesi, Z. (2022, December). A Full-Stack Neuromorphic Prototype Architecture for Low-Power Wireless Sensors. In *2022 IEEE Globecom Workshops (GC Wkshps)* (pp. 353-358). IEEE. DOI: 10.1109/GCWkshps56602.2022.10008616

Ren, J., Yu, Z., Xing, T., Cui, H., Chen, Y., & Guo, B. (2023, August). EnergySense: A Fine-Grained Energy Analysis Framework for DNN Processing with Low-Power Ubiquitous Sensors. In *2023 IEEE Smart World Congress (SWC)* (pp. 1-8). IEEE. DOI: 10.1109/SWC57546.2023.10449264

Saberi Anari, M. (2022). A Hybrid Model for Leaf Diseases Classification Based on the Modified Deep Transfer Learning and Ensemble Approach for Agricultural AIoT-Based Monitoring. *Computational Intelligence and Neuroscience, 2022*(1), 6504616. DOI: 10.1155/2022/6504616 PMID: 35422854

Samriya, J. K., Kumar, M., & Gill, S. S. (2023). Secured data offloading using reinforcement learning and Markov decision process in mobile edge computing. *International Journal of Network Management, 33*(5), e2243. DOI: 10.1002/nem.2243

Sarkozi, A. (2019). *New standards to curb the global spread of plant pests and diseases*. Food and Agriculture Organization of the United Nations.

Schranz, M., Di Caro, G. A., Schmickl, T., Elmenreich, W., Arvin, F., Şekercioğlu, A., & Sende, M. (2021). Swarm intelligence and cyber-physical systems: Concepts, challenges and future trends. *Swarm and Evolutionary Computation, 60*, 100762. DOI: 10.1016/j.swevo.2020.100762

Schwab, K. (2017). *The fourth industrial revolution*. Crown Currency.

Shaik, R., Raju, D., Behera, P. C., Changala, R., Mary, S. S. C., & Balakumar, A. (2024, March). Real-Time Anomaly Detection in 5G Networks Through Edge Computing. In *2024 Third International Conference on Intelligent Techniques in Control, Optimization and Signal Processing (INCOS)* (pp. 1-6). IEEE. DOI: 10.1109/INCOS59338.2024.10527501

Shanthakumar, C. S. T., Harish, N., & Giridharan, A. (2023, January). Internet of things and edge computing for real time applications. In *2023 International Conference on Intelligent and Innovative Technologies in Computing, Electrical and Electronics (IITCEE)* (pp. 1137-1141). IEEE.

Sharphathy, M. N., & Sumalatha, V. (2023, July). SSS-EC: Cryptographic based Single-Factor Authentication for Fingerprint Data with Machine Learning Technique. In *2023 2nd International Conference on Edge Computing and Applications (ICECAA)* (pp. 308-315). IEEE.

Shen, Z., Jin, J., Zhang, T., Tagami, A., Higashino, T., & Han, Q. L. (2021). Data-driven edge computing: A fabric for intelligent building energy management systems. *IEEE Industrial Electronics Magazine*, *16*(2), 44–52. DOI: 10.1109/MIE.2021.3120235

Siam, S. I., Ahn, H., Liu, L., Alam, S., Shen, H., Cao, Z., & Zhang, M. (2024). Artificial Intelligence of Things: A Survey. *ACM Transactions on Sensor Networks*.

Spicher, N., Klingenberg, A., Purrucker, V., & Deserno, T. M. (2021). Edge computing in 5G cellular networks for real-time analysis of electrocardiography recorded with wearable textile sensors. *arXiv preprint arXiv:2107.13767*. DOI: 10.1109/EMBC46164.2021.9630875

Stanko, A., Duda, O., Mykytyshyn, A., Totosko, O., & Koroliuk, R. (2024). *Artificial Intelligence of Things (AIoT)*. Integration Challenges and Security Issues.

Stankovic, M., Gupta, R., & Figueroa, J. E. Tambourine Innovation Ventures, Department of Trade, Investment and Innovation of UNIDO, Calzadilla-Sarmiento, B., Memedovic, O., Authried, O., & Rueth, T. (2021). INDUSTRY 4.0. In *Tambourine Innovation Ventures*. https://www.unido.org/sites/default/files/files/2020-06/UNIDO%20Background%20Paper%20on%20Industry%204.0_FINAL_TII.pdf

Tariq, M. U. (2025). Bridging Generations: Digital Transformation and Its Multifaceted Impact Across Societal Sectors. In Anshari, M., Almunawar, M., & Ordóñez de Pablos, P. (Eds.), *Impacts of Digital Technologies Across Generations* (pp. 1–22). IGI Global Scientific Publishing., DOI: 10.4018/979-8-3693-6366-9.ch001

Tariq, M. U. (2025). Integrating Digital Technologies to Optimize Sustainable Supply Chains. In Koç, E. (Ed.), *Developing Dynamic and Sustainable Supply Chains to Achieve Sustainable Development Goals* (pp. 33–64). IGI Global Scientific Publishing., DOI: 10.4018/979-8-3693-6284-6.ch002

Tariq, M. U. (2025). Navigating the Convergence of IoMT and Generative AI in Global Healthcare: Opportunities, Challenges, and Ethical Considerations. In Kumar, V., Katina, P., & Zhao, J. (Eds.), *Convergence of Internet of Medical Things (IoMT) and Generative AI* (pp. 513–534). IGI Global Scientific Publishing., DOI: 10.4018/979-8-3693-6180-1.ch022

Tariq, M. U. (2025). Gamification and Virtual Reality: Transforming Early Childhood Language Learning. In Manditereza, B. (Ed.), *Digital Pedagogy in Early Childhood Language Development* (pp. 25–52). IGI Global Scientific Publishing., DOI: 10.4018/979-8-3693-7437-5.ch002

Tariq, M. U. (2025). Leveraging Artificial Intelligence to Enhance Diversity and Drive Business Innovation. In Margaretha van der Poll, H., Andrew van der Poll, J., & Ngwakwe, C. (Eds.), *Diversity, AI, and Sustainability for Financial Growth* (pp. 79–96). IGI Global Scientific Publishing., DOI: 10.4018/979-8-3693-6011-8.ch004

Tariq, M. U. (2025). AI-Powered Breakthroughs: Revolutionizing Cognitive Psychology and Neuropsychology With Machine Learning. In Bansal, R., Maqableh, T., Shuklaa, G., Rabby, F., & Lathabhavan, R. (Eds.), *Transforming Neuropsychology and Cognitive Psychology With AI and Machine Learning* (pp. 65–92). IGI Global Scientific Publishing., DOI: 10.4018/979-8-3693-9341-3.ch003

Tian, Z., Wang, J. W., Li, J., & Han, B. (2021). Designing future crops: Challenges and strategies for sustainable agriculture. *The Plant Journal*, *105*(5), 1165–1178. DOI: 10.1111/tpj.15107 PMID: 33258137

Tulkinbekov, K., & Kim, D. H. (2022). Blockchain-enabled approach for big data processing in edge computing. *IEEE Internet of Things Journal*, *9*(19), 18473–18486. DOI: 10.1109/JIOT.2022.3160838

Tyagi, A. K., & Sreenath, N. (2021). Cyber Physical Systems: Analyses, challenges and possible solutions. *Internet of Things and Cyber-Physical Systems*, *1*, 22–33. DOI: 10.1016/j.iotcps.2021.12.002

Udutalapally, V., Mohanty, S. P., Pallagani, V., & Khandelwal, V. (2020). sCrop: A novel device for sustainable automatic disease prediction, crop selection, and irrigation in Internet-of-Agro-Things for smart agriculture. *IEEE Sensors Journal*, *21*(16), 17525–17538. DOI: 10.1109/JSEN.2020.3032438

Vaidya, S., Ambad, P., & Bhosle, S. (2018). Industry 4.0–a glimpse. *Procedia Manufacturing*, *20*, 233–238. DOI: 10.1016/j.promfg.2018.02.034

Verma, S., Kumar, P., & Singh, J. P. (2024). A unified lightweight CNN-based model for disease detection and identification in corn, rice, and wheat. *Journal of the Institution of Electronics and Telecommunication Engineers*, *70*(3), 2481–2492. DOI: 10.1080/03772063.2023.2181229

Wikipedia contributors. (2024, July 30). *Artificial intelligence of things*. Wikipedia. https://en.wikipedia.org/wiki/Artificial_intelligence_of_things

Wu, K., Xu, J., & Zheng, M. (2024). Industry 4.0: Review and proposal for implementing a smart factory. *International Journal of Advanced Manufacturing Technology*, *133*(3), 1331–1347. DOI: 10.1007/s00170-024-13839-7

Yang, L. (2024). Heterogeneous Internet of Things Big Data Analysis System Based on Mobile Edge Computing. *Journal of Information & Knowledge Management*, 2450047.

Zhang, Q., Cui, M., Liu, Y., Chen, W., & Yu, Z. (2024). Low-Power and Low-Cost AI Processor with Distributed-Aggregated Classification Architecture for Wearable Epilepsy Seizure Detection. *IEEE Transactions on Biomedical Circuits and Systems*. PMID: 39196752

Zheng, Z., Xie, S., Dai, H. N., Chen, X., & Wang, H. (2018). Blockchain challenges and opportunities: A survey. *International Journal of Web and Grid Services*, *14*(4), 352–375. DOI: 10.1504/IJWGS.2018.095647

KEY TERMS AND DEFINITION

Agriculture 4.0: The modern phase of agricultural transformation that leverages advanced technologies such as AI, IoT, robotics, and cloud computing to achieve precision, efficiency, and sustainability in farming.

Artificial Intelligence of Things (AIoT): The integration of artificial intelligence (AI) with the Internet of Things (IoT), enabling intelligent data analysis and automated decision-making from interconnected agricultural devices.

Precision Agriculture: A farming approach that uses data-driven technologies to monitor and optimize field-level management regarding crop health, resource use, and productivity.

Crop Disease and Pest Management: Techniques and strategies, increasingly driven by AIoT, to identify, monitor, and control diseases and pest infestations that threaten agricultural productivity.

Industry 4.0: The fourth industrial revolution characterized by the fusion of digital technologies—including AI, IoT, and automation—applied across various sectors, including agriculture, to enhance operational efficiency and innovation.

Chapter 13
Application of AIoT in Smart Retailing and Consumer Insights

Shikha Mittal
https://orcid.org/0000-0002-1092-1765
Raj Kumar Goel Institute of Technology, Ghaziabad, India

Manisha Singhal
Teerthanker Mahaveer Institute of Management and Technology, India

Mani Dublish
Ajay Kumar Garg Engineering College, Ghaziabad, India

Shaista Noor
Teesside University, UK

ABSTRACT

Rapid developments in technology are causing a revolution in retail. In order to remain competitive and enhance the shopping experience for customers, retailers are utilizing new technologies. These technical advancements are helping retailers to stay ahead of the competition, retailers are increasingly using Artificial Intelligence of Things (AIoT) to help them comprehend the millions of data points that are present in their stores and transform them into useful information that will enable them to align the business more quickly and effectively for the required changes. At a staggering CAGR of 21.8%, the smart retail market is expected to rise at a quick pace, from roughly $35.4 billion in 2023 to $140.6 billion by 2030. This chapter illustrates how retail establishments can benefit from a potent digital transformation experience through the combination of AI & IoT (AIoT). Additionally, this chapter

DOI: 10.4018/979-8-3693-8547-0.ch013

explores the advantages, difficulties, and prospects of AIoT in consumer insights and smart retailing, emphasizing its influence on the direction of the retail sector.

INTRODUCTION

Smart Retailing has gone through a paradigm shift with the emergence of big data, AI, and advanced technologies. Moreover, as digital technology is developing, the retail environment is evolving. To provide a seamless, integrated consumer experience, retailers are finding new dimensions in smart retail. Amazon Go, the first ever smart retail strategy to be used offline, was tested internally by the company in December 2016. Customers are no longer required to scan products in Amazon Go stores. Customers can just scan their smartphone as they enter the stores, select the things they want, and can depart from the store. Amazon tracks the items in virtual shopping carts, using machine vision, sensors, and big data analysis technologies to find out by default when an article is sold from or refilled back to the shelf. Based on these, a customer is automatically charged and given a receipt as they leave the store. Customers just need the Amazon Go app, an Amazon account, and a smartphone. This kind of decentralized use of advanced technology in retail is only one aspect of the whole retail environment, which is referred to as "Smart Retail". Smart retail has changed the whole customer experience, a fully advanced retail system integrating several smart retailers into an offline shopping environment. Previous research has shown that smart shopping increases business profitability and lowers operating costs (Dacko, 2017). Customers, however, are more concerned with the overall smooth service experience, integrating omni-channel in the retailing 4.0 era. Researchers and retailers are exploring whether an offline smart retail setup can be used to maximize the overall shopping experience of customers and whether integrating smart technology can be used to produce the "1 + 1 > 2" synergistic effect. Studying the factors driving consumer engagement in the context of smart retail is crucial because, in order to achieve seamless customer purchasing experience, engaging new customers has become a new opportunity for smart retailers. Retailing has developed into a dynamic industry in the era of the Internet and communication technologies. Customers' growing reliance on technology is one factor contributing to this (Zhitomirsky-Geffet & Blau, 2016). Organizations are becoming more conscious of the significance of IT adoption and how its use is a prerequisite for attaining greater IT productivity as they continue to raise their IT expenditure (Halilovic & Cicic, 2013). As predicted by (Browne et al., 2004), the way people shop has changed significantly over time, and the number of people who shop online has skyrocketed. Multiple touch points like smartphones, laptops, and tablets are used by society to share information, and retail uses a variety of cutting-edge (smart) technology to enhance the shopping experience for customers (Fotiadis & Stylos, 2017). Retail chains, for instance, have made significant investments in implementing self-service setups, including self-service cash desks, interactive and informative touch points with touch screens, digital signages, and mobile apps. These are enabled by Radio Frequency Identification (RFID) tags. Other merchants have created fully virtual stores where customers can find products and make purchases using their phones (Pantano & Timmermans, 2014).

Smart retail refers to an offline intelligent retail system that transforms physical establishments intelligently through connectivity and by becoming highly interactive. Marketing professionals use contactless, omnichannel, omnipresent technology and mobile applications to rebuild retail businesses. According to (Roy et al., 2018), front-end stores use the Internet of Things, intelligent technology-enabled shelves, and intelligent hardware (such as interactive fitting rooms) to reimagine the store experience and layout. The foundation for smart retail is technological integration, enabling systems using customer databases to facilitate omni-channel marketing, which can be achieved with back-end digitization. Intelligent technology (such as social fitting rooms, virtual shelves, interactive screens, and in-store mobile apps) is being used in retail establishments to improve customer experience and supplement interactive touchpoints between customers and retailers (Voropanova, 2015). Omni-touchpoint interaction makes it easier for customers to access goods and services and provides essential information. In order to integrate the digital and physical realms, smart retail uses intelligent technologies to enhance offline retail's perception, communication, and processing capacity (Pantano & Priporas, 2016). This gives consumers the apparent flexibility that traditional retail does not offer and enables real-time interactions between customers and retailers. Retailers can monitor, regulate, optimize, and offer autonomy with the use of smart retail. According to (Adapa et al., 2020), these competencies assist retailers in defining value propositions, creating consumer value, and improving the purchasing experience for customers.

BACKGROUND OF THE STUDY

The convergence of AI and IoT is a natural progression, as the capabilities of each technology complement and enhance the other. Companies can derive valuable insights from the enormous amount of data generated by such networked devices in real time by embedding AI algorithms in IoT devices. Predictive analytics, smarter decision-making, and personalized experiences are thus enabled. The foundations of AI and IoT, their respective contributions to retail, and the opportunities for collaboration that result from their convergence will all be addressed in this section.

The pros and cons of combining AI and IoT and their impact on society, companies, and technology will also be examined.

Smart Retailing

Smart retail is a technique that has revolutionized the retail industry significantly through the utilization of Artificial Intelligence of Things (AIoT) to facilitate simplification of the shopping process and improve the shopping experience. The primary goal of this revolution is to improve retailer efficiency while addressing the needs of modern consumers. Improved inventory management, consumer tracking, and targeted marketing result from the use by smart retail of AIoT to collect and analyze data in real time. For example, smart shelves can inform employees when items need to be replenished, and RFID tags can aid in monitoring stock levels. Customers can buy without having to queue using technologies such as self-service checkout kiosks and mobile-based barcode scanning. This reduces merchants' operating costs and enhances customer satisfaction. AI systems analyze consumer data based on consumers' preferences and buying habits to provide personalized recommendations and offers. By sending relevant offers directly to customers' phones, this personalization increases sales and fosters customer loyalty. Merchants can gain more insight into customer behavior, traffic patterns, and sales forecasts by using advanced analytics systems. Product placements, marketing strategies, and store displays are all enhanced by this data-driven strategy.

Artificial Intelligence of Things

The Internet of Things (IoT) and Artificial Intelligence (AI) are two of the most groundbreaking technologies of the 21st century, transforming whole industries and how we interact with the world around us. Artificial Intelligence of Things is a hybrid of artificial intelligence (AI) and the Internet of Things (IoT). AI links the devices with the internet for data collection and gives robots the capacity to learn, evaluate, and plan. A wide spectrum of industries, including manufacturing, healthcare, smart homes, and transportation, use AIoT. It enhances industry modernization, automation, personalization, and people's quality of life. Each technology has already achieved significant prominence on its own in several fields (Chen et al., 2022). However, additional creativity and efficiency in a range of applications could result from their consolidation. Artificial intelligence is essentially the capacity of robots to mimic human intelligence processes to assess data, make inferences, and take autonomous action. AI has impacted almost every facet of contemporary life, from natural language processing models that can comprehend and produce human language to machine learning algorithms that drive recommendation systems.

However, the Internet of Things is the term used for the network of interlinked devices using sensors, software, and other technologies to collect and exchange data. These gadgets can be anything from wearables and smartphones to industrial gear, home appliances, and even whole smart cities. By seamlessly merging the digital and physical worlds, IoT enables previously unimaginable levels of automation, efficiency, and ease (Tariq & Sergio, 2025).

Research Objectives

- To examine how smart retailers can benefit from AIoT.
- To know the value creation logic of AIoT applications in smart retail.

Research Methodology

A qualitative research approach was chosen to obtain consumer insight into AIoT applications in smart retailing. The author has investigated the tools that marketers use to boost efficiency, improve personalization, and enable data-driven decision-making, which ultimately improves marketing performance and return on investment. This study is descriptive, and examples are referenced from secondary sources found on different blogs and journals.

LITERATURE REVIEW

The technical roadmap for AIoT applications in the nascent retail sector is examined in this paper. The worldwide retail industry is quickly changing due to digital technology, automation, robots, and artificial intelligence of things (AIoT). Two fundamental technologies are AI and IoT, and a new third interactive use case that combines the two has surfaced. Organizations are utilizing this new technology these days. To identify people and objects without requiring a lot of sophisticated calculations or the installation of numerous sensors, they combine this new technology with an intelligent screening system. This technology manages the entire buying process and makes it easy to connect people, things, and consumption. Vending machines have also been on the market for a long time. Consider the F5 Future Store in China, which resembles a huge vending machine (Zhang et al., 2019). The main selling feature is that it sells fresh food products, and robotic arms are utilized to pick up stuff. Green Taste's "O2O Unmanned Convenience Store," which is situated in Taipei, Taiwan's Wanhua District, sells food and drinks through several vending machines and requires Easy Cards for customer identification. To put it briefly, AIoT technologies like vision sensors, deep learning, facial or biological identification, and RFID are the mainstays of unmanned convenience stores. Integrating and linking different intelligent devices and AI platforms to do data analysis and provide cloud solutions is the main opportunity. The industry is being severely disrupted by the growth of e-commerce and omni-channel retail, the gathering and analysis of vast amounts of data to create detailed consumer profiles, the escalation of labor due to automated management systems and surveillance, and numerous other applications. There are three stages of consumer shopping: pre-purchase, purchase, and post-purchase (Hoyer et al., 2020). The study developed enterprise reactions to various stages of customer purchasing behavior, using checkout behavior as the boundary of a shopping process.

Smart retail stores are physical, unsupervised enterprises that provide self-service and innovative shopping experiences via the use of smart technology. Retailer-facing and consumer-facing in-store smart technology are the two types found in smart retail establishments (Shankar et al., 2021). Examples of retailer-facing technologies are the systems utilized inside the store that customers cannot directly see or touch, including inventory management technology, customization and suggestion systems, the Internet of Things (IoT), and other advanced infrastructure for smart retail (Chen & Chang, 2023). Examples of consumer-facing technologies that are near customers and intended to promote customer interaction include digital screens, smart interactive devices, RFID tags, QR codes, smart shelves, smart mirrors, and self-checkouts (Grewal et al., 2020). Traditional offline and internet merchants are not the same as smart retail stores. Regarding physical retail, smart retail establishments differ from both conventionally attended retail establishments and digitally generated or transformed retail establishments. The primary difference is that (1) traditional attended retail establishments solely depend on the management and operation handled by in-store staff, starting from handling customer service to checkout. (2) Digitally transformed retail stores are simply an upgraded version of the former using e-service touch points (Barann et al., 2022) or implementing partial advance technology that reduce, rather than replacing, manual operation, such as self-service checkouts, mobile payments, and retail information systems (e.g., inventory management, retail enterprise resource planning). In other words, even with their digital transformations, retail establishments continue to offer their patrons a stifled shopping experience (Tariq, 2025).

Furthermore, vending machines and self-service business frameworks that do not include an in-store shopping experience that is engaging and uses a plethora of embedded smart technologies are not embraced in smart retail stores (Stoyanov, 2021). It seems that the "brick and mortar" aspect also sets smart retail establishments apart from internet merchants, who are unable to satisfy customers' desire for a tactile shopping experience. Academics expressed hope for smart retail powered by technology. Technology applications like self-service technologies, according to

(Huang & Rust, 2021), will replace an increasing number of mechanical operations that retail salespeople have long performed and transform conventional service interactions. Similarly, (Lee & Lee, 2020) named this no-staffed service approach—which involves little to no human interaction—the "untact" service, which can be described as "service provided to customer using advance technology without any face-to-face interaction between employees and customers." The COVID-19 changes have made technology-driven retail more crucial than ever (Niemeier et al., 2013). According to (Grewal & Roggeveen, 2020), smart retail stores are one of the futuristic retail modes. They offer lower social presence due to unmanned store environments that allow for pure self-service purchases and make the whole experience convenient using various smart technologies that assist consumer shopping journeys (Roy et al., 2020). Additionally, in order to support both utilitarian and hedonistic purchasing experiences, smart retail success also depends on consumers who are becoming more tech-savvy (Chang & Chen, 2021). With a focus on the distinctive value that technology creates, a wide use of smart technology in the retail sector has attracted various scholarly attention. For instance, RFID technology makes smart store environment creation by tracking the movement of products automatically (Hauser et al., 2021); IoT applications support experiential elements in the consumer journey (Roe et al., 2022); technology-enabled personalization helps customers make decisions in-store (Riegger et al., 2022); smart mirrors that use augmented reality (AR) enable customers to virtually try on three-dimensional clothing (Ogunjimi et al., 2021); and interactions with in-store technology enhance the effectiveness of consumer shopping (Roy et al., 2017). In terms of buying demands, smart technology also supports traditional values like fair prices and high quality (Lee et al., 2021). Smart retail establishments typically offer uniform products at lower prices than their conventional rivals because of the unstaffed business model's reduction of manual operation costs; the enhanced product value may also serve as their competitive edge. As a result, smart retail establishments enhance traditional value as seen in product cost-effectiveness in addition to offering customers the rare convenience and novelty of technology. The studies mentioned above, however, have only highlighted the special value that comes from adopting smart technology; they have not considered the strong traditional or common value of the product offerings that are common to those offered by traditional retail. As a result, the outlook on how smart technology empowers customers in smart retail stores is limited. All things considered, smart retail stores use smart technology to empower customers at every step of the purchasing process. Customers must register at the entrance stage by scanning QR codes to enter the store, and transaction convenience is crucial to this process. Since lower frontline staff costs lead to more competitive pricing, item quality and price are important factors in how consumers assess a product's worth throughout the product selection phase. Self-checkout is required to finish the transaction stage, and in this case, transaction convenience is crucial. Lastly, customers depart the business by going through a smart door that has anti-theft detection built into it. Additionally, smart technology is essential for helping customers along the entire buying process, and the interaction's usefulness and convenience of use are crucial. Consumers are required to perform every stage of the buying process individually; utilizing smart technologies to make purchases may necessitate a high degree of technological preparedness, and a lack of it may even prevent purchases (Park & Zhang, 2022).

AIOT TECHNOLOGIES IN SMART RETAILING

Smart retailing integrates several cutting-edge technologies to improve operational efficiency and the shopping experience. The development of smart commerce is being propelled by the incorporation of digital technologies, including AIoT, automated systems, advanced analytics, augmented reality, and improved security measures. In addition to increasing operational effectiveness, these technologies give customers more individualized and interesting purchasing experiences (Tariq, 2025).

Figure 1. AIoT technologies

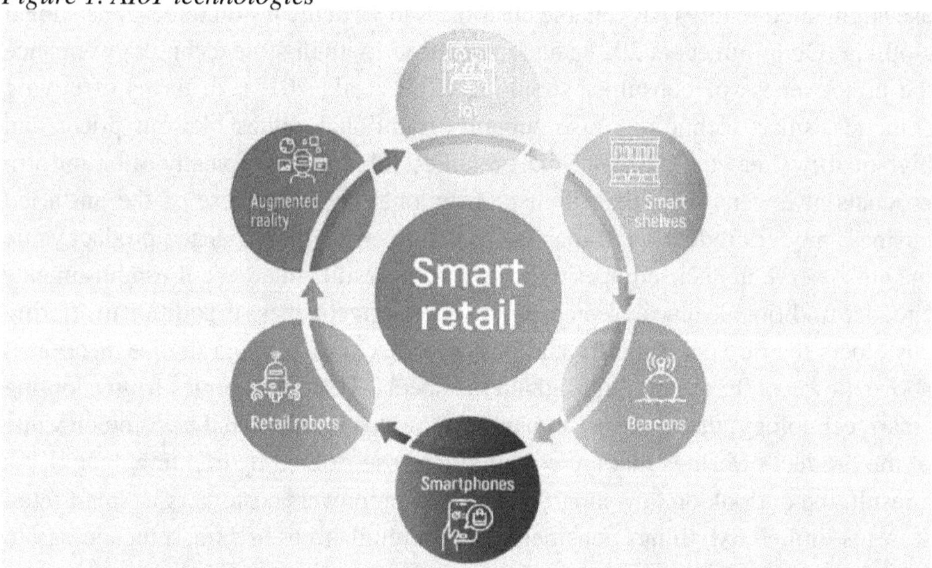

Source: https://inoxoft.com/blog/smart-retail-solutions-changing-shopping-experience/

The benefits of enhanced customer shopping experiences and the advantages of streamlining current retail company procedures are the main emphases of smart retail technologies. They are primarily divided into three categories.

Service-Oriented Smart Retailing Technologies

The service-oriented category technology that is primarily intended to enhance the in-store shopping experience for customers is included in the category of smart retailing technology. This category includes smart mirrors, smart dressing rooms, and mobile apps.

Mobile Apps

Mobile applications can be utilized both inside and outside of a store, but they must first be loaded on customers' mobile devices. Although there are many potential uses for these apps, their main goal is to gather information from users (Narang & Shankar, 2019). Some applications provide a cross-channel experience, while others just provide typical features like a store finder (Jeon et al., 2018), integrated loyalty cards, or access to exclusive deals (Inman & Nikolova, 2017). In these situations, shoppers can use a virtual store map to find their location within a store, scan products in-store to get more information, or check offers linked to the product (Adkar et al., 2018). However, individual store advertising is made possible by mobile apps, which open a new channel of engagement with consumers (Bues et al., 2017). Customers frequently consent to get personalized in-store notifications when they download the app, which is made possible by the app's data interchange with beacons. The significance of beacon technology in the retail industry is covered in detail by (Voelz et al., 2021). Beacons are tiny, affordable gadgets, while within range of the beacon, continuously send out small amounts of data via Bluetooth. If a related app is loaded and Bluetooth is enabled, the clients' mobile devices can then get this data (Zaim et al., 2019). An app may be prompted to send a personalized push notification to the user's device upon getting a signal from the beacon when a customer comes within range of that beacon placed near a product. The customer's purchasing experience can be enhanced by these communications, which may include helpful reminders, targeted advertising texts, or promotions (Inman & Nikolova, 2017). However, consumers are choosing to install fewer apps on their smartphones rather than more due to the plethora of accessible apps (Cordiglia & Van Belle, 2017). Customers would, therefore, prefer a single, comprehensive app, which is why shops must overcome the difficulty of gaining broad approval for their particular app. In addition to beacons, other SR technologies can facilitate further consumer engagements through mobile apps, such as Augmented Reality (AR) in conjunction with smart shelves

(Poushneh, 2018). Augmented reality (AR) is an interactive communication system that creates 3D virtual illustrations depicting pictures, an object, or information and projects it onto the user's reality. As they present the best chance for putting AR markers, they must be combined with other stationary technologies. Customers can use a related application to scan such a marker, which will display the shelf in front of them digitally on their mobile device. This allows for the highlighting of products or the acquisition of further product information (Rashid et al., 2015).

Smart Dressing Rooms

The purpose of smart dressing rooms is to provide clients with individualized shopping experiences by identifying and supplying information on the clothing articles brought into the dressing room and making recommendations based on the selected clothing products. Products are recognized using a technology known as radio-frequency identification (RFID), which allows data to be collected by contactless sensor reading. To accurately identify a particular product, these sensors are affixed to the corresponding items in the store and are read by an RFID reader at the changing area (Wong et al., 2012). According to (Mukherjee et al., 2018), recognized goods can be shown on an LCD touchscreen panel in the changing room together with product information, including color options, sizes offered, costs, and any associated discounts. Additionally, an intelligent product cross-selling system (IPCS) can be used to offer product recommendations on these screens. IPCS is a software program that allows customers to mix and match products in this case, apparel with other products.

Smart Mirrors

Smart mirrors are crucial instruments inside a smart dressing room. It can be placed independently on a store's sales floor or incorporated into the design of intelligent changing rooms. These are enabled to recognize a customer's face and body using technology during the trial process and then graphically imitate wearing a certain selected product, the mirrors are developed integrating hardware and software technologies (Poushneh, 2018). Once more, the objects the consumer is holding in front of the mirror are detected by RFID sensors.

Figure 2. The smart mirror

Source: https://www.reviewed.com/laundry/news/this-smart-mirror-aims-to-digitize-the-fitting-room

A 360° view on an integrated display uses AR and face and body recognition to replicate how the appearance would fit the customer without requiring them to change their attire (Roy et al., 2020). Additionally, an IPCS makes recommendations bas Ed on the customer selection, which customer holds facing the mirror, for goods that can be paired with the apparel items, just like smart dressing rooms do. Smart mirrors and smart dressing rooms are both customer-focused technologies that aim to create a distinctive and customized shopping experience, regardless of whether they are utilized in tandem or individually in real-world applications.

Business Process-Oriented Smart Retailing Technologies

Optimizing retail operations is the primary goal of smart retailing technologies, which fall under the business process-oriented group.

Smart Shelves

Retailers are able to leverage intelligent shelving solutions in a variety of ways. Using RFID sensors attached to a product or weighing sensors attached to a shelf where products are placed will primarily enhance the rapid communication and the anticipation of out-of-stock situations. Store employees no longer must physically inspect the inventory on the shelves because they are notified beforehand, which significantly reduces their effort. Additionally, by integrating the shelf data with the inventory management system of a retailer, out-of-stock situations can be virtually completely prevented. This can help prevent losses from out-of-stocks and consumer unhappiness (Inman & Nikolova, 2017). Additionally, digital price tags or so-called Electronic Shelf Labels (ELS) on the shelves allow for remote control of specific item pricing (Garaus et al., 2016). On the one hand, this reduces the amount of labor that employees would need to do to change pricing (for example, when promotions are included). Digital price tags can be used to ensure the dynamic pricing based on the customer willingness to pay more using demand and supply data, enabling a retailer to capitalize the higher revenue. For instance, the latter may increase the cost of its prepared meals during dinnertime, when patrons are pressed for time and are prepared to pay more for convenience. Smart shelves combined with ELS illustrate how adaptability can be used for saving money and generating higher revenue, making the operation of the retail convenient in very complex situations. However, if such pricing differentiations are viewed as unjust, the unique situation of temporal price modification through ELS runs the risk of losing the trust and approval of customers (Cordigli & Van Belle, 2017). The global smart shelves market is expected to develop significantly, reaching an estimated USD 7,268.82 million in 2023, according to the Global Smart Shelves Market Research Report (2021 to 2026). By 2030, it is anticipated to have grown at a compound annual growth rate (CAGR) of 26.61% to reach a staggering USD 38,123.51 million. One of the best examples of a shop that has successfully used smart shelves to monitor inventory levels and speed up the restocking process is Walmart. In 70 of its Canadian locations, the retailer tested an AI-based solution. To automatically scan the shelves at regular intervals, computer vision cameras were placed strategically in high-traffic areas. Due to the success of the pilot phase, the system was decided to be implemented in all the retailer's Canadian locations. One of the first uses of AIoT technology for tracking on-shelf availability in Canada's retail industry is this development.

BLE Beacons

Proximity marketing is made possible by Bluetooth Low Energy (BLE) beacons, which use a customer's location within the business to send customized offers and notifications to their smartphone. This promotes impulsive purchases and improves customer involvement (Lemon & Verhoef, 2016). For example, Reliance Retail has implemented BLE beacons in its stores to facilitate personalized marketing. By using the JioMart app, customers receive notifications about ongoing promotions and product information as they navigate through the store. This approach enhances customer engagement by delivering relevant content based on their location.

Hybrid Smart Retailing Technologies

According to their technological features in connection to mobility (Pantano & Viassone, 2014), smart retailing technologies are categorized and introduced to the concept of hybrids. According to their research, hybrid technologies belong to the retailer but can be utilized by the consumer while in the store.

Smart Shopping Carts

Among them, we categorize smart shopping carts that use real-time shopping feedback to communicate with customers directly (Roy et al., 2020). These shopping carts' primary feature is their capacity to track the overall cost of the purchase, which benefits both the buyer and the business (Sharmila et al., 2021). Products can be detected using RFID sensors as soon as they are added to or taken out of the shopping cart (Premananthan et al., 2020). The cart total is then instantly shown on an LCD screen that is connected to the cart.

Figure 3. Smart shopping cart

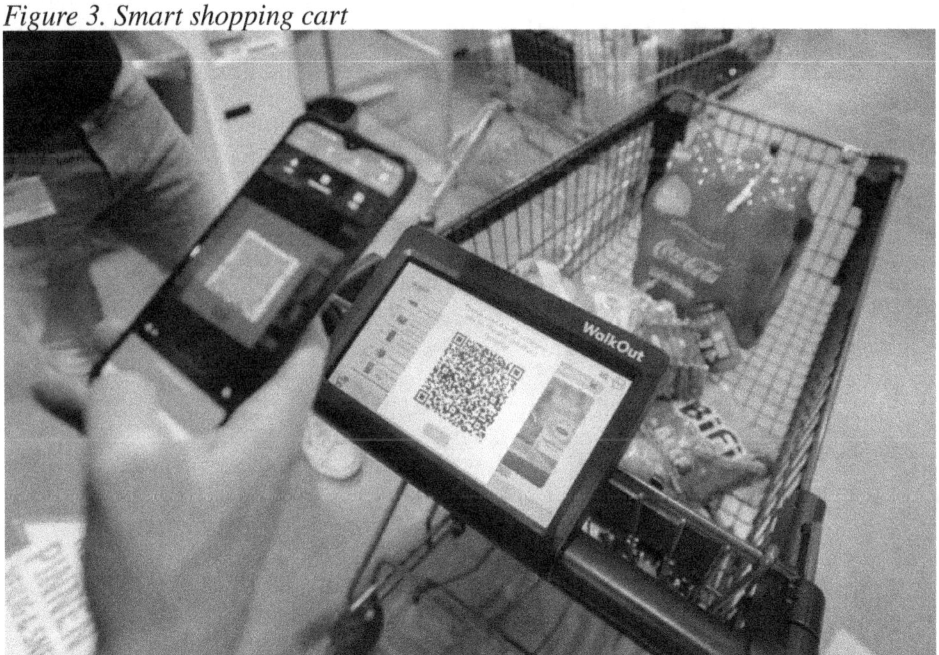

Source: https://www.retaildetail.eu/news/food/jumbo-tests-smart-shopping-cart/

When a customer eventually makes it to the checkout procedure, the billing information has already been sent there and linked to the appropriate shopping cart ID (Roy et al., 2020). Because they don't have to empty and reload their whole shopping basket for scanning at the checkout, customers save time and effort when making payments. Because there is less labor required for the checkout procedure, the retailer also needs fewer employees. In addition, technology can occasionally give consumers more details about goods or special offers, make tailored product recommendations, or help blind persons with voice control while they purchase (Sharmila et al., 2021).

Self-Checkout Stations and Go-Stores

Self-checkout stations eliminate the need for a cashier by enabling consumers to scan, bag, and pay for their goods at a terminal. Using the required information, a computer-assisted user interface walks clients through the checkout process step by step (Inman & Nikolova, 2017). An extension of these checkout terminals, known as "Go-Stores," can take many different forms. Customers can use an app to pay after scanning the items they wish to purchase with their smartphone. As an alternative, a combination of tech systems (such as computer vision and RFID sensors) detects when goods are taken off or put back on the shelf and maintains a virtual shopping cart with the items in it.

Figure 4. Self-service checkouts

Source: https://en.wikipedia.org/wiki/Self-checkout

The retailer's digital payment system then immediately charges the customer the purchase price (Grewal et al., 2017). BingoBox and Amazon Go are well-known examples of Go-Store technologies. As a result, the advantages of these technologies are quite comparable to those of smart shopping carts, offering customers greater convenience through shorter wait times and saving the retailer's staff savings.

Digital Signage

Digital signage technology is another example of a hybrid technology. According to Bauer et al. (2011), it is a private screen network made up of several LCD panels that show a variety of material, including ads and other pertinent information. Digital signage solutions give retailers centralized content administration for all of the network's screens, unlike offline signage (Bauer et al., 2018). As a result, retailers can show more and more precisely targeted ads in-store and rapidly and easily switch between different types of content (Garaus et al., 2021). This reduces expenses because the store employees have less labor to do while also creating new revenue streams because more advertising can be done. By providing engaging, educational, and amusing material, digital signage is largely utilized by stores to enhance the store's atmosphere and raise customer satisfaction. (Garaus & Wagner, 2019) Retailers were also able to demonstrate how digital signage at checkout areas improves customers' shopping experiences by lowering their perceived waiting times (Tariq, 2025).

Energy Management Systems

An EMS's capabilities are improved by the incorporation of AIoT devices, which offer extremely fine control over energy usage. Smart sensors can monitor temperature and air quality in real time, allowing for adjustments that optimize performance without sacrificing comfort. EMS helps retailers monitor, control, and optimize energy consumption across their facilities. Retailers can monitor, manage, and maximize energy use throughout their facilities with the use of EMS. This is especially important in an energy-hungry business where lighting, HVAC (heating, ventilation, and air conditioning), and refrigeration all carry high costs. By adjusting lighting and climate control in response to store population or time of day, IoT-capable devices can adjust energy consumption for maximum efficiency. This promotes sustainability as well as reduces operating costs. Energy monitoring sensors monitor real-time energy consumption patterns, allowing retailers to identify inefficiencies and rectify them.

FACTORS UNDERLYING THE SMART RETAIL GROWTH

The growth is driven by various interlinked factors, reflecting technological, consumer behavior, and economic changes.

Technological Innovations

AI and the internet of things (IoT) are used to enable personalized and efficient shopping experiences. AI allows retailers to process consumer data for personalized recommendations, while IoT allows for smart inventory management and operational efficiencies through networked devices. Augmented and virtual reality technologies are increasing customer interaction by enabling virtual try-ons and immersive shopping. For example, it is being used by retailers to enable customers to see products within their own space, which greatly improves decision-making and satisfaction. The contactless payment option has accelerated, thanks to consumer tastes in convenience and hygiene, especially after the COVID-19 pandemic. Services such as mobile wallets and self-checkouts are fast becoming the norm, pushing efficiency in payments.

Changing Consumer Preferences

Consumers are increasingly demanding more personalized shopping experiences that reflect their requirements. This demand is forcing retailers to adopt technologies that maximize customer engagement and satisfaction. Today's consumer values convenience, which has translated into the trend toward quicker shopping processes enabled by intelligent technologies. Retailers are implementing solutions that automate processes and minimize wait time. Conventional retail activities are redefining the dynamics of shopping for a unified omni-channel interface that provides flexible and accessible usage as per user demands.

ECONOMIC FACTORS

Smart retail technologies save operations costs through optimized inventory control and focused marketing tactics. Stock can be managed with maximum utilization for maximum profitability, minimizing waste and losses. Increasing disposable incomes and retail infrastructure investments are making it easier for smart retail solutions to gain traction, especially in emerging economies such as Asia-Pacific, where urbanization is happening at a fast pace.

AIoT Applications in Smart Retail

The fusion of Artificial Intelligence of Things (AIoT) with smart retailing is revolutionizing the sector by tapping into AI and IoT to optimize consumer insights and operational effectiveness. The combination provides real-time data capture and analysis, enabling retailers to maximize inventory, personalize customer experiences, and enhance in-store experiences. AIoT use cases like electronic shelf labels (ESLs), intelligent kiosks, and automated checkouts are changing retail by automating pricing, facilitating targeted promotions, and designing seamless shopping experiences.

- **Smart Video Technology:** AIoT enables the deployment of intelligent video systems that analyze in-store traffic patterns, manage queues, and enhance overall shopping experiences. They make use of high-definition cameras along with AI analytics to deliver actionable insights, enhancing customer care and business efficiency.
- **Remote Auditing and Inspections:** Physical store inspections can be done remotely by retailers using AIoT video technology, which streamlines processes and verifies compliance across multiple sites. It cuts costs drastically for physical audits while keeping the business under watch.
- **Inventory Management and Supply Chain Optimization:** AI algorithms examine IoT device data to predict demand, optimize supply chains, and manage inventory levels. This not only makes processes more efficient but also enables higher responsiveness to change in the marketplace, enabling retailers to hold optimum stock levels.
- **Enhanced Customer Personalization:** Intelligent retailers utilize AIoT to deliver automated checkout processes and tailored suggestions for personalized shopping experiences. Real-time data analysis powers such personalization, making the retailers smarter in understanding customers' behavior.
- **Parking Management Solutions:** Smart parking direction systems and automatic number plate recognition are two such AIoT applications that increase customer satisfaction through reduced waiting time and improved parking efficiency. The proper management of parking lot turnover rates is facilitated through these technologies.

ROLE OF AIOT IN IMPROVING CUSTOMER EXPERIENCE

Personalization of Shopping Experiences

AIoT allows retailers to provide highly personalized shopping experiences. Retailers can learn more about the preferences and habits of their customers through the use of data from IoT devices such as beacons, RFID tags, and smart shelves. This allows for product suggestions, promotions, and marketing strategies that are tailored to specific customers. For example, consumers can receive messages on their mobile phones offering them discounts on products they shop for regularly or are browsing.

Improved In-Store Navigation

It is easy for customers to get lost in big retail stores. AIoT technologies employ indoor positioning systems (IPS) and mobile applications to give customers real-time navigation guidance. Customers can be guided to a particular

1. product or department, making the shopping experience more enjoyable. Not only is it easier to find products, but it also stimulates store exploration.

Simplified Checkout Processes

Long checkout lines are a widespread annoyance for consumers. AIoT technologies like cashier-less shops, such as Amazon Go, enable customers to grab products off the shelves and leave without customary checkout processes. The system automatically monitors purchases with sensors and cameras, cutting wait times dramatically while improving convenience.

Smart Inventory Management

AIoT enhances inventory management via real-time stock level tracking and customer interaction with products. RFID-based smart shelves can alert employees when products have an expiration date or need replenishment. This enhances customer satisfaction and loyalty by ensuring bestsellers are always in stock.

Data-Driven Decision-Making for Improved Decisions

Retailers can make valuable observations regarding the preferences and conduct of their customers with the help of AIoT's analytics function. Retailers can enhance staffing levels, product displays, and store layouts based on actual traffic flows by accessing information collected from a number of IoT devices. Improved decision-making is facilitated through this data-driven approach, enhancing the shopping experience.

Enhanced Customer Interaction using Interactive Technologies

Interactive technologies like intelligent mirrors in dressing rooms can offer complementary items or sizes considering customer choices. Also, customized digital signage may provide meaningful offers based on customer demographics or purchase history, increasing interaction with shoppers and their experience in-store.

Effective Operations Processes

AIoT enables workers to spend more time with customers and less time on backend tasks through repetitive operations, such as inventory monitoring and price adjustment, that are automated. This efficiency of operations leads to a more interactive retail space wherein customer requirements may be attended to promptly.

Digital Transformation Examples in Smart Retail Stores

AIoT (Artificial Intelligence of Things) is revolutionizing retail experiences by leveraging innovative uses that improve customer interaction, optimize operations, and tailor marketing. A few actual smart retail store examples are presented below:

Amazon Go

Amazon Go transforms shopping with its "Just Walk Out" technology. Customers enter the store, pick products, and leave without undergoing a typical checkout process. IoT sensors, cameras, and artificial intelligence algorithms monitor purchases in real time and charge customers' accounts as they leave. This frictionless experience removes lengthy checkout queues and maximizes convenience for consumers.

Walmart Smart Inventory Management

Walmart uses AIoT to streamline inventory management in its vast store network. The company utilizes intelligent shelves that have RFID tags to monitor the level of goods in real-time and image recognition technology at cash counters to detect theft. This enhances the whole shopping experience as it allows Walmart to efficiently maintain restocking and ensure that highly demanded products are always in stock.

Lowe's LoweBot

Lowe's introduced LoweBot, an AI-based robot that helps shoppers find products within the store. The robot interacts with consumers, responding to inquiries and offering guidance, as well as keeping tabs on stock levels. This boosts customer service and helps ensure proper stock management.

Neiman Marcus's Snap. Find. Shop

Neiman Marcus has created an app named Snap. Find. Shop. This enables customers to snap pictures of products they spot somewhere else and discover similar products in their collection. This AI-based technology enriches the customer experience by making it easy to locate desired products without having to search much.

Interactive Fitting Rooms in American Eagle

American Eagle incorporates interactive fitting rooms that enable shoppers to scan items they want to try on. The system can alert staff in case more sizes are required and recommend complementary items depending on what the shopper is trying on. This is an individualized touch that makes the fitting room more enjoyable and motivates further purchases.

Beacon Technology for Targeted Offers

Bluetooth beacons are employed by retailers like Redbox to push targeted offers and messages to customers' phones when they are near specific products or kiosks. By giving customers relevant content based on their location and previous interactions, this technology drives sales through targeted promotions.

Smart Shelves

RFID-enabled smart shelves offer retailers real-time information on customer interactions and product availability. The data is critical for inventory management and enables retailers to optimize product placement based on customer behavior, thereby improving the shopping experience.

Taco Bell's Tacobot

Taco Bell has introduced Tacobot, an artificial intelligence-based ordering system that enables customers to order through messaging apps such as Slack. This new way of ordering makes the process simpler, faster, and efficient for consumers who wish to personalize their orders.

Benefits of AIoTin Smart Retail

Smart retailing has been influenced immensely by the proliferation of AIoT. Machine learning, computer vision, and natural language processing are some of the technologies that rely on AI to help merchants analyze vast amounts of data and get to know their customers' preferences and behavior better. Personalized shopping experiences, improved product recommendations, and optimized inventory management are all achieved with the data. Businesses' perceptions of consumer behavior, inventory management, and marketing plans are all changing due to the synergy of artificial intelligence (AI) and the internet of things (IoT), particularly within the realm of smart retail.

Improved Customer Insights

AI-based behavioral analysis goes deep into customer behavior patterns, preferences, and buying decisions, giving retailers a detailed understanding of their customers. Retailers can better tailor their products to meet the needs of each customer by understanding how they behave.

Tailored Shopping Experience

Behavior analysis can help retailers build tailored marketing messages and optimize store experiences. Leverage AI-powered analysis of customers' previous purchasing behavior and site visits to allow online and store-specific product recommendations. In-store digital signage could also display offer recommendations to individual shoppers based on shopping history or loyalty program member data, a highly personalized store visit.

Optimized Store Layout and Product Placement

Behavioral analysis gives insight into the way customers navigate a store and engage with products. This is crucial information for making informed decisions regarding store layout and product placement. Retailers can plan their stores to maximize the shopping experience, putting high-demand items in convenient locations or setting up items to promote additional purchases.

Enhanced Inventory Management

Predictive analytics, a primary component of behavioral analysis, enables retailers to anticipate future buying patterns based on previous customer actions. Retailers can streamline their inventory levels and ensure that they have the right products available when they require them due to this predictive ability. By limiting stock-out cases and reducing surplus inventory, retailers can save money and enhance customer satisfaction.

Increased Customer Sales and Loyalty

By marketing strategies, store layouts, and inventory management getting aligned with customer behavior insights, retailers experience a dramatic increase in sales and customer loyalty. The customers are happier and likely to come back when they are treated special and understood because of targeted promotions and personalized experiences.

Challenges of AIoT in Smart Retail

The convergence of Artificial Intelligence (AI) and the Internet of Things (IoT), referred to as AIoT, holds great promise for smart retail. Some of the challenges in implementing AIoT in smart retailing are as follows:

Cybersecurity Threats

With smart retail spaces becoming more and more dependent on connected devices, the potential for cyber attacks rises. Every IoT device is a possible avenue of entry for nefarious players, and thus, data breaches and operational failures occur. Retailers have to implement robust cybersecurity to protect confidential consumer data and maintain trust.

Data Management and Privacy Issues

AIoT systems collect huge amounts of data, for which effective data management mechanisms are needed. Processing and analyzing the data poses problems for retailers in compliance with privacy regulations. Fears regarding collection, storage, and usage of customer data may generate distrust from customers if they are not treated transparently.

Integration Complexity

Implementing AIoT technologies within current retail infrastructures can be complicated and expensive. Interoperability issues between various devices and systems frequently challenge retailers, making seamless operation difficult. Implementing common standards and protocols will help ensure diverse AIoT components function properly together.

Extremely High Costs of Implementation

Installation of AIoT systems might require a huge initial investment. For most retailers, particularly small ones, the cost of special technology, software, and educated employees might be prohibitive. To underwrite these costs, an effective business case that demonstrates a potential ROI is required.

Ethical Considerations

Ethical concerns regarding algorithmic bias and job displacement due to automation are raised by the application of AIoT. Making sure that AI systems work equally and in a transparent manner is essential to prevent detrimental effects on society. Retailers must overcome these ethical issues while taking advantage of AIoT technologies.

Scalability Challenges

With growing retail operations, it may become challenging to scale AIoT solutions. The systems need to be built in a way that accepts higher and higher levels of data volumes and device connections without compromising on performance or security. Approaches like distributed data storage and scalable processing frameworks are required to mitigate these scalability issues.

Shortage of Talented Manpower

There are few specialists in the sector who have the ability to implement and manage AIoT systems correctly. This human skills shortage might hinder the implementation of AIoT solutions in the retail sector since companies might not be able to obtain competent staff who know both AI and IoT systems.

Ethical Consideration in Adopting AIoT in Smart Retailing

Adoption of AIoT in smart retailing introduces various ethical considerations, which are mainly on privacy, data security, transparency, bias, and employment impact.

Privacy and Surveillance

The foremost ethical issue with AIoT in retailing is the possibility of intrusive surveillance. AIoT systems gather massive amounts of data through numerous touch points like sensors, cameras, and other IoT devices, in many cases containing personal details such as in-store activity, facial reactions, and buying habits (Shekhawat, 2022). This causes problems regarding consumer privacy since consumers may not always know the full amount of data they have recorded about them. Ethical AIoT implementation demands transparency, such that customers are informed about what data is being harvested and how it is being applied.

Data Security and Consumer Trust

In AIoT systems, extensive amounts of consumer data are stored, processed, and transmitted over networks. This data can be exposed to breaches, which is a major risk for consumer trust (Zhang & Tao, 2020). Retailers need to have robust cybersecurity practices and adhere to data protection best practices to protect against unauthorized access. They need to be compliant with the regulatory framework regarding data protection, e.g., GDPR in Europe, assuring ethical and legitimate data handling.

Transparency and Consent

Ethical embracing of AIoT necessitates transparency on how data will be utilized and obtaining explicit consumer consent. Shoppers must have the option of opting-in or opting-out of data collection and know how their data will drive their shopping behavior. Mistrust and destruction of the reputation of the retailer can result from a lack of transparency and consent.

Bias and Fairness of Algorithms

AI algorithms incorporated within AIoT systems are liable to present bias, causing some groups of consumers to receive discriminatory treatment. Personalization algorithms, for example, may promote preferred demographic sections to the disadvantage of others and give rise to biased shopping experience. Technology developers have to ensure that AI systems implemented, developed and tested on principles of fairness while considering inclusiveness to eliminate discriminations and biases.

Effect on Jobs

AIoT technologies can replace some jobs, like cashiers or stock handlers, with machines, which could result in job loss. Though this can enhance efficiency, it is an ethical concern regarding the future of retail jobs. Retailers embracing AIoT must think about how to assist workers who are impacted by automation, for example, through retraining initiatives or establishing new positions.

Environmental and Sustainability Issues

AIoT systems use large amounts of energy because of ongoing data collection, processing, and network usage, which can have environmental sustainability implications. Retailers must balance the advantages of AIoT with its environmental effects, possibly by restructuring energy use within stores or procuring energy-saving IoT devices to reduce carbon emissions.

Future of AIoT in Smart Retail

The prospects for AIoT in retail are bright, and there are several important developments expected. The world AIoT market is projected to expand from $1.26 trillion in 2023 to around $1.32 trillion during the next decade, driven by increasing adoption of IoT and connected devices in every segment, including retail. Retailers will be able to derive deeper insights from data gathered with IoT devices as AI algorithms become increasingly powerful. This will facilitate more strategic and informed decisions about inventory management, staffing, and marketing campaigns. AIoT can make retail more sustainable by optimizing the use of resources and minimizing waste through improved inventory management and energy-efficient operations. As connected devices become more prevalent comes the requirement for strong cybersecurity practices. AIoT can assist in identifying and preventing threats by monitoring patterns of data traffic across networks. Smart retail is revolutionizing the way consumers engage with products and services in brick-and-mortar stores. Through the integration of AIoT technologies, retailers can design a smooth shopping experience that not only satisfies consumer demands but also fuels business development. The continued innovation in AI, IoT, and data analytics will further influence this vibrant ecosystem, necessitating retailers to innovate and adjust continuously. Smart retailing has accelerated the demand for AIoT. Smart retail is a tool driven by enhanced technology that enables a store to create a more personalized experience for a customer. It also addresses some operational issues like designing the most appropriate manpower level usage to get the enhanced merchandising for mall crowd management and for supply chain management. It is not only appropriate for retail store operations but has enhanced safety and management of data. It helps in anticipating consumers' needs and likelihood of buying something. Smart retail can also be used to offer tailor-made solutions to the customer for a specific need. Retailers must strive for customer mind share by staying competitive in today's ever-changing and digital environment. Here, we also tried to reflect on the changes in the customer need and what impact this change will have on the smart retail environment. Thus, continuously enhancing customer experience using smart retailing is very important for meeting the customer expectation and giving exceeding experience for customer expectation.

CONCLUSION

The modern retail industry is propelled by new dimensions of digitization technology. The impact of further advancements in the retail-oriented technologies will only grow. Although smart retail is a cutting-edge retail model with an increasing share in overall retail sales, merchants have recently not been able to see its potential for growth. AIoT is becoming the technology of the future, with the integration of multiple touch points using advanced technology, smart sensors, strengthened connection, ease of interaction, and smart devices. The development of a multichannel strategy that uses multiple channels to communicate with customers is aided by artificial intelligence. New retail outlets are increasingly incorporating smart technologies and are using AIoT to make the consumer's purchase experience exceed the level of past experiences. AIot integrates various other smart technologies like robotics, augmented reality (AR) and virtual reality (VR), digital traceability, block data, Big data and drones, to capture the various input and integrating these with artificial intelligence (AI) and machine learning, the AI of Things is one of the technologies that will have the biggest impact on retailers' operations in the future. By using innovative technologies like IoT, AI, and ML, smart retail is changing the retail landscape and enhancing customer engagement while streamlining operations. This change improves customer satisfaction and streamlines corporate procedures to meet the demands of the digital age. This observation suggests that when merchants keep coming up with new ideas, integrating these technologies becomes essential to preserving their competitive edge and promoting expansion.

REFERENCES

Adapa, S., Fazal-e-Hasan, S. M., Makam, S. B., Azeem, M. M., & Mortimer, G. (2020). Examining the antecedents and consequences of perceived shopping value through smart retail technology. *Journal of Retailing and Consumer Services, 52*, 101901. DOI: 10.1016/j.jretconser.2019.101901

Adkar, N., Talele, A., Mundhe, C., & Gunjal, A. (2018, February). Bluetooth beacon applications in the retail market. In *2018 International Conference On Advances in Communication and Computing Technology (ICACCT)* (pp. 225-229). IEEE. DOI: 10.1109/ICACCT.2018.8529470

Barann, B., Betzing, J. H., Niemann, M., Hoffmeister, B., & Becker, J. (2022). Exploring customers' likeliness to use e-service touchpoints in brick and mortar retail. *Electronic Markets, 32*(2), 1–23. DOI: 10.1007/s12525-020-00445-0

Bauer, C., Dohmen, P., & Strauss, C. (2011, September). Interactive digital signage-an innovative service and its future strategies. In *2011 International Conference on Emerging Intelligent Data and Web Technologies* (pp. 137-142). IEEE. DOI: 10.1109/EIDWT.2011.29

Bauer, C., Garaus, M., Strauss, C., & Wagner, U. (2018). Research directions for digital signage systems in retail. *Procedia Computer Science, 141*, 503–506. DOI: 10.1016/j.procs.2018.10.135

Browne, G. J., Durrett, J. R., & Wetherbe, J. C. (2004). Consumer reactions toward clicks and bricks: Investigating buying behaviour online and at stores. *Behaviour & Information Technology, 23*(4), 237–245. DOI: 10.1080/01449290410001685411

Bues, M., Steiner, M., Stafflage, M., & Krafft, M. (2017). How mobile in-store advertising influences purchase intention: Value drivers and mediating effects from a consumer perspective. *Psychology and Marketing, 34*(2), 157–174. DOI: 10.1002/mar.20981

Chang, Y. W., & Chen, J. (2021). What motivates customers to shop in smart shops? The impacts of smart technology and technology readiness. *Journal of Retailing and Consumer Services, 58*, 102325. DOI: 10.1016/j.jretconser.2020.102325

Chen, J., & Chang, Y. W. (2023). How does smart technology empower consumers in smart retail stores? The perspective of technology readiness and situational factors. *Electronic Markets, 33*(1), 1. DOI: 10.1007/s12525-023-00635-6 PMID: 37035262

Chen, X., Su, X., Li, Z., Wu, J., Zheng, M., & Xu, A. (2022). The impact of omni-channel collaborative marketing on customer loyalty to fresh retailers: the mediating effect of the omni-channel shopping experience. *Operations Management Research : Advancing Practice Through Research, 15*(3), 983–997. DOI: 10.1007/s12063-022-00319-y

Cordiglia, M., & Van Belle, J. P. (2017, March). Consumer attitudes towards proximity sensors in the South African retail market. In *2017 Conference on Information Communication Technology and Society (ICTAS)* (pp. 1-6). IEEE. DOI: 10.1109/ICTAS.2017.7920651

Dacko, S. G. (2017). Enabling smart retail settings via mobile augmented reality shopping apps. *Technological Forecasting and Social Change, 124*, 243–256. DOI: 10.1016/j.techfore.2016.09.032

Fotiadis, A. K., & Stylos, N. (2017). The effects of online social networking on retail consumer dynamics in the attractions industry: The case of 'E-da'theme park, Taiwan. *Technological Forecasting and Social Change, 124*, 283–294. DOI: 10.1016/j.techfore.2016.06.033

Garaus, M., & Wagner, U. (2019). Let me entertain you–Increasing overall store satisfaction through digital signage in retail waiting areas. *Journal of Retailing and Consumer Services, 47*, 331–338. DOI: 10.1016/j.jretconser.2018.12.008

Garaus, M., Wagner, U., & Rainer, R. C. (2021). Emotional targeting using digital signage systems and facial recognition at the point-of-sale. *Journal of Business Research, 131*, 747–762. DOI: 10.1016/j.jbusres.2020.10.065

Garaus, M., Wolfsteiner, E., & Wagner, U. (2016). Shoppers' acceptance and perceptions of electronic shelf labels. *Journal of Business Research, 69*(9), 3687–3692. DOI: 10.1016/j.jbusres.2016.03.030

Grewal, D., Hulland, J., Kopalle, P. K., & Karahanna, E. (2020). The future of technology and marketing: A multidisciplinary perspective. *Journal of the Academy of Marketing Science, 48*(1), 1–8. DOI: 10.1007/s11747-019-00711-4

Grewal, D., & Roggeveen, A. L. (2020). Understanding retail experiences and customer journey management. *Journal of Retailing, 96*(1), 3–8. DOI: 10.1016/j.jretai.2020.02.002

Grewal, D., Roggeveen, A. L., & Nordfalt, J. (2017). The future of retailing. *Journal of Retailing, 93*(1), 1–6. DOI: 10.1016/j.jretai.2016.12.008

Halilovic, S., & Cicic, M. (2013). Antecedents of information systems user behaviour–extended expectation-confirmation model. *Behaviour & Information Technology, 32*(4), 359–370. DOI: 10.1080/0144929X.2011.554575

Hauser, M., Flath, C. M., & Thiesse, F. (2021). Catch me if you scan: Data-driven prescriptive modeling for smart store environments. *European Journal of Operational Research, 294*(3), 860–873. DOI: 10.1016/j.ejor.2020.12.047

Hoyer, W. D., Kroschke, M., Schmitt, B., Kraume, K., & Shankar, V. (2020). Transforming the customer experience through new technologies. *Journal of Interactive Marketing, 51*(1), 57–71. DOI: 10.1016/j.intmar.2020.04.001

Huang, M. H., & Rust, R. T. (2021). Engaged to a robot? The role of AI in service. *Journal of Service Research, 24*(1), 30–41. DOI: 10.1177/1094670520902266

Inman, J. J., & Nikolova, H. (2017). Shopper-facing retail technology: A retailer adoption decision framework incorporating shopper attitudes and privacy concerns. *Journal of Retailing, 93*(1), 7–28. DOI: 10.1016/j.jretai.2016.12.006

Jeon, K. E., She, J., Soonsawad, P., & Ng, P. C. (2018). Ble beacons for internet of things applications: Survey, challenges, and opportunities. *IEEE Internet of Things Journal, 5*(2), 811–828. DOI: 10.1109/JIOT.2017.2788449

Lee, J., Lee, Y., & Kim, S. (2021). The effects of consumers' in-store technology experience on perceived interactivity, retail Brand commitment, and revisit intention in a Korean beauty store. *International Journal of Human-Computer Interaction, 37*(6), 534–546. DOI: 10.1080/10447318.2020.1834730

Lee, S. M., & Lee, D. (2020). "Untact": A new customer service strategy in the digital age. *Service Business, 14*(1), 1–22. DOI: 10.1007/s11628-019-00408-2

Lemon, K. N., & Verhoef, P. C. (2016). Understanding customer experience throughout the customer journey. *Journal of Marketing, 80*(6), 69–96. DOI: 10.1509/jm.15.0420

Mukherjee, A., Smith, R. J., & Turri, A. M. (2018). The smartness paradox: The moderating effect of brand quality reputation on consumers' reactions to RFID-based smart fitting rooms. *Journal of Business Research, 92*, 290–299. DOI: 10.1016/j.jbusres.2018.07.057

Narang, U., & Shankar, V. (2019). Mobile app introduction and online and offline purchases and product returns. *Marketing Science, 38*(5), 756–772. DOI: 10.1287/mksc.2019.1169

Niemeier, S., Zocchi, A., & Catena, M. (2013). *Reshaping retail: Why technology is transforming the industry and how to win in the new consumer driven world.* John Wiley & Sons.

Ogunjimi, A., Rahman, M., Islam, N., & Hasan, R. (2021). Smart mirror fashion technology for the retail chain transformation. *Technological Forecasting and Social Change, 173*, 121118. DOI: 10.1016/j.techfore.2021.121118

Pantano, E., & Priporas, C. V. (2016). The effect of mobile retailing on consumers' purchasing experiences: A dynamic perspective. *Computers in Human Behavior, 61*, 548–555. DOI: 10.1016/j.chb.2016.03.071

Pantano, E., & Timmermans, H. (2014). What is smart for retailing? *Procedia Environmental Sciences, 22*, 101–107. DOI: 10.1016/j.proenv.2014.11.010

Pantano, E., & Viassone, M. (2014). Demand pull and technology push perspective in technology-based innovations for the points of sale: The retailers evaluation. *Journal of Retailing and Consumer Services, 21*(1), 43–47. DOI: 10.1016/j.jretconser.2013.06.007

Park, H. J., & Zhang, Y. (2022). Technology readiness and technology paradox of unmanned convenience store users. *Journal of Retailing and Consumer Services, 65*, 102523. DOI: 10.1016/j.jretconser.2021.102523

Poushneh, A. (2018). Augmented reality in retail: A trade-off between user's control of access to personal information and augmentation quality. *Journal of Retailing and Consumer Services, 41*, 169–176. DOI: 10.1016/j.jretconser.2017.12.010

Premananthan, G., Nagaraj, B., & Divya, N. (2020). WITHDRAWN: Sensor based integrated smart trolley system using Zigbee-experimental analysis.

Rashid, Z., Peig, E., & Pous, R. (2015, October). Bringing online shopping experience to offline retail through augmented reality and RFID. In *2015 5th International Conference on the Internet of Things (IOT)* (pp. 45-51). IEEE. DOI: 10.1109/IOT.2015.7356547

Riegger, A. S., Merfeld, K., Klein, J. F., & Henkel, S. (2022). Technology-enabled personalization: Impact of smart technology choice on consumer shopping behavior. *Technological Forecasting and Social Change, 181*, 121752. DOI: 10.1016/j.techfore.2022.121752

Roe, M., Spanaki, K., Ioannou, A., Zamani, E. D., & Giannakis, M. (2022). Drivers and challenges of internet of things diffusion in smart stores: A field exploration. *Technological Forecasting and Social Change, 178*, 121593. DOI: 10.1016/j.techfore.2022.121593

Roy, S. K., Balaji, M. S., & Nguyen, B. (2020). Consumer-computer interaction and in-store smart technology (IST) in the retail industry: The role of motivation, opportunity, and ability. *Journal of Marketing Management*, *36*(3-4), 299–333. DOI: 10.1080/0267257X.2020.1736130

Roy, S. K., Balaji, M. S., Sadeque, S., Nguyen, B., & Melewar, T. C. (2017). Constituents and consequences of smart customer experience in retailing. *Technological Forecasting and Social Change*, *124*, 257–270. DOI: 10.1016/j.techfore.2016.09.022

Roy, S. K., Shekhar, V., Lassar, W. M., & Chen, T. (2018). Customer engagement behaviors: The role of service convenience, fairness and quality. *Journal of Retailing and Consumer Services*, *44*, 293–304. DOI: 10.1016/j.jretconser.2018.07.018

Shankar, V., Kalyanam, K., Setia, P., Golmohammadi, A., Tirunillai, S., Douglass, T., Hennessey, J., Bull, J. S., & Waddoups, R. (2021). How technology is changing retail. *Journal of Retailing*, *97*(1), 13–27. DOI: 10.1016/j.jretai.2020.10.006

Sharmila, G., Ragaventhiran, J., Islabudeen, M., & Kumar, B. M. (2021). WITHDRAWN: RFID Based Smart-Cart system with automated billing and assistance for visually impaired.

Shekhawat, S. (2022, December). Use of AI and IoT to make Retail Smarter. In *2022 3rd International Informatics and Software Engineering Conference (IISEC)* (pp. 1-5). IEEE. DOI: 10.1109/IISEC56263.2022.9998202

Stoyanov, D. (2021). The role of vending channels in marketing: A systematic review and taxonomy of studies. *The Journal of Consumer Affairs*, *55*(2), 654–679. DOI: 10.1111/joca.12362

Tariq, M. U. (2025). Unlocking Competitive Edge: Harnessing the Power of Collaborative Innovation. In Martínez-Falcó, J., Sánchez-García, E., & Marco-Lajara, B. (Eds.), *Open Innovation Strategies for Effective Competitive Advantage* (pp. 315–344). IGI Global Scientific Publishing., DOI: 10.4018/979-8-3693-9266-9.ch011

Tariq, M. U. (2025). Revolutionizing Retail: Enhancing Customer Experiences With the Metaverse. In Gonçalves Rodrigues, M., Carvalho, M., & Monteiro Pratas, J. (Eds.), *Cases on Metaverse and Consumer Experiences* (pp. 175–202). IGI Global Scientific Publishing., DOI: 10.4018/979-8-3693-7245-6.ch007

Tariq, M. U. (2025). *AI-Driven Learning and Engagement in Higher Education*. IGI Global., DOI: 10.4018/979-8-3693-4074-5

Tariq, M. U., & Sergio, R. (Eds.). (2025). *Cases on AI-Driven Solutions to Environmental Challenges*. IGI Global, 2025. https://doi.org/DOI: 10.4018/979-8-3693-7483-2

Tariq, M. U., & Sergio, R. (Eds.). (2025). *Convergence of AI, Education, and Business for Sustainability*. IGI Global., DOI: 10.4018/979-8-3373-1917-9

Voelz, A., Mladenow, A., & Strauss, C. (2021). Beacon technology for retailers-tracking consumer behavior inside brick-and-mortar-stores. In *Database and Expert Systems Applications: 32nd International Conference, DEXA 2021, Virtual Event, September 27–30, 2021* [Springer International Publishing.]. *Proceedings*, *32*(Part I), 380–390.

Voropanova, E. (2015). Conceptualizing smart shopping with a smartphone: Implications of the use of mobile devices for shopping productivity and value. *International Review of Retail, Distribution and Consumer Research*, *25*(5), 529–550. DOI: 10.1080/09593969.2015.1089304

Wong, W. K., Leung, S. Y. S., Guo, Z. X., Zeng, X. H., & Mok, P. Y. (2012). Intelligent product cross-selling system with radio frequency identification technology for retailing. *International Journal of Production Economics*, *135*(1), 308–319. DOI: 10.1016/j.ijpe.2011.08.005

Zaim, D., Benomar, A., & Bellafkih, M. (2019). Developing a geomarketing solution. *Procedia Computer Science*, *148*, 353–360. DOI: 10.1016/j.procs.2019.01.043

Zhang, H., Li, D., Ji, Y., Zhou, H., Wu, W., & Liu, K. (2019). Toward new retail: A benchmark dataset for smart unmanned vending machines. *IEEE Transactions on Industrial Informatics*, *16*(12), 7722–7731. DOI: 10.1109/TII.2019.2954956

Zhang, J., & Tao, D. (2020). Empowering things with intelligence: A survey of the progress, challenges, and opportunities in artificial intelligence of things. *IEEE Internet of Things Journal*, *8*(10), 7789–7817. DOI: 10.1109/JIOT.2020.3039359

Zhitomirsky-Geffet, M., & Blau, M. (2016). Cross-generational analysis of predictive factors of addictive behavior in smartphone usage. *Computers in Human Behavior*, *64*, 682–693. DOI: 10.1016/j.chb.2016.07.061

ADDITIONAL READING

Chang, Y. W., Hsu, P. Y., Chen, J., Shiau, W. L., & Xu, N. (2023). Utilitarian and/or hedonic shopping–consumer motivation to purchase in smart stores. *Industrial Management & Data Systems*, *123*(3), 821–842. DOI: 10.1108/IMDS-04-2022-0250

Grewal, D., Gauri, D. K., Roggeveen, A. L., & Sethuraman, R. (2021). Strategizing retailing in the new technology era. *Journal of Retailing*, *97*(1), 6–12. DOI: 10.1016/j.jretai.2021.02.004

Li, L. H., Cheung, K. S., & Tse, W. S. (2023). Understanding the shoppers' perception in retail shopping malls: A self-determination theory perspective. *Journal of Strategic Marketing*, *31*(1), 58–73. DOI: 10.1080/0965254X.2020.1870046

Lin, S. W., Huang, E. Y., & Cheng, K. T. (2023). A binding tie: Why do customers stick to omnichannel retailers? *Information Technology & People*, *36*(3), 1126–1159. DOI: 10.1108/ITP-01-2021-0063

Noble, S. M., Mende, M., Grewal, D., & Parasuraman, A. (2022). The Fifth Industrial Revolution: How harmonious human–machine collaboration is triggering a retail and service [r] evolution. *Journal of Retailing*, *98*(2), 199–208. DOI: 10.1016/j.jretai.2022.04.003

KEY TERMS AND DEFINITION

Omni-Channel Marketing: It refers to a customer-focused strategy that unifies all platforms to provide a cohesive and uniform brand experience across websites, applications, and physical stores.

Smart Retail: Smart retail is the next evolution of retail, when traditional shopping techniques give way to an environment where AIoT technology assist consumers in making purchases.

Retail 4.0: Digitalizing the physical shopping experience by combining new retail and data collection technology is known as retail 4.0.

RFID (Radio-Frequency Identification): RFID is a system that uses radio chips to tag products in order to track inventories and prevent theft.

Beacon Technology: Small devices that send signals to cellphones in close proximity in order to deliver tailored messages, promotions, or location-based services.

Big Data Analytics: This is a process of extracting valuable insights that includes market trends, customer preferences, hidden patterns, and unidentified relationships.

360 Degree Customer View: The idea of combining data from several client touchpoints and systems in one location is known as a 360-degree view.

Advanced Analytics: Using complex techniques like ML and Predictive modeling for analysing the data to find new trends, forecasting future trends, making market intelegance report and using data for making decision.

ENDNOTES

1. https://www.fortunebusinessinsights.com/artificial-intelligence-of-things-market-107836

2. https://www.iotm2mcouncil.org/iot-library/news/smart-retail-news/white-paper-shows-how-aiot-can-help-retailers/

3. https://www.indianretailer.com/article/technology/digital-trends/how-amazon-is-amping-up-the-future-of-retail-through-just-walk-out-stores.

4. https://www.india.gov.in/topics/industries/retail

Chapter 14
The Evolution of Civil Engineering Field With the Emergence and Incorporation of Artificial Intelligence and Internet of Things

Aditya Singh
https://orcid.org/0000-0001-9347-5627
Amrita Vishwa Vidyapeetham, India

ABSTRACT

Civil Engineering is the oldest branch of engineering which was essential in the development of any civilization in the human history and eventually led to the development of other branches of engineering with the progress of any civilization in the pages of history. The same goes for the current times, but technological developments and implementation are usually seen at a slower rate in this branch of engineering compared to current existing branches of engineering. Over the recent decade, AI & IoT have developed at a very fast pace. Their applications and effect could be noticed in the field of civil engineering as well, which will be covered in this chapter. Then, some important new developments in this area because of AI and IoT will be discussed in order to understand the evolution and future developments of the mentioned field. Then, graphical analyses based on the available data will be performed to support the study and in understanding the future prospects.

DOI: 10.4018/979-8-3693-8547-0.ch014

INTRODUCTION

These days, two advanced technologies have been combined to form AIoT, known as Artificial Internet of Things, but it is necessary to first understand the root technologies of AI as well as IoT before moving to AIoT. From the study of Singh (2023), it could be understood that AI is an area that has branched out from the computer science field, which is about systems that are smart enough to mimic the intelligence of people up to a certain extent, at least. In other words, Artificial Intelligence allows computers to have abilities like understanding, reasoning, perception, and so on, similar to humans. That's why highly advanced Artificial Intelligence abilities are the basis of many systems that are intelligent in nature in various industries to not only develop services as well as novel products but also to raise the efficiency of the industries. On the other hand, IoT is considered to be a system that is linked to several devices or objects, which can not only gather data but also transfer them in real time with the assistance of implanted sensors or software inside them. To automate several tasks in industries, IoT is being applied at a high level. With input from the users or via sensors, the devices that are part of the IoT network can make a huge amount of data to proceed further, which is beneficial in smart systems. Then, when these two technologies are combined together, they are known as AIoT, meaning that the system of IoT will gather data, whereas Artificial Intelligence's ability will help in the processing of that gathered data. Hence, ML models in such systems are merged with not only data transfer ability but also the connectivity of IoT to boost AI. Simply put, when Artificial Intelligence is added to the system of the Internet of Things, its operation is not only about gathering and transmitting data but also the ability to really analyse and understand the given data. This enhances the interactions between machines and humans as well as improves not only analytics but also the management of data. In the true form, it adds Artificial Intelligence acting on a device like Edge Computing or Edge, with no requirement of external links, meaning that the internet might not be required in it, simply evolving IoT systems further. Now, the question comes. How does AIoT work in the mind? So, in simple terms, Artificial Intelligence is inserted into the infrastructure parts in AIoT devices, like chipsets, as well as programs that are all linked utilizing the Internet of Things networks. Then, APIs, which are known as application programming interfaces, are utilized to make sure all platform parts, software, and hardware cannot only communicate but also operate without any assistance from the end user to run properly. IoT devices, during their operation period, are able to not only make but also collect data, which is analysed by Artificial Intelligence in order to give insights as well as enhance productivity in addition to efficiency. Data learning is one of the processes utilized by AI systems to obtain insights.

Types of AIoT Systems

Mainly, systems like AIoT are set up on the basis of two things, which are either edge-based or cloud-based systems.

Edge-Based AIoT Systems

In these AIoT systems, at the edge, the processing of data is possible, indicating that the data obtained from IoT-based devices have their processing near to the said devices to decrease the bandwidth required to transmit the data, at the same time preventing conceivable delays during analysis of the data. This type of system comprises of the subsequent layers, which are.

- Collection terminal layer
- Connectivity layer
- Edge layer

    Collection Terminal Layer. This layer includes various kinds of hardware devices like cars, sensors, manufacturing equipment, mobility devices, and so on, which are linked to the gateway over the current power lines.

    Connectivity Layer. This layer comprises the field gateways, which act as the collection terminal layer and are linked to the current power lines.

    Edge Layer. This layer comprises amenities for processing and storage of data, in addition to generating insight.

Then, it is time to understand the other kind of AIoT system, which is a Cloud-based one, covered next in this subsection.

Cloud-Based AIoT Systems

These AIoT systems are known as IoT cloud, which is basically not only the way the data is processed but also the way data is managed from IoT-based devices with the assistance of platforms that are cloud computing ones. That's why IoT-based devices must be linked to the cloud, as data is not only processed and stored in the cloud but also accessed from the cloud through several services in addition to applications. These systems comprise the subsequent layers, which are as follows.

- Device layer
- Connectivity layer
- Cloud layer
- User communication layer

Device Layer. This layer is composed of various kinds of hardware, involving beacons, tags, production equipment, equipment for fitness as well as health, sensors, implanted devices, and cars.
Connectivity Layer. This layer includes cloud gateways as well as fields that contain elements of software or hardware that are able to connect cloud storage to sensors, controllers, and different smart devices.
Cloud Layer. This layer comprises processing of data through an Artificial Intelligence engine, data visualization, data access, data storage, as well as analytics through an API.
User Communication Layer. This Layer is built of applications in the mobile phones as well as web portals.

Main Factors Affecting AIoT

Nevertheless, of the role of the industry, processing of high amounts of massive data sets generated from IoT-based devices are important, as they aid in monitoring in real time, obtaining significant insights, improved experience of the users, in addition to the decreased cost of maintenance. These crucial factors are:

- ***Data collection.*** The system linked to IoT networks should collect data from various devices in order to help in the training of the model based on Artificial Intelligence to detect faults and reject biases in addition to correction of data during the processing of data over time.
- ***Training.*** Not only sophisticated neural networks but also procedures of training of numerous kinds are often required in models based on AI. Such arrangements need highly strong processing abilities in machinery as well as tools. As a consequence, it can aid as well as not only analyse highly considerable amounts of data but also perform parallel operations.
- ***Inferencing.*** Ultimately, the model based on AI, which is trained earlier, can produce predictive insights in addition to inferences. Due to this, these models can enhance as well as raise their gathering of data and analysis in addition to processing efficiency.

AIoT's Main Uses

This subsection will discuss the common utilization of AIoT, which are as follows.

- Predictive maintenance
- Inventory management
- Video surveillance

- Robust asset management
- Energy consumption management
- Real-time monitoring of machinery's condition
- Supply chain management

Predictive Maintenance

When AIoT is applied, then it is possible to utilize data from the machines to make applications that help in checking the status of the assets available as well as identifying the need for service for any particular asset. This helps throughout the lifecycle of the available assets, and only in the case of emergencies, repairs in addition to examination of assets are required to perform. This reduces the chances of sudden maintenance costs as well as unexpected outages. This helps not only in prolonging the life of the equipment but also in maximising the performance. This is not limited to the manufacturing sector but is also helpful in the construction industry, where machinery as well as tools could be maintained properly.

Inventory Management

When the Internet of Things platform and AI are incorporated, then inventories are managed in a better way than the conventional ways in the concerned facilities, as analytical abilities are provided by them that are appropriate for different uses. This also includes the improvement of the prediction of resources as well as just-in-time solutions to the management of inventories. Managing inventories is important not only in manufacturing industries but also in the construction industry (Tariq, 2025).

Video Surveillance

When IoT and AI are implemented, the video surveillance system becomes highly smart as well as efficient, which in turn strengthens security. Human operators are needed in the conventional Video Management Systems to watch numerous video feeds, which might affect the accuracy over time due to subjective judgement, as well as attentiveness. However, in the case of Smart Video Surveillance, AIoT uses ML algorithms, identifying objects, performing real-time analysis of the video feeds, and objectively detecting events in addition to humans. This might be helpful in many places, including in the field of traffic engineering.

Robust Asset Management

The performance of assets in comparison to the key performance indicators aids in enhancing the operational as well as performance efficiencies, along with finding out whether the present key performance indicators are appropriate or not. The AIoT platform helps in the development of apps, which are performance management ones to aid in observing any unusual behaviour of assets. Placing a trigger will help in permitting this platform to send automatic warning messages to the user at the time when any deviations are noticed. This will be helpful in various places, including construction sites.

Energy Consumption Management

With the use of highly energy-efficient substitutes, it is possible to decrease the use of energy for the linked devices. AIoT helps in not only tracing the use of energy but also detecting the areas to be developed with the passage of time. Further, AIoT aids in detecting patterns as well as prohibits strange leakage of energy, in addition to allowing the monitoring of the energy peaks to formulate strategies to decrease the consumption of energy. This might be helpful in many areas, including manufacturing industries but also at construction sites.

Real-time Monitoring of Machinery's Condition

The flow of data takes place in a single direction, as early as the devices are linked to the concerned platform. When AIoT is implemented, then monitoring variables like light, moisture, and temperature at the sites becomes possible. The predefined key performance indicators monitoring becomes easier, and the arrangement of automatic warning messages becomes possible in the case of specific parameters being exceeded or when the assets perform badly.

Supply Chain Management

The supply chains are dynamic. When AIoT is applied, it raises the control as well as transparency over the quality of the outputs of the suppliers. The AIoT permits the tracing of end-to-end assets from the start till the end of the supply chain as well as optimizing the routes aiming for shipment in addition to delivery to be optimized in the process. Not to forget that this could also be useful in the management of the supply chain is also essential in the construction sector mentioned in Singh (2024), which is also known as construction supply chain management.

Utilization of AI and IoT in the Civil Engineering Field

This subsection will discuss the particular areas in which AI and IoT are helpful in the domain of Civil Engineering, which are as follows.

- Infrastructure maintenance & management
- Environmental & sustainability assessment
- ITS
- Geotechnical engineering
- Automated construction
- Water resource management
- Structural health monitoring
- Smart cities
- Smart homes
- Smart office buildings
- Smart highways
- AVs
- Cobots
- City brains

Infrastructure Maintenance and Management

The life of infrastructure is being prolonged with the assistance of predictive maintenance led by AI. Then, using nonstop analysis of data from the IoT-based devices, as well as sensors, the Artificial Intelligence systems can forecast the time and location of maintenance requirements, which ultimately decreases the downtime but also increases the lifespan of many structures, including tunnels, bridges, and buildings. For example, the data comprising structural stress might have a pattern that will be analyzed by AI, leading to the advanced detection of areas needing reinforcement in order to stop any possible failure from occurring.

Environmental and Sustainability Assessment

The task of AI is considered to be innovative in the case of environmental impact assessment, as these models can perform analysis of complicated datasets to forecast the ecological footprint of projects taking place at the construction sites, involving features such as depletion of resources, usage of energy, as well as emissions of carbon dioxide, etc. Different scenarios at the construction sites are simulated by AI to aid engineers in deciding not only the materials but also the design to reduce the environmental impact of the ongoing projects, leading to development in a sustainable manner.

ITS

ITS is commonly known as an Intelligent Transportation System, which uses sensors as well as smart devices to manage traffic and improve transportation systems, as mentioned in the studies of Bhowmik et al. (2019) and Singh (2018). The system, powered by Artificial Intelligence, aids in improving not only the traffic flow and efficiency but also decreasing the congestion, optimizing the timing of the traffic lights, as well as improving the transport routes for the public. AIoT could help in gathering essential data on the roads and help in analysing it at the same time to improve the transport system.

Figure 1. ITS in Thailand

Source. Adirach Toumlamoon, Wikimedia

Geotechnical Engineering

The behavior of soil as well as its properties is being analyzed by AI, which plays an important role in this subfield of Civil Engineering. ML models help in processing of data gathered from different sources, which comprise of ground surveys in addition to satellite imagery, to forecast the liquefaction potential, stability of soil, as well as other important factors needed in projects at the site, especially for the safe foundation design in areas prone to landslides as well as earthquakes.

Automated Construction

In this case, it can be said that Artificial Intelligence is not restricted to design and planning, but AI algorithms are being used in construction robots to transform construction practices in Civil Engineering. This includes improving the safety of workers, speeding up construction time, and increasing the accuracy of work while maintaining quality. It could be seen in the handling of materials, bricklaying, and so on.

Figure 2. Construction robots

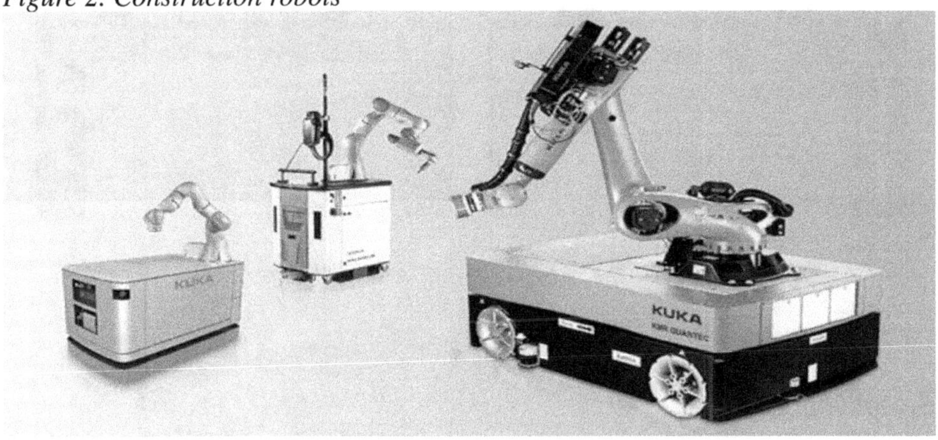

Source. RealAWS, Wikimedia

Water Resource Management

In the projects related to Civil Engineering, the optimization of the management of water resources is being done by Artificial Intelligence systems. The sensors can gather required data, and then AI can analyse the weather data and water use patterns, in addition to the conditions of the environs. Then, AI-supported models aid in forecasting demand, designing highly efficient systems to distribute water, and managing the process to treat water.

Structural Health Monitoring

The sensors and IoT devices can collect useful information concerning the given structures, and then AI can assess the building's status nonstop, or it might be the status of any other structure. The material stresses, temperature, and vibration are being considered in order to monitor the given structure in real-time, whereas the

Artificial Intelligence algorithms help in analysing the collected data to not only identify abnormalities but also to suggest essential interventions from time to time, along with forecasting the possible failures.

Figure 3. Structural health monitoring process of a bridge

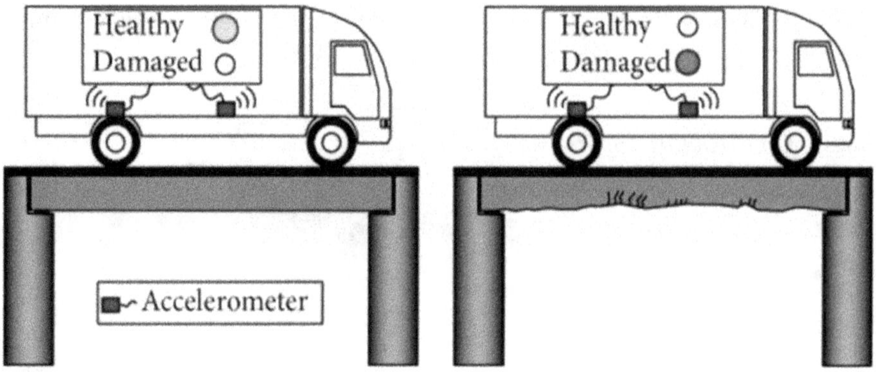

Source. Abdollah Malekjafarian, Patrick J. McGetrick, Eugene J. Obrien, Wikimedia

Smart Cities

They are cities that use smart technologies like meters, lights, and sensors to gather data, which is analysed to aid in increasing the economic growth of the cities, enhance the efficiency of operations of the cities, and enhance the quality of life of people living in smart cities. Here, AI and IoT have ample uses.

Figure 4. Smart City, Graz, Austria

Source. Armin Ademovic, Wikimedia

Smart Homes

They are residential places, where appliances in the home of a person learn via the interaction of the owner or occupants as well as via their responses. When AIoT is added, they can learn the habits of the owner to give personalized assistance.

Figure 5. Smart Home

Source. TP-Link Deutschland, Wikimedia

Smart Office Buildings

They are commercial places, where buildings are used as offices of an organization. IoT and AI could be merged to be applied to these smart buildings to transform the offices. Companies or organizations might choose to use a network of smart sensors fitted inside their offices in order to identify the people's presence as well as automatically change the temperature and lighting to save energy as much as possible. Further, facial recognition technology allows the above-mentioned types of buildings to control access via connected cameras as well as Artificial Intelligence to decide the rightful individuals who only obtain access to the building.

Figure 6. Smart building in Edinburg, UK

Source. Anne Burgess, Wikimedia

Smart Highways

Based on the study of Singh (2024), it could be understood that they are a type of highway using electronic and smart technology to enhance the operation of the linked AVs, street lighting as well as traffic lights. They further monitor the vehicle speed, traffic level, as well as highway's condition. Definitely, IoT and AI could be used here together to make the operation smoother.

Figure 7. Smart highway

Source. Tina Dekkers, Wikimedia

AVs

They are known as Autonomous Vehicles, which depend on numerous sensors as well video camera systems to collect data related to vehicles which are close by on the roads, look for people walking nearby in addition to monitor the situation of driving. When AI and IoT are both used, the AVs become even smarter and better, which is useful in improving the transportation system.

Figure 8. Mobileye autonomous shuttle

Source. Alexander Migl, Wikimedia

Cobots

They are also known as Collaborative Robots, which are meant to help humans not only in the assembly but also in the manufacturing of parts. They help people in numerous tasks like packaging, production, and quality control, in addition to the assembly of the products, with the assistance of AI tools and IoT-based devices. However, in the construction industry, they can install fasteners regularly, precisely, and accurately at the sites, improving the efficiency and saving time drastically.

Figure 9. Collaborative robot lifting column

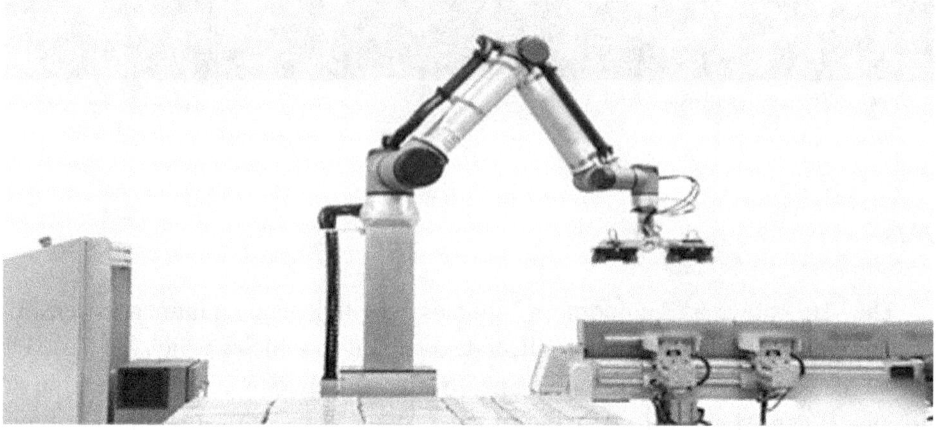

Source. CollaborativePalletizer, Wikimedia

City Brains

They are meant to encourage the development of urban areas by incorporating municipal data in real time with machine intelligence. For instance, Artificial Internet of Things systems can process enormous amounts of data streams, videos, and logs obtained from sensors in addition to systems present in the whole urban centre to identify problems like traffic light changes, accidents on the roads, and illegal parking.

Construction Industry

The industry can be transformed with the application of AI and IoT, as they help in various tasks like enhancing scheduling, planning, construction design, as well as aiding the construction robots or driverless heavy vehicles at the site, and so on. This makes the sites safer for humans and speeds up the projects without compromising the quality, leading to sustainable practices.

Objectives

There are various objectives of this chapter, which are as follows.

- To understand the concept of IoT in addition to AI as well as AIoT.
- To understand the need for AIoT and details regarding its uses in general, as well as in Civil Engineering.
- To understand areas of Civil Engineering being affected by AI and IoT, as well as some real-life case studies.
- To understand the current trends of IoT as well as AI in Civil Engineering and their future in this engineering field.

What is the Requirement and Utility of AI as Well as IoT in the Evolution of Civil Engineering?

In the study of Singh (2022), Fuzzy Logic could be used to improve the traffic and transportation system by reducing accidents. Also, ANN utility and scope in Civil Engineering in the future was considered in the study of Singh (2023). Then, Singh (2023) discussed the way AI could help encourage sustainable construction practices. Furthermore, Singh and Srivastava's (2024) study talked about the way Green AI could be helpful in Civil Engineering in accomplishing sustainable development. Basically, advanced technologies like AI are really helpful in transforming the Civil Engineering field, and in the case of IoT, the latter is helpful in gathering important data around the target in addition to transmitting the data to the destination for processing. Smart technologies require the use of IoT for smooth data collection and transmission. When AI and IoT are both applied in the Civil Engineering field, then the used smart devices become even smarter, and faster data collection, processing, analysis, and transmission of data takes place, enhancing this engineering field further.

MOTIVATION

The author performed the study on IoT and AI implementation in Civil Engineering because, in recent years, AIoT has emerged as an advanced technology that is attracting the attention of the masses. Since AIoT is considered to have vast potential and make the existing smart devices and systems even smarter, the author felt the need to investigate the way AI and IoT could help in the transformation of this field of engineering as well as the areas it could affect.

LITERATURE REVIEW

Thakur et al. (2024) studied the infrastructure of smart homes, and they worked on making them secure with a framework where the synergy of AI, Edge Computing, and IoT were used. They stated that such synergy is useful in surveillance through a camera, particularly in smart cities, as it gives several benefits in the allocation of resources. Their accuracy rate in outdoor situations was eighty-five percent, whereas in indoor situations, it was ninety-one percent.

Prabhakar et al. (2023) studied the industry known as construction, and they worked on incorporating IoT and artificial Intelligence, in addition to Blockchain, in their review study, which discussed solutions as well as challenges in the process. They talked about the way these three technologies can be combined, leading towards Industry 4.0. Kaginalkar et al. (2021) studied the services in smart cities, and they worked on the management of the quality of air using urban computing through their review study, where the perspective of cloud technology, Artificial Intelligence, and IoT were combined together. They stated that the above-mentioned cities, which are driven by data, have the prospect to permit the decrease of emissions in addition to assisting in mitigating climate change. Kapoor et al. (2024) studied civil engineering and worked on an engaging view while incorporating AI in the mentioned studied area. They mentioned about the techniques based on Artificial Intelligence, which offer a substitute method in comparison to the existing conventional methods, which are intended for extensive series of difficult problems, especially in the areas of structural health monitoring, construction management, concrete technology, architectural engineering, irrigation, structural analysis, space structures, transportation, environmental, in addition to geotechnical engineering. Jayaraman et al. (2024) studied models based on ML as well as IoT, and they worked on analyzing the quality of water by providing their decisive review. They stated that they not only reviewed but also detected various models on water quality indices in their study and reviewed data in real time on the research associated with GIS aimed at the quality of water. Quang et al. (2025) studied quality control of air in indoor environments, and they worked on improving its privacy protection aspects with the assistance of management platforms based on Artificial Intelligence. They then proceeded with a privacy-centred platform proposition to maintain the quality of air in the above-mentioned environments, and they investigated methods that are driven by AI to balance not only safeguarding the privacy of the user but also the performance of the quality of air at the same time. Moudgil et al. (2023) studied the energy infrastructure of buildings, and they worked on incorporating the Internet of Things in it through their decisive review study on solutions as well as challenges on the said matter. They then proceeded with the behavioural as well as technological interferences aimed at building the cognitive intelligence. They stated that for buildings in the future, there is a need for a faultlessly integrated framework based on IoT (Tariq, 2025).

Rayabharapu et al. (2022) studied control techniques to work on managing pollution using the aid of sensors as well as IoT. They proceeded with the complete solution to the pollution problem in the current civilization, which will allow them to not only discuss but also trace major environmental issues, societal problems, and significant problems with general health. They used different sensors to estimate various types of contaminants on the planet in their proposed methodology. Mor et al. (2024) studied construction, and they worked on applying AI to make it sustainable in nature. They discussed the modern techniques in the civil engineering area and investigated the searing concept of AI as well as its growth, starting from the past studies to possible developing themes with well-directed future guidelines. They strongly suggested that Artificial Intelligence must be utilized in sustainable as well as smart construction, based on their study outcomes. Alotaibi et al. (2024) studied intelligent homes, and they worked on making them environmentally friendly ones by integrating AI and 3D printing in addition to IoT to build them. They stated that AI can improve the operations of the system, whereas 3D printing can improve construction by reducing wastage and increasing speed, leading to sustainability, and IoT behaves as the main catalyst for the above-mentioned homes (Tariq, 2025).

Lakhouit (2025) studied the management of solid waste and worked on transforming it further in urban areas using IoT in addition to AI implementation through their review study to provide intelligent solutions to sorting, collecting, and recycling waste. They stated that the waste processes could be optimized and forecasted by smart systems. Rangasamy and Yang (2025) studied prefabricated construction, and they worked on transforming it for the future by merging technologies like IoT and artificial Intelligence in addition to BIM. They stated that this assimilation of the above-stated technologies in prefabricated construction is still in the initial stages and can considerably grow in the future. Wang et al. (2024) studied smart cities, and they worked on the way to safeguarding the load management of such cities particularly in the networks linked Internet of Things, through an Artificial Intelligence improved multiple stage learning-to-learning method. They stated that their proposed method controls MMStranformer, and their experimental results showed its effectiveness, making their research aid in the progress of Artificial Intelligence applications aimed at the management of energy in addition to the development of urban areas in a sustainable manner (Tariq, 2025).

Naji et al. (2023) studied concrete columns and worked on identifying the degradation as well as localization of its base cover on the basis of IoT as well as Artificial Intelligence, with the assistance of techniques based on deep learning. They then proposed a new automatic algorithm to proceed further, and they claimed that the VGG19 network has performed the best in comparison to other models, with an accuracy of one hundred percent to classify health conditions in the context of the column's base cover and only 0.33% of RMSE. Nikpour et al. (2025) studied smart cities, and they worked on managing energy intelligently in them with a framework based on the Internet of Things, as well as applying intelligent analysis to accomplish their research. They proceeded with ML approaches, which were applied to complicated systems in addition to networks, to get fruitful results. Ghoushchi et al. (2024) studied autonomous vehicles, and they worked on a unified multi-criteria decision-making method to improve their efficiency with the assistance of combined IoT as well as augmented intelligence. They used not only MCDM techniques but also fuzzy sets to rank as well as examine situations in order to enhance IoT in addition to augmented intelligence in the above-mentioned type of cars. Fan et al. (2024) studied carbon dioxide emissions and worked on monitoring them in real time by utilizing the power of the Internet of Things as well as Artificial Intelligence. They considered one hundred thirty-seven nations to analyse their data from the year 2020 till the year 2020, to provide solid proof that policies of states centred on economic growth in a sustainable manner, healthy ecosystems, in addition to excellent legislative alterations can reduce the above-mentioned emissions.

Elrifaee et al. (2024) studied the sites in construction projects, and they worked on their safety aspects by examining the roles of the Internet of Things in it. They then performed a complete review of limitations and the latest developments, in addition to recommendations to direct future research on it. They claimed that their systematic review not only disclosed 3 important safety dimensions in construction but also examined the impact of the Internet of Things on the safety of people at the site. Severino et al. (2024) studied infrastructures, and they worked on monitoring them with the assistance of reliable Artificial Intelligence, as well as using a method based on blockchain technology. They proposed a framework to be implemented on the basis of a technological sol named Hybrid Distributed Ledger Technology to enhance the credibility of AI, particularly in critical sectors including civil infrastructure management. Essamlali et al. (2024) studied a system to manage stormwater, and they worked on it with the assistance of combined ML as well as IoT technology to proceed with a novel architecture of low-impact development to obtain favorable outcomes. They mentioned the way fast urbanization in Morocco's Bouznika is creating serious problems of managing stormwater, and their proposed study could help optimize the said management in the mentioned place.

Mousavi et al. (2025) studied construction as well as unground mining, and they worked on the fusion of IoT-Bayes in order to monitor the risk related to the safety of the environment in real-time associated with their studied area. They considered the coal mines, which are present underground, having complicated underground situations for their research, and they mentioned new risk management to deal with their safety problems. Shaharuddin et al. (2023) studied smart buildings, and they especially focused on the situation of fire hazard in indoor conditions for their studied area as well as the way IoT based sensors could help in it, through their thorough review study of fifty-four interdisciplinary past papers over last 10 years, to obtain fruitful outcomes. Dai et al. (2023) studied buildings and worked on improving the quality of indoor air in their studied area, particularly the upcoming ones, with the assistance of IoT systems. They stated that with the above-mentioned technology, it is possible to get dependable monitoring results as well as algorithms that are driven through data and can induce the management of indoor air quality. Mohammadi et al. (2024) studied the interactions between building as well as people, and they worked to make mentioned interactions immersive, by incorporating IoT based sensor networks which are wireless in nature as well as immersive technology like AR, to control HVAC, thermal comfort visualization in addition to spatial-temporal mapping in real-time to obtain suitable outcomes. Wettewa et al. (2024) studied civil infrastructures as well as buildings, and they worked on improving their maintenance in addition to operation with the assistance of GNN. They mentioned optimizing the field's particular attribute engineering, hyperparameter, in addition to architecture. Reasonable techniques based on AI were incorporated by them to get desired results. Kheder et al. (2024) studied the system regarding the monitoring of road traffic, and they worked on DL techniques, as well as robotics powered by IoT to support their studied area in real-time. They claimed that the models proposed by them were supported by the test results to have considerable enhancement in accuracy.

Waqar et al. (2024) studied construction engineering, and they worked on systems aided by intelligent decisions in their studied area through the ML as well as AI methods. They performed their review study with the aim to accomplish a thorough analysis of ML as well as AI approaches in the above-mentioned field, with a particular focus on their practical benefits, applications, and limitations. Mukhti et al. (2024) studied damage to concrete brought by the corrosion of steel, and they worked on their programmed categorization through their analysis based on ultrasonic waves supported by Artificial Intelligence. They stated that when the training of AI is done, then the above-mentioned analysis will be able to improve the said categorization. Aljebreen et al. (2023) studied vehicles, and they worked on categorizing as well as identifying them accurately with the assistance of ensemble learning on the basis of algorithms related to the honey badger in addition to Internet of Things incorporation. They stated that a combination of DL and IoT approaches is recognized to be helpful in automatically identifying vehicles, and they tested the result of the HBOAEL-VDC method on standard databases of remote sensing images to accomplish their study. He et al. (2025) studied structural design, and they worked on making it intelligent as well as programmed by incorporating generative Artificial Intelligence as well as BIM. They considered human drawing to be encouraged to design a framework, which was a 2-stage generation one, and they developed a sophisticated model named the physics-based conditional diffusion model while taking physical situations into account. Dong et al. (2021) studied a system to manage pavement on the roads, and they worked on creating a framework for their studied area on the basis of big data in addition to IoT. In their research, they claimed to develop a pavement management system that will be able to deal with the sophisticated aspects of the road, which is its maintenance.

Songhorabadi et al. (2023) studied smart cities powered by IoT networks, and they worked on a method called fog computing to support their studied area. They then proposed a new fog-based method for the above-mentioned cities, and they took different perspectives into consideration. Thorough as well as unique open challenges and problems were discussed.

Guo et al. (2022) studied the construction of a subway station, and they worked not only on the modeling but also on the monitoring of the concentration of PM2.5 at their studied area, on the basis of optimized LSTM algorithm as well as the Internet of Things. Gbadamosi et al. (2021) studied the rail industry present in the United Kingdom, and they worked on predictive asset maintenance in addition to monitoring in order to use an execution plan for their studied area with the assistance of IoT.

Hostetter et al. (2024) studied fire engineering, and they worked on the function of Artificial Intelligence chatbots, which act as large language models, in their studied area. They examined the way Bard and ChatGPT could be answered by Bard, in addition to ChatGPT, to compare them and to produce desired study outcomes. Sarkar et al. (2024) studied concrete, and they worked on transforming their analysis by performing an intense survey of insights driven by Artificial Intelligence along with methods based on images on thorough quality control, determining the property of concrete, in addition to identifying cracks in an advanced manner, to accomplish their research. Hariri-Ardebili et al. (2023) studied dam engineering, and they worked on finding out the function of digital technologies as well as AI in their studied area. They mentioned the summary of Artificial Intelligence, and then its particular applications in dam as well as hydropower engineering, along with the present as well as latest technologies being executed in the said industry.

Mai et al. (2024) studied the construction industry, and they worked on finding out the growth of AI in communication, security, and maintenance in their studied area. They considered the period from the year 2014 till the year 2023, and they mentioned Artificial Intelligence's move to Virtual Reality, IoT, BIM, blockchain, and digital twins, along with the details about predictive analytics. Giannakidou et al. (2024) studied forest fire, and they worked on using AI as well as IoT in their studied area to identify and prevent fire hazards as well as restore forest through their complete survey in order to avoid environmental damage.

Fortin et al. (2024) studied road transportation, and they worked on a system to identify potholes present on roads on the basis of IoT as well as AI technologies in the Philippines. A new solution was proposed by them while the system called EyeWay was developed, which was a prototype of Artificial Internet of Things and was particularly designed to identify potholes in real-time better than earlier conventional methods. Bibri et al. (2024) studied City Brain, and they worked on understanding the combination of AI as well as IoT technologies used behind their studied area to propose an innovative environmental governance driven by data, which they claimed to have real application. Bibri et al. (2024) studied environmental sustainability, and they worked on smarter ecological cities as well as innovative AIoT solutions that were intended for their studied area, through their thorough methodological review, to accomplish their desired objectives. Seyyedi et al. (2024) studied waste management, and they worked on incorporating circular economy as well as digitalization in their studied area through a thorough review, in addition to adopting AI methods, to proceed in the direction of simulation model, along with fulfillment of their research goals. Pala et al. (2025) studied civil infrastructures, and they worked on detecting cracks as well as quality assurance optimization by utilizing AI to improve their studied area. They also focused on the sophisticated cognitive processes of Artificial Intelligence models as well as uses in the above-mentioned type of infrastructures. Ushakov et al. (2022) studied transportation engineering, particularly public transport systems, and they focused on understating the ways IoT affects the smart transport systems related to their studied area. They stated that companies in the aviation industry are inclined to utilize IoT in their operations associated with aviation, which include flight simulation, schedule, and weather monitoring. Mishra et al. (2022) studied structures related to the civil engineering field, and they utilized IoT in performing structural health monitoring of their studied area through their review paper. They discussed the various sensors linked to IoT networks that could be applied, and numerous lab examinations along with case studies for SHM were explained.

RESEARCH GAPS

There were many scientific and research studies published in journals and research books, as well as conference proceedings, that were taken into account, but mostly the recent years were considered further. However, it was noted that not too many studies are done on using AI and IoT both technologies in Civil Engineering field, compared to many other existing advanced technologies in other fields. Then, this study not only focused on the above-mentioned technologies but also on their uses as well as some real case studies in the world related to the area of Civil Engineering.

MAIN FOCUS OF THE CHAPTER

The chapter focussed on explaining the basic concepts of AI as well as IoT and then their merge. Then, it discussed the need and their implementation in the Civil Engineering field, as well as highlighted some real case studies globally. It also covered some problems and issues associated with it, as well as some graphical analysis to observe the current status and future of these advanced technologies in the area of Civil Engineering.

ISSUES, CONTROVERSIES, PROBLEMS

The emergence of AI and IoT merged together, making AIoT a solution to many existing problems and definitely a great way to make intelligent systems and devices smarter and even more efficient in nature. This makes them have high potential to transform the Civil Engineering field, but several problems and issues can't be overlooked. The initial cost will be high, and maintenance of such sophisticated systems and devices will not be easy at the sites. Then, trained people or workers will be required to work along with these advanced technologies, who are generally ignorant in the area of Civil Engineering projects. Data privacy, quality, incorporation, and so on will be further problems that need to be addressed. The harsh environment of the projects in some places might pose a difficulty in operating these sophisticated devices and systems.

SOME MAJOR AI AND IoT CASE STUDIES AROUND THE WORLD

This section will discuss some of the real-world case studies where AI and IoT have been incorporated in the area of Civil Engineering, which are as follows.

- Lendlease
- PCL Construction
- The Edge

- Turner Construction Company
- Boston Dynamic Spot
- ET City Brain
- London City Airport
- Tesla's self-driving vehicles

Lendlease

This is an Australian-based construction and real estate company in multiple countries, known for infrastructure, founded in 1958 in Sydney. The company utilizes the Internet of Things to improve the efficiency and safety of its operations at the sites during construction projects. They incorporated wearables, which were acting as IoT devices to monitor the condition of environs as well as the health of workers at the site, to obtain data in real time, which will, in the case of possible dangers, help in alerting the concerned site supervisors to take immediate action. In other words, the mentioned technology aided in making sure that the safety rules are being implemented strictly as well as in inhibiting accidents at the sites. Moreover, the company uses the sensors, which are part of IoT networks, to monitor their construction sites in order to trace several factors like weather conditions, vibrations, and noise to not only make sure safety standards are followed but also to optimize working environs.

Figure 10. Satellite view of lendlease headquarters in Sydney

Source. Google Earth

Figure 11. Lendlease office in Townsville

Source. Greditdesu, Wikimedia

PCL Construction

This is a private construction company that was founded in 1906 in Canada and later also opened its headquarters in the USA in 1975, leading to have 2 headquarters at present, one in Canada and the other in the USA. This company has adopted Internet of Things technology to enhance not only the safety but also the efficiency of their company's operations. They utilize GPS trackers in addition to RFID tags, which are part of IoT devices, to monitor the real-time status as well as the location of materials, machinery, and tools. It allows the system to stop unwanted replacements of misplaced or missing objects, as well as considerably decreases the spent time to search for the earlier mentioned objects, which leads to significant saving of cost. Further, this company hires predictive maintenance with the assistance of IoT sensors, which helps in detecting the optimum interval at which the equipment requires servicing as well as in monitoring the performance of equipment, which avoids sudden downtime as well as breakdowns, leading to smooth operation.

Figure 12. Satellite view of PCL construction headquarters in Edmonton

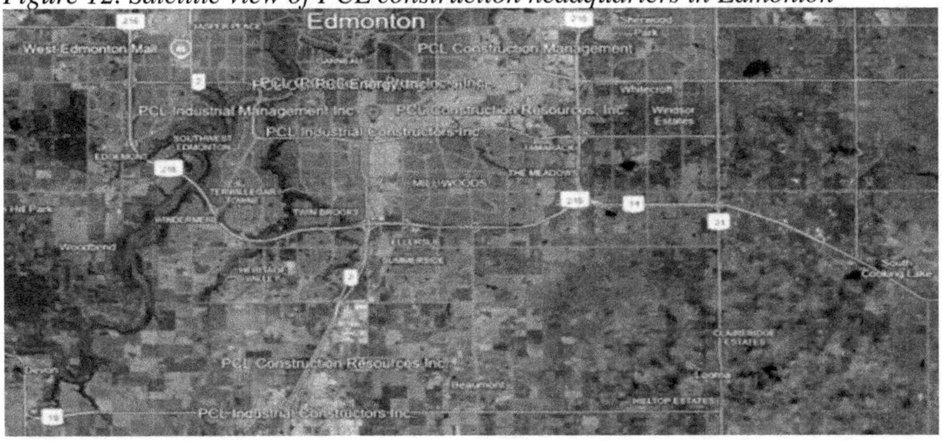

Source. Google Earth

The Edge

This is located in Amsterdam, and it is famous as the most sustainable office building across the globe, with a BREEAM score of 98.36% and an outstanding rating during its completion. The building uses sensors as part of an IoT network to not only adjust but also monitor temperature and lighting in order to use the energy in an optimum manner. There is an app in smartphone which is linked to these sensors, acting as the PA for the people inside the building, to improve the productivity in addition to the experience of the users in the office. The implementation of IoT technology here has improved the productivity of office workers as well as decreased the emissions of carbon by the building, showing the benefits and prospects of modernized construction with the assistance of smart technologies.

Figure 13. Satellite view of the edge building in Amsterdam

Source. Google Earth

Figure 14. Front view of the edge office building

Source. AValečka, Wikimedia

Turner Construction Company

This is a USA-based construction company, which is present in twenty countries in the world and was founded in 1902. Also known as the largest domestic contractor in the USA based on the info available in 2020. The company has incorporated sensors, which are part of IoT networks, into the operations of their cranes in order to change them into smart devices to obtain several benefits in the process. The mentioned sensors, in real time, analyse and gather data on the activities of cranes to decrease the idle times of the cranes, improving safety during crane operations, as well as to make sure the cranes are used in an optimum manner. This execution permits the operations of the cranes to be managed efficiently, as well as monitoring to be done in a precise manner, along with considerable enhancement of safety standards in addition to the timelines of the associated projects.

Figure 15. Satellite view of turner construction headquarters in New York

Source. Google Earth

Boston Dynamic Spot

Among the various sectors, the industrial sector is famous for using advanced technologies to update its industrial operations. A few of the latest projects in the direction of Industry 4.0 comprise robots for particular operations and services. Robots, especially, are currently able to adapt to the present demand of factories and industries to not only improve the efficiency of the operations but also provide smarter solutions. Due to the emergence of AIoT, it was possible to make robots even smarter than before, as well as highly responsive to various processes in industries. Boston Dynamics, which is a US-based company known for engineering as well as design of robots, founded in 1992, revealed many of the robotic systems including Spot. This is a mobile robot that is attracting the attention of people in the world due to its various services. They can move through various terrains with exceptional agility, securely gather data, and program the tasks related to inspecting the given place. These robots provide great ways to implement things in a highly effective as well as certain manner in industries and factories. However, it is noteworthy to understand that factories are not the only types of industries; construction is also a type of industry, so the way Spot can help in the construction industry must be taken into account. These robots are not limited to the floors in the factories but are also able to move properly at the sites during the course of construction projects, as well as laboratories and so on. They can work to aid the concerned team to outclass their conventional past performance, as well as give valued insights in relation site health, routine operations, in addition to info regarding possible dangerous circumstances.

Figure 16. Spot robot by Boston dynamics

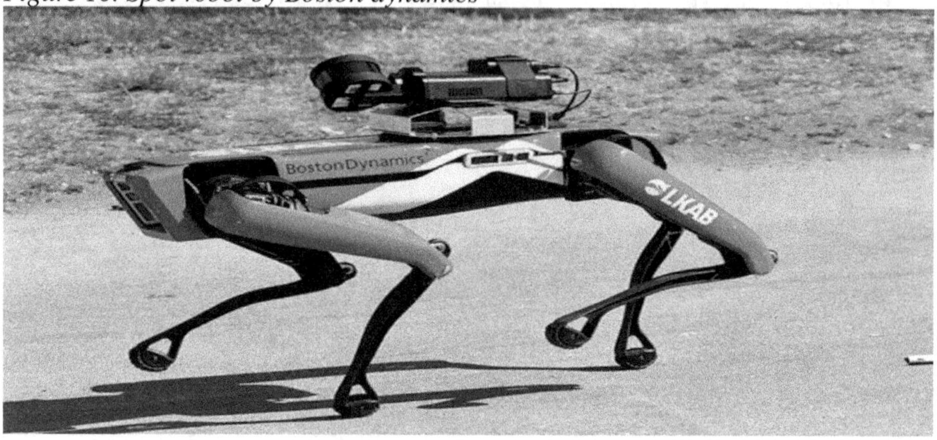

Source. Tore Danielsson (WMSE), Wikimedia

ET City Brian

Alibaba Cloud, which is a China-based company founded in 2009, developed this AI-driven technology in order to maximize the usage of public resources in metropolitan cities. With the assistance of deep neural networks as well as big data, in an urbanized centre, several sensors in addition to machines present in the said centre provide data streams as well as video logs for this system to process them. This system was implemented originally in the Chinese city named Hangzhou to find several benefits like the arrival times of ambulances were reduced to around 50%, wallowing aid to reach the desired destination in lesser time than traditionally. Then, the automation of traffic signals in the district named Xiaoshan saw an increase of fifteen percent in the travel speed of vehicles, as commuting time on a daily basis was decreased by three minutes. Further, the accuracy rate to detect incidents or accidents reached ninety-two percent, which speeded the process of reporting road accidents and led to faster emergency responses to save lives as well as take care of situations. This again transformed the traffic and transportation system in the aforementioned Chinese city.

Figure 17. Map of China showing location of Hangzhou city

Source. Dagvidur, Wikimedia

London City Airport

This airport is considered to be the first one to incorporate cross-technology networking, the Internet of Things, and Artificial Intelligence in order to provide passengers with accurate info regarding the statuses of flights, as well as to monitor all parts of the airport. The cabin crew is able to monitor the queue of passengers during boarding, the location of the passengers, the tracking of baggage, and many other important activities with the assistance of the above-mentioned technological devices. A digital engine model based on dependable IoT technology is embedded in this airport, which comprises Constrained Application Protocol, Industrial IoT, and Application Program Interfaces, in addition to Web Sockets. This allows for increasing the business delivery speed with the assistance of Business Intelligence as well as IoT dashboard solutions in an efficient manner.

Figure 18. London City airport

Source. N Chadwick, Wikimedia

Tesla's Self-Driving Vehicles

These vehicles are cars made by the USA-based automotive company, based company Tesla, which was founded in the year 2003. They utilize innovative driver assistance technology known as autopilot, which means automatic pilot in other words. They possess external cameras and strong onboard computers, in addition to ultrasonic sensors to gather data. Then, a model based on a deep neural network investigates the collected data, aiding the car in making the decision regarding its next action to be taken. By commencing the autopilot technology, the company has reached new heights in the context of self-driving abilities of vehicles. Since the automotive industry's next logical move was considered to be hands-free driving, the company's invention was not unexpected to decrease stress as well as increase the safety of driving. The AIoT has a major area to grow in this case to utilize such vehicles on public roads in order to transform the traffic & transportation engineering.

Figure 19. Tesla showroom in Dadeland Mall in Miami

Source. Phillip Pessar, Wikimedia

Figure 20. Tesla Model SB at Geneva, an example of AV

Source. Matti Blume, Wikimedia

METHODOLGY

This section discusses the various major problems and obstacles faced on the path of the above case studies in implementing AI and IoT technologies.

- Lendlease

- PCL Construction
- The Edge
- Turner Construction Company
- Boston Dynamic Spot
- ET City Brain
- London City Airport
- Tesla's self-driving vehicles

Lendlease. Here, the company observed challenges like training of manpower, collection as management of data problems, latency, maintenance of devices, etc.

PCL Construction. The company faced considerable obstacles like latency issues, connectivity issues at the site, skill gaps of workers and training to work side by side, high initial investment, durability of devices at the site, and so on.

The Edge. The building saw noteworthy hurdles to overcome, like environmental as well as regulatory compliances, adaptation as well as usability by occupants, risk of cyberattacks, processing as well as management of data problems, data privacy issues, high initial cost and connectivity issues, etc.

Turner Construction Company. The significant hindrances were management as well as processing of data, hacking risks, data privacy issues, chances of malfunction as well as operational risks, maintenance cost, and initial investment.

Boston Dynamic Spot. Here, the major obstacles were technical constraints, high initial cost, integration with present systems, real-time processing, security issues related to the protection of data, and adaption to work on challenging terrains.

ET City Brain. It faced problems in the management of data as well as integration from heterogeneous sources, technical challenges, data privacy as well as cybersecurity concerns, initial cost, compliance with the existing regulations, people acceptance as well as their participation, were the major hurdles which were faced.

London City Airport. In this case, the airport faced problems with data privacy as well as data volumes of passengers, regulatory compliance including data privacy laws, initial high financial investment, staff management and training, and the impact of weather on AIoT devices as major obstacles.

Tesla's Self-Driven Vehicles. On the other hand, the company has to work on the hindrances like accidents as well as system failures not to occur, if possible, technological limitations, market competition from BYD of China, and so on.

RESULTS AND DISCUSSION

In this section, data was obtained from various sources, including Statista, etc., to create graphs to analyze the market related to AI and IoT technologies.

Table 1. Growth of AIoT in the world

Market Size of AIoT	In USD
Year 2023 By TBI	5,090,000,000
Year 2024 By TBRC	9,980,000,000
Year 2024 By GlobalCIO (TrueAIoT)	9,980,000,000
Year 2028 By GlobalCIO	31,050,000,000
Year 2029 By TBRC	41,540,000,000
Year 2033 By TBI	124,870,000,000

Source. Global CIO, The Brainy Insights, The Business Research Company, and OpenPR

Table 2. Growth of North American AIoT market

North American AIoT Market Growth	In USD
Year 2024	5,600,000,000
Year 2030	21,660,000,000

Source. MarketsandMarkets

Table 3. Share of AIoT component segments

AIoT Component Segment Share	In (%)
Software in 2023	55.31
Other Components in 2023	44.69

Source. Brainy Insights

Table 4. Share of AIoT deployment type segments

AIoT Deployment Type Segment Share	In (%)
Cloud Segment in 2023	53.66
On-premise Segment in 2023	46.34

Source. Brainy Insights

Table 5. Share of AIoT end-user segments

AIoT End User Segment Share	In (%)
Manufacturing in 2023	35.87
Others in 2023	64.13

Source. Brainy Insights

Table 6. Share of AIoT by application

AIoT By Application Share	In (%)
Video Surveillance in 2022	27.1
Others (SCM, PM, IM, RAM, ECM, & RTMCM) in 2022	72.9

Source. Fortune Business Insights

Table 7. Growth of AIoT devices in the world

AIoT Devices Global Growth	Number
Year 2017	9,000,000,000
Year 2025 (Expected)	55,000,000,000

Source. SAS

Table 8. Share of IoT Technologies

IoT Technologies Share	In (%)
WiFi Share	31
Bluetooth + Cellular IoT	46
Others	33

Source. IoT Analytics

Table 9. Growth of technological investment in the initiative of Smart Cities in the world

Technology Investment in Global Smart City Initiative	In USD
Year 2018	81,000,000,000
Year 2023	189,500,000,000

Source. Statista

Table 10. Growth of annual revenue of IoT in the world

Global IoT Annual Revenue	In USD
Year 2020	181,500,000,000
Year 2033 (Expected)	934,200,000,000

Source. Statista

Table 11. IoT's market size growth in the world

Market Size of IoT	In USD
Year 2024 By GlobalCIO	714,480,000,000
Year 2032 By GlobalCIO	4,062,340,000,000

Source. Global CIO

Table 12. Growth of AIoT software vendors

AIoT Software Vendor Growth	In 10s
Year 2019	17.8
Year 2021	38.9

Source. IoT Analytics

Table 13. Comparison and growth of market share between North America and rest of the world

AIoT Market	**In (%)**
North America in 2022 By FB	35.6
Rest of the World in 2022 By FB	64.4
North America in 2023 By TBI	34.11
Rest of the World in 2023 By TBI	65.89
North America in 2024 By GVR	41
Rest of the World in 2024 By GVR	59

Source. The Brainy Insights, Grand View Research, and Fortune Business Insights

Table 14. IIoT benefits

IIoT	**In (%)**
Minimum Equipment Downtime Reduction	20
Maximum Equipment Downtime Reduction	30
Unscheduled Equipment Downtime Reduction	12
Increased Usage Rate of Equipment	40

Source. Global CIO

Figure 21. Growth of AIoT in the world

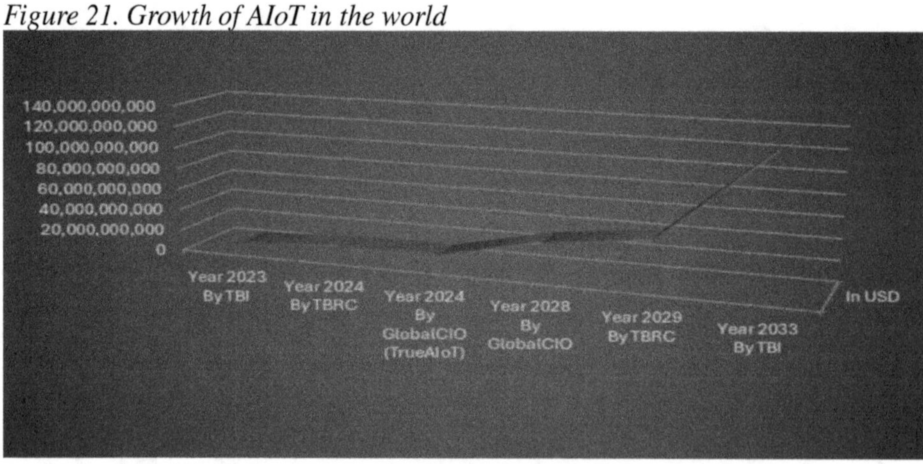

Source. Global CIO, The Brainy Insights, The Business Research Company, and OpenPR

Figure 22. Growth of North American AIoT market

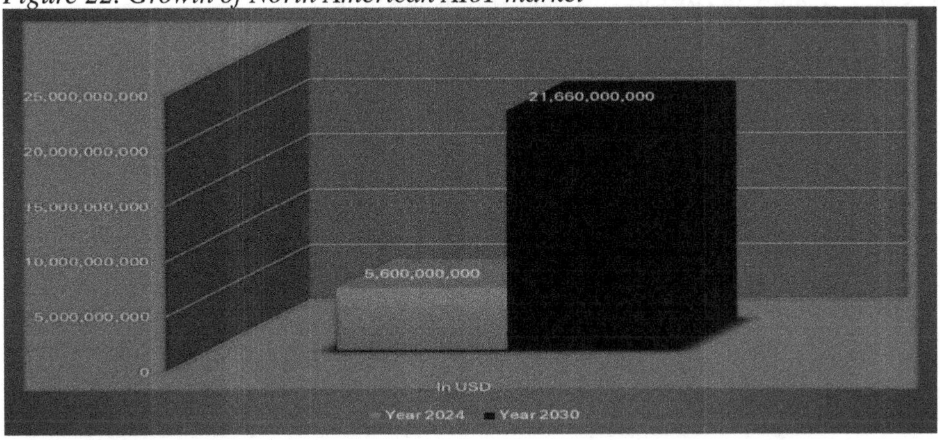

Source. MarketsandMarkets

Figure 23. Share of AIoT component segments

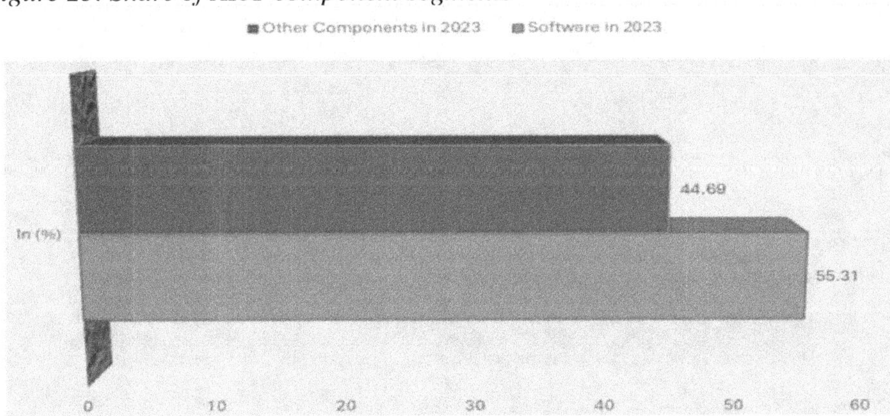

Source. The Brainy Insights

Figure 24. Share of AIoT deployment type segment

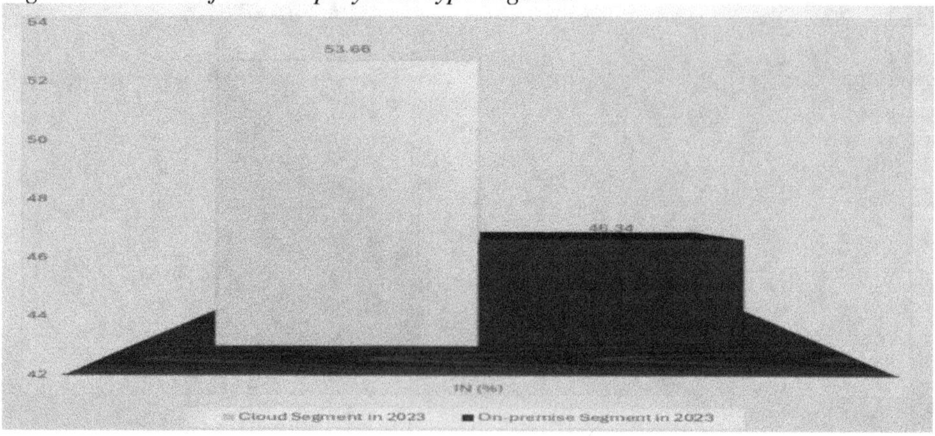

Source. The Brainy Insights

Figure 25. Share of AIoT end user segments

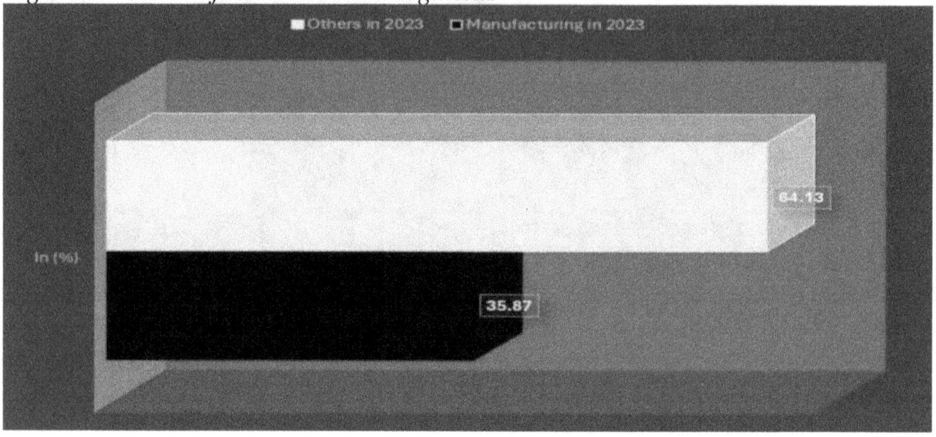

Source. The Brainy Insights

Figure 26. Share of AIoT by application

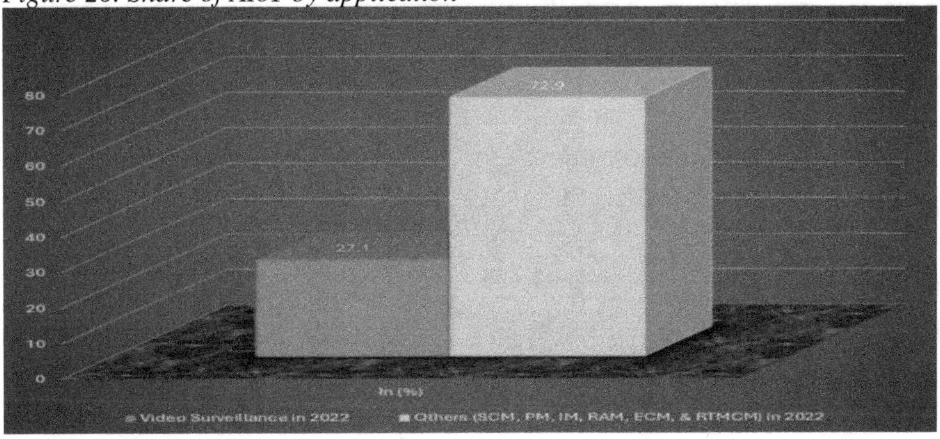

Source. Fortune Business Insights

Figure 27. Growth of AIoT devices in the world

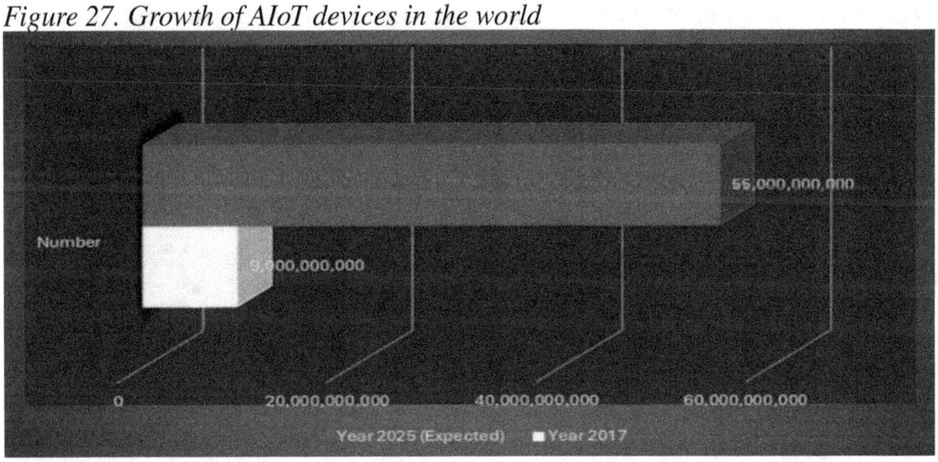

Source. SAS

Figure 28. Share of IoT Technologies

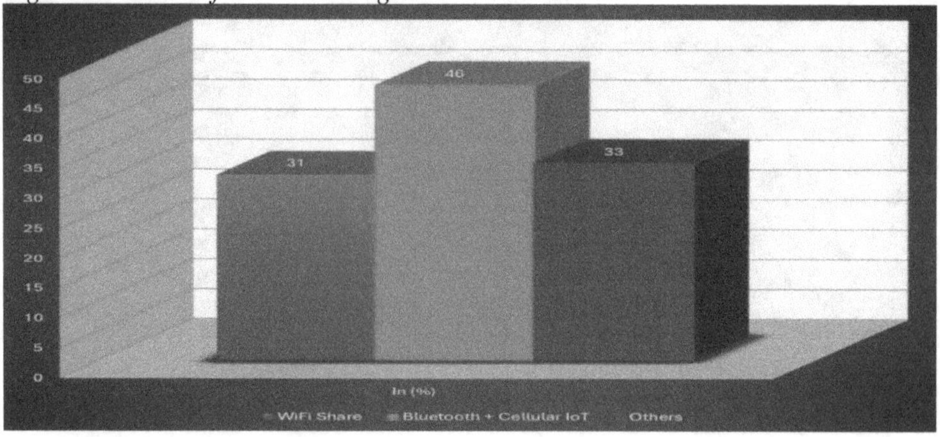

Source. IoT Analytics

Figure 29. Growth of technological investment in the initiative of Smart Cities in the world

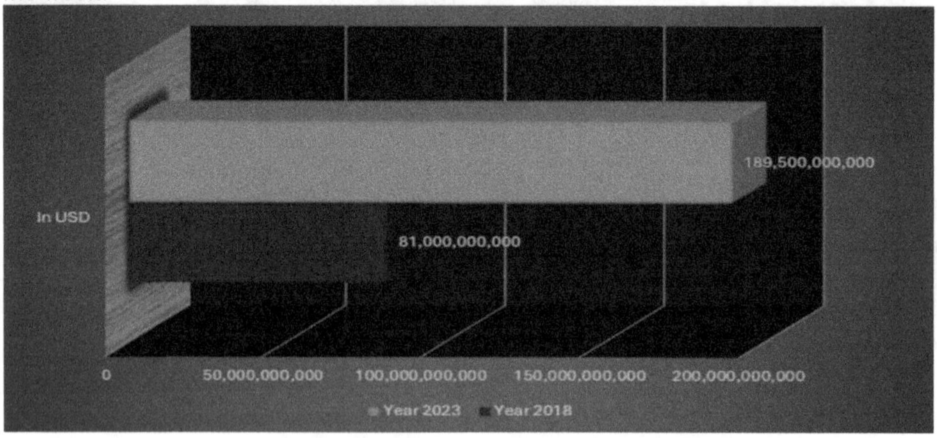

Source. Statista

Figure 30. Growth of annual revenue of IoT in the world

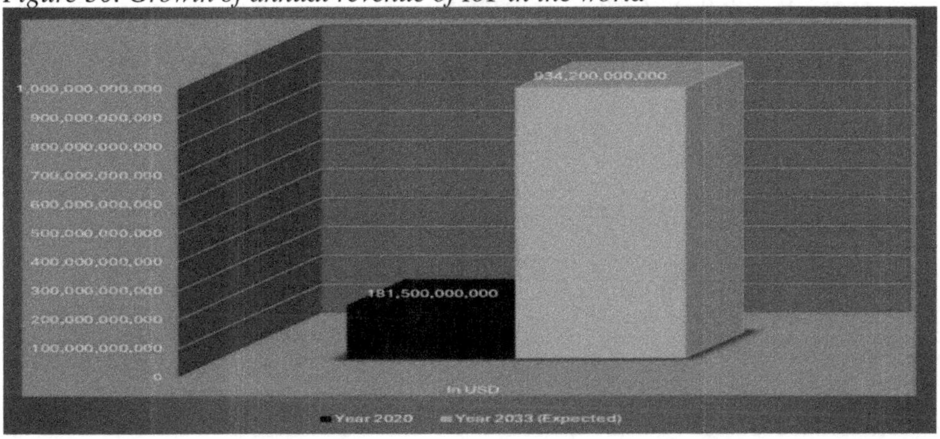

Source. Statista

Figure 31. IoT's market size growth in the world

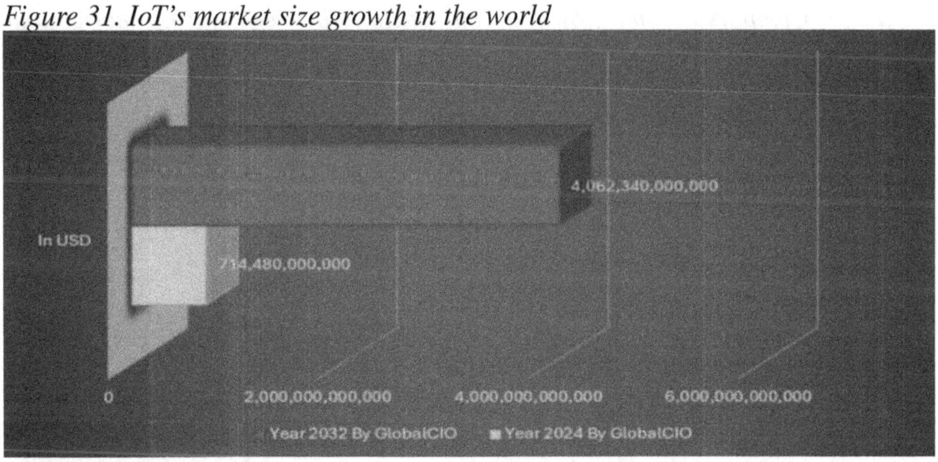

Source. Global CIO

Figure 32. Growth of AIoT software vendors

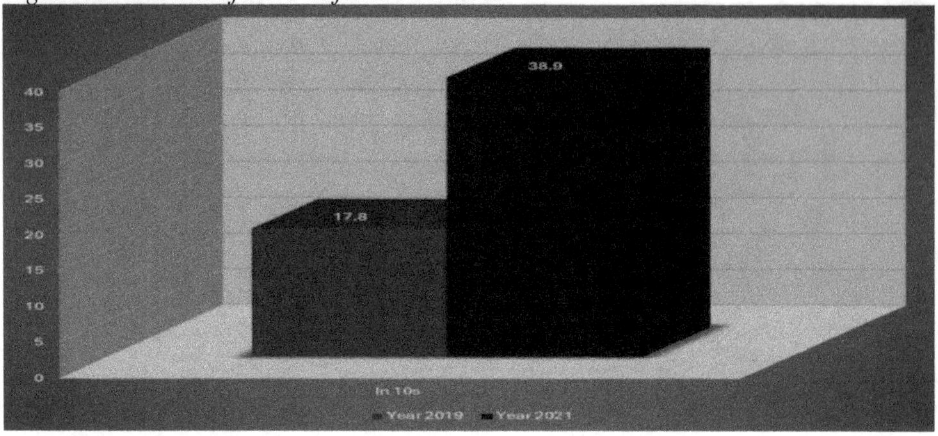

Source. IoT Analytics

Figure 33. Comparison and growth of market share between North America and the rest of the world

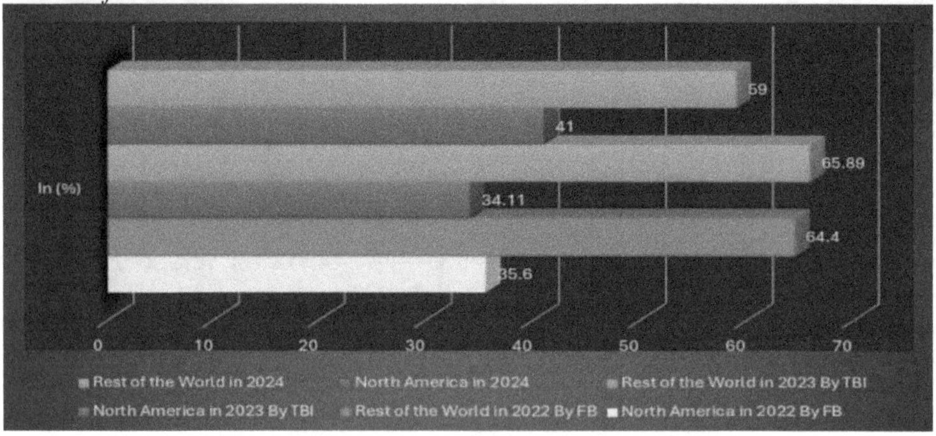

Source. The Brainy Insights, Grand View Research, and Fortune Business Insights

Figure 34. IIoT benefits

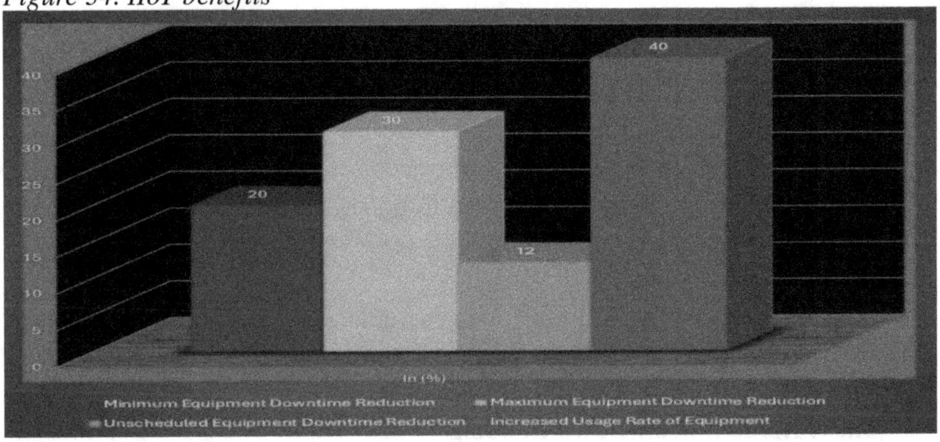

Source. Global CIO

Major Advantages and Challenges of AI as well as IoT in Civil Engineering

In this subsection, the analysis of the above graphs was performed, which are as follows.

- According to Fig. 21, the market value of AIoT in the year 2023 was over USD 5 billion, but by the year 2029, it is expected to grow by over 8 times, and by the year 2023, it is expected to grow by over 22 times. It is safe to say that the AIoT market is growing at a fast rate and has a bright future, meaning it will be wise for Civil Engineers to invest in it to transform their areas.
- Based on Fig. 22, the North American AIoT market is $5.6 billion USD in 2024, and by 2030, it is expected to reach over USD 21 billion, meaning a rise of roughly 4 times over 6 years. This means that the North American continent will continue to dominate the AIoT market, and investment in Civil Engineering areas in the continent might grow further or will be a wise option to do so.
- As per Fig. 23, the software component in AIoT has a market share of 55.31%, meaning the software component has dominated other components in AIoT. It is safe to say that AI will have high demand in the AIoT technology for fast processing and analysis of data, meaning that the technology will be useful for Civil Engineering areas, where not only data collection and transmission is needed, but also fast processing and analysis of data is essential.

- According to Fig. 24, the cloud segment in AIoT had a market share of over 53% in the year 2023, indicating that the cloud segment has more demand than the on-premise ones. This means that the cloud segment could be preferred more in Civil Engineering areas as well because of the lower initial cost than on-premise ones.
- Based on Fig. 25, manufacturing as the end user segment has 35.87% market share in AIoT, the highest compared to other segments, indicating that for Civil Engineering to evolve further, higher investment is required to implement AIoT technology.
- As per Fig. 26, by application, video surveillance has a 27.1% market share in the year 2022, the highest in comparison to other applications in AIoT. This means that it will definitely have higher demand and could be used in Smart Homes, Smart Office Buildings, Smart Highways, and so on in Civil Engineering areas.
- According to Fig. 27, the AIoT devices was around 9 billion in the year 2017, but by this year, 2025, it is expected to reach 55 billion, indicating around a 6 times increase in the number of devices in the span of 8 years. This means that AIoT devices are growing at a tremendous rate and have great demand because of their utility. Then, it is safe to say that in the future, these devices are expected to increase further, meaning that it will be wise to use more such devices in Civil Engineering areas as well, apart from their uses in different fields.
- Based on Fig. 28, Wi-Fi has a 31% share in technology in IoT, the highest compared to other types of technologies, including Bluetooth and cellular phones. This means that at the site, Wi-Fi technology could be given higher preference while implementing IoT networks before other technologies.
- As per Fig. 29, the technological investment in the initiative of Smart Cities in the world was USD 81 billion in the year 2018, and by the year 2023, it reached over USD 189 billion, meaning that the smart city initiative increased by over 2 times in 5 years. This also shows that AIoT technology has good scope and utility in this Smart Cities initiative across the globe.
- According to Fig. 30, the annual revenue of IoT was over USD 181 billion in the year 2020, and by the year 2033, it is expected to reach over $934 billion USD, meaning the annual revenue is expected to increase more than 5 times in 13 years. This means that it will be wise to invest in IoT technology, and the same can be said for Civil Engineering areas to take benefit of it.
- Based on Fig. 31, the market size of IoT was over USD 714 billion in the year 2024, and by the year 2032, it is expected to reach over USD 4 trillion, meaning that the market size of IoT devices is expected to increase by almost 6 times in 8 years. This means that the IoT technology might have more ap-

plications in the future, and several fields might transform considerably with its help. Then, it might be possible to see more applications of IoT technology in Civil Engineering areas, including way more projects than now.

- As per Fig. 32, the major vendors of AIoT were 178 in the year 2019, but by the year 2021, it reached 389, meaning that the vendors of AIoT increased more than twice in the span of 2 years only. It shows that due to the demand and utility of AIoT technology, the significant vendors are increasing rapidly in the world.
- According to Fig. 33, the North American continent had a market share in AIoT technology of over 34% in the year 2022 & 2023, but by 2024, its market share is 41%. Even though the North American continent has been dominating the AIoT market in the world, it is safe to say that despite the technology growing in other parts of the world, the North American continent will continue to dominate the market over the coming years. Then, the implementation of AIoT might be seen more in the Civil Engineering areas in the North American continent in the coming years in comparison to the developing parts of the world.
- Based on Fig. 34, the benefits of IIoT for industries regarding reduction in downtime as well increase in productivity, is eye catching, as IIoT might also be useful for the construction industry similarly. It is safe to say that advanced technologies like AI and IoT will improve the construction industry when implemented.

LIMITATIONS

This chapter discusses some of the major case studies related to the field of Civil Engineering where technologies like AI and IoT were incorporated, but there must be other case studies that might not be covered here. The book chapter focused on the ways AI and IoT technologies were transforming this engineering field. However, other fields have evolved thanks to AIoT, which aren't mentioned in this chapter. In Civil Engineering, the discussed areas that evolved with the above-mentioned technologies could be explained in more detail, which is another limitation of the chapter.

SOLUTIONS AND RECOMMENDATIONS

Technical hindrances will be there while implementing technologies like AI and IoT, but with proper training of people, it is possible to overcome them in the Civil Engineering areas. Then, technological and high initial cost related obstacles could be solved with more research, and with time, the related devices might become cheaper in the future, or the researchers might work to reduce the cost of these devices and systems in the future, which will help in their implementation in projects without worry. The durability problems in the harsh terrain of these sophisticated systems and devices might be solved later on with continuous research. People need to be encouraged and taught to accept as well as adopt these technologies wherever necessary in projects.

FUTURE RESEARCH DIRECTIONS

Research could be done in advancing the area and applications of AI as well as IoT merged together or AIoT, in other words, especially in the Civil Engineering fields. Then, research in the future could be done to make the AIoT systems and devices more durable irrespective of the terrain, including harsh terrain. Then, scientists and researchers might work on making these devices and systems work smoothly in rough weather, which projects naturally often in the world. Further, research could be done in the future to reduce the cost of AIoT systems and devices, which might increase their adoption at a faster rate.

CONCLUSION

This book chapter explained the concept of AI as well as IoT, in addition to AIoT, when the first two technologies are merged. It also mentioned the need behind the adoption of AIoT technology and its uses. Then, the way AI as well as IoT technologies could affect the areas of Civil Engineering was taken into account, and those areas were explained in detail. Then, gaps in the current literature were mentioned in the chapter. Moreover, real-life case studies related to Civil Engineering where advanced technologies like IoT and AI were implemented were discussed, and the challenges and obstacles they faced were covered. The chapter also talked about the issues and problems related to these technologies, and graphical analyses were performed based on the available data to understand the market of AIoT and its future scope, in addition to what it has stored for Civil Engineering areas. By application, video surveillance has a 27.1% market share in the year 2022, the highest in comparison to other applications in AIoT. This means that it will definitely have higher demand and could be used in Smart Homes, Smart Office Buildings, Smart Highways, and so on in Civil Engineering areas. The IoT technology might have more applications in the future, and several fields might transform considerably with its help. Then, it might be possible to see more applications of IoT technology in Civil Engineering areas, including projects way more than now. Even though the North American continent has been dominating the AIoT market in the world, it is safe to say that despite the technology growing in other parts of the world, the North American continent will continue to dominate the market over the coming years. Then, the implementation of AIoT might see more in the Civil Engineering areas in the North American continent in the coming years in comparison to the developing parts of the world. It is safe to say that advanced technologies like AI and IoT will definitely improve the construction industry when implemented.

ACKNOWLEDGEMENT

This research received no specific grant from any funding agency in the public, commercial, or not-for-profit sectors.

REFERENCES

Aljebreen, M., Alabduallah, B., Mahgoub, H., Allafi, R., Hamza, M. A., Ibrahim, S. S., Yaseen, I., & Alsaid, M. I. (2023). Integrating IoT and honey badger algorithm-based ensemble learning for accurate vehicle detection and classification. *Ain Shams Engineering Journal, 14*(11), 102547. DOI: 10.1016/j.asej.2023.102547

Alotaibi, B. S., Shema, A. I., Ibrahim, A. U., Abuhussain, M. A., Abdulmalik, H., Dodo, Y. A., & Atakara, C. (2024). Assimilation of 3D printing, Artificial Intelligence (AI) and Internet of Things (IoT) for the construction of eco-friendly intelligent homes. An explorative review. *Heliyon, 10*(17), e36846. DOI: 10.1016/j.heliyon.2024.e36846 PMID: 39286162

Bhowmik, S., Singh, A., & Misengo, C. (2019). A case study on intelligent transport system using traffic lights. *Our Heritage*, *67*(7), 96–110.

Bibri, S. E., Huang, J., & Krogstie, J. (2024). Artificial intelligence of things for synergizing smarter eco-city brain, metabolism, and platform. Pioneering data-driven environmental governance. *Sustainable Cities and Society*, *108*, 105516. DOI: 10.1016/j.scs.2024.105516

Bibri, S. E., Krogstie, J., Kaboli, A., & Alahi, A. (2024). Smarter eco-cities and their leading-edge artificial intelligence of things solutions for environmental sustainability. A comprehensive systematic review. *Environmental Science and Ecotechnology*, *19*, 100330. DOI: 10.1016/j.ese.2023.100330 PMID: 38021367

Dai, X., Shang, W., Liu, J., Xue, M., & Wang, C. (2023). Achieving better indoor air quality with IoT systems for future buildings. Opportunities and challenges. *The Science of the Total Environment*, *895*, 164858. DOI: 10.1016/j.scitotenv.2023.164858 PMID: 37343873

Dong, J., Meng, W., Liu, Y., & Ti, J. (2021). A framework of pavement management system based on IoT and big data. *Advanced Engineering Informatics*, *47*, 101226. DOI: 10.1016/j.aei.2020.101226

Elrifaee, M., Zayed, T., Ali, E., & Ali, A. H. (2024). IoT Contributions to The Safety of Construction Sites. A Comprehensive Review of Recent Advances, Limitations, And Suggestions for Future Directions. *Internet of Things : Engineering Cyber Physical Human Systems*, •••, 101387.

Essamlali, I., Nhaila, H., & El Khaili, M. (2024). A new architecture of Low Impact Development (LID)-based stormwater management system through Internet of Things (IoT) and Machine Learning integration. *Case Studies in Chemical and Environmental Engineering*, *10*, 100942. DOI: 10.1016/j.cscee.2024.100942

Fan, K., Li, Q., Le, Z., Li, Q., Li, J., & Yan, M. (2024). Harnessing the power of AI and IoT for real-time CO2 emission monitoring. *Heliyon*, *10*(17), e36612. DOI: 10.1016/j.heliyon.2024.e36612 PMID: 39281600

Fortin, L. V., Santos, A. R. V. D., Cagud, P. J. B., Castor, P. R., & Llantos, O. E. (2024). Eyeway. An Artificial Intelligence Of Things Pothole Detection System With Map Visualization. *Procedia Computer Science*, *251*, 216–223. DOI: 10.1016/j.procs.2024.11.103

Fortune Business Insights, https.//www.fortunebusinessinsights.com/artificial-intelligence-of-things-market-107836

Gbadamosi, A.-Q., Oyedele, L. O., Delgado, J. M. D., Kusimo, H., Akanbi, L., Olawale, O., & Muhammed-yakubu, N. (2021). IoT for predictive assets monitoring and maintenance. An implementation strategy for the UK rail industry. *Automation in Construction*, *122*, 103486. DOI: 10.1016/j.autcon.2020.103486

Ghoushchi, S. J., Haghshenas, S. S., Vahabzadeh, S., Guido, G., & Geem, Z. W. (2024). An integrated MCDM approach for enhancing efficiency in connected autonomous vehicles through augmented intelligence and IoT integration. *Results in Engineering*, *23*, 102626. DOI: 10.1016/j.rineng.2024.102626

Giannakidou, S., Radoglou-Grammatikis, P., Lagkas, T., Argyriou, V., Goudos, S., Markakis, E. K., & Sarigiannidis, P. (2024). Leveraging the power of internet of things and artificial intelligence in forest fire prevention, detection, and restoration. A comprehensive survey.[[Global CIO, https.//]. *Internet of Things : Engineering Cyber Physical Human Systems*, *26*, 101171. globalcio.com/articles/main/from-iiot-to-aiot-what-is-the-smart-industrial-internet-of-things/. DOI: 10.1016/j.iot.2024.101171

Grand View Research, https.//www.grandviewresearch.com/industry-analysis/artificial-intelligence-of-things-aiot-market-report

Guo, X., Wang, Y., Mei, S., Shi, C., Liu, Y., Pan, L., Li, K., Zhang, B., Wang, J., Zhong, Z., & Dong, M. (2022). Monitoring and modelling of PM2.5 concentration at subway station construction based on IoT and LSTM algorithm optimization. *Journal of Cleaner Production*, *360*, 132179. DOI: 10.1016/j.jclepro.2022.132179

Hariri-Ardebili, M.A., Mahdavi, G., Nuss, L.K., & Lall, U. (2023). The role of artificial intelligence and digital technologies in dam engineering. Narrative review and outlook. *Engineering Applications of Artificial Intelligence*, Volume 126, Part A, 106813.

He, Z., Wang, Y.-H., & Zhang, J. (2025). Generative AIBIM. An automatic and intelligent structural design pipeline integrating BIM and generative AI. *Information Fusion*, *114*, 102654. DOI: 10.1016/j.inffus.2024.102654

Hostetter, H., Naser, M. Z., Huang, X., & Gales, J. (2024). The role of large language models (AI chatbots) in fire engineering. An examination of technical questions against domain knowledge. *Natural Hazards Review*, *4*(4), 669–688. DOI: 10.1016/j.nhres.2024.06.003

HyScaler, https.//hyscaler.com/insights/ai-in-civil-engineering/.

Intuz, https.//www.intuz.com/blog/use-cases-and-advantages-of-aiot

IoT Analytics, https.//iot-analytics.com/number-connected-iot-devices/.

IoT Analytics, https.//iot-analytics.com/rise-of-industrial-ai-aiot-4-trends-driving-technology-adoption/.

Jayaraman, P., Nagarajan, K. K., Partheeban, P., & Krishnamurthy, V. (2024). Critical review on water quality analysis using IoT and machine learning models. *International Journal of Information Management Data Insights*, *4*(1), 100210. DOI: 10.1016/j.jjimei.2023.100210

Kaginalkar, A., Kumar, S., Gargava, P., & Niyogi, D. (2021). Review of urban computing in air quality management as smart city service. An integrated IoT, AI, and cloud technology perspective. *Urban Climate*, *39*, 100972. DOI: 10.1016/j.uclim.2021.100972

Kapoor, R., Kumar, A., Kumar, A., Kumar, A., & Arora, H. C. (2024). *1 - Artificial intelligence in civil engineering. An immersive view. Artificial Intelligence Applications for Sustainable Construction.* Woodhead Publishing Series in Civil and Structural Engineering.

Kheder, M. Q., & Mohammed, A. A. (2024). Real-time traffic monitoring system using IoT-aided robotics and deep learning techniques. *Kuwait Journal of Science, 51*(1), 100153. DOI: 10.1016/j.kjs.2023.10.017

Lakhouit, A. (2025). Revolutionizing urban solid waste management with AI and IoT. A review of smart solutions for waste collection, sorting, and recycling. *Results in Engineering, 25*, 104018. DOI: 10.1016/j.rineng.2025.104018

Mai, T. G., Nguyen, M., Ghobakhlou, A., Yan, W. Q., Chhun, B., & Nguyen, H. (2024). Decoding a decade. The evolution of artificial intelligence in security, communication, and maintenance within the construction industry. *Automation in Construction*, Volume 165, 105522. MarketsandMarkets, https.//www.marketsandmarkets .com/Market-Reports/ai-in-iot-market-43388726.html

Merit Data and Technology, https.//www.meritdata-tech.com/resources/blog/code -ai/ai-revolution-construction-applications/

Mishra, M., Lourenco, P. B., & Ramana, G. V. (2022). Structural health monitoring of civil engineering structures by using the internet of things. A review. *Journal of Building Engineering, 48*, 103954. DOI: 10.1016/j.jobe.2021.103954

Mohammadi, M., Assaf, G., & Assaad, R. H. (2024). Real-time spatial-temporal mapping and visualization of thermal comfort and HVAC control by integrating immersive augmented reality technologies and IoT-enabled wireless sensor networks. Towards immersive human-building interactions. *Journal of Building Engineering, 94*, 109887. DOI: 10.1016/j.jobe.2024.109887

Mor, N., & Kumar, P. Madhu, Jat, G.L., & Kumar, A. (2024). 2 - Application of artificial intelligence in sustainable construction. A secret eye toward the latest civil engineering techniques. Artificial Intelligence Applications for Sustainable Construction. *Woodhead Publishing Series in Civil and Structural Engineering*, Pages 75-91.

Moudgil, V., Hewage, K., Hussain, S. A., & Sadiq, R. (2023). Integration of IoT in building energy infrastructure. A critical review on challenges and solutions. *Renewable & Sustainable Energy Reviews, 174*, 113121. DOI: 10.1016/j.rser.2022.113121

Mousavi, M., Shen, X., Zhang, Z., Barati, K., & Li, B. (2025). IoT-Bayes fusion. Advancing real-time environmental safety risk monitoring in underground mining and construction. *Reliability Engineering & System Safety, 256*, 110760. DOI: 10.1016/j.ress.2024.110760

Mukhti, J. A., Gucunski, N., & Kee, S.-H. (2024). AI-assisted ultrasonic wave analysis for automated classification of steel corrosion-induced concrete damage. *Automation in Construction*, *167*, 105704. DOI: 10.1016/j.autcon.2024.105704

Naji, K., Gowid, S., & Ghani, S. (2023). AI and IoT-based concrete column base cover localization and degradation detection algorithm using deep learning techniques. *Ain Shams Engineering Journal*, *14*(11), 102520. DOI: 10.1016/j.asej.2023.102520

Nikpour, M., Yousefi, P. B., Jafarzadeh, H., Danesh, K., Shomali, R., Asadi, S., Lonbar, A. G., & Ahmadi, M. (2025). Intelligent energy management with IoT framework in smart cities using intelligent analysis. An application of machine learning methods for complex networks and systems. *Journal of Network and Computer Applications*, Volume 235, 104089. OpenPr, https.//www.openpr.com/news/3847849/global-artificial-intelligence-of-things-aiot-market-to-reach

Pala, G. K., Kesana, N. S., & Gopalapurapu, K. S. (2025). *25 - Advancements in optimizing the quality assurance and crack detection by leveraging the application of emerging artificial intelligence trends for enrichment of civil infrastructure-a recapitulation. Recent Developments and Innovations in the Sustainable Production of Concrete*. Woodhead Publishing Series in Civil and Structural Engineering.

Prabhakar, V. V., Xavier, C. S. B., & Abubeker, K. M. (2023). A Review on Challenges and Solutions in the Implementation of Ai, IoT and Blockchain in Construction Industry. *Materials Today: Proceedings*. Advance online publication. DOI: 10.1016/j.matpr.2023.03.535

Quang, T. V., Doan, D. T., Ngarambe, J., Ghaffarianhoseini, A., Ghaffarianhoseini, A., & Zhang, T. (2025). AI management platform for privacy-preserving indoor air quality control. Review and future directions. *Journal of Building Engineering*, *100*, 111712. DOI: 10.1016/j.jobe.2024.111712

Rangasamy, V., & Yang, J.-B. (2024). The convergence of BIM, AI and IoT. Reshaping the future of prefabricated construction. *Journal of Building Engineering*, *84*, 108606. DOI: 10.1016/j.jobe.2024.108606

Rayabharapu, V. K., Rampur, V., Jyothi, N. M., Tripathi, V., Bhaskar, T., & Glory, K. B. (2022). IOT sensor-based pollution management control technique. *Measurement. Sensors*, *24*, 100513. DOI: 10.1016/j.measen.2022.100513

Sarkar, K., Shiuly, A., & Dhal, K. G. (2024). Revolutionizing concrete analysis. An in-depth survey of AI-powered insights with image-centric approaches on comprehensive quality control, advanced crack detection and concrete property exploration. [[SAS, https.//]. *Construction & Building Materials*, *411*, 134212. www.sas.com/en_in/explore/resources/aiot.html. DOI: 10.1016/j.conbuildmat.2023.134212

Severino, F., Canciani, A., Felicioli, C., Gervasi, V., Pelosi, A., Natali, A., Salvatore, W., & Russo, S. (2024). Trustworthy AI for infrastructure monitoring. a blockchain-based approach. *Procedia Structural Integrity*, *62*, 276–284. DOI: 10.1016/j.prostr.2024.09.043

Seyyedi, S. R., Kowsari, E., Gheibi, M., Chinnappan, A., & Ramakrishna, S. (2024). A comprehensive review integration of digitalization and circular economy in waste management by adopting artificial intelligence approaches. Towards a simulation model. *Journal of Cleaner Production*, *460*, 142584. DOI: 10.1016/j.jclepro.2024.142584

Shaharuddin, S., Maulud, K. N. A., Rahman, S. A. F. S. A., Ani, A. I. C., & Pradhan, B. (2023). The role of IoT sensor in smart building context for indoor fire hazard scenario. A systematic review of interdisciplinary articles. *Internet of Things : Engineering Cyber Physical Human Systems*, *22*, 100803. DOI: 10.1016/j.iot.2023.100803

Singh, A. (2018). Use of Geographical Information System in Intelligent Transport. *International Journal of Research and Analytical Reviews*, *5*(4), 882–890.

Singh, A. (2022). Importance of Fuzzy Logic in Traffic and Transportation Engineering. In. Vasant, P., Zelinka, I., Weber, GW. (eds) Intelligent Computing & Optimization. ICO 2021. Lecture Notes in Networks and Systems, vol 371. Springer, Cham. https.//DOI: 10.1007/978-3-030-93247-3_10

Singh, A. (2023). The Present and Future Role of Artificial Intelligence in the Promotion of Sustainable Practices in the Construction Sector. In. Kahraman, C., Sari, I.U., Oztaysi, B., Cebi, S., Cevik Onar, S., Tolga, A.Ç. (eds) Intelligent and Fuzzy Systems. INFUS 2023. Lecture Notes in Networks and Systems, vol 759. Springer, Cham. https.//DOI: 10.1007/978-3-031-39777-6_2

Singh, A. (2023). The Recent Trend of Artificial Neural Network in the Field of Civil Engineering. In. Vasant, P., *et al.* Intelligent Computing and Optimization. ICO 2023. Lecture Notes in Networks and Systems, vol 855. Springer, Cham. https.// DOI: 10.1007/978-3-031-50158-6_32

Singh, A. (2024). The Current Status and Scope of Smart Highways in India. In L. Taha & S. Anwar (Eds.), *Principles and Applications in Speed Sensing and Energy Harvesting for Smart Roads* (pp. 1-41). IGI Global Scientific Publishing. https.// DOI: 10.4018/978-1-6684-9214-7.ch001

Singh, A. (2025). Chapter 7 The role of supply chain management in the construction industry. In P. Vasant, J. Thomas, V. Panchenko & G. Weber (Ed.), Smart Green Energy Production (pp. 95-120). Berlin, Boston. De Gruyter. https.//DOI: 10.1515/9783110717655-007

Singh, A., & Srivastava, A. (2024). Impact of Artificial Intelligence Techniques and Green AI Applications. In *Artificial Intelligence Techniques for Sustainable Development* (pp. 44-63). CRC Press. http.//DOI: 10.1201/9781003546382-3

Songhorabadi, M., Rahimi, M., Farid, A. M. M., & Kashani, M. H. (2023). Fog computing approaches in IoT-enabled smart cities.[[Sphere, https.//]. *Journal of Network and Computer Applications*, *211*, 103557. www.sphereinc.com/blogs/ai-and-iot-in-construction-unlocking-the-value/. DOI: 10.1016/j.jnca.2022.103557

Statista, https.//www.statista.com/statistics/1194709/iot-revenue-worldwide/

Statista, https.//www.statista.com/statistics/884092/worldwide-spending-smart-city-initiatives/

Tariq, M. U. (2025). Integrating Digital Technologies to Optimize Sustainable Supply Chains. In E. Koç (Ed.), *Developing Dynamic and Sustainable Supply Chains to Achieve Sustainable Development Goals* (pp. 33-64). IGI Global Scientific Publishing. https.//DOI: 10.4018/979-8-3693-6284-6.ch002

Tariq, M. U. (2025). Navigating the Convergence of IoMT and Generative AI in Global Healthcare. Opportunities, Challenges, and Ethical Considerations. In V. Kumar, P. Katina, & J. Zhao (Eds.), *Convergence of Internet of Medical Things (IoMT) and Generative AI* (pp. 513-534). IGI Global Scientific Publishing. https.// DOI: 10.4018/979-8-3693-6180-1.ch022

Tariq, M. U. (2025). Leveraging Artificial Intelligence to Enhance Diversity and Drive Business Innovation. In H. Margaretha van der Poll, J. Andrew van der Poll, & C. Ngwakwe (Eds.), *Diversity, AI, and Sustainability for Financial Growth* (pp. 79-96). IGI Global Scientific Publishing. https.//DOI: 10.4018/979-8-3693-6011-8.ch004

Tariq, M. U. (2025). Integrating Theory and Practice. Transformative Approaches in Practice-Led Research for Professional Development. In S. Kwok, P. Yu, & J. Le Corre (Eds.), *Exploring Practice-Led Research for Professional Development* (pp. 419-436). IGI Global Scientific Publishing. https.//DOI: 10.4018/979-8-3693-6376-8.ch016

Tariq, M. U. (2025). AI-Powered Breakthroughs. Revolutionizing Cognitive Psychology and Neuropsychology With Machine Learning. In R. Bansal, T. Maqableh, G. Shuklaa, F. Rabby, & R. Lathabhavan (Eds.), *Transforming Neuropsychology and Cognitive Psychology With AI and Machine Learning* (pp. 65-92). IGI Global Scientific Publishing. https.//DOI: 10.4018/979-8-3693-9341-3.ch003

TechTarget, https.//www.techtarget.com/iotagenda/definition/Artificial-Intelligence-of-Things-AIoT

Thakur, P., Goel, S., & Puthooran, E. (2024). Edge AI Enabled IoT Framework for Secure Smart Home Infrastructure. *Procedia Computer Science*, *235*, 3369–3378. DOI: 10.1016/j.procs.2024.04.317

The Brainy Insights, https.//www.thebrainyinsights.com/report/aiot-platforms-market-14367?srsltid=AfmBOor0tJ9wZ74FHeGYHiARfVYpInZ35zOHRjpYg9S7C6vKLjes5SAF

Ushakov, D., Dudukalov, E., Kozlova, E., & Shatila, K. (2022). The Internet of Things impact on smart public transportation. *Transportation Research Procedia*, *63*, 2392–2400. DOI: 10.1016/j.trpro.2022.06.275

Viso Suite, https.//viso.ai/edge-ai/artificial-intelligence-of-things-aiot/.

Wang, B., Dabbaghjamanesh, M., Kavousi-Fard, A., & Yue, Y. (2024). AI-enhanced multi-stage learning-to-learning approach for secure smart cities load management in IoT networks. *Ad Hoc Networks*, *164*, 103628. DOI: 10.1016/j.adhoc.2024.103628

Waqar, A. (2024). Intelligent decision support systems in construction engineering. An artificial intelligence and machine learning approaches. *Expert Systems with Applications*, Volume 249, Part A, 123503.

Wettewa, S., Hou, L., & Zhang, G. (2024). Graph Neural Networks for building and civil infrastructure operation and maintenance enhancement. *Advanced Engineering Informatics*, Volume 62, Part D, 102868. Wikimedia, https.//commons.wikimedia.org/wiki/File.London_City_Airport_-_geograph.org.uk_-_6895772.jpg

KEY TERMS AND DEFINTIONS

AIoT (Artificial Intelligence of Things): The integration of Artificial Intelligence with the Internet of Things to enable data-driven insights and autonomous decision-making.

Edge-based AIoT System: An AIoT architecture where data is processed locally near the source device to reduce latency and improve real-time responsiveness.

Cloud-based AIoT System: A system where IoT devices send data to cloud platforms for centralised processing, storage, and analytics via AI.

Predictive Maintenance: The use of AIoT technologies to anticipate equipment failures and schedule maintenance before breakdowns occur.

Structural Health Monitoring (SHM): An AIoT-enabled process of continuously assessing the condition of infrastructure through real-time sensor data analysis.

Compilation of References

Abbasi, R., Martinez, P., & Ahmad, R. (2022). The digitization of the agricultural industry–a systematic literature review on agriculture 4.0. *Smart Agricultural Technology*, *2*, 100042. DOI: 10.1016/j.atech.2022.100042

Abd Razak, S., Nazari, N. H. M., & Al-Dhaqm, A. (2020). Data anonymization using a pseudonym system to preserve data privacy. *IEEE Access : Practical Innovations, Open Solutions*, *8*, 43256–43264. DOI: 10.1109/ACCESS.2020.2977117

Abduljabbar, R., Dia, H., & Kwok, S. R. (2019). AI empowers conservation biology. *Nature*, *567*(7746), 133–135. DOI: 10.1038/d41586-019-00746-1 PMID: 30833739

Abduljabbar, R., Dia, H., Liyanage, S., & Bagloee, S. A. (2019). Applications of artificial intelligence in transport: An overview. *Sustainability (Basel)*, *11*(1), 189. DOI: 10.3390/su11010189

Abed, A. K., & Anupam, A. (2022). Review of security issues in the Internet of Things and artificial intelligence-driven solutions. *Security and Privacy*, *6*(3), e285. DOI: 10.1002/spy2.285

Abuladel, A., & Bamasag, O. (2020). Data and location privacy issues in IoT applications. *2020 3rd International Conference on Computer Applications & Information Security (ICCAIS)*, Riyadh, Saudi Arabia, 2020, pp. 1-6. https://doi.org/ DOI: 10.1109/ICCAIS48893.2020.9096837

Abusukhon, A. (2023). IOT bracelets for guiding blind people in an indoor environment. *Journal of Communications Software and Systems*, *19*(2), 114–125. DOI: 10.24138/jcomss-2022-0160

Aceto, G., Persico, V., & Pescapé, A. (2019). A survey on information and communication technologies for industry 4.0: State-of-the-art, taxonomies, perspectives, and challenges. *IEEE Communications Surveys and Tutorials*, *21*(4), 3467–3501. DOI: 10.1109/COMST.2019.2938259

Adapa, S., Fazal-e-Hasan, S. M., Makam, S. B., Azeem, M. M., & Mortimer, G. (2020). Examining the antecedents and consequences of perceived shopping value through smart retail technology. *Journal of Retailing and Consumer Services*, *52*, 101901. DOI: 10.1016/j.jretconser.2019.101901

Adkar, N., Talele, A., Mundhe, C., & Gunjal, A. (2018, February). Bluetooth beacon applications in the retail market. In *2018 International Conference On Advances in Communication and Computing Technology (ICACCT)* (pp. 225-229). IEEE. DOI: 10.1109/ICACCT.2018.8529470

Adli, H. K., Remli, M. A., Wan Salihin Wong, K. N. S., Ismail, N. A., González-Briones, A., Corchado, J. M., & Mohamad, M. S. (2023). Recent Advancements and Challenges of AIoT Application in Smart Agriculture: A Review. *Sensors (Basel)*, *23*(7), 3752. DOI: 10.3390/s23073752 PMID: 37050812

Afzal, M. K., Zikria, Y. B., Mumtaz, S., Rayes, A., Al-Dulaimi, A., & Guizani, M. (2018). Unlocking 5G spectrum potential for intelligent IoT: Opportunities, challenges, and solutions. *IEEE Communications Magazine*, *56*(10), 92–93. DOI: 10.1109/MCOM.2018.8493125

Afzal, M., Sah, A. K., Agarwal, S., Tanzeel, A., Elshaikh, R. H., Alobeidli, F. A., Alfeel, A. H., Choudhary, R. K., & Choudhary, A. (2024). Advancements in the treatment of autoimmune diseases: Integrating artificial intelligence for personalized medicine. *Trends in Immunotherapy*, *8*(2), 8970. DOI: 10.24294/ti8970

Ahmad, S., Arya, S. K., Gupta, S., Singh, P., & Dwivedi, S. K. (2023, May). Study of Cryptographic Techniques Adopted in Blockchain. In *2023 4th International Conference on Intelligent Engineering and Management (ICIEM)* (pp. 1-6). IEEE. DOI: 10.1109/ICIEM59379.2023.10166591

Ahmad, B., Syed, J. S., Shah, M. A., Khan, M., Khan, A., Hasnain, B., & Mumtaz, T. (2022). Security threats and research challenges of IoT -. *RE:view*, 1–10. Advance online publication. DOI: 10.1109/ICETECC56662.2022.10069706

Ahmed, E., Islam, A., Ashraf, M., Chowdhury, A. I., & Rahman, M. M. (2020). Internet of Things (IoT): Vulnerabilities, security concerns and things to consider. https://doi.org/DOI: 10.1109/ICCCNT49239.2020.9225283

Ahmed, S., ... (2022). An intelligent and multi-functional stick for blind people using IoT. In *2022 3rd International Conference on Intelligent Engineering and Management (ICIEM)*. IEEE. DOI: 10.1109/ICIEM54221.2022.9853012

Ahmed, F. (2017). An Internet of Things (IoT) application for predicting the quantity of future heart attack patients. *International Journal of Computer Applications*, *164*(6), 36–40. DOI: 10.5120/ijca2017913773

Ahmed, K., Dubey, M. K., Kumar, A., & Dubey, S. (2024). Artificial intelligence and IoT driven system architecture for municipality waste management in Smart Cities: A review. *Measurement. Sensors*, *101395*, 101395. Advance online publication. DOI: 10.1016/j.measen.2024.101395

Ahvar, E., Ahvar, S., & Lee, G. M. (2023). Artificial Intelligence of Things: Architectures, Applications, and Challenges. *Springer Handbook of Internet of Things*, 443-462.

Ahvenniemi, H., Huovila, A., Pinto-Seppä, I., & Airaksinen, M. (2017). What are the differences between sustainable and smart cities? *Cities (London, England)*, *60*, 234–245. DOI: 10.1016/j.cities.2016.09.009

Al Hossain, F., Lover, A. A., Corey, G. A., Reich, N. G., & Rahman, T. (2020). FluSense: A contactless syndromic surveillance platform for influenza-like illness in hospital waiting areas. *Proceedings of the ACM on Interactive, Mobile, Wearable and Ubiquitous Technologies*, *4*(1), 1–28. DOI: 10.1145/3381014 PMID: 35846237

Alaba, F. A. (2024). Definition of IoT. In *Internet of Things: A Case Study in Africa* (pp. 19–40). Springer Nature Switzerland. DOI: 10.1007/978-3-031-67984-1_2

Alaba, F. A., Othman, M., Hashem, I. A. T., & Alotaibi, F. (2017). Internet of Things security: A survey. *Journal of Network and Computer Applications*, *88*, 10–28. DOI: 10.1016/j.jnca.2017.04.002

Alagasan, K., Alkawaz, M. H., Iqbal Hajamydeen, A., & Mohammed, M. N. (2021). A review paper on advanced attendance and monitoring systems. In *2021 IEEE 12th Control and System Graduate Research Colloquium (ICSGRC)* (pp. 195–200). https://doi.org/DOI: 10.1109/ICSGRC53186.2021.9515249

Alahi, M. E. E., Sukkuea, A., Tina, F. W., Nag, A., Kurdthongmee, W., Suwannarat, K., & Mukhopadhyay, S. C. (2023). Integration of IoT-enabled technologies and artificial intelligence (AI). for smart city scenario: Recent advancements and future trends. *Sensors (Basel)*, *23*(11), 5206. DOI: 10.3390/s23115206 PMID: 37299934

Alam, T., & Gupta, R. (2022). Federated learning and its role in the privacy preservation of IoT devices. *Future Internet*, *14*(9), 246. Advance online publication. DOI: 10.3390/fi14090246

Albahri, A. S., Duhaim, A. M., Fadhel, M. A., Alnoor, A., Baqer, N. S., Alzubaidi, L., Albahri, O. S., Alamoodi, A. H., Bai, J., Salhi, A., Santamaría, J., Ouyang, C., Gupta, A., Gu, Y., & Deveci, M. (2023). A systematic review of trustworthy and explainable artificial intelligence in healthcare: Assessment of quality, bias risk, and data fusion. *Information Fusion*, *96*, 156–191. DOI: 10.1016/j.inffus.2023.03.008

Albino, V., Berardi, U., & Dangelico, R. M. (2015). Smart cities: Definitions, dimensions, performance, and initiatives. *Journal of Urban Technology*, *22*(1), 3–21. DOI: 10.1080/10630732.2014.942092

Albouq, S. S., Abi Sen, A. A., Almashf, N., Yamin, M., Alshanqiti, A., & Bahbouh, N. M. (2022). A survey of interoperability challenges and solutions for dealing with them in IoT environment. *IEEE Access : Practical Innovations, Open Solutions*, *10*, 36416–36428. DOI: 10.1109/ACCESS.2022.3162219

Albraheem, L., Alajlan, H., Aljenedal, N., Alkhair, L. A., & Gwead, S. B. (2023). An IoT-based smart plug energy monitoring system. *International Journal of Advanced Computer Science and Applications*, *14*(10). Advance online publication. DOI: 10.14569/IJACSA.2023.0141038

Aldowah, H., Ul Rehman, S., Ghazal, S., & Naufal Umar, I. (2017). Internet of things in higher education: A study on future learning. *Journal of Physics: Conference Series*, *892*, 012017. DOI: 10.1088/1742-6596/892/1/012017

Alghofaili, Y., Albattah, A., Alrajeh, N., Rassam, M. A., & Al-rimy, B. A. (2021). Secure cloud infrastructure: A survey on issues, current solutions, and open challenges. *Applied Sciences (Basel, Switzerland)*, *11*(19), 9005. DOI: 10.3390/app11199005

Ali, Z. H., Ali, H. A., & Badawy, M. M. (2015). Internet of Things (IoT): Definitions, challenges and recent research directions. *International Journal of Computer Applications*, *128*(1), 37–47. DOI: 10.5120/ijca2015906430

Aljebreen, M., Alabduallah, B., Mahgoub, H., Allafi, R., Hamza, M. A., Ibrahim, S. S., Yaseen, I., & Alsaid, M. I. (2023). Integrating IoT and honey badger algorithm-based ensemble learning for accurate vehicle detection and classification. *Ain Shams Engineering Journal*, *14*(11), 102547. DOI: 10.1016/j.asej.2023.102547

Allioui, H., & Mourdi, Y. (2023). Exploring the full potentials of IoT for better financial growth and stability: A comprehensive survey. *Sensors (Basel)*, *23*(19), 8015. DOI: 10.3390/s23198015 PMID: 37836845

Allmendinger, R. W., Siron, C. R., & Scott, C. P. (2017). Structural data collection with mobile devices: Accuracy, redundancy, and best practices. *Journal of Structural Geology*, *102*, 98–112. DOI: 10.1016/j.jsg.2017.07.011

Almada-Lobo, F. (2015). The Industry 4.0 revolution and the future of Manufacturing Execution Systems (MES). *Journal of innovation management, 3*(4), 16-21.

Almotairi, K. H. (2023). Application of Internet of Things in healthcare domain. *Journal of Umm Al-Qura University for Engineering and Architecture, 14*(1), 1–12. DOI: 10.1007/s43995-022-00008-8

Alotaibi, B. S., Shema, A. I., Ibrahim, A. U., Abuhussain, M. A., Abdulmalik, H., Dodo, Y. A., & Atakara, C. (2024). Assimilation of 3D printing, Artificial Intelligence (AI) and Internet of Things (IoT) for the construction of eco-friendly intelligent homes. An explorative review. *Heliyon, 10*(17), e36846. DOI: 10.1016/j.heliyon.2024.e36846 PMID: 39286162

Alowais, S. A., Alghamdi, S. S., Alsuhebany, N., Alqahtani, T., Alshaya, A. I., Almohareb, S. N., Aldairem, A., Alrashed, M., Saleh, K. B., Badreldin, H. A., Yami, M. S. A., Harbi, S. A., & Albekairy, A. M. (2023). Revolutionizing healthcare: The role of artificial intelligence in clinical practice. *BMC Medical Education, 23*(1), 689. Advance online publication. DOI: 10.1186/s12909-023-04698-z PMID: 37740191

Alzoubi, Y. I., Al-Ahmad, A. S., Kahtan, H., & Jaradat, A. (2022). Internet of Things and blockchain integration: Security, privacy, technical, and design challenges. *Future Internet, 14*(7), 216. Advance online publication. DOI: 10.3390/fi14070216

Anayat, S., & Rasool, G. (2022). Artificial intelligence marketing (AIM): Connecting-the-dots using bibliometrics. *Journal of Marketing Theory and Practice*, •••, 1 22.

Anderson, M. M. (2024). AI as Philosophical Ideology: A Critical Look Back at John McCarthy's Program. *Philosophy & Technology, 37*(2), 44. DOI: 10.1007/s13347-024-00731-1

Antico, T. M., Moreira, L. F. R., & Moreira, R. (2024). Evaluating the potential of federated learning for maize leaf disease prediction. *arXiv preprint arXiv:2412.07872*.

Anubha, A., & Shome, S. (2021). Intentions to use travel eWOM: Mediating role of Indian urban millennials' attitude. *International Journal of Tourism Cities, 7*(3), 640–661. DOI: 10.1108/IJTC-04-2020-0073

Ao, W., Fu, S., Zhang, C., Huang, Y., & Xia, F. (2019). A secure identity authentication scheme based on blockchain and identity-based cryptography. In Proceedings of *2019 IEEE 2nd International Conference on Computer and Communication Engineering Technology (CCET),* Beijing, China. DOI: 10.1109/CCET48361.2019.8989361

Aouedi, O., Vu, T. H., Sacco, A., Nguyen, D. C., Piamrat, K., Marchetto, G., & Pham, Q. V. (2024). A survey on intelligent Internet of Things: Applications, security, privacy, and future directions. *IEEE Communications Surveys and Tutorials*, 1. DOI: 10.1109/COMST.2024.3430368

Apanavičienė, R., & Shahrabani, M. M. N. (2023). Key factors affecting smart building integration into smart city: Technological aspects. *Smart Cities*, *6*(4), 1832–1857. DOI: 10.3390/smartcities6040085

Araújo, S. O., Peres, R. S., Barata, J., Lidon, F., & Ramalho, J. C. (2021). Characterising the agriculture 4.0 landscape—Emerging trends, challenges and opportunities. *Agronomy (Basel)*, *11*(4), 667. DOI: 10.3390/agronomy11040667

Arena, F., Collotta, M., Pau, G., & Termine, F. (2022). An overview of augmented reality. *Computers*, *11*(2), 28. DOI: 10.3390/computers11020028

Arowolo, M. E., Aaron, W. C., Eteng, U. S., Divine, I. L. O. H., Aguma, C. P., & Olagunju, A. O.Modupe Ebunoluwa ArowoloWilliam Clement AaronAdeniyi olusegun kugbiyiUbi Solomon EtengDivine ILOHChimaoge Peace AgumaAdeyemi Oyetoro Olagunju. (2024). Integrating AI enhanced remote sensing technologies with IOT networks for precision environmental monitoring and predicative ecosystem management. *World Journal of Advanced Research and Reviews*, *23*(2), 2156–2166. DOI: 10.30574/wjarr.2024.23.2.2573

Arsenyan, J., & Piepenbrink, A. (2023). Artificial intelligence research in management: A computational literature review. *IEEE Transactions on Engineering Management*, *71*, 2088–5100.

Aslam, A., Qureshi, K. N., & Newe, T. (2024). Future Privacy and Trust Challenges for AIoT Networks. In *Artificial Intelligence of Things (AIoT)* (pp. 198–216). CRC Press. DOI: 10.1201/9781003430018-14

Augustin, A., Yi, J., Clausen, T., & Townsley, W. (2016). A Study of LoRa: Long Range & Low Power Networks for the Internet of Things. *Sensors (Basel)*, *16*(9), 1466. DOI: 10.3390/s16091466 PMID: 27618064

Awaisi, K. S., Ye, Q., & Sampalli, S (2024). A Survey of Industrial AIoT: Opportunities, Challenges, and Directions. IEEE Access.

Awaisi, K. S., Ye, Q., & Sampalli, S. (2024). A Survey of Industrial AIoT: Opportunities, Challenges, and Directions. *IEEE Access : Practical Innovations, Open Solutions*, *12*, 96946–96996. DOI: 10.1109/ACCESS.2024.3426279

Ayaz, M., Ammad-Uddin, M., Sharif, Z., Mansour, A., & Aggoune, E. H. M. (2019). Internet-of-Things (IoT)-based smart agriculture: Toward making the fields talk. *IEEE Access : Practical Innovations, Open Solutions*, *7*, 129551–129583. DOI: 10.1109/ACCESS.2019.2932609

Azimi, I., Pahikkala, T., Rahmani, A. M., Niela-Vilén, H., Axelin, A., & Liljeberg, P. (2019). Missing data resilient decision-making for healthcare IoT through personalization: A case study on maternal health. *Future Generation Computer Systems*, *96*, 297–308. DOI: 10.1016/j.future.2019.02.015

Badr, Y., Zhu, X., & Naser, M. (2021). Security and privacy in the Internet of Things: Threats and challenges. https://doi.org/DOI: 10.1007/s11761-021-00327-z

Badshah, A., Ghani, A., Daud, A., Jalal, A., Bilal, M., & Crowcroft, J. (2023). Towards smart education through Internet of Things: A survey. *ACM Computing Surveys*, *56*(2), 1–33. DOI: 10.1145/3610401

Bahrin, M. A. K., Othman, M. F., Azli, N. H. N., & Talib, M. F. (2016). Industry 4.0: A review on industrial automation and robotics. *Jurnal Teknologi*, *78*, 6–13.

Bai, X., Cheng, Z., Duan, Z., & Hu, K. (2018). Formal modeling and verification of smart contracts. In *Proceedings of the 2018 7th International Conference on Software and Computer Applications,* Kuantan, Malaysia. DOI: 10.1145/3185089.3185138

Bajic, B., Suzic, N., Moraca, S., Stefanović, M., Jovicic, M., & Rikalovic, A. (2023). Edge computing data optimization for smart quality management: Industry 5.0 perspective. *Sustainability (Basel)*, *15*(7), 6032. DOI: 10.3390/su15076032

Baker, S., & Xiang, W. (2023). Artificial intelligence of things for smarter healthcare: A survey of advancements, challenges, and opportunities. *IEEE Communications Surveys and Tutorials*, *25*(2), 1261–1293. DOI: 10.1109/COMST.2023.3256323

Balaram, V. (2019). Rare earth elements: A review of applications, occurrence, exploration, analysis, recycling, and environmental impact. *Geoscience Frontiers*, *10*(4), 1285–1303. DOI: 10.1016/j.gsf.2018.12.005

Baligodugula, V. V., Ghimire, A., & Amsaad, F. (2024). An overview of secure network segmentation in connected IIoT environments. *Computing & AI Connect*, *1*(1), 1–12. DOI: 10.69709/CAIC.2024.193182

Balogh, S., Gallo, O., Ploszek, R., Špaček, P., & Zajac, P. (2021). IoT Security Challenges: Cloud and Blockchain, Postquantum Cryptography, and Evolutionary Techniques. *Electronics (Basel)*, *10*(21), 2647. DOI: 10.3390/electronics10212647

Bansal, G. (2016). Distinguishing between privacy and security concerns: An empirical examination and scale validation. *Journal of Computer Information Systems*, *57*(4), 330–343. DOI: 10.1080/08874417.2016.1232981

Barani, B. S., Pandey, A., Abiko, A. T., Vijaykumar, J., Rastogi, U., Genale, A. H., & Karthika, P. (2022). Analysis of machine learning data security in the Internet of Things (IoT) circumstance. https://doi.org/DOI: 10.1007/978-981-16-2126-0_20

Barann, B., Betzing, J. H., Niemann, M., Hoffmeister, B., & Becker, J. (2022). Exploring customers' likeliness to use e-service touchpoints in brick and mortar retail. *Electronic Markets*, *32*(2), 1–23. DOI: 10.1007/s12525-020-00445-0

Barns, S. (2018). Smart cities and urban data platforms: Designing interfaces for smart governance. *City, Culture and Society*, *12*, 5–12. DOI: 10.1016/j.ccs.2017.09.006

Barto, A. G. (2012). *Intrinsic motivation and reinforcement learning*. https://people.cs.umass.edu/~barto/IMCleVer-chapter-totypeset2.pdf

Batty, M., Axhausen, K. W., Giannotti, F., Pozdnoukhov, A., Bazzani, A., Wachowicz, M., & Portugali, Y. (2012). Smart cities of the future. *The European Physical Journal. Special Topics*, *214*(1), 481–518. DOI: 10.1140/epjst/e2012-01703-3

Bauer, C., Dohmen, P., & Strauss, C. (2011, September). Interactive digital signage-an innovative service and its future strategies. In *2011 International Conference on Emerging Intelligent Data and Web Technologies* (pp. 137-142). IEEE. DOI: 10.1109/EIDWT.2011.29

Bauer, C., Garaus, M., Strauss, C., & Wagner, U. (2018). Research directions for digital signage systems in retail. *Procedia Computer Science*, *141*, 503–506. DOI: 10.1016/j.procs.2018.10.135

Belenguer, L. (2022). AI bias: Exploring discriminatory algorithmic decision-making models and the application of possible machine-centric solutions adapted from the pharmaceutical industry. *AI and Ethics*, *2*(4), 771–787. DOI: 10.1007/s43681-022-00138-8 PMID: 35194591

Bender, E. M., Gebru, T., McMillan-Major, A., & Shmitchell, S. (2021, March). On the dangers of stochastic parrots: Can language models be too big? In *Proceedings of the 2021 ACM conference on fairness, accountability, and transparency* (pp. 610-623). DOI: 10.1145/3442188.3445922

Bera, B., Das, A. K., Obaidat, M. S., Vijayakumar, P., Hsiao, K., & Park, Y. (2021). AI-enabled blockchain-based access control for malicious attacks detection and mitigation in IoE. *IEEE Consumer Electronics Magazine*, *10*(5), 82–92. DOI: 10.1109/MCE.2020.3040541

Bergmann, J., Bott, O. J., Pretschner, D. P., & Haux, R. (2007). An e-consent-based shared EHR system architecture for integrated healthcare networks. *International Journal of Medical Informatics*, *76*(2-3), 130–136. DOI: 10.1016/j.ijmedinf.2006.07.013 PMID: 16971171

Bernardo, M. D. R. M. (2019). Smart city governance: From e-government to smart governance. In *Smart cities and smart spaces: Concepts, methodologies, tools, and applications* (pp. 196–232). IGI Global. DOI: 10.4018/978-1-5225-7030-1.ch009

Bessen, J. (2019). *AI and jobs: The role of demand.* National Bureau of Economic Research., DOI: 10.3386/w24235

Bharadwaj, H. K., Agarwal, A., Chamola, V., Lakkaniga, N. R., Hassija, V., Guizani, M., & Sikdar, B. (2021). A review on the role of machine learning in enabling IoT based healthcare applications. *IEEE Access : Practical Innovations, Open Solutions*, *9*, 38859–38890. DOI: 10.1109/ACCESS.2021.3059858

Bhardwaj, A., Subramanyam, G., Avasthi, V., & Sastry, H. (2016). Review of solutions for securing end user data over cloud applications. *International Journal of Advanced Computer Research*, *6*(27), 222–229. DOI: 10.19101/IJACR.2016.626005

Bhatia, G., Joshi, N., Iyengar, S., Rajpal, S., & Mahadevan, K. (2021). Crop Prediction Based on Environmental Conditions and Disease Prediction. In *Information and Communication Technology for Intelligent Systems:Proceedings of ICTIS 2020*, Volume 1 (pp. 335-344). Springer Singapore. DOI: 10.1007/978-981-15-7078-0_31

Bhise, A., Munshi, A., Rodrigues, A., & Sawant, V. (2022). Overview of AI in education. In *Artificial Intelligence in Higher Education* (pp. 31–62). https://doi.org/ DOI: 10.1201/9781003184157-2

Bhowmik, S., Singh, A., & Misengo, C. (2019). A case study on intelligent transport system using traffic lights. *Our Heritage*, *67*(7), 96–110.

Bibri, S. E., Alexandre, A., Sharifi, A., & Krogstie, J. (2023). Environmentally sustainable smart cities and their converging AI, IoT, and big data technologies and solutions: An integrated approach to an extensive literature review. *Energy Informatics*, *6*(1), 9. DOI: 10.1186/s42162-023-00259-2 PMID: 37032812

Bibri, S. E., Huang, J., Jagatheesaperumal, S. K., & Krogstie, J. (2024). The synergistic interplay of artificial intelligence and digital twin in environmentally planning sustainable smart cities: A comprehensive systematic review. *Environmental Science and Ecotechnology*, *20*, 100433. DOI: 10.1016/j.ese.2024.100433 PMID: 38831974

Bibri, S. E., Huang, J., & Krogstie, J. (2024). Artificial intelligence of things for synergizing smarter eco-city brain, metabolism, and platform. Pioneering data-driven environmental governance. *Sustainable Cities and Society*, *108*, 105516. DOI: 10.1016/j.scs.2024.105516

Bibri, S. E., Krogstie, J., Kaboli, A., & Alahi, A. (2024). Smarter eco-cities and their leading-edge artificial intelligence of things solutions for environmental sustainability: A comprehensive systematic review. *Environmental Science and Ecotechnology*, *19*, 100330. DOI: 10.1016/j.ese.2023.100330 PMID: 38021367

Biswas, D., Dutta, A., Ghosh, S., & Roy, P. (2024). Future trends and significant solutions for intelligent computing resource management. In *Computational Intelligence for Green Cloud Computing and Digital Waste Management* (pp. 187–208). IGI Global. DOI: 10.4018/979-8-3693-1552-1.ch010

Blanco-Carmona, P., Baeza-Moreno, L., Hidalgo-Fort, E., Martín-Clemente, R., González-Carvajal, R., & Muñoz-Chavero, F. (2023). AIoT in Agriculture: Safeguarding Crops from Pest and Disease Threats. *Sensors (Basel)*, *23*(24), 9733. DOI: 10.3390/s23249733 PMID: 38139579

Blumenstock, J. (2018). *Don't forget people in the use of big data for development*. Nature Publishing Group.

Bogue, R. (2013). Robotic vision boosts automotive industry quality and productivity. *The Industrial Robot*, *40*(5), 415–419. DOI: 10.1108/IR-04-2013-342

Bolici, R., & Mora, L. (2016). The development process of smart city strategies: the case of Barcelona. In RE-CITY Future City-Combining Disciplines (pp. 155-181). Juvenes print.

Bonnefon, J. F., Shariff, A., & Rahwan, I. (2016). The social dilemma of autonomous vehicles. *Science*, *352*(6293), 1573–1576. DOI: 10.1126/science.aaf2654 PMID: 27339987

Borgia, E. (2014). The Internet of Things vision: Key features, applications, and open issues. *Computer Communications*, *54*, 1–31. DOI: 10.1016/j.comcom.2014.09.008

Bouraga, S. (2021). A taxonomy of blockchain consensus protocols: A survey and classification framework. *Expert Systems with Applications*, *168*, 114384. DOI: 10.1016/j.eswa.2020.114384

Browne, G. J., Durrett, J. R., & Wetherbe, J. C. (2004). Consumer reactions toward clicks and bricks: Investigating buying behaviour online and at stores. *Behaviour & Information Technology*, *23*(4), 237–245. DOI: 10.1080/01449290410001685411

Bues, M., Steiner, M., Stafflage, M., & Krafft, M. (2017). How mobile in-store advertising influences purchase intention: Value drivers and mediating effects from a consumer perspective. *Psychology and Marketing*, *34*(2), 157–174. DOI: 10.1002/mar.20981

Bugeja, J., Jacobsson, A., & Davidsson, P. (2021). PRASH: A framework for privacy risk analysis of smart homes. *Sensors (Basel)*, *21*(19), 6399. DOI: 10.3390/s21196399 PMID: 34640718

Buil-Gil, D., Kemp, S., Kuenzel, S., Coventry, L., Zakhary, S., Tilley, D., & Nicholson, J. (2023). The digital harms of smart home devices: A systematic literature review. *Computers in Human Behavior*, *145*, 107770. DOI: 10.1016/j.chb.2023.107770

Business Wire. (2022). PathAI and Cleveland Clinic announce collaboration to build digital pathology infrastructure and evolve the use of AI-powered pathology algorithms in research and clinical care. Business Wire. Retrieved January 6, 2025, from https://www.businesswire.com/news/home/20220310005017/en/PathAI-and-Cleveland-Clinic-Announce-Collaboration-to-Build-Digital-Pathology-Infrastructure-and-Evolve-Use-of-AI-Powered-Pathology-Algorithms-in-Research-and-Clinical-Care

Bzai, J., Alam, F., Dhafer, A., Bojović, M., Altowaijri, S. M., Niazi, I. K., & Mehmood, R. (2022). Machine learning-enabled internet of things (iot): Data, applications, and industry perspective. *Electronics (Basel)*, *11*(17), 2676. DOI: 10.3390/electronics11172676

Callicott, J. B., & Mumford, K. (1998). Ecological sustainability as a conservation concept. In: *Ecological Sustainability and Integrity,* Concepts and Approaches. Springer; p. 31–45. DOI: 10.1007/978-94-017-1337-5_3

Calzada, I. (2018). (Smart) citizens from data providers to decision-makers? The case study of Barcelona. *Sustainability (Basel)*, *10*(9), 3252. DOI: 10.3390/su10093252

Cannavacciuolo, L., Ferraro, G., Ponsiglione, C., Primario, S., & Quinto, I. (2023). Technological innovation-enabling industry 4.0 paradigm: A systematic literature review. *Technovation*, *124*, 102733. DOI: 10.1016/j.technovation.2023.102733

Caragliu, A., Del Bo, C., & Nijkamp, P. (2011). Smart cities in Europe. *Journal of Urban Technology*, *18*(2), 65–82. DOI: 10.1080/10630732.2011.601117

Cardullo, P., & Kitchin, R. (2019). Smart urbanism and smart citizenship: The neoliberal logic of 'citizen-focused' smart cities in Europe. *Environment and Planning C. Politics and Space*, *37*(5), 813–830.

Castillo-Atoche, A., Caamal-Herrera, K., Atoche-Enseñat, R., Estrada-López, J. J., Vázquez-Castillo, J., Castillo-Atoche, A. C., Palma-Marrufo, O., & Espinoza-Ruiz, A. (2022). Energy efficient framework for an AIoT cardiac arrhythmia detection system wearable during sport. *Applied Sciences (Basel, Switzerland)*, *12*(5), 2716. DOI: 10.3390/app12052716

Catuogno, L., & Galdi, C. (2023). Secure Firmware Update: Challenges and Solutions. *Cryptography*, *7*(2), 30. DOI: 10.3390/cryptography7020030

Celesti, A., Fazio, M., Galletta, A., Carnevale, L., Wan, J., & Villari, M. (2019). An approach for the secure management of hybrid cloud–edge environments. *Future Generation Computer Systems*, *90*, 1–19. DOI: 10.1016/j.future.2018.06.043

Chadha, R., & Chaudhary, A. (2023, December). Advancing patient care and monitoring through the fusion of artificial intelligence and the Internet of Things in healthcare. In *International Conference on Intelligent Systems Design and Applications* (pp. 472-480). Cham: Springer Nature Switzerland.

Chanal, P. M., & Kakkasageri, M. S. (2020). Security and privacy in IoT: A survey. *Wireless Personal Communications*, *115*(2), 1667–1693. DOI: 10.1007/s11277-020-07649-9

Chang, Y. W., & Chen, J. (2021). What motivates customers to shop in smart shops? The impacts of smart technology and technology readiness. *Journal of Retailing and Consumer Services*, *58*, 102325. DOI: 10.1016/j.jretconser.2020.102325

Chassignol, M., Khoroshavin, A., Klimova, A., & Bilyatdinova, A. (2018). Artificial intelligence trends in education: A narrative overview. *Procedia Computer Science*, *136*, 16–24. DOI: 10.1016/j.procs.2018.08.233

Chatterjee, P. S., Ray, N. K., & Mohanty, S. P. (2021). LiveCare: An IoT-based healthcare framework for livestock in smart agriculture. *IEEE Transactions on Consumer Electronics*, *67*(4), 257–265. DOI: 10.1109/TCE.2021.3128236

Chatterjee, P., Bhadoria, R. S., & Pathak, Y. (Eds.). (2022). *5G and beyond: the future of IoT*. CRC Press. DOI: 10.1201/9781003045809

Chen, C. J., Huang, Y. Y., Li, Y. S., Chang, C. Y., & Huang, Y. M. (2020). An AIoT based smart agricultural system for pests detection. *IEEE Access : Practical Innovations, Open Solutions*, *8*, 180750–180761. DOI: 10.1109/ACCESS.2020.3024891

Chen, J., & Chang, Y. W. (2023). How does smart technology empower consumers in smart retail stores? The perspective of technology readiness and situational factors. *Electronic Markets*, *33*(1), 1. DOI: 10.1007/s12525-023-00635-6 PMID: 37035262

Chen, S. W., Gu, X. W., Wang, J. J., & Zhu, H. S. (2021). AIoT used for COVID-19 pandemic prevention and control. *Contrast Media & Molecular Imaging, 2021*(1), 3257035. DOI: 10.1155/2021/3257035 PMID: 34729056

Chen, W. L., Lin, Y. B., Ng, F. L., Liu, C. Y., & Lin, Y. W. (2019). RiceTalk: Rice blast detection using Internet of Things and artificial intelligence technologies. *IEEE Internet of Things Journal, 7*(2), 1001–1010. DOI: 10.1109/JIOT.2019.2947624

Chen, X., Su, X., Li, Z., Wu, J., Zheng, M., & Xu, A. (2022). The impact of omni-channel collaborative marketing on customer loyalty to fresh retailers: the mediating effect of the omni-channel shopping experience. *Operations Management Research : Advancing Practice Through Research, 15*(3), 983–997. DOI: 10.1007/s12063-022-00319-y

Cheruvu, S., Kumar, A., Smith, N., & Wheeler, D. M. (2019). Connectivity Technologies for IoT. In *Apress eBooks* (pp. 347–411). DOI: 10.1007/978-1-4842-2896-8_5

Chiradeja, P., & Yoomak, S. (2023). Development of a public lighting system with smart lighting control systems and internet of things (IoT). technologies for smart city. *Energy Reports, 10*, 3355–3372. DOI: 10.1016/j.egyr.2023.10.027

Cho, S. B. (2016). Exploiting machine learning techniques for location recognition and prediction with smartphone logs. *Neurocomputing, 176*, 98–106. DOI: 10.1016/j.neucom.2015.02.079

Choudhary, A. (2024). Internet of Things: A comprehensive overview, architectures, applications, simulation tools, challenges and future directions. *Discover Internet of Things, 4*(1), 31. Advance online publication. DOI: 10.1007/s43926-024-00084-3

Christidis, K., & Devetsikiotis, M. (2016). Blockchains and smart contracts for the Internet of things. *IEEE Access : Practical Innovations, Open Solutions, 4*, 2292–2303. DOI: 10.1109/ACCESS.2016.2566339

Chui, M., Yee, L., Hall, B., & Singla, A. (2023). The state of AI in 2023: Generative AI's breakout year.

Cirani, S., Ferrari, G., & Veltri, L. (2013). Enforcing security mechanisms in the IP-based Internet of things: An algorithmic overview. *Algorithms, 6*(2), 197–226. DOI: 10.3390/a6020197

Collins, C., Dennehy, D., Conboy, K., & Mikalef, P. (2021). Artificial intelligence in information systems research: A systematic literature review and research agenda. *International Journal of Information Management, 60*, 102383. DOI: 10.1016/j.ijinfomgt.2021.102383

Commey, D., Mai, B., Hounsinou, S. G., & Crosby, G. V. (2024). Securing blockchain-based IoT systems: A review. *IEEE Access : Practical Innovations, Open Solutions*, *12*, 98856–98881. DOI: 10.1109/ACCESS.2024.3428490

Cordiglia, M., & Van Belle, J. P. (2017, March). Consumer attitudes towards proximity sensors in the South African retail market. In *2017 Conference on Information Communication Technology and Society (ICTAS)* (pp. 1-6). IEEE. DOI: 10.1109/ICTAS.2017.7920651

Cui, L., Yang, S., Chen, F., Ming, Z., Lu, N., & Qin, J. (2018). A survey on application of machine learning for Internet of Things. *International Journal of Machine Learning and Cybernetics*, *9*(8), 1399–1417. DOI: 10.1007/s13042-018-0834-5

Cully, A., Clune, J., Tarapore, D., & Mouret, J. B. (2015). Robots that can adapt like animals. *Nature*, *521*(7553), 503–507. DOI: 10.1038/nature14422 PMID: 26017452

Culot, G., Nassimbeni, G., Orzes, G., & Sartor, M. (2020). Behind the definition of Industry 4.0: Analysis and open questions. *International Journal of Production Economics*, *226*, 107617. DOI: 10.1016/j.ijpe.2020.107617

Cyber-Physical Systems (CPS). (2024, June 3). NSF - National Science Foundation. https://www.nsf.gov/funding/pgm_summ.jsp?pims_id=503286

Dabir, A., Solkar, R., Kumbhar, M., & Narayanan, G. (2018, April). GPS and IoT equipped smart walking stick. In *2018 International Conference on Communication and Signal Processing (ICCSP)* (pp. 322–326). IEEE. DOI: 10.1109/ICCSP.2018.8524472

Dacko, S. G. (2017). Enabling smart retail settings via mobile augmented reality shopping apps. *Technological Forecasting and Social Change*, *124*, 243–256. DOI: 10.1016/j.techfore.2016.09.032

Dai, H., Zheng, Z., & Zhang, Y. (2019). Blockchain for Internet of Things: A survey. *IEEE Internet of Things Journal*, *6*(5), 8076–8094. DOI: 10.1109/JIOT.2019.2920987

Dai, X., Shang, W., Liu, J., Xue, M., & Wang, C. (2023). Achieving better indoor air quality with IoT systems for future buildings. Opportunities and challenges. *The Science of the Total Environment*, *895*, 164858. DOI: 10.1016/j.scitotenv.2023.164858 PMID: 37343873

Danbatta, S. J., & Varol, A. (2019). Comparison of Zigbee, Z-Wave, Wi-Fi, and bluetooth wireless technologies used in home automation. In *2019 7th International Symposium on Digital Forensics and Security (ISDFS)* (pp. 1-5). IEEE.

Davari, M., & Bertino, E. (2019, December). Access control model extensions to support data privacy protection based on GDPR. In *2019 IEEE International Conference on Big Data (Big Data)* (pp. 4017-4024). IEEE. DOI: 10.1109/BigData47090.2019.9006455

Dayana, D. S., Shanthi, T., Wali, G., Pramila, V. P., Sumitha, T., & Sudhakar, M. (2024). Enhancing usability and control in artificial intelligence of things environments (AIoT) through semantic web control models. In *Advances in Web Technologies and Engineering Book Series*. https://doi.org/DOI: 10.4018/979-8-3693-1487-6.ch009

De Clercq, M., Vats, A., & Biel, A. (2018). Agriculture 4.0: The future of farming technology. *Proceedings of the world government summit,* Dubai, UAE, 11-13.

De Fauw, J., Hughes, D. L., Coombs, C., Constantiou, I., Duan, Y., & Edwards, J. S. (2018). Clinically applicable deep learning for diagnosis and referral in retinal disease. *Nature Medicine*, *24*(9), 1342–1350. DOI: 10.1038/s41591-018-0107-6 PMID: 30104768

Deep, S., Zheng, X., Jolfaei, A., Yu, D., Ostovari, P., & Bashir, A. K. (2020). A survey of security and privacy issues in the Internet of Things from the layered context. https://doi.org/DOI: 10.1002/ett.3935

Deepak, G., Gulia, P., Gill, N. S., Yahya, M., Gupta, P., Shukla, P. K., & Shukla, P. K. (2024). Exploring the potential of blockchain technology in an IoT-enabled environment: A review. *IEEE Access : Practical Innovations, Open Solutions*, *12*, 31197–31227. DOI: 10.1109/ACCESS.2024.3366656

Demertzi, V., Demertzis, S., & Demertzis, K. (2023). An overview of privacy dimensions on the industrial Internet of Things (IIoT). *Algorithms*, *16*(8), 378. Advance online publication. DOI: 10.3390/a16080378

Demirci, M., Ünes¸ F., & Korlü, S. (2019). Modeling of groundwater level using artificial intelligence techniques: a case study of Reyhanli region in Turkey.

Devi, K. V. R., Koithyar, A., Lakhanpal, S., Parmar, A., Sethi, V. A., & Ftaiet, A. A. (2023, December). Edge Computing and 5G Integration for Real-time Analytics in Interoperable Smart Grids. In *2023 International Conference on Power Energy, Environment & Intelligent Control (PEEIC)* (pp. 419-424). IEEE. DOI: 10.1109/PEEIC59336.2023.10451199

Dey, A., & Boleng, J. (n.d.). *An Introduction to Context-Aware Computing (Suzanne Miller, Interviewer)*. SEI Podcast Series. In Carnegie Mellon University Software Engineering Institute., https://insights.sei.cmu.edu/documents/4992/2015_016_100_439312.pdf

Di Vaio, A., Palladino, R., Hassan, R., & Escobar, O. (2020). Artificial intelligence and business models in the sustainable development goals perspective: A systematic literature review. *Journal of Business Research, 121*, 283–314. DOI: 10.1016/j.jbusres.2020.08.019

Dia, I., Ahvar, E., & Lee, G. M. (2022). Performance evaluation of machine learning and neural network-based algorithms for predicting segment availability in AIoT-based smart parking. *Network (Bristol, England), 2*(2), 225–238.

Dian, F. J., Vahidnia, R., & Rahmati, A. (2020). Wearables and the Internet of Things (IoT)., Applications, Opportunities, and Challenges: A survey. *IEEE Access : Practical Innovations, Open Solutions, 8*, 69200–69211. DOI: 10.1109/ACCESS.2020.2986329

Diène, B., Rodrigues, J. J., Diallo, O., Ndoye, E. H. M., & Korotaev, V. V. (2020). Data management techniques for Internet of Things. *Mechanical Systems and Signal Processing, 138*, 106564. DOI: 10.1016/j.ymssp.2019.106564

Din, I. U., Almogren, A., & Rodrigues, J. J. P. C. (2024). AIOT integration in autonomous vehicles: Enhancing road cooperation and traffic management. *IEEE Internet of Things Journal, 11*(22), 35942–35949. DOI: 10.1109/JIOT.2024.3387927

Dong, J., Meng, W., Liu, Y., & Ti, J. (2021). A framework of pavement management system based on IoT and big data. *Advanced Engineering Informatics, 47*, 101226. DOI: 10.1016/j.aei.2020.101226

Dong, Y. (2020, November). Research on Logistics Talents Cultivation Strategy Against the Background of Artificial Intelligence and Internet of Things. In *2020 Conference on Education, Language and Inter-cultural Communication (ELIC 2020)* (pp. 1-6). Atlantis Press. DOI: 10.2991/assehr.k.201127.001

Drath, R., & Horch, A. (2014). Industrie 4.0: Hit or hype? [industry forum]. *IEEE Industrial Electronics Magazine, 8*(2), 56–58. DOI: 10.1109/MIE.2014.2312079

Dupont, L., Morel, L., & Guidat, C. (2015). Innovative public-private partnership to support smart city: The case of "Chaire REVES". *Journal of Strategy and Management, 8*(3), 245–265. DOI: 10.1108/JSMA-03-2015-0027

Duraipandi, S., Divyadharshini, R., Janani, M., & Samyuktha, P. (n.d.). *Smart Traffic Management System using IoT*. https://api.semanticscholar.org/CorpusID:264557309

Dwivedi, Y. K., Hughes, D. L., Coombs, C., Constantiou, I., Duan, Y., Edwards, J. S., Gupta, B., Lal, B., Misra, S., Prashant, P., Raman, R., Rana, N. P., Sharma, S. K., & Upadhyay, N. (2020). Impact of COVID-19 pandemic on information management research and practice: Transforming education, work and life. *International Journal of Information Management, 55*, 102211. DOI: 10.1016/j.ijinfomgt.2020.102211

Eghtesadi, A., Jarraya, Y., Debbabi, M., & Pourzandi, M. (2014). Preservation of security configurations in the cloud. In *Proceedings of the 2014 IEEE International Conference on Cloud Engineering,* 17-26. DOI: 10.1109/IC2E.2014.14

Elassy, M., Al-Hattab, M., Takruri, M., & Badawi, S. (2024). Intelligent transportation systems for sustainable smart cities. *Transportation Engineering*, *16*, 100252. DOI: 10.1016/j.treng.2024.100252

Elliott, D., Keen, W., & Miao, L. (2019). Recent advances in connected and automated vehicles. [English Edition]. *Journal of Traffic and Transportation Engineering*, *6*(2), 109–131. DOI: 10.1016/j.jtte.2018.09.005

Elrifaee, M., Zayed, T., Ali, E., & Ali, A. H. (2024). IoT Contributions to The Safety of Construction Sites. A Comprehensive Review of Recent Advances, Limitations, And Suggestions for Future Directions. *Internet of Things : Engineering Cyber Physical Human Systems*, •••, 101387.

Eminify. (2023, April 12). An Introduction to Industry 4.0 | emnify Blog. *An Introduction to Industry 4.0.* https://www.cmnify.com/blog/industry-4-0

Enshaei, N., & Naderkhani, F. (2024). The role of data quality for reliable AI performance in medical applications. *IEEE Reliability Magazine*, *1*(3), 24–28. DOI: 10.1109/MRL.2024.3430192

Esenogho, E., Djouani, K., & Kurien, A. M. (2022). Integrating artificial intelligence Internet of Things and 5G for next-generation smart grid: A survey of trends challenges and prospect. *IEEE Access : Practical Innovations, Open Solutions*, *10*, 4794–4831. DOI: 10.1109/ACCESS.2022.3140595

Espina-Romero, L., Gutiérrez Hurtado, H., Ríos Parra, D., Vilchez Pirela, R. A., Talavera-Aguirre, R., & Ochoa-Díaz, A. (2024). Challenges and Opportunities in the Implementation of AI in Manufacturing: A Bibliometric Analysis. *Sci*, *6*(4), 60. DOI: 10.3390/sci6040060

Essamlali, I., Nhaila, H., & El Khaili, M. (2024). A new architecture of Low Impact Development (LID)-based stormwater management system through Internet of Things (IoT) and Machine Learning integration. *Case Studies in Chemical and Environmental Engineering*, *10*, 100942. DOI: 10.1016/j.cscee.2024.100942

Ezeugwa, F. A. (2024). Evaluating the integration of edge computing and serverless architectures for enhancing scalability and sustainability in Cloud-based Big Data Management. *Journal of Engineering Research and Reports*, *26*(7), 347–365. DOI: 10.9734/jerr/2024/v26i71214

Fang, H., Qi, A., & Wang, X. (2020). Fast authentication and progressive authorization in large-scale IoT: How to leverage AI for security enhancement. *IEEE Network*, *34*(3), 24–29. DOI: 10.1109/MNET.011.1900276

Fan, K., Li, Q., Le, Z., Li, Q., Li, J., & Yan, M. (2024). Harnessing the power of AI and IoT for real-time CO2 emission monitoring. *Heliyon*, *10*(17), e36612. DOI: 10.1016/j.heliyon.2024.e36612 PMID: 39281600

Ferrara, E. (2023). Fairness and bias in artificial intelligence: A brief survey of sources, impacts, and mitigation strategies. *Sci*, *6*(1), 3. DOI: 10.3390/sci6010003

Ferrer, J.-R. (2017). Using edge computing for real-time processing in IoT systems. OpenEdition. Retrieved January 9, 2025, from https://journals.openedition.org/factsreports/4367

Fontes, C., Hohma, E., Corrigan, C. C., & Lütge, C. (2022). AI-powered public surveillance systems: Why we (might). need them and how we want them. *Technology in Society*, *71*, 102137. DOI: 10.1016/j.techsoc.2022.102137

Forbes (2023). Investment Trends in the Smart Home Industry. Retrieved from Forbes https://www.forbes.com/home-improvement/internet/smart-home-tech-trends/

Forkan, A. R. M., Kang, Y. B., Marti, F., Banerjee, A., McCarthy, C., Ghaderi, H., Costa, B., Dawod, A., Georgakopolous, D., & Jayaraman, P. P. (2024). Aiot-citysense: Ai and iot-driven city-scale sensing for roadside infrastructure maintenance. Springer. *Data Science and Engineering*, *9*(1), 26–40. DOI: 10.1007/s41019-023-00236-5

Fortin, L. V., Santos, A. R. V. D., Cagud, P. J. B., Castor, P. R., & Llantos, O. E. (2024). Eyeway. An Artificial Intelligence Of Things Pothole Detection System With Map Visualization. *Procedia Computer Science*, *251*, 216–223. DOI: 10.1016/j.procs.2024.11.103

Fortune Business Insights, https.//www.fortunebusinessinsights.com/artificial-intelligence-of-things-market-107836

Fotiadis, A. K., & Stylos, N. (2017). The effects of online social networking on retail consumer dynamics in the attractions industry: The case of 'E-da'theme park, Taiwan. *Technological Forecasting and Social Change*, *124*, 283–294. DOI: 10.1016/j.techfore.2016.06.033

Fraga-Lamas, P., Lopes, S. I., & Fernández-Caramés, T. M. (2021). Green IoT and edge AI as key technological enablers for a sustainable digital transition towards a smart circular economy: An industry 5.0 use case. *Sensors (Basel), 21*(17), 5745. DOI: 10.3390/s21175745 PMID: 34502637

Frank, B. (2021). Artificial intelligence-enabled environmental sustainability of products: Marketing benefits and their variation by consumer, location, and product types. *Journal of Cleaner Production, 285*, 125242. DOI: 10.1016/j.jclepro.2020.125242

Gai, K., Qiu, M., Zhao, H., & Dai, W. (2015, November). Anti-counterfeit scheme using Monte Carlo simulation for E-commerce in cloud systems. In *2015 IEEE 2nd International Conference on Cyber Security and Cloud Computing* (pp. 74–79). IEEE. DOI: 10.1109/CSCloud.2015.75

Gao, R. X., Krüger, J., Merklein, M., Möhring, H., & Váncza, J. (2024). Artificial Intelligence in manufacturing: State of the art, perspectives, and future directions. *CIRP Annals, 73*(2), 723–749. DOI: 10.1016/j.cirp.2024.04.101

Garaus, M., & Wagner, U. (2019). Let me entertain you–Increasing overall store satisfaction through digital signage in retail waiting areas. *Journal of Retailing and Consumer Services, 47*, 331–338. DOI: 10.1016/j.jretconser.2018.12.008

Garaus, M., Wagner, U., & Rainer, R. C. (2021). Emotional targeting using digital signage systems and facial recognition at the point-of-sale. *Journal of Business Research, 131*, 747–762. DOI: 10.1016/j.jbusres.2020.10.065

Garaus, M., Wolfsteiner, E., & Wagner, U. (2016). Shoppers' acceptance and perceptions of electronic shelf labels. *Journal of Business Research, 69*(9), 3687–3692. DOI: 10.1016/j.jbusres.2016.03.030

Garg, S., Singh, A., Kaur, K., Aujla, G. S., Batra, S., Kumar, N., & Obaidat, M. S. (2019). Edge computing-based security framework for big data analytics in VANETs. *IEEE Network, 33*(2), 72–81. DOI: 10.1109/MNET.2019.1800239

Gartner. (2023). Top Strategic Technology Trends for 2023. Retrieved from Gartner https://www.gartner.com/en/articles/gartner-top-10-strategic-technology-trends-for-2023

Gbadamosi, A.-Q., Oyedele, L. O., Delgado, J. M. D., Kusimo, H., Akanbi, L., Olawale, O., & Muhammed-yakubu, N. (2021). IoT for predictive assets monitoring and maintenance. An implementation strategy for the UK rail industry. *Automation in Construction, 122*, 103486. DOI: 10.1016/j.autcon.2020.103486

Ghosal, A., Majumdar, A., Dhar, P., Kundu, A., Mondal, A., Biswas, A., & Ghosh, P. (2020). Smart Stick for Blind using IoT. *IJIRT, 7*(5), 12–14.

Ghosh, M., & Thirugnanam, A. (2021). Introduction to artificial intelligence. *Artificial Intelligence for Information Management: A Healthcare Perspective*, 23-44.

Ghosh, S., Roy, P., Sarkar, S. K., Podder, A., & Roy, B. (2024). Challenges and barriers to integrating AI in library environments. In *Applications of Artificial Intelligence in Libraries* (pp. 109–138). https://doi.org/DOI: 10.4018/979-8-3693-1573-6.ch005

Ghoushchi, S. J., Haghshenas, S. S., Vahabzadeh, S., Guido, G., & Geem, Z. W. (2024). An integrated MCDM approach for enhancing efficiency in connected autonomous vehicles through augmented intelligence and IoT integration. *Results in Engineering*, *23*, 102626. DOI: 10.1016/j.rineng.2024.102626

Giannakidou, S., Radoglou-Grammatikis, P., Lagkas, T., Argyriou, V., Goudos, S., Markakis, E. K., & Sarigiannidis, P. (2024). Leveraging the power of internet of things and artificial intelligence in forest fire prevention, detection, and restoration. A comprehensive survey.[[Global CIO, https.//]. *Internet of Things : Engineering Cyber Physical Human Systems*, *26*, 101171. globalcio.com/articles/main/from-iiot-to-aiot-what-is-the-smart-industrial-internet-of-things/. DOI: 10.1016/j.iot.2024.101171

Ginantra, N. L. W. S. R., Indradewi, I. G. A. D., & Hartono, E. (2020, February). Machine learning approach for acute respiratory infections (ISPA) prediction: Case study Indonesia. []. IOP Publishing.]. *Journal of Physics: Conference Series*, *1469*(1), 012044. DOI: 10.1088/1742-6596/1469/1/012044

Giordano, G., Palomba, F., & Ferrucci, F. (2022). On the use of artificial intelligence to deal with privacy in IoT systems: A systematic literature review. *Journal of Systems and Software*, *193*, 111475. Advance online publication. DOI: 10.1016/j.jss.2022.111475

Gligorea, I., Cioca, M., Oancea, R., Gorski, A.-T., Gorski, H., & Tudorache, P. (2023). Adaptive learning using artificial intelligence in e-learning: A literature review. *Education Sciences*, *13*(12), 1216. DOI: 10.3390/educsci13121216

Gonzalez Ordiano, J. A., Waczowicz, S., Hagenmeyer, V., & Mikut, R. (2018). Energy forecasting tools and services. *Wiley Interdisciplinary Reviews. Data Mining and Knowledge Discovery*, *8*(2), e1235. DOI: 10.1002/widm.1235

González-Granadillo, G., González-Zarzosa, S., & Diaz, R. (2021). Security information and event management (SIEM): Analysis, trends, and usage in critical infrastructures. *Sensors (Basel)*, *21*(14), 4759. DOI: 10.3390/s21144759

Gopinath, V., Rao, K. V., & Rao, S. K. (2023). A comprehensive analysis of IoT security towards providing a cost-effective solution: A layered approach. *International Journal of Information Technology : an Official Journal of Bharati Vidyapeeth's Institute of Computer Applications and Management*, *15*(7), 3813–3826. DOI: 10.1007/s41870-023-01405-5

Gøthesen, S., Haddara, M., & Kumar, K. N. (2023). Empowering homes with intelligence: An investigation of smart home technology adoption and usage. *Internet of Things : Engineering Cyber Physical Human Systems*, *24*, 100944. DOI: 10.1016/j.iot.2023.100944

Gowda, V. D., Kaur, M., Srinivas, D., Prasad, K. D. V., & Shekhar, R. (2024). AIoT Integration Advancements and Challenges in Smart Sensing Technologies for Smart Devices. In *AIoT and Smart Sensing Technologies for Smart Devices* (pp. 42–65). IGI Global. DOI: 10.4018/979-8-3693-0786-1.ch003

Grand View Research, https.//www.grandviewresearch.com/industry-analysis/artificial-intelligence-of-things-aiot-market-report

Grandview Research Report (2024). Smart Home Market Size, Share and Trends Report, 2030. Available at: https://www.grandviewresearch.com/industry-analysis/smart-homes-industry

Grewal, D., Hulland, J., Kopalle, P. K., & Karahanna, E. (2020). The future of technology and marketing: A multidisciplinary perspective. *Journal of the Academy of Marketing Science*, *48*(1), 1–8. DOI: 10.1007/s11747-019-00711-4

Grewal, D., & Roggeveen, A. L. (2020). Understanding retail experiences and customer journey management. *Journal of Retailing*, *96*(1), 3–8. DOI: 10.1016/j.jretai.2020.02.002

Grewal, D., Roggeveen, A. L., & Nordfalt, J. (2017). The future of retailing. *Journal of Retailing*, *93*(1), 1–6. DOI: 10.1016/j.jretai.2016.12.008

Groumpos, P. P. (2021). A critical historical and scientific overview of all industrial revolutions. *IFAC-PapersOnLine*, *54*(13), 464–471. DOI: 10.1016/j.ifacol.2021.10.492 PMID: 38620687

Grover, P., Kar, A. K., & Dwivedi, Y. K. (2022). Understanding artificial intelligence adoption in operations management: Insights from the review of academic literature and social media discussions. *Annals of Operations Research*, *308*(1–2), 177–213. DOI: 10.1007/s10479-020-03683-9

Gubbi, J., Buyya, R., Marusic, S., & Palaniswami, M. (2013). Internet of Things (IoT).: A vision, architectural elements, and future directions. *Future Generation Computer Systems*, *29*(7), 1645–1660. DOI: 10.1016/j.future.2013.01.010

Guha, A., Grewal, D., Kopalle, P. K., Haenlein, M., Schneider, M. J., Jung, H., Moustafa, R., Hegde, D. R., & Hawkins, G. (2021). How artificial intelligence will affect the future of retailing. *Journal of Retailing*, *97*(1), 28–41. DOI: 10.1016/j.jretai.2021.01.005

Guo, S., Hu, X., Guo, S., Qiu, X., & Qi, F. (2020). Blockchain meets edge computing: A distributed and trusted authentication system. *IEEE Transactions on Industrial Informatics*, *16*(3), 1972–1983. DOI: 10.1109/TII.2019.2938001

Guo, X., Wang, Y., Mei, S., Shi, C., Liu, Y., Pan, L., Li, K., Zhang, B., Wang, J., Zhong, Z., & Dong, M. (2022). Monitoring and modelling of PM2.5 concentration at subway station construction based on IoT and LSTM algorithm optimization. *Journal of Cleaner Production*, *360*, 132179. DOI: 10.1016/j.jclepro.2022.132179

Guo, Y., Zhang, J., Yin, C., Hu, X., Zou, Y., Xue, Z., & Wang, W. (2020). Plant disease identification based on deep learning algorithm in smart farming. *Discrete Dynamics in Nature and Society*, *2020*(1), 2479172. DOI: 10.1155/2020/2479172

Gupta, A. K., & Srivastava, M. K. (2024). Framework for AI adoption in health care sector: Integrated DELPHI, ISM-MICMAC approach. *IEEE Transactions on Engineering Management*, *71*, 8116–8131. DOI: 10.1109/TEM.2024.3386580

Gupta, A., Gupta, S., Memoria, M., Kumar, R., Kumar, S., Singh, D., & Ansari, N. (2022, May). Artificial intelligence and smart cities: A bibliometric analysis. In *2022 International Conference on Machine Learning, Big Data, Cloud and Parallel Computing (COM-IT-CON)* (Vol. 1, pp. 540-544). IEEE. DOI: 10.1109/COM-IT-CON54601.2022.9850656

Gurung, A., & Raja, M. K. (2016). Online privacy and security concerns of consumers. *Information and Computer Security*, *24*(4), 348–371. DOI: 10.1108/ICS-05-2015-0020

Haber, S., & Stornetta, W. S. (1991). *How to time-stamp a digital document*. Springer Berlin Heidelberg. DOI: 10.1007/3-540-38424-3_32

Haenlein, M., Kaplan, A., Tan, C. W., & Zhang, P. (2019). Artificial intelligence (AI) and management analytics. *Journal of Management Analytics*, *6*(4), 341–343. DOI: 10.1080/23270012.2019.1699876

Haghi, M., Thurow, K., & Stoll, R. (2017). Wearable devices in medical Internet of Things: Scientific research and commercially available devices. *Healthcare Informatics Research*, *23*(1), 4. DOI: 10.4258/hir.2017.23.1.4 PMID: 28261526

Halilovic, S., & Cicic, M. (2013). Antecedents of information systems user behaviour–extended expectation-confirmation model. *Behaviour & Information Technology*, *32*(4), 359–370. DOI: 10.1080/0144929X.2011.554575

Hao J. (2021). Outlook for the Future of the Internet of Things in the 5G Era. Application of Microcontrollers and Embedded Systems. 21 (7).

Hariri-Ardebili, M.A., Mahdavi, G., Nuss, L.K., & Lall, U. (2023). The role of artificial intelligence and digital technologies in dam engineering. Narrative review and outlook. *Engineering Applications of Artificial Intelligence*, Volume 126, Part A, 106813.

Harrison, C., & Donnelly, I. A. (2011, September). A theory of smart cities. In *Proceedings of the 55th Annual Meeting of the ISSS-2011,* Hull, UK.

Hasan, N., Chamoli, A., & Alam, M. (2020). Privacy challenges and their solutions in IoT. https://doi.org/DOI: 10.1007/978-3-030-37468-6_11

Hauser, M., Flath, C. M., & Thiesse, F. (2021). Catch me if you scan: Data-driven prescriptive modeling for smart store environments. *European Journal of Operational Research*, *294*(3), 860–873. DOI: 10.1016/j.ejor.2020.12.047

Helbing, D. (2019). *Towards Digital Enlightenment 73–98*. Springer International Publishing., DOI: 10.1007/978-3-319-90869-4

He, Z., Wang, Y.-H., & Zhang, J. (2025). Generative AIBIM. An automatic and intelligent structural design pipeline integrating BIM and generative AI. *Information Fusion*, *114*, 102654. DOI: 10.1016/j.inffus.2024.102654

Hojlo, J. (2021). Future of Industry Ecosystems: Shared Data and Insights. Available at: https://blogs.idc.com/2021/01/06/future-of-industry-ecosystems-shared-data-and-insights/

Hong, J., & Kim, K. (2024). Impact of AIoT education program on digital and AI literacy of elementary school students. *Education and Information Technologies*. Advance online publication. DOI: 10.1007/s10639-024-12758-0

Hossain, T., Ahad, M. A. R., Tazin, T., & Inoue, S. (2018, October). Activity recognition by using LoRaWAN sensor. In *Proceedings of the 2018 ACM International Joint Conference and 2018 International Symposium on Pervasive and Ubiquitous Computing and Wearable Computers* (pp. 58–61).

Hosseinzadeh, A., Chen, F. F., Shahin, M., & Bouzary, H. (2023). A predictive maintenance approach in manufacturing systems via AI-based early failure detection. *Manufacturing Letters*, *35*, 1179–1186. DOI: 10.1016/j.mfglet.2023.08.125

Hostetter, H., Naser, M. Z., Huang, X., & Gales, J. (2024). The role of large language models (AI chatbots) in fire engineering. An examination of technical questions against domain knowledge. *Natural Hazards Review*, *4*(4), 669–688. DOI: 10.1016/j.nhres.2024.06.003

Hou, K. M., Diao, X., Shi, H., Ding, H., Zhou, H., & de Vaulx, C. (2023). Trends and challenges in AIoT/IIoT/IoT implementation. *Sensors (Basel)*, *23*(11), 5074. DOI: 10.3390/s23115074 PMID: 37299800

Hoyer, W. D., Kroschke, M., Schmitt, B., Kraume, K., & Shankar, V. (2020). Transforming the customer experience through new technologies. *Journal of Interactive Marketing*, *51*(1), 57–71. DOI: 10.1016/j.intmar.2020.04.001

Hsiao, S. J. (2022). Employing a wireless sensing network for AIoT based on a 5G approach. *Electronics (Basel)*, *11*(5), 827. DOI: 10.3390/electronics11050827

Hua, H., Li, Y., Wang, T., Dong, N., Li, W., & Cao, J. (2023). Edge computing with artificial intelligence: A machine learning perspective. *ACM Computing Surveys*, *55*(9), 1–35. DOI: 10.1145/3555802

Huang, Z. (2022). Research on artificial intelligence-related technologies for Internet of Things applications. https://doi.org/DOI: 10.1109/IIoTBDSC57192.2022.00029

Huang, C. H., Chou, T. C., & Wu, S. H. (2021). Towards convergence of AI and IoT for smart policing: A case of a mobile edge computing-based context-aware system. [JGIM]. *Journal of Global Information Management*, *29*(6), 1–21. DOI: 10.4018/JGIM.20211101.oa2

Huang, M. H., & Rust, R. T. (2021). Engaged to a robot? The role of AI in service. *Journal of Service Research*, *24*(1), 30–41. DOI: 10.1177/1094670520902266

Huang, Y. P., & Khabusi, S. P. (2025). Artificial Intelligence of Things (AIoT). Advances in Aquaculture: A Review. MDPI. *Processes (Basel, Switzerland)*, *13*(1), 73. DOI: 10.3390/pr13010073

Hui, C. X., Dan, G., Alamri, S., & Toghraie, D. (2023). Greening smart cities: An investigation of the integration of urban natural resources and smart city technologies for promoting environmental sustainability. *Sustainable Cities and Society*, *99*, 104985. DOI: 10.1016/j.scs.2023.104985

Hussain, A., Iqbal, A., Irfan, M. A., Ahmed, I., & Khalil, A. (2024). AIoT-based telehealth system using Healthy Pi. In *Impact of Artificial Intelligence on Society* (p. 143).

HyScaler, https.//hyscaler.com/insights/ai-in-civil-engineering/.

IBM. (2024, October 28). What is the IoT? *What is the IoT?*https://www.ibm.com/topics/internet-of-things#:~:text=The%20Internet%20of%20Things%20(IoT)%20refers%20to%20a%20network%20of,to%20collect%20and%20share%20data

IBM. (2024a, August 29). Industry 4.0. *What is Industry 4.0?*https://www.ibm.com/topics/industry-4-0

Ibrahim, A. M., Jose, R. R., Rabie, A. N., Gerstle, T. L., Lee, B. T., & Lin, S. J. (2015). Three-dimensional printing in developing countries. *Plastic and Reconstructive Surgery. Global Open*, *3*(7), e443. DOI: 10.1097/GOX.0000000000000298 PMID: 26301132

Ibrahim, H. T., Mazher, W. J., & Ucan, O. N. (2022, December). AIoT in healthcare: a systematic mapping study. In *2022 International Conference on Artificial Intelligence of Things (ICAIoT)*. (pp. 1-6). IEEE. DOI: 10.1109/ICAIoT57170.2022.10121743

Idrissi, Z. K., Lachgar, M., & Hrimech, H (2024a). Blockchain, IoT and AI in logistics and transportation: A systematic review. *Transport Economics and Management*. DOI: 10.1016/j.team.2024.09.002

Indolia, S., Goswami, A. K., Mishra, S., & Asopa, P. (2018). Conceptual understanding of Convolutional Neural Network- a deep learning approach. *Procedia Computer Science*, *132*, 679–688. DOI: 10.1016/j.procs.2018.05.069

Industry 4.0: The Future of Manufacturing | SAP. (n.d.). SAP. https://www.sap.com/india/products/scm/industry-4-0/what-is-industry-4-0.html#:~:text=Industry%204.0%20definition&text=Industry%204.0%20allows%20for%20smart,manufacturing%20and%20supply%20chain%20operations

Inman, J. J., & Nikolova, H. (2017). Shopper-facing retail technology: A retailer adoption decision framework incorporating shopper attitudes and privacy concerns. *Journal of Retailing*, *93*(1), 7–28. DOI: 10.1016/j.jretai.2016.12.006

International Energy Agency. (2017). *Digitalization & Energy (International Energy, 2017)*. Agency.

Intuz, https.//www.intuz.com/blog/use-cases-and-advantages-of-aiot

IoT Analytics, https.//iot-analytics.com/number-connected-iot-devices/.

IoT Analytics, https.//iot-analytics.com/rise-of-industrial-ai-aiot-4-trends-driving -technology-adoption/.

Issaoui, A., Örtensjö, J., & Islam, M. S. (2023). Exploring the General Data Protection Regulation (GDPR) compliance in cloud services: Insights from Swedish public organizations on privacy compliance. *Future Business Journal*, *9*(1), 107. DOI: 10.1186/s43093-023-00285-2

ISTAT. *Digitalizzazione e Tecnologia Nelle Imprese Italiane, Censimenti Permanenti Imprese*; Roma, Italy, 2020. Available online: https://www.istat.it/it/archivio/246548

Ivan, C., Vujic, M., & Husnjak, S. (2016). Classification of security risks in the IoT environment. In *Proceedings of the 26th DAAAM International Symposium,* Vienna, Australia. DOI: 10.2507/26th.daaam.proceedings.102

Jadhav, A., & Jadhav, V. S. (2022). A review on 3D printing: An additive manufacturing technology. *Materials Today: Proceedings*, *62*, 2094–2099. DOI: 10.1016/j.matpr.2022.02.558

Jasman, N., Jalil, M. F. I. M., Mukhtar, A., Sahari, K. S. M., & Rusli, M. E. (2022). IoT-based obstacle detection system for visually impaired person with smartphone module. *Journal of Advances in Information Technology*, *13*(4). Advance online publication. DOI: 10.12720/jait.13.4.368-373

Jawad, L. A. (2024). Security and privacy in digital healthcare systems: Challenges and mitigation strategies. https://doi.org/DOI: 10.1177/09702385241233073

Jayaraman, P., Nagarajan, K. K., Partheeban, P., & Krishnamurthy, V. (2024). Critical review on water quality analysis using IoT and machine learning models. *International Journal of Information Management Data Insights*, *4*(1), 100210. DOI: 10.1016/j.jjimei.2023.100210

Jeon, K. E., She, J., Soonsawad, P., & Ng, P. C. (2018). Ble beacons for internet of things applications: Survey, challenges, and opportunities. *IEEE Internet of Things Journal*, *5*(2), 811–828. DOI: 10.1109/JIOT.2017.2788449

Jha, K., Doshi, A., Patel, P., & Shah, M. (2019). A comprehensive review on automation in agriculture using artificial intelligence. *Artificial Intelligence Agriculture*, *2*, 1–12. DOI: 10.1016/j.aiia.2019.05.004

Jhaveri, R. H., Patel, N. M., Zhong, Y., & Sangaiah, A. K. (2018). Sensitivity analysis of an attack-pattern discovery based trusted routing scheme for mobile ad-hoc networks in industrial IoT. *IEEE Access : Practical Innovations, Open Solutions*, *6*, 20085–20103. DOI: 10.1109/ACCESS.2018.2822945

Jiang, P., Chen, Y., Liu, B., He, D., & Liang, C. (2019). Real-time detection of apple leaf diseases using deep learning approach based on improved convolutional neural networks. *IEEE Access : Practical Innovations, Open Solutions*, *7*, 59069–59080. DOI: 10.1109/ACCESS.2019.2914929

Ji, B., Liu, Y., Xing, L., Li, C., Zhang, G., Han, C., Wen, H., & Mumtaz, S. (2022). Survey of secure communications of Internet of Things with artificial intelligence. *IEEE Internet of Things Magazine*, *5*(3), 92–99. Advance online publication. DOI: 10.1109/IOTM.001.2100178

Jnr, B. A. (2024). Artificial Intelligence of Things and Distributed Technologies as Enablers for Intelligent Mobility Services in Smart Cities-A Survey. *Internet of Things : Engineering Cyber Physical Human Systems*, •••, 101399.

Jobin, A., Ienca, M., & Vayena, E. (2019). The global landscape of AI ethics guidelines. *Nature Machine Intelligence*, *1*(9), 389–399. DOI: 10.1038/s42256-019-0088-2

Johns Hopkins Medicine. (2020). Practical uses for artificial intelligence in health care. Johns Hopkins Medicine. Retrieved January 6, 2025, from https://www.hopkinsmedicine.org/news/articles/2020/02/practical-uses-for-artificial-intelligence-in-health-care

Jo, J., Park, K., Lee, D., & Lim, H. (2014). An integrated teaching and learning assistance system meeting requirements for smart education. *Wireless Personal Communications*, *79*(4), 2453–2467. DOI: 10.1007/s11277-014-1765-4

Jones, D. E., Alimi, T. O., Pordell, P., Tangka, F. K., Blumenthal, W., Jones, S. F., Rogers, J. D., Benard, V. B., & Richardson, L. C. (2021). Pursuing data modernization in cancer surveillance by developing a cloud-based computing platform: Real-time cancer case collection. *JCO Clinical Cancer Informatics*, *5*(5), 24–29. DOI: 10.1200/CCI.20.00082 PMID: 33411623

Kabashkin, I., & Shoshin, L. (2024). Artificial intelligence of things as new paradigm in aviation health monitoring systems. *Future Internet*, *16*(8), 276. DOI: 10.3390/fi16080276

Kaginalkar, A., Kumar, S., Gargava, P., & Niyogi, D. (2021). Review of urban computing in air quality management as smart city service: An integrated IoT, AI, and cloud technology perspective. *Urban Climate*, *39*, 100972. DOI: 10.1016/j.uclim.2021.100972

Kamruzzaman, A., Ismat, S., Brickley, J. C., Liu, A., & Thakur, K. (2022). A comprehensive review of endpoint security: Threats and defenses. In *Proceedings of the 2022 International Conference on Cyber Warfare and Security (ICCWS),* New York, USA. DOI: 10.1109/ICCWS56285.2022.9998470

Kaplan, A. (2022). Social Media Powered by Artificial Intelligence, Violence and Nonviolence. In Encyclopedia of Violence, Peace, & Conflict (Third Edition).

Kaplan, A., & Haenlein, M. (2019). Siri, Siri, in my hand: Who's the fairest in the land? On the interpretations, illustrations, and implications of artificial intelligence. *Business Horizons*, *62*(1), 15–25. DOI: 10.1016/j.bushor.2018.08.004

Kapoor, R., Kumar, A., Kumar, A., Kumar, A., & Arora, H. C. (2024). *1 - Artificial intelligence in civil engineering. An immersive view. Artificial Intelligence Applications for Sustainable Construction*. Woodhead Publishing Series in Civil and Structural Engineering.

Karar, M. E., Alsunaydi, F., Albusaymi, S., & Alotaibi, S. (2021). A new mobile application of agricultural pests recognition using deep learning in cloud computing system. *Alexandria Engineering Journal*, *60*(5), 4423–4432. DOI: 10.1016/j.aej.2021.03.009

Kasat, K., Shaikh, N., Rayabharapu, V. K., & Nayak, M. (2023). *Implementation and Recognition of Waste Management System with Mobility Solution in Smart Cities using Internet of Things, 2023 Second International Conference on Augmented Intelligence and Sustainable Systems*. ICAISS., Available at https://ieeexplore.ieee.org/document/10250690/, DOI: 10.1109/ICAISS58487.2023.10250690

Kaur, R., Gabrijelčič, D., & Klobučar, T. (2023). Artificial intelligence for cybersecurity: Literature review and future research directions. *Information Fusion*, *97*, 101804. DOI: 10.1016/j.inffus.2023.101804

Kayikci, S., & Khoshgoftaar, T. M. (2024). Blockchain meets machine learning: A survey. *Journal of Big Data*, *11*(1), 9. DOI: 10.1186/s40537-023-00852-y

Kazi, K. (2024b). Modelling and Simulation of Electric Vehicle for Performance Analysis: BEV and HEV Electrical Vehicle Implementation Using Simulink for E-Mobility Ecosystems. *In L. D., N. Nagpal, N. Kassarwani, V. Varthanan G., & P. Siano (Eds.), E-Mobility in Electrical Energy Systems for Sustainability (pp. 295-320). IGI Global.* Available at: https://www.igi-global.com/gateway/chapter/full-text-pdf/341172DOI: 10.4018/979-8-3693-2611-4.ch014

Kazi, K. (2024a). AI-Driven IoT (AIIoT) in Healthcare Monitoring. In Nguyen, T., & Vo, N. (Eds.), *Using Traditional Design Methods to Enhance AI-Driven Decision Making* (pp. 77–101). IGI Global., available at https://www.igi-global.com/chapter/ai-driven-iot-aiiot-in-healthcare-monitoring/336693, DOI: 10.4018/979-8-3693-0639-0.ch003

Kazi, K. (2025). Machine Learning-Powered IoT (MLIoT) for Retail Apparel Industry. In Tarnanidis, T., Papachristou, E., Karypidis, M., & Manda, V. (Eds.), *Sustainable Practices in the Fashion and Retail Industry* (pp. 345–372). IGI Global Scientific Publishing., DOI: 10.4018/979-8-3693-9959-0.ch015

Kazi, K. S. (2025). Advancing Towards Sustainable Energy With Hydrogen Solutions: Adaptation and Challenges. In Özsungur, F., Chaychi Semsari, M., & Küçük Bayraktar, H. (Eds.), *Geopolitical Landscapes of Renewable Energy and Urban Growth* (pp. 357–394). IGI Global Scientific Publishing., DOI: 10.4018/979-8-3693-8814-3.ch013

Kazi, K. S. (2025). AI-Driven IoT (AIIoT)-Based Decision-Making System for High BP Patient Healthcare Monitoring: KSK1 Approach for BP Patient Healthcare Monitoring. In Mzili, T., Arya, A., Pamucar, D., & Shaheen, M. (Eds.), *Optimization, Machine Learning, and Fuzzy Logic: Theory, Algorithms, and Applications* (pp. 71–102). IGI Global Scientific Publishing., DOI: 10.4018/979-8-3693-7352-1.ch003

Kazi, S. (2024). Machine Learning-Based Pomegranate Disease Detection and Treatment. In Zia Ul Haq, M., & Ali, I. (Eds.), *Revolutionizing Pest Management for Sustainable Agriculture* (pp. 469–498). IGI Global., DOI: 10.4018/979-8-3693-3061-6.ch019

Kazi, S. (2024a). Computer-Aided Diagnosis in Ophthalmology: A Technical Review of Deep Learning Applications. In Garcia, M., & de Almeida, R. (Eds.), *Transformative Approaches to Patient Literacy and Healthcare Innovation* (pp. 112–135). IGI Global., Available at https://www.igi-global.com/chapter/computer-aided-diagnosis-in-ophthalmology/342823, DOI: 10.4018/979-8-3693-3661-8.ch006

Kazi, S. (2024b). IoT Driven by Machine Learning (MLIoT) for the Retail Apparel Sector. In Tarnanidis, T., Papachristou, E., Karypidis, M., & Ismyrlis, V. (Eds.), *Driving Green Marketing in Fashion and Retail* (pp. 63–81). IGI Global., DOI: 10.4018/979-8-3693-3049-4.ch004

Kazi, S. (2024d). Artificial Intelligence (AI)-Driven IoT (AIIoT)-Based Agriculture Automation. In Satapathy, S., & Muduli, K. (Eds.), *Advanced Computational Methods for Agri-Business Sustainability* (pp. 72–94). IGI Global., DOI: 10.4018/979-8-3693-3583-3.ch005

Kazi, S. (2025). Machine Learning-Driven Internet of Medical Things (ML-IoMT)-Based Healthcare Monitoring System. In Soufiene, B., & Chakraborty, C. (Eds.), *Responsible AI for Digital Health and Medical Analytics* (pp. 49–86). IGI Global Scientific Publishing., DOI: 10.4018/979-8-3693-6294-5.ch003

Kazi, S. (2025a). Transformation of Agriculture Effectuated by Artificial Intelligence-Driven Internet of Things (AIIoT). In Garwi, J., Dzingirai, M., & Masengu, R. (Eds.), *Integrating Agriculture, Green Marketing Strategies, and Artificial Intelligence* (pp. 449–484). IGI Global Scientific Publishing., DOI: 10.4018/979-8-3693-6468-0.ch015

Kazi, S. (2025c). AI-Driven-IoT (AIIoT)-Based Decision Making in Drones for Climate Change: KSK Approach. In Aouadni, S., & Aouadni, I. (Eds.), *Recent Theories and Applications for Multi-Criteria Decision-Making* (pp. 311–340). IGI Global., DOI: 10.4018/979-8-3693-6502-1.ch011

Keerthana, R. K. V., Bhagyalakshmi, K., Papinaidu, M. V. V., & Liyakat, K. K. S. (2025). Machine learning based risk assessment for financial management in big data IoT credit. SSRN *Electronic Journal.* DOI: 10.2139/ssrn.5086671

Keramitsoglou, I., Cartalis, C., & Kiranoudis, C. T. (2006). Automatic identification of oil spills on satellite images. *Environmental Modelling & Software*, *21*(5), 640–652. DOI: 10.1016/j.envsoft.2004.11.010

Khadake, S. B., Chounde, A. B., & Suryagan, A. A., M. H. M. and M. R. Khadatare, (2024). AI-Driven-IoT(AIIoT) Based Decision Making System for High-Blood Pressure Patient Healthcare Monitoring, *2024 International Conference on Sustainable Communication Networks and Application (ICSCNA)*, Theni, India, 2024, pp. 96-102, DOI: 10.1109/ICSCNA63714.2024.10863954

Khan, N., & Gupta, K. (2022, October). IOT: Applications, Challenges and Latest Trends. In *2022 1st IEEE International Conference on Industrial Electronics: Developments & Applications (ICIDeA)* (pp. 181-186). IEEE.

Khan, F. S., Khan, S., Mohd, M. N. H., Waseem, A., Khan, M. N. A., Ali, S., & Ahmed, R. (2022, October). Federated learning-based UAVs for the diagnosis of Plant Diseases. In *2022 International Conference on Engineering and Emerging Technologies (ICEET)* (pp. 1-6). IEEE. DOI: 10.1109/ICEET56468.2022.10007133

Khan, J. I., Khan, J., Ali, F., Ullah, F., Bacha, J., & Lee, S. (2022a). Artificial intelligence and internet of things (AI-IoT) technologies in response to COVID-19 pandemic: A systematic review. *IEEE Access : Practical Innovations, Open Solutions*, *10*, 62613–62660. DOI: 10.1109/ACCESS.2022.3181605

Khan, M. A., & Salah, K. (2018). IoT security: Review, blockchain solutions, and open challenges. *Future Generation Computer Systems*, *82*, 395–411. DOI: 10.1016/j.future.2017.11.022

Khan, S. N., Loukil, F., Ghedira-Guegan, C., Benkhelifa, E., & Bani-Hani, A. (2021). Blockchain smart contracts: Applications, challenges, and future trends. *Peer-to-Peer Networking and Applications*, *14*(5), 2901–2925. DOI: 10.1007/s12083-021-01127-0

Khan, W. Z., Ahmed, E., Hakak, S., Yaqoob, I., & Ahmed, A. (2019). Edge computing: A survey. *Future Generation Computer Systems*, *97*, 219–235. DOI: 10.1016/j.future.2019.02.050

Kheder, M. Q., & Mohammed, A. A. (2024). Real-time traffic monitoring system using IoT-aided robotics and deep learning techniques. *Kuwait Journal of Science*, *51*(1), 100153. DOI: 10.1016/j.kjs.2023.10.017

Khodayar, M. E., & Wu, H. (2015). Demand forecasting in the smart grid paradigm: Features and challenges. *The Electricity Journal*, *28*(6), 51–62. DOI: 10.1016/j.tej.2015.06.001

Khokhar, R. (2022). Internet of Things privacy security protection access control research. https://doi.org/DOI: 10.1109/ITOEC53115.2022.9734497

Khowaja, S. A., Dev, K., Faseeh, M. N., Khuwaja, P., & Foschini, L. (2021). Towards industrial private AI: A two-tier framework for data and model security. *arXiv: Cryptography and Security*.

Kim, B., & Shin, K. S. (2024). Integration of Beyond 5g and Artificial Intelligence of Things (Aiot). with Non-Terrestrial Networks (Ntn).: Access to 5g and Low Earth Orbit (Leo). Telecommunications Facility in Korea. Available at *SSRN* 4978353. DOI: 10.2139/ssrn.4978353

Kim, J., Lee, S., Lee, G., Park, Y., & Hong, Y. (2016). Using a method based on a modified K-means clustering and mean shift segmentation to reduce file sizes and detect brain tumors from magnetic resonance (MRI) images. *Wireless Personal Communications*, *89*(3), 993–1008. DOI: 10.1007/s11277-016-3420-8

Kiran, D. R. (2019). Chapter 35-internet of things. *Production Planning and Control*, •••, 495–513.

Kitcharoen, P., Howimanporn, S., & Chookaew, S. (2024). Enhancing teachers' AI competencies through artificial intelligence of things professional development training. [IJIM]. *International Journal of Interactive Mobile Technologies*, *18*(02), 4–15. DOI: 10.3991/ijim.v18i02.46613

Kovelan, P., Thisenthira, N., & Kartheeswaran, T. (2019). Automated attendance monitoring system using IoT. In *2019 International Conference on Advancements in Computing (ICAC)* (pp. 376–379). https://doi.org/DOI: 10.1109/ICAC49085.2019.9103412

Krishnan, K. N., Jenu, R., Joseph, T., & Silpa, M. L. (2018). Blockchain based security framework for IoT implementations. In *Proceedings of the 2018 International CET Conference on Control, Communication, and Computing (IC4)*, Trivandrum, India. DOI: 10.1109/CETIC4.2018.8531042

Kudyba, S., & Kudyba, S. (2014). *Big data, mining, and analytics*. Auerbach Publications. DOI: 10.1201/b16666

Kuguoglu, B. K., van der Voort, H., & Janssen, M. (2021). The giant leap for smart cities: Scaling up smart city artificial intelligence of things (AIoT) initiatives. *Sustainability (Basel)*, *13*(21), 12295. DOI: 10.3390/su132112295

Kulkarni, P. (2023, November 7). *Evolution of Internet of Things (IoT) - A Brief History*. Bytebeam. https://bytebeam.io/blog/a-brief-history-of-internet-of-things/

Kumar, N., Madhuri, J., & ChanneGowda, M. (2017, May). Review on security and privacy concerns in Internet of Things. In 2017 International Conference on IoT and Application (ICIOT) (pp. 1-5). IEEE.

Kumar, N. M., & Mallick, P. K. (2018). Blockchain technology for security issues and challenges in IoT. *Procedia Computer Science*, *132*, 1815–1823. DOI: 10.1016/j.procs.2018.05.140

Kumar, N. M., & Mallick, P. K. (2018). The Internet of Things: Insights into the building blocks, component interactions, and architecture layers. *Procedia Computer Science*, *132*, 109–117. DOI: 10.1016/j.procs.2018.05.170

Kumar, S., Tiwari, P., & Zymbler, M. (2019). Internet of Things is a revolutionary approach for future technology enhancement: A review. *Journal of Big Data*, *6*(1), 1–21. DOI: 10.1186/s40537-019-0268-2

Kuo, Y. H., & Wu, E. H. K. (2023). Advanced, innovative AIoT and edge computing for unmanned vehicle systems in factories. *Electronics (Basel)*, *12*(8), 1843. DOI: 10.3390/electronics12081843

Kuppuswamy, A., Rajan, P. V., Selvaraj, S. K., Sankarappan, S., & Subramaniam, M. (2023). Object detection and facial recognition for the blind using deep learning and IoT. *AIP Conference Proceedings*, *2854*, 020044. DOI: 10.1063/5.0153559

Kurdi, M. Z. (2017). *Natural Language Processing and Computational Linguistics 2: semantics, Discourse, and Applications, 2*. John Wiley & Sons. DOI: 10.1002/9781119419686

Kutubuddin (2024). Explainable AI in Healthcare. In: Explainable Artificial Intelligence in healthcare System, editors: *A. Anitha Kamaraj, Debi Prasanna Acharjya*. ISBN: 979-8-89113-598-7. DOI: https://doi.org/DOI: 10.52305/GOMR8163

Kutubuddin. (2024a). Machine Learning (ML)-Based Braille Lippi Characters and Numbers Detection and Announcement System for Blind Children in Learning, *In Gamze Sart (Eds.), Social Reflections of Human-Computer Interaction in Education, Management, and Economics, IGI Global*. https://doi.org/DOI: 10.4018/979-8-3693-3033-3.ch002

Lakhouit, A. (2025). Revolutionizing urban solid waste management with AI and IoT. A review of smart solutions for waste collection, sorting, and recycling. *Results in Engineering*, *25*, 104018. DOI: 10.1016/j.rineng.2025.104018

Langa, R., Moeti, M. N., & Maubane, T. (2024). An AIoT-Based Automated Farming Irrigation System for Farmers in Limpopo Province. [JINITA]. *Journal of Innovation Information Technology and Application*, *6*(1), 12–27. DOI: 10.35970/jinita.v6i1.2187

Lee, J., Lee, Y., & Kim, S. (2021). The effects of consumers' in-store technology experience on perceived interactivity, retail Brand commitment, and revisit intention in a Korean beauty store. *International Journal of Human-Computer Interaction*, *37*(6), 534–546. DOI: 10.1080/10447318.2020.1834730

Lee, S. M., & Lee, D. (2020). "Untact": A new customer service strategy in the digital age. *Service Business*, *14*(1), 1–22. DOI: 10.1007/s11628-019-00408-2

Lemon, K. N., & Verhoef, P. C. (2016). Understanding customer experience throughout the customer journey. *Journal of Marketing*, *80*(6), 69–96. DOI: 10.1509/jm.15.0420

Leo Kumar, S. P. (2019). Knowledge-based expert system in manufacturing planning: State-of-the-art review. *International Journal of Production Research*, *57*(15-16), 4766–4790. DOI: 10.1080/00207543.2018.1424372

Leszczynski, A. (2016). Speculative futures: Cities, data, and governance beyond smart urbanism. *Environment and Planning A. Environment & Planning A*, *48*(9), 1691–1708. DOI: 10.1177/0308518X16651445

Li, H., Li, S., Yu, J., Han, Y., & Dong, A. (2022a, April). Plant disease and insect pest identification based on vision transformer. In *International conference on internet of things and machine learning (IoTML 2021)* (Vol. 12174, pp. 194-201). SPIE. DOI: 10.1117/12.2628467

Li, H., Li, S., Yu, J., Han, Y., & Dong, A. (2022b, January). AIoT platform design based on front and rear end separation architecture for smart agricultural. In *Proceedings of the 2022 4th Asia Pacific Information Technology Conference* (pp. 208-214). DOI: 10.1145/3512353.3512384

Lim, E. H., & Chai, Y., T., Muniandy, M. A., Fui Yong, T., Ooi, B. Y., & Lin, J. (2023). Edge computing and AI for IoT: Opportunities and challenges. In *Proceedings of the 2023 International Conference on Consumer Electronics - Taiwan (ICCE-Taiwan),* Pingtung, Taiwan. DOI: 10.1109/ICCE-Taiwan58799.2023.10226787

Li, S., Iqbal, M., & Saxena, N. (2022). Future industry internet of things with zero-trust security. *Information Systems Frontiers*, •••, 1–14.

Li, S., Xu, L. D., & Zhao, S. (2014). The Internet of things: A survey. *Information Systems Frontiers*, *17*(2), 243–259. DOI: 10.1007/s10796-014-9492-7

Little, S. G., & Akin-Little, A. (2008). Psychology's contributions to classroom management. *Psychology in the Schools*, *45*(3), 227–234. DOI: 10.1002/pits.20293

Liu, C., Yang, Z., Zhang, X., Zhu, Z., Chu, H., Huan, Y., & Zou, Z. (2023). A Low-Power Hybrid-Precision Neuromorphic Processor With INT8 Inference and INT16 [-nm CMOS. *IEEE Transactions on Circuits and Systems I: Regular Papers.*]. *Online Learning : the Official Journal of the Online Learning Consortium*, •••, 40.

Liu, L., Wang, R., Xie, C., Yang, P., Wang, F., Sudirman, S., & Liu, W. (2019). PestNet: An end-to-end deep learning approach for large-scale multi-class pest detection and classification. *IEEE Access : Practical Innovations, Open Solutions*, *7*, 45301–45312. DOI: 10.1109/ACCESS.2019.2909522

Liu, Q., Wang, G., Hu, J., & Wu, J. (2022). Preface of special issue on artificial intelligence: The security & privacy opportunities and challenges for emerging applications. *Future Generation Computer Systems*, *133*, 169–170. Advance online publication. DOI: 10.1016/j.future.2022.03.021

Liu, Y., Chen, Y., Ye, W., & Gui, Y. (2022). FPGA-NHAP: A general FPGA-based neuromorphic hardware acceleration platform with high speed and low power. *IEEE Transactions on Circuits and Systems. I, Regular Papers*, *69*(6), 2553–2566. DOI: 10.1109/TCSI.2022.3160693

Liu, Y., Ma, X., Shu, L., Hancke, G. P., & Abu-Mahfouz, A. M. (2020). From industry 4.0 to agriculture 4.0: Current status, enabling technologies, and research challenges. *IEEE Transactions on Industrial Informatics*, *17*(6), 4322–4334. DOI: 10.1109/TII.2020.3003910

Liu, Y., Yu, S., Zhu, Y., Wang, D., & Liu, J. (2018). Modeling, planning, application, and management of energy systems for isolated areas: A review. *Renewable & Sustainable Energy Reviews*, *82*, 460–470. DOI: 10.1016/j.rser.2017.09.063

Liu, Z., & Zeng, X. (2021). Hybrid intelligence in big data environment: Concepts, architectures, and applications of intelligent service. *Data and Information Management*, *5*(2), 262–276. DOI: 10.2478/dim-2020-0051

Li, X., Wang, Q., Lan, X., Chen, X., Zhang, N., & Chen, D. (2019). Enhancing cloud-based IoT security through trustworthy cloud service: An integration of security and reputation approach. *IEEE Access : Practical Innovations, Open Solutions*, *7*, 9368–9383. DOI: 10.1109/ACCESS.2018.2890432

Li, X., & Ye, B. (2021). Latency-Aware Computation Offloading for 5G Networks in Edge Computing. *Security and Communication Networks*, *2021*(1), 8800234. DOI: 10.1155/2021/8800234

Li, Y., Zuo, Y., Song, H., & Lv, Z. (2021). Deep learning in security of internet of things. *IEEE Internet of Things Journal*, *9*(22), 22133–22146. DOI: 10.1109/JIOT.2021.3106898

Liyakat (2024). ChatGPT: An Automated Teacher's Guide to Learning. *In R. Bansal, A. Chakir, A. Hafaz Ngah, F. Rabby, & A. Jain (Eds.), AI Algorithms and ChatGPT for Student Engagement in Online Learning* (pp. 1-20). IGI Global. https://doi.org/ DOI: 10.4018/979-8-3693-4268-8.ch001

Liyakat, (2025a). Heart Health Monitoring Using IoT and Machine Learning Methods. In A. Shaik (Ed.), *AI-Powered Advances in Pharmacology* (pp. 257-282). IGI Global. https://doi.org/DOI: 10.4018/979-8-3693-3212-2.ch010

Liyakat, S. (2024n). Impact of Nanotechnology on Battlefield Welfare: A Study. International Journal of Nanobiotechnology. 2024; 10(2): 19– 32p.

Liyakat. (2023). Detecting Malicious Nodes in IoT Networks Using Machine Learning and Artificial Neural Networks, *2023 International Conference on Emerging Smart Computing and Informatics (ESCI)*, Pune, India, 2023, pp. 1-5, . Available at: https://ieeexplore.ieee.org/document/10099544/DOI: 10.1109/ESCI56872.2023.10099544

Liyakat. (2025). IoT Technologies for the Intelligent Dairy Industry: A New Challenge. In S. Thandekkattu & N. Vajjhala (Eds.), *Designing Sustainable Internet of Things Solutions for Smart Industries* (pp. 321-350). IGI Global. https://doi.org/ DOI: 10.4018/979-8-3693-5498-8.ch012

Liyakat. (2025d). AI-Driven-IoT(AIIoT)-Based Decision Making in Kidney Diseases Patient Healthcare Monitoring: KSK Approach for Kidney Monitoring. In L. Özgür Polat & O. Polat (Eds.), *AI-Driven Innovation in Healthcare Data Analytics* (pp. 277-306). IGI Global Scientific Publishing. https://doi.org/DOI: 10.4018/979-8-3693-7277-7.ch009

Liyakat, K. K. S. (2023a). Machine Learning Approach Using Artificial Neural Networks to Detect Malicious Nodes in IoT Networks. In Shukla, P. K., Mittal, H., & Engelbrecht, A. (Eds.), *Computer Vision and Robotics. CVR 2023. Algorithms for Intelligent Systems*. Springer., DOI: 10.1007/978-981-99-4577-1_3

Liyakat, K. K. S. (2024). Machine Learning Approach Using Artificial Neural Networks to Detect Malicious Nodes in IoT Networks. In Udgata, S. K., Sethi, S., & Gao, X. Z. (Eds.), *Intelligent Systems. ICMIB 2023. Lecture Notes in Networks and Systems* (Vol. 728). Springer., available at https://link.springer.com/chapter/10.1007/978-981-99-3932-9_12, DOI: 10.1007/978-981-99-3932-9_12

Liyakat, S. (2024g). Nanotechnology in BattleField: A Study. Journal of Nanoscience. *Nanoengineering & Applications*, *14*(2), 18–30p.

Liyakat, S. (2024j). Nanotechnology in BattleField: A Study. *Journal of Nanoscience. Nanoengineering & Applications.*, *14*(2), 18–30p.

Lorenzo, N., Gallon, R., Palau, R., & Mogas, J. (2021). New objectives for smart classrooms from Industry 4.0. *Technology. Knowledge and Learning*, *26*(4), 719–731. DOI: 10.1007/s10758-021-09527-0

Loureiro, S. M. C., Guerreiro, J., & Tussyadiah, I. (2021). Artificial intelligence in business: State of the art and future research agenda. *Journal of Business Research*, *129*, 911–926. DOI: 10.1016/j.jbusres.2020.11.001

Ltd, H. T. C. (2022). *Artificial Intelligence Technology*. Springer Nature.

Lund, B. D., Wang, T., Mannuru, N. R., Nie, B., Shimray, S., & Wang, Z. (2023). ChatGPT and a new academic reality: Artificial Intelligence-written research papers and the ethics of the large language models in scholarly publishing. *Journal of the Association for Information Science and Technology*, *74*(5), 570–581. DOI: 10.1002/asi.24750

Lv, Y., Duan, Y., Kang, W., Li, Z., & Wang, F. (2014). Traffic flow prediction with Big Data: A Deep learning approach. *IEEE Transactions on Intelligent Transportation Systems*, •••, 1–9. DOI: 10.1109/TITS.2014.2345663

Machida, T., Yamamoto, D., Iwamoto, M., & Sakiyama, K. (2015, January). Implementation of double arbiter PUF and its performance evaluation on FPGA. In *The 20th Asia and South Pacific Design Automation Conference* (pp. 6–7). IEEE. DOI: 10.1109/ASPDAC.2015.7058919

Mahant, M. A. (2025). Machine Learning-Driven Internet of Things (MLIoT)-Based Healthcare Monitoring System. In Wickramasinghe, N. (Ed.), *Digitalization and the Transformation of the Healthcare Sector* (pp. 205–236). IGI Global Scientific Publishing., DOI: 10.4018/979-8-3693-9641-4.ch007

Mahmud, U., Hussain, S., Sarwar, A., & Toure, I. K. (2022). A distributed emergency vehicle transit system using artificial intelligence of things (DEVeTS-AIoT). *Wireless Communications and Mobile Computing*, *2022*, 1–12. Advance online publication. DOI: 10.1155/2022/9654858

Mai, T. G., Nguyen, M., Ghobakhlou, A., Yan, W. Q., Chhun, B., & Nguyen, H. (2024). Decoding a decade. The evolution of artificial intelligence in security, communication, and maintenance within the construction industry. *Automation in Construction*, Volume 165, 105522. MarketsandMarkets, https.//www.marketsandmarkets.com/Market-Reports/ai-in-iot-market-43388726.html

Maier, H. R., & Dandy, G. C. (2000). Neural networks for the prediction and forecasting of water resources variables: A review of modeling issues and applications. *Environmental Modelling & Software*, *15*(1), 101–124. DOI: 10.1016/S1364-8152(99)00007-9

Maiti, M., Priyaadharshini, M., & Vinayaga Sundaram, B. (2021). Augmented reality in virtual classroom for higher education during COVID-19 pandemic. In *Intelligent Computing* (pp. 399–418). https://doi.org/DOI: 10.1007/978-3-030-80129-8_29

Mala, N. S., Thushara, S. S., & Subbiah, S. (2017, February). Navigation gadget for visually impaired based on IoT. In *2017 2nd International Conference on Computing and Communications Technologies (ICCCT)* (pp. 334–338). IEEE. DOI: 10.1109/ICCCT2.2017.7972298

Manickam, S., & Kooy, A. (2020). Internet of Things for smart cities: Challenges, security, and privacy issues. *Social Science Research Network*. https://doi.org/DOI: 10.2139/SSRN.3713677

Marinescu, D. C. (2022). *Cloud computing: theory and practice*. Morgan Kaufmann.

Markets and Markets. (2022). Smart Home Market - Global Forecast to 2027. Retrieved from Markets and Markets https://www.marketsandmarkets.com/Market-Reports/european-smart-homes-market-1290.html

Marques, J. F., & Bernardino, J. (2020). Analysis of Data Anonymization Techniques. In *KEOD* (pp. 235-241). DOI: 10.5220/0010142302350241

Martin, K., Shilton, K., & Smith, J. ery. (2022). Business and the ethical implications of technology: Introduction to the symposium. In *Business and the Ethical Implications of Technology* (pp. 1–11). https://doi.org/DOI: 10.1007/978-3-031-18794-0_1

Martínez-García, M., & Hernández-Lemus, E. (2022). Data integration challenges for machine learning in precision medicine. *Frontiers in Medicine*, *8*, 784455. DOI: 10.3389/fmed.2021.784455 PMID: 35145977

Martino, R., & Cilardo, A. (2020). Designing a SHA-256 processor for blockchain-based IoT applications. *Internet of Things : Engineering Cyber Physical Human Systems*, *11*, 100254. DOI: 10.1016/j.iot.2020.100254

Martsenyuk, V. P., Klos-Witkowska, A., Sverstiuk, A., Bahrii-Zaiats, O., Bernas, M., & Witos, K. (2021). Intelligent Big Data System Based on Scientific Machine Learning of Cyber-physical Systems of Medical and Biological Processes. In *CMIS* (pp. 34-48). DOI: 10.32782/cmis/2864-4

Matin, A., Islam, M. R., Wang, X., Huo, H., & Xu, G. (2023). AIoT for sustainable manufacturing: Overview, challenges, and opportunities. *Internet of Things : Engineering Cyber Physical Human Systems*, *24*, 100901. DOI: 10.1016/j.iot.2023.100901

Mayo Clinic. (2025). Artificial intelligence and informatics - Overview. Mayo Clinic. Retrieved January 6, 2025, from https://www.mayo.edu/research/departments-divisions/artificial-intelligence-informatics/overview

McKinsey. (2024). What is AI (artificial intelligence)? Available at: https://www.mckinsey.com/featured-insights/mckinsey-explainers/what-is-ai

Mendez, D. M., Papapanagiotou, I., & Yang, B. (2017). Internet of Things: Survey on security and privacy. *arXiv: Cryptography and Security*. https://doi.org/DOI: 10.1080/19393555.2018.1458258

Merit Data and Technology, https.//www.meritdata-tech.com/resources/blog/code-ai/ai-revolution-construction-applications/

Merizalde, Y., Hern'andez-Callejo, L., Duque-Perez, O., & Alonso-G'omez, V. (2019). Maintenance models applied to wind turbines. *A comprehensive overview. Energies*, *12*(2), 225. DOI: 10.3390/en12020225

Merlec, M. M., & In, H. P. (2024). SC-CAAC: A smart-contract-Based context-aware access control scheme for blockchain-enabled IoT systems. *IEEE Internet of Things Journal, 11*(11), 19866–19881. DOI: 10.1109/JIOT.2024.3371504

Milovanovic, D. A., & Pantovic, V. (2023). 5G-AIoT artificial intelligence of things: Opportunity and challenges. In *Driving 5G Mobile Communications with Artificial Intelligence Towards 6G* (pp. 253–276). CRC Press. DOI: 10.1201/9781003205494-8

Mishra, M., Lourenco, P. B., & Ramana, G. V. (2022). Structural health monitoring of civil engineering structures by using the internet of things. A review. *Journal of Building Engineering*, *48*, 103954. DOI: 10.1016/j.jobe.2021.103954

Mishra, N., & Pandya, S. (2021). Internet of things applications, security challenges, attacks, intrusion detection, and future visions: A systematic review. *IEEE Access : Practical Innovations, Open Solutions*, *9*, 59353–59377. DOI: 10.1109/ACCESS.2021.3073408

Mohajan, H. (2021). Third industrial revolution brings global development.

Mohamadi, A., Heidarizadi, Z., & Nourollahi, H. (2016). Assessing the desertification trend using neural network classification and object-oriented techniques. *Journal ofFaculty.Istanbul University*, *66*, 683–690.

Mohammadi, M., Assaf, G., & Assaad, R. H. (2024). Real-time spatial-temporal mapping and visualization of thermal comfort and HVAC control by integrating immersive augmented reality technologies and IoT-enabled wireless sensor networks. Towards immersive human-building interactions. *Journal of Building Engineering*, *94*, 109887. DOI: 10.1016/j.jobe.2024.109887

Mok, W. K., Tan, Y. X., & Chen, W. N. (2020). Technology innovations for food security in Singapore: A case study of future food systems for an increasingly natural resource-scarce world. *Trends in Food Science & Technology*, *102*, 155–168. DOI: 10.1016/j.tifs.2020.06.013 PMID: 32834499

Mor, N., & Kumar, P. Madhu, Jat, G.L., & Kumar, A. (2024). 2 - Application of artificial intelligence in sustainable construction. A secret eye toward the latest civil engineering techniques. Artificial Intelligence Applications for Sustainable Construction. *Woodhead Publishing Series in Civil and Structural Engineering*, Pages 75-91.

More, P., Sakhare, S., & Mahalle, P. (2023, December). Identity-Based Access Control in IoT: Enhancing Security through Mutual Cryptographic Authentication and Context Awareness. In *2023 3rd International Conference on Mobile Networks and Wireless Communications (ICMNWC)* (pp. 1-6). IEEE.

Moudgil, V., Hewage, K., Hussain, S. A., & Sadiq, R. (2023). Integration of IoT in building energy infrastructure. A critical review on challenges and solutions. *Renewable & Sustainable Energy Reviews*, *174*, 113121. DOI: 10.1016/j.rser.2022.113121

Mouha, R. A. R. A. (2021). Internet of things (IoT). *Journal of Data Analysis and Information Processing*, *9*(02), 77–101. DOI: 10.4236/jdaip.2021.92006

Mousavi, M., Shen, X., Zhang, Z., Barati, K., & Li, B. (2025). IoT-Bayes fusion. Advancing real-time environmental safety risk monitoring in underground mining and construction. *Reliability Engineering & System Safety*, *256*, 110760. DOI: 10.1016/j.ress.2024.110760

Moussa, W., & Konstantas, D. (2018). IoT and security-privacy concerns: A systematic mapping study. *International Journal of Network Security & its Applications*, *10*(6), 25–33. Advance online publication. DOI: 10.5121/ijnsa.2018.10603

Mseer, N. I., & Ahmed, S. M. (2023). Artificial intelligence and security challenges. https://doi.org/DOI: 10.1007/978-3-031-35828-9_13

Mughal, A. A. (2018). The Art of Cybersecurity: Defense in Depth Strategy for Robust Protection. *International Journal of Intelligent Automation and Computing*, *1*(1), 1–20.

Muhammed, D., Ahvar, E., Ahvar, S., Trocan, M., Montpetit, M. J., & Ehsani, R. (2024). Artificial Intelligence of Things (AIoT) for smart agriculture: A review of architectures, technologies and solutions. *Journal of Network and Computer Applications*, *228*, 103905. DOI: 10.1016/j.jnca.2024.103905

Mukherjee, A., Smith, R. J., & Turri, A. M. (2018). The smartness paradox: The moderating effect of brand quality reputation on consumers' reactions to RFID-based smart fitting rooms. *Journal of Business Research*, *92*, 290–299. DOI: 10.1016/j.jbusres.2018.07.057

Mukhopadhyay, S. C., Tyagi, S. K. S., Suryadevara, N. K., Piuri, V., Scotti, F., & Zeadally, S. (2021). Artificial Intelligence-Based Sensors for next generation IoT Applications: A review. *IEEE Sensors Journal*, *21*(22), 24920–24932. DOI: 10.1109/JSEN.2021.3055618

Mukhti, J. A., Gucunski, N., & Kee, S.-H. (2024). AI-assisted ultrasonic wave analysis for automated classification of steel corrosion-induced concrete damage. *Automation in Construction*, *167*, 105704. DOI: 10.1016/j.autcon.2024.105704

Mulani, A. O., Bang, A. V., Birajadar, G. B., Deshmukh, A. B., & Jadhav, H. M. (2024). IoT Based Air, Water, and Soil Monitoring System for Pomegranate Farming. *Annals of Agri Bio Research*, *29*(2), 71–86.

Mulani, A. O., Liyakat, K. K. S., Warade, N. S., Patil, A., Kolte, M. T., Kinage, K., Rana, M., Salunkhe, S. S., Jadhav, V. S., & Nagrale, M. (2025). ML-powered Internet of Medical Things Structure for Heart Disease Prediction. *Journal of Pharmacology & Pharmacotherapeutics*, *0*(0), 0976500X241306184. Advance online publication. DOI: 10.1177/0976500X241306184

Murugamani, C., Shitharth, S., Hemalatha, S., Kshirsagar, P. R., Riyazuddin, K., Naveed, Q. N., Islam, S., Mazher Ali, S. P., & Batu, A. (2022). Machine Learning Technique for Precision Agriculture Applications in 5G-Based Internet of Things. *Wireless Communications and Mobile Computing*, *2022*(1), 6534238. DOI: 10.1155/2022/6534238

Muts, I. (2023). IoT in manufacturing: Revolutionizing production processes. Euristiq. Retrieved January 6, 2025, from https://euristiq.com/iot-in-manufacturing/

Nachbauer, M., & Kyriakides, L. (2019). A review and evaluation of approaches to measure equity in educational outcomes. *School Effectiveness and School Improvement*, *31*(2), 306–331. DOI: 10.1080/09243453.2019.1672757

Nagaty, K. A. (2023). Iot commercial and industrial applications and AI-powered IoT. In *Frontiers of Quality Electronic Design (QED) AI, IoT and Hardware Security* (pp. 465–500). Springer International Publishing. DOI: 10.1007/978-3-031-16344-9_12

Najafabadi, M. M., Villanustre, F., Khoshgoftaar, T. M., Seliya, N., Wald, R., & Muharemagic, E. (2015). Deep learning applications and challenges in big data analytics. *Journal of Big Data*, *2*(1), 1. Advance online publication. DOI: 10.1186/s40537-014-0007-7

Naji, K., Gowid, S., & Ghani, S. (2023). AI and IoT-based concrete column base cover localization and degradation detection algorithm using deep learning techniques. *Ain Shams Engineering Journal*, *14*(11), 102520. DOI: 10.1016/j.asej.2023.102520

Nakamoto, S. (2008). *Bitcoin: A peer-to-peer electronic cash system.* Satoshi Nakamoto.

Nam, T., & Pardo, T. A. (2011, June). Conceptualizing smart city with dimensions of technology, people, and institutions. In *Proceedings of the 12th Annual International Digital Government Research Conference: Digital Government Innovation in Challenging Times* (pp. 282-291). DOI: 10.1145/2037556.2037602

Naphade, M., Banavar, G., Harrison, C., Paraszczak, J., & Morris, R. (2011). Smarter cities and their innovation challenges. *Computer*, *44*(6), 32–39. DOI: 10.1109/MC.2011.187

Narang, U., & Shankar, V. (2019). Mobile app introduction and online and offline purchases and product returns. *Marketing Science*, *38*(5), 756–772. DOI: 10.1287/mksc.2019.1169

Nathan, S. S.Shelena Soosay NathanKuan Jung YingLim Hui WenLim Xin Weoi. (2023). Design of smart walking shoe for visually impaired people. *Journal of Advanced Research in Applied Mechanics*, *101*(1), 53–61. DOI: 10.37934/aram.101.1.5361

Nazar, W., He, X., & Usman, M. (2020). Security & privacy in IoT using machine learning & blockchain: Threats & countermeasures. *arXiv: Cryptography and Security*.

Nazarevich, D. (2023). AI and IoT at the crossroads: the rise of AIoT and its impact on the future. Available at: https://innowise.com/blog/artificial-intelligence-of-things/

Nazer, L. H., Zatarah, R., Waldrip, S., Ke, J. X. C., Moukheiber, M., Khanna, A. K., Hicklen, R. S., Moukheiber, L., Moukheiber, D., Ma, H., & Mathur, P. (2023). Bias in artificial intelligence algorithms and recommendations for mitigation. *PLOS Digital Health*, *2*(6), e0000278. DOI: 10.1371/journal.pdig.0000278 PMID: 37347721

Neeraja, P., Kumar, R. G., Kumar, M. S., Liyakat, K. K. S., & Vani, M. S. (2024). *DL-Based Somnolence Detection for Improved Driver Safety and Alertness Monitoring. 2024 IEEE International Conference on Computing, Power and Communication Technologies (IC2PCT)*. Greater Noida., Available at https://ieeexplore.ieee.org/document/10486714, DOI: 10.1109/IC2PCT60090.2024.10486714

Nerkar, P. M., & Dhaware, B. U. (2023). Predictive Data Analytics Framework Based on Heart Healthcare System (HHS) Using Machine Learning, *Journal of Advanced Zoology*, 2023, Volume 44, Special Issue -2, Page 3673:3686. Available at: https://jazindia.com/index.php/jaz/article/view/1695

Ngo, T. D., Kashani, A., Imbalzano, G., Nguyen, K. T., & Hui, D. (2018). Additive manufacturing (3D printing): A review of materials, methods, applications and challenges. *Composites. Part B, Engineering*, *143*, 172–196. DOI: 10.1016/j.compositesb.2018.02.012

Nguyen, D. C., Ding, M., Pathirana, P. N., Seneviratne, A., Li, J., Niyato, D., Dobre, O., & Poor, H. V. (2021). 6G Internet of Things: A comprehensive survey. *IEEE Internet of Things Journal*, *9*(1), 359–383. DOI: 10.1109/JIOT.2021.3103320

Nicodeme, C. (2021). Ai legitimacy for sustainability. In: 2021 IEEE Conference on Technologies for Sustainability (SusTech), pp. 1–5. IEEE, Ochoa, V., & Urbina-Cardona, N. (2017). Tools for spatially modeling ecosystem services: publication trends, conceptual reflections, and future challenges, *Ecosystem Servey, 26*, 155–169.

Niemeier, S., Zocchi, A., & Catena, M. (2013). *Reshaping retail: Why technology is transforming the industry and how to win in the new consumer driven world.* John Wiley & Sons.

Nikolov, N. (2020). Research of MQTT, CoAP, HTTP and XMPP IoT Communication protocols for Embedded Systems. In *Proceedings of the 2020 XXIX International Scientific Conference Electronics (ET)*, Sozopol, Bulgaria. DOI: 10.1109/ET50336.2020.9238208

Nikpour, M., Yousefi, P. B., Jafarzadeh, H., Danesh, K., Shomali, R., Asadi, S., Lonbar, A. G., & Ahmadi, M. (2025). Intelligent energy management with IoT framework in smart cities using intelligent analysis. An application of machine learning methods for complex networks and systems. *Journal of Network and Computer Applications*, Volume 235, 104089. OpenPr, https.//www.openpr.com/news/3847849/global-artificial-intelligence-of-things-aiot-market-to-reach

Nishant, R., Kennedy, M., & Corbett, J. (2020). Artificial intelligence for sustainability: Challenges, opportunities, and a research agenda. *International Journal of Information Management*, *53*, 102104. DOI: 10.1016/j.ijinfomgt.2020.102104

Nofer, M., Gomber, P., Hinz, O., & Schiereck, D. (2017). Blockchain. *Business & Information Systems Engineering*, *59*(3), 183–187. DOI: 10.1007/s12599-017-0467-3

Noori, N., Hoppe, T., & de Jong, M. (2020). Classifying pathways for smart city development: Comparing design, governance and implementation in Amsterdam, Barcelona, Dubai, and Abu Dhabi. *Sustainability (Basel)*, *12*(10), 4030. DOI: 10.3390/su12104030

Norori, N., Hu, Q., Aellen, F. M., Faraci, F. D., & Tzovara, A. (2021). Addressing bias in big data and AI for health care: A call for open science. *Patterns (New York, N.Y.)*, *2*(10), 100347. DOI: 10.1016/j.patter.2021.100347 PMID: 34693373

Noura, M., Atiquzzaman, M., & Gaedke, M. (2018). Interoperability in Internet of things: Taxonomies and open challenges. *Mobile Networks and Applications*, *24*(3), 796–809. DOI: 10.1007/s11036-018-1089-9

Nozari, H., Tavakkoli-Moghaddam, R., Ghahremani-Nahr, J., & Najafi, E. (2023). A conceptual framework for artificial intelligence of medical things (AIoMT). In *Computational Intelligence for Medical Internet of Things (MIoT) Applications* (pp. 175-189). Academic Press.

Nozari, H., Szmelter-Jarosz, A., & Ghahremani-Nahr, J. (2022). Analysis of the challenges of artificial intelligence of things (AIoT) for the smart supply chain (Case study: FMCG industries). *Sensors (Basel), 22*(8), 2931. Advance online publication. DOI: 10.3390/s22082931 PMID: 35458916

Nuanmeesri, S., & Poomhiran, L. (2020). Developing of intelligence walking stick and mobile application for elderly health care using the internet of things.

Obaidat, M. A., Obeidat, S., Holst, J., Al Hayajneh, A., & Brown, J. (2020). A comprehensive and systematic survey on the Internet of things: Security and privacy challenges, security frameworks, enabling technologies, threats, vulnerabilities and countermeasures. *Computers, 9*(2), 44. DOI: 10.3390/computers9020044

Odnala, S., Shanthy, R., Bharathi, B., Pandey, C., Rachapalli, A., & Liyakat, K. K. S. (2025). Artificial Intelligence and Cloud-Enabled E-Vehicle Design with Wireless Sensor Integration. SSRN *Electronic Journal*. DOI: 10.2139/ssrn.5107242

Ogunjimi, A., Rahman, M., Islam, N., & Hasan, R. (2021). Smart mirror fashion technology for the retail chain transformation. *Technological Forecasting and Social Change, 173*, 121118. DOI: 10.1016/j.techfore.2021.121118

Oh, J., Lee, J., Park, Y., & Park, Y. (2022, December). A secure data processing system in edge computing-powered AIoT. In *2022 IEEE Asia-Pacific Conference on Computer Science and Data Engineering (CSDE)*. (pp. 1-4). IEEE. DOI: 10.1109/CSDE56538.2022.10089302

Olawade, D. B., Wada, O. Z., Ige, A. O., Egbewole, B. I., Olojo, A., & Oladapo, B. I. (2024). Artificial intelligence in environmental monitoring: Advancements, challenges, and future directions. *Hygiene and Environmental Health Advances, 100114*, 100114. Advance online publication. DOI: 10.1016/j.heha.2024.100114

Omrany, H., Al-Obaidi, K. M., Hossain, M., Alduais, N. A., Al-Duais, H. S., & Ghaffarianhoseini, A. (2024). IoT-enabled smart cities: A hybrid systematic analysis of key research areas, challenges, and recommendations for future direction. Springer. *Discover Cities, 1*(1), 2. DOI: 10.1007/s44327-024-00002-w

Ortega, A. (2023). A survey of machine and deep learning methods for privacy protection in the Internet of Things. *Sensors (Basel), 23*(3), 1252. Advance online publication. DOI: 10.3390/s23031252 PMID: 36772292

Ortega-Fernández, A., Martín-Rojas, R., & García-Morales, V. J. (2020). Artificial intelligence in the urban environment: Smart cities as models for developing innovation and sustainability. *Sustainability (Basel), 12*(19), 7860. DOI: 10.3390/su12197860

Osservatori.net. *Smart Agrifood: Condivisione e Informazione, Gli Ingredienti Per L'innovazione*; Politecnico di Milano: Milan, Italy, 2021; Available online: www .osservatori.net

Ourad, A. Z., Belgacem, B., & Salah, K. (2018). Using blockchain for IOT access control and authentication management. *Lecture Notes in Computer Science, 10972*, 150–164. DOI: 10.1007/978-3-319-94370-1_11

Pala, G. K., Kesana, N. S., & Gopalapurapu, K. S. (2025). *25 - Advancements in optimizing the quality assurance and crack detection by leveraging the application of emerging artificial intelligence trends for enrichment of civil infrastructure-a recapitulation. Recent Developments and Innovations in the Sustainable Production of Concrete*. Woodhead Publishing Series in Civil and Structural Engineering.

Pallagani, V., Khandelwal, V., Chandra, B., Udutalapally, V., Das, D., & Mohanty, S. P. (2019, December). *DCrop: A deep-learning based framework for accurate prediction of diseases of crops in smart agriculture. In 2019 IEEE international symposium on smart electronic systems (iSES)(formerly inis)*. IEEE.

Panduman, Y. Y. F., Funabiki, N., Fajrianti, E. D., Fang, S., & Sukaridhoto, S. (2024). A Survey of AI Techniques in IoT Applications with Use Case Investigations in the Smart Environmental Monitoring and Analytics in Real-Time IoT Platform. *Information (Basel), 15*(3), 153. DOI: 10.3390/info15030153

Pani, S., Pattnaik, O., & Pattanayak, B. K. (2024, February 2). *Predictive maintenance in Industrial IoT using Machine Learning approach*. https://www.ijisae.org/index.php/IJISAE/article/view/4689

Pantano, E., & Priporas, C. V. (2016). The effect of mobile retailing on consumers' purchasing experiences: A dynamic perspective. *Computers in Human Behavior, 61*, 548–555. DOI: 10.1016/j.chb.2016.03.071

Pantano, E., & Timmermans, H. (2014). What is smart for retailing? *Procedia Environmental Sciences, 22*, 101–107. DOI: 10.1016/j.proenv.2014.11.010

Pantano, E., & Viassone, M. (2014). Demand pull and technology push perspective in technology-based innovations for the points of sale: The retailers evaluation. *Journal of Retailing and Consumer Services, 21*(1), 43–47. DOI: 10.1016/j.jretconser.2013.06.007

Paoletti, M. (2021). Industrial Internet of Things: State-of-the-art and directions of future development.

Parihar, V., & Malik, A. Bhawna, Bhushan, B., & Chaganti, R. (2023). From smart devices to smarter systems: the evolution of artificial intelligence of things (AIoT) with characteristics, architecture, use cases and challenges. In AI models for blockchain-based intelligent networks in IoT systems: Concepts, methodologies, tools, and applications (pp. 1-28). Cham: Springer International Publishing.

Park, H. J., & Zhang, Y. (2022). Technology readiness and technology paradox of unmanned convenience store users. *Journal of Retailing and Consumer Services, 65*, 102523. DOI: 10.1016/j.jretconser.2021.102523

Patel, K. K., Patel, S. M., & Scholar, P. (2016). Internet of things-IOT: definition, characteristics, architecture, enabling technologies, application & future challenges. *International journal of engineering science and computing, 6*(5).

Patel, K., & Patel, H. B. (2020). A state-of-the-art survey on recommendation system and prospective extensions. *Computers and Electronics in Agriculture, 178*, 105779. DOI: 10.1016/j.compag.2020.105779

Pathak, A., Adil, M., Rafa, T. S., Ferdoush, J., & Mahmud, A. (2020). An IoT based voice controlled blind stick to guide blind people. *Int. J. Eng. Invent, 9*, 9–14.

Patton, R. M., & Buffington, M. L. (2016). Keeping up with our students: The evolution of technology and standards in art education. *Arts Education Policy Review, 117*(3), 1–9. DOI: 10.1080/10632913.2014.944961

Petit, M. (2018). Towards a critique of algorithmic reason. A state-of-the-art review of artificial intelligence, its influence on politics, and its regulation. Quadratic Deletion CAC, 44.

Piantadosi, V., Rosa, G., Placella, D., Scalabrino, S., & Oliveto, R. (2022). Detecting functional and security-related issues in smart contracts: A systematic literature review. *Software, Practice & Experience, 53*(2), 465–495. DOI: 10.1002/spe.3156

Picton, C., & Kahu, E. R. (2021). 'I knew I had the support from them': Understanding student support through a student engagement lens. *Higher Education Research & Development, 41*(6), 2034–2047. DOI: 10.1080/07294360.2021.1968353

Pise, A. A., Almusaini, K. K., & Ahanger, T. A. (2022). Research article enabling artificial intelligence of things (AIoT) healthcare architectures and listing security issues.

Pise, A., Almuzaini, K. K., Ahamed, T., Ahanger, A., Farouk, A., Pant, K., Kumar, P., Pareek, P., & Nuagah, S. J. (2022). Enabling artificial intelligence of things (AIoT) healthcare architectures and listing security issues. *Computational Intelligence and Neuroscience*, *2022*, 1–14. Advance online publication. DOI: 10.1155/2022/8421434 PMID: 36911247

Poria, S., Cambria, E., Bajpai, R., & Hussain, A. (2017). A review of affective computing: From unimodal analysis to multimodal fusion. *Information Fusion*, *37*, 98–125. DOI: 10.1016/j.inffus.2017.02.003

Pourrahmani, H., Yavarinasab, A., Zahedi, R., Gharehghani, A., Mohammadi, M. H., Bastani, P., & Van Herle, J. (2022). The applications of Internet of Things in the automotive industry: A review of the batteries, fuel cells, and engines. *Internet of Things : Engineering Cyber Physical Human Systems*, *19*, 100579. DOI: 10.1016/j.iot.2022.100579

Poushneh, A. (2018). Augmented reality in retail: A trade-off between user's control of access to personal information and augmentation quality. *Journal of Retailing and Consumer Services*, *41*, 169–176. DOI: 10.1016/j.jretconser.2017.12.010

Prabhakar, V. V., Xavier, C. S. B., & Abubeker, K. M. (2023). A Review on Challenges and Solutions in the Implementation of Ai, IoT and Blockchain in Construction Industry. *Materials Today: Proceedings*. Advance online publication. DOI: 10.1016/j.matpr.2023.03.535

Pradeepa, M., ... (2022). Student Health Detection using a Machine Learning Approach and IoT, *2022 IEEE 2nd Mysore sub section International Conference (MysuruCon)*, 2022. Available at: https://ieeexplore.ieee.org/document/9972445

Praitheeshan, P., Pan, L., & Doss, R. (2020). Security evaluation of smart contract-based on-chain Ethereum wallets. *Lecture Notes in Computer Science*, *12570*, 22–41. DOI: 10.1007/978-3-030-65745-1_2

Prakash, A., Avasthi, S., Agarwal, K., & Hussain, M. (2024). Modern healthcare systems: Unveiling the possibility of AIoT for remote patient monitoring. In *Developments Towards Next Generation Intelligent Systems for Sustainable Development* (pp. 180–203). IGI Global.

Prasad, K. R., Karanam, S. R., Ganesh, D., Liyakat, K. K. S., Talasila, V., & Purushotham, P. (2024, May). AI in public-private partnership for IT infrastructure development. *The Journal of High Technology Management Research*, *35*(1), 100496. DOI: 10.1016/j.hitech.2024.100496

Prashant, K. Magadum (2024). Machine Learning for Predicting Wind Turbine Output Power in Wind Energy Conversion Systems, *Grenze International Journal of Engineering and Technology,* Jan Issue, Vol 10, Issue 1, pp. 2074-2080. Grenze ID: 01.GIJET.10.1.4_1 Available at: https://thegrenze.com/index.php?display=page&view=journalabstract&absid=2514&id=8

Prathima, K. M., & Navya, B. S. (2021). AIoT - Artificial Intelligence of Things. https://doi.org/DOI: 10.48175/IJARSCT-V4-I3-013

Premananthan, G., Nagaraj, B., & Divya, N. (2020). WITHDRAWN: Sensor based integrated smart trolley system using Zigbee-experimental analysis.

Priya Nerkar and Sultanabanu. (2024). IoT-Based Skin Health Monitoring System [IJBPAS]. *International Journal of Biology, Pharmacy and Allied Sciences, 13*(11), 5937–5950. DOI: 10.31032/IJBPAS/2024/13.11.8488

Pydala, B., Kumar, T. P., & Baseer, K. K. (2023). Smart_Eye: A navigation and obstacle detection for visually impaired people through smart app. [JAETS]. *Journal of Applied Engineering and Technological Science, 4*(2), 992–1011. DOI: 10.37385/jaets.v4i2.2013

Qi, W., Xu, X., Qian, K., Schuller, B. W., Fortino, G., & Aliverti, A. (2024). A Review of AIoT-based Human Activity Recognition: From Application to Technique. *IEEE Journal of Biomedical and Health Informatics*. PMID: 38809724

Quang, T. V., Doan, D. T., Ngarambe, J., Ghaffarianhoseini, A., Ghaffarianhoseini, A., & Zhang, T. (2025). AI management platform for privacy-preserving indoor air quality control. Review and future directions. *Journal of Building Engineering, 100*, 111712. DOI: 10.1016/j.jobe.2024.111712

Rácz, A., Veres, A., Hága, P., Borsos, T., & Kenesi, Z. (2022, December). A Full-Stack Neuromorphic Prototype Architecture for Low-Power Wireless Sensors. In *2022 IEEE Globecom Workshops (GC Wkshps)* (pp. 353-358). IEEE. DOI: 10.1109/GCWkshps56602.2022.10008616

Raghu, N., Mahesh, T. R., Vivek, V., Kumaran, S. Y., Kannanugo, N., & Vishwanatha, S. (2025). IoT-Enabled Safety and Secure Smart Homes for Elderly People. In *Future of Digital Technology and AI in Social Sectors* (pp. 297–328). IGI Global.

Rahi, P., Sood, S., Dandotiya, M., Kalhotra, S. K., & Khan, I. R. (2023). Artificial intelligence of things (AIoT) and metaverse technology for brain health, mental health, and wellbeing. In *Advances in Healthcare Information Systems and Administration Book Series*. https://doi.org/DOI: 10.4018/978-1-6684-8913-0.ch019

Rahman, M. U., Guidi, B., Baiardi, F., & Ricci, L. (2020). Context-aware and dynamic role-based access control using blockchain. *Advances in Intelligent Systems and Computing*, 1449-1460.

Raj, E., Buffoni, D., Westerlund, M., & Ahola, K. (2021, October). Edge mlops: An automation framework for aiot applications. In 2021 IEEE International Conference on Cloud Engineering (IC2E). (pp. 191-200). IEEE.

Ramlowat, D. D., & Pattanayak, B. K. (2019). Exploring the Internet of Things (IoT) in education: A review. In *Information Systems Design and Intelligent Applications* (pp. 245–255). https://doi.org/DOI: 10.1007/978-981-13-3338-5_23

Rangasamy, V., & Yang, J.-B. (2024). The convergence of BIM, AI and IoT. Reshaping the future of prefabricated construction. *Journal of Building Engineering*, *84*, 108606. DOI: 10.1016/j.jobe.2024.108606

Ransbotham, S., Kiron, D., Gerbert, P., & Reeves, M. (2017). Reshaping business with artificial intelligence: Closing the gap between ambition and action. *MIT Sloan Management Review*, •••, 59.

Rantos, K., Spyros, A., Papanikolaou, A., Kritsas, A., Ilioudis, C., & Katos, V. (2020). Interoperability challenges in the cybersecurity information sharing ecosystem. *Computers*, *9*(1), 18. DOI: 10.3390/computers9010018

Rashid, Z., Peig, E., & Pous, R. (2015, October). Bringing online shopping experience to offline retail through augmented reality and RFID. In *2015 5th International Conference on the Internet of Things (IOT)* (pp. 45-51). IEEE. DOI: 10.1109/IOT.2015.7356547

Ratasich, D., Khalid, F., & Geissler, F.. (2019). A roadmap to resilient IoT for cyber-physical systems. *IEEE Access : Practical Innovations, Open Solutions*, *7*, 13260–13283. DOI: 10.1109/ACCESS.2019.2891969

Raut, R., …. (2022). IoT-assisted smart device for blind people. In *Intelligent Systems for Rehabilitation Engineering* (pp. 129–150). DOI: 10.1002/9781119785651.ch6

Rawat, D. B., & Reddy, S. R. (2017). Software defined networking architecture, security and energy efficiency: A survey. *IEEE Communications Surveys and Tutorials*, *19*(1), 325–346. DOI: 10.1109/COMST.2016.2618874

Rayabharapu, V. K., Rampur, V., Jyothi, N. M., Tripathi, V., Bhaskar, T., & Glory, K. B. (2022). IOT sensor-based pollution management control technique. *Measurement. Sensors*, *24*, 100513. DOI: 10.1016/j.measen.2022.100513

Ray, P. P. (2018). A survey on Internet of Things architectures. *Journal of King Saud University. Computer and Information Sciences*, *30*(3), 291–319. DOI: 10.1016/j.jksuci.2016.10.003

Rejeb, A., Rejeb, K., Treiblmaier, H., Appolloni, A., Alghamdi, S., Alhasawi, Y., & Iranmanesh, M. (2023). The Internet of Things (IoT). in healthcare: Taking stock and moving forward. *Internet of Things : Engineering Cyber Physical Human Systems*, *22*, 100721. DOI: 10.1016/j.iot.2023.100721

Ren, J., Yu, Z., Xing, T., Cui, H., Chen, Y., & Guo, B. (2023, August). EnergySense: A Fine-Grained Energy Analysis Framework for DNN Processing with Low-Power Ubiquitous Sensors. In *2023 IEEE Smart World Congress (SWC)* (pp. 1-8). IEEE. DOI: 10.1109/SWC57546.2023.10449264

Reyna, A., Martín, C., Chen, J., Soler, E., & Díaz, M. (2018). On blockchain and its integration with IoT. Challenges and opportunities. *Future Generation Computer Systems*, *88*, 173–190. DOI: 10.1016/j.future.2018.05.046

Riegger, A. S., Merfeld, K., Klein, J. F., & Henkel, S. (2022). Technology-enabled personalization: Impact of smart technology choice on consumer shopping behavior. *Technological Forecasting and Social Change*, *181*, 121752. DOI: 10.1016/j.techfore.2022.121752

Roberts, M. E., Stewart, B. M., Tingley, D., & Airoldi, E. M. (2013). The structural topic model and applied social science. *Advances in neural information processing systems workshop on topic models: Computation, application, and evaluation*

Rodriguez-Soto, C., Velazquez, A., Monroy-Vilchis, O., Lemes, P., & Loyola, R. (2017). A joint ecological, geographical and cultural approach to identify territories of opportunity for large vertebrates conservation in Mexico. *Biodiversity and Conservation*, *26*(8), 1899–1918. DOI: 10.1007/s10531-017-1335-7

Roe, M., Spanaki, K., Ioannou, A., Zamani, E. D., & Giannakis, M. (2022). Drivers and challenges of internet of things diffusion in smart stores: A field exploration. *Technological Forecasting and Social Change*, *178*, 121593. DOI: 10.1016/j.techfore.2022.121593

Rogers, R., & Dhatariya, K. K. (2021). Bilateral Charcot neuroarthropathy in pregnancy: A case report and review of the influence of pregnancy hormones on ligament laxity. *AACE Clinical Case Reports*, *7*(1), 57–60. DOI: 10.1016/j.aace.2020.11.015 PMID: 33851021

Rouhani, S., & Deters, R. (2019). Security, performance, and applications of smart contracts: A systematic survey. *IEEE Access : Practical Innovations, Open Solutions*, *7*, 50759–50779. DOI: 10.1109/ACCESS.2019.2911031

Roy, S. K., Balaji, M. S., & Nguyen, B. (2020). Consumer-computer interaction and in-store smart technology (IST) in the retail industry: The role of motivation, opportunity, and ability. *Journal of Marketing Management*, *36*(3-4), 299–333. DOI: 10.1080/0267257X.2020.1736130

Roy, S. K., Balaji, M. S., Sadeque, S., Nguyen, B., & Melewar, T. C. (2017). Constituents and consequences of smart customer experience in retailing. *Technological Forecasting and Social Change*, *124*, 257–270. DOI: 10.1016/j.techfore.2016.09.022

Roy, S. K., Shekhar, V., Lassar, W. M., & Chen, T. (2018). Customer engagement behaviors: The role of service convenience, fairness and quality. *Journal of Retailing and Consumer Services*, *44*, 293–304. DOI: 10.1016/j.jretconser.2018.07.018

Ruhela, S., Chaudhary, P., Shrivas, R., & Chopra, D. (2021). AIoT application for food recommendation based on emotion analysis. https://doi.org/DOI: 10.48175/IJARSCT-928

Saberi Anari, M. (2022). A Hybrid Model for Leaf Diseases Classification Based on the Modified Deep Transfer Learning and Ensemble Approach for Agricultural AIoT-Based Monitoring. *Computational Intelligence and Neuroscience*, *2022*(1), 6504616. DOI: 10.1155/2022/6504616 PMID: 35422854

Sadhu, P. K., Yanambaka, V. P., & Abdelgawad, A. (2022). Internet of things: Security and solutions survey. *Sensors (Basel)*, *22*(19), 7433. DOI: 10.3390/s22197433 PMID: 36236531

Saha, B., & Srivastava, D. (2014, March). Data quality: The other face of big data. In *2014 IEEE 30th International Conference on Data Engineering* (pp. 1294-1297). IEEE.

Sahni, V., & Singh, M. (2024). Smart Indian agriculture farm using an IoT dashboard. *Educational Administration: Theory and Practice*. https://doi.org/DOI: 10.53555/kuey.v30i5.3215

Sahoo, T., Mondal, A., Roy, P., & Podder, A. (2024). Artificial intelligence and its application in engineering: A comprehensive review. In *Emerging Engineering Technologies and Industrial Applications* (pp. 1-20). DOI: 10.4018/979-8-3693-1335-0.ch001

Said, S., Rowan, I., Hesham, O., Abou Tabl, I., Nu, M., Youssef, S. M., & Elagamy, M. (2021). AIOT-Arch: Furthering artificial intelligence in big data IoT applications. *IOP Conference Series. Materials Science and Engineering*, *1051*(1), 012008. Advance online publication. DOI: 10.1088/1757-899X/1051/1/012008

Saisubramanyam, K., & Jhansi Rani, A. (2020). IoT based smart walking stick for blind or old aged people with GPS tracking location. *Journal of Engineering Science*, *11*(1), 501–505.

Salama, A. K., & Abdellatif, M. M. (2022, December). AIoT-based Smart Home Energy Management System. In *2022 IEEE Global Conference on Artificial Intelligence and Internet of Things (GCAIoT)*. (pp. 177-181). IEEE.

Samriya, J. K., Kumar, M., & Gill, S. S. (2023). Secured data offloading using reinforcement learning and Markov decision process in mobile edge computing. *International Journal of Network Management*, *33*(5), e2243. DOI: 10.1002/nem.2243

Santhi, V., Sabareesh, Y. N. S., Sudheer, P. P., & Krishna, V. P. S. (2024). Trends and Challenges in AIoT Implementation for Smart Home, Smart Buildings, and Smart Cities in Cloud Platforms. *Artificial Intelligence of Things (AIoT) for Productivity and Organizational Transition*, 240-319.

Sarikaya, R. (2017). The technology behind personal digital assistants: An overview of the system architecture and key components. *IEEE Signal Processing Magazine*, *34*(1), 67–81. DOI: 10.1109/MSP.2016.2617341

Sarkar, K., Shiuly, A., & Dhal, K. G. (2024). Revolutionizing concrete analysis. An in-depth survey of AI-powered insights with image-centric approaches on comprehensive quality control, advanced crack detection and concrete property exploration. [[SAS, https.//]. *Construction & Building Materials*, *411*, 134212. www.sas.com/en_in/explore/resources/aiot.html. DOI: 10.1016/j.conbuildmat.2023.134212

Sarker, I. H. (2021). Deep Learning: A comprehensive overview on techniques, taxonomy, applications and research directions. *SN Computer Science*, *2*(6), 420. Advance online publication. DOI: 10.1007/s42979-021-00815-1 PMID: 34426802

Sarker, I. H., Furhad, M. H., & Nowrozy, R. (2021). AI-driven cybersecurity: An overview, security intelligence modeling and research directions. *SN Computer Science*, *2*(3), 1–18. DOI: 10.1007/s42979-021-00557-0

Sarkozi, A. (2019). *New standards to curb the global spread of plant pests and diseases*. Food and Agriculture Organization of the United Nations.

Sasi, T., Lashkari, A. H., Lu, R., Xiong, P., & Iqbal, S. (2024). A comprehensive survey on IoT attacks: Taxonomy, detection mechanisms and challenges. *Journal of Information and intelligence, 2*(6), 455-513.

Sasi, T., Lashkari, A. H., Lu, R., Xiong, P., & Iqbal, S. (2024). A comprehensive survey on IoT attacks: Taxonomy, detection mechanisms and challenges. *Journal of Information and Intelligence*, *2*(6), 455–513. DOI: 10.1016/j.jiixd.2023.12.001

Sathya, D., Nithyaroopa, S., Betty, P., Santhoshni, G., Sabharinath, S., & Ahanaa, M. J. (2018). Smart walking stick for blind person. *International Journal of Pure and Applied Mathematics*, *118*(20), 4531–4536.

Sayed, S. A., Abdel-Hamid, Y., & Hefny, H. A. (2023). Artificial intelligence-based traffic flow prediction: A comprehensive review. *Journal of Electrical Systems and Information Technology*, *10*(1), 13. Advance online publication. DOI: 10.1186/s43067-023-00081-6

Sayyad (2025b). AI-Powered IoT (AI IoT) for Decision-Making in Smart Agriculture: KSK Approach for Smart Agriculture. In S. Hai-Jew (Ed.), *Enhancing Automated Decision-Making Through AI* (pp. 67-96). IGI Global Scientific Publishing. https://doi.org/DOI: 10.4018/979-8-3693-6230-3.ch003

Sayyad (2025c). KK Approach to Increase Resilience in Internet of Things: A T-Cell Security Concept. In D. Darwish & K. Charan (Eds.), Analyzing Privacy and Security Difficulties in Social Media: New Challenges and Solutions (pp. 87-120). IGI Global Scientific Publishing. https://doi.org/DOI: 10.4018/979-8-3693-9491-5.ch005

Sayyad (2025d). Healthcare Monitoring System Driven by Machine Learning and Internet of Medical Things (MLIoMT). *In V. Kumar, P. Katina, & J. Zhao (Eds.), Convergence of Internet of Medical Things (IoMT) and Generative AI* (pp. 385-416). IGI Global Scientific Publishing. https://doi.org/DOI: 10.4018/979-8-3693-6180-1.ch016

Sayyad, (2018). Significance of Projection and Rotation of Image in Color Matching for High-Quality Panoramic Images used for Aquatic study, *International Journal of Aquatic Science*, 9(2), pp. 130 – 145.

Sayyad, (2025). KK Approach for IoT Security: T-Cell Concept. In Rajeev Kumar, Sheng-Lung Peng, & Ahmed Elngar (Eds.), *Deep Learning Innovations for Securing Critical Infrastructures.* IGI Global Scientific Publishing.

Sayyad. (2025a). AI-Powered-IoT (AIIoT)-Based Decision-Making System for BP Patient's Healthcare Monitoring: KSK Approach for BP Patient Healthcare Monitoring. *In S. Aouadni& I. Aouadni (Eds.), Recent Theories and Applications for Multi-Criteria Decision-Making (pp. 205-238). IGI Global.*https://doi.org/DOI: 10.4018/979-8-3693-6502-1.ch008

Schranz, M., Di Caro, G. A., Schmickl, T., Elmenreich, W., Arvin, F., Şekercioğlu, A., & Sende, M. (2021). Swarm intelligence and cyber-physical systems: Concepts, challenges and future trends. *Swarm and Evolutionary Computation*, *60*, 100762. DOI: 10.1016/j.swevo.2020.100762

Schwab, K. (2017). *The fourth industrial revolution*. Crown Currency.

Selvarani, S., Ganeshan, M. K., & Vethirajan, C. Ashok Kumar, & Arumugam, U (2023). Artificial intelligence and machine learning in smart manufacturing in industry 4.0. In *International Journal of Research Publication and Reviews* (Vol. 4, Issue 11, pp. 2053–2058).https://ijrpr.com/uploads/V4ISSUE11/IJRPR19316.pdf

Sen, P. C., Hajra, M., & Ghosh, M. (2019). Supervised Classification Algorithms in Machine Learning: A Survey and review. In *Advances in intelligent systems and computing* (pp. 99–111). DOI: 10.1007/978-981-13-7403-6_11

Severino, F., Canciani, A., Felicioli, C., Gervasi, V., Pelosi, A., Natali, A., Salvatore, W., & Russo, S. (2024). Trustworthy AI for infrastructure monitoring. a blockchain-based approach. *Procedia Structural Integrity*, *62*, 276–284. DOI: 10.1016/j.prostr.2024.09.043

Seyyedi, S. R., Kowsari, E., Gheibi, M., Chinnappan, A., & Ramakrishna, S. (2024). A comprehensive review integration of digitalization and circular economy in waste management by adopting artificial intelligence approaches. Towards a simulation model. *Journal of Cleaner Production*, *460*, 142584. DOI: 10.1016/j.jclepro.2024.142584

Shafik, W. (2024). Smart health revolution: Exploring artificial intelligence of internet of medical things. In *Healthcare Industry Assessment: Analyzing Risks, Security, and Reliability* (pp. 201–229). Springer Nature Switzerland. DOI: 10.1007/978-3-031-65434-3_9

Shafique, K., Khawaja, B. A., Sabir, F., Qazi, S., & Mustaqim, M. (2020). Internet of things (IoT) for next-generation smart systems: A review of current challenges, future trends and prospects for emerging 5G-IoT scenarios. *IEEE Access : Practical Innovations, Open Solutions*, *8*, 23022–23040. DOI: 10.1109/ACCESS.2020.2970118

Shaharuddin, S., Maulud, K. N. A., Rahman, S. A. F. S. A., Ani, A. I. C., & Pradhan, B. (2023). The role of IoT sensor in smart building context for indoor fire hazard scenario. A systematic review of interdisciplinary articles. *Internet of Things : Engineering Cyber Physical Human Systems, 22*, 100803. DOI: 10.1016/j.iot.2023.100803

Shaik, R., Raju, D., Behera, P. C., Changala, R., Mary, S. S. C., & Balakumar, A. (2024, March). Real-Time Anomaly Detection in 5G Networks Through Edge Computing. In *2024 Third International Conference on Intelligent Techniques in Control, Optimization and Signal Processing (INCOS)* (pp. 1-6). IEEE. DOI: 10.1109/INCOS59338.2024.10527501

Shamsuzzoha, A., Nieminen, J., Piya, S., & Rutledge, K. (2021). Smart city for sustainable environment: A comparison of participatory strategies from Helsinki, Singapore, and London. *Cities (London, England), 114*, 103194. DOI: 10.1016/j.cities.2021.103194

Shankaranarayanan, G., & Cai, Y. (2006). Supporting data quality management in decision-making. *Decision Support Systems, 42*(1), 302–317. DOI: 10.1016/j.dss.2004.12.006

Shankar, V., Kalyanam, K., Setia, P., Golmohammadi, A., Tirunillai, S., Douglass, T., Hennessey, J., Bull, J. S., & Waddoups, R. (2021). How technology is changing retail. *Journal of Retailing, 97*(1), 13–27. DOI: 10.1016/j.jretai.2020.10.006

Shanthakumar, C. S. T., Harish, N., & Giridharan, A. (2023, January). Internet of things and edge computing for real time applications. In *2023 International Conference on Intelligent and Innovative Technologies in Computing, Electrical and Electronics (IITCEE)* (pp. 1137-1141). IEEE.

Sharghivand, N., & Derakhshan, F. (2021). Data security and privacy in industrial IoT. In A. B. Editor & C. D. Editor (Eds.), *Industrial IoT: Challenges, Design Principles, Applications, and Business Models* (pp. 35–50). Springer. DOI: 10.1007/978-3-030-76613-9_3

Sharifi, A. (2019). A critical review of selected smart city assessment tools and indicator sets. *Journal of Cleaner Production, 233*, 1269–1283. DOI: 10.1016/j.jclepro.2019.06.172

Sharma, S. (2024). Benefits or concerns of AI: A multistakeholder responsibility. *Futures, 157*, 103328. DOI: 10.1016/j.futures.2024.103328

Sharmila, G., Ragaventhiran, J., Islabudeen, M., & Kumar, B. M. (2021). WITHDRAWN: RFID Based Smart-Cart system with automated billing and assistance for visually impaired.

Sharphathy, M. N., & Sumalatha, V. (2023, July). SSS-EC: Cryptographic based Single-Factor Authentication for Fingerprint Data with Machine Learning Technique. In *2023 2nd International Conference on Edge Computing and Applications (ICECAA)* (pp. 308-315). IEEE.

Shaveta, X. (2024). Federated learning in edge computing environments: Opportunities, challenges, and future directions. [IJSR]. *International Journal of Scientific Research, 13*(9), 275–278.

Shekhawat, S. (2022, December). Use of AI and IoT to make Retail Smarter. In *2022 3rd International Informatics and Software Engineering Conference (IISEC)* (pp. 1-5). IEEE. DOI: 10.1109/IISEC56263.2022.9998202

Shekhawat, S. (2023). Smart retail: How AI and IoT are revolutionising the retail industry. Journal of AI. *Robotics & Workplace Automation*, *2*(2), 145–152. DOI: 10.69554/TCLG1264

Shemshack, A., & Spector, J. M. (2020). A systematic literature review of personalized learning terms. *Smart Learning Environments*, *7*(1), 33. Advance online publication. DOI: 10.1186/s40561-020-00140-9

Shen, Z., Jin, J., Zhang, T., Tagami, A., Higashino, T., & Han, Q. L. (2021). Data-driven edge computing: A fabric for intelligent building energy management systems. *IEEE Industrial Electronics Magazine*, *16*(2), 44–52. DOI: 10.1109/MIE.2021.3120235

Shinde, S. S., Nerkar, P. M., Kazi, S. S., & Kazi, V. S. (2025). Machine Learning for Brand Protection: A Review of a Proactive Defense Mechanism. In Khan, M., & Amin Ul Haq, M. (Eds.), *Avoiding Ad Fraud and Supporting Brand Safety: Programmatic Advertising Solutions* (pp. 175–220). IGI Global Scientific Publishing., DOI: 10.4018/979-8-3693-7041-4.ch007

Shi, Q., Zhang, Z., Yang, Y., Shan, X., Salam, B., & Lee, C. (2021). Artificial intelligence of things (AIoT) enabled floor monitoring system for smart home applications. *ACS Nano*, *15*(11), 18312–18326. DOI: 10.1021/acsnano.1c07579 PMID: 34723468

Shi, W., Cao, J., Zhang, Q., Li, Y., & Xu, L. (2016). Edge computing: Vision and challenges. *IEEE Internet of Things Journal*, *3*(5), 637–646. DOI: 10.1109/JIOT.2016.2579198

Shollo, A., Hopf, K., Thiess, T., & Müller, O. (2022). Shifting ml value creation mechanisms: A process model of ml value creation. *The Journal of Strategic Information Systems*, *31*(3), 101734. DOI: 10.1016/j.jsis.2022.101734

Shukla, S., George, J. P., Tiwari, K., & Kureethara, J. V. (2022). Data ethics and challenges. In *Springer Briefs in Applied Sciences and Technology* (pp. 61–72). Springer Nature.

Siam, S. I., Ahn, H., Liu, L., Alam, S., Shen, H., Cao, Z., & Zhang, M. (2024). Artificial Intelligence of Things: A Survey. *ACM Transactions on Sensor Networks*.

Sibanda, M., Bhero, E., & Agee, J. (2023, January). Ai edge processing-a review of distributed embedded systems. In 2023 31st Southern African Universities Power Engineering Conference (SAUPEC). (pp. 1-6). IEEE. DOI: 10.1109/SAUPEC57889.2023.10057624

Sicari, S., Rizzardi, A., Grieco, L., & Coen-Porisini, A. (2015). Security, privacy and trust in Internet of things: The road ahead. *Computer Networks*, *76*, 146–164. DOI: 10.1016/j.comnet.2014.11.008

Siddiqi, M. A., Yu, H., & Joung, J. (2019). 5G Ultra-Reliable Low-Latency Communication Implementation Challenges and Operational Issues with IoT Devices. *Electronics (Basel)*, *8*(9), 981. DOI: 10.3390/electronics8090981

Silva, D., Inocêncio, L., Soares, J., & Sofia, R. (2021). A Performance Analysis of Internet of Things Networking Protocols: Evaluating MQTT, CoAP, OPC UA. *Applied Sciences (Basel, Switzerland)*, *11*(11), 4879. DOI: 10.3390/app11114879

Silva, M. M. D., & Guerreiro, J. (2020). On the 5G and Beyond. MDPI. *Applied Sciences (Basel, Switzerland)*, *10*(20), 7091. DOI: 10.3390/app10207091

Singh, A. (2022). Importance of Fuzzy Logic in Traffic and Transportation Engineering. In. Vasant, P., Zelinka, I., Weber, GW. (eds) Intelligent Computing & Optimization. ICO 2021. Lecture Notes in Networks and Systems, vol 371. Springer, Cham. https.//DOI: 10.1007/978-3-030-93247-3_10

Singh, A. (2023). The Present and Future Role of Artificial Intelligence in the Promotion of Sustainable Practices in the Construction Sector. In. Kahraman, C., Sari, I.U., Oztaysi, B., Cebi, S., Cevik Onar, S., Tolga, A.Ç. (eds) Intelligent and Fuzzy Systems. INFUS 2023. Lecture Notes in Networks and Systems, vol 759. Springer, Cham. https.//DOI: 10.1007/978-3-031-39777-6_2

Singh, A. (2023). The Recent Trend of Artificial Neural Network in the Field of Civil Engineering. In. Vasant, P., *et al.* Intelligent Computing and Optimization. ICO 2023. Lecture Notes in Networks and Systems, vol 855. Springer, Cham. https.// DOI: 10.1007/978-3-031-50158-6_32

Singh, A. (2024). The Current Status and Scope of Smart Highways in India. In L. Taha & S. Anwar (Eds.), *Principles and Applications in Speed Sensing and Energy Harvesting for Smart Roads* (pp. 1-41). IGI Global Scientific Publishing. https.// DOI: 10.4018/978-1-6684-9214-7.ch001

Singh, A. (2025). Chapter 7 The role of supply chain management in the construction industry. In P. Vasant, J. Thomas, V. Panchenko & G. Weber (Ed.), Smart Green Energy Production (pp. 95-120). Berlin, Boston. De Gruyter. https.//DOI: 10.1515/9783110717655-007

Singh, A., & Srivastava, A. (2024). Impact of Artificial Intelligence Techniques and Green AI Applications. In *Artificial Intelligence Techniques for Sustainable Development* (pp. 44-63). CRC Press. http.//DOI: 10.1201/9781003546382-3

Singh, R., Prabha, C., & Sharma, N. (2023). Artificial internet of things (AIoT) and its momentous impact and challenges in modern agriculture. In Proceedings of the *2023 International Conference on Intelligent Computing and Information Systems* (pp. 123–130). IEEE. DOI: 10.1109/icicis56802.2023.10430232

Singh, A. (2018). Use of Geographical Information System in Intelligent Transport. *International Journal of Research and Analytical Reviews*, *5*(4), 882–890.

Singh, A., Kapoor, D., & Bose, R. (2021). Enhancing Home Security Using AIoT: A Case Study of Indian Households. *Indian Journal of Technology and Engineering*, *27*(3), 145–160.

Singha, R., & Singha, S. (2024). AIoT concepts and integration: Exploring customer interaction, ethics, policy, and privacy. In *Artificial Intelligence of Things (AIoT) for Productivity and Organizational Transition* (pp. 26–51). IGI Global. DOI: 10.4018/979-8-3693-0993-3.ch002

Singh, R. P., Javaid, M., Haleem, A., & Suman, R. (2020). Internet of Things (IoT) applications to fight against COVID-19 pandemic. *Diabetes & Metabolic Syndrome*, *14*(4), 521–524. DOI: 10.1016/j.dsx.2020.04.041 PMID: 32388333

Singh, S., & Kumar, D. (2020). Perceptions of security and privacy in Internet of Things. In Proceedings of the *2020 International Conference on Information and Communication Technology* (pp. 45–52). IEEE. DOI: 10.1109/ICICT48043.2020.9112462

Sithembiso, S., Kekana, T. A., & Sibiya, A. (2022). Strategies for Internet of Things data privacy and security using systematic review. In *Advances in Cyber-Physical Systems and Security* (pp. 78–85). ECCWS., DOI: 10.34190/eccws.21.1.194

Songhorabadi, M., Rahimi, M., Farid, A. M. M., & Kashani, M. H. (2023). Fog computing approaches in IoT-enabled smart cities.[[Sphere, https.//]. *Journal of Network and Computer Applications*, *211*, 103557. www.sphereinc.com/blogs/ai-and-iot-in-construction-unlocking-the-value/. DOI: 10.1016/j.jnca.2022.103557

Sood, S. K., & Mahajan, I. (2017). Wearable IoT sensor based healthcare system for identifying and controlling chikungunya virus. *Computers in Industry*, *91*, 33–44. DOI: 10.1016/j.compind.2017.05.006 PMID: 32287550

Soori, M., Arezoo, B., & Dastres, R. (2023). Internet of things for smart factories in industry 4.0, a review. *Internet of Things and Cyber-Physical Systems*, *3*, 192–204. DOI: 10.1016/j.iotcps.2023.04.006

Spicher, N., Klingenberg, A., Purrucker, V., & Deserno, T. M. (2021). Edge computing in 5G cellular networks for real-time analysis of electrocardiography recorded with wearable textile sensors. *arXiv preprint arXiv:2107.13767*. DOI: 10.1109/EMBC46164.2021.9630875

Stankovic, M., Gupta, R., & Figueroa, J. E. Tambourine Innovation Ventures, Department of Trade, Investment and Innovation of UNIDO, Calzadilla-Sarmiento, B., Memedovic, O., Authried, O., & Rueth, T. (2021). INDUSTRY 4.0. In *Tambourine Innovation Ventures*. https://www.unido.org/sites/default/files/files/2020-06/UNIDO%20Background%20Paper%20on%20Industry%204.0_FINAL_TII.pdf

Statista (2016). Internet of Things (IoT) connccted devices installed base worldwide from 2015 to 2025. Available at: https://www.statista.com/statistics/471264/iot-number-of-connected-devices-worldwide/

Statista (2023a). Smart Home – India. Available at: https://www.statista.com/outlook/cmo/smart-home/india

Statista, https.//www.statista.com/statistics/1194709/iot-revenue-worldwide/

Statista, https.//www.statista.com/statistics/884092/worldwide-spending-smart-city-initiatives/

Statista. (2023b). Consumer Interest in Smart Home Solutions. Retrieved from Statista https://www.statista.com/statistics/1130403/smart-home-revenue-distribution-forecast-in-north-america-by-segment/

Stergiou, C., Psannis, K. E., Kim, B. G., & Gupta, B. (2018). Secure integration of IoT and cloud computing. *Future Generation Computer Systems*, *78*, 964–975. DOI: 10.1016/j.future.2016.11.031

Stippich, A. (2017). Key components of modular propulsion systems for next generation electric vehicles. *CPSS Transactions on Power Electronics and Applications*, *2*(4), 249–258. DOI: 10.24295/CPSSTPEA.2017.00023

Stockholm Resilience Centre's (SRC) contribution to the 2016 Swedish 2030 Agenda HLPF report (Stockholm University, 2017).

Stolojescu-Crisan, C., Crisan, C., & Butunoi, B. P. (2021). An IoT-based smart home automation system. *Sensors (Basel)*, *21*(11), 3784. DOI: 10.3390/s21113784 PMID: 34070717

Stopps, H., & Touchie, M. F. (2021). Residential smart thermostat use: An exploration of thermostat programming, environmental attitudes, and the influence of smart controls on energy savings. *Energy and Building*, *238*, 110834. DOI: 10.1016/j.enbuild.2021.110834

Stoyanov, D. (2021). The role of vending channels in marketing: A systematic review and taxonomy of studies. *The Journal of Consumer Affairs*, *55*(2), 654–679. DOI: 10.1111/joca.12362

Strelkova, O., & Pasichnyk, O. (2017). Three Types of Artificial Intelligence, Khmelnytskyi National University: Khmelnytskyi, Salcedo-Sanz, S., Cuadra, L., & Vermeij, M.J.A. (2016). A review of computational intelligence techniques in coral reef-related applications. *Ecological Informatics*, *32*, 107–123.

Subramaniyan, M., Skoogh, A., Bokrantz, J., Sheikh, M. A., Thürer, M., & Chang, Q. (2021). Artificial intelligence for throughput bottleneck analysis – State-of-the-art and future directions. *Journal of Manufacturing Systems*, *60*, 734–751. DOI: 10.1016/j.jmsy.2021.07.021

Sui, Q., & Liu, X. (2023). Edge computing and AIoT based network intrusion detection mechanism. *Internet Technology Letters*, *6*(5), e324. DOI: 10.1002/itl2.324

Sun, Y., Zhang, J., Xiong, Y., & Zhu, G. (2014). Data security and privacy in cloud computing. *International Journal of Distributed Sensor Networks*, *10*(7), 190903. DOI: 10.1155/2014/190903

Susan, J., Subashini, P., & Krishnaveni, M. (2023). Artificial Intelligence of Things for Smart Healthcare Development: An Experimental Review. *Handbook of Research on Deep Learning Techniques for Cloud-Based Industrial IoT*, 29-60.

Sylla, T., Mendiboure, L., Chalouf, M. A., & Krief, F. (2021). Blockchain-based context-aware authorization management as a service in IoT. *Sensors (Basel)*, *21*(22), 7656. DOI: 10.3390/s21227656

Szeliski, R. (2014). *Concise Computer Vision: An Introduction Into Theory and Algorithms*. Springer London.

Taimoor, N., & Rehman, S. (2021). Reliable and resilient AI and IoT-based personalised healthcare services: A survey. *IEEE Access : Practical Innovations, Open Solutions, 10*, 535–563. DOI: 10.1109/ACCESS.2021.3137364

Talaghzi, J., Bennane, A., Himmi, M. M., Bellafkih, M., & Benomar, A. (2020). Online adaptive learning. In *Proceedings of the 13th International Conference on Intelligent Systems: Theories and Applications*. https://doi.org/DOI: 10.1145/3419604.3419759

Talukder, A., & Haas, R. (2021, June). AIoT: AI meets IoT and web in smart healthcare. In Companion Publication of the 13th ACM Web Science Conference 2021 (pp. 92-98).

Tamboli, D. A., & Sawant, V. A. M. H. M. and S. Sathe, (2024). AI-Driven-IoT(AIIoT) Based Decision-Making- KSK Approach in Drones for Climate Change Study, *2024 4th International Conference on Ubiquitous Computing and Intelligent Information Systems (ICUIS)*, Gobichettipalayam, India, 2024, pp. 1735-1744, DOI: 10.1109/ICUIS64676.2024.10866450

Tang, H., Shi, J., & Lei, K. (2016, June). A smart low-consumption IoT framework for location tracking and its real application. In *2016 6th International Conference on Electronics Information and Emergency Communication (ICEIEC)* (pp. 306–309). IEEE. DOI: 10.1109/ICEIEC.2016.7589744

Tariq, M. U. (2024). Harnessing Persuasive Technologies for Enhanced Learner Engagement and Motivation. In M. Sanmugam, D. Lim, N. Mohd Barkhaya, W. Wan Yahaya, & Z. Khlaif (Eds.), *Power of Persuasive Educational Technologies in Enhancing Learning* (pp. 30-62). IGI Global. https://doi.org/DOI: 10.4018/979-8-3693-6397-3.ch002

Tariq, M. U. (2024). Integrating AI and Blockchain in EV Charging: Innovations and Challenges. In L. D., N. Nagpal, N. Kassarwani, V. Varthanan G., & P. Siano (Eds.), *A Sustainable Future with E-Mobility: Concepts, Challenges, and Implementations* (pp. 253-269). IGI Global Scientific Publishing. DOI: 10.4018/979-8-3693-5247-2.ch013

Tariq, M. U., & Sergio, R. (Eds.). (2025). *Cases on AI-Driven Solutions to Environmental Challenges*. IGI Global, 2025. https://doi.org/DOI: 10.4018/979-8-3693-7483-2

Tariq, M. U. (2024). Application of blockchain and Internet of Things (IoT) in modern business. In Sinha, M., Bhandari, A., Priya, S., & Kabiraj, S. (Eds.), *Future of customer engagement through marketing intelligence* (pp. 66–94). IGI Global., DOI: 10.4018/979-8-3693-2367-0.ch004

Tariq, M. U. (2024). Generative AI in Curriculum Development in Higher Education. In Fields, Z. (Ed.), *Impacts of Generative AI on Creativity in Higher Education* (pp. 227–258). IGI Global., DOI: 10.4018/979-8-3693-2418-9.ch009

Tariq, M. U. (2024). Integration of IoMT for Enhanced Healthcare: Sleep Monitoring, Body Movement Detection, and Rehabilitation Evaluation. In Liu, H., Tripathy, R., & Bhattacharya, P. (Eds.), *Clinical Practice and Unmet Challenges in AI-Enhanced Healthcare Systems* (pp. 70–95). IGI Global., DOI: 10.4018/979-8-3693-2703-6.ch004

Tariq, M. U. (2024). Multi-Agent Models in Healthcare System Design. In Dall'Acqua, L. (Ed.), *Bioethics of Cognitive Ergonomics and Digital Transition* (pp. 143–170). IGI Global., DOI: 10.4018/979-8-3693-2667-1.ch008

Tariq, M. U. (2024). Navigating the Personalization Pathway: Implementing Adaptive Learning Technologies in Higher Education. In Minh Tung, T. (Ed.), *Adaptive Learning Technologies for Higher Education* (pp. 265–291). IGI Global., DOI: 10.4018/979-8-3693-3641-0.ch012

Tariq, M. U. (2024). Smart Transportation Systems: Paving the Way for Sustainable Urban Mobility. In Munuhwa, S. (Ed.), *Contemporary Solutions for Sustainable Transportation Practices* (pp. 254–283). IGI Global., DOI: 10.4018/979-8-3693-3755-4.ch010

Tariq, M. U. (2024). Streamlining Operations Insights and Innovations From the Gulf Cooperation Council (GCC). In Ayed, T., Ali, I., Abdelhamid, H., & Mohamed, A. (Eds.), *Utilizing Case Studies in Business Education* (pp. 188–216). IGI Global., DOI: 10.4018/979-8-3693-3779-0.ch010

Tariq, M. U. (2024). The role of AI ethics in cost and complexity reduction. In Tennin, K., Ray, S., & Sorg, J. (Eds.), *Cases on AI ethics in business* (pp. 59–78). IGI Global., DOI: 10.4018/979-8-3693-2643-5.ch004

Tariq, M. U. (2025). AI and the Ethical Crossroads: Navigating Privacy, Personhood, and Autonomy in the Digital Age. In Chakraborty, S. (Ed.), *Human Values, Ethics, and Dignity in the Age of Artificial Intelligence* (pp. 49–72). IGI Global Scientific Publishing., DOI: 10.4018/979-8-3693-9035-1.ch003

Tariq, M. U. (2025). AI and Work-Life Balance: Transforming Employee Wellbeing in the Modern Workplace. In Ahmed, E., Babar, A., Samad, A., Ahmed, R., & Beydoun, G. (Eds.), *Strengthening Human Relations in Organizations With AI* (pp. 85–110). IGI Global Scientific Publishing., DOI: 10.4018/979-8-3693-6507-6.ch004

Tariq, M. U. (2025). *AI-Driven Learning and Engagement in Higher Education.* IGI Global., DOI: 10.4018/979-8-3693-4074-5

Tariq, M. U. (2025). AI-Driven Research Methodologies: Revolutionizing Data-Driven Discoveries in Engineering and Physical Sciences. In Basha, J., Alade, T., Al Khazimi, M., Vasudevan, R., & Khan, J. (Eds.), *Optimizing Research Techniques and Learning Strategies With Digital Technologies* (pp. 97–122). IGI Global Scientific Publishing., DOI: 10.4018/979-8-3693-7863-2.ch004

Tariq, M. U. (2025). AI-Enhanced Project-Based Learning: Revolutionizing Commerce Education With Generative AI. In ElSayary, A. (Ed.), *Prompt Engineering and Generative AI Applications for Teaching and Learning* (pp. 125–142). IGI Global Scientific Publishing., DOI: 10.4018/979-8-3693-7332-3.ch008

Tariq, M. U. (2025). AI-Powered Breakthroughs: Revolutionizing Cognitive Psychology and Neuropsychology With Machine Learning. In Bansal, R., Maqableh, T., Shuklaa, G., Rabby, F., & Lathabhavan, R. (Eds.), *Transforming Neuropsychology and Cognitive Psychology With AI and Machine Learning* (pp. 65–92). IGI Global Scientific Publishing., DOI: 10.4018/979-8-3693-9341-3.ch003

Tariq, M. U. (2025). AI-Powered Business Process Automation: Revolutionizing Firm Management. In Derbali, A. (Ed.), *AI, Economic Perspectives, and Firm Business Management* (pp. 199–224). IGI Global Scientific Publishing., DOI: 10.4018/979-8-3693-7357-6.ch010

Tariq, M. U. (2025). Beyond the Classroom: The Sustained Influence of Educators on Student Success. In West, E. (Ed.), *Former Educators' Roles in Supporting Student Growth and Learning* (pp. 321–346). IGI Global Scientific Publishing., DOI: 10.4018/979-8-3693-6427-7.ch013

Tariq, M. U. (2025). Bridging Cultures and Languages: Innovative Literacy Strategies for Inclusive and Engaged Classrooms. In Tussey, J., & Haas, L. (Eds.), *Supporting Cultural Differences Through Literacy Education* (pp. 257–282). IGI Global Scientific Publishing., DOI: 10.4018/979-8-3693-9271-3.ch010

Tariq, M. U. (2025). Bridging Generations: Digital Transformation and Its Multifaceted Impact Across Societal Sectors. In Anshari, M., Almunawar, M., & Ordóñez de Pablos, P. (Eds.), *Impacts of Digital Technologies Across Generations* (pp. 1–22). IGI Global Scientific Publishing., DOI: 10.4018/979-8-3693-6366-9.ch001

Tariq, M. U. (2025). Co-Living With Augmented Digital Beings-Navigating the Intersection of AI and Everyday Life. In Moutinho, L., & Martins, L. (Eds.), *Impacts of Sensetech on Society* (pp. 187–206). IGI Global Scientific Publishing., DOI: 10.4018/979-8-3693-7147-3.ch009

Tariq, M. U. (2025). Empowering Learning Through Networked and Connected Education: Case Studies in Digital Engagement. In Gierhart, A. (Ed.), *Cases on Enhancing P-16 Student Engagement With Digital Technologies* (pp. 169–198). IGI Global Scientific Publishing., DOI: 10.4018/979-8-3693-5633-3.ch007

Tariq, M. U. (2025). Empowering Patients With AI-Ethical Digital Tools for Health Data Management and Decision. In Pesqueira, A., & de Bem Machado, A. (Eds.), *Navigating Privacy, Innovation, and Patient Empowerment Through Ethical Healthcare Technology* (pp. 197–216). IGI Global Scientific Publishing., DOI: 10.4018/979-8-3693-7630-0.ch008

Tariq, M. U. (2025). Enhancing Pandemic Preparedness With AI-Driven Risk Prediction Models. In Shah, I., Sial, Q., & Fateh, S. (Eds.), *Generative AI Techniques for Sustainability in Healthcare Security* (pp. 77–94). IGI Global Scientific Publishing., DOI: 10.4018/979-8-3693-6577-9.ch005

Tariq, M. U. (2025). Gamification and Virtual Reality: Transforming Early Childhood Language Learning. In Manditereza, B. (Ed.), *Digital Pedagogy in Early Childhood Language Development* (pp. 25–52). IGI Global Scientific Publishing., DOI: 10.4018/979-8-3693-7437-5.ch002

Tariq, M. U. (2025). Harnessing Technology to Combat Bias: Innovative Tools and Techniques in HR. In Kanwal, S. (Ed.), *Navigating Bias in Human Resource Management* (pp. 155–184). IGI Global Scientific Publishing., DOI: 10.4018/979-8-3693-7132-9.ch006

Tariq, M. U. (2025). Integrating Digital Technologies to Optimize Sustainable Supply Chains. In Koç, E. (Ed.), *Developing Dynamic and Sustainable Supply Chains to Achieve Sustainable Development Goals* (pp. 33–64). IGI Global Scientific Publishing., DOI: 10.4018/979-8-3693-6284-6.ch002

Tariq, M. U. (2025). Integrating ICT for Enhanced Organizational Resilience: Strategies and Case Studies. In Carvalho, L., Reis, L., Neves de Almeida Baptista Figueiredo, A., & Russo, N. (Eds.), *Leveraging Technology for Organizational Adaptability* (pp. 59–80). IGI Global Scientific Publishing., DOI: 10.4018/979-8-3693-6045-3.ch004

Tariq, M. U. (2025). Integrating Theory and Practice: Transformative Approaches in Practice-Led Research for Professional Development. In Kwok, S., Yu, P., & Le Corre, J. (Eds.), *Exploring Practice-Led Research for Professional Development* (pp. 419–436). IGI Global Scientific Publishing., DOI: 10.4018/979-8-3693-6376-8.ch016

Tariq, M. U. (2025). Leveraging Artificial Intelligence to Enhance Diversity and Drive Business Innovation. In Margaretha van der Poll, H., Andrew van der Poll, J., & Ngwakwe, C. (Eds.), *Diversity, AI, and Sustainability for Financial Growth* (pp. 79–96). IGI Global Scientific Publishing., DOI: 10.4018/979-8-3693-6011-8.ch004

Tariq, M. U. (2025). Leveraging Libraries and Information Centers for Startup Innovation and Growth. In Gupta, V., & Gupta, C. (Eds.), *Navigating Strategic Partnerships for Sustainable Startup Growth* (pp. 1–28). IGI Global Scientific Publishing., DOI: 10.4018/979-8-3693-4066-0.ch001

Tariq, M. U. (2025). Navigating Public Administration 5.0: Embracing AI for Smarter Governance. In Wongmahesak, K., Ahmad, J., & Mustanir, A. (Eds.), *Public Governance Practices in the Age of AI* (pp. 167–186). IGI Global Scientific Publishing., DOI: 10.4018/979-8-3693-9286-7.ch008

Tariq, M. U. (2025). Navigating the Convergence of IoMT and Generative AI in Global Healthcare: Opportunities, Challenges, and Ethical Considerations. In Kumar, V., Katina, P., & Zhao, J. (Eds.), *Convergence of Internet of Medical Things (IoMT) and Generative AI* (pp. 513–534). IGI Global Scientific Publishing., DOI: 10.4018/979-8-3693-6180-1.ch022

Tariq, M. U. (2025). Quantum Algorithms and Predictive Analytics: Revolutionizing Consumer Insight. In Gajbhiye, P., Kannan, H., Rodriguez, R., & Rojas-Méndez, J. (Eds.), *The Quantum AI Era of Neuromarketing* (pp. 173–202). IGI Global Scientific Publishing., DOI: 10.4018/979-8-3693-7673-7.ch008

Tariq, M. U. (2025). Revitalizing Pedagogy: Integrating Indigenous Knowledge and Practices Into Higher Education Disciplines. In Kgari-Masondo, M. (Ed.), *Indigenous Teaching Disciplines and Perspectives for Higher Education* (pp. 379–400). IGI Global Scientific Publishing., DOI: 10.4018/979-8-3693-9296-6.ch018

Tariq, M. U. (2025). Revolutionizing Retail: Enhancing Customer Experiences With the Metaverse. In Gonçalves Rodrigues, M., Carvalho, M., & Monteiro Pratas, J. (Eds.), *Cases on Metaverse and Consumer Experiences* (pp. 175–202). IGI Global Scientific Publishing., DOI: 10.4018/979-8-3693-7245-6.ch007

Tariq, M. U. (2025). Smart Forecasting With AI: Revolutionizing Energy Consumption and Storage. In Derbali, A. (Ed.), *Integrating Artificial Intelligence Into the Energy Sector* (pp. 165–184). IGI Global Scientific Publishing., DOI: 10.4018/979-8-3693-7112-1.ch009

Tariq, M. U. (2025). Unlocking Competitive Edge: Harnessing the Power of Collaborative Innovation. In Martínez-Falcó, J., Sánchez-García, E., & Marco-Lajara, B. (Eds.), *Open Innovation Strategies for Effective Competitive Advantage* (pp. 315–344). IGI Global Scientific Publishing., DOI: 10.4018/979-8-3693-9266-9.ch011

Tariq, M. U. (2025a). Innovative Business Models: Integrating Social, Economic, and Environmental Goals in Rural Manufacturing. In Prabhakar, A., Yu, P., & Erokhin, V. (Eds.), *Rural Social Entrepreneurship Development: Network-Based Manufacturing System Model* (pp. 147–174). IGI Global Scientific Publishing., DOI: 10.4018/979-8-3693-7515-0.ch005

Tariq, M. U., & Sergio, R. (Eds.). (2025). *Convergence of AI, Education, and Business for Sustainability*. IGI Global., DOI: 10.4018/979-8-3373-1917-9

Tariq, M. U., & Sergio, R. P. (2025). Ethical Considerations and Social Impact of AI and Computational Intelligence in Society 5.0. In Pandey, R., Srivastava, N., Prasad, R., Prasad, J., & Garcia, M. (Eds.), *Open AI and Computational Intelligence for Society 5.0* (pp. 225–248). IGI Global Scientific Publishing., DOI: 10.4018/979-8-3693-4326-5.ch010

Tawalbeh, L. A., Muheidat, F., Tawalbeh, M., & Quwaider, M. (2020). IoT privacy and security: Challenges and solutions. *Applied Sciences (Basel, Switzerland)*, *10*(12), 4102. DOI: 10.3390/app10124102

TechTarget, https.//www.techtarget.com/iotagenda/definition/Artificial-Intelligence-of-Things-AIoT

Thakur, P., Goel, S., & Puthooran, E. (2024). Edge AI Enabled IoT Framework for Secure Smart Home Infrastructure. *Procedia Computer Science*, *235*, 3369–3378. DOI: 10.1016/j.procs.2024.04.317

Thapliyal, S., Wazid, M., Singh, D. P., Chauhan, R., Mishra, A. K., & Das, A. K. (2024). Secure Artificial Intelligence of Things (AIoT)-enabled authenticated key agreement technique for smart living environment. *Computers & Electrical Engineering*, *118*, 109353. DOI: 10.1016/j.compeleceng.2024.109353

The Brainy Insights, https.//www.thebrainyinsights.com/report/aiot-platforms-market-14367?srsltid=AfmBOor0tJ9wZ74FHeGYHiARfVYpInZ35zOH RjpYg9S7C6vKLjes5SAF

The Sun. (2023). World's first AI hospital unveiled in China with robot doctors who 'can treat 3,000 patients a day & will save millions'. The Sun. Retrieved January 6, 2025, from https://www.thesun.co.uk/tech/28190601/worlds-first-ai-hospital-china/

Tian, Z., Wang, J. W., Li, J., & Han, B. (2021). Designing future crops: Challenges and strategies for sustainable agriculture. *The Plant Journal*, *105*(5), 1165–1178. DOI: 10.1111/tpj.15107 PMID: 33258137

Tian, Z., Yan, B., Guo, Q., Huang, J., & Du, Q. (2020). Feasibility of identity authentication for IoT based on blockchain. *Procedia Computer Science*, *174*, 328–332. DOI: 10.1016/j.procs.2020.06.094

Toivonen, T., Heikinheimo, V., Fink, C., Hausmann, A., Hiippala, T., Jarv, O., Tenkanen, H., & Di Minin, E. (2019). Social media data for conservation science: A methodological overview. *Biological Conservation*, *233*, 298–315. DOI: 10.1016/j.biocon.2019.01.023

Torad, M. A., Bouallegue, B., & Ahmed, A. M. (2022). A voice controlled smart home automation system using artificial intelligent and internet of things. *Telkomnika*, *20*(4), 808. DOI: 10.12928/telkomnika.v20i4.23763

Tsai, C.-C., Cheng, Y.-M., Tsai, Y.-S., & Lou, S.-J. (2021). Impacts of AIoT implementation course on the learning outcomes of senior high school students. *Education Sciences*, *11*(2), 82. DOI: 10.3390/educsci11020082

Tulkinbekov, K., & Kim, D. H. (2022). Blockchain-enabled approach for big data processing in edge computing. *IEEE Internet of Things Journal*, *9*(19), 18473–18486. DOI: 10.1109/JIOT.2022.3160838

Tyagi, A. K., & Sreenath, N. (2021). Cyber Physical Systems: Analyses, challenges and possible solutions. *Internet of Things and Cyber-Physical Systems*, *1*, 22–33. DOI: 10.1016/j.iotcps.2021.12.002

Tyralis, H., Papacharalampous, G., & Langousis, A. (2019). A brief review of random forests for water scientists and practitioners and their recent history in water resources. *Water (Basel)*, *11*(5), 910. DOI: 10.3390/w11050910

Udutalapally, V., Mohanty, S. P., Pallagani, V., & Khandelwal, V. (2020). sCrop: A novel device for sustainable automatic disease prediction, crop selection, and irrigation in Internet-of-Agro-Things for smart agriculture. *IEEE Sensors Journal*, *21*(16), 17525–17538. DOI: 10.1109/JSEN.2020.3032438

Ullah, A., Anwar, S. M., Li, J., Nadeem, L., Mahmood, T., Rehman, A., & Saba, T. (2023). Smart cities: The role of Internet of Things and machine learning in realizing a data-centric smart environment. *Complex & Intelligent Systems*, *10*(1), 1607–1637. DOI: 10.1007/s40747-023-01175-4

Upadhyaya, A. N., Surekha, C., Malathi, P., Suresh, G., Suriyan, K., & Liyakat, K. K. S. (2025). Pioneering cognitive computing for transformative healthcare innovations. SSRN *Electronic Journal.* DOI: 10.2139/ssrn.5086894

Usama, M., Qadir, J., Raza, A., Arif, H., Yau, K. A., Elkhatib, Y., Hussain, A., & Al-Fuqaha, A. (2019). Unsupervised machine learning for networking: Techniques, applications and research challenges. *IEEE Access : Practical Innovations, Open Solutions*, *7*, 65579–65615. DOI: 10.1109/ACCESS.2019.2916648

Ushakov, D., Dudukalov, E., Kozlova, E., & Shatila, K. (2022). The Internet of Things impact on smart public transportation. *Transportation Research Procedia*, *63*, 2392–2400. DOI: 10.1016/j.trpro.2022.06.275

Uskov, V. L., Bakken, J. P., & Pandey, A. (2015). The ontology of next generation smart classrooms. In *Smart Education and Smart E-Learning* (pp. 3–14). https://doi.org/DOI: 10.1007/978-3-319-19875-0_1

Vaidya, S., Ambad, P., & Bhosle, S. (2018). Industry 4.0–a glimpse. *Procedia Manufacturing*, *20*, 233–238. DOI: 10.1016/j.promfg.2018.02.034

Vardakis, G., Hatzivasilis, G., Koutsaki, E., & Papadakis, N. (2024). Review of Smart-Home Security Using the Internet of Things. *Electronics (Basel)*, *13*(16), 3343. DOI: 10.3390/electronics13163343

Varghese, J. E. E. N. A., Vargheese, S. K., & Peter, E. L. D. H. O. (2020). A study on artificial intelligence of things: Techniques and applications. *A Journal of Composition Theory, 8*(3), 888-896.

Venkatesan, K., & Rahayu, S. B. (2024). Blockchain security enhancement: An approach towards hybrid consensus algorithms and machine learning techniques. *Scientific Reports*, *14*(1), 1149. DOI: 10.1038/s41598-024-51578-7

Verma, S., Kumar, P., & Singh, J. P. (2024). A unified lightweight CNN-based model for disease detection and identification in corn, rice, and wheat. *Journal of the Institution of Electronics and Telecommunication Engineers*, *70*(3), 2481–2492. DOI: 10.1080/03772063.2023.2181229

Verma, S., Sharma, R., Deb, S., & Maitra, D. (2021). Artificial intelligence in marketing: Systematic review and future research direction. *International Journal of Information Management Data Insights*, *1*(1), 100002. DOI: 10.1016/j.jjimei.2020.100002

Vermesan, O., & Friess, P. (2014). *Internet of things applications-from research and innovation to market deployment*. Taylor & Francis.

Verrest, H., & Pfeffer, K. (2019). Elaborating the urbanism in smart urbanism: Distilling relevant dimensions for a comprehensive analysis of smart city approaches. *Information Communication and Society*, *22*(9), 1328–1342. DOI: 10.1080/1369118X.2018.1424921

Vetitnev, A. M., Maznichenko, M. A., Lopatinskiy, D. B., & Aksenov, I. A. (2020). Traditional and digital technologies in professional education: Integration opportunities. *Journal of Physics: Conference Series*, *1691*(1), 012135. DOI: 10.1088/1742-6596/1691/1/012135

Vinuesa, R., Fdez. De Arévalo, L., Luna, M., & Cachafeiro, H. (2016). Simulations and experiments of heat loss from a parabolic trough absorber tube over a range of pressures and gas compositions in the vacuum chamber. *Journal of Renewable and Sustainable Energy*, *8*, 342–354. DOI: 10.1063/1.4944975

Viso Suite, https.//viso.ai/edge-ai/artificial-intelligence-of-things-aiot/.

Voelz, A., Mladenow, A., & Strauss, C. (2021). Beacon technology for retailers-tracking consumer behavior inside brick-and-mortar-stores. In *Database and Expert Systems Applications: 32nd International Conference, DEXA 2021, Virtual Event, September 27–30, 2021* [Springer International Publishing.]. *Proceedings*, *32*(Part I), 380–390.

Voigt, P., & Bussche, A. v. d (2017). *The GDPR: Principles, rights, and obligations*. Springer. DOI: 10.1007/978-3-319-57959-7

Voropanova, E. (2015). Conceptualizing smart shopping with a smartphone: Implications of the use of mobile devices for shopping productivity and value. *International Review of Retail, Distribution and Consumer Research*, *25*(5), 529–550. DOI: 10.1080/09593969.2015.1089304

Wale, A. D., & Dipali, R.. (2019). Smart Agriculture System using IoT. *International Journal of Innovative Research in Technology*, *5*(10), 493–497.

Walia, G. K., Kumar, M., & Gill, S. S. (2024). AI-empowered fog/Edge resource management for IoT applications: A comprehensive review, research challenges, and future perspectives. *IEEE Communications Surveys and Tutorials*, *26*(1), 619–669. DOI: 10.1109/COMST.2023.3338015

Wang, C., Ma, C., Li, M., Gao, N., Zhang, Y., & Shen, Z. (2021). Protecting data privacy in federated learning combining differential privacy and weak encryption. In M. X. Editor & Y. Z. Editor (Eds.), *Federated Learning: Advances and Applications* (pp. 101–115). Springer. DOI: 10.1007/978-3-030-89137-4_7

Wang, P., & Goertzel, B. (2017). Introduction: aspects of artificial general intelligence, in Proceedings of the 2007 conference on Advances in Artificial General Intelligence: Concepts, Architectures, and Algorithms: Proceedings of the AGI Workshop 2007, 2006, pp. 1–16 Ukraine, pp. 1–4.

Wang, B., Dabbaghjamanesh, M., Kavousi-Fard, A., & Yue, Y. (2024). AI-enhanced multi-stage learning-to-learning approach for secure smart cities load management in IoT networks. *Ad Hoc Networks*, *164*, 103628. DOI: 10.1016/j.adhoc.2024.103628

Wang, C. X., Di Renzo, M., Stanczak, S., Wang, S., & Larsson, E. G. (2020). Artificial intelligence enabled wireless networking for 5G and beyond: Recent advances and future challenges. *IEEE Wireless Communications*, *27*(1), 16–23. DOI: 10.1109/MWC.001.1900292

Wang, L. (2021). The challenge and prospect of scalability of blockchain technology. In *Proceedings of the 5th International Conference on Computer Science and Artificial Intelligence,* Beijing, China. DOI: 10.1145/3507548.3507594

Wang, W., Hoang, D. T., Hu, P., Xiong, Z., Niyato, D., Wang, P., Wen, Y., & Kim, D. I. (2019). A survey on consensus mechanisms and mining strategy management in blockchain networks. *IEEE Access : Practical Innovations, Open Solutions*, *7*, 22328–22370. DOI: 10.1109/ACCESS.2019.2896108

Wang, Z., & Srinivasan, R. S. (2017). A review of artificial intelligence based building energy use prediction: Contrasting the capabilities of single and ensemble prediction models. *Renewable & Sustainable Energy Reviews*, *75*, 796–808. DOI: 10.1016/j.rser.2016.10.079

Waqar, A. (2024). Intelligent decision support systems in construction engineering. An artificial intelligence and machine learning approaches. *Expert Systems with Applications*, Volume 249, Part A, 123503.

Wei, W., Piuri, V., Pedrycz, W., & Ahmed, S. H. (2022). Special issue on Artificial Intelligence-of-Things (AIoT): Opportunities, challenges, and solutions-Part II: Artificial-intelligence-powered Internet of Things. *Future Generation Computer Systems*. Advance online publication. DOI: 10.1016/j.future.2022.07.019

Wei, Z., Zhu, M., Zhang, N., Wang, L., Zou, Y., Meng, Z., Wu, H., & Feng, Z. (2022). UAV-assisted data collection for Internet of Things: A survey. *IEEE Internet of Things Journal*, *9*(17), 15460–15483. DOI: 10.1109/JIOT.2022.3176903

Weng, X., Ye, H., Dai, Y., & Ng, O. (2024). Integrating artificial intelligence and computational thinking in educational contexts: A systematic review of instructional design and student learning outcomes. *Journal of Educational Computing Research*, *62*(6), 1640–1670. DOI: 10.1177/07356331241248686

Wettewa, S., Hou, L., & Zhang, G. (2024). Graph Neural Networks for building and civil infrastructure operation and maintenance enhancement. *Advanced Engineering Informatics*, Volume 62, Part D, 102868. Wikimedia, https.//commons.wikimedia.org/wiki/File.London_City_Airport_-_geograph.org.uk_-_6895772.jpg

Wiafe, I., Koranteng, F. N., Obeng, E. N., Assyne, N., Wiafe, A., & Gulliver, S. R. (2020). Artificial intelligence for cybersecurity: A systematic mapping of literature. *IEEE Access : Practical Innovations, Open Solutions*, *8*, 146598–146612. DOI: 10.1109/ACCESS.2020.3013145

Wijesundara, W. M. A. B., Lee, J. S., Tith, D., Aloupogianni, E., Suzuki, H., & Obi, T. (2024). Security-enhanced firmware management scheme for smart home IoT devices using distributed ledger technologies. *International Journal of Information Security*, *23*(3), 1–11. DOI: 10.1007/s10207-024-00827-x

Wikipedia contributors. (2024, July 30). *Artificial intelligence of things*. Wikipedia. https://en.wikipedia.org/wiki/Artificial_intelligence_of_things

Williamson, B. (2015). Digital education governance: Data visualization, predictive analytics, and 'real-time' policy instruments. *Journal of Education Policy*, *31*(2), 123–141. DOI: 10.1080/02680939.2015.1035758

Wong, W. K., Leung, S. Y. S., Guo, Z. X., Zeng, X. H., & Mok, P. Y. (2012). Intelligent product cross-selling system with radio frequency identification technology for retailing. *International Journal of Production Economics*, *135*(1), 308–319. DOI: 10.1016/j.ijpe.2011.08.005

World Economic Forum (WEF). 2018. Fourth Industrial Revolution for the Earth Series Harnessing Artificial Intelligence for the Earth.

Wu, Y. C., Wu, Y. J., & Wu, S. M. (2019). An outlook of a future smart city in Taiwan from post–Internet of Things to artificial intelligence Internet of Things. In *Smart Cities: Issues and Challenges* (pp. 263-282). Elsevier. DOI: 10.1016/B978-0-12-816639-0.00015-6

Wu, H., Han, H., Wang, X., & Sun, S. (2020). Research on artificial intelligence enhancing Internet of things security: A survey. *IEEE Access : Practical Innovations, Open Solutions, 8*, 153826–153848. DOI: 10.1109/ACCESS.2020.3018170

Wu, K., Xu, J., & Zheng, M. (2024). Industry 4.0: Review and proposal for implementing a smart factory. *International Journal of Advanced Manufacturing Technology, 133*(3), 1331–1347. DOI: 10.1007/s00170-024-13839-7

Wu, Y. (2021). Cloud-edge orchestration for the Internet of things: Architecture and AI-powered data processing. *IEEE Internet of Things Journal, 8*(16), 12792–12805. DOI: 10.1109/JIOT.2020.3014845

Xiao, Y., Zhang, N., Lou, W., & Hou, Y. T. (2020). A survey of distributed consensus protocols for blockchain networks. *IEEE Communications Surveys and Tutorials, 22*(2), 1432–1465. DOI: 10.1109/COMST.2020.2969706

Xie, T., Li, R., Zhang, X., Zhou, B., & Wang, Z. (2019, October). Research on heartbeat classification algorithm based on CART decision tree. In *2019 8th International Symposium on Next Generation Electronics (ISNE)* (pp. 1–3). IEEE. DOI: 10.1109/ISNE.2019.8896650

Xu, H., Seng, K. P., Ang, L. M., & Smith, J. (2024). Decentralized and distributed learning for AIoT: A comprehensive review, emerging challenges and opportunities. *IEEE Access : Practical Innovations, Open Solutions, 12*, 101016–101052. DOI: 10.1109/ACCESS.2024.3422211

Yadav, V. (2024). The future of smart homes: Trends and predictions for the next decade India. Available at: https://etedge-insights.com/technology/innovation/the-future-of-smart-homes-trends-and-predictions-for-the-next-decade-india/

Yang, L. (2024). Heterogeneous Internet of Things Big Data Analysis System Based on Mobile Edge Computing. *Journal of Information & Knowledge Management*, 2450047.

Yan, J. (2024). AIoT in Smart Homes: Challenges, Strategic Solutions, and Future Directions. *Highlights in Science. Engineering and Technology, 87*, 59–65.

Yu, Y., Li, Y., Tian, J., & Liu, J. (2018). Blockchain-based solutions to security and privacy issues in the Internet of things. *IEEE Wireless Communications, 25*(6), 12–18. DOI: 10.1109/MWC.2017.1800116

Zadeh, L. A. (1975). Fuzzy logic and approximate reasoning. *Synthese, 30*(3-4), 407–428. DOI: 10.1007/BF00485052

Zaim, D., Benomar, A., & Bellafkih, M. (2019). Developing a geomarketing solution. *Procedia Computer Science*, *148*, 353–360. DOI: 10.1016/j.procs.2019.01.043

Zanella, A., Bui, N., Castellani, A., Vangelista, L., & Zorzi, M. (2014). Internet of Things for smart cities. *IEEE Internet of Things Journal*, *1*(1), 22–32. DOI: 10.1109/JIOT.2014.2306328

Zhang, C., Xie, Y., Bai, H., Yu, B., Li, W., & Gao, Y. (2021). A survey on federated learning. *Knowledge-Based Systems*, *216*, 106775. DOI: 10.1016/j.knosys.2021.106775

Zhang, F., Pan, Z., & Lu, Y. (2023). AIoT-enabled smart surveillance for personal data digitalization: Contextual personalization-privacy paradox in smart home. *Information & Management*, *60*(2), 103736. DOI: 10.1016/j.im.2022.103736

Zhang, H., Li, D., Ji, Y., Zhou, H., Wu, W., & Liu, K. (2019). Toward new retail: A benchmark dataset for smart unmanned vending machines. *IEEE Transactions on Industrial Informatics*, *16*(12), 7722–7731. DOI: 10.1109/TII.2019.2954956

Zhang, J., & Goyal, S. B. (2024). AI-driven decision support system innovations to empower higher education administration. *Journal of Computers. Mechanical and Management*, *3*(2), 35–41. DOI: 10.57159/gadl.jcmm.3.2.24070

Zhang, J., & Tao, D. (2021). Empowering things with intelligence: A survey of the progress, challenges, and opportunities in artificial intelligence of things. *IEEE Internet of Things Journal*, *8*(10), 7789–7817. DOI: 10.1109/JIOT.2020.3039359

Zhang, Q., Cui, M., Liu, Y., Chen, W., & Yu, Z. (2024). Low-Power and Low-Cost AI Processor with Distributed-Aggregated Classification Architecture for Wearable Epilepsy Seizure Detection. *IEEE Transactions on Biomedical Circuits and Systems*. PMID: 39196752

Zhao, J., Hu, H., Huang, F., Guo, Y., & Liao, L. (2023). Authentication technology in Internet of things and privacy security issues in typical application scenarios. *Electronics (Basel)*, *12*(8), 1812. DOI: 10.3390/electronics12081812

Zheng, Z., Xie, S., Dai, H. N., Chen, X., & Wang, H. (2018). Blockchain challenges and opportunities: A survey. *International Journal of Web and Grid Services*, *14*(4), 352–375. DOI: 10.1504/IJWGS.2018.095647

Zheng, Z., Xie, S., Dai, H., Chen, W., Chen, X., Weng, J., & Imran, M. (2020). An overview on smart contracts: Challenges, advances and platforms. *Future Generation Computer Systems*, *105*, 475–491. DOI: 10.1016/j.future.2019.12.019

Zhitomirsky-Geffet, M., & Blau, M. (2016). Cross-generational analysis of predictive factors of addictive behavior in smartphone usage. *Computers in Human Behavior, 64*, 682–693. DOI: 10.1016/j.chb.2016.07.061

Zhou, J., Cao, Z., Dong, X., & Vasilakos, A. V. (2017). Security and privacy for cloud-based IoT: Challenges. *IEEE Communications Magazine, 55*(1), 26–33. DOI: 10.1109/MCOM.2017.1600363CM

Zhu, Z., Sun, Y., & Riezebos, P. (2016). Introducing the smart education framework: Core elements for successful learning in a digital world. *International Journal of Smart Technology and Learning, 1*(1), 53. DOI: 10.1504/IJSMARTTL.2016.078159

Zovko, K., Šerić, L., Perković, T., Belani, H., & Šolić, P. (2023). IoT and health monitoring wearable devices as enabling technologies for sustainable enhancement of life quality in smart environments. *Journal of Cleaner Production, 413*, 137506. DOI: 10.1016/j.jclepro.2023.137506

Zuo, C., Lin, Z., & Zhang, Y. (2019). Why does your data leak? Uncovering the data leakage in cloud from mobile apps. In *Proceedings of the 2019 IEEE Symposium on Security and Privacy (SP),* San Francisco, USA. DOI: 10.1109/SP.2019.00009

About the Contributors

Muhammad Usman Tariq has more than 16+ year's experience in industry and academia. He has authored more than 200+ research articles, 110+ case studies, 150+ book chapters and several books other than 4 patents. He is founder and CEO of The Case HQ, a unique repository for courses, narrative and video case studies. He has been working as a consultant and trainer for industries representing six sigma, quality, health and safety, environmental systems, project management, and information security standards. His work has encompassed sectors in aviation, manufacturing, food, hospitality, education, finance, research, software and transportation. He has diverse and significant experience working with accreditation agencies of ABET, ACBSP, AACSB, WASC, CAA, EFQM and NCEAC. Additionally, Dr. Tariq has operational experience in incubators, research labs, government research projects, private sector startups, program creation and management at various industrial and academic levels. He is Certified Higher Education Teacher from Harvard University, USA, Certified Online Educator from HMBSU, Certified Six Sigma Master Black Belt and has been awarded PFHEA, SFSEDA, SMIEEE, and CMBE.

***

Anubha Anubha is a Professor of Marketing at Jaipuria Institute of Management, Ghaziabad, India. Her research interests include social media marketing, Islamic marketing, electronic word of mouth, advertising, and consumer behaviour. She has published many scholarly "ABS 3 level", "ABDC" and "Scopus-indexed research papers in various journals of Wiley, Emerald, Taylor & Francis, and Sage publications including Psychology and Marketing, Current Issues in Tourism, Journal of Islamic Marketing, Journal of Internet Commerce, Global Knowledge, Memory & Communication. She has been an active reviewer of journals of Elsevier and Emerald. She has presented papers at various National and International conferences at MDI Murshidabad, IIM Indore, IIT Delhi, XLRI Jamshedpur, and Curtin University. Recently her edited book, indexed in Scopus was published by IGI Global.

Anu Disney D holds a PhD degree from Anna University. She has obtained her master's and bachelor's degrees in Computer Science and Engineering from Anna University. She is currently serving as an Assistant Professor at Sathyabama Institute of Science and Technology in Chennai. Her research interests encompass Wireless Communications, IoT (Internet of Things), and Artificial Intelligence. She has published her research findings in various reputed international journals/ conferences. Her academic journey underscores a strong commitment to advancing these fields through research and teaching.

Renuka Devi D currently serves as an Assistant Professor in the Department of Computer Science at Stella Maris College(Autonomous) in Chennai, India. With over 15 years of extensive teaching experience, she holds a Ph.D. from the University of Madras. Her academic expertise spans areas such as Data Mining, Machine Learning, Big Data, and Artificial Intelligence. She has authored a book titled "Research Practitioner's Handbook on Big Data Analytics," published by Apple Academic Press, CRC Press, USA, and has contributed articles to various publications, including IEEE, Springer, Scopus, and Web of Science. In addition, she holds patents in the fields of virtual network security, sentiment analysis application using an ensemble incremental deep multiple layer perceptron model, a smart walking stick for the visually impaired, and an AI-based interactive web and voice application. She presented papers at international conferences, earning accolades such as the Best Paper Award and the Best Researcher Award. She is associated with various international societies, including the International Computer Science and Engineering Society (ICSES) and the International Association of Engineers (IAENG). Additionally, Dr. Renuka Devi serves as a reviewer for prestigious Scopus indexed and web of science journals. She is also an editorial member of the Journal of Advances in Management Sciences & Information Systems and has represented India as a panelist in the "Global Perspectives on Artificial Intelligence in Higher Education - A virtual roundtable on AI" in 2023 organized by Alamo Colleges District, San Antonio, USA.

Mitra Tithi Dey received her B.Sc., M.Sc. and M.Tech in Computer Science. She is Currently working as Assistant Professor and HOD in Department of Computer Science at Netaji Nagar Day College, affiliated to University of Calcutta. She is a research scholar at Jadavpur University at School of Mobile Computing and Communication. Her research interests include Internet of Things, Deep Learning,

Digital Image Processing etc. She has published many research papers in reputed international conference proceedings, journals and book chapter.

Shivnath Ghosh is a Professor and Head of the Department of Computer Science and Engineering at Brainware University. With 20+ years of academic experience, he has made significant contributions to research and development. He has published over 50 research papers, holds 7 patents, authored 12 books, and contributed to 14 book chapters. Currently, he is guiding six Ph.D. research scholars, with two having already been awarded their Ph.D. under his supervision.

Tamilselvan K. S., working as Professor at KPR Institute of Engineering and Technology. I completed my BE Degree in ECE at Bharathiar University, M.E Degree in Embedded System Technologies and PhD in Medical Image Fusion at Anna University. I have 33 years of teaching experience and 2 years of industrial experience and published 75 research papers in various International journals and conferences. Currently I am guiding 7 research scholar under Anna University.

Kazi Kutubuddin Sayyad Liyakat has completed his B.E., M.E., and Ph.D. in E&TC Engineering and is nowadays working as a Professor & Head of Department, E&TC Engineering Department and was Dean R&D. He is Post-Doctoral worked on "IoT in Healthcare Applications". His area of Interest is IoT, AI and ML. He has published more than 110+ papers in various Journals. Also published 11 books in the field of Engineering. He has published 15 Indian Patents, 2 South African Grant Patent, 2 Indian Copyright Patents and 8 UK Grant Patent. He worked as a Reviewer for Scopus Conferences and Journal. Also work as Editorial Board Member for various Journals. He got 2 Best Researcher Award, Best Faculty Award and Appreciation Letter from MoE's Innovation Cell, Govt. of India.

Harshavardhan Kurtkoti, is pursuing BTech in Information Science and Technology. His keen interests are in the domain of MLOps and Data Science. His achievements include finalist at two national level hackathons and winning a University level IEEE hackathon. He is an enthusiastic learner who constantly upskills and innovates.

Swetha Margaret is an accomplished professional with a diverse background in academia, research, and industry, specializing in Cyber and Network Security, Cloud Computing, Computer Networks, IoT, IIoT, Big Data, and Artificial Intelligence. With 12 years of experience, she currently serves as an Assistant Professor in the Department of Computer Science at Stella Maris College, bringing seven years of dedicated teaching expertise. Dr. Margaret holds a Ph.D., earned during her three-year tenure as a full-time Doctoral Research Scholar at Quaid E Millath College,

Chennai. Prior to her academic pursuits, she gained valuable industry experience with IBM and Citrix, focusing on IBM mainframe back- end support, task management, and load creation. Her commitment to professional development is evident through various international certifications, including those from IBM, Big Data University, and Udemy, covering Cloud Computing, Data Science Methodology, and more. As the Chief Information Security Officer (CISO) at Stella Maris College since 2023, she has demonstrated leadership in securing information assets. Dr. Margaret's research contributions extend to over 20 publications in international journals, including Scopus, IEEE, and Springer. Her expertise has been recognized through accolades such as the "Best Researcher Award" from D K International Research Foundation and the 'Young Faculty in Science' Award during the Contemporary Academic Meet-CAM by Venus International Foundation, both in 2018-2019. Her commitment to innovation is evident through patents, including Innovation patent for "Un Nanban," an AI-based interactive web and voice application, and a Design patent for a "Smart Walking Stick" for visually impaired individuals in 2023. Represented India as a panelist in the "Global Perspectives on Artificial Intelligence in Higher Education - A virtual roundtable on AI" in 2023 organised by Alamo Colleges District, San Antonio, USA

Sucharita Mitra(Sarkar) received B.Sc. [Physics (H)], M.Sc.[Electronic Science] and Ph.D.(Tech)[Measurement and Instrumentation] degree from University of Calcutta[CU]. At present, she is Associate Professor and HOD in Department of Electronics of Netaji Nagar Day College, affiliated under CU. Also attached at Electronic Science Department as Guest Faculty. Formerly, she attached to the Indian Statistical Institute as a Post Doctoral Fellow (IISC-DBT). She visited University of Oxford as Post-Doctoral fellow under the DBT-CREST award scheme of Govt. of India. Obtained INSA Visiting Scientist Award in 2022. Recipient of Dr. K.S. Krishnan Memorial Award 2023 from IETE for best system-oriented paper. Her research interests include Soft Computing and AI based biomedical signal and image analysis, telemedicine etc., She published more than 60 research papers in reputed international and national journals and conference proceedings including 1 book and 7 book chapters. Life Member of the Bio-medical Engineering Society of India.

Aashna Nishad is pursuing BTech in Information Science and Technology. Her keen interests are in the domain of Machine Learning and Data Science. Her achievements include finalist at two national level hackathons and winning a University level IEEE hackathon. She is an enthusiastic learner who constantly upskills and innovates.

Shaista Noor is a distinguished academic who earned her Ph.D. in Business from Taylor's University, Malaysia, where she was honored with the Taylor's Excellence Research Award. Her research interests encompass women entrepreneurship, commercialization, leadership, management, aging, higher education institutions, and Sustainable Development Goals (SDGs).

Poornima Pandian pursuing her research in the field of Cognitive Radio Networks from the Anna University. She currently serves as an Assistant Professor in the Department of ECE at Sri Sai Ram Engineering College. Her research interests include Wireless Networks, Machine learning techniques, Quantum Computing and Optimization techniques.

Sri Suman Patra received B.Sc. [Physics (H)] and M.Sc. degree in Physics from Jadavpur University, Kolkata. At present, he is Assistant Professor in the Department of Physics of Netaji Nagar Day College, affiliated to University of Calcutta, Kolkata, India.

Piyal Roy is an accomplished academician in the field of Computer Science & Engineering. He has completed his BSc in Computer Science, MSc in Computer Science and MTech in Computer Science & Engineering. Currently, he is working as an Assistant Professor at Computer Science & Engineering department at Brainware University, India.

Saptarshi Kumar Sarkar is an Assistant Professor at Brainware University. With a dedication to academic excellence, he brings a wealth of knowledge and experience to his students. His research interests include AI, ML and Social Networking, contributing significantly to advancements in his field.

Aditya Singh is an Independent Researcher, Editorial Review Board Member in 6 American International Journals (IJSSMET, IJSDS, IJPAEI, IJESGT, IJDSST, IJRLEDM), Reviewer in 8 American, 4 Singaporean & 1 Indonesian International Journals (IJUPSC, IJCVIP, IRMJ, JTA, IJAIBM, IJCEWM, JITR, IJSSSP, JDSIS, AAES, JCCE, SWT, & IJEECS) these 19 International Journals include some Scopus & WoS indexed ones, Mentor (Research) at Academy Innova World, Kalipur, India & Ex-Alumni Mentor (LPU) at present. He had completed his regular B. Tech degree in Civil Engineering from Lovely Professional University, India, in 2020. He is currently affiliated with Amrita Vishwa Vidyapeetham, Coimbatore, India. He has 29 publications under his name, in which he is a single author in 20 of them, whereas in 6 of them he is the main author. Most of his publications are Indexed in Scopus. He had also worked as a Reviewer/Editorial Review Board Member for 149 times in the evaluation of manuscripts so far in Conferences, Research Books and

Journals of International stature. His global presence as a professional could also be seen with 25 Paper Presentations in 22 Conferences in 9 countries (Thailand, Sri Lanka, Egypt, India, Cambodia, Bangladesh, Turkey, United Kingdom, & Germany); as well as his position as Program Committee Member, and Scientific Committee Member in International Conferences, and Reviewer in total 8 International Conferences (including countries Thailand, Cambodia, USA, India, and UK), and Keynote Speaker in Faculty Development Programme, and so on. He had also won 2 International Awards((Thailand) & (Cambodia)) as a Reviewer in 2023. He had worked on 52 positions so far in his professional career, including positions in Journals, Conferences, Research Books of International stature.

Manisha Singhal currently works at the Department of Management, MMH Collage Ghaziabad (CCS University). Manisha does research in Organizational Psychology/Human resource management. She is currently working on Corporate practices, psychological contract fulfillment, competency management practices, employer branding and management of healthcare organizations.

Y Mohamadi Begum is currently working as a professor in the department of CSE at Swamy Vivekananda Yoga Anusandhana Samsthana (Deemed to be University), Bangalore. She has a Doctorate in CSE awarded by Anna University, Chennai. She has about 30 years of teaching experience in various capacities. She is credited with publications in international journals and conferences. Her areas of research include Cloud resource management, Parallel Computing, Blockchain Technology, Machine Learning and Information Management.

Index

Symbols

5G 23, 33, 34, 35, 41, 59, 64, 65, 67, 69, 72, 74, 126, 140, 141, 186, 191, 198, 199, 248, 252, 260, 262, 264, 285, 300, 327, 382, 388, 391, 392, 393, 394

A

Advanced Analytics 60, 400, 404, 429
Advanced Encryption 78, 83, 84, 85, 95, 102
AI 1, 2, 3, 14, 18, 24, 29, 30, 33, 34, 35, 36, 37, 38, 39, 40, 42, 43, 44, 45, 46, 47, 48, 49, 50, 51, 52, 53, 54, 55, 56, 57, 58, 59, 60, 61, 62, 63, 64, 65, 66, 67, 68, 69, 71, 72, 73, 74, 75, 76, 77, 78, 79, 80, 81, 82, 83, 84, 85, 86, 87, 88, 89, 90, 91, 92, 93, 94, 95, 96, 98, 100, 101, 102, 103, 104, 105, 109, 110, 115, 116, 122, 123, 124, 125, 126, 127, 128, 130, 131, 132, 133, 135, 139, 142, 145, 150, 151, 152, 153, 154, 155, 156, 157, 158, 159, 161, 164, 165, 167, 168, 169, 170, 171, 172, 173, 174, 175, 176, 177, 178, 179, 181, 182, 183, 185, 186, 187, 188, 191, 193, 195, 197, 198, 199, 200, 201, 203, 205, 206, 207, 208, 210, 211, 212, 213, 218, 219, 220, 221, 222, 230, 231, 232, 233, 234, 235, 236, 239, 240, 241, 242, 243, 244, 246, 247, 248, 249, 250, 251, 252, 256, 257, 258, 259, 261, 262, 263, 264, 265, 266, 267, 269, 270, 271, 275, 276, 277, 278, 279, 280, 281, 284, 285, 287, 290, 291, 292, 293, 294, 295, 296, 297, 299, 300, 301, 305, 306, 307, 308, 309, 313, 314, 318, 320, 321, 322, 323, 325, 326, 327, 329, 330, 331, 332, 333, 334, 335, 336, 337, 338, 339, 340, 341, 342, 343, 344, 345, 346, 347, 348, 349, 350, 351, 352, 353, 354, 355, 357, 358, 359, 360, 361, 362, 363, 364, 369, 370, 373, 376, 377, 378, 379, 380, 382, 383, 384, 385, 386, 388, 390, 392, 394, 395, 396, 397, 398, 399, 400, 401, 402, 408, 412, 413, 416, 417, 418, 419, 420, 421, 422, 425, 427, 428, 431, 432, 434, 435, 437, 438, 439, 440, 442, 443, 444, 445, 446, 447, 448, 449, 450, 451, 452, 458, 461, 463, 473, 475, 476, 477, 478, 479, 480, 481, 482, 483, 484, 485
AI Competencies 318, 320, 323
AI-driven Security 78, 85, 86, 87, 102, 115, 248
AIoT 33, 58, 59, 66, 67, 68, 69, 70, 71, 73, 75, 76, 77, 78, 79, 80, 81, 82, 83, 84, 85, 86, 87, 88, 89, 90, 91, 92, 93, 94, 95, 96, 97, 98, 99, 100, 101, 102, 167, 168, 169, 170, 171, 172, 173, 174, 175, 176, 177, 178, 179, 180, 181, 182, 183, 184, 185, 186, 187, 188, 189, 190, 191, 192, 193, 194, 195, 196, 198, 199, 200, 239, 240, 241, 246, 247, 248, 249, 250, 251, 252, 253, 254, 255, 256, 257, 258, 259, 260, 261, 262, 263, 264, 265, 266, 267, 269, 270, 273, 275, 278, 284, 285, 287, 289, 290, 292, 293, 294, 295, 296, 297, 299, 300, 301, 302, 305, 307, 314, 318, 319, 321, 323, 324, 326, 327, 329, 360, 361, 362, 363, 364, 365, 373, 376, 377, 378, 379, 380, 381, 382, 383, 384, 385, 386, 387, 388, 389, 391, 392, 393, 394, 396, 397, 398, 400, 401, 404, 408, 411, 413, 414, 415, 417, 418, 419, 420, 421, 422, 429, 430, 432, 433, 434, 435, 436, 438, 441, 445, 451, 452, 457, 460, 462, 463, 464, 465, 466, 473, 474, 475, 476, 477, 479, 480, 482, 484, 485
AIoT Systems 58, 77, 78, 79, 80, 81, 82, 83, 84, 85, 86, 87, 88, 89, 90, 91, 93, 94, 95, 96, 102, 169, 170, 174, 176, 179, 180, 181, 185, 186, 190, 191,

192, 193, 194, 195, 241, 246, 247, 248, 258, 270, 297, 302, 321, 377, 378, 379, 380, 382, 383, 384, 418, 419, 420, 421, 433, 476
Artificial Intelligence 1, 2, 3, 33, 34, 35, 37, 38, 44, 46, 47, 48, 49, 50, 51, 52, 53, 55, 58, 59, 60, 64, 65, 66, 68, 69, 70, 71, 72, 73, 74, 75, 76, 78, 79, 80, 81, 83, 92, 95, 97, 98, 99, 100, 101, 102, 103, 127, 129, 133, 135, 137, 139, 141, 164, 167, 173, 175, 177, 179, 181, 182, 183, 185, 188, 193, 197, 198, 199, 200, 207, 208, 209, 210, 211, 212, 218, 219, 222, 231, 233, 236, 239, 240, 241, 242, 243, 246, 247, 249, 251, 260, 261, 262, 263, 264, 265, 266, 267, 270, 271, 275, 276, 278, 280, 281, 283, 287, 290, 292, 293, 294, 295, 296, 299, 300, 307, 308, 311, 318, 322, 323, 324, 326, 327, 329, 330, 331, 332, 333, 334, 335, 336, 337, 338, 339, 341, 342, 343, 344, 345, 347, 348, 349, 350, 351, 352, 354, 355, 356, 357, 358, 359, 360, 361, 362, 364, 369, 388, 389, 390, 391, 392, 394, 395, 396, 397, 400, 401, 413, 415, 417, 418, 422, 428, 431, 432, 434, 437, 438, 439, 440, 442, 446, 447, 448, 449, 450, 451, 459, 478, 479, 480, 481, 482, 483, 484, 485
Artificial Intelligence (AI) 369
Artificial Intelligence of Things 58, 65, 68, 69, 76, 78, 80, 81, 83, 92, 95, 97, 98, 99, 101, 197, 198, 199, 200, 246, 251, 260, 262, 263, 264, 265, 266, 267, 293, 294, 295, 296, 323, 324, 326, 360, 362, 364, 392, 394, 395, 396, 397, 400, 401, 413, 415, 428, 478, 479, 485
Artificial Internet of Things 100, 246, 267, 299, 432, 444, 451

B

Blockchain 33, 34, 35, 67, 69, 96, 97, 99, 101, 103, 104, 105, 110, 111, 115, 116, 117, 118, 119, 120, 121, 122, 123, 124, 126, 127, 128, 129, 130, 131, 132, 133, 134, 140, 141, 264, 272, 274, 276, 278, 281, 330, 345, 371, 376, 384, 385, 386, 390, 395, 396, 446, 448, 450, 482, 483

C

Civil Engineering 431, 437, 438, 439, 445, 446, 447, 451, 452, 473, 474, 475, 476, 477, 480, 481, 483
Cloud Computing 2, 20, 28, 34, 56, 59, 60, 72, 106, 131, 134, 185, 269, 285, 292, 296, 318, 330, 332, 362, 363, 371, 376, 390, 391, 396, 433
Cloud Security 104, 105, 108, 115, 121
Consumer Insights 397, 398, 413
Cybersecurity 11, 89, 96, 102, 105, 113, 123, 129, 130, 131, 133, 180, 188, 189, 190, 191, 193, 205, 209, 229, 236, 272, 274, 275, 280, 294, 296, 345, 351, 418, 420, 421, 462

D

Data Analytics 17, 70, 91, 169, 188, 191, 193, 233, 240, 271, 272, 296, 338, 343, 370, 371, 377, 389, 421, 429
Data Privacy 33, 55, 56, 64, 75, 76, 77, 78, 79, 80, 81, 82, 83, 84, 85, 87, 88, 89, 90, 91, 92, 93, 94, 95, 96, 100, 101, 102, 116, 126, 160, 167, 170, 174, 179, 180, 189, 192, 194, 248, 254, 259, 273, 277, 279, 301, 385, 386, 388, 452, 462
Decision Making 37, 203, 206, 207, 208, 218, 220, 221, 223, 230, 231, 233, 302, 312
Digital Policy Tools 319
Disease Management 362, 363, 376, 379, 381, 385

E

Edge Computing 19, 33, 34, 35, 56, 59, 65, 68, 69, 70, 73, 74, 93, 96, 109,

115, 125, 126, 128, 130, 131, 140, 141, 158, 185, 186, 191, 219, 247, 248, 293, 296, 320, 382, 384, 385, 387, 388, 389, 391, 393, 394, 395, 396, 432, 446
Educational Equity 320
Energy Efficiency 45, 119, 120, 126, 131, 137, 140, 167, 169, 170, 171, 174, 239, 249, 253, 258, 259, 289, 332, 336, 337, 348
Ethical AI 92, 94, 95, 244, 350

F

Federated Learning 24, 78, 87, 88, 93, 95, 97, 101, 102, 116, 126, 131, 133, 386, 390

G

GPS 47, 51, 53, 55, 137, 139, 140, 142, 143, 146, 149, 150, 152, 154, 155, 158, 159, 163, 164, 312, 454
GSM 137, 139, 142, 143, 146, 149, 376

H

Healthcare 2, 4, 5, 9, 10, 11, 14, 15, 17, 18, 23, 26, 28, 29, 30, 31, 33, 34, 38, 44, 51, 52, 53, 55, 56, 58, 59, 60, 63, 64, 66, 68, 69, 71, 73, 76, 77, 78, 79, 80, 81, 82, 83, 84, 85, 86, 87, 90, 95, 98, 99, 100, 101, 102, 108, 109, 112, 126, 136, 164, 168, 169, 171, 187, 192, 193, 195, 199, 217, 230, 231, 233, 234, 235, 236, 241, 243, 245, 248, 260, 265, 269, 270, 271, 272, 273, 274, 275, 276, 277, 278, 279, 280, 281, 284, 285, 286, 287, 290, 291, 292, 293, 294, 295, 296, 300, 318, 319, 324, 352, 368, 369, 371, 374, 377, 378, 379, 387, 389, 394, 400, 484

I

Impact of AI 44, 165, 329, 343, 344
Industrial IoT 3, 33, 49, 71, 86, 88, 100, 123, 129, 265, 459
Industry 4.0 34, 72, 265, 288, 312, 323, 361, 362, 363, 366, 386, 387, 388, 389, 391, 394, 395, 396, 446, 457
Intelligent Connectivity 33, 34, 35, 36, 37, 38, 43, 44, 55, 56, 57, 58, 61, 64, 65, 74, 240
Intelligent Transportation System 438
Internet of Things 1, 2, 3, 9, 11, 12, 13, 15, 17, 19, 20, 21, 28, 29, 30, 31, 33, 35, 38, 40, 47, 48, 50, 51, 52, 55, 58, 60, 64, 66, 67, 68, 69, 71, 72, 73, 75, 76, 79, 97, 98, 99, 100, 101, 104, 127, 128, 129, 130, 131, 133, 134, 135, 136, 138, 163, 165, 167, 173, 175, 177, 179, 181, 182, 183, 185, 188, 193, 198, 200, 204, 207, 208, 209, 210, 211, 218, 219, 222, 230, 231, 232, 233, 234, 236, 239, 240, 241, 244, 245, 246, 249, 251, 260, 261, 262, 263, 264, 265, 266, 267, 270, 273, 275, 278, 281, 283, 284, 287, 288, 293, 294, 299, 300, 301, 307, 313, 318, 322, 324, 326, 330, 360, 361, 362, 372, 374, 386, 387, 388, 390, 392, 393, 395, 396, 399, 400, 401, 402, 412, 417, 418, 425, 426, 428, 431, 432, 435, 444, 447, 448, 449, 450, 451, 453, 454, 459, 478, 479, 481, 483, 485
Inventory Management 50, 51, 54, 59, 400, 402, 408, 412, 413, 414, 415, 416, 417, 418, 421, 434, 435
IoBT 203, 204, 205, 206, 207, 208, 209, 210, 211, 212, 213, 214, 218, 219, 220, 221, 222, 223, 229, 236, 237
IoT 1, 2, 3, 5, 6, 7, 9, 10, 11, 12, 13, 14, 15, 16, 17, 18, 19, 20, 21, 22, 23, 24, 25, 26, 27, 28, 29, 30, 31, 33, 34, 35, 36, 37, 38, 40, 41, 42, 43, 44, 45, 46, 47, 48, 49, 50, 51, 52, 53, 54, 55, 56, 57, 58, 59, 60, 61, 62, 63, 64, 65, 66, 67, 68, 69, 70, 71, 72, 73, 74, 75, 76, 77, 78, 80, 81, 82, 84, 85, 86, 87, 88, 91, 92, 95, 97, 98, 99, 100, 101, 103, 104, 105, 106, 107, 108, 109, 110, 111, 112, 113, 114, 115, 116, 118,

119, 120, 121, 122, 123, 124, 125, 126, 127, 128, 129, 130, 131, 132, 133, 134, 135, 136, 137, 138, 139, 140, 141, 142, 143, 144, 145, 146, 147, 149, 152, 159, 163, 164, 165, 167, 168, 169, 170, 171, 172, 173, 175, 176, 177, 178, 179, 181, 182, 183, 185, 186, 188, 189, 193, 195, 197, 198, 200, 204, 208, 210, 212, 213, 218, 219, 220, 223, 230, 231, 232, 233, 234, 235, 236, 239, 240, 241, 244, 245, 246, 247, 248, 249, 251, 252, 253, 254, 256, 258, 259, 260, 262, 263, 264, 265, 266, 267, 268, 269, 270, 271, 273, 275, 278, 280, 281, 282, 283, 284, 285, 286, 288, 290, 291, 292, 293, 295, 296, 297, 299, 300, 301, 305, 306, 307, 313, 314, 318, 320, 322, 323, 324, 326, 327, 330, 343, 360, 361, 362, 363, 364, 367, 370, 372, 373, 374, 375, 376, 377, 378, 379, 380, 382, 384, 385, 386, 387, 388, 389, 390, 392, 396, 397, 399, 400, 401, 402, 403, 411, 412, 413, 414, 415, 417, 418, 419, 420, 421, 422, 426, 427, 430, 431, 432, 433, 434, 435, 437, 439, 440, 442, 443, 444, 445, 446, 447, 448, 449, 450, 451, 452, 453, 454, 455, 456, 459, 461, 463, 464, 465, 466, 473, 474, 475, 476, 477, 478, 479, 480, 481, 482, 483, 484, 485

IoT Networks 20, 25, 26, 27, 56, 86, 88, 103, 107, 108, 109, 112, 115, 116, 120, 122, 123, 125, 126, 232, 245, 292, 434, 450, 451, 453, 456, 474, 485

IoT Security 12, 15, 24, 26, 105, 106, 110, 112, 122, 124, 125, 127, 128, 129, 223, 234, 273

K

KSK Approach 203, 218, 220, 221, 224, 225, 226, 229, 231, 233, 234, 235

M

Machine Learning 2, 4, 8, 10, 16, 17, 18, 20, 24, 25, 26, 27, 28, 29, 30, 31, 36, 38, 39, 42, 43, 59, 68, 71, 72, 73, 74, 86, 87, 97, 99, 102, 122, 124, 132, 137, 147, 150, 152, 165, 198, 206, 208, 209, 219, 230, 231, 232, 233, 234, 235, 246, 247, 248, 261, 269, 270, 275, 278, 281, 283, 284, 285, 286, 290, 291, 293, 295, 296, 304, 308, 330, 331, 332, 333, 334, 338, 339, 340, 342, 343, 345, 346, 360, 363, 387, 390, 391, 392, 394, 395, 400, 417, 422, 479, 480, 482, 484, 485

Machine Learning Algorithms 4, 8, 16, 36, 59, 122, 152, 208, 278, 291, 330, 334, 338, 342, 400

Microcontroller system 135

P

Personalization 28, 38, 44, 248, 267, 320, 325, 400, 401, 403, 413, 414, 420, 426

Pests 345, 361, 365, 379, 380, 388, 390, 393

Predictive Analytics 20, 43, 46, 47, 48, 51, 54, 58, 59, 63, 64, 80, 85, 86, 87, 92, 100, 110, 126, 171, 172, 186, 191, 201, 209, 277, 319, 326, 362, 365, 371, 373, 376, 378, 384, 399, 418, 451

Privacy 11, 12, 13, 14, 21, 23, 24, 25, 30, 31, 33, 55, 56, 58, 59, 64, 75, 76, 77, 78, 79, 80, 81, 82, 83, 84, 85, 87, 88, 89, 90, 91, 92, 93, 94, 95, 96, 97, 98, 99, 100, 101, 102, 104, 108, 109, 116, 117, 124, 126, 127, 128, 130, 131, 133, 134, 140, 160, 167, 170, 174, 179, 180, 183, 184, 189, 190, 192, 194, 195, 196, 200, 234, 244, 247, 248, 249, 254, 256, 257, 259, 260, 261, 266, 267, 272, 273, 274, 277, 279, 287, 288, 289, 295, 299, 301, 306, 314, 315, 321, 322, 351, 382, 383, 385, 386, 388, 389, 418, 420, 425, 446, 452, 462, 482

Public Safety 46, 56, 58, 60, 61, 82, 167, 168, 169, 170, 171, 173, 177, 187,

190, 191, 193, 196, 319, 378

R

Remote Monitoring 142, 217, 269, 290

S

Security 1, 3, 11, 12, 13, 14, 15, 16, 18, 19, 20, 21, 22, 23, 24, 25, 26, 27, 28, 30, 31, 35, 41, 42, 46, 47, 48, 49, 55, 56, 59, 65, 66, 75, 76, 77, 78, 79, 80, 81, 82, 83, 84, 85, 86, 87, 88, 89, 90, 91, 92, 93, 94, 95, 96, 97, 98, 99, 100, 102, 103, 104, 105, 106, 107, 108, 109, 110, 111, 112, 113, 114, 115, 116, 118, 119, 120, 121, 122, 124, 125, 126, 127, 128, 129, 130, 131, 132, 133, 134, 167, 173, 174, 175, 179, 180, 181, 189, 190, 192, 194, 199, 204, 205, 212, 213, 223, 229, 234, 239, 241, 244, 245, 247, 248, 249, 250, 252, 254, 256, 257, 258, 259, 260, 261, 263, 264, 265, 266, 272, 273, 274, 276, 277, 279, 280, 294, 296, 299, 301, 302, 306, 311, 314, 315, 319, 321, 322, 324, 345, 361, 362, 363, 365, 371, 372, 377, 381, 382, 383, 385, 389, 391, 392, 394, 404, 419, 420, 435, 450, 462, 481

Sensors 2, 3, 6, 9, 10, 12, 17, 20, 31, 35, 36, 37, 40, 41, 42, 44, 45, 46, 47, 48, 49, 50, 51, 53, 54, 55, 56, 59, 60, 61, 62, 66, 70, 76, 80, 81, 82, 84, 86, 87, 91, 92, 99, 105, 122, 123, 128, 132, 135, 136, 137, 138, 139, 140, 142, 145, 146, 149, 150, 152, 153, 155, 157, 158, 159, 161, 165, 168, 169, 170, 171, 172, 173, 175, 176, 177, 178, 180, 183, 185, 186, 187, 191, 197, 200, 203, 204, 205, 206, 207, 208, 212, 214, 215, 216, 217, 218, 219, 222, 223, 224, 225, 226, 229, 236, 240, 243, 244, 245, 246, 247, 248, 250, 256, 261, 264, 265, 278, 286, 287, 289, 290, 296, 314, 318, 322, 331, 337, 338, 340, 343, 344, 347, 354, 365, 373, 374, 376, 377, 378, 380, 384, 385, 386, 387, 388, 389, 392, 393, 394, 395, 398, 401, 406, 407, 409, 410, 411, 414, 415, 420, 422, 424, 432, 433, 434, 437, 438, 439, 440, 442, 443, 444, 447, 449, 451, 453, 454, 455, 456, 457, 458, 460, 482

Smart Agriculture 234, 235, 263, 363, 373, 386, 387, 392, 395

Smart Cities 1, 15, 19, 33, 34, 42, 44, 46, 55, 58, 60, 64, 66, 68, 70, 73, 76, 82, 86, 88, 91, 98, 126, 167, 168, 169, 171, 177, 180, 181, 182, 183, 184, 185, 186, 188, 193, 195, 196, 197, 198, 199, 200, 230, 241, 252, 253, 262, 264, 287, 299, 318, 319, 365, 378, 401, 437, 440, 446, 447, 448, 450, 465, 474, 482, 484, 485

Smart City Technologies 198

Smart Healthcare 10, 11, 17, 73, 79, 81, 195, 241, 265, 278, 281, 295, 318

Smart Homes 26, 41, 44, 47, 48, 49, 87, 88, 95, 101, 112, 174, 239, 240, 241, 245, 248, 249, 250, 251, 252, 253, 254, 255, 256, 257, 258, 259, 261, 264, 266, 400, 437, 441, 446, 474, 477

Smart Retail 72, 241, 397, 398, 399, 400, 401, 402, 403, 405, 412, 413, 415, 417, 418, 421, 422, 423, 424, 429

Smart stick 135, 145, 147, 149, 150, 151, 152, 153, 154, 155, 156, 157, 161, 162, 163

Structural Health Monitoring 437, 439, 446, 451, 481, 485

Sustainable Development 193, 194, 294, 331, 335, 347, 349, 351, 356, 362, 379, 394, 445, 484

T

Techniques 2, 3, 8, 14, 21, 28, 38, 49, 71, 73, 74, 78, 83, 84, 85, 87, 88, 89, 92, 93, 95, 100, 102, 108, 114, 115, 116, 120, 124, 127, 132, 219, 246, 265, 266, 275, 277, 279, 283, 284, 290, 293, 302, 309, 314, 317, 332, 334,

339, 340, 342, 348, 352, 354, 355, 357, 358, 363, 376, 379, 382, 383, 386, 391, 393, 396, 429, 446, 447, 448, 449, 481, 482, 484
Telehealth Devices 269
Transportation 28, 33, 34, 38, 43, 45, 53, 55, 60, 61, 64, 68, 69, 70, 91, 95, 101, 136, 160, 164, 168, 169, 170, 171, 173, 175, 177, 178, 183, 187, 190, 241, 245, 329, 330, 332, 335, 340, 354, 369, 378, 379, 400, 438, 443, 445, 446, 451, 458, 460, 483, 485

U

Urban Challenges 168, 195
Urban Infrastructure 34, 44, 47, 61, 167, 173, 186, 195, 200
Urbanization 168, 252, 412, 448

V

Vocational Training 317
Voice Playback Module 136, 137

W

Wearable Technology 10, 138, 139, 204, 208, 222, 289, 296, 374